MW00989873

MVS
Concepts and Facilities

MVS
Concepts and Facilities

Robert H. Johnson

Intertext Publications
McGraw-Hill Book Company

New York St. Louis San Francisco Auckland Bogotá
Hamburg London Madrid Mexico Milan Montreal
New Delhi Panama Paris São Paulo
Singapore Sidney Tokyo Toronto

To my wife, Marie
for her love, support, and friendship

Library of Congress Catalog Card Number 88-83705

10 9 8 7 6 5 4 3 2 1

ISBN 0-07-032673-8

Intertext Publications/Multiscience Press, Inc.
One Lincoln Plaza
New York, NY 10023

McGraw-Hill Book Company
1221 Avenue of the Americas
New York, NY 10020

Composed in Ventura Publisher by Context, Inc.

Contents

Preface

The International Business Machine Corporation (IBM) manufactures and sells computers. IBM has offices in most countries in the world. Like the British Empire of yesteryear, the sun never sets on IBM. IBM's largest and most powerful computers are the System/370 Processor Complexes. This book is about the software and hardware of those IBM computers.

System/370s are usually located at corporate headquarters or in some large companies at division or regional locations. The System/370, or "mainframe," computers are capable of supporting hundreds or thousands of terminals. Almost every American is affected by an IBM computer.

In the early 1980s, IBM and many other companies reported growth in computer capacity at a rate of 50–60 percent annually. At first, this seems like too high a rate. I have observed this growth rate all through the 1980s at data centers that I have worked in or studied. With such a growth rate comes a large responsibility to manage the growth.

The computer industry has changed drastically in the last 20 years. When I started as a computer programmer in the late 1960s, the "mainframe" computer I used was housed in a room by itself. Today, I am using a Personal Computer on my desk that can process instructions as fast and has eight times the available storage for programs as did my old mainframe.

The documentation for my first mainframe computer was in a bookshelf by my desk. The volume of documentation for my current mainframe computer is so large that my company does not even have it all — it is too expensive to manage documentation for the parts we do not use. *What documentation we need requires an entire room to house it!*

That first mainframe computer could run one operating system at a time. We ran DOS for a while, stopped it, and ran MVT for a while. The 3090 you can buy today can run in single image mode, physically partitioned mode, VM/XA mode, VM/XA mode with Multiple Preferred Guests, or Logically Partitioned Mode. You can buy PR/SM to divide it up like a Thanksgiving turkey. Help!

I have taught the concepts in this book since the early 1970s as a part of my duties for large Fortune 500 companies as well as for government installations. The most often asked question is "Where do I begin?"

The answer is not easy — each month brings new, excellent manuals from the IBM forest-to-books factory. The documentation is interdependent on the version and release of the software and hardware. Over the years I have created and taught introductory courses which provide an overview of the architecture and an introduction to the Multiple Virtual Storage (MVS) operating system. The result of my teaching is this book.

The motto of the IBM Corporation is THINK. That is an appropriate motto for anyone, but it is a requirement for understanding the computer industry. One goal of this book is to get you to think and ask questions — about your job, about MVS, about IBM.

FOR WHOM THIS BOOK WAS WRITTEN

This text is designed for the data processing person who may be in several skill areas that use the IBM System/370 family of computers. The origin of this book is a two-day in-depth course on MVS. I have structured the book to fit a college or technical school semester.

Application programmers write COBOL or other programs that are instructions to the IBM computers. While programmers can write good, efficient programs without the concepts in this book, the really successful ones who move up in the programming hierarchy understand these concepts. Programmers have been the most successful audience of these concepts. They directly apply the concepts in this book to real problems at work. The results are massive savings, better programs, and much better systems.

Systems Analysts must know these concepts. Unfortunately, until now, they were not written in one place, so the Analyst must either dig through the mounds of manuals, try to find educational introductions, or just wing it.

Systems Programmers deal with these concepts every day. The problem is that many Systems Programmers have been promoted through the ranks of programmers and operators. This is GREAT! They already have a great background to do the job and excel at running the mainframe computer. Where do they get concepts training? Probably from one or two "seminars" or from the excellent IBM user groups such as SHARE or GUIDE. Mostly, though, Systems Programmers just wing it.

Operations and Production Control personnel have all the responsibility to keep the monster running. Unfortunately, most companies "forget" to provide the training to understand the nature of the computer. This group has provided me with the second most gratifying and productive audience for these concepts. In three large computer centers, I have had the privilege of teaching these concepts to Operations and Production Control personnel. The result has been many excellent systems managers and workers. My work was not entirely unselfish. Teaching these concepts, my 3:00 A.M. calls all but disappeared.

Managers and supervisors of data centers that have or are thinking of having IBM mainframe computers are the most fertile ground for the concepts in this book. Most line managers in the computer industry have been promoted from within. Usually these persons were very good at what they did and were made managers to capitalize on that success. Again, who trained the trainers? I invite this group to learn these concepts and pass them on to their people.

OPERATING SYSTEM ENVIRONMENT

This book has been written primarily for MVS/370, MVS/XA, and MVS/ESA, but since the concepts are similar for VM, DOS/VSE, and ACP, those users will also benefit from the book.

A WORD ON THE STYLE USED

The style of the book has been kept simple. The complexity of the System/370 and Multiple Virtual Storage (MVS) environment and the limited space in this text makes it a challenge for all.

WHAT YOU NEED TO KNOW TO READ THIS BOOK

This book is an introduction and assumes that the reader does not have detailed knowledge about all pieces of the architecture. The reader should at least "be in the business" or "be studying to be in the business." The reader should have knowledge of or be studying Job Control Language (JCL).

In many cases, the reader is referred to the IBM reference documents for complete information on subjects. These manuals are exhaustive and should be studied by the reader for either more detailed explanations or when actually working with the MVS component.

The reader is cautioned to check the documentation that is published and be sure it matches the version of MVS running at the data center. IBM changes commands and adds functions with each release. I have attempted to note major conflict areas throughout the book, but the final reference should be the documentation for your system.

WHY THIS BOOK IS COMPLETE

Each section, and each chapter within a section, has been used over the years to teach MVS concepts. The organization has been tested, changed, and tested again. There are other successful ways to organize the material, but this version at least anticipates the questions that students of MVS ask.

You will find that this book treats some topics superficially and others in (somewhat extreme) depth. I could have appealed to those who value aesthetics over utility, but you cannot increase your value much through generalities.

This book is not so much an MVS reference work as a cross-reference. You could use it as a departure point into the otherwise overwhelming MVS documentation, which may list in exhaustive detail what you may specify but not why. This book presents the "what" with a lot of "why."

HOW YOUR INSTALLATION BENEFITS

One goal of this book is to help you understand the underlying architecture of MVS to help you do your job better and more efficiently, and to guide you to the correct decisions for your company. Decisions in the System/360 and System/370 environment cost in the tens of thousands to millions of dollars.

You can affect these decisions in a positive way. The penalty for not understanding these concepts is, at a minimum, unnecessary expenses, outages, or problems. The maximum penalty is total system failures, which cost companies millions of dollars.

WHAT IS INCLUDED

Part A is an introduction to the System/360 and System/370. The history of the architecture is important because that is the key to the success of this family of processors. But there is another reason:

WHAT IS PAST, IS PROLOGUE

The above is carved on the National Archives building in Washington, D.C. What it means is that we must study the past to know what our future is. If we know the truth about the past, it will set us free to change our course. If we ignore the past, we are doomed to repeat the past.

For the Multiple Virtual Storage (MVS) architecture, each step in the development of the architecture is still there. Much of the code of the previous systems is identical to what is in the operating system today. Some feel that MVS/ESA was a "new operating system." It is not. It is an extension of what was there before.

Part A also establishes a theme used throughout: The reason you improve yourself, apart from increasing your self-esteem, is to better serve your company. You do that by better use of the resources if you are an end user, better application design if a programmer, better awareness if an operator, and better maintenance if a systems programmer.

Part B thoroughly investigates the System/370 hardware, because the hardware has determined the structure of the software. Without this base in reality, discussion of software would require abstract generalization. Processor Complexes, Central Storage management, and input/output devices are covered there.

Part C discusses MVS software. Many descriptions of operating systems give a "top-down" view, progressing from abstract to concrete, and never quite get around to saying what happens when the system is turned on! I begin with that, then proceed to MVS services available once the system is running.

MVS/XA and MVS/ESA are compared and contrasted so the remaining discussion can directly address the consequences of these distinctions. The subsystem which controls initiation and termination of work, JES, is then considered, followed by data access mechanisms, program management, and access to data communications facilities. Part 3 ends with a discussion of the utility programs that are provided with MVS.

Part D contains information and techniques to get the most performance out of an MVS system. Chapter 15, an in-depth look at input/output, is probably the most important in the book because with it anyone who writes or modifies JCL or defines data set parameters can favorably affect system throughput.

The last two chapters detail how MVS manages system resources and what feedback exists for measuring and improving performance and for diagnosing software and hardware malfunctions.

The appendices not only have a glossary and an index but also have statistical tables and useful information about MVS such as explanations of MVS messages and Abend codes.

Take time now to read the Table of Contents. You should reread it periodically as you progress through the book: There is much information here, and the Table of Contents will help to remind you of its organization. Know where you have been and where you are going.

SUMMARY

There are three types of people in this world. Those who make things happen, those who notice that something has happened, and those who ask "what happened?" While this society needs all three types, it is more fun to be the one who makes things happen. The goal of this book is to help you make things happen.

After finishing this book, you should be able to perform your job better. You should have more confidence because you will have specific knowledge of how the MVS operating system works with the hardware. You should be able to use the tools of your trade better. These could be software monitors, compilers, utilities, or the reference materials.

And finally, a word of caution. The concepts presented in this book are background and an introduction to MVS and the hardware that forms the basis of one of the most successful operating systems the computer industry has seen. It is a very dynamic and powerful system. Because of its ever-changing nature, you should constantly verify and question decisions you are asked to make concerning

MVS. It is best if you install the product, build benchmarks, and examine the output. Of course you cannot do this for every system that you work on, but you can do it for every important business system.

ACKNOWLEDGMENTS

I would first like to thank my wife, Marie, for the support she has given me, not only in this endeavor, but throughout our life together. She has always been on my team. I thank God for sending Marie to me.

I thank my son, Tom Johnson, for giving up a summer of fun in the sun to help design and create the drawings for the figures. I thank my oldest son, Dan Johnson, for editing the manuscript and giving me guidance to make the script more readable. His pen was merciless! I thank my daughter, Tracy Johnson Monahan, for running errands and giving me an example of persistent and consistent attention to details.

I thank Bill Mosteller for his support and friendship over the years. His encouragement and assistance made this a much more readable book. If it has flaws, those are mine, but if it flows smoothly, the credit is due to his mighty, sharp pen. Bill is widely known as a JES guru, but his work with VM and human factors issues are even more important to the industry.

Rick Rooney helped me understand the politics of data processing. Thanks to Bill Fairchild for his assistance on the DASD topics. Bill is a technician, leader, and teacher.

I thank Gordon Stauffer for his support as a supervisor and a friend always. Many of my organizational skills are due to his fine example. I am honored to call him a friend.

Probably much of my technical talent I owe to the three musketeers of Mead Data Central: Dale Waddell, Jim Hirst, and Jack Kelly were a wonder to behold. I profited much in that brief period.

I thank all the people at Morino Associates who have helped me understand and control MVS. To Mario Morino who has seen and sees the future as no one I have ever known. Special thanks go to Brian Currah, who taught me that if you read the microfiche, you can understand how MVS really works, and to Jim Bowerman, who taught me the real value of VM, capacity planning, and modeling.

Thanks to the Candle Corporation and their OMEGAMON products for a window into MVS. Without OMEGAMON, I would never have seen the results of many of my tuning and modification efforts on MVS.

I thank the many people who have assisted me to get to my current level, especially my co-workers and staff. Charlie Mitchell and Charles Chamberlain are two of the most dedicated directors I have ever known. Charles and Curtis Townsend have given me the best operational support I have had.

Tom Stanley helped with the portions on ICF catalogs. Neil Stevens, Carolyn Barnett, Miles Lucas, John Geluso, and Candy Reynolds made my days easy so my nights could be filled with visions of MVS. Rick Milazzo, Tom Horvath, Jim Thompson, and Michele Berger used the tuning techniques to build one of the most efficient financial systems. Sue Courter and Kathy Calabrese and the rest of their staff redesigned their VSAM applications using these techniques and saved our company hundreds of thousands of dollars.

Many of the people who lifted my knowledge were brave enough to ask a question. Once the question was asked, we found the answer and were lifted to a new height of knowledge. Many were supervisors who pushed me to new adventures. Larry Shute asked me the one question that fanned my desire to understand the Input/Output system. Bill Deterding gave me the true grit determination to maintain 110 percent integrity and demand from my software and hardware vendors the same integrity and price performance. Howard Wolvington showed me the excitement of modifying MVS. Dave Hardy showed me the leadership necessary for highly technical people. Bob Weir gave me an understanding of financial implications of the data processing industry and taught me that any contract can be changed to make it more equitable for our side.

A special thanks to Tony Carlson for showing me the world and giving me an appreciation for my country that I would never have had if he had not provided the channel for me to visit Europe and Africa. Dave Halbig was a vital partner for those trips. Their support for the first *MVS: Concepts and Facilities* laid the foundation for this journey.

And finally, my thanks to Jay Ranade, who started me on this journey and provided the support and guidance that were needed to keep me on the track.

So I wish you good luck to an exciting future. To paraphrase my reply to "How are you," I reply, *"It's GREAT, but it's getting better!"*

Trademarks and Copyrights

A

Introduction to Multiple Virtual Storage (MVS)

Part A of *MVS: Concepts and Facilities* is an introduction to the System/360 and System/370 architecture. The environment we run today in modern data centers is to a large degree exactly like the environment of 20 years ago, except now everything is bigger, more complex, and much faster.

The history of the operating systems that have run on System/360 and System/370 hardware is included because much of what was, is. If you understand where you came from, you can more easily understand where you are. What is the fifth point on the compass? Where you are now. If you understand where you are, you can plot a course to where you are going.

1

Introduction to the MVS Environment

1.1. SYSTEMS ARCHITECTURE

Systems architecture is the term used to describe the relationship between the parts of the computer and the operating system that executes on the computer. The implementation of the systems architecture is what is seen by the programmer or analyst.

The systems architecture is usually defined in a Principles of Operation (POP) manual (e.g., *IBM System/370 Extended Architecture — Principles of Operation*, SA22 7085). The POP provides a detailed reference of the machine functions performed by the computer system. Each version of MVS has a POP to describe the architecture.

The systems architecture includes a list of computer instructions that can be executed, how a program can read and write data (Input/Output), how many concurrent instructions can be executed (Multiprocessing), and how the computer memory is accessed (real or virtual accesses).

IBM competitors use the Principles of Operation to make hardware that will exactly emulate the IBM hardware. These

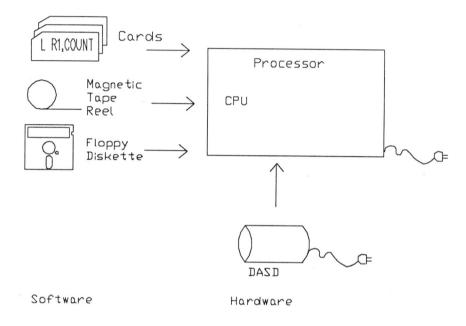

Figure 1.1 Software and hardware. Software is the computer program that can be run on the hardware. Hardware is the physical box that can be plugged into the wall, or at least has batteries somewhere. **Note:** Software may require specific hardware. The hardware must have an Input/Output device to get the software into the hardware before the program can be executed.

manufacturers, called Original Equipment Manufacturers (OEM) or Plug Compatible Manufacturers, produce excellent, cost-effective hardware. Examples are AMDAHL, NAS, Memorex, and Storage Technology Corporation. While there are differences in the method of implementing the architecture, the differences are beyond the scope of this book. When considering new hardware, you should review the OEM vendors and understand their implementation in order to make a good, cost-effective decision for your company.

There are two parts to architecture — the software side and the hardware side. Figure 1.1 shows software as the programs that are executed on the hardware. Software is delivered on magnetic tape, floppy diskettes, or other "soft" media. Hardware is the physical boxes that a customer buys and plugs into the electrical outlets. The software is "loaded" into the hardware.

1.2. HISTORY OF SYSTEM/360 TO SYSTEM/370 ARCHITECTURE

1.2.1. Introduction

Before we look at all the components of the System/360/System/370, it is important to view the history that led to the development of such a successful system.

1.2.2. Computers Before the System/360 Architecture

The era of the "big computers" began in the early 1960s. IBM had three categories of computers:

Scientific Computers The scientific family of computers was primarily designed to perform calculations with large numbers. The computer term for large number processing is **floating point arithmetic.**

Floating point arithmetic allows very large (or small) numbers to be represented and manipulated. The IBM 704, 709, 7090, 7040-44, and 7094 were examples of this type of computer. Universities and very large companies bought this type of computer.

Decimal Computers The decimal family of computers was primarily designed to perform calculations with dollars and cents. The numbers may have been in the billions, but more than two digits to the right of the decimal point were rarely needed. The computer term for this type of calculation is **decimal arithmetic.**

The IBM 7070 and 7080 were examples of decimal computers. Businesses that wanted to process financial data were the customers.

Most authors group a "family" of computers together and give them a name to refer to any or all of the models in the family. All the above models are usually called the 70xx family, where "xx" implies that there were several different models. Later we will discuss the 308x family (such as the 3083, 3081, and 3084) and the 309x family (such as the 3090-200, 3090-400, and 3090-600).

Character Computers Some computer families were character oriented. These were more general purpose. Character–oriented meant that the computer was designed to address single characters such as names and addresses.

The IBM 1401, 1410, and 7010 were examples of character computers. Generally, smaller businesses purchased these computers. In some cases, the 1401 ran side by side with the 70xx family. The 70xx did the processing and the 1401 did the tape-to-tape and tape-to-print functions. The 1401 was a "slave" processor to the 70xx family.

Problems with Multiple Architectures While all of these families could perform decimal, number and character manipulation, the **architecture** was slanted toward one function or the other. If a company chose a family and their processing changed, then major changes would be needed in the application programs.

Each family used different instructions to perform the same function. Figure 1.2 shows that even adding to a counter required different instructions. Not only were the instructions different, but the 14xx and 70xx hardware used **word marks** to separate fields and even instructions. So, looking through a listing of a program was very difficult. Many fields and even instructions were implied, so the listings did not contain all the necessary detail to understand what was going on.

The conversion from one software system to another was traumatic for all involved. Every application program had to be completely rewritten from scratch to use the new hardware. IBM learned it's lesson: It is easier to sell new computers if the customers do not have to change their application software.

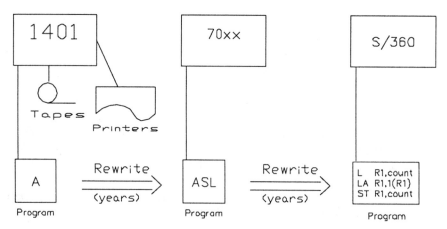

Figure 1.2 Progression from early IBM to S/360. The progression from the 1401 in the early 1960s to the S/360 architecture was a difficult one. Each step was accomplished by rewriting most application software. This example shows that even a single add was different.

1.2.3. System/360: One Last Architecture

In the summer of 1964, IBM announced the System/360 architecture. *The System/360 unified machine architectures.* The System/360 models all had binary, decimal, floating point (including single and double precision), character, and word orientation, *all in a single, profitable computer.*

The software conversion would be just as hard from the 70xx to the System/360 as it was from the 14xx to the 70xx, but the industry was promised this was the last time. IBM promised even more — larger and faster computers would allow the customers to grow their computers without rewriting their code. *The System/360 unified the IBM computing industry to a single set of instruction.*

The System/360 model 30 was designed to handle minimum processing requirements. The model 75 was 50 times as fast as the model 30, but the *instruction set was the same!* Speed improvements were made by changing the hardware, not the user programs. All models were **program compatible**.

What is this promised compatibility? A program written for one model of the System/360 (or System/370) will run on the next version of the hardware. For example, a program that executes on a System/360 model 50 will run on the System/370 model 3090. There may be some limitations, for example:[1]

- The program does not depend on operating facilities that are not on the next fastest computer.
- The program does not depend on instructions executing in a particular period of time.
- The program is not dependent on hardware that is not included in the next fastest computer.
- The program is not dependent on facilities being absent when the facilities are included in the next highest computer (e.g., the program must not depend on interruptions caused by invalid instruction operation codes if they are present on the next computer).
- The program is not dependent on results or functions that are defined in the Principles of Operation manual as being unpredictable or model dependent.

---

1. See *IBM 3084 Functional Characteristics* (GA22-7088) pages 1-2 through 1-3 for an example.

- The program is not dependent on results or functions that are defined as being deviations from the POP.

I started my career by converting 7074 assembler programs to IBM System/360 assembler. These System/360 programs are still running 20 years later. I replaced a System/360 model 50 with a System/370 model 155 with no changes to the application code. It really works!

The goal of the System/360 was to allow the sales and marketing divisions of IBM to go into an account with System/360 architecture, sell the newest System/360 architecture machine, and be able to guarantee to the customer that no software changes would be required to use the new hardware. To the author's knowledge, IBM has kept that promise. Applications may need to do *extra things* to take advantage of the architectural improvements, but more on that later.

IBM was saying that if an application ran on one System/360 processor, it would run on the *next highest* processor offering. IBM, being a manufacturing company, will protect your investment as you move forward. This concept is called **upward compatibility**.

1.2.4. Terminology

Some criticize the computer industry for its acronyms, secret words, or "buzz" words. What is an MFT? What is an MVT? If we are talking about football, MVT may be Most Valuable Tackle. We are talking about computers, so it is perfectly obvious to the most casual observer that it must be Multiprogramming with Variable number of Tasks! Ha! Not to most of us anyway.

There is hope! Most computer buzz words have a logical basis for their existence, and it is one of the goals of this book to give the background for the terms so that the reader can better understand them — not just the words behind the letters, but the ideas behind the words. Hardware and software is an excellent example. Once you know the background, it is easy to see that hardware refers to anything that is "hard." This even carries over to the personal computer (PC) world. Hardware refers to the cards that go inside the PC to perform certain functions. Software comes on floppy diskettes or micro floppy disks.

Computer professionals speak of "executing" programs. We do not kill programs by cutting off the head in a guillotine. We "perform" or "carry out" the program instructions by "running" the program.

In defense of our industry, have you talked to anyone in the military recently? What is a NIPSICOMSI? Nurses have their own language, too. Come here STAT! What if my name is not "STAT"? The society of the 1980s and the 1990s is complex. The English language has been expanded to include special meanings words for each industry. In order to survive, we must learn to speak the dialects of our professions or avocations.

The hardest task in writing this book was to make sense out of the various words IBM has used for the same thing. IBM has called the read/write storage that is available inside the computer several different names:

1. **Core Storage** is the term for the doughnut-shaped device called a toroid or "core." Twists of wire ran around the core rings and current indicated on or off. The inventor, An Wang, discovered in the late 1940s that if you passed the electronic current in one direction, it set the magnetic flux to positive (a "one") and a current in the other direction set the magnetic flux to negative (a "zero").

2. The term **Main Storage** may be used to distinguish from auxiliary or Direct-Access Storage Devices (DASD) storage. It is currently being used in the documentation for the 43xx family of computers and in the Principles of Operation (POP).

3. IBM uses the term **Central Storage** to represent the storage inside the 309x family of computers. RMF monitor displays are being changed to use Central Storage.

4. **Processor Storage** is used on the configuration screen frame of the 309x family of computers.

5. IBM offers optional Central Storage, called **Expanded Storage**, that has limited use under MVS. The application program does not normally access Expanded Storage, but can use supervisor services to directly or indirectly address Expanded Storage. IBM even called Expanded Storage "Extended Storage" for a while!

6. The term **Real Storage (RS)** is used to contrast with virtual storage.

7. **Random-Access Memory (RAM)** is storage that is available to be written to and read from.

My first choice for this book was to use "real storage." Real implies that you could go and touch the storage. You could ask your IBM

Customer Engineer to hand you the hardware card that contains a certain amount of "real" storage.[2] You cannot do that with "virtual" storage. "Real" is the term IBM uses for the modules that control Central Storage — "Real Storage Manager." The IBM manual *MVS/Extended Architecture System Programming Library: Initialization and Tuning* (GC28-1149) uses the term "Real Storage Overview."

It may seem that IBM cannot get the name straight. Part of it may be documentation that is being carried from generation to generation. A light appears at the end of the tunnel, however. IBM changed its software monitor — Resource Monitor Facility (RMF) version 4.1.1 — to use the term "Central Storage." IBM seems to have settled on Central Storage as the name for its "real" storage.

This book will use the term **Central Storage** to define the storage that is used to hold instructions and data while executing for an application. I hope, for our sakes, Central Storage is the final name.

1.2.5.   System/360 vs System/370 Architecture

The System/370 is different from the System/360 architecture in five areas:

1. Dynamic Address Translation (DAT). The MVS Software chapter will discuss how and why DAT is used by MVS to free up the application programmer from concerns about the hardware on which the application is running.
2. Multiprocessing. MVS is designed for multiprocessing systems. Applications that can take advantage of multiple CPUs in a computer are going to operate at maximum efficiency under MVS.
3. Protection Facilities. Applications can benefit from the System/370 extensions to the System/360 protection facilities.
4. Extended Real Addressing. The System/370 computers are designed to remove Central Storage considerations from the

---

2. Most hardware is delivered on "cards" or "boards" which can be plugged into the computer. This packaging allows the Customer Engineer or service person to replace a component quickly. The cards plug into a "mother board" with slots for the "cards."

application. The MVS/XA and MVS/ESA chapter will discuss this.

5. Channel Indirect Addressing. The System/370 has vastly different channel capabilities and Channel Indirect Addressing is the first of a series of hardware architecture changes that will enable the System/370 to grow into the 1990s. (We will discuss "channels" later; for now, consider them to be low-level paths for communication between pieces of hardware.)

1.3. OPERATING SYSTEMS

The goal of the System/360 architecture was to be able to use the same operating system on small to large hardware configurations. The software developers, however, created several operating systems to run on the System/360 architecture.

The System/360 and System/370 hardware have lived up to the promise. The software mainly has been upward compatible, but, as we shall see, the conversion from DOS to MVT to MVS was a little messy. The problems were not with application programs, but in the systems and operations areas. The conversion from MVS/370 to MVS/XA was relatively easy and should be accomplished by most installations in 2–3 months. The conversion from MVS/XA to MVS/ESA is as easy.

The question each company eventually will ask is "Should we convert from MVS/370 to MVS/XA (or from MVS/XA to MVS/ESA)?" In order to answer that question, you will have to understand the architecture.

The architecture defines the hardware and the operating system that can run on the hardware. When you understand the architecture, you can decide if the architecture (and therefore the operating system) will give the return on investment needed for the conversion.

1.3.1. Early Operating Systems

To place MVS into historical context, we will look at some alternatives to it and its predecessors. These operating systems were designed for and ran on much smaller computers than MVS, but their evolution is the basis for many of the MVS functions we see today.

Tape Operating System In the early 1960s the 140x and 70xx family of computers used a Tape Operating System (TOS). Guess where the operating system was in TOS? On magnetic tape, of course!

The Tape Operating System was loaded from tape into the computer, and the data center could then run the programs that the data center had developed to process the data center's tasks. Almost all programs were written at the data center for specific data center needs.

Disk Operating System (DOS) In the late 1960s and early 1970s the Disk Operating System (DOS) was used to run small System/360 machines. They were called **Disk** Operating Systems because the software was placed on a round platter (disk) in a Direct-Access Storage Device (DASD).

Figure 1.3 shows the storage map of DOS. The DOS system is loaded from DASD into the System/360 hardware. In DOS, the data center could have two applications running at the same time — Foreground (FG) and Background (BG). Why two partitions? Because once you get a single job started in a partition, you have resources — computer operators, DASD, tape drives — sitting idle. In many shops

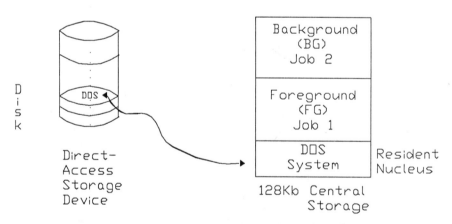

Storage Map of DOS

Figure 1.3   Disk Operating Systems (DOS). Disk Operating Systems have a very small operating system and two partitions. Each partition can run one "job" — one or more programs that read files and/or output files. DOS has a "Resident Nucleus" which contains the operating system programs. It also has areas for DOS to dynamically load modules for additional functions.

the Foreground ran an online terminal application and the Background ran test and production jobs.

It is interesting to note that the current PCs are as powerful as the early System/360s, but the developers of the Personal Computer DOS did not learn from the System/360 developers and create at least two partitions.

1.3.2. Operating System (OS) Types

As computers grew larger, the hardware was capable of running more than two applications at a time. Several versions of operating systems were conceived to use the larger machines.

IBM already had a DOS, so IBM used the term Operating System (OS) to distinguish the "new" from the old. OS was placed on a DASD and then loaded into the computer in order to run the data center's jobs.

Primary Control Program (PCP) Now, with all that buildup, I introduce the first OS — Primary Control Program (PCP). It ran just one application program at a time! Application programs were started one at a time. When each one was finished, another could be started. PCP did introduce the supervisor services that would be expanded to today's MVS. (Substitute PC/DOS for PCP and it remains true today! History *does* repeat.)

Probably the largest user of PCP was a large government agency. This was an excellent example of a PCP application — very large files, large amounts of processing during April, and important enough to warrant a medium to large computer.

With PCP, the application program was *never delayed* by another application program. PCP was the last mainframe operating system that could make that claim.

The last statement is a very important one and one often missed by people in the computer industry. The terms "multitasking" or "multiprogramming" are used to refer to having more than one set of application programs to choose from to turn control over to the computer resources. Once a choice is possible, the possibility for delay exists.

It takes time to turn control back to the waiting program. The first program's registers and program status word (PSW) must be saved. The second program's registers and PSW must be reloaded.

All other multitasking systems will delay a single application program. Certain applications can be given priority, but as the operat-

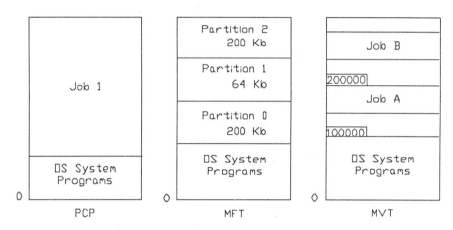

Figure 1.4   OS type Operating Systems. Primary Control Program (PCP) ran one application at a time. Multiprogramming with Fixed number of Tasks (MFT) ran installation-defined number of tasks at one time (up to 15). Multiprogramming with Variable number of Tasks (MVT) ran up to 15 tasks at a time.

ing system services other tasks, even the highest priority will be delayed slightly.

Multiprogramming with Fixed Number of Tasks (MFT)   Figure 1.4 shows PCP versus MFT. The greatest benefit of MFT was that the data center could run more than one task or application at a time.

The "fixed" part of this operating system was because the installation defined fixed size partitions to run work. The first partition was named P0, the second P1, and so forth to a maximum of 15. Numbering from zero is very typical in the computer industry. In most cases in System/370 architecture, the first of a list will be 0. Here is how a hypothetical data center might have defined their MFT partitions:

1. P0 is a 200K partition and can run programs that need up to 204,800 bytes of Central Storage.
2. P1 is a 64K partition and can run programs that need up to 65,536 bytes of Central Storage to run.
3. P2 is a 200K partition that can run programs that need up to 204,800 bytes of Central Storage

While one program waited (for a tape mount or even a tape read), the other program could execute instructions.

Multiprogramming with Variable Number of Tasks (MVT) A third type of OS operating system was MVT. Under MVT the data center did not have to decide in advance what sizes of programs could run. The application programmer specified what size to use, and MVT would allocate that size "region."

There is very little difference between a "partition" and a "region." This early example of different names for similar functions was a warning of things to come.

MVT was, therefore, much more flexible and was used by most large System/360 and System/370 computer centers. MVT grew up to become MVS. Figure 1.4 shows MVT tasks. The name "task" comes from the MVT control block that was used to maintain information about a program running under MVT — the **Task Control Block** (TCB). A **task** is any one unit of work running under an operating system. In most of these early operating systems a job only had one task. **Multitasking** is the term used to represent more than one task (and therefore TCB) running inside a single job.

Spooling Components There were other components which quickly became an integral part of the operating systems. Spooling components became the interface to the operating system — and therefore represented it to the users. The first of these was developed for the U.S. space exploration program just beginning in Houston, Texas. System/360 computers were an integral part of the preparation for launch. The software developers discovered that the productivity of all the people would improve if the computer center could deliver printed reports and cards faster. Say "spool," and for most people, an image of a spool of thread comes to mind, but **spool** is an acronym for **Simultaneous Peripheral Operation OnLine**.

The Houston Automatic Spooling Program II (HASP) was created to provide card read/punch and printer services. HASP was an optional part of the early MVT systems. Its successor is Job Entry Subsystem 2 (JES2).

A second method of controlling batch jobs and spooling systems was created. The Asymmetric Multiprocessing System Version 3 (ASP3) is another philosophy of how you control the system. ASP3 was used with MVT. The successor to ASP3 is Job Entry Subsystem 3 (JES3).

Although HASP or ASP were optional parts of previrtual operating systems, either JES2 or JES3 are required components of MVS. JES2 and JES3 are fully described in a separate chapter.

1.3.3.   Virtual Operating Systems

Even with all these combinations of operating systems and options, the hardware engineers were creating computers that were bigger and faster than the software developers could effectively use. Also, the companies who purchased these large, relatively expensive computers were writing large, complex application systems to be executed.

The first constraint reached was that insufficient Central Storage was available to certain large applications. (Refer back to Figure 1.4.) In the MVT system shown, unallocated storage that begins at location 100000 cannot be used together with storage starting at location 200000. The reason is that the two unallocated areas of memory are not contiguous. Job A is in between the two Central Storage addresses. This is called **memory fragmentation**. Memory fragmentation is the first problem overcome by virtual operating systems.

Another problem was recognized. If my program required a megabyte of storage to run on my computer, and you only had a half-megabyte of storage installed in your computer, then you could not run my program. The feature of the System/370 that overcomes this problem is virtual storage. IBM created a number of virtual operating systems.

DOS/VS and VSE   The developers of DOS added virtual storage to their systems. DOS/VS was the first version. DOS/VS Extended (DOS/VSE) was the follow-on product and is in use today.

Some installations are now considering converting from DOS/VSE to MVS. The instructions in your programs will run under MVS (they are on the same hardware) *but the supervisor service calls will not work*! Opens, closes, reads, writes, and other service requests are different for DOS/VSE and MVS. Usually you will only need to recompile the programs to get them to work, but to do that, you will need an environment that has both DOS/VSE and MVS.

IBM recommends very few Original Equipment Manufacture (OEM) products. The Computer Associates/University Computing Company package UCC TWO (or DUO as it was originally called) is an exception. IBM recommended UCC TWO as one method of running DOS programs under OS. (See IBM document DOS/VSE to MVS General Information Manual — GG24-1524-1).

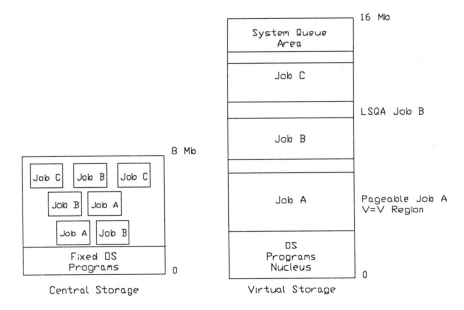

Figure 1.5   Single Virtual Storage (SVS). The Virtual Storage of 16 Mb was divided as needed by job partitions.

VS1: Virtual Storage 1   OS/VS1 is similar to MFT above with virtual storage. The operator can dynamically redefine partitions. Up to a maximum of 15 problem program "partitions" can be used to execute "jobs."

VS1 supports Customer Information Control System (CICS) and Information Management System (IMS) for online transaction processing functions. VS1 has a high level of compatibility with MVS and is an attractive distributed processing environment for MVS.

VS1 was "stabilized" effective February 23, 1984, which means that IBM will not make substantial enhancements to the operating system. The OS/VS1 Basic Programming Extensions (BPE) was created to add support under VS1 for additional hardware (e.g., 3848 Cryptographic Unit and 3375 DASD).

VS2: Single Virtual Storage (SVS)   Virtual Storage 2 is the name IBM gave to the virtual storage that was similar to MVT above with virtual storage. The operating system managed virtual storage dynamically — the operator did not have to "set partitions."

Figure 1.5 shows the virtual storage layout of OS/VS2 Single Virtual Storage (SVS).[3] Note that it is similar to MVT only now there seems to be 16 Mb of storage for application and system programs regardless of the size of Central Storage. In this example, 16 Mb of the programs and operating system can be run on an 8 Mb computer. Now we both have the "same size computers."

Memory fragmentation is also less of a problem because the application is made to believe that memory is contiguous, while it is really scattered throughout Central Storage. The operating system, not the application program, can manage the resources.

How does the Operating System do this? No program needs all of its memory all of the time, so the Operating System breaks the memory into equal-sized blocks called "pages," then ensures that only the pages needed at any given time are in Central Storage — the rest are saved on DASD. By shuffling pages between Central Storage and DASD in a complex "shell game," the Operating System gives the illusion that there is more Central Storage than exists.

The Operating System can now run more programs than would fit into real storage. This concept will be fully explained in later chapters, but for now recognize that job A, job B, and job C would not fit into the box labeled "Central Storage.", they would fit into the box labeled "Virtual Storage."

VS2: Multiple Virtual Storage (MVS) Figure 1.6 shows the virtual storage map of OS/VS1 Version 2 or MVS. MVS introduced the concept of **address spaces**. An address space is the complete range of computer addresses that a program can use. The program could be an application batch program, a terminal task or a system task. The term **Address Space Identifier** (ASID) is used to identify an address space.

Each address space or application program can access up to 16 megabytes of storage regardless of the amount of Central Storage. This is different from SVS above where *the sum of all* address spaces could not total more than 16 megabytes. The limit is raised to 2 gigabytes by MVS/XA and to 16 terabytes by MVS/ESA. There I go with those buzz words again! These terms will be explained in detail

---

3. SVS was called "VS2 Release 1" in some places. IBM now starts a series of programs with "Version," and "Release" is used to identify subsequent distributions.

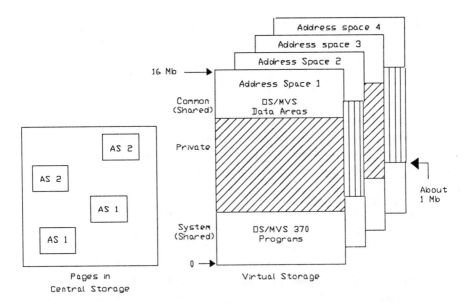

Figure 1.6 Multiple Virtual Storage (MVS). Each address space could access up to 16 Mb of address space. The Operating System uses the top and bottom of each 16-Mb address space.

in other chapters. For now, what is a megabyte? Big. What is a gigabyte? Really BIG! What is a terabyte? HUGE!

You will see in later chapters that the application programs do not really get 16 Mb (more like one-fourth to one-half that number) because the Operating System shares the upper and lower portions of virtual storage among all address spaces.

In Figure 1.6, the shaded areas are unique to an address space. The "OS/MVS Data Areas" and the "OS/MVS 370 Programs" area are *exactly the same* for each address space. These *common* areas are the areas MVS uses to communicate from one address space to another.

IBM has had many versions and releases of MVS. Two of the following are very important: MVS 3.8 (the base for all current MVS operating systems) and MVS System Product (the base for all additions to 3.8).

MVS Releases 1 and 2: MVS Release 1 was the first of the MVS Operating Systems.[4] It had many reliability problems. The system

---

4. Note that "version" was not used in those days.

would run for a few hours and then need total restart (called Initial Program Load (IPL)), but MVS provided many benefits to a data center:

1. "Unlimited" tasks (application programs and terminal tasks).
2. "Unlimited" virtual storage. The problems of managing partitions and shifting work were gone.
3. Fewer operator commands that involved structuring the Operating Systems environment. MVS came with management techniques that were needed in a large data center.

The definition of "unlimited" was subject to the amount of hardware a data center purchased or leased. Release 2 was a complete redistribution of MVS to fix a number of these problems.

MVS Release 3: In 1975, IBM bundled many changes into MVS and announced Release 3 of MVS. From 1975 to 1979 there were about a dozen subreleases of MVS which IBM numbered 3.1, 3.2, and so forth. In the spring of 1979 the most stable release — Release 3.8 — was announced. This release was not without its problems, as problems were discovered and fixes created daily.

One of the things not understood by most people in the profession — including most systems programmers — is that MVS 3.8 is *still* the base release of all subsequent releases of MVS. If you order MVS/XA version 2.2, you get MVS 3.8 plus some additional software.

During this time, IBM added functions to MVS by combining modifications or whole replacements of functional components under the name of **Selectable Units (SUs)**. Several of the most important ones were:

1. SU 04: Scheduler Improvements — these allowed more work to be performed efficiently.
2. SU 05 and 06: Supervisor Performance — improved the performance of the MVS supervisor routines.
3. SU 09: Sequential Access Method – Extended (SAM-E) — improved the performance of sequential access methods, mainly by increasing the default number of I/O buffers from 2 to 5.
4. SU 60: This addition placed the date in the VTOC entry of each data set that was accessed by MVS. The date would be used to record the last day a data set was used by a program.

DASD management programs use this today to archive data sets that have not been accessed in a specific period of time.[5]

MVS / Systems Extensions: A number of enhancements were developed to improve the Operating System. IBM bundled a number of these into a package and sold them as "Systems Extensions." Thus, MVS/3.8 SE was born. There were two versions — SE 1 and SE 2.

MVS / SP System Product Release 1 and 2: The second wave of for-a-price enhancements were called System Product, or SP. SP1 was referred to as Release 1. SP2 was referred to as SP Release 2. SP Release 2 was not delivered to the general public.

MVS / SP Version 1 Release 3: The developers released SP Release 3 in such a short time that most installations installed Release 3 and skipped Release 2. IBM called this MVS "Version 1 Release 3." The sharp observer started asking "What will Version 2 be?" MVS/SP Version 1 Release 3 is also called MVS/370 or MVS/SP 370.

1.3.4. eXtended Addressing (XA)

MVS SP Version 2 turned out to be the Operating System to support Extended Architecture. Figure 1.7 shows eXtended Addressing. Instead of 16 Mb, an address space is 2 Gb. The upper and lower portions are shared — just like MVS/370. You will see that MVS/370 is the basis for MVS/XA and MVS/ESA. As data processing needs grew, the need to access more data required larger processor complexes, more DASD online, and it became more important to the corporations that the data be accessible. IBM had learned its lessons well. The "next system" would emphasize Reliability, Availability, and Serviceability (RAS). It would be easy to install. The data center would not require a large volume of changes to install MVS/XA. First, IBM made it easy to add new hardware by making new hardware transparent to the application programmers. Now

---

5. The technique used is to let MVS save the date last used and turn on a bit to say the data set has been changed. The data set management system can back up data sets only if they have been changed and archive the data set based on rules established by the data center.

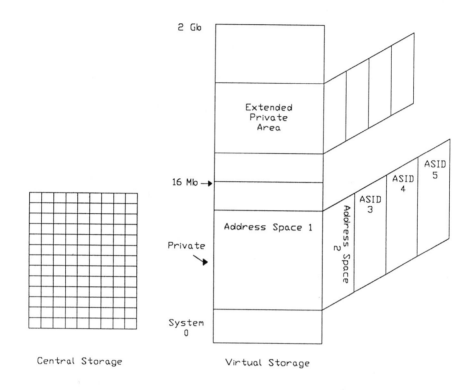

Figure 1.7   eXtended Virtual Storage (XA). "Extended Virtual" refers to 2 Gb of storage.

(MVS/XA 2.2) IBM is making it easier for the systems programmers to install new hardware.

In the fall of 1982, IBM selected several companies to install a new Operating System. These sites were called Early Support Program (ESP) sites. A company that participates in an ESP program agrees to install the software before the program is generally available and works with IBM and OEM vendors to test their applications running with the new IBM program. During the spring of 1983, MVS/XA became generally available.

The conversion from MVS/370 to MVS/XA is relatively easy — in the order of a few months of effort — *if your installation is prepared.* IBM calls this preparation "positioning." The hard, time-consuming part is getting "positioned."

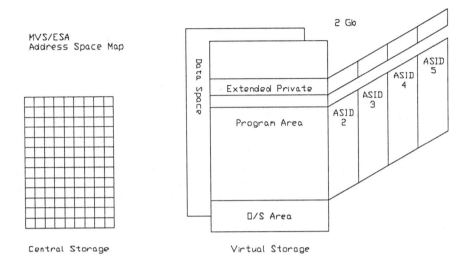

Figure 1.8   MVS/SP Version 3: Enterprise Systems Architecture. The next progression was to more Virtual Storages.

1.3.5.   MVS SP Version 3: Enterprise Systems Architecture

Figure 1.8 shows the MVS/ESA address space map. The same 2-Gb address space that was in MVS/XA is also available for programs and data. What is new is that there are up to 15 additional 2-Gb address spaces for data only. A subsequent chapter will discuss this format in detail.

MVS/ESA is no revolution in Operating Systems. The conversion from MVS/XA to MVS/ESA is as easy as the conversion from MVS/370 to MVS/XA. Much of the improvement is implemented in the microcode — the instructions in the computer that perform the work that application instructions want done. Much of ESA is designed to eliminate software piracy and discourage hardware manufacturers from copying IBM's developments.

1.3.6.   Other Operating Systems

MVS has a number of sister Operating Systems that are included here for your understanding that MVS is not the only operating system to run on System/370 architecture.

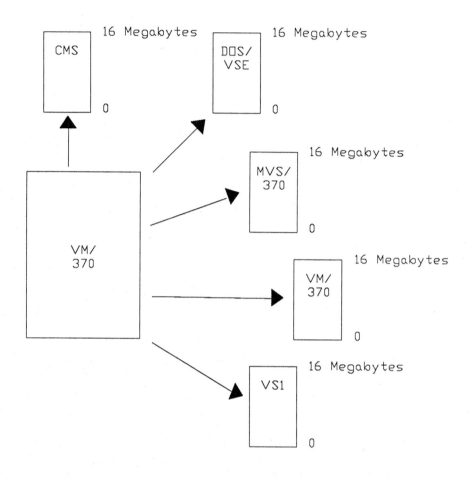

Figure 1.9   Virtual Machines. Virtual Machines refer to the emulation of an entire address space available to the software. For instance, an entire MVS operating system could occupy one virtual machine. A VM system could occupy one virtual machine under control of another virtual machine.

Virtual Machines Both IBM and the user community use Virtual Machine (VM) for production time sharing. VM plays an important part in MVS development and should be understood by anyone knowledgeable with MVS. MVS can run in a Virtual Machine (Address Space) under VM. The best use of this environment is for testing MVS, which is very productive. I have run production MVT and MVS systems under VM, and while it is difficult to tune, it can be done.

Figure 1.9 shows the map of VM/370. Note that each application under VM/370 has control of its own 16-Mb address space (or 2 Gb for VM/XA). Each of these Operating Systems are referred to as **guest** Operating Systems.

This makes VM an important production and testing tool. For example, one of those Virtual Machines could be a DOS/VSE Operating System running production DOS/VSE applications. Another could be a VS1 Operating System. Another could be a test MVS/370 Operating System. Another could be the Conversational Monitor System, a single-user mini Operating System written expressly for VM (actually CP-67 but that goes way back). This "CMS" should not be confused with "Cross Memory Services," discussed later.

Another guest Virtual Machine could be a test VM/370. Yes, for the first time an Operating System was designed to run a second copy of itself. What a wonderful testing and training tool!

Remember that IBM recommended DUO as a way to run DOS applications under MVS. VM is an even better way.

1.3.7. Airline Control Program/Transaction Processing Facility(TPF)

The first major need in the computer industry was to process transactions. The airline and hotel industry needed to track reservations. Credit card companies needed to process charge transactions and payments. Car rental agencies needed to reserve, rent, and return cars. Police departments needed to track responses. Electronic funds transfer agencies needed to track money transfers.

The common profile of these industries was that they all had thousands of transactions to process from thousands of terminals. The loss of a single transaction would be very costly. The cost of computer outage could be measured in hundreds or thousands of dollars for every minute of outage.

In the late 1950s and early 1960s, these needs could not be met by any of the existing Operating Systems. Between 1958 and 1963, IBM and American Airlines created the SABRE online reservation system for the airline industry. That system was the first to use the Airline Control Program (ACP). The ACP is another Operating System that is not MVS, but is included here briefly as it is an Operating System that runs on the same System/360 and System/370 hardware. Between 1970 and 1979, hardware and software enhancements were made to the existing system. In 1979, IBM introduced the Airline

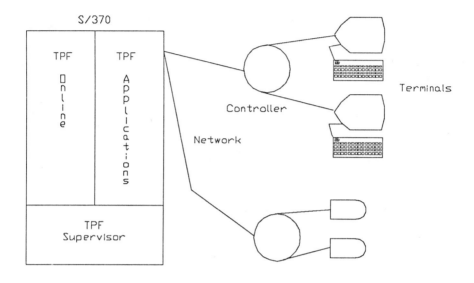

Figure 1.10   ACP/TPF. The Airline Control Program (ACP) /Transaction Processing Facility (TPF) processes thousands of terminals and gives very quick response. The TPF Supervisor is the Operating System on the System/370 hardware. The TPF Online modules control the processing for the network and the TPF applications run the transactions.

Control Program/Transaction Processing Facility ACP/TPF. In 1983, IBM introduced TPF version 2, which supported more than one computer (loosely coupled) and the 308x hardware.

In Figure 1.10 the ACP is controlling thousands of transactions per minute. Terminals spread across the country in a network access the same data and can reserve flights within a few seconds.

One of the hallmarks of the ACP is that the system can be interrupted and restarted within seconds with little or no loss of data. This feature is called **checkpoint/restart**. Of course, an outage occurs exactly when you are trying to straighten out your flight plans.

Figure 1.10 shows the layout of ACP and ACF/TPF. The TPF supervisor controls the TPF online processor and the TPF application programs. Each application is designed to be very short in duration. Applications are written in assembler language for the fastest possible processing.

TPF has some features that MVS does not now have. TPF can synchronize multiple computers' time-of-day clocks. TPF has sophisticated record processing and complete recovery of all file updates.

1.4. SUMMARY

Systems architecture characterizes the nature of hardware and software. Prior to System/360, hardware architectures were designed for specific tasks, which necessitated different software architectures. Improvements to architectures required costly conversions.

System control software for early machines was characterized by the peripherals used: TOS loaded applications from tape and DOS from disk.

In 1964, IBM announced System/360, a single hardware architecture to serve all needs. Having unified hardware meant that unified software could be written. Hardware improvement centered on performance rather than function; software improvement centered on function rather than conversion to new hardware.

Central Storage, upon which the central processor operated, was a costly and scarce resource. (Several other terms were used for Central Storage, including core, main, processor, and real storage.) It is no surprise that System/360 system control software (Operating Systems) was characterized primarily by techniques for managing Central Storage: PCP dedicated it to one application program; MFT split it into several fixed pieces, or "partitions"; MVT varied the number and size of these pieces, calling them "regions."

The invention of virtual storage freed systems from the constraints of Central Storage by supplementing them with less expensive, though slower, external storage devices in a manner transparent to most software by employing Direct Address Translation (DAT) hardware.

DAT's transparency allowed migration of existing Central Storage operating systems to a virtual storage environment: DOS became DOS/VS, MFT became OS/VS1, and MVT became OS/VS2, also known as "SVS" (Single Virtual storage.) OS/VS2 still had regions like MVT, but the regions were carved out of a single large (though virtual) address space.

The second version of OS/VS2 was the first MVS. MVS is similar to PCP, in that a single job sees itself and MVS in a single address space. MVS, of course, controls many more than just one address space.

MVS has had a long life. Obtaining adequate reliability required three releases, and the third release, version 3.8 System Product (SP), is the base for all releases to date and is also called MVS/370.

MVS/SP Version 2 became MVS/XA, and MVS/SP Version 3 became MVS/ESA. This book is concerned primarily with MVS/370,

MVS/XA, and MVS/ESA, this group representing the major splits in MVS architecture.

Operating systems other than MVS can use System/370: VM is a hypervisor which not only sports virtual storage but extends the idea to virtual machines as well. VM is self-virtualizing, meaning it can even run itself. ACF/TPF is an Operating System optimized for reliable, fast transaction processing.

We will look into the depths of MVS for the remainder of the book. The reader is cautioned not to overlook the other Operating Systems. They are useful and in some cases may be the best choice for your company.

Do not get caught in the trap of always wanting the newest. The newest may not be the best. Beware that IBM will not support old systems for an indefinite time. You risk staying on an "old" system until IBM stops support of the Operating System.

Throughout the rest of the book, we will refer to the IBM hardware architecture as System/370. The reader should note that the hardware does have differences. The differences should not be noticeable by the application, but they are vital to the Operating System.

A large number of people are associated with the MVS environment. The following titles will be used throughout this book to indicate generic groups of people. Each group plays an integral part in the success of a data center:

1. **Data center users** are the customers of the data center. They may be programmers, accountants, clerks, vice presidents. Anyone who uses the services of the data center directly (usually on terminals) or indirectly (reports or information) is a data center user.

2. **Operations** personnel are the people who are in or near the hardware and are charged with the responsibility of issuing commands and using the MVS software and hardware to perform the goal of the data center, and often are positioned as the first to notice system problems.

3. **Production Control** personnel are responsible for the batch jobs and online systems that manipulate the "live" files for the corporation.

4. **Systems Analysts and Programmers** design the systems and write the programs that execute on the data center hardware. There are usually several levels, from the person

who only writes programs to the more senior person who designs and installs the systems.

5. **Systems Programmers** are responsible for the MVS software and hardware. They build MVS, apply modifications, install utilities, and ensure that the data center hardware and software can support the above people.

Before we start the technical discussions, we will investigate what an Operating System such as MVS should do for the end user and the data center, for it is very true — if you do not know where you are going, then any road will get you there, and you may not know where you are after you arrive (or what harm you may unknowingly have done).

2

End User and Data Center Considerations

2.1. END USER BENEFITS

The goal of a computer center is to accept commands/programs from the end users and produce reports or actions that are beneficial to the end user. While scurrying around to complete a day's work at the computer center, this goal must be kept in mind.

The user wants to manage — create, access, delete — files of information. The terminal that is used for online access should be able to share data and send messages from one to another. The cost of software should be shared among all its users. Figure 2.1 shows the most common of these, the **sort**. The sort will take a file in any sequence and rearrange it into another sequence.

2.1.1. Resource Management — Files

Figure 2.2 shows the most precious asset of a computer center, the files that store the data gathered by the end users. Once entered, the data can be displayed or used anywhere terminals are located that are attached to the computer. The easier it is for the end user to use and manipulate his data, the better the computer center is performing its directive. Subsecond response time at a terminal is useless if the message returned is "your data is gone."

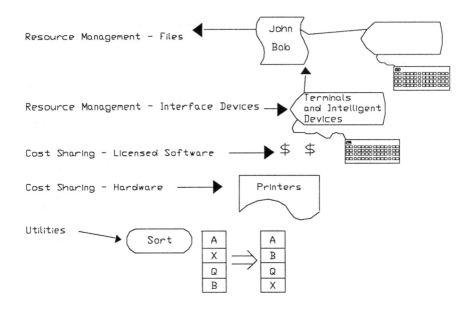

Figure 2.1   End user benefits: cost. The end user in the MVS environment benefits from several areas. The cost of providing services is shared by multiple departments or user groups. MVS is one of the most cost-effective systems to create this environment.

Efficient management of data consists of several components that should be agreed upon by the owners of the data and the data processing department:

1. Standard file formats. An Operating System should provide structured file formats to free the applications programmer from the need to design and program at too detailed a level. If the programmer/analyst chooses a nonstandardized file format, then each user of the data must know the format and write at a very detailed level (called physical I/O) to access the data. If the Programmer/Analyst selects a standard file format, such as the MVS partitioned access file format, then any other MVS user can access the data without knowing the structure of the data set. Application programmers need only to issue "READ" (or "GET") and "WRITE" (or "PUT") statements. The "READ" or "WRITE" instructions call MVS programs, which access the data. The name given to the modules that actually read or write the data is **access method.**

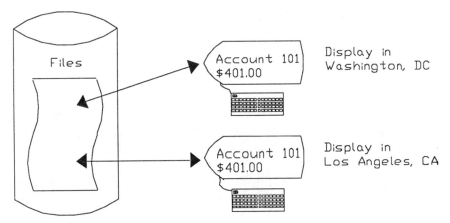

Figure 2.2   End user benefits: 1. Resource Management – files. Data files are the most important asset of a data center. The management of data is the primary concern of a data center. Data sharing is important. The figure shows that a terminal located in Washington, DC, can display the same information as a terminal in Los Angeles if the data base is "centralized" under MVS.

2. Standard allocation methods. Operating System routines should assist in the task of defining the area for the files to be placed. The definition of data areas or "data sets" under MVS is fairly complex, but there is great flexability.
3. Device independence. About every two years, IBM introduces new and improved Input/Output devices. One of the IBM goals is to have applications start using the new devices as soon as they are ready. If the application only uses standard access methods, then as soon as IBM changes the access method, the application can start using the new devices. MVS provides device independence.
4. Asset protection. There is a whole industry concerned with protection of an enterprise's assets in the form of security and audit of data processing. I agree with many of their premises and encourage an enterprise to ensure that business continuance plans are in place and tested. Another section of this chapter will discuss disaster recovery considerations.
    To paraphrase an old cartoon, I have seen the enemy and the enemy is us. Asset protection is much more than attacks from within or without. Accidental deletion, human errors, hardware and software errors really cause more problems than "the enemy." MVS provides *protection* only if the data center employees have the knowledge to implement all needed procedures and practices.

Absolute protection is impossible. Any protection costs real resources to implement. Each company must decide on the resources it wishes to pay for protection, then implement that level of protection.

Ironically, although the highest paid manager may have the ultimate responsibility for asset protection, it is often the troops in the trenches — operations staff and Systems Programmers — who execute this protection. It is therefore worthwhile to ensure that they are given effective training — formally or informally — toward that end. Involving them in the decision making and planning gives them a personal stake in the outcome. Quality is only number one when *every member of the team* is practicing quality. Systems programmers: Listen to your operators — *really* listen. Operators: Do not be afraid to speak up. You are the last line of defense in a very complex world. Programmer/Analysts: Ask questions, talk among yourselves. Become egoless![1] Managers: create an environment that does not emphasize blame. All employees of the data center are a team. If someone makes a mistake, find a way to prevent the mistake or minimize the consequences of the mistake.

2.1.2.   Resource Management — Interface Devices

Figure 2.3 shows that MVS provides the end user access to data, either by displaying the data on a terminal or downloading the data to a Personal Computer. The data center usually provides a Data Base/Data Communication (DB/DC) interface such as the Customer Information Control System (CICS), Information Management System (IMS), or Data Base 2.[2] Applications written for the DB/DC system display data on the screen in a format agreed upon by programming and user departments.

---

1. The term "egoless programming" describes the confidence to go to another and say "help." It was described in The Psychology of Computer Programming by Gerald Weinberg, pp 56-60; ISBN 0-442-29264-3; 1971; published by Nostrand Reinhold Company, N.Y.
2. IMS and CICS contain a "data communication" component to access terminals. IMS provides a hierarchical data base system. DB2 provides a relational data base system.

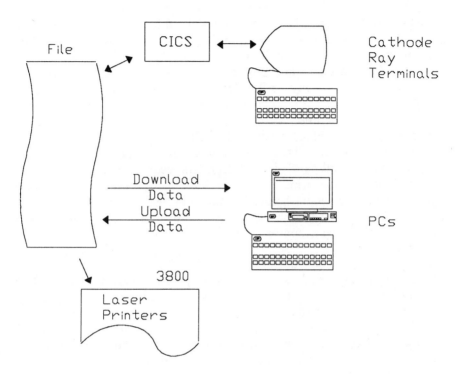

Figure 2.3 End user benefits: 2. Resource management – interface devices. To access the data, the end user needs interface to the computer center. The access may be a terminal, a "unit record" device such as printers, or intelligent workstation such as a Personal Computer (PC).

The first consideration in allowing the end user to access data is the interface devices used to access, process, and obtain output from the computer center.

Terminal Control In the 1960s and early 1970s, the computer industry was batch oriented. Programs were executed by reading in punched computer card decks. Output was printed reports or listings. In the 1980s, many homes have microprocessors that are more powerful than those early processors, and they have access to their data on cassette tape, floppy diskettes, and hard disks.

Desktop terminals are now a "normal" way to access the data stored at a computer center. The access may be via the IBM Customer Information Control System (CICS) or other Data Base/Data Communications (DB/DC) program using VTAM, TCAM, or Roll Your Own (RYO) terminal control programs.

The terminals may be Cathode Ray Terminals (CRTs), which are also called "nonintelligent" terminals. These hardware items attach to the system and display information that is formatted by the MVS system. CRTs are the most cost-effective way to access the MVS system. The terminal may be 24, 32, or 43 lines per screen and 80 or 132 characters per line. The terminal may be monochrome (black and white, amber and white, or green and white) or color (usually four colors — red, blue, green, and white).

The terminal may be a Personal Computer or "intelligent terminal." The "intelligent" derives from the requirement that the terminal have an Operating System and application programs inside to access a network. One benefit of the intelligent terminal is that it can **upload** data from the PC to the mainframe or it can **download** data from the mainframe to the PC.

Unit Record Device Scheduling and Control   Unit record devices are no longer only card readers, card punches, and impact printers. They are expensive laser printers that will produce high-quality pages and automate documentation.

These printers are the real workhorses of the MVS environment. While most data is viewed online on terminals, most organizations need volumes of printed material (reports to outside agencies, write paychecks, bills to customers). These print at *12,000 lines per minute* or *three pages per second.*

As the hardware became more expensive, it became necessary to gather it into a central location and control the devices by scheduling usage. For the most part, the control of these devices is performed automatically with JES2 and JES3.

2.1.3.   Cost Sharing — Licensed Software

Figure 2.4 shows that developmental programmers create programs that are of use to the general population. These software tools are sold or leased to companies to make them more productive. The same is true for the MVS Operating System itself. The charges can be:

1.   One-time charges. The developer can charge a single fee for the product. This is usually the largest fee. After all, the entire cost of development plus profit must be divided by the number of people who pay for software. The problem with this method is that the seller and buyer are separated after the payment.

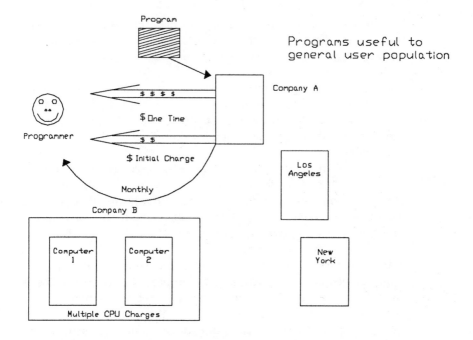

Figure 2.4   End user benefits: 3. Cost sharing – licensed software. All software that is used in computing costs money. The money is either spent on in-house written programs or purchased as part of a system from an outside vendor.

The application developer does not need to do any more work as there is no more money forthcoming. The buyer may need support for the software, but that would imply a new business transaction.

2. Initial charge with periodic maintenance fees. This is the most popular method of paying for MVS. The initial fee is to offset the development costs, and the monthly maintenance fees force both parties to maintain the product.

3. A monthly lease fee. There is usually no one-time charge (good to get started), but as with most leases, this is the most expensive prospect. Many of these lease plans include a minimum number of months to pay for the product. Twelve months is the most expensive, 24 is slightly less, and 36 is usually the least expensive.

   As with all contracts, be sure you read the fine print. The contract usually has clauses similar to the ones used with bank certificates of deposits — if nothing is done, the lease restarts for the same length of time as the original contract. Do you really want that contract to be automatically renewed for an additional 36 months by your inaction?

As computers got larger, and as data centers started having more than one computer in a facility, and as a company had more than one physical location for computing, there arose the opportunity to charge for these additional processing locations:

1. **Multiple computer charges.** Developers discovered that, if you charge a flat fee for a product, the purchaser may use the product on multiple computers. Thus, the additional charge per "CPU" at each site. IBM charges for second and subsequent computers at the same site at a discounted rate from the base price. The fee should always be discounted (probably more than many vendors do discount) because the vendor only has one group of people or applications to support. I believe the fee is valid because the more applications (requiring more CPU power), the more support a vendor is likely to be asked to do. One good management technique to minimize costs to an installation is to isolate function on one computer (MVS on computer 1, VM on computer 2) and only pay the license charges for that computer.

2. **Additional site charges.** Developers discovered that computer centers have multiple physical locations, thus the "additional site" fees. The same reasoning applies to these fees, but it may be more expensive for a vendor because there usually is a whole new audience for support at a different location.

3. **Computer system size changes.** As you will see later, computers come in all sizes. The difference in size between the smallest 370 and the largest 370 may be many orders of magnitude. IBM has begun to charge differently for different system sizes. This trend will continue and expand. The most affected part of a data center by this change is the budget. If the data center upgrades a computer, each contract should be studied to determine the software cost differentials, and the cost should be a part of the computer upgrade decision.

The average computer center has discovered that, as the cost of hardware is going down, the cost of the software to drive the hardware is increasing. Some years ago, the user could buy a small 370 computer for less than $300,000. If that value were prorated over 36 months, the charge would be $8,333 per month. The software license fees to run the operating system and all necessary software would be over $10,000 *per month* in licensing fees.

In spite of the recent interest in decentralized computing, two facts will ensure the survival of the large computer center: the cost of software and the need to share corporate data.

2.1.4. Cost Sharing — Hardware

Figure 2.5 shows specialized hardware, such as mass storage devices and laser printers, that have been around for some time. The ability to share these resources is well established.

The 1990s will increase the requirements for graphic and color representation of data. This will require the purchase of such new items as color printers which can produce graphic prints, color foils, and slides.

In the early 1980s it sometimes cost $50,000 to own hardware to produce color slides from graphic representations of online data. In the late 1980s Personal Computers could do the same for $10,000. The cost of producing graphics is coming down, but as they say in Congress, $10,000 here, $10,000 there, and pretty soon it adds up to real money!

2.1.5. Utilities

An enterprise can best select a utility only if it carefully evaluates — and tests — the vendor products. One of the first utilities that a computing center provides is the SORT/MERGE utility. Figure 2.6 shows the sort/merge as an example. The SORT feature will input one file and output a new file that is in a collating sequence — ascending or descending. The MERGE feature takes either multiple files or two files that are already in sorted order and merges them into a single file.

When the computer center evaluates the different sort/merge programs, the data center should use the sort programs at its own data center on its own data and compare the results. This procedure is called a **benchmark**.

Once selected, the data center should provide documentation and support for the utility.

Other utilities are usually available at each computer center. They may be written by the Systems Programmers or high-level applications programmers who do not accept "we do not have a utility to do

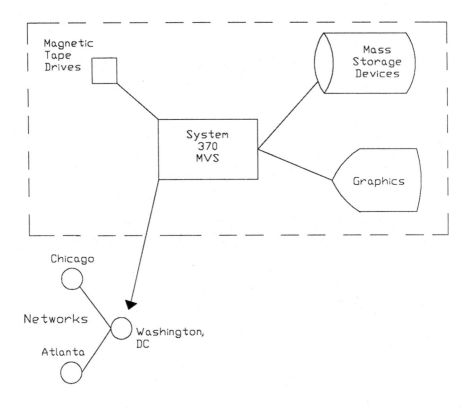

Figure 2.5 End user benefits: 4. Cost sharing – specialized hardware. Expensive hardware costs can be shared by many users if it is centrally located. In this example, if a PC user at the central computer center in Washington, DC, bought graphics software and a laser printer, then only that user could do graphics. If the data center purchased the software and printer and connected it to MVS, that user could do graphics. The MVS solution would be more expensive, but the second graphics user would not have to buy the software. Graphics could be used in Atlanta by just purchasing a printer.

that" for an explanation. These programs may not have documentation, or the documentation may exist only in the form of comments in the source of the language used to create the program. Utilities are the "hidden gold" of a computer center.

The users of the data center may have to go prospecting to find some of the hidden gold. The main reason I have found is that data center management does not provide time and facilities to document these utilities well enough for other users. The data center should provide the resources needed. The company gets better productivity,

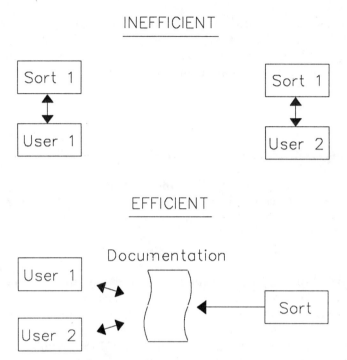

Figure 2.6   End user benefits: 5. Utilities. As specific requirements appear, the data center can provide customized routines and programs to accomplish the goals of the enterprise. In this example, the inefficient data center will have users writing or purchasing their own tools such as the sort. An efficient data center will select, document, train, and provide support for the user community for each utility.

the author gets pride of authorship, and the users get much better systems.

Another most important utility is the backup and restore utilities of a data center. Properly installed and maintained, a data center can have a series of jobs run each night to back up every data set that has been changed the previous day. Periodically, the entire DASD volume can be backed up. If data center users accidentally destroy data, the most they should lose is the last 24 hours. This process is called **incremental backup**. I have routinely recovered mainframe data sets after disaster struck. I recovered the entire source code for a large government agency's legal information retrieval system by having another backup and understanding Direct Access Storage Devices (DASD). A two-year project would have been lost!

The Personal Computer world, on the other hand, is a time bomb waiting to go off. I have seen the entire mailing list of a Fortune 500 company's publicity magazine lost because it was on a Personal Computer hard disk that was accidentally erased without having a back-up.

2.2. DATA CENTER MANAGEMENT BENEFITS

MVS provides many features that allow the data center management to operate a data center in a cost-effective manner. Accounting may not be used by every data center, but every data center should strive toward minimizing costs. Some sort of accounting is vital to that task. Error control can also be delegated a lower role, but eventually the data center will come to grips with errors. Errors are just too expensive. Work flow management is probably the first of these topics to be addressed by a data center. Nothing focuses the data center management like a batch test job locking out the vice president's reports. Disaster recovery is an often overlooked item until a disaster or near disaster happens. MVS provides data organizations that answer most needs. We will investigate them.

2.2.1. Accounting

All the costs of a data center must be paid for. If each user could afford a 512-Mb 309x to process his or her TSO, Batch, and DB/DC requirements, then we would not need accounting, but each user cannot afford the maximum processing he needs at any instant in time, so we have a need for accounting. The best accounting is to charge real money (coin of the realm) for the resources consumed, but within the company this may be impossible. Some companies utilize "funny money" as an internal allocation tool. Some attempt should be made to have the individual departments budget and accept responsibility for the decisions they make that cost resources. For any accounting, you will need several items:

1. Information collected about each user.
2. Cost of each resource.
3. An accurate, repeatable billing mechanism.

This book is on MVS concepts and not billing, so why do I bring up this topic? Because there are some MVS concepts (and hardware concepts) that affect **accountability**.

Accountability is being able to report who is using the resources of the data center. In Figure 2.7, user A, consuming only 1/21 of the computer resources, should "pay" for 1/21 of the cost of running the data center. What if user A returns twice user B's value to the company? That is a management problem.

Repeatability is the measure of consistency between a measurement today and a measurement at some future time *on the same hardware*. Said another way, a fixed usage of resources used today should cost the same as the same resources used a month later, assuming the same cost to provide those services.

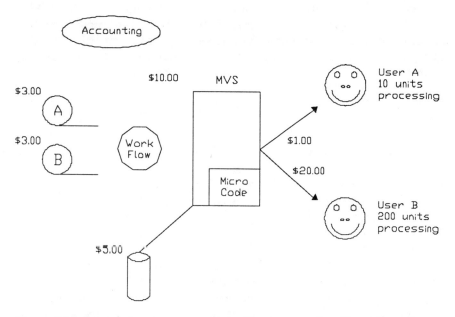

Figure 2.7 Data center management benefits — accounting. The data center management is charged with running an efficient data center. The user departments are charged with efficiently using the resources. Accounting for the resources used is necessary. In this example we see two tape drives that cost $3 per unit of time, a Processor Complex that costs $10 per unit of time, and DASD that costs $5 per unit of time. The total cost is $21 per unit of time. If user A uses 10 units and user B uses 200 units, then user A should be charged $1 and user B should be charged $20. In real life, of course, it is never that simple. Tapes get charged by the reel and tape mount. DASD gets charged by the track-day. CPU gets charged by the CPU second.

Variability is the measure of consistency between *executions on different hardware*. For example, a fixed amount of CPU cycles on a 4381 should be some multiple of the CPU cycles on a 3081. If the hardware changes, the cost should likewise change.

Repeatability and **variability** can also be affected by new MVS software, hardware, and the microcode that drives the hardware. A term often used to mean the combination of hardware and microcode is **firmware**.

As MVS is changed by IBM and the installation, these measures will change. The data center needs to understand and manage the software and firmware changes which affect repeatability and variability.

Firmware changes do affect the data center. Once, the microcode for 3083 processors at microcode level 208297A moved a half megabyte of hardware save area to below the 16-megabyte line. Data centers (and users) lost a half megabyte of Central Storage after that microcode level was applied. Is that worth tracking? I think so. If a program was run before the firmware change, it may cost more to run after the firmware change, depending on the methods used by the accounting routines.

2.2.2.   Error Logging and Recovery

Figure 2.8 shows the error logging and recovery process. Hardware and software errors are expensive to the end user and the data center. The data center usually does not get paid for jobs underway when the system crashes. Ideally, the errors should be nondisruptive.

At point 1 in the figure, a tape error occurs. MVS performs error recovery (2) and writes a record (to SYS1.LOGREC) recording the error. Software can also detect errors (3). Sometimes the recovery routine corrects the error and puts out an error message about the error. Sometimes the error cannot be overcome. A record is written and the task is abnormally terminated.

Hardware errors should not crash the system. In the figure, a tape drive encounters an error reading a tape. The problem could be with the tape drive, the tape itself, or the connectors that connect the tape drive to the hardware. MVS notes the error, writes an error to a logging data set (SYS1.LOGREC), and tries to recover.

Software errors should not crash the system. In Figure 2.8, suppose the program is trying to add one to a counter. The counter may

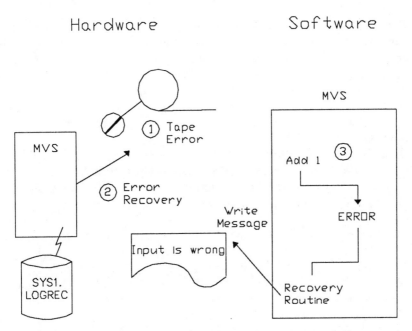

Figure 2.8   Data center management benefits — error logging and recovery. Errors in the software and/or hardware should be logged and recovery actions documented to minimize the impact, yet allow management of errors.

be defined improperly. MVS will record the error and try to recover from the error.

Neither software nor hardware errors should *ever* damage user data that existed before the processing began without forcing an abend to warn the user that the data is damaged. Recovery routines should ensure that the processing is completely recovered or the task abnormally terminated. Recovery job streams should ensure the data is restored correctly before continuing the task.

MVS error recovery is now so complete that the MVS system should not have to be restarted until a scheduled time. *Every* outage that is not scheduled should be tracked. What caused the crash should be fixed and not ignored. The computing industry is the very best at autopsies. We must never let our ability to explain what happened cloud our real goal of never letting errors happen in the first place.

A corollary to this is that the newest is not necessarily the best. The 3350 device was less reliable for its first four years than the 3330. The 3380 DASD is more reliable, but in its first four years, several manufacturing problems caused them to be unreliable.

Most catastrophic errors begin with warnings. The disk drive that is having soft errors will eventually have uncorrectable ones and damage data. The software error that terminates a user job and gets logged will eventually terminate one of the vital system components and crash the system. *Keep up with the warnings.*

Error logging and tracking is the responsibility of the data center. The MVS system utility that reports on errors is generically referred to as **LOGREC** or **EREP**.

I advise that the data center manage the error reporting. Do not just run the utility to print errors and merely give it to your vendor. Establish a separate tracking function in your organization. The following are functional areas of error recording and recovery:

1. Error logging is the responsibility of the operating system. In MVS system routines write to a data set — SYS1.LOGREC — whenever a software or hardware error is encountered.

2. Error recovery is the responsibility of the vendor. The software and hardware should attempt wherever possible to overcome the error and continue processing.

3. Hardware repair is the responsibility of the hardware vendor. There are a number of ways the vendor and data center management can agree on maintenance. Time and materials is the term used to identify the way most of us repair things in our house. If something breaks, we call a repair shop, wait for them to get there, and pay them for the time they spent and the cost of materials. Maintenance contracts ensure that you will get service for a fixed monthly fee. IBM generally will service its maintenance contract customers first.

4. Software repair is the responsibility of the software vendor. The software should have error detection and recovery built into it. You should scrutinize the contract very carefully. In most cases, you should be successful in negotiating contract additions and changes that will be less one-sided. Some things to consider for most software contracts are:

    a. A statement that the software will not open MVS to integrity exposures.

    b. A statement that the company will upgrade for new versions of MVS within a certain time period. Be specific about the number of months.

    c. A statement which ensures that your company is protected if the software company goes out of business or abandons the product. The U.S. government has a standard contract

clause which requires the company to place the source in
an escrow account in case of failure.

5. Software and hardware repair verification is the responsibility
of the data center. New devices should not be placed into service until they are certified — after installation — as being
functional. Repaired devices should be tested thoroughly after
they have been returned to the data center as "fixed" devices.
Testing should be done with tools obtained from the vendor,
from outside sources or by tools developed at the data center.
Do not do as one co-worker did in the early days — place the
volume in service so that a large number of users' temporary
data sets got allocated. His theory was, if the device was still
broken, people would notice and tell him!

The vendor should be held responsible for providing what the data
center is paying for. This includes hardware that is fixed correctly,
on the first attempt, in a reasonable period of time. Add up the
maintenance fees you are paying for all the hardware on the computer room floor. This is a good indicator of the level of service you
should be receiving.

2.2.3. Work Flow Management

Figure 2.9 shows the components of work flow management in the
data center. The data center should manage the work flow so that
the end user gets what he pays for in a timely manner within the
guidelines of the enterprise.

Maximize Utilization of Real Resources Resource utilization — CPU,
I/O, and Central Storage — should be maximized by the data center.
CPU and Central Storage are easily shared. MVS gives control to
one ASID and then to another. I/O devices are more complex to
share. Tape drives are the ultimate serial device. MVS address
spaces cannot share a tape drive, so MVS must assign a tape drive
to an ASID if the ASID needs to access a tape file.

In the example in Figure 2.9, the MVS system called "BATCH" has
three tape drives. A job running on the MVS system called "TSO1"
needs two tape drives. MVS JES2 systems cannot share tape drives
between Processor Complexes. (JES3 systems, as you will see, have a
Global Processor Complex controlling device assignment and do
share tape drives.) Non-IBM software vendors (sometimes called

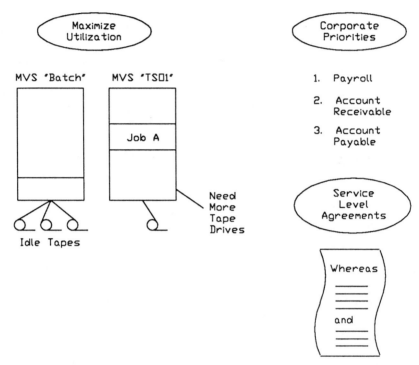

Figure 2.9   Work flow management. The goals of the corporation can be accomplished if the work flow is managed in the priority order of the importance of the work. In this example, the MVS system called "batch" has three tape drives. A job running on "TS01" needs two tape drives, but only one is available. The data center should provide for sharing devices. The corporate priorities (goals) and the service level agreements with the user community should be documented.

"Original Equipment Manufacturers" or OEMs, however, have software to provide this service for JES2.

Exercise Control over Corporate Priorities   The management of a data center and the users should agree on the priorities under which the work will be processed. Once agreed upon, MVS has numerous controls to effect these management decisions.

In most cases, the data center will want online access to have higher priority than batch work, because the online activity has a person waiting for the result and people are expensive resources. In most cases, the data center will want production work completed before test work. Within these broad classifications are exceptions the MVS software can and should handle.

Service Level Agreements Service Level Management is the process of agreeing upon the objectives of the corporation that is running the data center and supplying service. All data centers have Service Level Agreements: They are either specific or implied.

Too often, the data center staff looks on service level objectives as the enemy. There are several reasons for both sides (data center and user) to agree on these objectives and formalize them:

1. Service level objectives force agreement on the service which will be provided.
2. Service level objectives quantify the real, measurable human expectations about service. If you are waiting in line at the grocery counter in the "big basket" line, then you do not mind waiting several minutes. If you are in the express checkout line, however, any wait of more than a few minutes is intolerable.
3. Service level objectives minimize conflicts between data center and users. The last thing this team needs is to hotly contest what is "trivial" response time. Response time should be measured at the terminal, not at the Processor Complex. Network delays are delays to the user!

Service level agreements should have a method to measure and report on the success or failure of the data center to meet agreed levels. If you can measure something, you can manage it. Both sides are cautioned to avoid agreements which cannot be met. I have seen service level agreements which state that a system will be up 8:00 A.M. to 8:00 P.M. That is not possible 100 percent of the time. Some percentage must be stated — 95 percent of the time, for example. Otherwise, any outage is a violation of the agreement.

Some of the items which you should consider for Service Level Agreements are:

1. Establish tape mount service. The number of tape drives should be spelled out and a premium paid for requesting service that is above the normal ability of the data center to mount tapes. The policies for "foreign" tapes should be spelled out. The user should not expect to bring a tape to the data center and have it mounted in five minutes. Users should not keep tapes outside the data center.
2. Data set naming conventions. The data center should develop, document, and get agreement on data set naming conventions. All data sets must be cataloged.

3. Data set recovery procedures should be established. Recovery of the data set should be the user's responsibility except after a hardware failure. Verification of the data restored should be the user's responsibility.

4. Applications should be able to regress by a certain period of time (one day, one week) to recover from logical errors in the data. The user department should be responsible for maintaining changes made during that time.

The end user should agree to specify the resources which are expected to be used and should further agree that, if these limits are exceeded, then the job/session will either be cancelled or reduced in priority to a lower level. The drastic step of cancelling is usually done by JES or SMF exits. The action must be automatic to avoid unequal enforcement. The reduction in service is accomplished with SRM tuning parameters.

Processing should be classified by the user and data center into the type of workload the processing represents. If the job is an online Data Base or Data Communication system (such as the Customer Information Control System (CICS)), then an agreed-upon job name or account number can be set by MVS to get special treatment. Thus, CICS could be given resources ahead of a batch sort.

2.2.4. Disaster Recovery Considerations

The architecture of MVS allows the *properly prepared* data center to design, test, and implement a complete disaster recovery plan. Some of the things that should be considered for a disaster recovery plan are included here. The list cannot be complete, because a disaster recovery plan is unique for each installation. The data center should build the plan with the cooperation of all parties. The data center and the user departments should test the plan, either by physically going offsite and testing the plan or, at the very least, walking through the plan testing the pieces that the data center can test.

1. Choose between a **hot site** or a **cold site**. A hot site is a disaster location that contains most if not all of the hardware and software needed to run the data center applications. The site may be at another location owned and/or operated by your company, or some outside vendor may provide the hot site hardware. The hardware must match up with the software. If you are running MVS/ESA, you cannot have a 3084 at your "hot

site." (MVS/ESA does not run on a 3084.) A cold site is a location that provides air conditioning, raised floor, electrical connections, and water ready to install the needed equipment. The data center is responsible for finding and providing the equipment. The cold site is substantially less expensive than the hot site, but takes considerably longer to start up.

2.   Carefully choose a disaster recovery team to design and document the disaster recovery process.

3.   Document the disaster recovery procedures. The disaster recovery manual may have chapters such as:

   a.   Names and phone numbers for all key personnel. The data center personnel, the applications departments, software and hardware vendors, and emergency numbers for every service that is necessary to the data center should be included.

   b.   Escalation plan for notification purposes. Checklist and damage assessment procedures should spell out what should be done and how it should be accomplished for various types of disasters:

      i.   Utility disasters — outages of one or more utilities such as an electrical outage.

      ii. Equipment disasters — loss of one or more pieces of equipment. IBM has a series of procedures for isolating single points of failure called **Component Failure Identification Analysis (CFIA)**, which would focus on each piece of software and hardware and determine what could and should be done if that component failed. This was a marketing tool designed to encourage the data center to buy backup equipment, but it is a good idea. In one CFIA that I participated in, we identified that a large part of our MVS paging was dependent on a floppy diskette drive (to load the microcode) and there was not a spare in the region.

      iii. Building disasters — where the building is partially or completely destroyed.

      iv. Regional disasters — where substantial parts of the city or area where the data center is located are damaged. Flooding, hurricanes, ice, and snow are examples of regional disasters that could affect data processing.

      v.   Communications disasters — where the capability of communicating across phone lines is disrupted. A fire in a remote building could completely terminate the data center's ability to service its remote customers. That happened in Chicago during 1988. A fire in a suburban Chicago telephone switching building completely terminated telephone communication for thousands of subscribers for weeks and even months. What would happen to your business if your users could not access their data?

c. Backup storage — location and access. All offsite materials should be stored at a location other than the primary data center. The contents and usage of these backup media should be documented.

d. Lists. Lists of computer forms, types, and count of equipment needed. Lists of supplies and location from which they are ordered.

e. Copies of tested procedures that are used to restore whole DASD volumes and data sets.

4. Copies of manuals — IBM and other vendor documentation. The primary ones needed are Device Support Facilities (DSF) to initialize new volumes, Data Facility Data Set Services (DFDSS), or whatever backup programs your data center uses, and MVS utilities and messages manuals.

5. Think up ways to make disaster recovery easier:

a. Protect a second set of backup tapes. Keep them offsite or in a fireproof safe. Fireproof safes may not be waterproof. If there is the possibility of water damage, keep a second set of tapes.[3]

b. Keep spare cables above the raised floor. Many data centers are tempted to store extra computer cables below the floor. If water gets in there, the spares will be damaged with the active cables.

2.3. INTRODUCTION TO DATA

Before you learn about the specifics of the hardware and software of MVS, you will need to know several more definitions. Another chap-

---

3. If tapes do get wet, *keep the tapes wet*. There are vendors who will restore tapes but the tapes should be completely submerged in water to prevent uneven drying.

ter will discuss data set access methods, but some basics of data relationships are needed to discuss the hardware and software of MVS. If you are an experienced MVS user, you may want to fast forward directly to the hardware section.

2.3.1. Data Relationships

A **file** is a group of related physical blocks. Think of a file as a file cabinet that may be in your office or home. Files are made up of **blocks**. Blocks can be thought of as file folders within the file cabinet. Just like file folders, the blocks may all be the same size or of different sizes. Within each block are **logical records**. The logical records are similar to the sheets of paper in the file folder. Each logical record is made up of **fields**. Fields are like areas on the page — the top may be the title. The page number may be centered on the last line of the page. Fields may be made up of **subfields**. Subfields may be viewed as the areas within a field. **Characters** are the smallest entity — just like on the sheet of the page.

IBM often calls a file a **data set**.

2.3.2. Fixed-Length Data

Fixed-length data is defined as a record, field, or any of the above relationships which do not vary in number of characters from one entity to another. For example, if a file consists of fixed length blocks, and the first block is 8,000 characters, then by definition, all other blocks (except maybe the last one) are 8,000 characters long.

2.3.3. Variable-Length Data

Variable-length data can be defined as a block, record, or field which has a variable number of characters in the entity. If the first block in an entity contains 503 characters, the next record may be smaller, the same, or larger than 503 characters.

In MVS, variable length data has a counter associated with the block or record or field that gives the length of the data.

2.4. SUMMARY

MVS is one of the most successful Operating Systems ever created. One of the secrets is that the requirements of the end user have been satisfied. The end users originally needed to have data processed and reports placed on their desk the next morning. Today information is available in files that are accessible to the end users on terminals on their desk.

The Customer Information Control System (CICS) and Information Management System (IMS) control the terminals and databases that are used by the data center's end users. Original Equipment Manufacturers create software that also provides these services under MVS.

Cost sharing of software and hardware is another hallmark of MVS. The data center is charged with the responsibility to manage and contain costs of a data center. The end user community is charged with the responsibility to explicitly state what they need and help justify the cost to the company. You can equate this to mass transit in your city. Most people have a car of their own, but if everyone uses the car to drive to work, the roads are overloaded between 8:00–9:00 A.M. and 5:00–6:00 P.M. If the community provides mass transit to move hundreds of people at one time, everything runs much better.

Work flow management and service level agreements are an integral part of a successful data center. Disaster recovery is the responsibility of both the data center users and management.

If the data center users and management form a team, the goals of the enterprise can be accomplished. Your enterprise does have goals, doesn't it? Listen to what Lewis Carroll taught us about goals in *Alice's Adventures in Wonderland*. Alice was talking to Cheshire-Puss, the cat:[4]

"Would you tell me, please, which way I ought to go from here?" "That depends a good deal on where you want to get to," said the Cat. "I don't much care where —" said Alice. "Then it doesn't matter which way you go," said the Cat. "—so long as I get *some-*

---

4. Lewis Carroll, *The Works of Lewis Carroll*, ed. Edward Guiliano. Longmeadow Press, Avenel Books, Inc. and Crown Publishers, Inc., New York, 1982, pp. 39–40.

where," Alice added as an explanation. "Oh, you're sure to do that," said the Cat, "if you only walk long enough."

Be different from Alice, wandering from place to place. You will surely achieve something. It may not be what you want. Set goals, measure your progress, and adjust your goals. Some of the questions you may want to ask are:

1. Does my data center have effective management of the software and hardware?
2. Do we have effective documentation?
3. Do we have cost-effective resource management?
4. Does management provide adequate training budgets to improve the level of expertise for the data center personnel and end users?
5. Are service level agreements in place to define the common goals of the enterprise, and has the enterprise assigned resources to ensure the goals are measured and met where possible?
6. Has the data center developed a plan for disaster recovery and has management allocated resources to test the plan?

Data management is the real final product of the data center and the end user community. This chapter begins our study of MVS by supplying definitions of data relationships:

1. A file or data set is a group of related physical blocks.
2. Physical blocks contain one or more logical records.
3. Logical records contain one or more data fields.
4. Fields may have subfields — or areas within the field — that can be considered separately.
5. Characters are the smallest entity of a file.

B

System 370 Hardware Concepts

The second part of *MVS Concepts and Facilities* is the System/370 hardware. The System/370 contains all the functions of the System/360. The terms System/360 and System/370 may be interchanged. In this section, we will cover the processor complexes that Multiple Virtual Storage (MVS) operates on. What makes MVS so successful is Virtual Storage. Since Virtual Storage is another view of the central storage which is in the Processor Complex, it is presented here.

One of the most important parts of any MVS introduction is the Input/Output subsystem. The channels, Direct-Access Storage Devices (DASD), and other devices are discussed here.

Before we proceed to these wondrous things, though, we will briefly digress to ensure we know all about the simpler things. It is amazing how many computer professionals do not know what happens when they press a key on a keyboard. We use terms like "byte," "parity," and "megabyte" every day and take them for granted, but do we really understand their precise meaning?

3

Processor Complexes

3.1. NUMBERING SYSTEMS — HOW COMPUTERS COUNT

Most computer texts assume the reader knows different numbering systems and how they are used in computers. But I have found that it helps to have a review. If you know all about numbering systems, feel free to skip forward to the section on Processor Complex components. You do so at your own risk because the rest of the book builds on the information in this section.

3.1.1. Introduction to Numbers

Sand: As you walk along the beach, your bare feet feel sand flowing through your toes; it sticks to your clothes and gets into your picnic lunch. The same sand, heated to its melting point, forms the silicon from which semiconductor chips are sliced. These chips are the building blocks of Twentieth-Century computers, and computers are very good counters.

Why should you be concerned with how computers count? Because computers have changed the way people think. Computers have changed the way humans do everything. Some day, count the number of "computers" you encounter. Almost every purchase will be recorded by a computer terminal. Your watch is probably run by one or more "chips." Have you looked under the hood of your car? You may not need to deal directly with any of these "chips," but it is almost a certainty that your profession will have you work with a computer.

Although the electrical engineering of a computer system is beyond the scope of this book, it is important to understand the basis of all computers before we discuss the specific architecture of the System/370. This basis is the binary numbering system — not because some wild, hairy scientist decided that the binary system (base 2) should be used, but because of the sand. Sand becomes computer chips, which are nothing more than repositories for on/off switches.

A computer is built of hundreds, millions, and even more switches. A switch may be on (represented by a one) or off (represented by a zero). With only two numbers to represent the numbering system, the language of computers is binary. Before we try to understand the computer language of binary, let's start with the numbering system we all know — decimal.

3.1.2. Decimal Numbers

The decimal system is so named because it has 10 possible symbols (see Figure 3.1). The symbols range from zero to nine.

Numbers can be used to count or to address something. One number we are familiar with, but often overlook, is zero. Zero represents a count of "none." Zero can represent a real entity. Have you ever known someone or some business that had an address that ended in a zero? 3400 Main Street. Computers addresses are no different than street addresses. Zero represents the first position or address, no units beyond the beginning.

Computers still count starting at one, just like we do. A "zero" is a lack of what you are counting, and a "one" is a single item. One plus one still is a "two." In different contexts, "zero" can have different meanings.

What happens when we get to 10? We only have the numbers 0–9 to represent a value, so we "create" a 10, which is a "10." What have we really done? We placed a zero in the far right field to say "no units" and placed a one in the second field to the left to say "one 10."

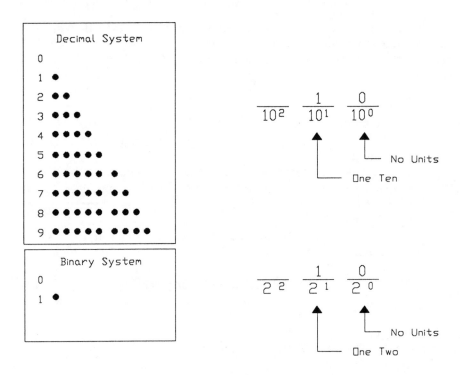

Figure 3.1   Numbering systems. The numbering system most people are familiar with is the decimal system — base 10. Note that digits 0 through 9 are used. The number system which computers use is the binary system — base 2. Digits 0 and 1 are used.

Mathematicians call this second field the first power or, in the case of decimal arithmetic, 10 raised to the first power. What would the third field from the right be? Ten to the second power, or hundreds.

3.1.3.   Binary Numbers

In the binary system, there are two numbers: zero and one. What happens when we need to count to two? The same thing we do with the decimal system: place a zero in the units field and a one in the next field to the left. If this field will represent a two, what is it? Two raised to the power of 1, of course. Two in the binary system is written as *10*.

The binary numbering system has a major drawback. It uses too many digits to represent values. A "10" in the decimal system is 10 items. A "10" in the binary system is only 2 items. Let's count to 13 in binary:

1. 00000. The first place to start counting is with nothing. Most people overlook this because in kindergarten they were taught to count 1, 2, 3, etc. The idea of "zero" or "none" was implied, not stated.
2. 00001. The first item has a one in the "units" position.
3. 00010. When you add 1 in the units position to 1, you get a number that cannot be represented (with a single binary digit), so it becomes "10."
4. 00011. The third item and fourth possibility is a count of three. The number can be viewed as "one unit of one" and "one unit of two" or three.
5. 00100. The fourth item is another number not in the binary system, so we move one position to the left (two to the power of two, or four) to represent a count of four.
6. 00101. The fifth is one one and one four.
7. 00110. The sixth is one four and one two.
8. 00111. The seventh is one four, one two, and one one.
9. 01000. The eighth is one eight.
10. 01001. The ninth is one eight and one one.
11. 01010. The tenth is one eight and one two.
12. 01011. The eleventh is one eight, one two, and one one.
13. 01100. The twelfth is one eight and one four.
14. 01101. The thirteenth is one eight, one four, and one one.

3.1.4. Hexadecimal Numbers

What did the computer architects do with the problem that binary has too many digits? The language of their computer was base 2. That is too clumsy. The language of people is base 10. That does not fit, so they moved on. The next numbering system chosen was octal — base 8. Base 8 uses three bits to represent zero through seven. Base 8 has some problems:

1. IBM selected a word size of 32 bits. Eight divided by three is not a whole number. Thirty-two divided by 4 is a whole number.

2. IBM selected floating point arithmetic to "normalize" on 4-byte groups, not bits like older systems.[1]
3. The byte selected is 8 bits. Eight divided by four is an even number. Eight divided by 3 bits is not an even number.
4. Octal still requires more digits than base 10 to represent large numbers.

Octal was chosen by some non-IBM mainframe designers. That they chose octal is not wrong, just different. IBM chose hexadecimal — base 16 — as the base for the System/370 architecture.

Hexadecimal requires 16 symbols for its numbers. Obviously, 0 to 9 work for the first 10, but what about 11 through 15? Remember, the highest number in a number system is one less than the base to account for zero, so the letters A for 10, B for 11, C for 12, D for 13, E for 14, and F for 15 were chosen (see Figure 3.2). (It is customary to write the base of a number as a subscript unless the assumed base is clear from the context.)

How do we count to 19 in hexadecimal? Zero through 9 are identical to decimal. Ten through 19 are:

1. 000A. The tenth item and eleventh possibility. *Note:* The A goes in the "units" position.
2. 000B. The eleventh item and the twelfth possibility.
3. 000C. The twelfth item.
4. 000D. The thirteenth item.
5. 000E. The fourteenth item.
6. 000F. The fifteenth item.
7. 0010. We rolled over: One "16" and no units!
8. 0011. The seventeenth item. One 16 and one.
9. 0012. The eighteenth item. One 16 and two.
10. 0013. The nineteenth item. One 16 and three.

This book will not explain how to convert from one numbering system to another. That is a topic for another course. Anyway, there are a number of excellent calculators that will do the conversion for you at a touch of a button. My suggestion is to learn how to do the conversion, then invest in a good calculator.

---

1. A normalized floating point number has a nonzero leftmost hexadecimal digit. The reason for normalization is to provide the most precision.

Count	Hexadecimal		Count	Hexadecimal
0	0		1 0	A
1	1		1 1	B
2	2		1 2	C
3	3		1 3	D
4	4		1 4	E
5	5		1 5	F
6	6		1 6	1 0
7	7		1 7	1 1
8	8		1 8	1 2
9	9		1 9	1 3

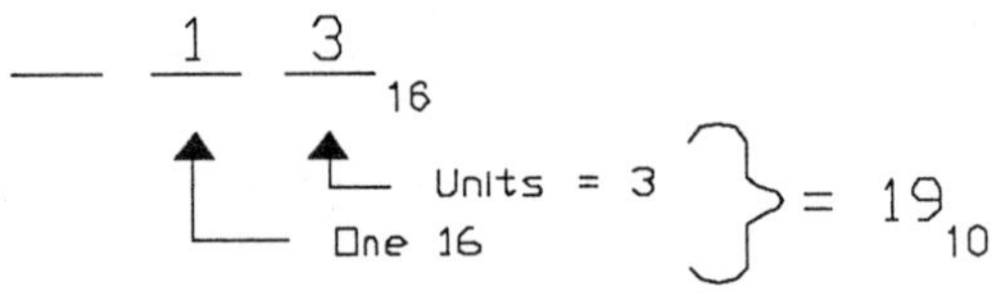

$$1 \quad 3 _{16}$$

Units = 3
One 16
$\Big\} = 19_{10}$

Figure 3.2   Hexadecimal numbering system. Because binary requires a large number of digits to represent even small numbers, IBM chose hexadecimal — base 16 system. *Note:* 0 through 9 and "A" through "F" are used to represent the numbers. In this example we count to 19 (decimal). Nineteen in decimal is "13" in hexadecimal, that is, one 16 and three units. Note the subscripts "16" for hexadecimal and "10" for decimal.

One thing you should have concluded by now is that a number is an idea, and whether we write it in base 10, 2, 8, or 16 makes no difference. Numbers are used for calculation or identification, number bases are used to communicate numbers.

3.1.5.   Addressable Units — Words

Most computer architectures have an "addressable unit", which is the smallest unit of storage that can be addressed. In some architectures, this is called a **word**. The word may contain four, eight, ten or any number of binary digits as defined in the architecture of the computer.

The System/370 architecture is **byte** addressable. A byte is eight data bits and one parity bit. A **bit** is a contraction of the words "binary" and "digits" (see Figure 3.3). In the System/360, the byte actually has nine bits: The leftmost bit of a byte is the parity bit. In the System/370, the parity bits for eight bytes are combined into an **Error Correction Code (ECC)** byte or **Checking-Block Code (CBC)** associated with that eight-bit group. The length of the ECC is eight bits because it contains the parity bit for each byte of eight bytes. The length of the CBC varies with each model, which permits detection and/or correction of multiple bit errors in a single byte.

How does parity work? In the first example in Figure 3.3, a number four is stored in the byte. The parity is set to zero to keep the number of bits an odd number (one in this case). In the second example, a number five is stored in the byte. In this case, the parity is set to one so that the number of bits is an odd number (three bits).

You should know that the parity bit is usually not seen by the software but only by the error detection and correction hardware. When software refers to a "byte," this means the eight-bit data part and excludes the parity bit.

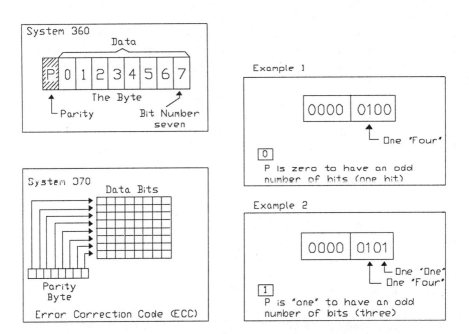

Figure 3.3   The byte. The byte is a combination of eight data bits and one parity bit. The number of bits that are "on" will always be an odd number (1, 3, 5, 7, or 9 bits) in odd parity mode.

System/370 uses odd parity. An odd number of bits in every byte (counting the parity bit) will be turned on or set. If a byte has an even number of bits turned on, then an error is detected and a **machine check** occurs. Bit errors are just one of several types of machine checks.

The term "machine check" introduces us to a new concept. What happens when the hardware detects something is wrong? Either the Processor Complex or the channels can detect a processing error. These errors are grouped into the generic term "check." The Processor Complex detects **machine checks**, and the channels detect **channel checks**. These terms will be discussed in more detail later. Different models in the System/370 line of computers implement single bit error detection and correction, double bit error detection and correction, and even triple bit error detection. Each new model series gets better at detection and correction of errors in storage.

MVS does not get involved in the processing of checks unless the hardware cannot "recover" or overcome the problem. In some cases, the MVS operator will see a message on the console. In most cases, MVS will write a record to a recording data set — SYS1.LOGREC — to record that the error has occurred.

The System/360, as previously stated, combined "scientific" processing with "business" processing. The byte access satisfies the business processing requirements. The System/370 can address words which satisfy the "scientific" processing needs.

Byte access is also called variable access. By this we mean that the computer can access (read or write to) a single byte of 8 bits. Bytes can be combined to form fixed length fields called words. Word access in System/370 is referred to as **Fixed Point** access.

Word access in System/370 is unlike most other computer architecture designation of "words" because the size of the word varies (see Figure 3.4).

The grouping of four bits of a byte is often referred to by another name — a **nibble**. The left four bits are referred to as the left nibble, high order nibble or zone bits. The rightmost four bits are referred to as the right nibble, low order nibble, or numeric bits.

A **halfword** is two bytes. The parity bit is not shown in this figure and will not be shown through the rest of this book. However, remember that every byte has a parity bit somewhere for checking purposes. There are 16 bits in a halfword. They are numbered from 0 to 15, left to right.

One of the most confusing things to new students of System/370 is bits. In Figure 3.4, the bits in a byte are labeled or numbered from zero to seven, but when two bytes are combined in a halfword, then

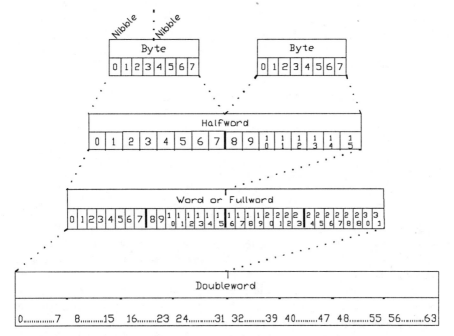

Figure 3.4 Combinations of bytes to make words. Two bytes make a halfword. The bits in a halfword are numbered 0 to 15. Four bytes make a word. The bits in a word are numbered 0 to 31. Eight bytes make a doubleword. The bits are numbered 0 to 63.

the same byte would be labeled 8 to 15 if it were the right byte in the halfword. Once the student understands that the relative position or context of a byte must be known before its bits can be labeled, then the task of identifying bit position becomes clear.

A **word** is four bytes. There are 32 bits in a word. The number 32 will have a lot of meaning when we discuss the System/370 architecture extended by MVS/XA and MVS/ESA. Eight bytes are a **doubleword**. There are 64 bits in a doubleword. The bits are numbered from 0 to 63, left to right.

There are special types of words and doublewords. These contain **floating point** values. Floating point is a term given to arithmetic operations involving a fraction and an exponent. For instance:

501,000 can also be expressed as .501 x 10 raised to the 6th power.
413,000 can also be expressed as .413 x 10 raised to the 6th power.

Fixed Point arithmetic would add the numbers:

```
   501,000
 +413,000
 ---------
   914,000
```

Floating point arithmetic would add the values:

```
 .501 × 10 to the 6th power
+.413 × 10 to the 6th power
 ------
 .914 × 10 to the 6th power
```

To perform arithmetic operations, floating point arithmetic logic adjusts the numbers until the exponents are equal before the value can be manipulated. Floating point is most useful for expressing very large numbers and is the basis of the System/370 claim to be a scientific processor.

Floating point can be single precision (each value is a word in size — 4 bytes), double precision (each value is a doubleword in size — 8 bytes), or extended floating point (each value is two doublewords). As you can see, one pattern of bits can be interpreted in several ways. Let's look at this idea a bit more closely.

3.1.6.   Code Systems.

You are probably wondering what a byte represents. Is the byte a character such as the letter z? Is it a binary number? Is it a decimal number? The words on this page were created on a computer. How did the computer know that when I pressed the shift key and the a key that the letter A should be stored? How did the computer tell the printer to print the letter A?

The answer is simple. The eight data bits of a byte can represent **characters**, **binary numbers**, or **anything** you want them to be. The eight data bits of a byte can represent binary numbers such as the four in Figure 3.3. They can represent characters. In Figure 3.5, the first byte has a value of 1100 0001 in binary, C1 in hexadecimal, and 193 in decimal. This could represent a counter of the number of widgets that were manufactured today. The value of 193 could also represent the uppercase letter A — the first letter of the alphabet.

The representation is the coding system. The System/370 architecture uses a form of Binary Coded Decimal (BCD) to define what a byte means. BCD code representation is a six-bit code. All characters

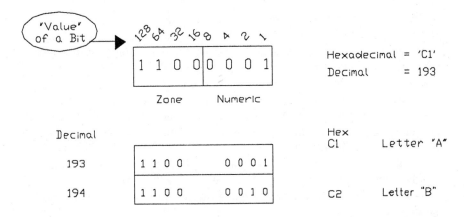

Figure 3.5   EBCDIC byte representation. A byte can represent a number such as the count of 193 widgets built in the factory today. A byte can contain a representation of the letter "A" as the hexadecimal value C1. The letter "B" is represented by the hexadecimal value "C2."

and numbers are represented by six bits. Six bits can contain only 64 combinations of characters and digits, however, so IBM extended BCD.

The System/370, then, uses the Extended Binary-Coded Decimal Interchange Code (EBCDIC). EBCDIC uses eight bits (just right for an IBM byte!), which can represent 256 characters. Upper- and lowercase alphabetic characters, special characters such as periods, commas, etc., and even control characters can be represented.

How do we determine what a byte represents in this coding system? To begin with, each bit in a byte is assigned a value. The leftmost four bits — called zone bits for historical reasons — are assigned the decimal values of 128, 64, 32, and 16. Said another way, the "zero" bit "on" is worth a decimal value of 128.[2]

The rightmost four bits — the numeric bits — are assigned the decimal values of 8, 4, 2, and 1. The value in a byte can be used to access a table of codes as defined for EBCDIC. In such a table the value x'C1' or binary 1100 0001 or decimal 193 is the capital letter A. Hexadecimal C2 is the capital letter B. An example is given in Figure 3.5. By pressing a "shift" and the letter a on the keyboard, the value x'C1' is loaded into the buffer for the keyboard.

---

2. A bit turned "on" is when the bit has a value of one.

This is a good time to mention single quotes and double quotes. Note above that I have written x'C1' in single quotes. The x indicates hexadecimal. Single quotes are used because in the System/370 assembler language and Job Control Language (JCL), single quotations are required. Double quotes are the standard when referring to something in English that is quoted or when you want something to stand out in a sentence. As my son, Dan, has pointed out to me: Use single quotes when talking to an IBM computer and use double quotes when talking to people.

A warning about keyboards. Some keyboards have more than one single quote. There is an "open quote" (' — x'79') and a "close quote" (' — x'7D'). Computers use the close quote only (') — even to open a quote!

A good reference source for codes is the "IBM green card." IBM publication X20-1703 was a green folding reference card that contained System/360 reference data. The assembler instructions were on the card as well as binary (called "System/360 8 bit code"), hexadecimal, BCD (called "BCDIC"), and EBCDIC. When the System/370 was announced, the green card became the yellow card and was given a new number (GX20-1850). This card has grown into a booklet of information on the System/370.

There is another coding system — The American Standard Code for Information Interchange (ASCII). IBM, for most of the 1970s and 1980s, tried to ignore ASCII.

ASCII is a seven-bit code developed by and for users of telecommunications and data processing networks. With seven bits, ASCII can represent 128 code patterns. IBM tried to develop an eight-bit ASCII to be used on the System/360 machines, but that was a little like developing a television set that could not receive any of the current television stations. IBM dropped ASCII/8.

The IBM personal computer was developed to communicate using ASCII. ASCII terminals can communicate with MVS, but all information processing inside the Processor Complex is done with EBCDIC.

Figure 3.6 shows a comparison between EBCDIC and ASCII. For the letter "A," note that the EBCDIC representation of x'C1' (binary 1100 0001) is the capital letter "A."

The ASCII representation — using seven bits and not eight — is binary '100 0001', which is almost the same as the EBCDIC. The leftmost or high order bit is missing. One could almost write a rule that says use only the rightmost seven bits to convert ASCII to EBCDIC. Whoa, it is not that simple!

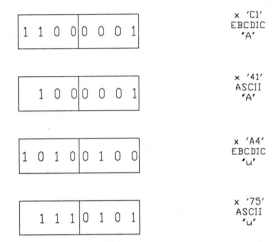

Figure 3.6 ASCII and EBCDID comparison. The representation of ASCII as compared to EBCDIC looks similar, but not for all characters. There is no way 256 characters can be mapped onto 128 possible combinations.

Look at the comparison of the lowercase "u." In EBCDIC it is x'A4' or a binary '1010 0100'. For ASCII, the binary code is '111 0101'. Not even close. There must be programmatic conversion of ASCII to EBCDIC or vice versa. ASCII sometimes uses the high bit for data transmission parity, and various vendors (including IBM) have "extended ASCII," using the 8th bit to get italics or graphics.

MVS will convert tape files from ASCII to EBCDIC as the tape file is being read into storage.

Data terminals which use ASCII can access MVS by using special hardware boxes called "protocol converters." These will be discussed later.

3.1.7. Kilobytes, Megabytes, Gigabytes, and Terabytes.

Just as we use scientific notation to simplify writing big numbers in decimal, we have invented a shorthand for big numbers in binary. Rather than using an exponent, we use words to represent multipliers. These multipliers seem strange at first, but then become almost like the decimal system in their familiarity. In fact, some computer professionals talk about multiples of the binary system as if they *were* decimal multiplications. They are not. Figure 3.7 shows the relative sizes.

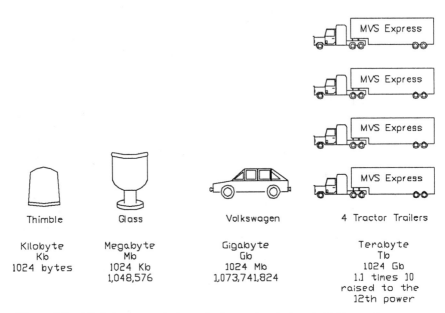

Thimble	Glass	Volkswagen	4 Tractor Trailers
Kilobyte Kb 1024 bytes	Megabyte Mb 1024 Kb 1,048,576	Gigabyte Gb 1024 Mb 1,073,741,824	Terabyte Tb 1024 Gb 1.1 times 10 raised to the 12th power

Figure 3.7   Kilobytes, megabytes, gigabytes, terabytes. 1,024 bytes is a kilobyte, 1,024 kilobytes is a megabyte, 1,024 megabytes is a gigabyte, 1,024 gigabytes is a terabyte. If we filled a thimble with 1,024 grains of sand and then counted out a megabyte of sand, it would take a glass to hold it. A gigabyte of sand might fit in a small car, and a terabyte would take several tractor trailers!

The first multiplier is the **Kilobyte (Kb)**. Kilo refers to the multiplier "to the power of 10," so a kilobyte is 1,024 bytes or two raised to the power of 10. Even though kilo is borrowed from the decimal "thousand," the numbering system is binary and we say "kilo" because 1,024 is close to 1,000. Kilobyte is abbreviated "K" or "Kb".

As the numbers get larger, there are other conventions used that cause some students problems. For instance, the value 65,536 is expressed as 64K and not 65 Kb. Why? Because 1,024 x 64 = 65,536. 65 Kb would equal 66,560.

A thousand and twenty-four kilobytes is a **Megabyte (Mb)** or 1,048,576 bytes (1,024 * 1,024). Mega is borrowed from the decimal for "million," and again, since we are counting in the binary system, we use the term for the nearest value to a 1,048,576.

A thousand twenty-four megabytes is a **Gigabyte (Gb)**, or 1,073,741,824 bytes. Giga is two raised to the power of 30.

A thousand twenty-four gigabytes is a **Terabyte (Tb)**, or 1,099,511,627,776 bytes. Tera is two raised to the power of 40. Soon we will be into some really big numbers!

How big are these numbers? Suppose in Figure 3.7, 1,024 grains of sand fit in the thimble. A megabyte of sand might fit in a glass. A gigabyte might fit in a VW car. A terabyte might fit inside four tractor trailers!

Another unit of measurement in computers is the speed of the processor. In this case we use the term **nanosecond**, which is one-thousand-millionth of a second. I once saw the great lady of COBOL — Rear Admiral Grace Hopper (USNR) — give a talk. In it she demonstrated a nanosecond. She, like most of us, cannot visualize these ultrasmall or ultralarge numbers, so she asked an engineer to demonstrate a nanosecond. If you have ever met Ms. Hopper, you know her requests could not be denied. The engineer brought her a piece of wire about 12 inches long: "A nanosecond is the time it takes electricity to get from one end of this wire to another," he said. Every time I see a 12-inch piece of wire, I think of that example and of a "nanosecond."

A **millisecond (MS)** is one-thousandth (1,000) of a second. A **microsecond (μS)** is a millionth (1,000,000) of a second. A **nanosecond (ns)** is one-thousand-millionth of a second. A **picosecond (ps)** is one-trillionth of a second — one-thousandth of a nanosecond.

Note that we have switched back to decimal multipliers because we are defining units of time, not units of storage.

3.2. PROCESSOR COMPLEX COMPONENTS

We now begin to look at the pieces of a computer. The discussion will be in general terms of the components so you can study the Processor Complex that you are supporting or using.

3.2.1. Basic Computer Concepts

"The computer": What a wonderful and all-encompassing term. The average person is beginning to use the term for almost any combination of data processing equipment. One of my most memorable commercial advertisements many years back was for one of the local "computer learning institutes."

The advertisement pictured people in front of a set of magnetic tape drives stating how they loved their new computer jobs. It appeared so clean and challenging. The tape drive was not the computer! Anyone in computer operations for a small or large computer center knows that peripheral operations is anything *but* a clean job.

What is a computer? Even the computer industry does not agree. Every manufacturer has its own names for the components. IBM, for example, has used:

1. **CPU.** The Central Processor Unit (CPU) is one of the components of a computer. It is confusing to refer to the combination of components by the name of one of the components.
2. **Central Electronic Complex (CEX).** This term is used with the 309x family. The combination is electronic in nature and again is complex. If we place a Central Electronic Complex at a city other than where the central computer is located, however, would it be called a "remote Central Electronic Complex"?
3. **Processor Complex.** The hardware does do data processing and it certainly is complex.

This book will use the term **Processor Complex** as the combination of all the basic components (see Figure 3.8). The generic components of the Processor Complex are:

1. **Central Storage.** Central Storage is the Random-Access Memory (RAM) that can be written to or read from. RAM contains computer programs and data fields. (The concepts of Central Storage will be expanded later as we learn of Virtual Storage, Expanded Storage, and other variations of storage.) Central Storage is measured in kilobytes (for System/360 models), megabytes (for System/370 models), and soon gigabytes. Terabytes are (at this writing) reserved for Direct-Access Storage Devices (DASD) that we will explore in later chapters.

   IBM says that the minimum Central Storage needed to run MVS is four megabytes. That is not totally accurate. You can IPL MVS with four megabytes Central Storage: You probably cannot do anything except test one or two applications, however. The practical minimum is probably eight megabytes. I would not try to run production MVS without 16 megabytes.
2. **Central Processor Unit (CPU).** The CPU is where the instructions are executed. There are several components in a CPU:

   a. **Registers:** Registers are special purpose areas in a computer which hold addresses or data. In the System/370, there are several types:

    i.   **General purpose registers.** There are 16 general purpose registers numbered from 0 to 15 (or x'0' to x'F' in hexadecimal). These registers are operated upon by the System/370 instruction set. Each register is a fullword in size — four bytes, 32 bits. The registers contain:

        1) Data, such as counters.

        2) Addresses, such as the address of a program or index pointers to lists of data.

    ii. **Floating point registers.** There are four floating point registers. They are numbered zero, two, four and six. Each register is a doubleword in size — 8 bytes, 64 bits.

        The floating point registers are *not the same* as the general purpose registers (that is, floating point and general purpose registers are distinctly different parts of the Processor Complex). Floating point registers load from or store to single words (single precision) or doublewords (double precision).

    iii. **Special purpose registers.** There are a number of other registers in the architecture that control expanded functions. For example, there are 16 **Control Registers (CR)**, which are used by MVS to control address spaces and pass information to the hardware. These will be explained as they are covered in the future chapters defining the expanded functions. There are 16 **Access Registers (AR)**, which are used by MVS/ESA to point to data spaces in use by a program.

  b. **Arithmetic and Logical Unit (ALU).** The ALU contains the circuits necessary for adding, subtracting, and comparing data fields as well as the circuits necessary to operate on data. The ALU accesses and stores information in the registers.

  c. **High speed buffer.** The high speed buffer is also called "cache." The purpose of the CPU cache is to speed up processing of instructions. CPU cache is used to "pipeline" or overlap instruction and data manipulation. In other words, it makes the processor "faster" than the raw speed. An application can defeat or ruin the performance of CPU cache with either of these techniques:

    i.   Process arrays out of order so that multidimensional arrays are randomly processed or processed in a manner to make each access to another page. I have observed a FORTRAN program running on a 370/168 processor which *increased the CPU requirements* of all other work on the processor.

ii. Jump from module to module so that the "working set" is very large. The advantage of using structured programming is the ability to segment work into manageable segments, but if the movement from program to program consumes resources out of proportion to the work accomplished, then the result is inefficient processing.

d. **Computer Systems Controller.** The Computer Systems Controller is responsible for all access outside the CPU. The following are the functions of the Computer Systems Control section:

i. Coordinate all references to Central Storage for both instructions and data.

ii. Oversee the execution of instructions. There are two subfunctions to instruction processing:

1) The first part of instruction execution, called **I mode**, is to cause the instruction to be fetched from Central Storage.

2) The second part of instruction execution, called **E mode**, is to decode the instruction to determine the type of instruction and what "operands" are required. If the instruction needs information from the registers, then that data is made available. If the instruction needs information from or written to Central Storage, then that access is made.

3. **Channels.** The channels are the electronic components that control the movement of data from outside the Processor Complex to inside the Processor Complex.

Refer again to Figure 3.8. As the CPU executes instructions, the general purpose registers, floating point registers, access registers (if MVS/ESA), high speed buffers, and Central Storage are used in the execution. Since each CPU has only one set of these, the entire CPU is dedicated to the instructions and data of a single task.

Implied here is that the operating system — MVS — has loaded the registers and storage with the data and instructions for a single task. The operating system is also instructions and data. What really happens is:

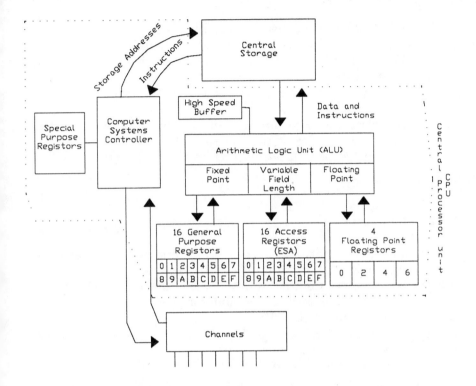

Figure 3.8   Generic Processor Complex components. The major components of a Processor Complex are the CPU, the channels, and Central Storage. The CPU consists of the Arithmetic Logic Unit (ALU), the registers, the high speed buffer, and the Computer Systems Controller.

1. MVS selects a task to which it wants to transfer control. The task may be a terminal running under TSO, CICS, a batch job, or a Started Task.
2. MVS saves its own registers and data.
3. MVS loads the registers of the new task.
4. MVS "transfers control" to the program. One of the System/370 instructions is the Load Program Status Word (LPSW). The Program Status Word (PSW) is one of the "special registers" that the CPU uses to keep track of what instruction is being executed.
5. As each instruction is executed, the PSW is either incremented to the next instruction (sequential processing) or completely changed (branching) to another location.

6. The program either gives up control:
   a. Voluntarily by issuing a "Supervisor Call" (SVC) such as waiting for an event to occur such as an I/O operation or a timed event.
   b. Involuntarily by using up a fixed length of time. The time is model dependent but in the range of 200 milliseconds.
7. MVS reloads its registers and data areas to either perform some system service or transfer control to another task. Control could also be returned to the task that was interrupted.

3.2.2. Uniprocessors

The prefix "uni" means one. The term "uniprocessor" means a Processor Complex that contains one central processing unit to share and control one set of Central Storage and one set of channels.

Early System/360 processors were uniprocessors. Some System/370 processors are uniprocessors. The 3083 is an example of a uniprocessor in the System/370 308x model line. Figure 3.9 shows an example of a uniprocessor complex.

Note that the CPU is labeled "2." In all uniprocessors up to the 3083, the CPU was marked "0." Remember that in the world of computers, the "zero" address is just like street addresses — the first one is zero and the zero address may or may not be used. In this case, the physical location of the CPU was on the bottom of a six-foot swing-out frame. This gave sharp observers of the architecture an indication that the same frame would hold a second CPU. The 3081 was introduced with two CPUs, but they were labeled "0" and "2." Was CPU "1" the System Controller?

The 308x and 309x Processor Complex systems have changed the architecture from previous System/370 models. In Figure 3.9, the following are new components:

1. **System Controller (SC).** One new major component of both the 308x and 309x families is the System Controller. The major function of the System Controller is similar to the Computer System Controller in the CPU above — to provide the paths and controls for communication between the CPU, the channels, and Central Storage. The SC is more complex because data is stored directly into the high-speed buffer associated with each CPU and because the SC is designed to handle multiple CPUs.

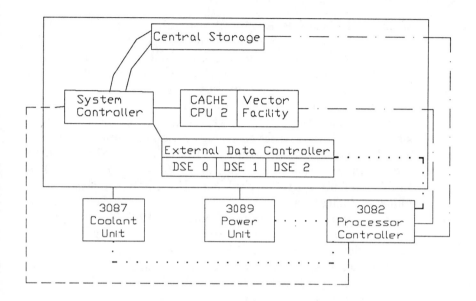

Figure 3.9   Uniprocessors. Uniprocessors have one CPU, one block of central storage, and one set of channels. In this diagram, we see the 3083 architecture. Note that a system controller is now external to the CPU. The 3082 is dedicated to the functions associated with monitoring, controlling and maintaining the processor complex. The 3083 CPU is labeled "2."

2. **Vector Processing Facility or Enhanced Vector Facility.** The 309x Processor Complex family has a new processor called the vector facility. Vector Processing is designed for the "cn gineering" type instructions. The Vector Facility is the IBM entry into large-scale engineering applications. Business applications written in COBOL cannot benefit yet from this additional, relatively expensive hardware addition because the compiler must build object code to take advantage of the vector processor and the programmer must write programs that allow vectorization.

   As of this writing the IBM VS Fortran compiler Version 2 and the Engineering and Scientific Subroutine Library (ESSL) are required.

   Most processors in the System/370 family have been **scalar** processors. Scalar refers to instructions that operate on a pair of operands (such as A and B) and produce a single output (such as C). Vector processing performs operations on "sets" of elements (a vector) instead of a single pair. Thus A1, A2, A3, A4, and A5 could be added to B1, B2, B3, B4, and B5 in a single operation. The vector processor is faster in these special cases because only a single instruction has to be fetched (I mode) and executed (E mode). The vector processor is an extension of the CPUs instruction and execution elements.

3. **The External Data Controller (EXDC).** The EXDC replaces the Channels from the previous Processor Complexes. The EXDC controls up to 24 channels. The EXDC consists of the following logical elements:

   a. One Channel Processing Element (CPE). The CPE is a computer that handles the control of I/O operations and handles up to three Data Server Elements (DSEs).

   b. The Data Server Element (DSE) is another computer that handles up to eight (8) channels. The channels are now called Interface Adapter Elements (IAE).

   c. The Interface Adapter Element (IAE) controls the I/O operations for all devices on the channel.

4. **Processor Controller (PC).** The 3082 or 3092 processor controller provides error recording, recovery, and diagnostic support for customer engineers and data center personnel. If the hardware cannot recover from the error, the PC performs error analysis and attempts to identify the **Field Replaceable Unit (FRU)**. The PC can also perform diagnostic routines to test components. The PC also has connections to call the IBM Large System Support Center for remote service.

5. **Coolant Distribution Unit.** The 3087 provides water cooling that is pumped into the **Thermal Conduction Modules (TCM)**. TCMs are the unit in the Processor Complex that contain all the chips and logic circuits that make up the hardware components of the 308x or 309x Processor Complex. TCMs are multilayered circuit boards which significantly reduce power consumption, space, and cooling requirements.

6. **Power Unit.** The 3089 Power Unit provides 400 Hz power to the Processor Complex. One 3089 is required for each side of a 3084. Another term that is used for the Power Unit is **Motor Generator**, because the early power distribution units were motors that were driven by electrical power and the motors created electrical power. The output was smoother, without spikes in the power which might be received from the local electric company.

3.2.3. Multiprocessors

Multiprocessor is the term used by IBM when the Processor Complex has more than one CPU inside the box. In the early days, IBM gave the user an opportunity to add CPUs to get more power. The speed of the individual CPU was not changed. Today, IBM gives the customer the opportunity to add CPUs and change the speed of the CPU itself. It is getting very difficult to understand and compare the Processor Complex offerings. We will start with a discussion of the CPU upgrades, and then discuss the numbers of CPUs in a Processor Complex.

Midlife Kickers — "Upgrades" When IBM announces a new series of Processor Complexes, it usually announces a model just about the size of the largest model in the previous series and one significantly faster. For example, when the 3090 family was announced, the 3090-200 was approximately the same total capacity of the 3084 and the 3090-400 was approximately double the capacity of the 3084.

The above strategy gives the company a place to grow to if they are constrained now, and gives the company adding or replacing a Processor Complex a forward-to-the-future path. IBM then fills in between, above and below those levels.

So far, IBM has also increased the speed of the ability of the Processor Complex to perform work. In the case of the 308x series these **midlife kickers** were called the **plus** and the **X** models, so a 3081 could be a 3081, a 3081+ or a 3081X. The speed difference was about 15 percent.

The 3090 midlife kickers were called **Enhanced**. The 3090 E was announced at about 12 percent faster, and the 3090 S was announced at about 15 percent faster than that. We will call these the "E/S" models. IBM calls the hardware **ESA/370**. At the same time, IBM announced that the E/S would have a "new" operating system — MVS/ESA. It became apparent that, as Central Storage and I/O devices became larger and more prevalent, the Processor Complex would have to become faster. There are two ways to do that: make the CPU execute instructions faster or put more CPUs inside the Processor Complex. **Multiprocessing** refers to this latter solution — more than one CPU in a Processor Complex. In a multiprocessing environment, one CPU is processing the instructions of one task while another CPU is processing the instructions of another task.

Multiprocessing is similar to, but not the same as, **parallel processing**, in which two or more sequences of instructions from the same task are executed simultaneously.

The term **Multiprogramming** refers to running two or more computer tasks (terminal handlers like TSO, batch jobs, or CICS regions) by interleaving instruction sequence execution. Do not be confused by these two terms.

Types of Multiprocessing When IBM combined more than one CPU in a physical piece of hardware, it gave that combination several names:

1. **Multiprocessor.** The term refers to the ability to have more than one task executing at the same time, not just two or more tasks running in the Processor Complex at the same time (alternating use of the CPU) as we have had since leaving behind Primary Control Program (PCP), but two instructions executing at the same point in time.

2. **Attached Processor.** This term was used in the System/370 family to indicate that there was a second CPU. The second CPU was limited. Usually the Attached Processor Unit (APU) could not do I/O instructions. The System/370 158, 168, and 303x families had APU options.

3. **Multiengine.** Multiengine implies that there can be more than one task at work at the same time. The comparison is to things we see in other areas of our lives — multiengine airplanes or boats.

4. **Dyadic.** Dyadic processors imply two-way processing. The Processor Complex contains two integrated central processors, each having access to a common Central Storage, Expanded Storage, and channels. The 3081 is a dyadic processor.

5. **Triadic.** Triadic processors imply three-way processing. The Processor Complex contains three integrated central processors, each having access to a common Central Storage, Expanded Storage, and channels. The 3090-300 is a triadic processor. You cannot use MVS/370 as the operating system on the triadic.

6. **Four-way.** The 3090-400 is a combination of two 3090-200s. The 3090 model 400 has four CPUs and thus can process up to four tasks at the same time. You may be able to use MVS/370 on the 3090-400 (see below).

7. **Five-way.** The 3090-500 is a combination of two 3090-300s. There are five CPUs in the five-way. You cannot use MVS/370 as the operating system on a five-way.

8. **Six-way.** The 3090-600 is a combination of two 3090-300s. There are six CPUs in the six-way. You cannot use MVS/370 as the operating system on a six-way.

As of this writing, the latest MVS implementation allows a maximum of from 16 to 4,096 CPUs — depending on which control blocks you look at — but the 4,096 is only a theoretical limit because of the overhead of passing control from one task to another.

This book will use the term **multiprocessors** to include all of the above. Let's look at some configurations. The Dyadic has two CPUs that share one Central Storage and one (or more) channel sets. Figure 3.10 shows an example of a Dyadic Processor Complex.

Above, I stated the MVS/370 cannot operate certain 309x Processor Complexes. That meant "native" or as the primary operating system that runs the Processor Complex. The Processor Complex can be segmented to allow MVS/370 (or other Operating Systems that have limitations) to operate on the Processor Complex.

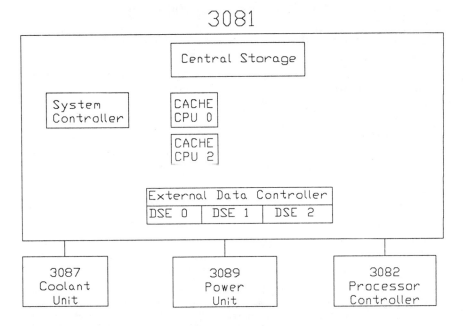

Figure 3.10   Multiprocessor — dyadic. Dyadic processors have two or more CPUs. They share a common Central Storage and channels. In the 3081 the CPUs are labeled "0" and "2."

The 3084Q or 3090-400 Processor Complexes contain four central processor units and can be used in **single image mode** (all the CPUs and other resources available to a single copy of MVS) or **partitioned mode** (some portion of the CPUs and other resources available to a single copy of MVS). As an example, MVS/370 can IPL on one side of the 3084, because MVS/370 can support a two-CPU environment.

The 3090 E/S models have a feature called **Processor Resource/Systems Manager** (PR/SM), which allows the processor to be divided into logical partitions. The 3090-600 contains six CPUs and can be used in either single image, partitioned mode (three CPUs on each side), or (if you purchase the additional features) partitioned in up to six logical partitions (12 if you physically partition the Processor Complex). The number six can change as IBM distributes new microcode support. Most of the 3090 E/S models support PR/SM partitioning.

Figure 3.11 shows a 3084 (four-way) in single image mode. In this mode, all processors share all the Central Storage and channels. Single image mode requires MVS/XA version 2 Release 1.7 or later. You cannot use MVS/370 to operate in single image mode on the 3084.

If a batch job or CICS region were operating under MVS/XA in single image mode, the instructions for the address space could be executing in any one of the CPUs at any given time. If you were trying to evaluate the relative speed of one System/370 Processor Complex to another, you would need to understand multiprocessing. For example, in Figure 3.11, if the speed of each CPU was 7.5 Millions of Instructions per Second (MIPS), then the total power would be 7.5 * 4 or approximately 30 MIPS. Any one task would only run at the speed of 7.5 MIPS.[3]

There is a method that a single address space can use to take advantage of these multiple CPUs — **multitasking**. A multitasking

---

3. There are volumes written about how you calculate the speed of an individual CPU in a Processor Complex. One of the quickest methods is to write a program to get the time the program starts, execute a known number of instructions, and calculate the elapsed time. The calculation of instructions per second is then the measure. The problem with this is that the type of instruction affects the outcome. If one evaluator uses one instruction and another uses another instruction, then they might report that the same CPU has different rates.

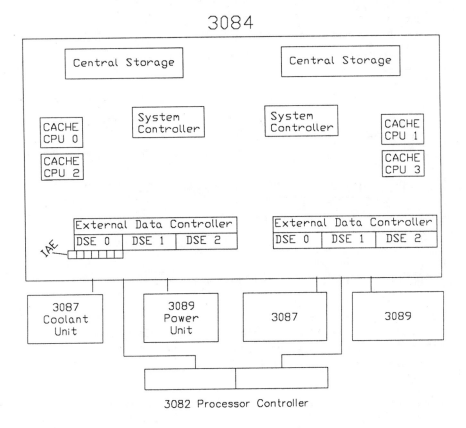

Figure 3.11 Multiprocessor — single image. Multiprocessors can execute in "single image" mode where all CPUs are available to the same copy of MVS. The 3084 CPUs are labeled 0, 1, 2, and 3.

address space is initialized to have two Task Control Blocks (TCBs) to allow MVS to dispatch the two tasks in two different CPUs inside the Processor Complex. Most batch jobs do not use multitasking. Most TSO sessions do not use multitasking. Many database systems *do* use multitasking. CICS uses multitasking for VSAM I/O operations and some other system level tasks, but not generally for any application transactions.

Figure 3.12 shows a 3090-400 (four-way) in partioned mode. In this mode, two processors, half the channels, and half the Central Storage are allocated to each side. There is a separate copy of MVS running on each side.

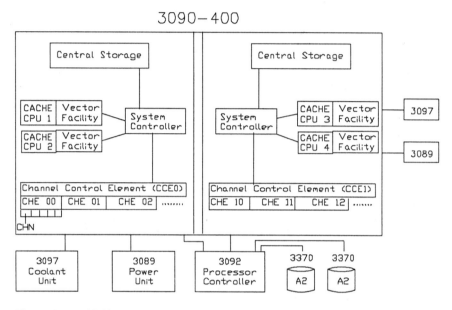

Figure 3.12   Multiprocessor — partitioned. Multiprocessor dyadic Processor Complexes can operate like two independent Processor Complexes. The 3090-400 is shown. Note the different names for the channel subsystem. Note the CPUs are labeled 1, 2, 3, and 4.

Note the channel subsystem has different names. The **Channel Control Elements** (CCE) are the same as the **External Data Controllers** in the 3084. Each CCE controls up to 32 **Channel Elements** (CHE). A CHE serves the same function as a Data Server Element on the 3084. The difference is that the 3090-400 CHE controls four Channel Server Elements (CHN) and the DSE serves eight Interface Adapter Elements (IAEs). This may indicate that the channels on the 3090 are designed for six megabytes per second instead of the three megabytes per second on the 308x hardware. As of this writing, only 4.5 megabytes per second are supported on the 3090 hardware. N-way Processor Complexes are divisible in a fixed manner: Four CPU Processor Complexes must be split in half, two CPUs per side. You cannot partition one and three. (With PR/SM, the 3 to 1 division can be accomplished.)

While the partitioned mode looks like two completely separate processing systems, *it is not two processing systems*. There are common circuits. If one of these circuits has a problem, both sides may be affected. There are, however, two good reasons for running in partitioned mode:

1. Your data center is using MVS/370. Two 3081 processors have been joined together to form a 3084Q and the data center is converting from MVS/370 to MVS/XA to combine the processing into single image mode.

2. The data center must run separate versions of MVS:

    a. Virtual Storage constraint problems require it. There are data centers which have not been able to run all the work of the data center on one copy of MVS. (See the Virtual Storage chapter for more complete information on Virtual Storage constraint.)

    b. Security regulations require it. Even though MVS is a very secure environment, some military and business requirements will force a data center to have separate copies of MVS running.

    c. The data center wants to run a copy of MVS that may not be production quality. If the data center is testing modifications to MVS or a new subsystem, it is safest to run a separate copy of MVS and control the jobs and users that run on the second copy. You are not putting all your eggs in one basket!

There are several financial considerations to running MVS on a single Processor Complex. IBM will only charge one licensing fee for the 3084 or 3090-400 even if the Processor Complex is run in partitioned mode. Many OEM software vendors will want to charge multiple licensing fees if the Processor Complex runs in partitioned mode.

3.3. CENTRAL STORAGE MANAGEMENT

We will now look at the storage that MVS uses to service applications. The Read-Only Memory (ROM) that is available to the hardware will be introduced. The storage in the Processor Complex — Central Storage and Expanded Storage and the storage outside the Processor Complex that is used to support virtual storage — will be discussed.

3.3.1. Hardware Addressable: Read-Only Memory

Read-Only Memory (ROM) usually contains the instructions called **microcode**, which processes the System/370 instructions.

Microcode is the term used for the microinstructions in the hardware that tell the hardware how to execute the instructions designated in the Principle of Operations. Microcode is installed by the IBM customer engineer when *engineering changes* are made to the hardware.

Microcode is installed in a part of the Processor Complex that is not addressable by the operating system (MVS) or the application programs. Microcode is an alternative to electronic circuitry to implement function in the Processor Complex. For example, MVS could clear a 4-Kilobyte (Kb) page of Central Storage to zeros by using one or several instructions in the POP to write zeros to the Central Storage frame, or MVS could let the microcode clear a new page the first time it was accessed by a new address space. The latter is much faster because it is implemented in the microcode.

3.3.2. User Addressable: Central Storage

The MVS/XA architecture supports up to two gigabytes of Central Storage. The maximum available will increase from time to time as IBM doles out "Central Storage support."

Central Storage is allocated in 4-Kb blocks. Each block of Central Storage is referred to as a **page frame**. Each frame is assigned to a specific task in MVS. The frame could have one of three attributes: fixed, pageable, or available (see Figure 3.13).

Fixed pages are pages that some task has had assigned to it and then issued an MVS supervisor call to request that the page be "fixed" in storage. The page is marked as not available for any other task and the page must stay in exactly the place that it is when the supervisor call is issued.

An example of a fixed page is one used to store part of the MVS list of tasks or jobs that are executing. These pages are **long-term fixed** pages. The page will probably be fixed for a relatively long time — maybe for many weeks or as long as this copy of MVS is running this Processor Complex.

A second type of page fixing is for I/O operations. The System/370 architecture requires all buffer space to be "fixed" while the I/O operation is going on. It is reasonable that the I/O operation require that the page frame not "move" while the I/O subsystem is trying to move data from a tape, DASD, or other drive to a Central Storage frame. Just imagine the I/O processor trying to chase a Central Storage frame around 64 Mb of Central Storage to load it up with 800 bytes from a tape drive!

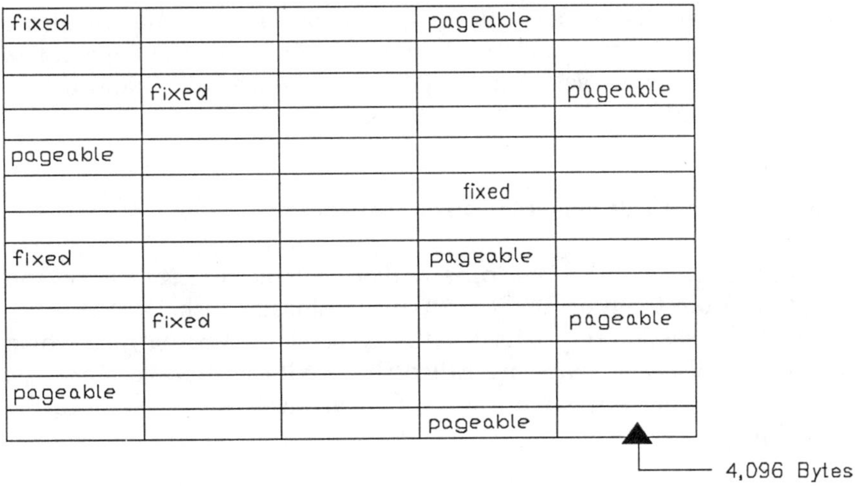

fixed			pageable		
	fixed				pageable
pageable					
				fixed	
fixed			pageable		
	fixed				pageable
pageable					
			pageable		

                                                    ▲
                                            └────── 4,096 Bytes

Figure 3.13   Central storage. Central Storage consists of pages that have been locked into storage ("fixed"), pages that are being used but are available for "page out," and available pages that can be used to satisfy requests for new pages. There are many available pages in this example to emphasize that MVS runs best with lots of available pages.

Therefore, if a program has a 32-Kb block to read, then 32Kb of Central Storage is fixed, the I/O is started, and once the I/O is completed, the 64-Kb pages are reset to "pageable." This is an example of **short-term fixed** pages. The pages will be fixed for only a relatively short time, such as one-tenth of a second.

A page is said to be pageable when the page is in Central Storage, and it is not short-term or long-term fixed.

MVS routines control the use of Central Storage and request the movement of Central Storage frames to Expanded Storage and auxiliary storage. The MVS routines that control Central Storage — Real Storage Manager (RSM) — assign Central Storage frames from an available pool called the "available frame queue." Frames are placed on the available frame queue when:

1. The address space terminates. All pages in use by the address space are made "available."
2. The page is freed by an address space.
3. The address space is swapped out and most of the pages that belonged to the address space are made available.

4. The page is "stolen." RSM "steals" pages when the available frame queue is below a minimum. RSM copies the page out to a system data set (Auxiliary Storage — see below) and marks it available.

3.3.3. System Addressable: Auxiliary Storage

What happens when MVS runs out of Central Storage pages and needs to store them on DASD? Auxiliary Storage is the DASD space that MVS uses for the "paged out" pages. The MVS routines which control DASD page space are called the Auxiliary Storage Manager. Figure 3.14 shows auxiliary storage. There are two types of DASD page space:

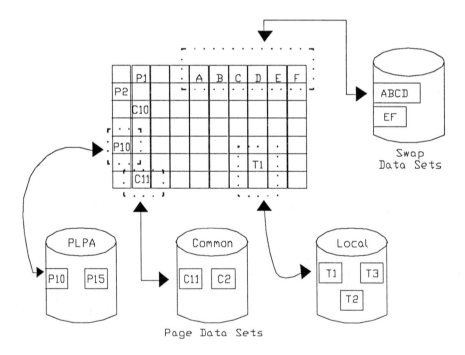

Figure 3.14   MVS Auxiliary Storage. MVS Central Storage is written to and read from two types of direct access data sets. The first type is **page** data sets. The second is **swap** data sets. Note page T1 is in Central Storage and also on the local page data set. This represents a page that was paged out at some previous time and has been brought back in. It exists in both places.

1. Page data sets contain single pages or blocks of pages assigned to a task. There are three types of page data sets:
   a. The Pageable Link Pack Area (PLPA) data set contains only the pages of the MVS modules which are in the "link pack area." PLPA will be described in detail later. Only one PLPA data set is allowed.
   b. The Common data set contains only the MVS data area pages which are common to all address spaces. Common will be described in detail later. Only one Common data set is allowed.
   c. The Local data set contains the pages of any address space which are not in Central Storage. More than one Local data set is recommended.
2. Swap data sets contain blocks of pages which are assigned to a task. Swap data sets will be described in detail later.

3.3.4. System Addressable: Expanded Storage

The 309x model series added a new type of internal storage. Expanded Storage is optional storage which provides more resources to the operating environment. As of this writing, the I/O subsystem does not do I/O operations to Expanded Storage.

Look at Figure 3.15. Page P1 can be moved from Central Storage to Expanded Storage very quickly — in approximately 75 microseconds. This is much quicker than an I/O to the auxiliary storage LOCAL data set, which might take 40 milliseconds, so the first use of Expanded Storage is to be a large repository for pages which are not needed now but have a good probability of being requested soon.

If page P2 was moved to Expanded Storage and was to be paged out, the page would have to be moved to Central Storage and then paged out to the LOCAL data set.

Expanded Storage is limited in its use and will be fully explained in the chapter on MVS/XA and MVS/ESA.

3.4. MULTIPROCESSING CONCEPTS

Many System/370 Processor Complexes are single processor models, but the trend is to more than one CPU to process the workload for MVS. MVS is a big Operating System. It seems natural that larger

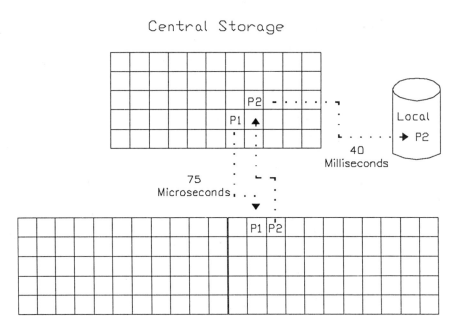

Figure 3.15   Expanded Storage. Expanded Storage is a second type of internal storage that is available only in the 309x family of Processor Complexes. Note page P2 had to be transferred from Expanded Storage back into Central Storage before being transferred to the Local page data set.

Processor Complexes will be used with MVS. There are several concepts that are needed for multiprocessing.

3.4.1.   Central Storage Access

The data a CPU needs to process may be program instructions, data in the form of Input/Output buffers that contain records from devices or "data areas" needed by programs. When a CPU does not find data in the cache, it sends a request to the Systems Controller. The data may be in Central Storage or in the cache of another CPU (if multiprocessing). The speed of access is increased by a concept called "pipelining."

Pipelining Data Access   In parallel, the Systems Controller looks at Central Storage and the cache of the other CPUs. The first request to finish cancels the other requests and reads the data into the cache of the CPU requesting the data. This parallel access is called **pipelining**.

If the data had been fetched as **exclusive** — the program in that CPU wanted to update the data — the buffer that has the requested data is instructed to **buffer cast out** the data. The data in the "from" buffer is moved to Central Storage for all CPUs to access.

The method of pipelining, and therefore its effectiveness, is usually proprietary to the individual Processor Complex. Because it is, a data center evaluating multiple vendors' Processor Complexes would do well to benchmark[4] their jobstreams to see how their data will be processed.

Data Transfer Size   Each Processor Complex has different sizes of data transfer. The size started somewhere around 16 bytes and has worked up to at least 128 bytes. Much of the method and size of the pipelining operation is proprietary information about the Processor Complex.

3.4.2. System Time of Day (TOD) Clock and Clock Comparator

Each physical "side" of a Processor Complex has its own TOD clock and clock comparator. The 3083 has one, as do the single CPU 3090s. The 3090-400 and the 3084 have two — one for each "side." A separate clock is needed in case the data center is running in "partitioned" mode. If the Processor Complex is in single image mode, the clocks are synchronized to give the same value from all CPUs in the complex.

In addition to these "operating system" clocks, there is a hardware clock associated with each "side." The hardware clock is used by the Processor Complex to time stamp information kept by the diagnostic

---

4. The term "benchmark" is used to describe the process of collecting programs, data, and the JCL required to run the programs into a portable package that can be run with different software or hardware. The output should be identical (the function is the same), and the performance and resources consumed should be compared to see how the new software or hardware performed.

portions of the Processor Complex. The operating system cannot access these clocks, which are powered by a battery inside the Processor Complex much like the battery in your Personal Computer or watch.

One of the great questions that has plagued many data centers is why the Processor Complex cannot set the TOD clocks from the hardware clock. The TOD clocks are reset to "invalid" when the Processor Complex performs a **Power On Reset**. MVS (and other operating systems) discover the TOD clock is invalid and ask the operator to "set the TOD clock" when an IPL is performed after a Power-On Reset.

The TOD clock synchronization problem becomes more serious with multiple Processor Complexes. One Processor Complex could receive a task to process at 11:00 A.M. (according to its clock) and process it on another Processor Complex at 10:59 A.M. (according to that Processor Complex's clock).

Over the years, several home-grown solutions have tried to address this situation. Some placed a quartz clock (or even link to the National Bureau of Standards!) as a "device" attached to the Processor Complex. The IPL was interrupted to "read" the time and set the TOD clock.

IBM now has a TOD clock enabling mechanism with the 3090 E/S models. SEC 223670 will enable the TOD setting from "a battery operated PCE battery." If your data center has a need to synchronize clocks, you may want to investigate these solutions.

One warning to the data center: When you automate anything, implement checking routines. The hardware clock may not be set correctly to begin with. The hardware clock may not be accurate. It may gain or lose time over a period of days, weeks, or months. Create a procedure to "check the clocks" periodically.

3.4.3. Input/Output Interrupts

When an Input/Output operation is requested, the device will want to signal that the process is complete. In the case of MVS/370 operation, the CPU which initiated the request must be interrupted. In the case of MVS/XA and MVS/ESA, although any CPU can be interrupted, MVS controls which one actually will be interrupted. The method of control is to turn on bits in the control registers that allow or disallow interruptions by the Input/Output subsystem.

3.5. CENTRAL STORAGE PROTECTION

There are a number of storage protection methods designed into the System/370 architecture and implemented in MVS. Protection of Central Storage is vital to keeping one application from intentionally or accidentally harming another application — including MVS and its subsystems.

3.5.1. Types of Protection

Central Storage contains data from all tasks in the system. The System/370 architecture must be able to protect one task's storage from another task's access — either read or write.

Central Storage protection is implemented by assigning attributes to Central Storage page frames. There are several types of protection, presented here in the order that IBM introduced them:

1. Storage Key protection.
2. Segment protection.
3. Low Address Protection.
4. Page protection.

3.5.2. Storage Key Protection

Each block of Central Storage has an additional — hidden — byte associated with it called the **storage protection key**. This is similar to the parity bit but is another byte altogether and is one byte per 2048 bytes and not one bit per byte like the parity bit.

A key is associated with each 2048 bytes (2Kb) of Central Storage. In DOS systems, Central Storage is allocated, and thus protected, in 2-Kb increments. In all MVS systems, storage is allocated, and thus protected, in 4,096 byte (4-Kb) increments. There are still two protect keys; MVS just sets them both to the same value.

Figure 3.16 shows the eight bits of a storage key. The leftmost four bits are allocated to the protection key. With 4 bits, we can have storage keys from 0 to 15 or a total of 16 possibilities. If all the bits were 0, that block would have a storage key of 0. Key 0 is reserved to protect MVS storage. In the example, the storage key is 1000 (binary), a value of eight.

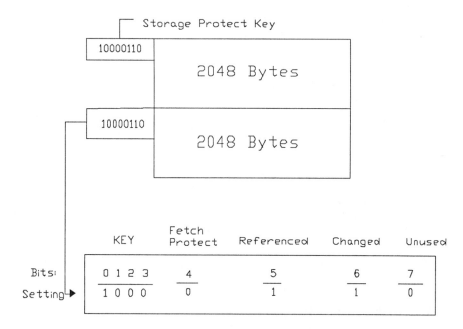

Figure 3.16   Storage key protection. A physical block of Central Storage (2 Kb in both DOS and MVS) contains an extra byte called a storage key. The key contains information about the block: A protection key, a fetch protection bit, a referenced bit, and a changed bit. MBS combines two 2-Kb "blocks" into one 4-Kb "frame."

The total number of nonzero protection keys is 15. In all of the previrtual systems, such as MVT and MFT, there was a limitation of 15 initiators — each initiator required its own storage protection key. The limit of 15 jobs running at one time was acceptable for a System/360 model 40, but is not acceptable for a 308x or 309x processor.

The remaining bits of the protection key indicate the status of the storage block. The CPU and channels change these bits as a matter of course when processing instructions.

Bit 4, the fifth bit from the left, is the fetch protection bit. If this bit is set, then only the operating system, not application code, can read or "fetch" data from this block.

Bit 5, the sixth bit from the left, is the referenced bit. If a program references any data (reads data or executes instructions in the block), then the hardware turns on this bit to show MVS that the block has been used.

Bit 6, the seventh bit from the left, is the changed bit. If any bits in this block of data are changed, the hardware turns on this bit to indicate to the operating system that some data has changed. In this manner, MVS can detect if it is necessary to write a copy of this block of Central Storage to auxiliary storage (paging or swapping).

Bit 7, the eighth bit from the left, is unused.

In previrtual operating systems, the operating system used key zero for itself and assigned another key to a job or task as it was initiated. (Remember these operating systems were limited to 15 tasks — the number of "other" keys.) In MVS, the keys are assigned differently:

1. Key 0 is storage used by MVS for control blocks (nucleus) and reentrant modules.
2. Key 1 is storage used by the job scheduler (JES2, JES3).
3. Key 2 is storage used by the **Virtual Storage Personal Computing** (VSPC) subsystem — a timesharing system which supports multiple terminals under one address space.
4. Key 3 is reserved.
5. Key 4 is reserved.
6. Key 5 is storage used by data management (IOS, OPEN/CLOSE).
7. Key 6 is storage used by TCAM and VTAM.
8. Key 7 is storage used by Information Management System/Virtual Storage (IMS/VS) — a database/data communications system.
9. Key 8 is used by all batch jobs and all TSO address spaces. In JCL this key is assigned for "V=V" address spaces — Virtual=Virtual.
10. Keys 9–15 are reserved for Virtual=Real jobs. A V–R job is a batch job or started task that requires contiguous Central Storage to operate. There are almost no tasks left which have this requirement, but MVS is an upward compatible system and keeps function around forever.

A Storage Protection key value is associated with each Central Storage page frame, but how does MVS associate that page with a specific task? For the answer we need to look closer at the Program Status Word, or PSW (see Figure 3.17). The PSW contains a protection key as part of the PSW. For MVS/370, MVS/XA, and MVS/ESA, bits 8–11 contain a storage key. Any time the CPU attempts to store data into Central Storage, the storage keys are compared:

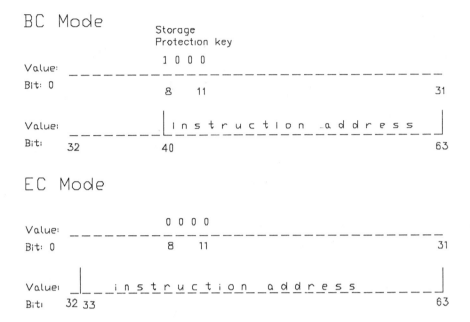

Figure 3.17   Program Status Word (PSW). There are two types of PSW. The BC mode is used for non-MVS operating systems. The EC mode is used for MVS. MVS/370 uses 24 bits for the address in EC mode. MVS/XA and MVS/ESA uses 31 bits for the address.

1. The **protection key** in the "current PSW" is matched against the **storage key** of the block before a write takes place.
2. The write is allowed if the keys match or if the protection key in the PSW is zero. A PSW key of zero can store in any block (see restrictions below).
3. A protection exception will result in a program error interrupt if the keys do not match and the protection key in the PSW is not zero.

From above, remember that MVS uses a key of 0 to protect most of its data areas. The application code — executing with a PSW protection Key of eight — cannot modify MVS (or other operating system) data areas.

What prevents the application from modifying its PSW to key 0? The answer is that to modify the "current" PSW is a **privileged instruction**. Only MVS supervisor routines are in privileged mode.

What about other tasks' Central Storage blocks? After all, all jobs, TSO sessions, CICS regions, etc., are in the key of eight. Therefore,

all Central Storage pages are in key 8. What keeps them from clob-
bering each other?

The answer is in the Central Storage Management operating system programs' control blocks: **segment and page tables**. The inter-
nals of Real Storage Manager (RSM) are beyond the scope of this
book, but until you take a good MVS structure and flow class, suffice
it to say that when a Central Storage page frame is assigned to an
address space, it is noted in MVS control blocks. If a program tries to
address a Central Storage block that is not assigned to the address
space, then a program interruption will occur and the access will be
prevented.

This program interrupt is an x'0C4' abend and usually causes confusion among application programmers. Just remember, an x'0C4'
abend is accessing any area which is not assigned to your task. Look
for index registers or table pointers which did not stop while looping
through a table or that were not initialized.

While we are looking at Figure 3.17, note that the instruction address is 24 bits long in BC mode and 31 bits long in EC mode.

3.5.3. Segment Protection

The second type of storage protection is Segment protection. Figure
3.18 shows segment protection. All of MVS/370 Virtual Storage is
divided into 64Kb segments. MVS/XA and MVS/ESA Virtual Storage
is divided into one-megabyte segments. If the program or system has

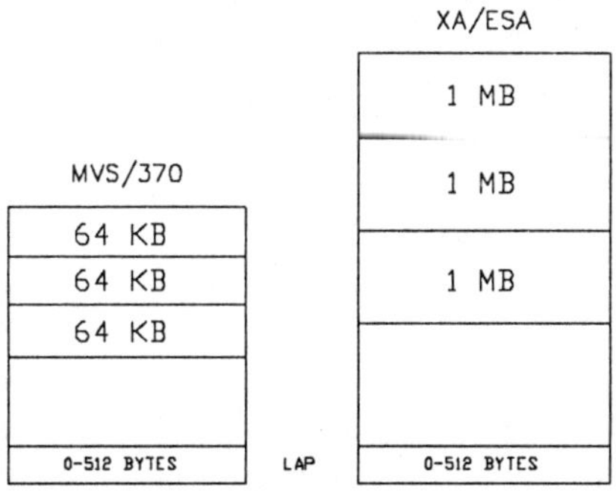

Figure 3.18   Segment protection and LAP. Segment protection is the second
method by which the System/370 architecture allows the MVS operating system
to protect itself and other users from damage. In MVS/370 the segments are 1
Mb so page protection is used. Low address protection is a method of
protecting MVS from itself.

not obtained storage from the segment, or if the segment is not included as part of the common area, then that entire 64-Kb segment is unavailable to the program. A segment may be marked read only to prevent either applications programs or systems programs from modifying areas that should be read only.

3.5.4.   Low Address Protection (LAP)

The third type of protection is Low Address Protection (LAP). Low Address Protection is designed to protect Central Storage addresses x'00000000' to x'00000200' (the first 512 bytes) from damage.

These addresses are important because this area is used by the hardware to control timer interrupts, supervisor calls, program checks, machine checks, and Input/Output interrupts. The hardware stores the address of the program interrupted and loads the address of the MVS routine that will handle the interrupt.

We have learned that any task operating with a PSW key of zero could store in any Central Storage page frame, regardless of its protection key. In order to make MVS even more reliable, the hardware was changed to require an additional bit in one of the special registers in order to allow the alteration of the first 512 bytes of Central Storage, making this act a very deliberate one.

Let's examine one use of this Low Address area. (For reasons described later, this is also called the "Prefixed Save Area.") From above, we said that an application program could request a service from MVS. Well, how does that happen? The application program could execute one of the instructions in the System/370 Principles of Operation called Supervisor Call (SVC). The Supervisor Call NEW PSW is located at hex location x'68'.

The System/370 architecture stores the current PSW (which includes the current address) in **Supervisor Call Old PSW** and loads the PSW from the **Supervisor Call New PSW**. The protection key is set (zero), the "problem state" bit is turned off so that MVS can execute privileged operations. The address in the Supervisor Call NEW PSW is called the **First Level Interrupt Handler** (FLIH).

This "branching" has a new name: **state change** (more generally known in literature as "context switching"). The state of the System/370 has changed from "application" to "system."

In Figure 3.19, note that the application program is executing instructions and needs some supervisor service. An SVC is issued which "state changes" to MVS to perform the service. MVS returns to the program by reloading the old PSW.

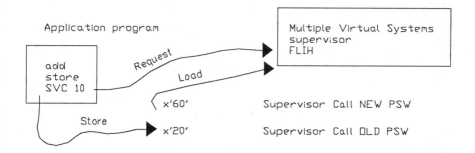

Figure 3.19   State change — First Level Interrupt Handler. An application
program asks MVS for supervisor services by issuing an SVC. The System/370
architecture states that the current PSW is stored in the OLD PSW location and
the new PSW is loaded. Control is transferred to the First Level interrupt
handler.

3.5.5. Page Protection of System Areas

MVS/XA continued the quest to protect system areas better than its
predecessor MVS/370. Page protection is implemented in MVS/XA
and MVS/ESA to protect system areas that are not protected by segment protection or Low Address Protection. Page protection is in addition to storage protection keys — we are protecting MVS from itself, not from application programs.

Page protection in MVS/XA and MVS/ESA helps prevent acciden-
tal or intentional changing of Central Storage pages by marking
specific pages as being "read-only."

Let's look at one reason to make a single page "read-only." A
reentrant program is one that has been written so that it does not
modify any area inside the program. All data — counters, addresses,
values — are changed in areas outside the program.

The program could be used concurrently by two or more tasks in
the same or different address spaces. The savings are substantial.
One (or several) Central Storage page frames could service many
tasks.

Example   What if a program marked reentrant actually modifies itself? This could cause system software errors. For example, in Figure
3.20:

1. Program A (running in job DATA01) is executing to apply pay
    raises.

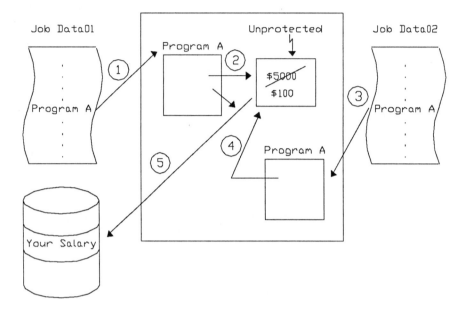

Figure 3.20   Module Storage Protection. This example shows why Central Storage pages need to be marked "read only" to prevent programming errors from using the same virtual storage (mapped onto Central Storage) for two purposes at the same time.

2. Program A stores a pay raise for you in the amount of $5,000 into some common Virtual Storage that is unprotected. Program A is interrupted.
3. Job DATA02 starts to execute program A to give a $100 pay raise to the office clown.
4. Program A, in job DATA02, stores the $100 in the same common Virtual Storage.
5. Program A, in job DATA01, is dispatched and writes to the payroll file, not knowing that your pay raise of $5,000 has been lowered to $100.

Now do you know why protection is desirable? While this example may seem far-fetched, it happens. Usually, applications do not share common Virtual Storage, but this can happen — and sometimes does with system modules.

Bypassing protection As with all security, there is a way around page protection. When MVS/XA was first installed, many IBM modules and data center accounting modules were discovered to violate this rule. The modules protected themselves in various ways — system locks, disabling, etc. — but MVS/XA was going to be delayed as developers discovered and changed the offending code.

A work-around was created for these situations. Page protection is optional on the Fixed Link Pack Area (FLPA) and the Modified Link Pack Area (MLPA). To remove the protection, specify in SYS1.PARMLIB member IEASYSxx: **MLPA=(,,NOPROT)** and/or **FIX=(,,NOPROT)**.

It is okay to disable the protection until the problem is corrected, but be sure the protection is reinstated. Look at all members of IEASYSxx MLPA and FIX members. If any of them specify no protection, ask your systems programmer why. If you are your systems programmer, remove them and see what happens — in a test environment at first, of course.

3.6. SUMMARY

The computers that MVS runs on are based on the binary numbering system, but people use the hexadecimal numbering system because it is compact. The System/370 architecture combines eight bits — from "Binary digIT" — to form a byte. Two bytes are a halfword. Four bytes are a word. Eight bytes are a doubleword.

A kilobyte (Kb) is 1,024 bytes. A megabyte (Mb) is 1,024 kilobytes or 1,048,576 bytes. A gigabyte (Gb) is 1,024 megabytes or 1,073,741,824 bytes. A terabyte (Tb) is 1,024 gigabytes or 1,099,511,627,776 bytes.

The Processor Complex contains Central Storage to hold programs and data for MVS. One or more Central Processor Units (CPUs) actually process instructions. General purpose registers hold data, counters, or addresses. Floating point registers are used for large (or small) mathematical processing. Special purpose registers, such as control registers and access registers, are set by MVS to control how the hardware operates.

MVS supports uniprocessors (one CPU) and multiprocessors (two or more CPUs in a Processor Complex). Some multiprocessors can be divided into partitioned mode so that two copies of MVS (or other operating system) can be running concurrently. Multitasking is the term for a single address space that has more than one program active at one time. A multitasking address space can benefit when operating on a multiprocessing Processor Complex because there is concurrent instruction execution with multiple CPUs.

Some memory in the Processor Complex is read-only and not accessible by MVS. Central Storage is accessible by all MVS tasks and is referenced by addresses as small as a byte. Central Storage is "paged" in and out of system data sets grouped together on Auxiliary Storage. An option for the 309x series of Processor Complexes is Expanded Storage, which is similar to an overflow for Central Storage pages.

MVS uses a number of protection methods to keep applications, and MVS itself, from reading from or writing to areas in Central Storage. Storage key protection flags a Central Storage page frame as belonging to a logical group of programs. Segment protection allows MVS to flag units of 1 megabyte (MVS/370) or 64 megabytes (MVS/XA or MVS/ESA) of storage as "read-only." Low Address Protection and page protection assist MVS in protecting units of 4,096 bytes (that is, pages).

The next chapter will show the MVS implementation of Virtual Storage and the contents of Virtual Storage in the MVS environment.

4

Virtual Storage

4.1. INTRODUCTION TO VIRTUAL STORAGE

Virtual Storage is what the application programmer can access. Each
MVS task — address space — has its own copy of Virtual Storage.
This chapter will look at Virtual Storage in depth, from the contents
of the various versions of MVS to the services that MVS performs, to
the auxiliary storage that maps Virtual Storage.

4.1.1. Central Storage to Virtual Storage

Before virtual Operating Systems such as MVS/370, MVS/XA, and
MVS/ESA, the Operating System loaded programs in their entirety
into Central Storage as the program or job was selected for execution. If the program required 400Kb of storage at any time during
the execution of the program, then all 400Kb of storage was allocated
at the start of the program and freed up at program termination.

Remember from previous chapters that Virtual Storage or Central
Storage is measured in thousands of bytes but because all computers
are based on the binary system (base 2), we measure in thousands in
base two, or 1,024 bytes or characters. A kilobyte is 1,024 bytes. A
megabyte is 1,024 * 1,024 or 1,048,576 bytes. In this book and most
others, we speak in terms of "K" or "Kb," which is short for kilobytes.

One technique used in Operating Systems before MVS to alleviate
a storage crunch was called **overlays**. The design of overlays was to
have a **root** segment of some size with all commonly used routines

and segments that would overlay each other as functions were needed. Overlays required extra personnel time to set up and extra Operating System time was needed to run an "overlay" program. There may be overlay programs in your data center, but they should be removed. Overlay should not be needed in an MVS environment.

Most programs require different sizes of Central Storage to run. Most programs also require different elapsed time or wall clock time to execute. This caused several problems in systems without Virtual Storage.

1. **Infrequently Used Central Storage.** Some portions of Central Storage were not efficiently used:
   a. Some Central Storage was never used because some storage within programs is reserved for a rare event to happen. An example is in a payroll program. In Figure 4.1, Job A could be processing a weekly payroll. A routine is required to process an employee that left for some reason. If Job A were run once a week and only one person left during the year, the Central Storage would be allocated for the length of the payroll job for each of the 52 weeks but used only during one week.
   b. Some Central Storage was used once and not used again. In our payroll job, there is a routine to calculate the number of days in this month. Once used, the value is available for all other routines. The Central Storage to hold that part of the program would remain allocated until the entire payroll program finished.
2. **Fragmented Central Storage.** Some portions of Central Storage were not used due to fragmentation. In Figure 4.1:
   a. Job A starts and uses 200K or 204,800 bytes.
   b. Job B starts and uses 50K or 51,200 bytes.
   c. Job C starts and uses 200K or 204,800 bytes.
   d. Job B ends, freeing 50K or 51,200 bytes.
   e. Job D tries to start, requiring 100K or 102,400 bytes, but cannot because the Central Storage must be contiguous. There is 50K in the middle and 62K at the end, but not 100K in contiguous central storage, so job D must wait for job C to finish.

The data center would run more smoothly if, in Figure 4.1, the free portions could be pushed together to form one 112K region. The result was that programmers and systems analysts devised many ways to reduce the Central Storage requirements. Many hours were

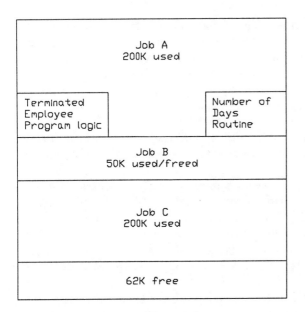

Figure 4.1   Central Storage without Virtual Storage. Fragmentation of Central Storage is much worse in an architecture that does not include Virtual Storage.

spent rewriting programs and systems to improve Central Storage efficiency.

4.1.2. Address Spaces

The goal of Virtual Storage is to free the programmer and the data center from Central Storage management issues. The concept of an **address space** was developed to accomplish this.

An **address space** is a range of virtual addresses that is accessible to **a program**. This range of addresses is a contiguous area that is available for the program to access program instructions, data areas, I/O buffers, etc. The range of addresses is from 0 to either 16 Mb or 2 Gb, depending on the MVS version.

Virtual Storage can be thought of as a glass that is filled by adding things to the bottom. One example of adding things is the loading of the program. The program could be "poured" into the bottom of the glass — like soda — then executed. A second example of adding could be defining I/O buffers to read in or write out data. One could think of this as adding whipped cream to the top of the glass.

The first virtual systems (SVS—Single Virtual Systems) used only a single virtual address space for the entire system. The benefit that SVS gave the IBM user was that it partially overcame the problem in Figure 4.1 above. No matter how much Central Storage the processor complex had, the user community could allocate up to 16 Mb among the running jobs. Figure 4.2 shows the jobs of Figure 4.1 running under SVS; job D can now start.

Some people thought that SVS was a stopgap to allow larger processor complexes to run more efficiently while IBM completed the real goal: MVS.

As Processor Complexes became more powerful, Central Storage was too expensive to waste. A single address space used Central Storage more efficiently, but it quickly became clear that multiple address spaces were the solution to growing program demands. With MVS, each job has its own address space, and each address space could be as large as 16 Mb (MVS/370) or two Gb (MVS/XA and MVS/ESA).

As MVS starts up, it creates a single address space (the MASTER address space) and several other "Operating System" address spaces. Examples are CATALOG (to manage VSAM catalog requests), CONSOLE (to manage communication to OS consoles in the computer room), and GRS (to manage queuing resources across address spaces and across multiple computers).

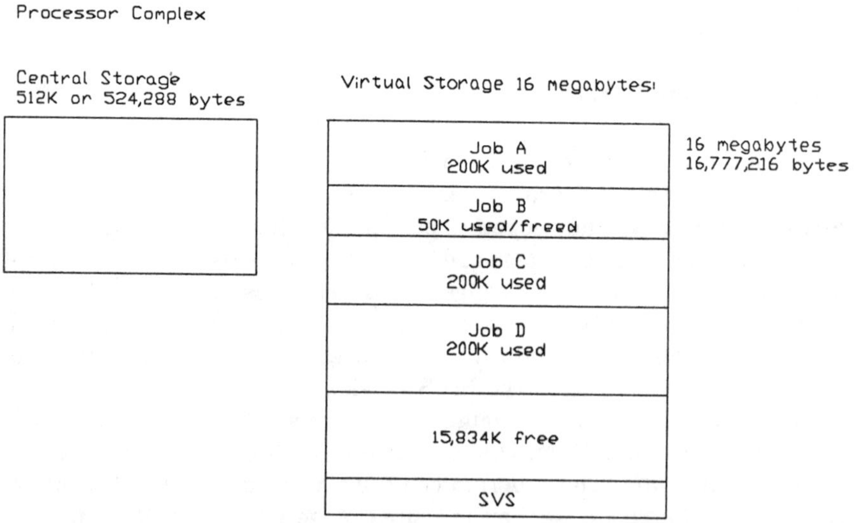

Processor Complex

Central Storage
512K or 524,288 bytes

Virtual Storage 16 megabytes

Job A 200K used	16 megabytes 16,777,216 bytes
Job B 50K used/freed	
Job C 200K used	
Job D 200K used	
15,834K free	
SVS	

Figure 4.2   SVS — Single Virtual Space. SVS allowed a virtual storage of 16 Mb to be used for all programs.

4.1.3. Virtual Storage Sizes

Virtual Storage is a concept that *defines an address space for use in computing.* The "virtual" in "virtual storage" indicates that the size potentially extends beyond the computer's Central Storage. Virtual Storage size was originally designed to always exceed the Central Storage size, but as we will see, central storage caught up with and passed Virtual Storage in MVS/370. Central Storage options in MVS/XA and MVS/ESA are now equal to the Virtual Storage — 2 Gb.

In science and engineering, the prefix "mega-" means ten to the sixth power. When referring to storage capacity, it is two to the twentieth power. A megabyte is 1,048,576 bytes. For MVS/370, the range is from 0 through 16,777,215, or 16 megabytes. For MVS/XA and MVS/ESA, the range is from 0 through 2,147,483,647, or 2 gigabytes. The prefix "giga" means ten to the ninth power, but in the binary system it means two to the thirtieth power, or 1,073,741,824 (in decimal notation).

Computer manufacturers did not just sit in a smoke-filled back room and elect 16 megabytes and 2 gigabytes as the standard. Remember, computers are based on binary — power of 2 — because they are designed with silicon transistor-based logic: on and off, zero and one, so addresses (and everything else in computers) are defined in multiples of single bits. The 16 megabytes came from the S/370 architecture which defines 24 bits for an address — 24 bits is hex FFFFFF, which is 16,777,216, or 16 megabytes. The 2 gigabytes came from the S/370 eXtended Architecture that defines 31 bits for an address — 31 bits is hex 7FFFFFF, which is 2,147,483,647 bytes, or 2 gigabytes.

Virtual may be the same size as, or different from, the size of central storage:

1. In an MVS/370 system virtual is always 16 Mb:
   a. Virtual Storage could be exactly equal to Central Storage: 16 Mb of Central Storage and 16 Mb of virtual.
   b. Virtual Storage could be smaller than Central Storage: 24 Mb of Central Storage and 16 Mb of virtual.
   c. Virtual Storage could be larger than Central Storage: 8 Mb of Central Storage and 16 Mb of virtual.
2. In an MVS/XA and MVS/ESA, system Virtual Storage is 2 Gb:
   a. Virtual Storage could be exactly equal to Central Storage: 2 Gb of Central Storage and 2 Gb of virtual.

    b. Virtual Storage could be larger than Central Storage: 24 Mb of Central Storage and 2 Gb of virtual.

4.2. VIRTUAL STORAGE CONTENTS

In Figure 4.3, we see the types of areas that are used by MVS for your programs. Examples are:

1. The computer program. Usually a program consists of several parts:
   a. The program you want to execute. These are the "add" or "move" statements you want to execute to perform a certain task.
   b. Compiler runtime library programs. Most programs are compiled or assembled and include "calls" to subprograms supplied with the compiler. One example is to open a file for processing.
   c. Access method programs. As we explained in Part I, MVS contains many programs to help you accomplish the task at hand. One example is the programs that open, read or write to data sets. Another example is a spooler such as JES, which accepts and prints lines of output. Another example is error recovery modules to intercept and overcome hardware and software errors.

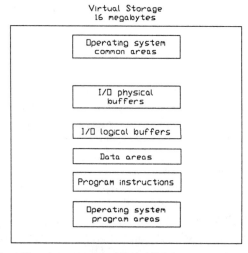

Figure 4.3   Virtual Storage contents. Virtual Storage contains parts of the Operating System — in this case MVS/370 — and areas for your program.

2. Data in the form of counters, names, etc.
3. I/O buffers for logical records (one record as you have defined it in your data), and I/O buffers for physical records (groups of one or more logical records that are the size transferred to and from I/O devices).
4. MVS/370, MVS/XA, and MVS/ESA Operating System code, data, and I/O buffers. Subsequent chapters will detail what is in these areas and how they support you.

4.2.1. Instructions

In Figure 4.4, instructions are System/370 machine instructions produced as a result of a compilation of programs written in COBOL, FORTRAN, PL/I, or Assembler. The programs may be utilities such as sorts, Operating System programs such as IDCAMS, or programs you write. In Figure 4.4, three instructions in a high level language are part of a program that was written for a specific application. The instructions are placed into a data set by the programmer, input to a compiler to generate assembler or machine instructions, processed by the Linkage editor program, and are now in "executable form."

The executable form is read into Virtual Storage by the Operating System. The Operating System allocates Central Storage frames and transfers the executable form of the program into Central Storage.

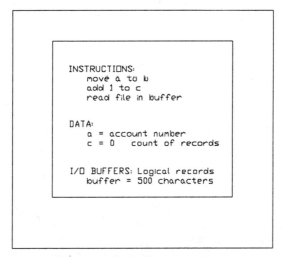

Figure 4.4   Virtual Storage. Virtual Storage can contain program instructions, data used by the program, or I/O buffers for reading and writing data from DASD, tapes, or other devices.

This Central Storage is now associated with, or "maps," the Virtual Storage of the program.

4.2.2. Data

Data is the report titles, counters, or other data areas that are used by programs. Data may be inside the program ("nonreentrant programming") or completely outside the program ("reentrant programming"). You will see later why reentrant programming is better.

4.2.3. Operating System Common Areas

The Operating System also needs areas within virtual storage for programs, data areas, I/O buffers, and hardware reserved areas:

1. **Program areas:** The Operating System (MVS/370, MVS/XA, MVS/ESA or any other Operating System) needs program areas. Examples are programs to communicate with the system consoles and programs to handle hardware interrupts.
2. **Data areas:** The Operating System executes in the Master address space, and user programs execute in other address spaces. Movement can only take place in controlled circumstances across address spaces. Thus, common data areas are required:
   a. User program puts a message in a common area.
   b. User program notifies the system, via supervisor call, that the message is there.
   c. Operating System receives and acts upon message, maybe returning some data through the common area.
3. **I/O buffers:** Most terminals are controlled by system communications software such as the Virtual Telecommunications Access Method (VTAM) or TeleCommunications Access Method (TCAM). In these cases, the I/O buffer for the terminal is in some other address space, and as you type on a terminal, the data is received by VTAM/TCAM and transferred to a TSO or CICS address space.
4. **Hardware area:** The hardware and software have common areas that both can read and write to pass information between each other.

The "first page frame" is one hardware "work area." In MVS, this area is called the **Prefixed Save Area** (PSA). The PSA is the first page (beginning at address zero) of Central Storage unless there is more than one CPU in a processor complex. In the case of two or more CPUs, the first page is "moved" to another area — one area for each CPU. When the PSA is moved, it is moved for all CPUs in the Processor Complex. The first 4K of Central Storage is "wasted" because it is not used by any CPU.

Another work area is the **Hardware Save Area** (HSA). In 308x and 309x models, the Processor Complex microcode interfaces with the MVS Operating System to define the hardware attached to the Processor Complex. This process is explained later.

4.2.4. I/O Buffers — Logical Records

Most programs access *one logical record* at a time. The logical record is the size of the record defined in the program. For example, 100 characters for name + 400 characters for address = 500 characters total (see Figure 4.5). Logical records are contained in contiguous areas of Virtual Storage. In this example, 500 bytes of Virtual Storage would be allocated to this one logical record.

4.2.5. I/O Buffers — Physical Records

Logical buffers are placed into physical buffers (physical referring to the actual blocks that are transferred from Central Storage to an I/O device). These blocks are very important to the way an application executes under MVS.

Name	Address
100 Bytes	400 Bytes

Figure 4.5   Logical records. One logical record is the size that the programmer/analyst determines at file design time. In this case, the logical record is 500 characters, or bytes, long. 100 bytes is for the name field and 400 bytes is for the access field.

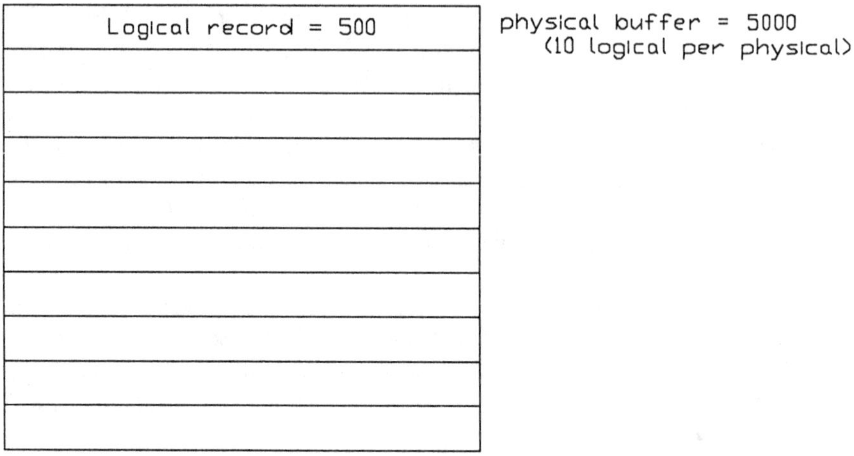

Logical record = 500

physical buffer = 5000
(10 logical per physical)

Figure 4.6   Logical vs. physical records. In this example, the logical record is 500 bytes long. The physical record is 5,000 bytes long. Each physical record can contain up to 10 logical records.

Logical Versus physical records   Physical records are groups of logical records (see Figure 4.6). Subsequent chapters will discuss each of these types of blocking and the "access methods" that are required to access each type.

1. There may be one logical record per physical record. This type is called **UNBLOCKED**.
2. There may be an integral number of logical records per physical record. This type is called **BLOCKED**. See Figure 4.6 for an example of a blocked record.
3. There may be parts of one logical record in multiple physical records. This type is called **SPANNED**. See Figure 4.7 for an example of a spanned record.

Physical Record Size   Physical record size is determined by rules of where the physical size is defined. Figure 4.8 illustrates the following:

1. The first place MVS looks to find the physical record size is from within the program. The program is deemed most important, because if the programmer placed the size in the pro-

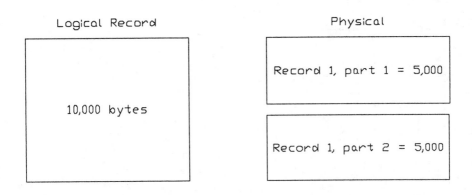

Figure 4.7 Spanned records. In this example, the logical record size is 10,000 bytes. The physical record size is 5,000 bytes. Each logical record requires two physical records.

gram, there must be a really good reason for him to have it in the program. If the size is specified (e.g., nonzero) in the program, the system does not look further for the physical record size.

Specifications within the program should only be used for very special cases. If the size is in the program, then you must recompile the program to change the block size.

I recommend that you do not let the program control the physical block size. In COBOL programs, use **BLOCK CONTAINS ZERO**. In Assembler, code **BLKSIZE=0** on DCB macros.

2. The second place MVS looks to find the physical record size is in the Job Control Language (JCL). The JCL DD card statement can specify the physical record size with the BLKSIZE parameter to determine the physical block size of the record. This is the preferred area for specification for all new files.

Warning: If a file is built with a block size of 4,000 bytes, you cannot magically change it by specifying 5,000 bytes on the JCL. If the file is an old or previously built file, then the block size must be specified as it was at the time the file was created. The only way to "change" the block size is to create a new file with the new block size and copy the contents of the old file to it.

There are special considerations for VSAM that will be discussed later.

```
┌─────────────────────┐       ╱──────────────────────────────────────────╲
│                     │      ╱  2. On the JCL                              │
│                     │     │      non VSAM:   DCB=BLKSIZE on DD Card      │
│                     │     │      VSAM:                                   │
│                     │     │         AMP=('BUFSP=nnn')                    │
│                     │     │            or                               │
│                     │     │         AMP=('BUFND=nnn','BUFNI=nnn')        │
│ 1. Within the program│     └──────────────────────────────────────────────┘
│                     │
│    -- Do not use.   │
│                     │           ╭────────────────────╮
│                     │          ╱                      ╲
│                     │         │                        │
│                     │         │  3. On the DASD VTOC   │
│                     │         │     or VSAM Catalog    │
│                     │         │    (at define time)    │
│                     │          ╲                      ╱
└─────────────────────┘           ╰────────────────────╯
```

Figure 4.8   Where MVS gets the physical block size. MVS first looks at the program control blocks. If MVS finds the physical block size there, that is the one it uses. It is not recommended that programs specify the physical block size, because any changes would require recompiling the program. The JCL parameters should be used for allocating files. After allocation, the VTDC or tape label will contain the physical block size.

3. The third place MVS looks for the physical block size is in the DASD Volume Table of Contents (VTOC), the tape label, or the VSAM catalog. This is the preferred place for old data sets. Once the file has been created, the system keeps attributes including the physical block size. Programs and JCL should not redescribe the size.

I/O Considerations   The MVS access method modules group one or more logical records into physical records. The size of the physical record is the size of the data transported to and from the I/O device. Blocking is the first method of tuning I/O processes.

The physical block size of the final output file may be constrained by the origin or destination of a file. For example, most microfiche machines and other "nonattached" peripherals will have block size constraints. These peripherals do not have sophisticated operating systems to perform blocking and deblocking routines.

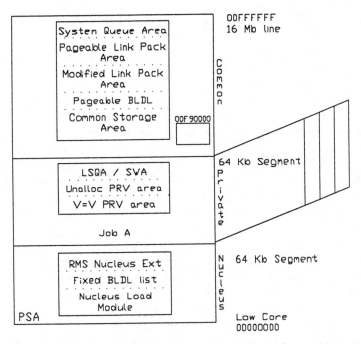

Figure 4.9   MVS/370 Virtual Storage Management. Virtual Storage is limited to 16 megabytes. It is segmented into three parts — common, private, and nucleus.

4.3.   MVS/370 VIRTUAL STORAGE CONTENTS

Now let's look at a detailed picture of MVS/370 virtual storage (see Figure 4.9). The areas discussed in MVS/370 will be in the MVS/XA and MVS/ESA Virtual Storage, only they will be mirrored above and below the 16-Mb line.

MVS Virtual Storage is logically divided into three parts. The top part is common area, the bottom part is common area and what is left in between is for the user's programs. *The middle part is replicated as many times as there are address spaces.* Each boundary is located on a 64-Kb boundary. Each section is an integral number of 64Kb bytes.

The middle part is where your program or job runs — called the **private area**. The space above and below is available for communication *by all jobs in the system*. That is, address x'00F90000' in job A's address space references *exactly* the same Central Storage byte as address x'00F90000' in all other address spaces.

4.3.1. MVS/370 Virtual Storage — Common (TOP)

Approximately the top one-half to one-third of virtual storage contains the common control block areas and the common MVS module areas (see Figure 4.10). The System Queue Area (SQA) is for control blocks shared across address spaces. The Pageable Link Pack Area (PLPA) contains the common MVS modules such as the access method modules. Performance of the whole system is improved by placing modules in the PLPA, which normally are in the system link libraries. For example, ISPF — the interactive TSO terminal monitor — can be placed in the PLPA and all TSO users share the modules. Central Storage usage is enhanced, terminal response is improved. Unfortunately, adding ISPF to PLPA takes away about 1 Mb of the private space in MVS/370.

The Modified Link Pack Area (MLPA) contains the modules that are included in the common area at IPL time in addition to PLPA modules. MLPA modules can also be new (changed) copies of modules in the PLPA. The data center may do this to install new products or install changes to existing products.

The Pageable BLDL area contains the directory entries for the modules specified in member IEABLDxx in SYS1.PARMLIB. The

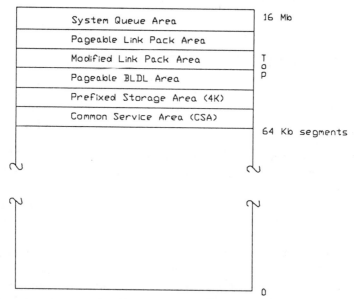

Figure 4.10   MVS/370 Virtual Storage — Common (TOP). The areas that are included at the top of common storage are either program or control block areas.

Prefixed Save Area is the multiprocessor/attached processor copy of the first 4,096 bytes of Central Storage.

The Common System Area (CSA) is a second area for control blocks used by several address spaces (e.g., VTAM, IMS, and CICS) for communication.

4.3.2. MVS/370 Virtual Storage — Private (Middle)

The middle third is unique to each address space (see Figure 4.11). The highest area is called the Local System Queue Area. Control blocks for this address space are in this area. The lowest area — the System Region — is used by MVS modules to control the address space (remember from MVT, an "address space" was called a "region"). Moving higher in storage, the user programs and the storage requested by these programs are allocated from the remainder of the middle area. There is an imaginary line separating the user area from the system control blocks — the dynamic boundary for the "region." This line is set by the REGION= keyword on the job or EXEC DD statement.

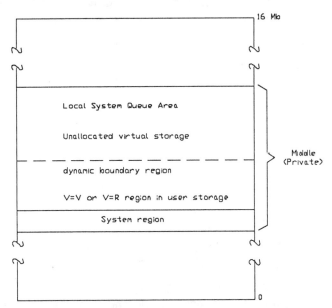

Figure 4.11   MVS/370 Virtual Storage — Private (middle). The middle of Virtual Storage is the "private" or user area. The "system region" is the area used by MVS routines that are controlling the address space.

The middle area is the area that the data center users have to execute their programs. One of the balancing acts that the data center must do is to ensure that the performance of the system is maximized (adding modules to the PLPA), while ensuring that the user has the virtual storage needed. It is much easier to expand this area than to shrink this area, because if you shrink the area, you might prevent some of your users from running.

I recommend that you have the next Virtual Storage change planned — stay one step ahead, if not to warn users, then at least to give yourself time to consider the ramifications. Some data centers even withhold some Virtual Storage in case an important user system gets into Virtual Storage constraint problems.

4.3.3.   MVS/370 Virtual Storage — Nucleus (Bottom)

The lowest third — Nucleus (for MVS/370) — contains the parts of storage that are required to be in Central Storage at all times ("fixed"); (see Figure 4.12). One example is the Recovery Manage-

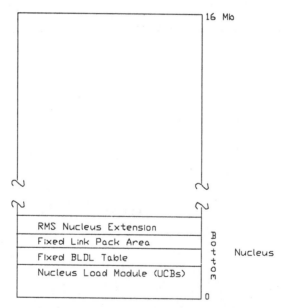

Figure 4.12   MVS/370 Virtual Storage — Nucleus (bottom). The lower part of Virtual Storage maps one for one into Central Storage and contains the nucleus load module and any modules or control blocks that need to be loaded into Central Storage and "fixed."

ment Support (RMS) area. Recovery areas must be in Central Storage at all times because recovery actions such as channel checks and machine checks may not allow the Operating System to read in modules and data areas.

The Fixed Link Pack Area (FLPA) contains modules that must be in fixed storage. FLPA modules are not restricted to reentrant requirements (probably to support old versions of data base SVCs) and are globally used or acquire a high level of system locks.

The Fixed BLDL table is a list of modules pointed to by the BLDLF parameter in the IEASYS00 member of SYS1.PARMLIB.

The Nucleus load module contains the Unit Control Blocks (UCBs), which point to the I/O devices attached to this system. The Nucleus load module also contains many MVS supervisory routines (SVCs).

4.3.4. MVS/370 — Virtual Storage Constraint

Virtual Storage Constraint is a situation where the Virtual Storage size causes problems: Jobs cannot run successfully, the data center cannot install new programs or functions because there is not enough Virtual Storage, etc. Virtual Storage is said to be constrained when:

1. You may not be able to add more Time Sharing Option (TSO) users to your information center.
2. You may have to split apart your Customer Information Control System (CICS) applications in order to get them to run.
3. You may not be able to define a larger terminal network or handle the current terminal activity without "crashing" the system.
4. You may not be able to run large batch applications.
5. You may not be able to install new products or features, or new releases of old products.

The 16-Mb constraint eventually becomes a major problem for MVS/370 systems. It may and will become a problem for MVS/XA and MVS/ESA systems:

1. All programs have not been rewritten to access virtual storage above and below the 16-Mb line. These programs will contribute to Virtual Storage constraint problems with MVS/XA and MVS/ESA.

2. Above the 16-Mb line, there are system parameters to limit the size of ESQA, etc. Until the IBM user community learns how, and begins to manage Virtual Storage, problems will develop in the data center.

4.4. MVS/XA AND MVS/ESA VIRTUAL STORAGE CONTENTS

In Figure 4.13 you see the MVS/XA Virtual Storage map. The Virtual Storage map of MVS/XA is similar to the MVS/370 except there is a piece of each type of storage above the 16-Mb line and a piece of each type of storage below the line.

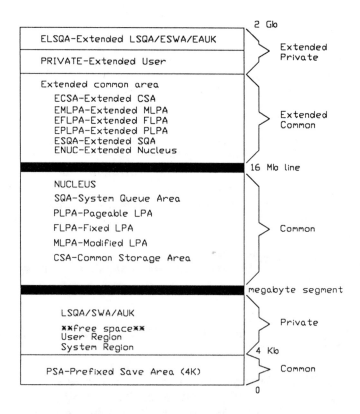

Figure 4.13   MVS/XA Virtual Storage Management. Virtual Storage is 2 Gb.

4.4.1. MVS/XA Above the Line

The areas above the 16-Mb line require special versions of programs to access this area. In general, they contain the same data and/or programs that exist below the line, only all references to the data and/or programs have been changed to support 31-bit access. The areas are:

1. The Extended Private (EPRIVATE) area. You can load entire, reasonably sized databases into storage with 31-bit addressing. How you get it there requires some compiler support. As of this writing, FORTRAN, VS COBOL Version 2, Assembler H, and PL/I Version 5 Release 1 have announced support for 31-bit programming, but you still have to write or rewrite programs that access the data — the compiler cannot do it all for you. The following areas make up Extended Private:
   a. Extended User (EUSER).
   b. Extended Local Systems Queue Area (ELSQA).
   c. Extended Scheduler Work Area (ESWA).
   d. Extended Authorized User Key (EAUK).
2. Extended Common.
   a. Extended Common Service Area (ECSA).
   b. Extended Pageable Link Pack Area (EPLPA).
   c. Extended Fixed Link Pack Area (EFLPA).
   d. Extended Modified Link Pack Area (EMLPA).
   e. Extended System Queue Area (ESQA).
   f. Extended Nucleus (ENUC).

4.4.2. MVS/XA Below the Line

The areas "below the line" are:

1. Common area.
   a. The NUCLEUS area.
   b. System Queue Area (SQA).
   c. Pageable LPA (PLPA).
   d. Fixed LPA (FLPA).
   e. Modified LPA (MLPA).
   f. Common Storage Area (CSA).
2. The private area. The major difference from MVS/370, is that the private area starts just after the Prefixed Save Area (PSA).

In MVS/370, the Nucleus (approximately 1 Mb) was in "low storage."

   a. Local System Queue Area (LSQA).
   b. Scheduler Work Area (SWA).
   c. Authorized User Key area (AUK).
   d. User Region — at last! This is where your program runs.
   e. System Region.
3. Common — low storage: Prefixed Save Area (PSA).

4.4.3.   Virtual Storage Constraint Relief

The main benefit of MVS/XA and MVS/ESA over MVS/370 is Virtual Storage Constraint Relief (VSCR). Throughout this book, you will see comparisons of MVS/370 and MVS/XA. Your company may even be considering conversion from MVS/370 to MVS/XA or from MVS/XA to MVS/ESA. Because MVS/XA is considerably more expensive in terms of actual dollars for leasing the software and in real resources used, you should choose MVS/XA only when it can benefit your company. The types of additional real resources required are about 1 Mb of Central Storage and some CPU cycles.

When there was only MVS/370 and MVS/XA, MVS/XA was the direction that IBM wanted all companies to go. IBM is not going to provide much VSCR for MVS/370. IBM will not supply MVS/370 with support for dates after December 31, 1999.[1] The support for the Twenty-first Century will only be in MVS/XA. Now that there is MVS/370, MVS/XA and MVS/ESA, MVS/ESA is the direction that IBM wants all companies to migrate to.

Nevertheless, some of the VSCR techniques can be used in MVS/370. You can remove unused function — eliminate TCAM from PLPA if you do not use TCAM in your data center, or you can split workload — divide CICS into multiple regions.

It is recommended that small companies delay upgrading to MVS/XA as long as is economically feasible. Large data centers should convert as soon as the company can afford the price and resources and when they have the manpower to work on the project.

---

1. Your data center must be converted well before 1999. Think of all the tape and DASD data sets that you have with expiration data sets equal to or greater than 1999!

The first area of VSCR provided by MVS/XA is moving the nucleus to straddle the 16-Mb boundary. The conversion to MVS/XA is stated to provide from 1.4–2.4 Mb of VSCR. Most of this comes from splitting the nucleus.

MVS / XA will not completely remove Virtual Storage constraint. As the MVS/XA Operating System grows, more Virtual Storage will be needed for the Operating System. Most of the "new" code and data areas will be "above the line." The real limitation will be application programs. As they are converted to fully utilize the 2-Gb address space, THEN VSCR will disappear. Or will it? Remember that at one time, 16 Mb was "more than anyone will ever use!"

4.5. VIRTUAL STORAGE SEGMENTS

Compare Figure 4.9 (MVS/370) with Figure 4.13 (MVS/XA). Note that the dividing line between the top common area and the private area has a segment value at the line. MVS/370 segments are 64K long. MVS XA segments are 1 Mb in size.

In MVS/XA, the areas below the 16-Mb line must be allocated in megabyte increments. If the common area is 6.1 Mb, then 7 Mb will be allocated and the private area would only be 9 Mb. *There are no small errors in laying out MVS / XA and MVS / ESA storage maps.*

4.6. VIRTUAL STORAGE SERVICES

Figure 4.14 shows the creation of a virtual address space. One is created each time a TSO user logs on or a new batch initiator is started.

4.6.1. Address Space Creation

The address space creation routine checks to ensure a new address space can be created. If there is not room (too many address spaces are running) the request is deferred until the system can find or make room. If so, the Virtual Storage Manager (VSM) is invoked to assign the Virtual Storage. This assignment is merely creation of control blocks and adding them to chains that indicate an address space exists. A Local System Queue Area (LSQA) is built in the address space.

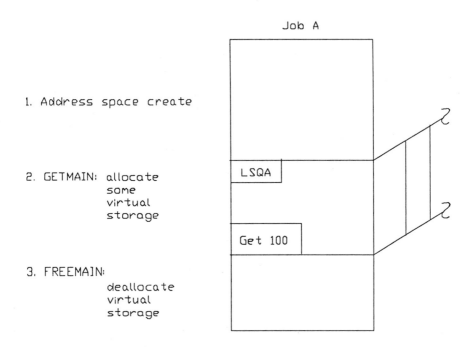

1. Address space create

2. GETMAIN: allocate
            some
            virtual
            storage

3. FREEMAIN:
            deallocate
            virtual
            storage

Figure 4.14   Virtual Storage processing. Virtual Storage is obtained by
GETMAIN processing and released by FREEMAIN processing.

The Region Control Task (RCT) control blocks, such as page tables,
are built in the LSQA. The RCT is dispatched and attaches the program or task. An example of a task is LOGON for TSO terminals.

4.6.2.   GETMAIN Service

Requests for allocation of Virtual Storage are serviced by the GET-
MAIN routines of VSM. Requests include all classes of virtual
storage: new address space, space within an address space, and common storage.

The Virtual Storage is divided into subpools of storage. Subpools
are numbered from 0 to 255. The subpool number indicates where
the storage is located and the attributes of the storage (protected or
not, fixed or pageable storage key, etc.).

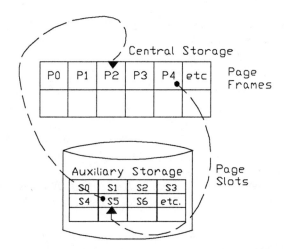

Figure 4.15   Central Storage vs. Auxiliary Storage. Central Storage is defined in 4,096-byte blocks called page frames. Auxiliary Storage is allocated in 4,096-byte blocks called page slots.

4.6.3. FREEMAIN Service

Requests to free Virtual Storage are serviced by the FREEMAIN routines of VSM. These routines update and combine control blocks to make Virtual Storage available to other requestors.

4.7. AUXILIARY STORAGE

Figure 4.15 shows the relationship of Central Storage to auxiliary storage. A 4,096-byte portion of a user's Virtual Storage is called a **PAGE**. When loaded into Central Storage it is called a **PAGE FRAME**. There are never enough Central Storage page frames available for all Virtual Storage pages. Auxiliary storage is used to hold pages until needed. The pages are stored in a **PAGE SLOT** on external DASD storage.

One of the MVS/370 and MVS/XA subsystems is the Auxiliary Storage Manager (ASM). ASM transfers Virtual Storage pages between Central Storage and auxiliary storage either as a paging operation (one or several pages at a time) or as a swapping operation (an entire address space at a time). ASM is called by the Real Storage Manager (RSM) and by the Virtual Block Processor (VBP). There are several types of paging operation:

1. **Demand page out:** In Figure 4.15, ASM would move Central Storage page frame P4 to slot S5. P4 would then be free to be given to some other job.
2. **Demand page in:** In Figure 4.15, ASM would move slot S5 to page frame P2. Slot S5 would *not* become free. Once a page has been written to Auxiliary Storage, it stays there until the address space is terminated.

   If page frame P2 were needed, ASM would check if the page had been altered. If the frame were altered, a page out would be required.

   If the page frame P2 were *not modified*, ASM would not have to page out P2 to slot S5 because there already is a copy in slot S5.

   This is the first way programmers benefit from reentrant code. If the program does not modify itself, then it is most unlikely that the page frame would be paged out if the page frame is needed. This cuts the paging time in half.

   The second way reentrant code is useful is that multiple address spaces can *share the page frame*. The page could be in a common part of storage, and multiple address spaces could execute the program from the same page frames.
3. **Swap out:** A swap out occurs when most of the address space pages are to be moved to Auxiliary Storage. Only the "private" pages of the address space are transferred. Once the pages are moved to Auxiliary Storage, the pages are placed on the available page queue. Some common pages remain in Central Storage because these pages contain the locations in Auxiliary Storage that have the swapped out pages. When an address space is "swapped out," the application program cannot execute instructions.
4. **Swap in:** A swap in occurs when some of the address space pages are to be moved to Central Storage to start execution again. An address space must be in Central Storage to execute.

4.8. SUMMARY

Virtual Storage is a technique in which the hardware uses available Central Storage and Auxiliary Storage (DASD) to create the illusion that there is a vast amount of Central Storage.

Data and the instructions which operate on it have addresses associated with them. Virtual Storage groups addresses into manageable units called "pages," shuffling these between Central Storage and Auxiliary Storage to ensure that only needed pages occupy Central Storage. Special "DAT" hardware dynamically translates virtual addresses in instructions to the real addresses of hardware memory (Central Storage).

Although Virtual Storage eliminates the need for development-intensive overlay techniques, prevents waste of Central Storage, and can "automatically" manage huge software, it does have complications.

For example, I/O only operates with real addresses — the operating system must translate addresses for I/O much like DAT does for CPU instructions. Having multiple virtual address spaces results in the problem of communicating between them, sharing data and code while maintaining protection and security. Shared virtual addresses in the SQA, PLPA, and Nucleus in MVS are used for this. Virtual Storage is more difficult to measure and control than Central Storage.

Even with "huge" virtual address spaces, the unthinkable happened — more Central Storage can be installed in a Processor Complex than could be addressed with 24-bit virtual addressing! The seven new address bits added to the Extended Architecture hardware had ramifications in the software, resulting in MVS/XA. The principle of upward compatibility meant that MVS/XA must maintain a distinction between old 24-bit and new 31-bit addresses and the "line" separating their addressability. The MVS Virtual Storage architecture has helped free most data centers and most programmers from concerns about the Central Storage a program or file requires. Unfortunately, many programmers and production jobs are still running with the limitations imposed by previous operating systems. It is not uncommon to find the production payroll job sorting thousands or millions of records in 512K of Virtual Storage. (This is the "if it ain't broke, don't fix it" syndrome.)

By increasing the Virtual Storage (the minimum recommended is 2048K for any job or TSO user), we can obtain large benefits for the programmer and the data center and reduce the cost of running the job. Who said there is no free lunch?!

Actually, someone does pay for the lunch, so let's look at the things to watch for:

1. Virtual Storage really maps onto Central Storage. Central Storage costs real dollars. There are many "war" stories to describe the Fortran programmer who decided to invert a matrix for the fun of it and caused many problems to all online users in a data center.

2. I/O buffers need real resources to fill. It is possible to have so many buffers as to cause the I/O subsystem to "burp" whenever a particular application runs. We will see why in the chapter on I/O tuning.

We now begin our look at the input/output devices that store and retrieve the data manipulated in and by address spaces.

5

Input-Output: Channels and Control Units

5.1. WHY INPUT/OUTPUT CONSIDERATIONS

Data Processing organizations strive to *process data* into *information* and output the information in a useful manner. Most people think of processing as programming, but there are really three important parts to processing:

1. INPUT: The data file(s) is (are) read into Central Storage in the Processor Complex so that each logical record is available to be processed.
2. PROCESS: The data is inspected and/or changed to another format. Calculations are made. The design specifications are applied and programming is done to follow those specifications. Data and Information could be treated as synonyms, but most data processing professionals consider data to be unprocessed and information to be "finished" in some manner. One person's information may be another's data.
3. OUTPUT: The data is written as defined in the specifications. The output could be only a condition code, which indicates that a file is in balance, or the output could be a whole new master file.

Many Systems Analysts and Programmers look only at the process part of the equation. Once the process part is correct, they consider the job is done. In some cases, this is fine. In other cases, this tunnel vision causes trouble.

One reason analysts and programmers overlook the I/O subsystem is that it is one of the most misunderstood parts of any application implementation. It need not be. When I/O considerations are ignored and the volume is high, the application may take very long to process, or the files may take too much room on external storage. Then someone screams to "fix" it. Wouldn't it be better to design the fix in at the start?

Take the example in Figure 5.1. The design of this program is to copy a file to an archive copy to be stored offsite — a common practice as part of a backup or disaster recovery plan. The only process to be done is to copy input records to the output file buffers. You learned from the chapter on Processor Complexes that machine instructions operate at nanosecond speed. High level language statements such as COBOL have several assembler instructions for each statement but still execute in nanoseconds.

I/O devices operate in the millisecond range, and a single millisecond is a thousand nanoseconds. *Input / Output operations require thousands of time units longer than instructions.*

The reason to tune I/O operations is to minimize elapsed or wall clock time of a batch job or online transaction. If you can reduce by 10 percent the number of I/O operations, you will probably improve by 10 percent not only elapsed time but the cost of the job. Would you be interested in saving your company 10 percent of all you do? Said another way, would you like to be known as a person who performs at 110 percent of capacity at your performance review time? Good. Let's begin.

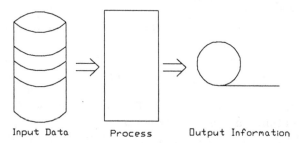

Input Data   Process   Output Information

Figure 5.1   Input/Output. A simplistic view of data processing is to get some data, process it, and output some information.

5.2. BALANCED SYSTEM CONSIDERATIONS

IBM has for years been a proponent of **Balanced** systems. Balanced systems take into consideration the relationships between the CPU, I/O subsystem, Central Storage, and virtual storage.

Why are balanced systems necessary? Consider the fire hose. A regulation fire hose is 2 1/2 inches in diameter and is able to pump hundreds of gallons of water a minute. An unbalanced system is similar to trying to fill your glass with water from a fire hose. You can do it, but it will make a mess in the attempt.

The opposite is also true. Try filling your 25,000-gallon swimming pool with a teacup. Balanced systems require that each resource in the Processor Complex should be in proportion to and respond accordingly to each of the other resources.

5.2.1. Central Processor Unit (CPU) Power

CPU power is the ability to perform machine language instructions which are part of higher level language instruction. The COBOL ADD and MOVE instructions need CPU cycles. (Refer again to Figure 5.1.)

Assume that a goal was to reduce the time it takes to make the backup file. One could try to "tune" the program. Program tuning efforts (changing the way the program is written) or use of optimizers (which change the machine instructions that are executed as a result of the higher level instructions) can lower the CPU resource required.

Remember, though, we are reducing the requirements for processes which require microseconds and nanoseconds. In this simple system, the program only needs to move the data from the input file buffer to the output file buffer.[1] Once the system is designed and programmed, the CPU time required will not vary much — the instruction pattern will not change very much.

There is another method to speed up instruction processing. The 3090 series of processors can be configured with an optional **Enhanced Vector Facility.** The Vector Facility is the IBM entry into

---

1. The input buffer can also be the output buffer, so movement is not necessary in Central Storage.

large-scale vector processing. Most applications cannot benefit from this additional, relatively expensive hardware addition because the compiler must build object code to take advantage of the vector processor and the computations in the program must be amenable to vector math. The IBM VS Fortran compiler Version 2 and the Engineering and Scientific Subroutine Library (ESSL) are required.

5.2.2. Central Storage

Instructions must be in Central Storage to execute. Data (including I/O buffers) must be in Central Storage to be accessed by instructions. By modifying the I/O process, Central Storage demand is changed. For example, if you request two buffers to be in read in at a time, and each buffer is 4,096 bytes long, then 8,192 bytes of Central Storage are required for a read. If, however, you request 10 buffers, then 40,960 bytes of real storage are required for a read.

5.2.3. Input/Output System

The Input/Output system is the most critical of all the pieces of the Balanced System concept. This is not to say that the others are not important — if you try to put 10 pounds of widgets in a 5-pound bag and find out you have run out of CPU or Central Storage, then elongated response time will be the uncomfortable result. You will find, however, that most of the things you can control (and adjust easily) will be in the I/O system. There are several aspects to the I/O system:

1. Access method choice: This important decision is made at program design time.
2. Access pattern: The way a program calls in logical records affects the way the I/O system reacts. Once coded, it is usually hard to change.
3. The blocking factors: The number of logical blocks per physical block is the easiest to change. Generally, it may be done at any time in the life cycle of an application. Blocking factors can be changed to alter the performance of a job. Fortunately, changes in block size can remedy many problems with design. Reblocking will not, however, help the analyst who reads the whole file sequentially to apply one update transaction.

5.2.4. Practical Considerations

Throughout this book, I tie technical information into information you can use to be better at your job. One way is to show practical methods to apply the information presented in this book for your situation. Two examples will be used in this book.

Monthly Job: 54 Hours! The first example in Figure 5.2 is a monthly job which produces microfiche of the company's transactions. The output is a year-to-date microfiche for each entity in the company. As the year proceeds, more and more data is processed. For the last month of the fiscal year, the job takes 54 hours elapsed time. That is a long time! What if there were an error in the processing or the hardware during the 54 hours? You would have to start all over!

Investigation reveals that the company has adequate CPU, Central Storage, and I/O subsystems. The job is limited to 4,096-byte blocks on the output tape because the tape will be carried to an offsite location to produce the microfiche. Later, you will learn how to tune this job.

Daily Job: 13 Hours! A second example in Figure 5.2 is a daily job to process business from the previous day. At the end of the year, it takes 13 hours to process yesterday's data. What happens if the job fails? Production may be so far behind, it will never catch up.

An associated problem with this job is that it must run *after* the online CICS system is down and *before* it comes up in the morning.

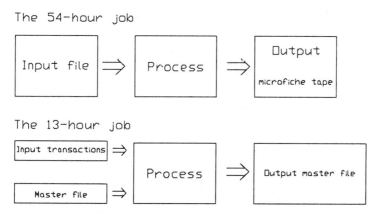

Figure 5.2 Practical considerations. In order to show practical considerations to the I/O subsystem, two typical production jobs will be used: a monthly job and a daily job.

The CICS is shut down at 6:00 P.M. and brought up at 8:00 A.M. That is 14 hours — one hour to spare if nothing goes wrong, goes wrong, goes wrong. Later this problem, too, will be solved — by understanding the basic I/O system. Before we can solve these problems, let's look at the IBM 370 I/O system in greater depth.

This will be a lengthy digression before we get back to these problems, but as you are reading, keep in mind that the ultimate purpose of this study is to learn how the hardware affects the performance of applications under MVS. A little knowledge goes a long way toward bringing real savings to you and your company.

5.3. DEVICE CONNECTION AND ADDRESSING

CPUs, Channels, Control Units, and I/O devices are electronically connected components of the Processor Complex (see Figure 5.3). The electronic connections between the Processor Complex and the control units are made with *BUS and TAG cables* or fiber optic cables. These cables can be thought of as electronic extension cords from the Processor Complex to the control units for Input/Output devices.

The BUS cable carries the data signals — the characters or bytes of data to and from the device. The TAG cables carry control information about the I/O operation. The technical aspects of channel cables are beyond the scope of this book. See your local IBM customer engineer if you would like to explore this topic further.

There is a very important but little known fact that, when the cables are strung under the computer room floor, the *gray* end connector (sometimes with a pink label) is away from the Processor Complex. Even experienced customer engineers or data center personnel forget this item and have to repull hundreds of feet of heavy, bulky cable. If you want to have some fun, wait until you hear hallway talk about expanding the DASD subsystem or adding DISK or tape devices. Casually remind them to place the *"gray away"* from the CPU! They will view you with new respect from that day on.

The channel connection can be viewed logically or physically:

1. The logical path is a three-digit hexadecimal device number: 2F0 is channel 2, control unit number F, and device 0.
   a. For MVS/370 systems, the logical device address is the same as the physical device address. MVS/370 has a maximum theoretical limit of 4,096 devices, because MVS/370 only uses the three-digit number. Remember your hexadecimal math: The maximum hexadecimal number

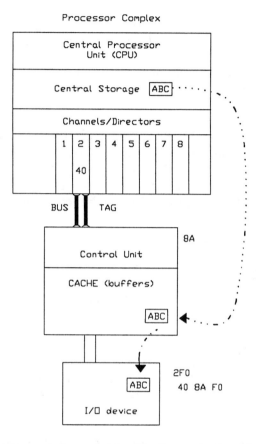

Figure 5.3   CPU/Channels/Control Units. The Processor Complex contains the Central Processor Unit(s), Central Storage, and channels or directors to interface to the I/O system. Connected to the Processor Complex by cables are the I/O Control Units. I/O devices are connected by cables to the control unit. Devices have logical addresses (2F0) and physical addresses (40 8A F0).

using three positions is x'FFF', or 4095. Devices can be numbered from 000 (yes you can have an address 000), to 4,095. The real MVS/370 limit is much smaller (approximately 1,800 devices) depending on how many of each type (DASD, tape, unit record, or teleprocessing devices) are defined.

b. MVS/XA and MVS/ESA use the logical path address for operator communication. So, for the above example, you would issue the operator command "mount 2F0 . . ." to identify that device.

2. The physical path is identified by a six-digit number: cp-cu-dv. Each piece is a two-digit hexadecimal number with values from 0 to 255 (hex 'FF').

   a. **cp**: Channel Path or Channel Path Identification (CHIPID). The architectural limit is 256 channels. The practical limit is Processor Complex model dependent.

   b. **cu**: Control unit number. The architectural limit for control unit numbers is 256. The actual limit depends on the configuration. Eight is the normal maximum number of control units on a CHIPID. Each control unit is assigned a unique number by the customer engineer at installation time.

   c. **dv**: Device address. The architectural and actual limit is 256 devices.

MVS/XA and MVS/ESA use the physical path to perform I/O instructions. The theoretical limit of the number of devices for MVS/XA is 65,536 (64K). The actual limit in MVS/XA started at 4,096 and is expanded as IBM changes MVS.

5.4. CHANNELS

The channel is the part of the Processor Complex that communicates with the control units which attach I/O devices to the Processor Complex.

The channel is a computer by itself. In the System/370 architecture, most channels are inboard (inside the Processor Complex). In the System/370 model 168 the channels were "outboard," or separate boxes. The 168 separation of channels from the rest of the Processor Complex was poor architecture and was not carried forward to the 303x family.

From the 303x series forward, IBM started controlling the channels with another processor. IBM renames this processor with each series of Processor Complexes. Examples are **directors** on the 3033, **External Data Controllers** (EXDC) on the 308x series, or **Channel Control Elements** (CCE) on the 309x series. This book uses the term "channel" to include all of the hardware and microcode in the channel subsystem.

The channel processes I/O requests from MVS and "interrupts" the CPU when an I/O operation is completed (successfully or unsuccessfully). The channel directs the flow of information between I/O devices and real storage. This allows some overlap of CPU processing with I/O operations.

Some older architectures allowed the channel to interfere with the CPU processing. This "cycle stealing" from the CPU has been replaced in the 308x and later architectures by the separate CPU dedicated to processing channel needs. Some interference is still present when the channel accesses Central Storage, however.

In most channel architectures, the channel transfers one byte at a time. In some older architectures, the data transfer was two bytes at a time. Because this latter design did not make it into the 1980s, it is assumed that the coordination of multiple bytes was not profitable.

5.4.1. Burst vs. Byte Mode

Figure 5.4 diagrams the two modes of I/O operations: burst mode and byte-multiplex mode.

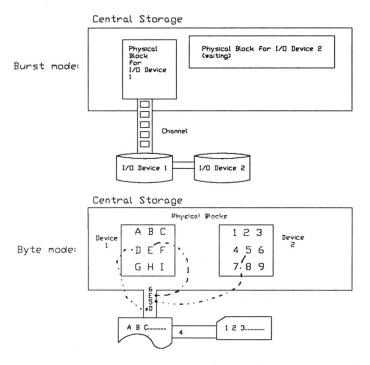

Figure 5.4   Burst vs. Byte mode. In burst mode, one I/O device monopolizes the channel for the duration of the whole block. In byte-multiplex mode, any one device only monopolizes for a short burst, or a byte at a time. The byte mode channel has characters for both devices.

1. **Burst mode** channel operation is where the I/O device monopolizes the channel during transmission of information. The burst can consist of a few bytes, a whole block of data, a sequence of blocks, or status information.
2. **Byte-multiplex mode** channel operation is where the I/O device monopolizes the channel for only a short interval of time. Byte multiplex mode is used where many I/O devices share the same channel, and each is given a short time slice of the channel's attention. Byte-multiplex is most efficient for very slow devices. It is mandatory for certain teleprocessing terminals and for slow card readers such as the 2501.

5.4.2. Subchannel

The portion of a channel that controls an I/O operation is called a **subchannel** (see Figure 5.5). The subchannel consists of internal storage, which is used to store:

1. I/O unit address of the current operation.
2. Byte count of data transferred.
3. Control information.
4. Status information.

In this example, device 401 has 105 bytes left to transfer out to the device (output operation) or has 105 bytes that have been transferred into Central Storage (input operation).

5.4.3. Types of Channels

There are three types of channels: byte multiplexor, selector, and block multiplexor:

1. **Byte multiplexor channels** operate on one byte at a time. Figure 5.6 illustrates byte multiplexor channels which handle teleprocessing and other byte-at-a-time devices such as slow impact printers and card readers. A byte multiplexor channel contains 256 subchannels and can operate at any one time in either byte or burst mode.

    Burst or byte is determined by the length of the operation. Whenever the burst causes the device to be connected to the channel for more than approximately 100 microseconds, the

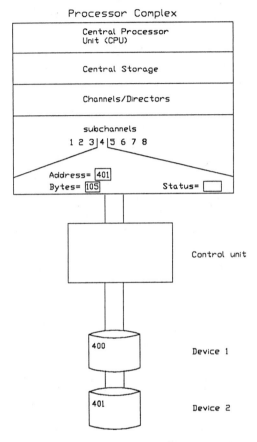

Figure 5.5 Subchannels. Subchannels are a combination of electronic hardware and microcode which are part of the channel. They contain hardware registers to keep information about each device physically attached to the channel.

channel is considered to be in burst mode. Pending I/O operations are delayed by the channel until the current mode is established. A byte-multiplexor channel is most efficient when running devices in byte-multiplex mode.

2. **Selector channels** operate with only one device at a time. After the I/O device is "attached" to the channel, one byte at a time is transferred to the channel until all the bytes in a block have been transferred. If there are multiple blocks, then the channel stays busy until the device is ready to accept data for the next block. This continues until all the channel commands are completed.

Byte Multiplexor Channels

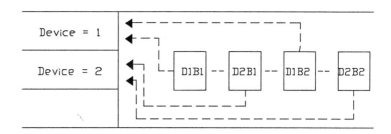

Figure 5.6   Byte multiplexor channel. Byte multiplexor channels contain one subchannel for each device because all information about the position of each device must be maintained at one time. In this example, two devices, D1 and D2, are transmitting data. Device 1 transmits byte 1, then device 2 transmits its byte 1, then device 1 transmits its byte 2, and then device 2 transmits its byte 2, and so on.

Figure 5.7 illustrates selector channels: They operate in burst mode. Selector channels have only one subchannel and always force the I/O device into burst mode. Selector channels were found on System/360 Processor Complexes.

In Figure 5.7, while drive 2 block 3 and block 4 are being written, drive 1 is prevented from receiving block 4.

3. **Block Multiplexor channels** interleave physical blocks of data to and from devices; they operate in burst mode. A Block Multiplexor channel is most efficient when running devices designed to operate in burst mode. Multiplexing is permitted when:

   a. Permitted by the channel — bit zero of control register zero is on.
   b. An operation is between bursts.
   c. An operation is between blocks when command chaining.
   d. An operation is in command retry.

In Figure 5.8, devices 1 and 2 have two blocks to be written at the same time. Since device 2 got started first, the first block for device 2 starts to transmit. When that block is completed, the channel can then transmit block 1 for device 1. This continues — interleaving blocks — until all blocks are written.

Block Multiplexor channels can operate in Selector Mode. The control unit determines whether to enter selector mode. In the case of

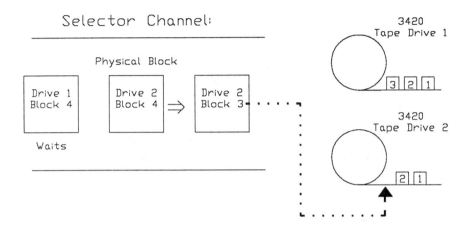

Figure 5.7   Selector channels. There are blocks available for each of two 3420-type tape drives. Once tape 2 has logically connected to the channel, all blocks for tape 2 must be transferred before tape 1 can perform I/O operations.

the 3803 tape control unit — for the 3420 tapes — it can operate only in selector mode. The 3420 operates in selector mode even on the 308x and 309x Processor Complexes, with all Block Multiplexor Channels.

5.4.4. Shared vs Nonshared

Both byte multiplexor and block multiplexor channels vary in the number of subchannels they contain. They can concurrently sustain one I/O operation for each subchannel up to the maximum limit of the channel. The subchannels may be:

1. **Shared** when data transfer to or from a set of devices implies the use of the same subchannel. The 3420 family of magnetic tape units are examples because the concurrency of I/O operations is limited by the control unit to one I/O at a time. At the top of Figure 5.9, the portion of the subchannel that holds the information about an I/O operation is called a **Unit Control Word** (UCW). Only one of all the tapes attached to a control unit can be reading, writing, or seeking at a time.

Block Multiplexor Channel

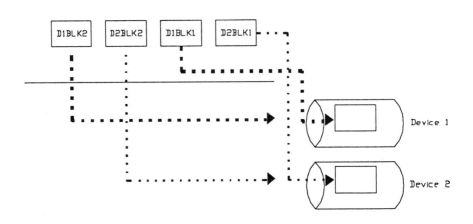

Figure 5.8   Block multiplexor channels. Block multiplexor channels operate in Burst mode and can be interrupted between transfers of blocks. Device 1 transfers block 1, device 2 transfers block 2, device 1 transfers block 2, device 2 transfers block 2, and so on.

2. **Nonshared** when they have a single I/O device associated with the subchannel. Direct-Access Storage Devices and the 3480 family of tape drives use nonshared subchannels. In Figure 5.9, each device has one UCW. In the case of the 3380 disk, each drive may be reading, writing, or seeking at the same time.

Each Processor Complex model has a different method of specifying shared and nonshared. **Warning:** In the IOCP for 308x and 309x Processor Complexes, you have an option on the CNTLUNIT macro, SHARED= parameter. SHARED=N should be selected for DASD and 3480 tape drives. These devices can have concurrent I/O operations to each device. Some installations discovered the wrong settings were coded after they discovered that I/O operations were taking over 60 milliseconds instead of the 20–25 milliseconds.[2]

2. Thanks to James C. Crane for documenting this for the rest of the computer industry.

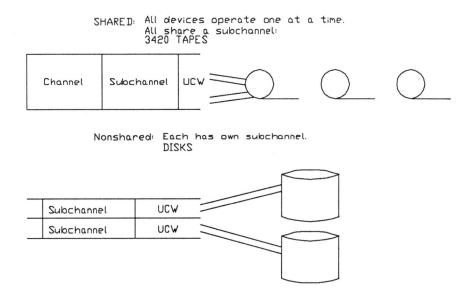

Figure 5.9   Shared vs. nonshared subchannels. There are two types of channel sharing. If a channel can process requests for more than one device at a time, the Unit Control Words (UCWs) are said to be "nonshared."

SHARED=Y should be selected for 3420 tape drives including the 3422.

5.5.   STORAGE CONTROL UNITS (SCU)

A Storage Control Unit is a computer which connects a channel to strings of I/O devices such as Direct-Access Storage Devices (DASD). The SCU can be thought of as a traffic cop between the channel and the devices attached to the control unit. Figure 5.10 shows a control unit such as the IBM 3880 or 3990.

The control program of this very powerful computer is called **microcode**. When a Control Unit is powered up, an Initial Microprogram Load (IML) is performed, which loads the microcode from a floppy disk drive in the control unit.

Microcode can be thought of as the operating system of the computer in the Storage Control Unit. Microcode accepts commands from the channel and changes the commands into specific electrical signals required by the device. Microcode controls the timing of data transfer to the Processor Complex, provides information concerning

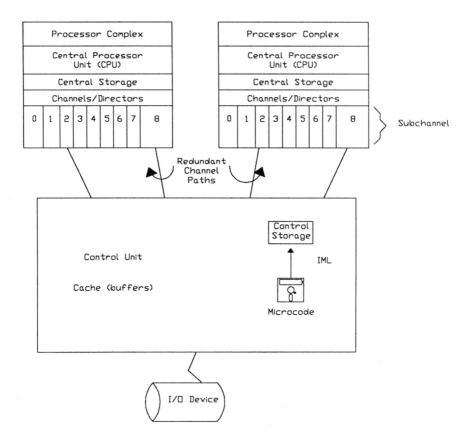

Figure 5.10   Storage control units. The storage control unit changes generalized commands into electrical signals. It is microcode controlled. It may have cache or Random-Access Memory to hold blocks in the control unit.

the devices attached, and maintains error recording information. For example, the 3880 will report that a device exists even if the device is powered down.

Changes to either the microcode or electronic components are called **Engineering Changes** (EC), or Engineering Change Order (ECO) with other vendors.

Because the control unit can operate only if the floppy diskette drive is operable, the diskette becomes a critical component of data access on that unit. The data center should ensure that the vendor maintains spare diskette drives!

In Figure 5.10, the microcode on the floppy diskette is provided by IBM. IBM may install the microcode as part of preventive maintenance operations, or the data center may install the microcode (in the case of the 3×74 terminal control units). In both cases, the recommended procedure for upgrading microcode is:

1. Schedule upgrades at least 6 months after release and not more than 12 months after release. This "slightly behind the bleeding edge" timing should keep you from experiencing old problems while not experiencing new ones.
2. Understand the changes to the new microcode. The changes may or may not affect the operation of the data center.
3. Schedule time to install and test the microcode.

Some control units may be attached to more than one channel. This is called **two channel switch feature**. Two channel switch feature is used for:

1. **Redundancy.** If a channel to a control unit fails, the data center can still access the data through the control unit.
2. **Multiple access by two or more Processor Complexes.** As the data processing needs of a company grow, there may come a time when two or more Processor Complexes will be required to service the needs of the data center. When this happens, two Processor Complexes will need to share access to data on a single control unit.

There is one slight problem with control units. Sometimes they get into microcode "loops." This condition is called a **hot I/O** condition. The control unit interrupts the CPU. The CPU disables, processes the I/O interruption, and prepares to continue. Just before the MVS Input/Output processor (IOS) prepares to go to the MVS dispatcher, it enables for interrupts again "just to see if another I/O is ready." In the case of the hot I/O condition, the acceptance of the first I/O did not satisfy the control unit, so it interrupts the CPU again. The control unit and MVS are now looping. MVS has time out conditions for this situation and will only tolerate a certain number of interrupts from the same control unit or device before it terminates the channel path that is causing the problem. The device is said to be **boxed** or in terminal error condition until the operator can vary the device back online — presumably after it has been fixed.

5.6.   CACHE

IBM architecture designates several areas as "cache." Figure 5.11 shows the three types. The first type of cache is covered in the chapter on Processor Complexes: CPU cache. There are two other areas where the term cache is used, both of which are housed in control units.

5.6.1.   Control Unit Cache

Let's now look in detail at the cache that is in the control unit. Both DASD and tape control units can have cache installed. It is important to understand, because future control units will probably all have cache features.

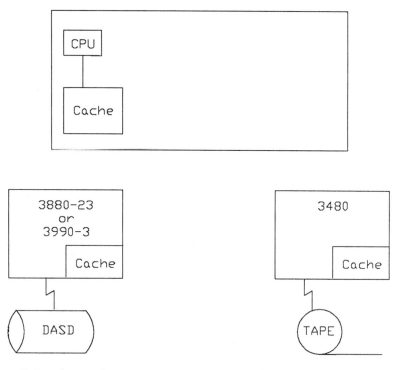

Figure 5.11   Cache. There are three general types of cache. All are high speed buffers in hardware devices.

DASD Cache A control unit with Random-Access Memory (RAM) which is used to buffer I/O operations is said to be **cached**. The IBM 3880 models 11, 21, 13, 23, and the IBM 3990 model 3 are examples of DASD cached control units (see Figure 5.12). A copy of the block is on the DASD device. A copy of the block may be in the control unit RAM. Some of the terms used with cache devices are as follows:

1. **Write Miss** is the term used when MVS asks to write a block and the block is not in the control unit storage. The control unit finds and assigns a block of storage in the control unit. This is the slowest of all I/O operations unless fast write is used (see below).

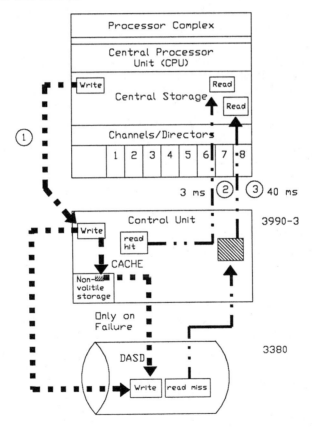

Figure 5.12 DASD cache. DASD cache is Random-Access Memory (RAM) inside the 3990-3 control unit. The 3990-3 is different from the 3880 cached control units because it can have nonvolatile storage to allow fast writes that protect data.

2. **Write Hit** is the term used when MVS asks to write a block and the block is in the control unit storage. The control unit updates the block with the new information.
3. **Read Hit** is the term used when MVS asks to read a specific block from a device and the block is in the cache in the control unit. This is the fastest read — the control unit immediately begins data transfer of the block. Figure 5.12, at location 2, shows an example of a read hit. The block begins transfer in about 3 ms.
4. **Read Miss** is the term used when MVS asks to read a specific block and the block is not in storage. The control unit must go to the device and read in the block. Figure 5.12, at location 3, shows a read miss when the storage control unit must go to the device to get a block.

Special considerations are in effect for write commands. Almost all DASD cache control units will not return to MVS to say the I/O operation is complete until the write commands have safely deposited the information on the disk surface. The theory is that if something happens in the few milliseconds between cache update and DASD update, then the integrity of the data is jeopardized. Thus, IBM takes a very conservative approach to DASD caching of data.

The IBM 3990 model 3 control unit introduces several new cache terms:

1. **DASD Fast Write** refers to an output operation where the data is written concurrently to cache storage and **nonvolatile storage** (NVS) in the control unit. MVS is notified that the I/O operation is complete and the data is scheduled for destaging to the DASD. Both copies of the data remain in the control unit until the data is completely written to the DASD. In Figure 5.12, at location 1, the block is written from Central Storage into the cache and NVS. MVS is notified that the I/O operation is complete. The control unit begins to transfer the block to the 3380. If the transfer does not complete, the 3990 will use the NVS copy of the block to write the record to DASD at the first opportunity.
2. **Cache Fast Write** is an option for special types of temporary data, such as sort intermediate work files. The write operation places the data in cache and returns to MVS immediately. The nonvolatile storage is not used. The data is written to DASD, if necessary.

When the program requests "fast write," it is saying that the data will not be necessary if any subsystem — or MVS itself — fails. Examples are SORT work areas. If the sort program fails to end, the output file is not completed and the work files will have to be recreated again when the sort is restarted.

3. **Dual Copy** is the ability of the 3990-3 to have a volume that is offline to MVS be a mirror image of another volume that is available to the 3990-2. Dual copy will cause a write to the primary volume to be stored in the cache, and the second copy will be written to the dual copy volume. Thus, important data can be duplexed onto two recording media. If one DASD is discovered to be defective, the other can be switched quickly. No DUMP/RESTORE is required.

The reader should inspect the manuals for the 3990: *IBM 3990 Introduction* (GA32-0098), *IBM 3990 Planning, Installation, and Storage Administration Guide (PISA)* (GA32-0100), *IBM 3990 Reference* (GA32-0099), and *IBM 3990 Installation Manual and Physical Planning (IMPP)* (GA22-7064).

One point that may be confusing to many people with the ability to connect up to eight (8) paths to a single 3380 is that *only four paths* are allowed to any one Processor Complex. The eight paths enable the two Processor Complexes to have four paths each.

Why is DASD cache so important? **Speed.** The average cached I/O will take approximately 3 milliseconds versus the 40 milliseconds for a noncached, well-tuned I/O operation. Since most applications and online response times are directly related to I/O speed, moving the I/O to a cached device could *reduce* the response time by *a factor of 13* — a very lucky number.

DASD cache always makes *read hit* operations faster. Select data sets for cache application that have a high read-to-write ratio.

In Figure 5.13, you see that the cache microcode stages some or all of a DASD track based on what the microcode predicts the pattern of the next I/O request will be. Manufacturers differ on this philosophy to speed up the process. Some cache microcode reads whole tracks in at one time. The logic here is that if you get a block on a track, you will probably want the whole track.

Some cache microcode reads from the point of read to the end of the track. The logic here is that the program would rarely back up — read block 4, then back up to block 3. Which is better for your data center? Well, which method do your applications utilize? You will see later in the chapter on monitoring and tracing facilities — CCWTRACE — how to do this.

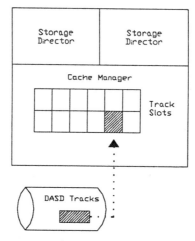

Figure 5.13   Cache differences. Some units read in whole tracks at a time. Some units read into cache only what is requested. Most cache units allow some data center specification of the data set or volumes that are cached. Note that the control unit pictured above has two "storage directors." Almost all 3880 and 3990 control units have two physical storage directors inside one physical box. The 3880 storage directors have common electronic components. The 3990 storage directors are electronically separate.

Tape Cache   You will see a complete discussion of magnetic tape in the chapter on Other Peripherals. For now, let's inspect the control unit that attaches those tape drives to the channel.

The IBM 3480 or 3422 tape controllers, or OEM controllers such as the Storage Technology Corporation (STC) 4800 Tape Accelerator, are designed to cache control and read operations. The 3480 **caches write operations**.

The programmer analyst must prevent the 3480 from caching write operations if the tape is going to be used in a recovery operation. If the MVS system crashes and all the recovery information is not on the tape, then recovery will be incomplete. To remove cache writing, place the DCB=OPTCD=W on the DD statement. MVS will use the Tape-Write-Immediate operation of the 3480. The 3480 cache is still used as a buffer, but the program is not given control until the data is safely written onto the magnetic surface of the tape.

Caching speeds up the I/O operation for tape drives just as it does for DASD. The 3480 tape drive is about *39 percent faster* than the 3420 model 8. Part of the speed improvement is due to the 3.0 Mb/s transfer rate (versus the 1.2 Mb for the fastest 3420), and part of the speed is due to the cache.

5.6.2. Tuning Cache

Control unit cache — specifically DASD cache — is the only type of cache that can be controlled by your data center. The following should be considered when configuring an I/O subsystem:

1. Cache is expensive. Control unit cache is similar in cost to Central Storage in the Processor Complex, but Central Storage at the end of a channel cable is more expensive than Central Storage in the Processor Complex. Plan cache usage wisely. Ensure that it benefits applications and systems to the extent that its cost is justified.
2. Manage cache usage. As part of the procurement process, you should do a financial justification of the hardware. You should ensure that the important tasks in MVS are actually using the cache. Monitor cache usage.
3. The real benefit of DASD cache is **read requests**. Make every effort to raise the read to write ratio.

5.7. CENTRAL STORAGE CONSIDERATIONS

Channels transfer data to and from Central Storage, and this section discusses things to consider when you think of the Input/Output subsystem. The I/O subsystem is one of the largest consumers of Central Storage. Some people believe that you (anyone in the data center) do not need to be concerned with the size of Central Storage *because you can order more Central Storage when you need it.*

What they overlook is that Central Storage is usually purchased with the Processor Complex, and additional Central Storage is a capital purchase that may have to be approved all the way to the board of directors. I realize that a company *can* purchase much more Central Storage as it is needed. I just feel that is not the way corporations work today, and I do not see them changing. Data processing is a part of the organizational team that accomplishes the task of the enterprise. Data processing does not get all the resources it wants or needs.

5.7.1. Page Frame Size

The I/O subsystem exists to fill physical data buffers in Central Storage which are placed in 4,096-byte **page frames**. Physical block size selection should consider Central Storage frame size. Examine Figure 5.14. Each logical record is 500 bytes, and the physical block size is set to 5,000. Thus, there are 10 logical records per physical block. What effect does this have on Central Storage? Each physical 5,000-byte block uses two real page frames — wasting 3,192 bytes.

Now examine Figure 5.15. Each logical record is 5,000 bytes long. The physical block is also 5,000 bytes long. Two Central Storage page frames are still required to hold a single physical block — again wasting 3,192 bytes.

In these two examples, both waste Central Storage. The solution:

1. In the example in Figure 5.14, the solution is to block the file at eight logical 500-byte records per physical record. This uses 4,000 of 4,096 bytes of Central Storage.
2. In the example in Figure 5.15, the solution is to block the file at three logical records per physical record. The result will be 15,000 of 16,384 Central Storage bytes, or a waste of 8.5 percent instead of 39.0 percent.

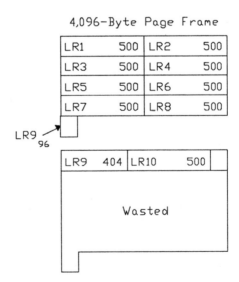

Figure 5.14   Central Storage considerations. Each logical record is less than 4,096 bytes: In this example each logical record is 500 bytes. The file is blocked at 10 logical records per physical record. The first eight and part of logical record 9 fit into the first Central Storage page. The rst of logical record 9 and logical record 10 fit into the second real storage frame. Since real storage is allocated in 4,096-byte blocks, a large portion of the second block is wasted.

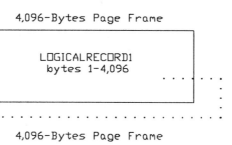

Figure 5.15   Central Storage considerations — page frames. In this example, one 5,000 logical record is unblocked. MVS uses two 4,096-byte page frames to hold the block.

5.7.2.   Central Storage Problems

Central Storage Constraint   In Figure 5.16 we have a 16-megabyte Central Storage Processor Complex. That is 4,096 page frames. The MVS operating system code probably uses about 2,048 page frames. Fifteen active TSO users use about 1,200 page frames, and eight batch jobs use about 800 frames with 48 page frames "left" available.

If one of the jobs had a file with a physical block size of 4,096 bytes, and we decide to increase the number of buffers from 40 to 100 for that job, then that batch job would require an additional 60 page frames of Central Storage for I/O operation.

In a constrained system your program may make things much worse:

1. The program loads 100 pages of I/O.
2. The system steals most of these pages because the system needs the page frames before your program can access the page frames.
3. The program finishes one 4,096-byte block and is forced to wait for MVS to read the page from the MVS paging data set.

Thus, improper overblocking may cause the job to run longer, not shorter! One I/O operation has been converted into three I/O operations, a feat similar to turning wine into water! (Turning water into wine is *much* better.)

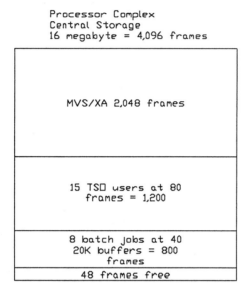

Figure 5.16   Central Storage constraint. It is possible to force MVS into a constraint situation. This figure shows one example of how MVS could fill up 16 Mb. There are eight batch jobs running. Another batch job could not run efficiently and may make them all run poorly

Warning: Very large block sizes, combined with large numbers of physical buffers grouped together, may cause **Central Storage constraint** problems.

Access Patterns   The second problem area for Central Storage is the access pattern that you use to scan the data. Remember that all three components of an operation must be in real storage:

1. The instruction: move, add, etc.
2. The input to the instruction: constants, data buffers, etc.
3. The output from the instruction: constants, data buffers, etc.

If any of the above are not in Central Storage, then the operation cannot continue.

Suppose the program in Figure 5.17 is reading a file of names and account numbers and needs 100 bytes of data — the name of a person on the payroll. The analyst chose to put all transactions concerning the person into one very large — 32 Kb — block. All 32,000 bytes of data must be read into Central Storage to get to the 100 bytes of data needed.

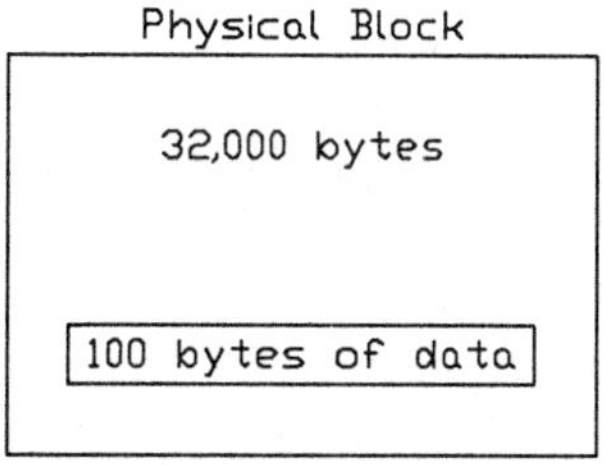

Physical Block

32,000 bytes

100 bytes of data

Figure 5.17 Example of a small amount of data in a large block. This block is 32,000 bytes long, but the data is the name of a person on the payroll. Only 100 bytes of data are needed from this I/O.

5.7.3. Solutions — Avoiding problems

There are many ways to solve these problems. Each application will need a unique solution. Some things to consider are:

1. Redesign the file.
    a. Separate the file into several files. Build a file of names and addresses and a second file of transactions. Each file could have smaller records. This is an often used solution.
    b. Write your own "access method" to read in parts of a block, using read with no data transfer for the parts of the block that are not needed. This is a very time-consuming and expensive solution.
    c. Choose a different access method. Is the file a good candidate for VSAM?
2. Redefine the block size.
    a. Select a block size that will efficiently transfer into storage only what you need. Your block size should approximate how much data you need for a given transaction or logical group of instructions.
    b. Use large block sizes for batch processing. If the file is only to be processed by batch programs, block the file as large as practical on the device.
    c. Use small block sizes for Online Interactive Programming. If the file will be used online, block the file as small as is feasible.
    d. Use large block sizes to conserve DASD and tape space. Records written to peripheral devices have interblock gaps that waste space on the recording media.
3. Redefine how the program accesses physical blocks. Fully utilize the data in a page frame before you go to another. Do not

skip from one record to another. Do not access a few pieces of a record, go off to another file, and return to the same record.

After an I/O operation, the data is in a buffer in one or more page frames. Each page frame is in Central Storage and available to process. If you do not use the page frame, the operating system (any Virtual system including VM, MVS/370, MVS/XA, DOS-VSE, etc.) will try to "recover" or "steal" the frame for others. The best access pattern is to start at the beginning of a page frame, process the data in the frame and never return to access the page frame.

5.8. SUMMARY

Information is data with meaning, data interpreted. Processing takes input data, gives or changes its meaning, and produces output. Our companies demand information and want it produced efficiently.

Many programmers believe the effort of writing efficient programs contributes much to overall system efficiency, but once those hours are spent making one program efficient, they are gone, and new hours are required to make the next one efficient.

Could those hours spent on one program be redirected to make many programs more efficient, all at once? With some understanding of the System/370 I/O architecture, they can. You may be able to make 50 production programs more efficient without altering a single program.

I/O often requires several magnitudes more time than the instructions which process the data: Improve the I/O efficiency (by blocking) of a file, and you improve the efficiency of every program that does I/O to that file.

This chapter and the following two give you information to do just that. Your new knowledge and the exercise of it may increase your value to your company — and perhaps later to another.

MVS contains "access methods" which perform I/O on behalf of application programs. An access method communicates with channels, each of which has a logical and physical path, or address. The CPU instruction which initiates an I/O operation, "Start I/O" ("Start Subchannel" in MVS/XA and MVS/ESA), specifies the path to the I/O device and the Central Storage of a "channel program." The channel, itself a specialized computer, effects the channel program by communicating with the addressed control unit, which in turn communicates with the addressed device. I/O operates concurrently with CPU processing.

(MVS/XA and MVS/ESA contain provisions for a new channel command format with 31-bit Central Storage data buffer addresses in addition to System/370 24-bit addresses. They also improve the concurrency of I/O and CPU processing.)

Channels are called "directors" on the 3033, "EXDCs" on the 308x series, and "CCEs" on the 309x series and can operate in either burst or byte mode. A subchannel directly interacts with the I/O controller.

Channels are of three types: byte multiplexor, selector, and block multiplexor. Byte and block multiplexor channels may be shared or nonshared.

Storage Control Units (SCUs) may contain cache storage to improve the performance of an I/O. Read and write "hits" are cache successes, and "misses" are failures, meaning only that the device had to be accessed. Several flavors of cache are available.

Cache is relatively small and expensive but can improve I/O throughput. SCU cache for DASD can be controlled and tuned by your data center.

SCUs interact with devices, and the next two chapters detail several kinds of devices.

Despite these details about I/O machinery, remember that the goal of the MVS I/O subsystem is to transfer data between devices and 4,096-byte page frames in Central Storage. If too few pages are allocated for I/O buffers, I/O will depend on processing speed: Too many pages could result in Central Storage constraint. Inappropriate choice of data set block size can result in wasted page fragments or wasted I/O operation or duration. The choices to be made are an exercise in balance and moderation.

Controlling allocation and use of DASD can be your most effective means of improving application program efficiency, and that is the subject of the next chapter.

6

Direct-Access Storage Devices (DASD)

6.1. INTRODUCTION TO DASD

6.1.1. History of DASD

In the 1950s and 1960s computers grew in importance and size. As they did, computer users required that more and more data be available. Users also demanded faster access to their data.

Many computer industry experts believe that growth in size and popularity of computers has occurred because of the invention of the transistor, the computer chip (sand!), or even the microprocessor. I believe that Direct-Access Storage Devices (DASDs) are the real reason for the growth of our industry. More data, readily accessible, produced the desire for more data.

Before the System/370, there was a direct access device called the **RAMAC 350** which could hold 5 million characters. RAMAC is an acronym for Random-Access Method of Accounting and Control. The RAMAC was not just a faster, prettier device. RAMAC was different.

Until RAMAC, data was processed sequentially using either punched cards or magnetic tape.

Sequential access was acceptable for file processing — sometimes called master file updating — because the data processing community really wanted to process sequentially. It was easy to learn, easy to do, and they had lots of practice. They wanted to read one copy of the master file, apply updates, and write a new copy of the master file to tape. To do master file updating, a program had to do the following:

1. Gather some changes or transactions.
2. Sort the transactions by some sequence such as last name or account number. The sequence is the same sequence as the master file.
3. Start reading the master file.
   a. If a transaction matches the master file record, make the changes, and write the record.
   b. If the transaction does not match the master file, write the unchanged master file record and read another master file record.
4. Continue until all master file records are copied to the new file with any changes necessary.

Updating master files was — and is — very important, but the user community quickly learned that sequential processing was not acceptable for information gathering when only a few records were required.

What if the data center wanted to read the 5,000th record? Read and skip 4,999 records, of course! What if the data center had one change to the 7,777th record, and that was all it had to do? Read 7,777 records, make one change, read the rest, and write a whole new file!

With the RAMAC, the record could be accessed directly, changed, and rewritten. No other records in the file had to be processed. Sure, the device was physically huge. The RAMAC had disks 24 inches in diameter, 20 tracks to the inch. The heads were 50/1,000 inch above the surface of the disk. The heads moved *several feet* in order to reach the furthest record, but it could hold *five million* characters. Wow!

In the 1950s, five million characters were a large amount of data. The personal computer I am using to type these words has 70 million characters on a three-inch disk, and I am running out of room.

6.1.2. Terminology

There are several terms used to refer to direct access devices. The first is Direct-Access Storage Devices (DASD). Another is **disk**. Disk really refers to a single rotating metal platter. Currently, one or both surfaces are covered with a magnetic ferrous-oxide coating. More than one platter is used in most DASDs.

A third name associated with this type of storage media is **Winchester Disks**. The name came from an IBM internal project name for the 3340 family of DASD and referred to a ski-like design of the read/write head that "floated" above the surface of the disk.

6.1.3. Storage Hierarchy

Whenever you get two or more things (magnetic tapes came first, DASD came second), you tend to want to name the "group." The name that IBM uses is storage hierarchy. Large, infrequently used files could be stored on sequential media (magnetic tapes). Small, frequently used files could be stored on DASD. But there is more to it than that — isn't that always the case?

A storage hierarchy is used to organize the areas on which data and computer program instructions might be stored. Some of the areas are used for very short periods of time — fractions of a second. Some of the areas are used for very long periods of time — years.

The storage hierarchy shown in Figure 6.1 is in the form of a pyramid. The top sections represent data areas that are electronic in nature. This storage is very expensive, so there is usually a relatively small amount. Electronic memory is measured in bytes, kilobytes, and megabytes.

The bottom of the hierarchy represents the least expensive storage media — magnetic and optically recorded data. The bottom section contains the most data and is measured in gigabytes and terabytes.

The following are components of the storage hierarchy:

1. **CPU cache** is inside the Processor Complex and is associated with the CPU executing instructions for the program. CPU cache contains data and instructions that are required for the window of instructions being executed by the program. These data areas are copied from Central Storage. Access to data and instructions is within the cycle time of the computer — generally in nanoseconds.

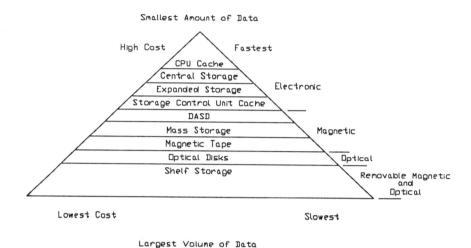

Figure 6.1 Storage hierarchy. Data is stored on many types of media. At the top is expensive, fast storage. At the bottom is inexpensive, slow media.

2. **Central Storage** is the storage that contains all of the data and instructions the program requires for execution. Both application programs and Multiple Virtual Storage (MVS) have data and instructions in Central Storage. Access time is within several cycles of the computer.

3. **Expanded Storage** is an extension of Central Storage on the 309x model series of processors. As MVS/ESA grows, Expanded Storage will become a very valuable area of storage for data.

4. **Storage Control Unit cache** contains copies of data records between the Processor Complex and the I/O device. If the data is in SCU cache, the access time is generally 3 milliseconds.

5. **DASD** is the spinning medium. By the end of this chapter you will see why DASD is the cornerstone of the storage hierarchy. DASD blocks can be retrieved into Central Storage in 40–100 milliseconds, depending on the type of device and the path delays.

6. **MASS Storage** devices, such as the IBM 3850 Mass Storage System, are a combination of DASD and tape units. The 3850 can store as much as 472,000 million bytes of data. Data is stored on **virtual DASD**. A virtual DASD looks like a 3330 device. Data is actually stored on three-inch-wide magnetic tape cartridges inside the 3850. When data is accessed

(OPEN), MVS in conjunction with the 3850 loads the data from cartridges onto real DASD. This process is called **staging**. Mass Storage access is generally in the 1-5 second range.

Either 3330 devices or 3350 devices (emulating 3330s) can be attached to the 3850 to be the "real" devices.

After the data is not needed (CLOSE), the data is moved back onto the data cartridge if the data has been modified. If the data has not been modified, then the copy already on the cartridge is correct, and no action is needed.

IBM has stopped selling the 3850. It was a very effective, if frustrating, device. I used one for five years, and when it was working, data would be available in less than a minute, but when it was not working, a huge volume of data was totally unavailable. In all fairness, I never personally lost a byte of data that was stored on the 3850. Still, I am glad I do not have to support one now. IBM has a manual to help users migrate from the 3850 — *3850 MSS Migration Guide* (GG24-1716).

7. **Magnetic Tape storage** contains the largest volume of data. Magnetic tape traditionally has been the place to store long-term data, but to retrieve the data gets more expensive each year. Access to tape data has several components:
   a. Wait for tape drive allocation.
   b. Wait for operator to find and mount the tape on the drive.
   c. Wait for the tape to start up and transfer the requested block of storage. Because tapes are sequential devices, the access is usually expressed in megabytes per second.

8. **Optical disks** have great promise for the future. Optical Disks are not supported by IBM on their mainframes as of this writing, although they have them in the laboratories. Because IBM does not support them, the ones offered by other vendors have to emulate a supported IBM device. Currently, the support emulates 3803 tape controllers and the optical platters "appear" as IBM 3420 or 3840 tape drives.

Optical disks use a technique called **Write Once Read Many** (WORM). The recording medium is physically or chemically altered by the write laser. The data cannot be "erased." Until the engineers find a way around the technical problem of writing to optical storage, some use the alternate track idea to just keep writing alternate tracks for "rewritten" data.

One advantage of Optical disks is a huge byte-to-floor space ratio. One 12-inch platter can hold several gigabytes of storage per side, depending on manufacturer. Also, the disks are amenable to mechanical handling — so called "jukeboxes."

One disadvantage is that access times can be relatively long. The platters rotate at a slower rate (54 versus 16.5 ms for real DASD). Write Verify is often used to ensure that the data written is exactly what was intended. Seeking to anything but adjacent tracks usually takes longer because the read/write assembly is generally much larger and more difficult to move and position.

Another disadvantage is that we do not have enough research to ensure that, once written, the "optical bubbles" will be the same after many years.

9. **Shelf Storage** is the part of the hierarchy that contains disks and tapes which can be removed and placed on a shelf. The cost of storage is the very lowest — the cost of the media and the square feet of storage space.

Shelf storage is also the slowest for retrieval. The time to retrieve might be hours or days if the medium is a magnetic tape stored at an offsite location. The data center should consider the time for retrieval as part of the cost — waiting for the operator to get the media and mount it on the tape or disk drive.

6.2. DASD COMPONENTS

Figure 6.2 contains a logical view of the components of DASD.

6.2.1. Storage Control Unit (SCU)

The chapter on Input-Output Channels and Control Units defined the control units relationship between the channel and the head of string. The IBM 3880 models 1, 2, and 3, and the 3990 models 1, 2, and 3 are examples of Storage Control Units. SCUs are reintroduced here to remind you that DASD requires control units.

The SCU is the traffic cop between the channel in the Processor Complex and the DASD. The SCU contains microcode programs and logic cards to accept commands from the channel (called **channel commands**), interpret the commands, control the timing of the data transfer to the Processor Complex, provide information concerning the status of the device, and maintain error recording information.

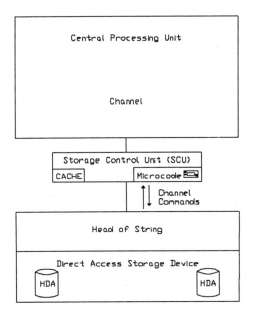

Figure 6.2 DASD components. The components of a hardware system to access data directly are hardware boxes on an electrical path from the Processor Complex to the direct access storage media.

6.2.2. Head of String (HOS)

The Head of String, or device controller, is the traffic cop between the SCU and the DASDs directly attached to the HOS. HOS is a term used for the first DASD device in a "string" (one or more DASD connected together). The HOS contains microcode programs and logic cards to interpret and execute commands received from the SCU, detect errors in data transfer, correct some data integrity errors, control device formatting, and translate data from the format on the DASD to data acceptable to the channel.

There may be several Heads of String attached to each Storage Control Unit.

6.2.3. Head Disk Assembly (HDA)

The Head Disk Assembly contains the recording media and the necessary physical read/write mechanisms to record and transfer data to and from the recording media.

Physical Components of the HDA   *Disks:* The HDA has several round platters coated with a magnetic surface. Each **platter** or **disk** is attached in the center by a column. The column and platters rotate in unison, relatively fast — 3,600 revolutions per minute.

Generally one of the surfaces is reserved for use by the drive itself. This servo surface is used by the drive to ensure the heads are centered over each data track as the arm is moved to a new set of tracks. The set of tracks corresponding to one radial head position is called a **cylinder**. The servo surface may also contain areas for additional read/write heads ("fixed heads"). The servo surface may also contain fixed head cylinders and/or data recovery information.

Actuator (Volume): The term **Actuator** refers to the set of read/write heads, access arms, and a motor to move the heads across the surface of the disk. The RAMAC had one head, and that head had to move several feet to access data. Then the engineers tried one head per track, but one head per track was too expensive to manufacture, so **movable heads** became the standard for the industry.

Actuator also refers to the DASD space accessible by one set of read/write heads. The IBM hardware documentation uses the term actuator for the read/write heads. The data center uses the term "volume," because the MVS Job Control Language (JCL) uses "VOLUME=" parameters to identify on what volume a data set resides. This book will use "actuator" and "volume" to mean the same thing — all the hardware that is concerned with DASD space and is addressable as a unit by MVS.

Some HDAs have one actuator and some have two actuators. Figure 6.3 is an example of two actuators per HDA. Until the early 1980s, before IBM introduced the 3370 and 3375 (337x) devices, IBM warned data centers that the combination of two volumes in one HDA should be avoided. Problems on the surface of one logical volume would destroy two logical volumes by spreading the dust and chips of magnetic medium to the other actuator.

Of course, what IBM was referring to were its competitors, such as the Storage Technology Corporation, which combined two volumes into one HDA for economy. After the introduction of the 337x, it "became OK" for the computer community to have multiple volumes per HDA. Progress marches on!

As the requirement for more online storage increased, manufacturers wanted to produce DASD with more bytes per actuator. Manufacturers found they could increase the number of bytes in several ways:

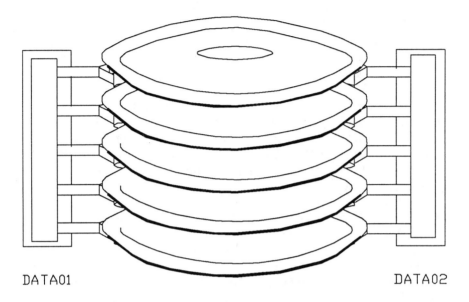

DATA01   DATA02

Figure 6.3   Volume. The "volume" is the logical collection of cylinders and tracks that are available to the Multiple Virtual Storage (MVS) system. Note that there can be two volumes per HDA — DATA01 and DATA02.

1. Change the surface coating of the disk. Finer material allows bits on the track to be closer. So far, IBM has not chosen this path.
2. Change the read/write head. IBM chose head technology because it promised the greatest return for the effort and required the least effort on the part of its users to remain compatible. The maximum number of bytes per track and the number of tracks per cylinder remained constant.

The size of the area where a single bit is stored — called a **bit cell** — is determined by:

1. The thickness of the coating on the disk.
2. The height of the read/write head as it flies above the surface of the disk.
3. The length of the gap in the read/write head to detect the bit.
4. Laws of physics. There are practical limits that cannot be surpassed with current technology.

5. Profitable manufacturing methods. This is one of the most important factors. If IBM or other vendors cannot make a profit building the item, it will probably not get past the research and development laboratories.

Read/Write Head Technology: IBM chose **thin head technology**. It addresses both items 2 and 3 above. The 3380 technology flies the head 11 millionths of an inch above a disk rotating at 3,600 Rotations per Minute (RPM). The speed and height compares to flying a Boeing 747 airplane 600 miles per hour and **less than one inch** over the runway.

The 3380 has improved head design to allow denser patterns of data stored on the disk than its predecessors. The head is no longer a hand-wound electromagnet. It is a fabricated, very light, aerodynamically designed piece of technical wizardry.

There should be little interference between two actuators in an HDA if there are separate arms for each actuator. Multiple actuators per HDA become a consideration when it is time to replace the HDA. Remember, it is not a question of *if* you will need to replace the HDA, but *when* you will need to replace the HDA. With the heads flying closer and closer, the probability of errors grows as the drive gets older.

In the example in Figure 6.3, assume MVS encounters errors on volume DATA01. You cannot just replace DATA01, because the HDA is a single **Field Replaceable Unit** (FRU). A FRU is the smallest item an IBM Customer Engineer can replace at the customer's site. You must move the data on both DATA01 and DATA02 to another HDA (if you can) and let IBM replace the HDA, which contains both DATA01 and DATA02.

Logical Components of an Actuator *Records:* What is recorded on the actuator or volume? The application designer and programmer develop logical record descriptions to contain the information needed for their "record." Logical records are written and read by the application. The logical records are grouped into a physical record to be written to and read from the DASDs.

In Figure 6.4, three logical records are combined into one physical record, or **block**.

Tracks — Groups of Blocks: On the recording surface of the DASD platter are areas which are defined as **tracks**. These areas are complete circles of space to record data.

In Figure 6.5, each block is placed on the recording medium in a circle. Some authors compare this to a phonographic record. Tracks

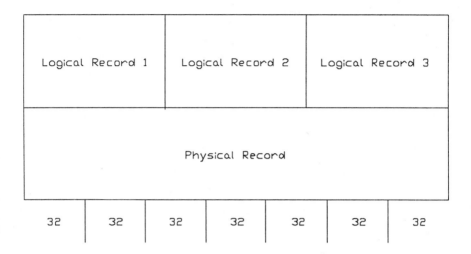

Figure 6.4   Physical record or block. A physical record or block is a group of one or more logical records. In this example, three logical records are contained in one physical record.

are similar (they are even called tracks on a phonographic record), but on a record, the groove is a **continuous line** which forms a spiral. The phonographic needle follows the groove around and around, moving from the outside of the platter to an area closer to the center of the platter. The phonographic needle does not pass over the same spot (unless the record is cracked and the needle skips). On a DASD, the read/write head has the same records pass under the head every rotation until the read/write head is moved.

Another difference from phonographic records is that you cannot see the tracks. Tracks are logical locations on a disk, not physical grooves on the platter.

There is an **interblock gap** between each block. Figure 6.5 has a list of several examples of the size of the gap. The gap differs from device type to device type, not because the platter is spinning faster (they all spin at the same rate — 3,600 RPM), but because the recording density differs. The electronics of the device require a certain amount of time to detect the end of a physical block and get prepared for another block.

The interblock gap is about 1 percent of the maximum track capacity for a device. Do not be fooled into thinking that 1 percent is too small a number to be concerned about. On a single-capacity 3380, there are 13,275 user tracks. If you could minimize the gaps to one per track, you would have 6,637,500 more bytes available on the

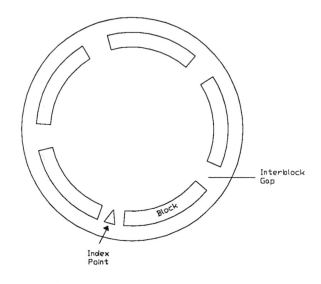

Device Type	Track Capacity (Bytes)	Gap (Bytes)
3330	13030	135
3350	19069	185
3380	47476	500

Figure 6.5   Track. Each track has one or more physical blocks to record data. Note that there is an *Interblock gap* between each block. In the table are some examples of different track capacities and gap lengths in bytes.

device. You cannot limit the device to one gap per track. You can, however, minimize the loss.

Each track on a particular device has the same maximum number of bytes per track. Although it may seem that the outer tracks could record more data because they are longer (much like a track and field race around a round track), every track records the same number of bytes. The data, on the inner tracks, is read and/or written at a higher transfer rate than the data on the outer tracks.

Since the data on the outermost tracks is recorded at a lower density than the data on the innermost tracks (the same amount of data, the maximum track capacity, is stored in a larger number of linear inches), the outermost track is the most reliable and the innermost track is the least reliable of all tracks. The IBM utility program ICKDSF, which is used to analyze DASD tracks, attempts to read data from the innermost track. If this least reliable track can be read successfully, then the reliability of the entire surface is assumed. Also, IBM stores the most critical data (used in DASD surface analysis) on the outermost track. Who cares? Where do you want your next pay raise stored?

Normally these facts do not make a difference. A track is a track, right? Wrong! User data which is deemed to be of very critical nature to your business should be stored on the outermost available track.

Cylinder — Groups of Tracks: Figure 6.6 shows a typical DASD. A Cylinder is a logical group of tracks on all the addressable platters. A Cylinder contains all the data that can be accessed without moving the read/write head.

A cylinder could be thought of as a stack of tracks — one track for each recording surface on the platter. Once the mechanism is positioned — at cylinder 10 for example — then head 0 (IBM starts at zero, of course) through head n (where n is the largest head number), can be used without moving the actuator. Remember, when numbering from zero, as we are doing here, the maximum head number is one less than the "count" of the heads. For example, the 3380 has 15 heads. The heads are numbered from 0 through 14. Head switching is relatively fast — at electronic speed.

Actuator movement — called **seeking** — is a time-consuming part of data access. The heads are moved across the surface of the disk to a new group of tracks. The time it takes for the read/write arm to move from its current position to the desired cylinder is called **seek delay**. Seek delay is usually measured in milliseconds.

The maximum seek time occurs when the head is positioned at either cylinder 0 or the highest cylinder and has to move across all

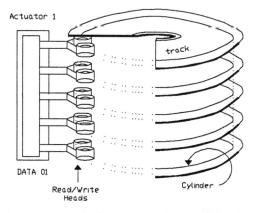

Figure 6.6   Cylinders. As the Actuator moves to a particular spot on the platter, the collection of data under all of the heads is called a cylinder.

the cylinders. The shortest seek time occurs when the head only needs to be moved to an adjacent cylinder (maybe as high as three cylinders away). The average seek is somewhere in between. IBM uses movement across one third of the cylinders in its performance statistics because the average seek distance, assuming a randomly chosen cylinder number, is equal to one-third of the maximum possible distance. For the 3330, the average seek time is 30 ms. For the 3350, the average is 25 ms. For the 3380, the average is 16 ms. Each new generation lowers the seek time by architectural improvements.

Some DASDs eliminate seek delay with a feature called **fixed-head cylinders**. Fixed-head cylinders have separate read/write heads for some (3350) or all (2305) cylinders. Access to any track under fixed heads does not have any seek time — the heads do not have to move. It was rumored that the 3380 was shipped later than planned because IBM could not get the fixed heads to work. Fixed heads on the 3380 were originally announced and then withdrawn by IBM.

Seek time was thought to be a major problem with I/O response time, and the fixed-head option was designed to allow the data center to allocate data under the fixed head to minimize delay to the data. The problem with this theory was that either too much data was required (more than two cylinders for the 3350) or the data moved as the data center allocated data sets, scratched them, and reallocated them. In any case, it looks as if fixed-head devices will not be offered on any future DASD.

6.2.4. Tracks

A track can be formatted in one of two manners:

1. **Fixed Block Architecture (FBA)** tracks are preformatted with fixed size blocks — usually 512 bytes. Every physical record on the track is the same size. If the application needs smaller or larger logical records, they are "fitted" into the fixed size by the operating system. IBM 3310, 3370, 9332, and 9335 are examples of FBA devices; VM/CMS supports FBA. MVS does not support FBA devices.
2. **Count Key Data (CKD)** architecture devices have a self-defining record structure which allows records from approximately 18 bytes up to the full track size to be recorded on the surface of the disk.

Track Cells and Block Sizes Some devices (e.g., 3375 and 3380), have the physical records recorded in small pieces called track cells. The 3380 is a CKD device, but each 3380 track is divided into 1,499 user data segments of 32 bytes each. Every physical block uses multiples of these 32-byte segments. (Refer back to Figure 6.4.) Note the 32-byte segments under the physical block. If a physical block were 3,200 bytes long, then the block would use a whole number of segments. If the physical block were 3,000 bytes, then 94 blocks, or 3,008 bytes of the track, would be used to store 3,000 bytes.

I do not mean to sound like a bit picker, but we quickly learn when dealing with any storage medium that the multipliers of records (usually thousands or millions of records) cause the smallest differences to make a big difference in DASD usage. Where possible, a MVS data set's block size should be a multiple of 32 bytes.

The theoretical maximum number of bytes on the track is 1,499 times 32, or **47,968** bytes, but if you look up block size in the 3380 device manuals, you will see that the maximum block which can be written is **47,476** bytes. What happened to the other 492 bytes? There must be some data on the track other than our blocks.

Do not confuse the maximum block that *can* be written to a 3380 with the maximum block that *is supported* by standard access methods in MVS. The maximum supported block is 32,760 bytes.

Remember, a halfword can be used to count up to 65,535 (or 64K − 1). A halfword used for the length of a block should support lengths up to 65,535 bytes, but most halfword arithmetic is made with an assembler instruction — Load Halfword. The Load Halfword instruction has a quirk. When two bytes of Central Storage are moved into a four-byte general purpose register and the high order bit (bit zero in the halfword) is on, the instruction propagates the bit to the left — bits 0 through 15 of the full word become "on." (See Figure 3.4 for the numbering of bits in halfword.)

The maximum block supported was the amount that could be represented by 15 bits — 32,767 — rounded down to 32,760. If IBM turned off the high order bits in the register after each load (or used the S/370 Insert Character under Mask instruction), two bytes could represent 64-Kb blocks. When OS/PCP was developed in the 1960s, however, 32 Kb were all the architects thought we would need. Now, of course, there are thousands of programs inside and outside of the operating system that assume a maximum of 32,760 bytes. Remember, all System/370 operating systems are **upward compatible**. The reluctance to change is one of the prices we pay for this upward compatibility. If you use a nonstandard access method (e.g., EXCP), you can write blocks of data that exceed 32,760 bytes in length.

Count Key Data Tracks Now let's look at the format of each physical block on the track. Figure 6.7 contains the structure of each block on a track:

1. **Count Area.** Each block has an eight-byte area which contains flags, the address of the record, the length of the key, and the data length of the following block(s). The length includes the size of the key area (if any) and the size of the data block.
2. **Key Area.** An optional key area may exist. The key area was used by two of the old data set architectures — Basic Direct Access Method (BDAM) and Indexed Sequential Access Method (ISAM) — to separate the key of a record from the rest of the record. Keyed data failed to be of much commercial value, because the key was usually needed inside each logical record — not outside the physical block. There are some specialized data sets that are keyed in Multiple Virtual Storage. The VTOC on a DASD volume is a keyed data set. Partitioned data sets have a directory at the beginning of the data set. The directory is a keyed area. The CVOL catalog structure also had a keyed area.
3. **Data Area.** The Data Area, which is also optional but usually present, contains the physical block of data. Each physical block can contain multiple logical records.

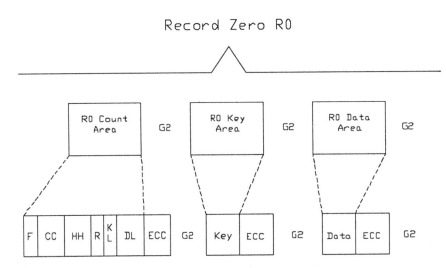

Figure 6.7 DASD record contents. Each "record" on DASD is a self-defining record — the record is in three parts: count, optional key area, and optional data area.

From now on, this book will not include the detail of the count-key-data portion of each record but will only discuss the data area.

Note in the diagram that some bytes are available to MVS (e.g., the Flag, the cylinder, and the head). Some, such as the Error Correction Codes (ECC) or Detection Code Bytes (DCB) are not available to MVS. The unavailable bytes are generated by the controller and the device and are used to detect and correct read errors. The unavailable bytes will not be shown throughout the rest of the book.

Figure 6.8 shows all the elements of a track:

1. The **Index Point** is the start of all tracks. Since a track is recorded in a circle, the Index Point also represents the end of the track. Each type of DASD has its own type of indicator to locate the start of a track, but one platter surface is usually used for a **servo** function to orient to the start of the track.
2. The **gap** (G1) is the space that separates the Index Point from the Home Address.
3. The **Home Address** (HA) contains the address of the track (CCHH), a flag indicating the condition of the track, and skip

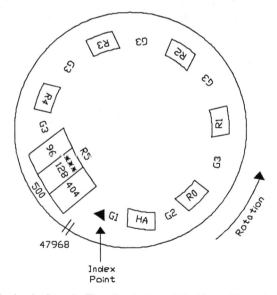

Figure 6.8   A physical track. The physical track begins with an Index Point to notify the read/write heads of the start of the track. The home address contains information about the track. Record zero (the track descriptor record) is used for end of file or to point to other tracks if this track is in error. Each data record contains a count area, an optional key area, and a data area.

displacement information if bad areas on the track have been detected and "flagged." This feature, called **self-defining**, has the track contain the address of the track. It is similar to having house numbers on your house. The hardware can check to see if it is in the right house!

If the data area at the start of any track that should contain the Home Address is bad, then the entire HDA should be replaced.

4. **Gap** (G2) separates the Home Address from the Record Zero.

5. **Record zero** (R0) is also called the track descriptor record. The count area of R0 is used to point to an alternate track if one has been assigned. Normally, MVS dictates that R0 have a count area and a data area but no key area. The data area should always be eight bytes long.

6. **Gap** (G3) separates the area between Record Zero and the count areas for the first data record.

7. **Data records** (R1 through Rn) are physical blocks as written by the access method. Different access methods of Multiple Virtual Storage will be discussed later. Remember, a Data record consists of a count area, a key area if needed, and data block (except for an end-of-file record). An end-of-file record is a data record with a count field with the data length equal to 0 bytes.

So back to the missing 492 bytes. The count and gaps just to get started are 15 32-byte segments, or 480 bytes. The Error Correction Control (ECC) bytes are 12 bytes long. Therefore, 480 + 12 + 47,476 is equal to the maximum of 47,968 bytes. Just the End-of-File (EOF) mark is 16 segments of 32 bytes, or 512 bytes.

Who cares? You and every MVS data processing professional should. As an example of why, allocate a VSAM file that has 512-byte blocks on a 3380 device. In the DASD Statistics appendix (Selected Small Physical Blocks) in the table for 3380 devices, there can be 46 blocks per track, if the blocks are 512 bytes. Write a one-gigabyte file — not an unusual size for a master file. Each track would hold 46 x 512 or 23,552 bytes of the file, and it would take 45,591 tracks, or 3.43 actuators of single capacity actuators.

Now reorganize that VSAM file to 4,096-byte physical blocks. Each track could hold 10 physical blocks, or 40,960 bytes of the file on each track. There are 36 fewer gaps *on each track*, or 500 x 36 = 18,000 bytes that are not wasted. The file would require 26,215 tracks, or 1.97 actuators of single capacity 3380s.

Assume that the cost of a 3380 single capacity actuator is $22,000. Now take the difference in the cost of the file:

$22,000 * 3.43 = \$75,460$
less $22,000 * 1.97 = \$43,340$

Net savings: $32,120

What if you went to your supervisor or the Director of Management Information Services at your data center and said something like "how would you like it if I saved you $32,000?" And those savings are just the beginning. How many resources are used as the file is being read and written for batch processing, backing up the file, and storing the file offsite for disaster recovery purposes?

Track Defects   When a data block is written to the disk surface, the actuator does not have a write head and a read head at the end of each arm, so a write command does not really know if the data was written properly. In the early versions of DASD, write failures had a larger probability of failure than today.

Job control language (JCL) allows the programmer to specify **write verify** (OPTCD=W). The access method will write the record and then read the record just written to ensure the record actually made it to the recording surface.

I do not recommend that this option be used for 3380 devices. The reliability of the write command is now so high that the price is not worth it. What is the price? The record is written on the track, but you told the access method to try to read the record. A **complete revolution** is required to read the record.

Each track can actually contain more than the 47,968 bytes. If any one 32-byte segment has a bad spot, then the 3380 can be instructed by MVS to skip the bad area. These **skip displacements** are 128-byte areas that are skipped if an error is detected. Think of them as a bandaid on the disk!

Look at Figure 6.8. Record 5 is 500 bytes long but 100 bytes into where the record is to be written, a bad spot is detected on the surface of the track. A skip displacement can be set to indicate "write 96 bytes, skip 128 bytes, write 404 bytes."

The one key thing you need to know is that **there is a limit to the number of skip displacements per track**. Once all the skip displacements are used up on a single track, then the track is marked bad. In order to use the track, an alternate track must be assigned.

The IBM utility Data Facility Product/Device Support Facilities (ICKDSF) is used to assign skip displacements and alternate tracks. Release 8.0 and later versions of Device Support Facilities can print a map of the primary and alternate track assignments. The NOCHECK, NOASSIGN, and ALLTRACKS parameters are used.

Each family of DASD has skip displacement hardware built in. The engineering aspects of this feature are beyond the scope of the book, but your vendor — IBM or OEM — can supply you with information to explain skip displacements.

Rotational Position Sensing (RPS)   Another aspect that distinguished one generation of DASD from another was the ability to "sense" where the heads were in relation to the Index Point. As the platter rotates, the device keeps a counter of the angular sector that the heads are passing. A "sector" is like a slice of pie — a wedge-shaped piece of the spinning platter.

In Figure 6.9, there are 222 sectors (numbered 0 to 221 for a 3380) which divide the circle. The head is positioned at sector 33. Record 5

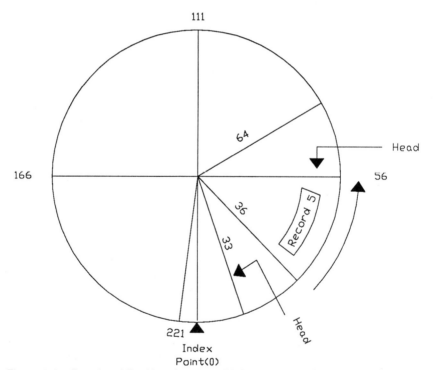

Figure 6.9   Rotational Position Sensing (RPS). The surface of a disk is divided into evenly spaced angular sectors. In this example, there are 222 sectors. If the head is positioned just over sector 33, record 5 starts to be read in sector 36. If the head is positioned at sector 56, an RPS miss would cause a 15.1-ms delay before data transfer can begin.

is located in sector 36. If the device were asked to transfer record 5 at this time, the delay would be only three sectors. At 3,600 rpm, a whole revolution would take 16.6 milliseconds (ms). The three-sector delay would only take 0.22 ms, but if the head were positioned in or just past sector 36, then the delay would require 15.1 ms.

Valid set sector arguments are listed in the DASD Statistics appendix. To see exactly how to calculate the sector number, see the appropriate storage control manual, such as *IBM 3880 Storage Control Description Manual* (GA26-1661), in the section on "Rotational Position Sensing."

This delay has improved from generation to generation: 16.8 ms is quoted for 3330, 16.7 ms for 3350, and 16.6 ms for 3380. Although they all rotate at 3,600 rpm and they all use the same size platter, the area needed to record the data is smaller, and thus a smaller rotational delay is claimed.

This **rotational delay**, also called **latency**, is the time it takes for the data on the track to reach a position so that the read/write head can read the data. Sometimes the distance is short and sometimes the distance is long, so the time used for most calculations is **8.3 ms**, or one half a rotation.

RPS allows the DASD device to disconnect from the channel and control unit while the heads were waiting to *come close* to the sector that was needed. In some devices this was three sectors before the requested sector. The drive would attempt to connect to the channel and control unit in the time it took for the three sectors to pass under the head.

RPS does not improve the speed of a single drive. All RPS can do is hurt the performance of a single drive. Too bad someone cannot invent disk brakes for DASD!

RPS improves the overall efficiency of the entire DASD subsystem because it allows multiple actuators to be active at the same time. When the activity reaches a certain point, then RPS miss penalties cause I/O response time to elongate to unacceptable values.

A word of caution to the readers who are writing channel programs that build the RPS set sector commands. As early as 1972 and as late as this writing, I have heard war stories about channel programs that calculated the RPS sector *just one sector late*. That is like being partially dead! One sector late is a guaranteed 16.6 ms delay for *every I/O*. I urge you to find those routines and verify the correct sector. Use GTF CCWTRACE to trace the I/O and print out the channel program and the data, and verify that the sectors are being calculated correctly.

6.2.5. Warning on HDA Reliability

The HDA is a spinning medium which uses air and possibly other lubricants to keep the head from scoring or affecting the surface that contains the magnetically stored data. Over the years, there have been a number of problems with this architecture. Although they are "fixed" now, you should be aware of their existence:

1. Certain chemical agents used in the air conditioning units (to prevent organisms from growing) actually plated the disk surfaces and caused head crashes. Ask your IBM Customer Engineer if you have or have had this problem.
2. Certain 3380 standard devices (AA4, B04) had manufacturing defects in the air flow mechanisms after the filtering surfaces. Particles broke off the plastic components and caused head crashes. Ask your IBM Customer Engineer if you have or have had this problem.
3. Some volumes rarely move the actuator (due to access patterns), which causes the HDA to "wear a hole" into the surface. One example is a JES checkpoint volume that only has a few cylinders of data, yet gets so many I/O requests that it is undesirable to place other data on the volume. Another example may be the index to a large data set in which the index is a small number of cylinders but gets a large volume of I/O requests.

    You may want to consider writing a program to "exercise" or move the actuator at intervals. If the data set is in the middle of the volume, it may be enough to just periodically list the VTOC (assuming the VTOC is far enough away from the constantly used data — on cylinder zero for instance). Watch that this "preventive maintenance" does not hurt the performance you need on the volume. Do not use ICKDSF ANALYZE to read the whole volume and delay the important application.

    It is possible that IBM will change the microcode in the drive to move the head. For example, the microcode could move the head every 38 seconds to a random spot away from the cylinder that the heads are positioned. Warning the standard for every DASD I/O is to begin with a SEEK command. MVS provides this command for any channel program that goes through the EXCP (SVC 0) interface. Other interfaces (STARTIO for example) do not prefix the channel program. Ensure your channel program begins with a SEEK if you use these other I/O drivers.

6.3. TYPES OF DASD

Having discussed DASD features in functional groups, we now take a look at DASD development by IBM. Some of the devices are not supported by the latest versions of MVS, but you will see the progression from one generation to another so you can plan for the unannounced generations.

6.3.1. Fixed-Head Storage Module: 2305

Figure 6.10 shows an abstract view of the 2305. The 2305 was a mixture of architectures and, in some ways, was similar to the original RAMAC. Because it was so different from the DASDs, which followed, it is presented before we get to movable head devices.

The 2305 Fixed-Head Storage Module was an example of the architecture that attempted to reduce the time to move the read/write heads over the storage. This device is no longer in production and was only used for MVS paging devices.

The 2305 had eight addresses of which seven could be used to access data. (The eighth access was used by MVS supervisor routines for control.)

The 2305 model 1 had 7,330 bytes per track. There were 48 cylinders and 8 tracks per cylinder for a total of 384 tracks. A model 2 track held 14,660 bytes. There were 96 cylinders and 8 tracks per cylinder for a total of 768 tracks. The data was transferred to the mainframe at 1.5 Mb per second. Both models had one alternate cylinder.

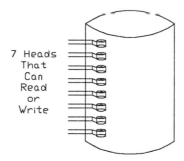

7 Heads
That
Can
Read
or
Write

Figure 6.10   Rotating devices: 2305. The 2305 was a fixed-head device. It was used mainly for MVS paging data sets. Most DASD responds to one address. The 2305 had eight addresses, and the device would process I/O instructions from seven of them.

6.3.2.   First Generation: 2311 and 2314

The first generation was characterized by removable media. The 2311 and 2314 (and an "enhanced 2314" called a 2319) had removable media. Because the heads remained in the DASD and the platters were removed, first-generation devices are not described by the term Head Disk Assembly (HDA).[1] The 2314 arm with the read/write heads stayed in the machine. The platters and spindle were removable.

The benefits of this architecture were that the data center could have more direct access files than they had hardware. You could have — and many did — an entire master file on one set of removable media and another entire master file on another set of removable media.

The liabilities were that the volumes were susceptible to dust and other contaminants (and being dropped or lost!). For that reason, the distance between the head and the surface of a single disk platter was relatively large. Think about this architecture. The read/write heads were not even in the same unit as the media. The heads moved in and out of completely different platters.

The 2311 device had a track size of 3,625 bytes with 10 heads per cylinder and 200 cylinders per module. One module held 7,250,000 bytes.

The 2314 device had a track size of 7,294 bytes with 20 heads per cylinder and 200 cylinders per module. One module held 29,176,000 bytes.

6.3.3.   Second-Generation 3330

The second generation of DASD was characterized by the addition of Rotational Position Sensing (RPS). The head of string and control unit were much "smarter": the control unit of the 3330 was approximately the power of a System/360 model 30. Second-generation DASD also separated heads (remained in the hardware box) from discs (removed) and are not described as HDAs.

---

1. There were other versions of DASD, such as 1301, 1311, 1401, but they are not considered MVS devices.

Figure 6.11 illustrates the 3330 device. The 3330 was the drive and the 3336 was the removable medium or disk pack. The 3330 was released in single capacity (100 megabytes per actuator) and dual capacity (200 megabytes per actuator). There were two actuators in each device — one on top of the other — but the actuators were independent of each other and electrically separated.

The 3330 single capacity had 411 cylinders with seven used for alternate tracks for 404 total user cylinders. There were 19 tracks per cylinder. A track held 13,030 bytes. A single module held 100 Mb per volume. The data was transferred to the mainframe at 806 Kb/s.

The 3330-11 dual capacity model had 815 cylinders — 7 for alternates and 808 for the user. There were 19 tracks per cylinder. A track held 13,030 bytes. A single module held 200 MB per volume. The data was transferred to the mainframe at 806 Kb/s.

6.3.4. Third Generation: 3340, 3344, 3350, 3370, 3375

Figure 6.12 shows an example of a third-generation DASD. Most third-generation DASDs have nonremovable media — the HDA and disks are fixed in place and can only be replaced by calling the vendor's customer engineer.

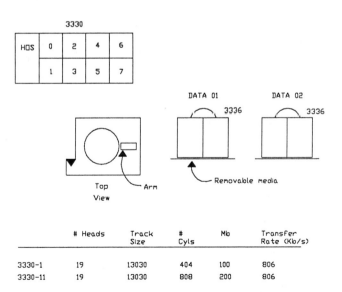

	# Heads	Track Size	# Cyls	Mb	Transfer Rate (Kb/s)
3330-1	19	13030	404	100	806
3330-11	19	13030	808	200	806

Figure 6.11   Second generation — removable media. The 330 devices represent the removable media devices with intelligence. RPS was introduced.

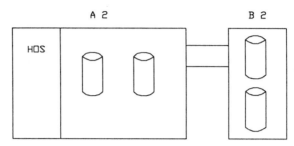

Figure 6.12   Third generation — nonremovable media. The third generation is characterized by actuators that are not removable by data center personnel. The 3340, 3344, 3350, 3370, and 3375 are examples.

The 3340 is a hybrid. The platters and heads are removable. The 3340 is the drive, and the 3348 is the removable medium. The 3348-35 has 348 cylinders. One cylinder holds alternate tracks. Each track holds 8,368 bytes. There are 12 tracks per cylinder. A single actuator holds 34,944,768 bytes. The data is transferred to the mainframe at 885 Kb/s.

The 3348-70 has 696 cylinders. Each track holds 8,368 bytes. There are 12 tracks per cylinder. Two cylinders are used for alternate tracks. A single actuator holds 69,889,536 bytes per volume. The data is transferred to the mainframe at 885 Kb/s.

The 3350 has 555 cylinders. Five additional cylinders are used for alternate tracks. Each track holds 19,069 bytes. There are 30 tracks per cylinder. A single actuator holds 317 MB per volume. The data is transferred to the mainframe at 1,198 Kb/s. An option is two cylinders under fixed heads — cylinders 1 and 2.

That the cylinders were one and two brings up a warning to the reader about checking the product specification for exact meanings of hardware specifications. In the early days of the 3350, a data center that I worked at had 3350s with fixed heads. We had set up data on cylinders zero and one and noticed that the response time of the data sets on cylinder zero was not what we expected. After we researched the problem, we discovered that the fixed cylinders were one and two, not zero and one. Who cares about such an "old" architecture?

Bring that question forward to the 1990s and tell me how much you know about your million dollar cached 3990 model 3! What data do you think is being cached? What data is actually benefiting from cache? You should know!

The 3350 could also be configured as two 3330s or a dual capacity 3330. The hardware mapped the 19 heads of the 3330 onto the 30 heads of the 3350. This was an expensive solution (to develop) to an upward compatibility issue. Do not expect IBM (or other vendors) to do this with future hardware.

The 3370 has 750 cylinders. Each track holds 31,744 bytes. There are 12 tracks per cylinder. A single actuator holds 286 Mb per volume. The data is transferred to the mainframe at 1.859 Mb/s. The 3370 is **Fixed-Block Architecture** (FBA). Although it is not supported by MVS, the 3370 is an integral part of one of the Processor Complexes that MVS runs on — the 309x. The 3370 is used to store the microcode and diagnostic programs for the 309x.

The 3375 has 960 cylinders with one used for alternate tracks, for a total of 959 user cylinders. Each track holds 35,232 bytes. There are 12 tracks per cylinder. A single actuator holds 409.8 Mb per volume. The data is transferred to the mainframe at 1.86 Mb/s.

Some models of the third generation — the 3370 and 3375 — are the first to introduce a diagnostic tool for the IBM customer engineer to use. The **Maintenance Device** (MD) is a hand-held microprocessor that plugs into the Storage Control Unit or the DASD. The MD leads the CE through diagnosis and replacement of actually or possibly failing Field Replaceable Units (FRU). It performs the following functions:

1. Automatically executes diagnostic routines.
2. Recreates and isolates failures.
3. Analysis of **Fault Symptom Codes** generated by the hardware.

6.3.5. Fourth Generation: 3380

The 3380 family of DASDs spans the 1980s and provides a wide range of storage devices that contain from 630 Mb to 1,890 Mb per actuator. The size range allows the data center to configure a device for either performance or capacity.

The 3380 is more reliable than any of the previous generations of DASD — an average of one trillion bits of information processed with only one error. In perspective, that is like publishing a 50-page daily newspaper for 2,000 years with only a single incorrect letter.

The model numbers of the 3380 family indicate the function of the unit:

1. The first character indicates whether a unit is a Head of String (HOS) or secondary unit:

    a. **A** or **C** indicates a head of string. An AE4 is a head of string and can attach directly to a Storage Control Unit.

    b. **B** indicates a secondary unit which must be attached to an HOS in order to be used. A BE4 must be attached behind an AD4 or AE4. This is called "filling out" the string.

2. The second character indicates the type and size of the unit:

    a. **0** or **A** indicates a single capacity Standard Model Group.

    b. **D** indicates a single capacity Extended Capability Model.

    c. **E** indicates a dual capacity Extended Capability Model.

    d. **J** indicates a single capacity Enhanced Subsystem Model.

    e. **K** Indicates a triple capacity Enhanced Subsystem Model.

3. The third character indicates the number of logical volumes or actuators that are in the unit:

    a. **4** indicates two HDAs, each with two actuators, for four logical volumes.

    b. **2** indicates one HDA with two actuators for two logical volumes.

Several features mark the transition into the fourth generation:

1. **Dynamic Path Selection** (DPS). Until the fourth generation, the HOS was little more than an electronic traffic cop to connect a DASD to a controller. With the 3380, the HOS became an intelligent controller in its own right.

    DPS is a combination of four functions for 3380 devices with at least two paths:

    a. Alternate Controller Selection is the ability of the 3380 to use two paths for transferring commands and data.

    b. Simultaneous data transfer over the two paths as long *as the actuators are on separate paths*.

    c. Volume reserve by group of paths. All DASD supports volume reserve to protect data when one Processor Complex is updating information in the VTOC and other common areas. The 3380 can be reserved on one path, have that path fail, and continue the operation on another path without interruption.

    d. Dynamic path reconnect (MVS/XA only) allows the 3380 to interrupt the control unit over any active path when trying to reconnect to transfer data or commands.

    All models except the A04 provide two or more paths to access the data on the actuators. Figure 6.13 shows two units of 3380: an AA4 and a B04. The physical representation shows each unit has two HDAs with two actuators to each HDA. The

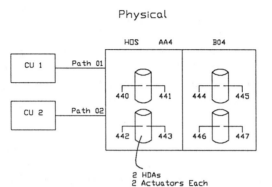

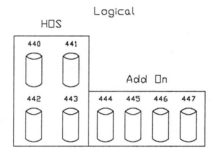

Figure 6.13   Fourth generation — 3380. The fourth generation of
Direct-Access Storage Devices continues the nonremovable media design, but
expands it by adding additional function in the Head of String.

logical representation shows eight actuators, or volumes, in
this diagram. If an I/O operation were in progress on device
4A0 using path 01, then another I/O operation could be started
to device 4A2 to proceed concurrently.

The logical configurations in these figures are not drawn to
scale. The physical size of the HOS is the same as the expansion units. The logical HOS representation is drawn to allow
room to discuss internal paths.

A single HOS can be connected through control units to multiple Processor Complexes (eight with the proper features). The
HOS must be informed of and keep track of which paths go to
which Processor Complex. Path information is kept in an area
in the HOS (for 3880 control units and 3380 devices) or the
control unit (for 3990 control units) called the **DPS Array**.

Operators and systems programmers should use the
DEVSERV command to display the paths as this command

actually issues an I/O instruction to verify the *current* condition of the path.

DPS is another name for **multiple pathing**. Several of the OEM second-generation devices allow multiple concurrent I/O operations to be actuators in a string. Almost all of the OEM third-generation 3350 equivalents supported Multiple Paths. Examples are:

- Control Data Corporation (CDC) called it's "Dual Access Facility."
- Storage Technology Corporation (STC) called it's "Dual Port Feature."
- Memorex called it's "Intelligent Dual Interface (IDI)."

The third-generation 3375 can be configured with a special "last" device — a D2 unit — which would allow two I/O operations for up to eight 3375 devices, but the IBM 3380 family was *designed* to allow multiple I/O operations on a single string. This "second path" is not the same as DPS.

Once an I/O operation is started, for all third-generation devices, the I/O operation must stay on the path selected at the start of the I/O operation. Normally this is not a problem, but what if there were a problem reconnecting at an RPS disconnect? The result would be a 16.7 ms delay.

With MVS/XA as the operating system driving the 3380, the RPS miss can be avoided by a feature of DPS called **Dynamic Path Reconnect** (DPR). With DPR, the 3380 attempts to reconnect to all paths attached to a single Processor Complex at the same time. The first path that responds will be used for the reconnect. This feature allows MVS/XA to attempt more I/O operations per second with a few long delays.

2. **Device Level Selection** (DLS). DLS is an extension of DPS, in that DLS allows two simultaneous I/O operations *on any path to the head of string*. DLS is available only on IBM models AD4, AE4, AJ4, and AK4. (Most of the OEM implementations include "true dual pathing" — no limitations on internal pathing — on their second- and third-generation hardware.)

Another very helpful feature of DLS 3380s are **Beejay switches and lights**. The Standard 3380 devices only have a power-on light and an enable/disable switch for the entire string. The DLS 3380s have a ready light and an enable/disable switch for *each actuator* on the string. In 1982, I visited the San Jose Laboratories in California to discuss my experiences with standard 3380s installed at a large data center. I explained to the engineers and IBM management that operators and data center managers needed to know which actuator had a problem, not just that some actuator had a problem.

The Beejay switches and lights appeared on the DLS devices shortly thereafter. I have numerous "war stories" about how the presence of the lights and switches minimized outages and diagnostic time. The most significant one happened when a JES2 SPOOL volume was damaged. JES (and therefore MVS) ABENDed, and JES would not run after IPL. By disabling the device with the Beejay switch, the system could be started, and service was restored to thousands of terminals. The volume was repaired with normally scheduled maintenance.

3. **Device Level Selection enhanced** (DLSE). DLSE is an extension of DLS. The IBM 3380 models AJ4 and AK4 can be connected to a second AJ4 or AK4 to permit four paths to a single actuator.

4. **Customer Maintenance**. IBM transferred the media maintenance to the data center. IBM Customer Engineers provided all maintenance functions for the first three generations. They installed devices and performed error correction by assigning alternate tracks and skip displacements. With the 3380, IBM provides an MVS utility — Data Set Facilities — to analyze and correct errors on the disk surface.[2]

That we would be responsible for media maintenance came as a surprise to most of us in the early 1980s. Today, IBM claims it is a "highlight" of the 3380 architecture, but just like freedom, it is a two-edged sword. With control comes responsibility.

User media maintenance requires that at least one person in every IBM facility understand the concepts in this book. The penalty for not understanding these concepts is, at a minimum, unnecessary disruption of operations when data errors occur. The maximum penalty could be severe outages for the data

---

2. DSF is used with the 3350 devices, but IBM performed skip displacement analysis with the 3350. The 3380 was the first "user"-maintained device, in my experience.

center — maybe days — while recovery operations can be accomplished.

As of this writing, there are 12 models of the 3380. Eleven of them are the standard architecture of HOS and attached Bxx boxes. One of them — CJ2 — has an integral control unit for direct attachment to a 4381, 9370, or 30xx family of processors. Selection and configuration is now much more complex than with the older, simpler drives.

Figure 6.14 illustrates that the three types are all the same physical box, and they are. The actuator and head design changed between models to allow the capacity to double and triple. The floor space and power requirements are similar, so the data center gets much more storage for the same utility cost.

Single Capacity   The 3380 single capacity has 887 cylinders, with one used for alternate tracks and one used for Servo functions for 885 user cylinders. Each track can hold 47,476 bytes. A single actuator could hold 630 Mb per volume. The data is transferred to the mainframe at 3.0 Mb/s.

The 3380 single capacity devices are models A04, AA4, B04, AD4, BD4, AJ4, BJ4, and CJ2. All but the CJ2 have four logical actuators. The CJ2 has two actuators.

Double Capacity   The 3380 double capacity has 1,772 cylinders, with one used for alternate tracks and one used for Servo functions for 1,170 user cylinders. Each track can hold 47,476 bytes. A single actuator could hold 1,280 Mb per volume. The data is transferred to the mainframe at 3.0 Mb/s.

The 3380 dual capacity devices are models AE4 and BE4.

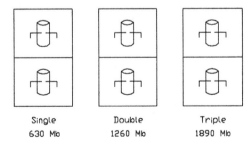

Single
630 Mb

Double
1260 Mb

Triple
1890 Mb

Figure 6.14   3380. The 3380 models have single, double, and triple capacity actuators.

Triple Capacity The 3380 triple capacity has 2,657 cylinders, with one used for alternate tracks and one used for Servo functions for 2,655 user cylinders. Each track can hold 47,476 bytes. A single actuator could hold 1,920 Mb per volume. The data is transferred to the mainframe at 3.0 Mb/s.

The 3380 triple capacity devices are models AK4 and BK4.

3380 Strings A Head of String device (such as the AD4) can have attached up to three add-on units. The group of units is referred to as a string. The HOS and the storage control unit to which it attaches determine whether the device can have one, two, or four data paths active at any one time.

Single-Path Strings: The A04 model can only have one connection to a storage control unit. Because this is the same architecture as the second-generation DASD, the only reason to consider A04 models is the price. Performance with an A04 HOS will not be as good as the rest of the 3380 family.

The reason is quite simple — servers. Did you ever go into a supermarket and find five people waiting for one checkout clerk? If you were fourth, you knew you could not get out before 1, 2, and 3 were finished; if there were two checkout clerks, you could choose the wrong one and wait much longer than if you chose the other one, but in the end two "servers" will outperform a single server.

In later chapters, we will see that MVS does have a way to butt into line with dispatching priorities and I/O queuing, but let's not get ahead of ourselves.

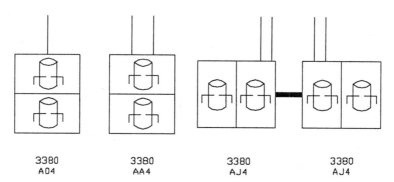

```
    3380         3380         3380         3380
    A04          AA4          AJ4          AJ4
```

Figure 6.15   Strings. The 3380 can be configured with single, dual, and four paths. Note with four paths, the HOS are butted together and the data center must plan the floor space carefully for this configuration. The two HOS must be touching.

Two-Path Strings: The 3380 AA4 shown in Figure 6.15 has two paths. Two devices can be active at the same time as long as they are not on the same path.

Four-Path Strings: Enhanced Subsystem 3380s (AJ4, BJ4, AK4, and BK4) can have two HOS, butted together, and then any four of the actuators on the two strings can have concurrent I/O operations. This feature is called **Device Level Selection Enhanced** (DLSE). Four path strings can be configured only when attached to a 3990 model 2 or 3 Storage Control Unit with the proper microcode and version of MVS.

There are rules about which units can be attached to which units. AD4s cannot have B04 units attached (DLS head of string needs DLS units). AD4s can have AE4s attached (both are DLS architecture). Be sure to consult your Customer Engineer in your planning stage to add new units. If the CE cannot hook it up, it probably is no use buying the unit.

Internal Paths   Each 3380 HOS (except the A04) contains two sets of control unit logic, and each control unit has four paths for accessing the devices on the string. There are two types of internal paths:

Standard Models: The Standard models (e.g., AA4) limit which actuator can have concurrent I/O operations. In Figure 6.16, the internal paths of the control units are shown. For side 1, path zero will be used to access both actuator zero and actuator one. Path one will be used to access both actuator two and actuator three.

The drawback to this architecture is that if you have I/O operations which might happen one right after the other, placing the data sets on actuator zero and actuator one would always cause a delay of the second I/O. We are back to the single checkout clerk. Yes, MVS would think it was doing a good job by scheduling two I/O operations, but they would be processed sequentially, or worse, they might interfere with one another. Remember RPS miss?

As you add B04 units, the situation gets a little bit better. Look at the whole string. If the HOS does random I/O operations for all the actuators on the string, then the probability of a bottleneck is slightly lower, but it remains a limiting architecture. None of the OEM manufacturers made this mistake.

Extended Capability and Enhanced Subsystems: The Extended Capability models (AD4, AE4) and the Enhanced Subsystem models (AJ4 and AK4) eliminated the architectural limit of the standard model. Any path can be used to access any actuator on the string. Figure 6.17 shows that either the A1 side or the A2 side can access any of the 16 actuators in a string.

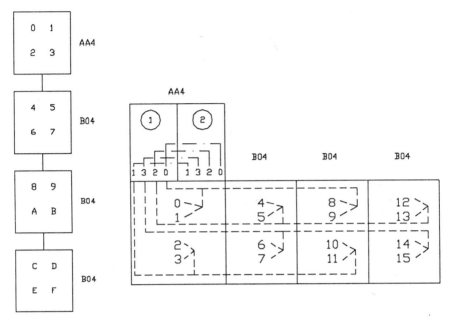

Figure 6.16   Standard model internal paths. Two views of the 3380 standard are shown. The left one is the physical view. The AA4 contains actuators zero, one, two, and three. The first B04 contains actuators four, five, six, and seven, and so forth. The view on the right shows the internal pathing. In the AA4, internal path zero accesses actuator zero and one. It also accesses actuators eight and nine if the B04 is attached. One, and only one, of those actuators can be active on both sides of the HOS. If actuator one is busy, then actuators zero, eight, and nine cannot be accessed by either side.

Upgrading IBM can upgrade certain single capacity devices (AD4 and BD4) to dual capacity devices (AE4 and BE4) and certain single capacity devices (AJ4 and BJ4) to triple capacity devices (AK4 and BK4). Upgrading is a cost-effective conversion, but it is less expensive to get the size you will need in the first place.

In addition, there is a very large penalty for upgrading in terms of timing and effort. The data center must remove all data from the single capacity device (2.56 Gb), wait approximately 24 hours (upgrade and reformat of the actuators), and restore the 2.56 Gb. The least painful time to accomplish upgrades is when the data center has at least four single capacity actuators as excess capacity at the time of the conversion. This is "the rich get richer" in the DASD world.

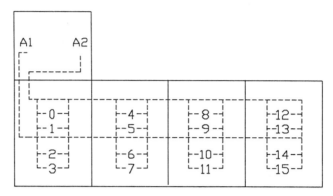

Figure 6.17　Extended Capability and Enhanced Subsystem Model internal paths. Either side of the Head of String can access any of the actuators (up to 16).

Recommendations　The hardest part of all is to decide what is required for your application. The easiest answer is, of course, to get all Enhanced Subsystem Model Group devices (AJ4, BJ4, AK4, and BK4) from day one, but that is also the most expensive option. You do not have to have all the same type. In fact, a mix and match philosophy is the most cost-effective method of managing your DASD resources.

Here are some guidelines for you to use to evaluate what is right for your situation:

1. Do not choose A04 unless you have to for financial reasons. The A04 is just not acceptable in an MVS environment because it only has one path for four actuators.
2. Select Standard Architecture (AA4, B04) when you are constrained for money. They are very good units, and although IBM no longer sells them, they can be obtained through third party leasing companies for the best price per megabyte. **Remember your goal: Price performance.**
3. Select double and triple capacity for very large files. Your company may have several files which are larger than 630 megabytes. The double and triple capacity actuators are ideal for these files. The theory behind this rule of thumb is that large files are normally accessed randomly, and the amount of data accessed is usually small — such as occasionally looking up history records for last year. Multiple volume data sets are harder to manage than data sets which fit on one DASD volume. Larger DASD will minimize the number of multiple

volume data sets or will minimize the number of volumes required for a single data set.

4. Select Enhanced Subsystem (AJ4, BJ4) for data that must be accessed with a minimum of delay. Usually, these files are read or written so often that every improvement in I/O access time can be seen by your end users. The concept here is I/O loading, that is, how much data you can put on a volume before you overrun the capability of the drive (and string, control unit, and channel) to deliver blocks of data in a timely manner?

5. Design some strings with only a single Ax4 HOS. These strings should contain data sets such as the MVS paging data sets or database indexes. You cannot afford to have any other I/O contending for the HOS of these high activity data sets.

6. Design all other strings as full strings — four units, 16 actuators. This rule applies in almost all data processing centers. The very small data processing center — 4381 — cannot afford to have too many control units. For purely economic reasons, the small data center will usually have full strings. Large data centers can afford to have many control units, because they usually have many 3380 devices. The random pattern of access to files will minimize the drawback of having so much data on four dual capacity or triple capacity devices on each HOS.

7. Upgrade single capacity units to dual or triple capacity when you are growing at a steady rate. By delaying the additional storage capacity, this results in substantial savings of lease/purchase money for the DASD space.

These are general guidelines and should be effected only if you have a firm grasp of the DASD considerations and the tools to monitor the response time, not only of your users, but of the DASD subsystem itself.

Be sure to keep up with the documentation. Complete information about the 3380 family of DASD can be obtained by asking your IBM SE to order **GBOF-1762**. This order number covers several manuals (now eleven) on the 3380 and associated control units.

6.3.6. Solid State Devices (SSD)

IBM has never shipped Solid State devices that read and write to Random-Access Memory (RAM) as the final I/O device. (Cached control units do use solid state memory for caching, but not to hold the data "permanently" like SSDs.) They are discussed here because most of the OEM suppliers have a Solid State offering. Examples are the Storage Technology 4305 and the Amdahl 6680.

Solid State technology improves the performance of an I/O operation by completely eliminating the seek time and latency associated with rotating disks. Instead of read/write heads, the SSD has microcode and associated RAM that *emulate* one of the supported MVS devices. In Figure 6.18, each track is represented by 48 Kb of RAM memory. There is no waiting for rotational delays.

The supported types are usually 2305, 3350, or 3380 type devices. The result is an I/O operation with a response time of 3 ms per I/O instead of the 25-40 ms for a rotating DASD.

In Figure 6.18, each track is represented by 48 Kb of memory. There is no wait for the disk to spin, only selection of the correct spot in memory. It performs like Central Storage at the end of a channel cable (because it is), and as such has the expense of Central Storage. Examples of the uses that some data centers have made of SSDs are:

1. MVS paging and swapping devices. These areas are relatively small yet very important to the overall performance of the Processor Complex. Since MVS does not support SSDs, effective use of SSDs for paging may require modifications of MVS to fully utilize the space on the SSD for active pages, not inactive ones.
2. JES checkpoint data sets. JES is discussed in another chapter, but for now, there is a small (1–10 cylinders) data set that is

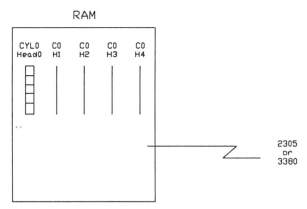

Figure 6.18   Solid State Devices (SSDs). Although IBM has not supplied Solid State Devices, other manufacturers do. The SSD is a piece of hardware with Random-Access Memory and microcode that emulate IBM hardware such as the 3380 or the 2305.

vital to the Job Entry Subsystem — the checkpoint data set. An SSD is an ideal medium.

3. Multiple Systems control data sets. Some OEM software packages maintain a system-wide global data set that is used for allocation and protection of resources.

One drawback to the SSD is that, like Central Storage in the Processor Complex, RAM only retains its memory as long as there is power applied to the circuits. Many SSDs have internal battery power supplies to keep the memory "alive" if the wall power goes off for any reason. If the unit does not have this feature, or if it fails, then all the data on the SSD is lost, or worse, randomized. In the case of MVS paging, this is not a problem. If you lose the power on a paging device, MVS will generally terminate abnormally.

6.3.7. Fifth Generation

The fifth generation of DASD has not been announced as of the writing of this book, but that does not matter. What matters is this: Are you prepared to evaluate the next generation? The fifth generation will not be the end of new hardware in our lifetime. Hardware technology is advancing at much too fast a pace for you to be satisfied with static knowledge. The most important thing this book can teach you is how to intelligently analyze and apply resources to reach your goals — especially when the resources change in form and function.

I suspect that IBM had the 3380 device in test in 1975 when the 3350s were announced. If that is true, then the 3380s should be replaced by the fifth generation soon. What will be different? The 3350 to 3380 change included changes in the track format — track size, number of heads, number of cylinders. The 3350 had 30 tracks per cylinder, and the 3380s have 15. Of course, IBM could not announce the change in tracks per cylinder to the computer industry — nor should they — but, using history as our teacher, we should make decisions today that will not cause us problems in the future. Try to avoid dependencies on 15 tracks per cylinder. Try to avoid dependencies on 47,476 bytes per track. Document dependencies which are unavoidable — such as block size — in such a way that they may be easily recalculated when drive architecture changes.

What about track size? Look at the number required to represent the number of tracks on a triple capacity 3380 — xK4:

$$2655 \text{ cyls (xK4)} \times 15 = 39825$$

The number used to count the number of tracks per actuator is growing. Remember OCTAL? Octal was not selected because the numbering system was too small to hold the values needed. Try to stay away from dependencies on 47,476 bytes per cylinder. Future generations may change the track size, the number of tracks per cylinder, or the number of cylinders.

The fifth generation may combine solid state technology and 3480 tape drives! No more backing-up devices — it will have its own tape drive built in.

The only thing for certain is that the fifth generation will be a new architecture. Determine what the new features will do to and for you. Will it help or hurt your installation's goals? Good luck!

6.4. SUMMARY

The IBM Direct Access Storage Devices present the greatest possibility for success or failure in a data center. DASD usually becomes the largest expense item. DASD usually is the most visible aspect of the data center.

One thing the data center is advised to do is to build a tool kit of programs and expertise on how to control DASD. Build DASD exercisor programs. Develop procedures to test repaired DASD HDAs.

The major points of this chapter are:

1. Direct Access Storage Devices are a critical part of any MVS data center. DASD is the major structural component of the storage hierarchy. Processor Complex storage and storage control unit CACHE are fed by the spinning direct access devices. Magnetic tape and optical storage media are used to house backups and very large files. The cost-conscious data center must learn to control the DASD growth.
2. The data center can understand the connection of DASD to the Processor Complex:
    a. Channels control the connection from the Processor Complex to the control units (or storage directors) for DASD.
    b. Heads of string are the electrical components inside the first device attached to the control unit which control access to other devices attached to the HOS.
    c. Head Disk Assemblies are the spinning media that have the recording surfaces used to store data.

    d. Actuator is the term used for a single addressable entity (or volume) that can be used to store MVS data sets or files.

Now we will look at some of the other devices connected to an MVS system's Storage Control Units.

7

Other Peripherals

7.1. MAGNETIC TAPE

Magnetic tape is the most popular storage medium for data and contains most of the data that is stored in the data processing environment. The reason is cost. Nothing is less expensive for mass storage of data in an acceptable format for retrieval.

Magnetic tape is made by taking a plastic tape and bonding a layer of magnetic material on the tape. A spot on the tape could be magnetized one way and would represent a *one*. Magnetized in the other direction, the spot would represent a *zero*. Groups of these spots can be combined to represent one byte. Groups of bytes are a physical block on the tape.

The beginning of data recorded on a tape is indicated by a metallic "reflector" strip (in the case of 3420 tapes) or by the tape drive "counting" to the start of the tape (in the case of 3480 tapes.)

Computer magnetic tape is similar to the tape recorder you have at your house for voice or music, with one major difference. The data tape is being read to or written to in physical I/O blocks. The "tape recorder" must therefore start up, get up to speed, read or write and stop "on a dime" — usually in 1/2 inch. Can you envision your favorite pop singer having to wait part of a second between each note?

Because of the likelihood of an error writing data on the magnetic tape, most magnetic tape units use a two-gap read/write head (see Figure 7.1). The data is written, and a half-inch later it is read and checked for valid characters.

If an error occurs, MVS is notified by an error completion code from the control unit. MVS error recovery routines retry the write. If several retries are attempted without success, the tape drive can be instructed — by channel command words — to attempt to skip over the bad spot. This write/read repetition is sometimes observed as a "rocking" motion of the 3420 tape reels.

The error checking is done both across the tape and down the length of the tape. Also displayed in Figure 7.1 is a portion of a tape. Each character has a parity bit associated with it to ensure that a bit is not dropped. If the tape is written with *even* parity, then the checking hardware ensures that each column contains an even number (0, 2, 4, 6, or 8) of bits. If the tape is written with *odd* parity, then the checking hardware ensures that each column contains an odd number (1, 3, 5, or 7) of bits. Most tapes in the MVS environment are odd parity.

In addition to parity, a **longitudinal redundancy check** is made. Each block of data ends with check bits to ensure that the block of data contains the correct number of bits. Each manufacturer and model has a block check mechanism and may call the block checking mechanism by another name.

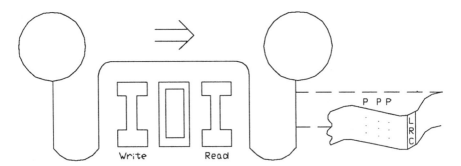

Figure 7.1 Magnetic tapes. Computer magnetic tapes usually use a tape recording mechanism that has both a write head and a read head. The tape is written and immediately read to verify the tape has been recorded properly. Magnetic tape uses two types of error checking to ensure that the data that was supposed to be written actually was: Parity and Longitudinal Redundance Checking (LRC).

The shelf life of data on magnetic tape is a variable that does not have a simple answer and is not agreed upon by experts in the industry. If you talk to members of the Customer Engineer staff, they are likely to tell you (as they have me) *six months*. If you talk to the manufacturer of the tape, it is many years. As with other areas, you should decide for yourself. I would not trust any data that has been on the shelf more than six months. If the data is that important, you should copy the data to a new tape every six months.

7.1.1. Performance Characteristics

The performance of a tape subsystem is measured by the throughput of the subsystem in megabytes per second. The throughput depends on a number of factors. Some factors are decided when the tapes are written — the architectural limits. Some factors are controlled by the application programmer. The following are architectural considerations:

1. **The number of active tape drives and channel paths.** The number of channel paths limits the number of drives transferring data. Most installations attach eight tape drives to a single control unit and connect two control units so two tapes of the 16 can be operating concurrently. Tape access is almost always associated with batch jobs, and instantaneous response is not needed by batch jobs.
2. **Buffering in the control unit** (tape cache). If the control unit does not have to wait for the tape to complete an action, the throughput of the subsystem will be better.
3. **The speed of the tape over the read/write heads.** The faster the tape moves, the faster data can be transferred.
4. **Channel speed.** The speed of the channel places an upper limit on the data transfer rate. If the channel operates at three megabytes per second, then the tape drive can operate at any speed up to and including three megabytes per second.
5. **Channel utilization.** Selector mode channels can operate up to 100 percent channel busy without degradation of the entire channel. With DASD channels and the possibility of RPS miss delays, a single DASD request could take 40 milliseconds (ms) at 30 percent busy and 90 ms at 60 percent busy. On tape channels, if a single I/O request takes 40 ms at 30 percent busy, it will also take 40 ms at 100 percent channel busy. The

total transfer of all blocks requested from the tape may take longer because the I/O is waiting for the channel to get started.

The following application design items can affect the throughput of the tape subsystem:

1. **Size of the data set.** Very large data sets can monopolize a tape subsystem. One example is a dump of all the data on a DASD volume to a tape drive. The dump program can read data at 3 megabytes per second (for 3380 devices) and attempt to write the data to tape immediately. If the tape channel is not 3 megabytes, the DASD channel always has data available for the tape channel. In this case, the data set (a whole DASD volume) can monopolize one channel path for the 15–20 minutes it takes to dump all of a 3380.

2. **Block size** of the data set being read or written. Small blocks waste tape (interblock gaps) and throughput. The channel, control unit, and tape drive perform the same work for a 4,096-byte block as they do for a 32,760-byte block in the areas of selection, setup, tape-up-to-speed, and stopping. Writing tape blocks less than 32 Kb is like driving four hours to the beach, only staying 10 minutes, then driving home again.

3. **Selection of write validity checking** (tape write immediate on 3480 devices). Caching is disabled when tape write immediate is selected. Things like tape forward spacing and small blocks return to the speed of the the 3420 tape drives. The only faster item is data transfer rate.

There are two types of magnetic tape architecture in use: round tapes and square tapes.

7.1.2. Round Tapes — 3420

The round tape reels are 10-1/2 inches in diameter. The magnetic tape is 1/2 inch wide and usually 2,400 feet long (for full-sized reels). The coating is generally iron oxide.

The invention that keeps the 3420 tape from breaking is the "vacuum column." As far back as 1950, IBM used a glass vacuum chamber that held several feet of tape — both in front of and after the read/write heads. The extra tape cushioned the shock of the tape starting and stopping. As with most vacuum implementations, breakdowns in this feature cause many problems with the 3420 tape drive family. Figure 7.2 shows the characteristics of the 3420 tape drive family. There are three major groups of 3420 tape drive options:

1. Tape density in bits per inch (bpi):
   a. 800 bits per inch.
   b. 1,600 bits per inch
   c. 6,250 bits per inch
2. Transport speed — the maximum speed of the tape across the heads in inches per second (ips). There are three options:
   a. 75 ips
   b. 125 ips.
   c. 200 ips.
3. There are two recording formats:
   a. 7 tracks of data across the one-half inch tape
   b. 9 tracks of data across the one-half inch tape

The subprocesses of a tape read are: start the I/O operation, get the tape up to speed, pass over the interrecord gap, and transfer the data.

It has been my experience that the units with 200 ips tape speed have more errors than the slower tape drives. *Caution:* That speed may be too fast for tape media.

One of the problems with the above was that as IBM introduced faster and denser tape drives, the installation was stuck with tape reels that were "not certified" for the denser recording. Many installations had whole tape libraries of tape reels that were "certified" at 1600 BPI when IBM announced the 6250 bpi tape drives. After a

Model	3	4	5	6	7	8
Speed in/sec	75	75	125	125	200	200
Start time in ms	1.8	1.4	1.4	1.1	1.3	0.8
Data Rate Kb/s						
1,600	120	120	200	200	320	320
6,250		470		780		1,250

Figure 7.2 3420 magnetic tape characteristics. The table shows the speed in inches per second, the startup for the tape to come to speed, and the resultant data transfer rate for each of the 3420 models. The model 8, at 200 inches per second and with a startup time of less than one millisecond, stretches the architecture — sometimes the tape.

while, the industry settled on 6250 bpi tape reels as the standard. I only mention that so that you can be alert to 1600 bpi tape reels used in a 6250 bpi environment. It may work but the probability of errors is greatly increased.

7.1.3.   Square Tapes — 3480

Differences Between 3420 and 3480   The 3480 Magnetic Tape Subsystem is a higher-performance, more reliable magnetic tape subsystem than the 3420 tape family. The major differences between the 3480 and the 3420 are:

1. 3480 data cartridges are four inches square and contain chromium-dioxide covered tape. Although the cartridge is one-fourth the size of the round tape, it can hold 20 percent more data — 200 million characters for the 3480 versus 160 million characters for the 3420.

   The architecture of the 3480 may allow 100 Kb-per-inch recording — up from the 38 Kb-per-inch today. IBM promises that the recording media being used today will support that denser recording *if the tape cartridges are manufactured by IBM or meet IBM standards.*

   Do not get caught with substandard media, no matter what the price.

2. The 3480s are microprocessor-controlled drives which move the tape without the need for capstans or complex vacuum columns.

3. Data can be transferred by the 3480 at either 1.5 Mb/s per second (Model B11) or 3.0 Mb/s per second (model B22). I recommend you match your channel speed to the tape control unit speed. If you have 308x or 309x channels — at 3.0 Mb/s — you should install 3.0-Mb models.

4. Data is recorded on 18 tracks by the 3480, not 9 as on the 3420. This recording technique may be similar to the one developed at IBM for the 3850 Mass Storage subsystem. If so, it should prove reliable.

5. The 3480 cartridge does not have reflector strips at the front and back of the tape. The drive measures travel to the logical start of tape and synchronizes the reading of the first block. The last block is "sensed" when the tape drive has passed a standard length.

There are two modes supported by MVS. Full function mode requires MVS/XA. Compatibility (with 3420) mode is used for MVS/370.

1. Full function mode:
   a. Read/write buffering. The 3480 is the first device to address a situation with write commands on a cached control unit. All cache controllers up to this time waited for the data to get to the medium before it signaled MVS that the I/O operation was successful. Although this ensured the data was written to the media, it also slowed down the write commands. The 3480 buffers the block and signals successful completion immediately. *The I/O block is in cache, not on the tape.* What if something in the complex fails (such as a power outage) before the block is written to the tape? IBM is saying that either the hardware will recover or the program will abend, which brings me to an important warning.

   When any program abends, the only recovery is to *not depend on files that were open at the time of the abend.* If a file is open and the task abends, MVS will not "close" the file. Logical records in the buffers are not "flushed" out to the output device. In the case of a tape on the 3480, the output tape should be discarded and the file rewritten. If you are a Systems Analyst, factor this into the error recovery plans in your system designs. If you are an operator or production control person, watch for job streams that do not restore files. The thing lost might be your $10,000 pay increase!

   b. Message display. The top of the 3480 device has a message display. Requests for mounts, unloads, and error messages are displayed in full function mode. There are a number of OEM attachments that capture MVS console commands and display similar messages for the 3420 family.

   c. Processor assignment. A string of tape drives (either type) can be attached to multiple Processor Complexes. With 3420 tape drives, either the data center had to have OEM software to protect the drives, or the operations staff had to be very careful about which drives were online to which Processor Complex.

   The problem starts with how MVS initializes a tape drive. MVS issues a rewind and unload Channel Command Word

(CCW) as it is mounting a new tape. If a particular drive is online to another Processor Complex (MVS, VM, or any other operating system), then the MVS rewind and unload command will be performed by the tape drive — even if it is in the middle of reading/writing a file. It usually only happens with very important tapes such as the payroll job.

The 3480 tape subsystem *assigns* devices to a particular Processor Complex. 3480s do not have the rewind and unload problem of the 3420 subsystem. The Assign facility is activated when the MVS VARY online command is issued. Once a drive is online to one Processor Complex, another operating system, such as MVS, cannot access the device until it is offline to the first Processor Complex.

d. High speed search. The application programmer can use the NOTE and POINT facilities to search for a specific relative block on the tape. This feature frees up the channel and control unit (similar to the seek on DASD) while the specific unit is moving the tape.

e. Tape-Write-Immediate Mode. Some applications require that the data be on the tape before successful completion is indicated. These applications are generally involved in recovery like CICS and IMS logging. The 3480 can be instructed to not signal successful completion until the physical block is successfully on the magnetic tape. Tape-write-immediate is used when the MVS, JCL contains **DCB=OPTCD=W** (write verify).

f. System mode on Automatic Cartridge Loader Feature (ACLF). An optional feature of 3480 devices is the Automatic Cartridge Loader Feature. In all data centers, there is a certain percentage of scratch tape mounts. Scratch tapes or "nonspecific" requests are tapes which are allocated for output data sets. Examination of several installations has shown that the percentage of scratch tapes is over 50 percent[1]

---

1. If the percentage is over 50 percent for scratch tapes, that means there are many tapes that are mounted, written to, and never used again. Though this may seem strange, you will find that data set backups in the form of applications writing their own backups, and system backups account for a large portion of tape access.

Multiple Virtual Storage open routines allocate tape drives with ACLF for scratch requests before other tape drives. Scratch tape requests are satisfied in four seconds — with no wait time for the operator to recognize that a request has been made which is one to three minutes for an efficient operations staff.

Sharp operators have discovered multivolume file performance can be improved (and labor reduced) by having large multivolume files allocated to tape drives with ACLF. They swap (using DDR below) the file to a drive with ACLF and then load the tapes in the order that the tapes will be requested by the application. Input operations benefit from auto loading, not just output operations!

g. Dynamic Device Reconfiguration (DDR) mode. DDR is a group of MVS recovery routines that intercept I/O errors and coordinate movement of the tape from a suspect drive to another drive. The coordination includes rewinding the tape from the current drive, allocating a new drive to the application, forward spacing the tape to the error location, and retrying the read or write operation. Operator requested swaps can also be performed. In the example above, the operator could swap the allocation of a multivolume file to a device with the ACLF. The application will not be delayed unless the hopper runs out of tapes.

2. Compatibility mode retains some, but not all, of the benefits of the 3480s:

a. Read/Write buffering is active. The benefits of lowered channel busy time and faster throughput remain.

b. Tape-write-immediate mode. If the device is going to signal completion ("device end") after buffering the data to be written, then the override must be available for those data sets which require which the block be written to the tape media.

Conversion from 3420 to 3480 Many installations convert from 3420 architecture to 3480 architecture. The conversion is relatively easy *if the installation is prepared.* The overall plan is to install the new tape drives, test them, and convert with few operational changes. The new tapes will be used with a "new generic name" for selected test jobs. After the drives have been tested, the generic names will be switched so that the "default" name will point to the 3480 drives.

As an example, take the installation in Figure 7.3. Devices 980-987 are production 3420 round tapes. Devices 920-927 are replacement

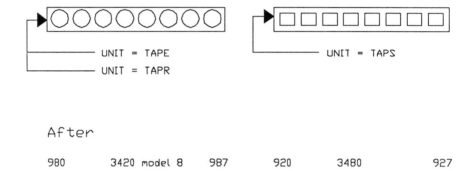

Figure 7.3   Conversion of 3420 to 3480. The top part of this figure shows the configuration before conversion, the bottom part after conversion.

3480 square tapes. Generic device name **TAPE** points to the round tapes before conversion. Generic device name **TAPS** points to the new square tapes. Generic device name **TAPR** also points to the round tapes.

After the conversion, TAPE will point to the new square tapes and TAPR will point to the old round tapes. The following is a simplified task plan to convert round to square:

1. Ensure that all tape data sets are cataloged. If for some reason your installation does not have a standard that all data sets must be cataloged, then now is the time to implement such a standard. There are very few acceptable reasons to not have all data sets cataloged. This "easy" conversion plan will not work if tape data sets are not cataloged.
2. Test the new 3480 devices by changing the JCL of specific jobs and specifying UNIT=TAPS.
3. Convert JCL that must be changed:
   a. Identify all data set names for tapes that are exported to another data center which requires round tapes (or for which square tape support is not known.) Examples are

tapes to be taken to microfiche developers and tapes that are sent to another facility.

b. If you have not done so, you may want to establish standards that these have unique data set name combinations. One example is uuuuu.FICHE.aaa.bbb.ccc, where FICHE is a required second field in the data set name of any tape to be taken to a microfiche unit. The unique name aids in identifying these "offsite" tapes.

c. Generate new copies of the JCL and/or write instructions to assist others in converting theirs. In this example, all special tape data sets will have to have the UNIT= parameter changed on the JCL which creates the tape data set from UNIT=TAPE to UNIT=TAPR. In the transition, TAPE and TAPR point to the round tapes so the change can be put into production and not have to be changed after this transition time.

4. Change the default to square tapes. Stop all processing and start a new copy of MVS which has UNIT=TAPE point to square tapes (devices 920 through 927) and UNIT=TAPR point to round tapes (devices 980-987.)

5. Decide whether you are going to copy groups of tapes from round tapes to square tapes. If you do decide to copy some, you must create JCL to copy from UNIT=TAPR to UNIT=TAPE.

What makes this approach work is that most applications have job steps which read a tape, process the data, and output a tape. The input to the job is a data set, and the volume and unit are obtained from the system catalog. The system catalog contains the real device name — in this case 3420 model 8. The generic output name of TAPE points to the new 3480 units. Without JCL or program changes, the old round tapes are copied to the new cartridges by just running the application job. Many installations employing this method report that after three months, almost all round tape usage is eliminated.

One of the most difficult problems to contend with in a data center is the problem of errors on tape I/O operations. The problem could be in one of several areas:

1. The tape could be bad. Replace the tape, recreate the data, and the problem is solved.

2. The tape drive could be bad. Turn the drive over to the Customer Engineer, let him fix it, test it after he gives it back, and the data center has finished.

3. A dirty tape with either dust, dirt, or the magnetic oxide itself flaking off contaminates a tape drive. The next tape on the drive is "bad." The culprit may get away scot-free! If the bad tape does not get errors, it may not be noticed. The tape may be a **foreign tape** that was used at some data center other than yours.
4. The tape media vendor is not up to the specifications of the tape drive vendor. The tape drive vendor blames all tape errors on a "bad tape library." (This often occurs as a result of buying tapes from the lowest bidder.)

Your data center may want to take advantage of the conversion from round tapes to square tapes to "put an end" to dirty tapes causing a problem for the whole data center. If you buy all your square tapes from an approved vendor and do not mix tape media vendors, you will isolate the problem to the tape vendor or the tape drive manufacturer. If you prevent "foreign" tape cartridges from being used on your new drives, you may be successful in reducing tape errors even further.

7.1.4. Tape Labels

MVS access methods support internal tape labels on magnetic reels and cartridges. Internal tape labels are blocks written on the tape before and after data sets to describe the data set name and attributes. The blocks are written and read by MVS access methods under the direction of the application JCL. A tape may have:

1. No label — the only blocks on the tape are data blocks.
2. IBM Standard labels — blocks at the front and end of a data set describe the data set.
3. User labels — the data center can write routines that are installed in MVS to process special labels. Most data centers do not find this a cost-effective solution.
4. American National Standard Institute (ANSI) labels — blocks at the front and end of a data set describe the data set.
5. Bypass Label Protection (BLP). Although BLP is not really a label option for the physical tape, it is included here for completeness. BLP tells MVS to ignore labels if they are on the tape. If they are, the program will read them like data, or the labels can be bypassed by specifying file numbers that include labels as if they were files on the tape.

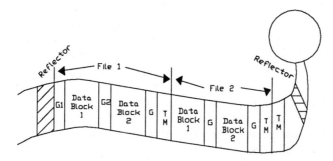

Figure 7.4 Nonlabeled tape. On a nonlabeled tape, the data blocks begin just after the reflector and Interblock Gap. The blocks continue until a Tape Mark is reached — indicating end of file.

Non Label (NL) The layout of a nonlabeled 3420 tape is shown in Figure 7.4. The beginning of a 3420 has a metallic reflector strip to indicate the Beginning of Tape (BOT). A gap separates the BOT from the first physical block. Two physical blocks, each separated by a gap, are shown.

The end of a file on tape is marked by a special bit pattern called a **Tape Mark** (TM). If the tape has a second data set, or **file**, then the process will be repeated until the last file on the tape is created. Two adjacent tape marks indicate a logical end of tape. The end of the usable tape is indicated by a second reflector strip.

IBM Standard Label (SL) Figure 7.5 shows an example of an IBM Standard labeled tape. A standard labeled tape requires the following format:

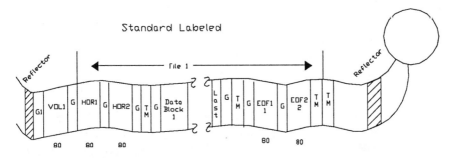

Figure 7.5 Standard Label (SL) tapes. This figure shows one file on a Standard Label tape. The VOL1, HDRx, and EOFx records are all 80 bytes. The data blocks can be any size.

1. Reflector strip to indicate logical start of tape. If the strip is damaged or falls off, then the relative location of the start of tape is lost. All the data on the tape may be lost.
2. A Volume (VOL1) record as the first 80-byte record on the tape.
3. Two Header (HDR1 and HDR2) 80-byte records to describe the file following these records. Note that HDR2 records are sometimes omitted by other operating systems, but are created by MVS in all cases.
4. Tape Mark.
5. Data blocks of the file. The blocks are whatever size the file specifications allow.
6. Tape Mark.
7. Two Trailer (EOF1 and EOF2) 80-byte records to contain information about the file. Trailers contain a count of the physical records (block count) on the file. If the block count in the trailer record does not match the block count that MVS accumulated while reading the file, then the program is ABENDed with code of x37, where "x" is a number assigned by MVS and "37" is the hexadecimal representation (decimal 55) of the Supervisor call for End of Volume (EOV). EOV is the part of MVS that is abending the program. The appendix "Abend Codes" explains this process further.
8. Tape Mark.
9. Repeat items 3 through 8 above for subsequent files, if any are on the tape.
10. Tape Mark. Two tape marks in a row indicate the logical end of volume.
11. Reflector strip to indicate the end of the usable part of the tape. The strip is used by the drive to stop writing before the program writes off the end of the tape. (The reflector strip is used to stop all types — standard label and nonlabeled.) The program is interrupted, MVS end of volume writes trailer records and switches to another volume for the program.

User Label (UL)   User Label (UL) files are very similar to Standard Label files, and many implementations of UL files have standard VOL1, HDRx, and TRLx records. The UL is implemented by data center routines added to MVS to process all tapes with user labels. Generally, the user labels are used for additional security for the data on the tape.

Very few MVS data centers use UL tapes.

ANSI Label (AL) ANSI Label (AL) files are supported for compatibility for the interchange of data among computers of various manufacturers. The support is described by the American National Standards Institute (ANSI) in the American National Standard Magnetic Tape Labels for Information Exchange, ANS X3.27 — 1969.

ANSI tapes are the only support MVS has for tapes written in any character set except EBCDIC. The ASCII label is converted to EBCDIC on read and EBCDIC is converted to ASCII on write.

ANSI labels are similar to standard IBM format but written in ASCII code and not EBCDIC codes. The following are the major differences:

1. An unlimited number of ANSI user labels may be at the beginning and end of the file. The labels may be greater than 80 characters.
2. The formats of the VOL1, HDR2, EOF2, and EOV2 may be different.
3. The ANSI labels HDR2, EOF2, and EOV2 are optional.

The "A" in "AL" stands for ANSI, not ASCII as is often misstated. Ironically, many vendors who only support AL tapes on their systems follow the standard imperfectly.

Very few MVS data centers use AL tapes. They are used by data centers that communicate by sending tapes to and from non-IBM computers.

Usually when a tape has an ANSI label, it contains ASCII data also. The DCB=OPTCD parameter is used to specify EBCDIC to ASCII conversion.

Label Considerations Nonlabeled tapes are dangerous. Think about the processing required for a nonlabeled tape. The data is created by some processing component. The data is written to a tape with some external marking. The tape is moved to the MVS Processor Complex. A batch job calls for the external serial number and specifies a device type. Any data set name can be used because there is no checking done for nonlabeled tapes. The computer operator reaches for the tape and mounts the tape. The job reads the blocks of data.

There are many opportunities for error here. The tape could be labeled wrong. There could be two tapes with the same external volume serial number. The only way the wrong tape will not cause problems is if the program's expectations do not match the contents of the tape. For example, if the program expects fixed 4,096-byte blocks and the tape contains 5,000-byte blocks, the job will not execute.

Many non-IBM Processor Complexes produce IBM standard tapes — even the Personal Computer. Standard label tapes contain several safeguards to ensure the application program is getting the data that was intended for the application:

1. MVS open routines read the header and ensure the data set name is the data set asked for in the JCL.
2. The trailer record ensures that the block count written to the tape and recorded in the trailer was read this time. Otherwise an x37 abend will be issued as MVS processes the trailer record.

Standard labeled tapes should be used unless the tape is coming from a non-MVS data center or is going to a non-MVS application that requires NL or will not permit standard labeled tapes.

Tape data sets should be cataloged unless they are nonlabeled tapes that are coming from a non-MVS data center or are going to a non-MVS application, and that application requires nonlabeled tapes.

7.1.5. Tape Control Unit Cache

Tape Control Unit cache such as the STC tape drives with the cache attachment or the IBM 3480 or 3422 tape devices are designed to buffer control unit commands (forward space file, rewind, and unload) and read requests. The IBM units also buffer **write requests**.

The IBM 3480, with one megabyte of cache, has been measured as approximately *39 percent faster* than the 3420 model 8, which was the fastest of the 3420 models. Part of this speed improvement is the 3.0-Mb/s transfer rate versus the 1.2-Mb/s transfer rate of the 3420, but a large part of the speed is due to caching the read/write operations.

The Programmer Analyst cannot alter the use of tape cache — other than overloading the cache with large block sizes or chained scheduling. In selecting a tape subsystem, however, cache size should be considered.

I worked with an OEM vendor in the early 1980s to size its tape cache. The suggestion from their engineering department was for a 64-Kb cache, but I ran some tests and determined that the DASD backup program wrote 32-Kb blocks to tape. With three blocks at a time, the cache would be overrun. To my knowledge, they selected 128-Kb cache, and it operated successfully.

IBM originally shipped the 3480 with 512 Kb of cache. The subsystem was changed in 1986 to include 1 Mb of cache for the A22 model control unit. In 1989 IBM announced 2 Mb cache. The additional cache resulted in performance improvements of approximately 20 percent for writes and 30 percent for reads.

In Figure 7.6, the IBM 3480 cached controller is pictured with its tape drives. A "2 by 16" configuration is shown — two A22 control units and 16 tape drives. The 3480 B22 units have two tape drives in each physical box.

Each Control unit has two channel paths for access by MVS. Each control unit attaches to four devices — eight tape drives. MVS can access tape drive 920 through path 01 because the control unit for path 01 connects to 920.

MVS can also access 920 through path 03. The two control units communicate because they are connected with cables or Dual Control

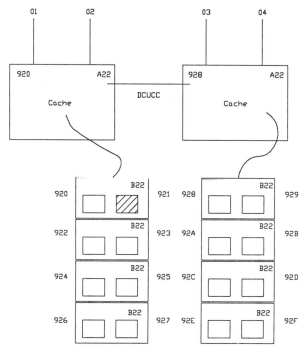

Figure 7.6   Tape Control Unit Cache. The 3480 Tape Control Unit and associated tape drives have cache buffers between the Processor Complex and the physical motion of the tape in the cartridge.

Unit Communications Capability (DCUCC). Another term used by IBM and OEM vendors for this interconnection of tape control units is **communicators**. Examine the following situation:

1. MVS writes block 1 to tape 920 through path 01. The block is really in the cache in control unit 920.
2. MVS writes block 2 to tape unit 920, but now path 01 is busy with some other tape and path 03 is selected.
3. The two 3420-A22 control units must synchronize writing from the cache to get block 1 on the tape first and block 2 second.

Perhaps that is why IBM recommends that the 3480 tapes be assigned *alternate preferred paths* on the **CNTLUNIT** macro that creates the system I/O generation. An example, using Figure 7.6, is code path 01 for device 920 and path 03 for device 921 and keep alternating paths through the string. MVS will always try to use path 1 for device 920 and path 3 for 921. If the "usual" happens, an input tape will be requested on 920 and an output on 921. The control units will be "dedicated" to separate tape drives. Of course, when more tapes start to be used, the benefit will become cloudy. I have coded 3480s using alternate preferred paths and it seems to work.

7.2. PRINTERS

7.2.1. Glossary of Printing Terms

Printing is a profession unto its own and is far beyond the scope of this book. However, the MVS environment has available some beautiful printers.

This introduction will lead you into the world of "in-house publishing." You may not think your company has or needs the ability to publish, but what about program documentation? What about internal standards and procedures? How many times have you sent "several copies" to "a few users?"

Presentation on the Page   In the good old days, when you wanted to print a line of data on the printer, you formatted 132 characters in a buffer and asked MVS to print it on a print device. That is still true for "line-at-a-time" printers, but laser printers can rotate the page and the characters on the page. Though it is possible to print in 90-degree rotation, 180-degree rotation, and 270-degree rotation, just two presentations are used most often.

Landscape: Landscape gets its name from a page that is viewed so that the widest dimension is across the page and the narrowest dimension is up and down. Landscape is what the good old printers printed. In Figure 7.7, two pages are represented. Landscape is best for reports and other printouts that require many columns of data.

Portrait: Portrait gets its name from photographic portraits which usually show people in pictures that are longer than they are wide (e.g., 8" by 10"). Portrait is best for the written word because the eye gets tired if it has to move too far. This book is printed in portrait orientation for that reason. If, for some reason, you must print text on landscape paper, you should consider a columnar layout — like a newspaper — to make the print easier on the eyes.

Lines Per Page: Almost all page layouts begin with the number of lines per page. In the MVS environment, JES and its print processors have defaults — generally 60 or 61 lines per page for "standard" printing. The 3800 printer will only print 60 lines per page in emulation mode (which emulates a line printer). Any number of lines per "page" can be specified for "special forms."

Pitch: Characters Per Inch: Another consideration for printing is pitch, expressed in Characters per Inch (CPI). The default is usually set by the standard paper width being used in a data center. If the paper is 14 inches wide, then 13 inches is usable, and the default will probably be 10 characters per inch. If the paper is 11 inches wide, 10 inches is usable, and the default will probably be 15 characters per inch. Each installation is different so you must check your data center's specifications.

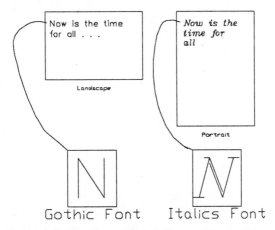

Figure 7.7 Presentation on the page. Landscape (on the left) and portrait (on the right) are the two major presentation styles. The characters, if printed by a laser printer, can be represented in several fonts, or type styles.

Fonts: Also presented in Figure 7.7 is the letter "N" in simple gothic style and italics. The study of the proper font to use for a specific text is also a profession unto itself. The beginner should select one or two fonts — not fancy ones — and start experimenting.

Program control over font changing is limited to laser printers and some dot matrix printers. Impact printers must have their print mechanism changed to change fonts.

Picture Elements (PELs): With line printers, the character is printed by a band or chain. The character is struck with a tiny hammer that presses the ribbon onto the paper, much like a typewriter. Laser printers formulate the character by depositing electronic charges on a drum, rotating the drum into some dry ink, and then fixing the ink onto the page. The page and ink are heated, or **fused**, to make the ink permanent. The characters are formed with tiny dots called **picture elements** (pels).

The more dots per inch, the finer the character looks. These dots also allow laser printers to combine text and graphics on the same page.

Carriage Control   The original line printers contained a paper tape loop that was an integral part of the printer, called a **carriage control tape**. The tape had holes punched in the paper tape to indicate certain positions on the paper. The holes were at fixed locations on the tape called "channels." The punches indicated positions such as top of form, bottom line of form, down one inch, and down to one inch above the bottom. Channel 1 was generally the top of the page.

The printer expected the print line contained carriage control characters as the first character of the print line. The printer read the character (and eliminates it from the line) and performed the indicated action. For example, to start a new page, a "skip to channel 1" command was needed.

There are three methods to provide carriage control characters. Two are for line mode printers. One is for laser printers such as the 3800.

ANSI—VBA and FBA: The most common is the American National Standard Control Characters as defined by x3.9-1978 ANSI Programming Language FORTRAN. Figure 7.8 shows the commonly used values.

The Programmer Analyst specifies DCB=RECFM=VBA for variable blocked records or DCB=RECFM=FBA for fixed blocked records and places an ANSI character in column 1 of the output. The printed output is placed in columns 2 through the end of the logical record.

```
CODE       Action before printing record
----       -----------------------------
blank      space one line
0          (zero) space two lines
-          space three lines
+          do not space--use this to overprint characters
1          skip to line 1 on a new page
```

Figure 7.8   ANSI defined Printer Control Characters. Place the appropriate character in the first position of each line. Place the characters to be printed on the second and subsequent positions of the line.

Machine—VBM and FBM: A second option to control printing is to use **machine carriage control**. The term "machine" is used because the hexadecimal value for the carriage control is the CCW command code that will be used to start the I/O operation. Figure 7.9 shows some of the commonly used codes.

The Programmer Analyst specifies DCB=RECFM=VBM for variable blocked records or DCB=RECFM=FBM for fixed blocked records and places one of the hexadecimal characters in column 1 of the output. The printed output is placed in columns 2 through the end of the logical record.

OPTCD=J: A third method, only used for laser printers such as the 3800 and 3820, is to provide two bytes of control. The first byte is the usual ANSI or machine carriage control. In the example in Figure 7.10, the line begins with characters "blank" and "one." In

```
Hex
Value      Action after printing record
-----      ----------------------------
09         space one line
11         (zero) space two lines
19         space three lines
01         do not space--use this to overprint characters
89         skip to line 1 on new page
```

Figure 7.9   Machine Carriage Control. Another method of telling MVS on what line on the page to print a given line of text is to use "machine" characters. The hexadecimal byte is the same value as used in the Channel Command Word to send to the line printer.

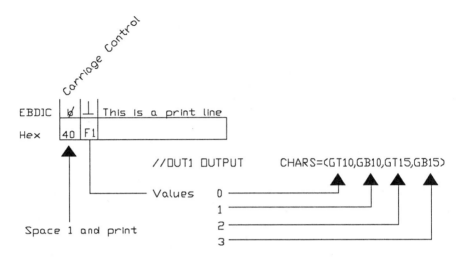

Figure 7.10   OPTCD=J. A third method of directing output text lines is to
specify DCB=OPTCD=J on the output DD statement. The line will then have
two bytes of control characters. The first is regular machine or ANSI control.
The second is a pointer to one of four fonts or the JCL parameter CHARS=.

hexadecimal, these values are x'40F1'. A blank ANSI carriage control
says space one line and print. A "+" (overprint) may or may not overprint depending on the laser implementation.

The second character — Table Reference Character — can have a
value from zero to three — four possible combinations to effect font
switching. Value zero indicates that the font for this line should be
selected from the first value in the DD or OUTPUT JCL statement
CHARS=. A "1" indicates the second positional value in the CHARS=
statement. A "2" indicates the third positional value in the CHARS=
statement. A "3" indicates the fourth positional value in the
CHARS= statement. In this figure, a "1" selects font GB10, or Gothic
Bold at 10 characters per inch.

7.2.2.   Local Printing

Local printing is the meat and potatoes of MVS. For most data
centers, the printed page is the culmination of all the teleprocessing
for input and query and batch processing. Reports and information
are conveyed on the printed page.

One of the major tasks of a data center and the end users is to **control** local print. It is a natural response to a problem to say "print it and we will look at it," but this response is probably a delay tactic. If we do not know what we need, why print everything? Why not take time to *think* about what you need and then print just that? Better still, view the output online and try not to print anything unless necessary.

The MVS versions of JES (JES2 and JES3) are finely tuned printing machines. Remember that is the origin of their history — to print volumes of paper for NASA as the space program was being developed. There are many publications to help fine tune JES from the SHARE and GUIDE organizations, and someone at the data center should be actively involved in one of the SHARE or GUIDE organizations. Let's look at the printers that JES supports:

Line Printers The IBM 1401 computer early in the 1960s had a "chain" printing mechanism that improved the speed and reliability of printing. The 1403 printer lasted well into the 1980s. The printer could print 600 lines per minute. On each link of the chain was a single character. The chain traveled 90 inches per second. Behind the chain were 132 tiny hammers positioned across the paper. When all the hammers had struck all the characters on the line, the paper was advanced per instructions from the channel control words.

Now you know the rest of the story of why the "standard" print line is 132 characters — 132 print positions on the paper was the most that the first printers could print with 132 little hammers! Remember, upward compatibility demands that once a standard is set, it will remain forever. It can be expanded, enhanced, or extended, but never decreased or removed.

Band Printers Band printers are extensions of the old chain printer technology with the link chains replaced by inexpensive metal bands of raised characters.

Laser Printers In the printer industry, laser printers provide excitement. They are popping up all over the place! For the mainframe, the 3800 Printing Subsystem printers print at 215 pages per minute:

1. The 3800 model 1 was the first of the laser printers and only printed by emulating line printers. The output is on single part continuous forms paper and the data center cannot use multiple part paper (there is no "hammer" to strike through carbon paper). You cannot print labels on these printers — the

temperature is too high. (OEM 3800-type printers can print labels because they use a cooler temperature.)

2. The 3800 models 3 and 6 are high speed Advanced Function Printers. The resolution for the model 3 and 6 is 240 x 240 picture elements (pels) per square inch. The 3800 model 3 is rated at over 200 *pages* per minute. The 3800-6 is rated at over 130 pages per minute. *Pages* can be printed pages, graphic images, or a combination of print and graphs.

3. The 3800 model 8 is only shipped to foreign countries such as Japan and will print text using "two-byte" fonts. There are so many characters in the alphabet that it requires one byte to represent a group of characters ("wards") and another byte to represent the character.

All except the 3800 model 1 can operate in two modes: page mode and compatibility mode.

Page Mode: The 3800-3 class printers are really built to operate in page mode. Another name for page mode is **All Points Addressability** (APA) mode. In page mode, the printers are sent a whole page at a time including control information to create images or electronic forms on the blank page. The IBM Document Composition Facility (DCF) and Graphical Data Display Manager (GDDM) systems can be used to build pages for page mode operation.

JES can use the 3800 in page mode by building a functional subsystem to control the printer. Functional Subsystem (FSS) mode allows the Programmer Analyst to print in any of four rotations: zero, 90, 180, and 270 degrees. Multiple fonts per line can be used without using OPTCD=J.

There are many pieces to the software JES uses to build the Functional Subsystem. The Print Services Facility (PSF) is the name of the software IBM sells to provide AFP services.

Compatibility Mode: The models 3 and 6 can be run in "compatibility" with the model 1. This line-at-a-time mode emulates the line printers — only much faster, clearer, and more reliable. The printer can also print 10 lines to the inch for really small, eye-hurting printouts.

Why big, fast laser printers? Consider a large company with 120,000 customers. The imaginary company is a $2,000,000,000 company. It is now time to send out invoices. If we print invoices on a line printer, it takes three days. If we print the invoices on a 3800 model 3, it takes one day. At $2 billion per year income, getting the money turned around and in the company banks "x" day(s) earlier could mean more than $200,000 in interest at 4 percent!

7.2.3. Remote Printing

Remote printing refers to printers that are not channel-attached to the Processor Complex. The physical location may be in the same building as the MVS Processor Complex, but the printer is attached via communications lines, not bus and tag cables.

General Types Remote printing is handled by JES or OEM products. There are three general classifications of remote printing:

1. 3274 remote printers. Remote 3274 or 3174 control units can have a printer attached. These printers now make up the vast majority of small remote printing configurations. They are relatively inexpensive, quick and easy to install.
2. Remote Job Entry (RJE)/Network Job Entry (NJE). The 43xx and 9370 class of Processor Complexes make a very acceptable remote configuration for large-volume remote printing. These small distributed MVS systems can have printers attached to spool and print large volumes of printed output. The user can even have a 3800 on one of these Processor Complexes if its cost is justified.
3. Laser printers
   a. The 3835 is similar to the 3800 but slower. It prints approximately 88 pages per minute.
   b. The 3820 is similar to a copy machine in that it uses cut sheet paper and is capable of 20 pages per minute. Since it was designed as a page printer, there is no compatibility mode and cannot recognize carriage control characters. See *IBM 3820 Introduction and Planning Guide* (GBOF-1189) for complete instruction on how to install a 3820.
   c. The 3827 is a cut sheet printer with a rated speed of 92 pages per minute. The print is at 240 pels per inch.
   d. The 4250 is a high-resolution, all points addressable printer, which prints 600 x 600 pels per square inch on continuous alumnized surface paper — the alumnized surface is burned off to leave the black varnish surface for the dots. The 4250 attaches to a 3x74 control unit for local or remote attachment.

      The output of the 4250 is camera-ready for direct use in copying or offset printing. The 4250 is only supported by the IBM program product *Composed Document Print Facility* (CDPF).

The 4250 is probably the most complex printer in the IBM arsenal, but if you need camera-ready copy quickly, then this is your printer. Quick is a relative term: Printing a single sheet may take approximately one and one-half minutes depending on what is printed on the page. The print head moves one meter per second (across the page!).

Tuning Remote Printing Remote printing does lend itself to some tuning by the Programmer Analyst. Each extra character, blank or not, must be transmitted over the phone line unless it can be compressed out. Telecommunications expenses are generally the largest expense of a distributed network. Some Tuning techniques are shown in Figure 7.11:

1. Keep your characters together and to the left of the page.
2. Select hardware that supports data compression. Oddly enough, the IBM 3820 does not support data compression, to the author's knowledge.
3. Select remote printing software that implements SNA (or other) data compression. The IBM Field Developed program

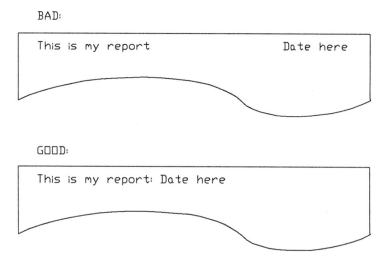

Figure 7.11   Tuning remotely printed output. The two examples of print lines above represent an efficient and an inefficient organization for print lines. Imbedded blanks are often not removed from printed lines. Do not force the end user to have a crowded, unusable report, but where possible consider the communication line.

(JES328x) and several OEM products, such as VTAM Printer Support System (VPS)[2] compress at least trailing blanks. If you are selecting remote printing software, be sure to benchmark the method of data compression.

7.3. SUMMARY

Understanding MVS peripheral equipment is an important part of your growth in the IBM environment. Tape drives come in two flavors: round and square. Round tapes will always be with us for compatibility and portability reasons. Do not underestimate the "sneaker network."[3]

You want the best performance and most reliable tape drives. As of this writing, that seems to be the IBM (or equivalent) 3480 tape drives.

As with DASDs, understand what you are asking the tape drive to do. Be careful of interblock gaps as they waste time and money.

Only use standard labels unless you are dragged kicking and screaming to use nonlabeled tapes.

If you can get control units that have cache, do so by all means. Tapes are sequential devices, and anything you can do to make them co-exist better with other devices is very good business. The 3480, which operates in block multiplex mode, is a cached device and combines all these good attributes.

Stretch your understanding and usage of your printers. Many installations have laser printers and still only use them as fast replacements for the 1403 printer.

It should go unsaid that your printed output should be professional in appearance. Uppercase characters are only for 1403 thinking people. Complete sentences are a must. Think, document, and report professionally. It should go unsaid, but just yesterday I saw a computer report from a large communications company that had all uppercase letters.

---

2. Product of Levi, Ray & Shoup, Inc., Springfield, IL
3. Sneaker network is the term used for placing data on a round (maybe square) tape and handing it to an employee in tennis shoes to run the data to its destination. You probably will send the tape via postal service, UPS, Federal Express, or other carrier, but you get the idea.

C

MVS Software Concepts

Part C of *MVS Concepts and Facilities* discusses the MVS software. The system services that MVS performs for the end user and the data center are introduced. Data set access methods are covered. Data set management is covered. MVS utilities are introduced, and sample JCL is included.

8

MVS Software

8.1. INTRODUCTION TO MVS SERVICES

MVS only runs on System/370 Processor Complexes. The operating system executes instructions which are only available on the System/370. Various releases of Multiple Virtual Storage (MVS) can run only on specific System/370 Processor Complexes. Remember, IBM promises upward compatibility. In fact, it strives to entice the data center management to buy new hardware by introducing software which will only run on the new equipment. If you want the new function, you generally have to buy the new hardware. One example is that MVS/ESA will only run on the 309x Expanded Processor Complexes (models E/S).

There are notable exceptions — MVS/370 will run on the 309x series of Processor Complexes. When the 3090 Processor Complex was announced, the user community had predicted that MVS/370 would not be allowed on the 309x series, but very few data centers had converted from MVS/370 to MVS/XA. IBM did not want to limit its population of potential customers. Also, IBM recognized that few data centers would want to convert both their hardware and software at the same time.

The MVS operating system provides a number of services for application programs. "Application" is used here to mean an application program such as a COBOL program, a utility program such as the SORT, a Data Base/Data Communication "system" such as IMS or CICS, a "system program" such as JES or VTAM, or even the MVS operating system itself. Any program which runs under the MVS operating system will eventually need these services — either explicitly (the application calls the supervisor service directly) or implicitly (some other program does the call on behalf of the application). Services are provided for the following areas:

1. **Dynamic Address Translation (DAT).** DAT requires certain control blocks in virtual storage. MVS constructs these control blocks.
2. **Multiprocessing.** MVS is *designed* to operate on a Processor Complex which has multiple CPUs. Many of the services provided by MVS support multiprocessing. Remember, multiprocessing is the term used when more than one instruction can be executed simultaneously.
3. **Multiprogramming** is the term used for many tasks appearing to use the resources of the Processor Complex. MVS supports tightly and loosely coupled multiprogramming.
4. **ENQUE and Locking.** Multiprogramming and multiprocessing environments require solutions to communications problems with two or more tasks operating at the same time. ENQUE and Locking services solve these problems.
5. **Timing.** Applications need an alarm clock to tell them the current time and "wake them up" at times in the future. MVS timing services are discussed in this chapter.
6. **System Operator Communication.** Applications need to notify the MVS operator of information. The MVS system itself is one of the largest users of operator communication. MVS Write-to-Operator communication and console support are discussed in this chapter.
7. **Address space management.** Applications are written as if they were the only task being executed in a Processor Complex. MVS manages task creation, control, and interruption processing. The MVS dispatcher and tasks are introduced in this chapter. The term **dispatch** is used to describe MVS operating system modules turning control of the CPU over to a task.

8. **Batch job management and spooled input and output.** As data center users submit work to the MVS system, the JES subsystem controls and manages these resources. JES is introduced in a separate chapter.

9. **Data set management and access methods.** There are several types of data sets or files in the MVS architecture. The type of file is determined by the MVS Access Method selected to build the file. MVS does a wonderful job of managing data sets. A separate chapter introduces the MVS services which allocate a data set, keep track of it in system catalogs, and retrieve the data set.

10. **Program management.** All of these services are provided by programs written by IBM and supplied as part of the IBM operating system. Additional programs are supplied by the data center. Applications have their own common "program libraries." How are these programs gathered and managed? The answer lies in a separate chapter — Program Management.

11. **Communications software and hardware.** The task of providing and servicing terminal access to MVS is provided by the communications software and hardware supported under MVS. The software — BTAM, TCAM, and VTAM as well as the 37x5 hardware — is discussed in a separate chapter — Telecommunications.

12. **Utilities.** The application and system utilities which are provided by IBM are discussed in a separate chapter. This introduction gives the reader a view of which utilities serve which purposes.

The processes MVS undergoes from the time power is applied to the system until it is fully operational is instructive from two standpoints. First, the process itself is fascinating, and knowing what is supposed to happen can help you understand what the causes might be if it fails. Second, it is one thing to know what services MVS supplies and how they work, but learning about the initialization process helps explain why some of them must exist.

Moreover, evidence of some MVS services appears on the system console during initialization. If you have the opportunity, look for these.

The section on multiprogramming is the pivotal point of the chapter where we consider most of the remaining services as a list of topics.

8.2.   MVS INITIALIZATION

This section concentrates on System/370 and MVS initialization.
After everything is initialized, we will be ready for work.

8.2.1.   Preparing the Hardware for Initialization — Power On

The data center must perform some preliminary functions to prepare
the hardware for MVS. The procedure is only necessary when starting a Processor Complex for the first time or after the IBM Customer
Engineer has performed maintenance on the Processor Complex. The
procedure is commonly called **power on**.

Power on may take up to 20 minutes as the Processor Complex
has to perform many functions. Some functions require operator interaction accomplished through the use of "frames," which are particular displays on the system console:

1. **Power on.** The power is applied to the processor complex. The
    operator presses the "power on" button. Figure 8.1 is a repre-
    sentation of a physical 3081 Processor Complex. Every 308x
    and 309x Processor Complex has similar buttons and consoles,
    so you should consult the manual appropriate for your Proces-
    sor Complex.

    During power on, each component has power applied, and
    diagnostics are run to determine if all circuits are operating
    correctly. This may take several minutes. The power-on button
    will be pink while the power-on sequence is taking place and
    will change to white after the power-up sequence is complete.

2. **Initial Microprogram Load (IML).** The processor complex
    loads the microcode instructions to enable the System/370 in-
    struction set. The microcode is loaded from floppy diskettes
    onto a hard disk inside the Processor Complex (for a 308x) or
    from 3370s (for a 309x).

3. **Release Configuration.** After an IOCP has been loaded, the
    Processor Complex is said to be "configured." Before another
    IOCP is used, a Release Configuration command is required.
    The Release Configuration step is not required if the Processor
    Complex has just been IMLed because there is no "configura-
    tion" to release.

4. **Power-On Reset.** At the hardware console, the operator
    selects the hardware configuration frame. The frame is used to
    configure ("place online") CPUs, Central Storage ("Storage Ad-

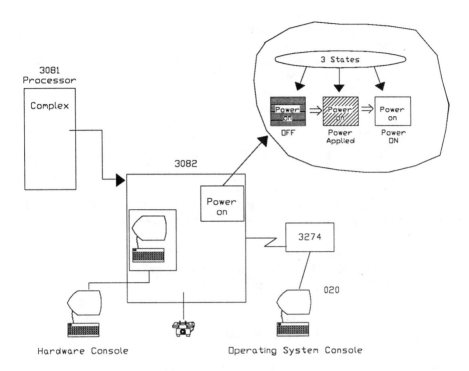

Figure 8.1 Preparing the Processor Complex for MVS. The above System/370 is a representation of a 3081 Processor Complex. There are two hardware consoles — one physically inside the 3082 (Processor Controller) and one outside the Processor Complex — usually sitting beside the MVS Operator Console. At least one 327x console is attached to a 3x74 controller for MVS use.

dresses"), and the channel configuration ("EXDC"). The frame is used to select the **Control Program** (CP) mode (MVS/370, MVS/XA or MVS/ESA), and other configuration options, such as what CPUs should be online and what Central Storage should be online.

The operator may need to select an Input/Output Configuration Data Set (IOCDS), which defines the configuration of hardware attached to the Processor Complex. Once the IOCDS is selected, it is "remembered" by the Processor Complex and need not be changed until the hardware changes and a new IOCDS is created.

The IOCDS is loaded into the highest half megabyte of Central Storage and describes the hardware attached to the Processor Complex. The area the IOCDS is loaded into is called the High Save Area (HSA). How the IOCP is created will be discussed in detail later in this chapter.

5. **Clear and Load.** On the hardware console, the operator selects the Operator Control frame and selects the **logical** Channel Control Unit (CCU) address of the Systems Residence Volume (SYSRES), which is placed in hardware registers to prepare for loading the operating system. I recommend two steps to load MVS:

   a. **System Reset and Clear.** This command resets all the channels and subchannels and clears Central Storage to hexadecimal zeros. A System Reset should always be performed because it resets control units to clear pending I/O operations and/or overcome some problems with control units. A System Reset does not guarantee all control units and/or devices are active: It just frees up the channel in case one is broken. Central Storage must be cleared to ensure that bits and addresses are not left "set" to cause MVS problems. For example, what if storage was not cleared, and MVS "found" a pointer to a batch job that finished several hours ago? Would MVS try to continue? No, MVS would probably terminate abnormally.

   b. **Load.** The system is reset (this is the second reset), and the operating system is loaded into storage. Because MVS clears storage as part of its initialization, the System Reset and clear (above) is not necessary all the time, but it may eliminate problems. I advise operators to perform both the explicit and implicit System Reset — it is worth committing to habit because problems from a missed reset (for whatever reason) would be difficult to diagnose.

8.2.2. Preparing the Hardware for Initialization — IOCP

After powering up a System/370 Processor Complex, the hardware and software need to be synchronized as to the hardware which is attached. The IOCP tells the Processor Complex what it needs to know about the devices attached to the Processor Complex. This process is called "IOCP," because the MVS program which creates the communication file is called the Input/Output Configuration Program. The communication file is the Input/Output Configuration Data Set.

IOCP is now supported by all operating systems, but when the 3081 was first shipped, MVS was the only operating system which could run the IOCP. If the 3081 were to be loaded with the Virtual Machine/370 operating system, MVS would have to be loaded first or loaded under control of VM to change the IOCDS. Figure 8.2 shows the MVS implementation of the IOCP:

1. The Systems programmer decides what equipment — types and number — will be configured. The equipment is defined in Assembler macros.
2. Assembler macros are written to describe the I/O devices attached to the Processor Complex. The macros are supplied as input to the Input/Output Configuration Program (IOCP). (These also input to the systems generation process.)
3. Output from IOCP are listings to report any errors and define the configuration and, optionally, an updated IOCDS on the Processor Complex which the IOCP is running on:
   a. On some models of the System/370, there are two IOCDS files per processor side. On others, there are four. Parameters on the "EXEC" statement tell IOCP if and where to write the IOCDS.
   b. There is a frame on the "hardware console" which permits or prohibits writing to the IOCDS. The target IOCDS must be enabled for updating.

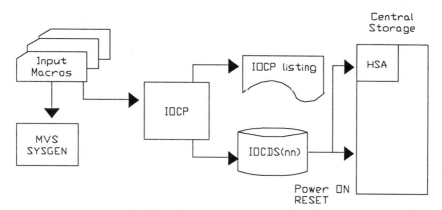

Figure 8.2   MVS IOCP generation. The systems programmer develops a set of assembler macros. These macros are used for both the MVS I/O generation and IOCP. From the IOCP program comes listings and the IOCDS in the Processor Complex. At Power On Reset, the microcode loads the IOCP into control blocks in the Hardware Save Area (HSA) in Central Storage. Both MVS and the Processor Complex use this area.

4. The same input file given to IOCP can be used by MVS to do the I/O generation.
5. Once the IOCDS has been created successfully, a Power-On Reset can be performed to effect the new IOCP.
6. Devices cannot be added to the system without terminating MVS. Therefore, it is generally a good idea to have extra devices generated before new hardware actually arrives.

There are two other ways to change the IOCDS. A stand-alone version is available and should be part of the disaster recovery plan for your data center. The IOCP is written to magnetic tape (or punched cards!). The stand-alone version of IOCP is shipped with each Processor Complex. A second method is to manually build an IOCDS from the hardware screens. See the manual *Input/Output Configuration Program Users Guide and Reference* (GC28-1027) for full details.

8.2.3. Initial Program Load (IPL)

The term Initial Program Load (IPL) has been used by IBM since the origin of operating systems on the System/360. It implies the system is prepared for productive application work to be performed. In the days of the Disk Operating System (DOS), the IPL could be performed in a matter of seconds. Most DOS applications were batch in nature, so once the operating system was available, jobs could be started. Today the Virtual Machine (VM) operating system also IPLs in a very few seconds.

As function increased and the operating system became more complex, the time to IPL grew until today, for MVS, it is measured in minutes. The IPL now has a number of components. For a reasonably sized Processor Complex with MVS as the operating system, a large VTAM network to initialize, and multiple CICS and/or IMS systems to initialize, the data center does well to ready the system for users in under 30 minutes.

SYSGEN the Systems Residence (SYSRES) Volume Before MVS can be loaded into a Processor Complex, a DASD volume must be prepared with the MVS modules and several required libraries. The process of building the system volume is called a **system generation** (SYSGEN).

In Figure 8.3, the volume is labeled "SYSRES." As part of the system volume creation, the REFORMAT command of the IBM Device

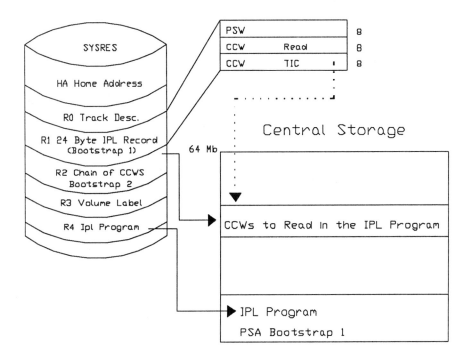

Figure 8.3   MVS IPL — hardware. The Processor Complex loads the two bootstrap records and turns control over to the channel program in the bootstrap to load the IPL program. The IPL program loads the Nucleus Initialization Program (NIP). NIP initializes MVS.

Support Facility (DSF) is used to place the IPL program on the volume.[1]

Initialization of MVS   There are differences between the initialization of MVS/370, MVS/XA, and MVS/ESA. These differences are mentioned here and expanded on in the chapter which compares MVS/370 to MVS/XA and MVS/XA to MVS/ESA — "MVS/XA and MVS/ESA." There are two stages to the IPL: hardware and software (see Figure 8.3).

---

1. DSF can also be used to place other "IPL" programs on DASD. **There can be only one IPL program on a single DASD volume.** One example is the stand-alone dump program, which is needed if all of MVS must be dumped to get diagnostic information.

Hardware phase of IPL:

1. The 24-byte IPL record (Bootstrap 1) is read into central storage location zero from Cylinder 0 Head 0 record 1 on the DASD volume. Record 0 is the track descriptor record required on every track.
2. Bootstrap 1 is executed to read the IPL program (Bootstrap 2) into Central Storage at an address above where the IPL program will be. Bootstrap 2 is read from Cylinder 0 Head 0 record 2 and contains a chain of Channel Command Words (CCWs) to read in the IPL program.
3. The channel subsystem turns control over to the bootstrap CCWs (with a Transfer in Channel (TIC) command), which read in a small program called Initial Program Load (IPL), located at Cylinder 0 Head 0 record 4 on the SYSRES DASD volume. IPL is read into Central Storage at location zero. The IPL program contains, as the first 512 bytes of the program, the constants which make up the Prefixed Save Area (PSA). Remember the PSA is just constants — PSW areas and status areas which the hardware uses to communicate with MVS.

    If the volume is not initialized with an IPL program, the Processor Complex will fail to complete the LOAD function. The operator will note little or no activity on the consoles and usually a "loading" indicator will be on the hardware console.

Software phase of IPL: The IPL program is the part of MVS which begins the initialization of MVS. Its two major functions are to prepare Central Storage and load the MVS modules which are linked together in a module in SYS1.NUCLEUS called IEANUCxx. IPL then loads and transfers control to the Nucleus Initialization Program (NIP).

Until IPL and NIP have fully initialized enough of MVS to communicate with the operator, any errors will result in a **disabled wait state**. A disabled wait state exists when all the CPUs in a Processor Complex are disabled for interruption and the PSW contains a wait state code. Wait state codes are documented in the message library-system codes manual (e.g., *MVS/Extended Architecture Message Library: System Codes* (GC28-1157) for MVS/XA).

IPL: The IPL program performs its functions to prepare for MVS (see Figure 8.4).

1. IPL clears and/or tests Central Storage and sets all the storage keys. IPL determines the size of Central Storage. IPL will only

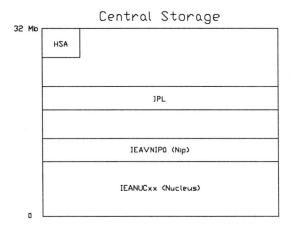

Figure 8.4   Central Storage After IPL. IPL relocates itself higher up in Central Storage and loads the nucleus (IEANUCxx) and NIP (IEAVNIPO). IPL turns control over to NIP. Note the high portion of Central Storage has the High Save Area (HSA) for communication between MVS and the hardware.

"find" what is configured by the power on reset. If the Processor Complex has 64 megabytes of Central Storage, but the configuration only "put online" 32 megabytes of Central Storage, then MVS will only have access to 32 megabytes of Central Storage.

2. IPL finds the selected NIP in SYS1.NUCLEUS and determines the size of the module. IPL relocates itself to make room in Central Storage for NIP. IPL then loads NIP.
3. For XA, IPL calls IPL Resource Initialization Modules (IRIMs) to set up the various resource managers. For example, the Real Storage Manager (RSM) initializes control blocks to map out the Central Storage of the machine.
4. IPL turns control over to the Nucleus Initialization Program (NIP).

NIP: The Nucleus Initialization Program continues the process of initializing MVS. The program — IEAVNIP0 — calls many other modules to perform parts of the initialization. These modules are collectively called Resource Initialization Modules (RIMs).

1. NIP initializes Central Storage. IPL has cleared all of Central Storage to hexadecimal zeros. NIP will now fill in the important areas. For MVS/370, the nucleus is loaded starting at real address zero, and the System Queue Area (SQA) and the Com-

mon Service Area (CSA) are loaded at the top of Central Storage. For MVS/XA and MVS/ESA, the nucleus is loaded at the top of virtual storage straddling the 16-megabyte line.

2. NIP initializes the Master Address Space. NIP uses the Master Space for its own address space. Virtual Storage is allocated for other MVS areas. The different versions of NIP set up the virtual storage areas which will be required. NIP uses member MSTRJCLxx of SYS1.NUCLEUS where "xx" is a two-digit number to "build" the address space. The member consists of constants which contain the "JCL" that is used for the Master Scheduler. The System User Attribute Data Set (UADS), the system message data set (SYS1.BRODCAST), the system procedure libraries (SYS1.PROCLIB), and other installation defined data sets are included.

3. NIP initializes the control blocks to describe the I/O devices. The MVS control block used for each I/O device is called a Unit Control Block (UCB). During this time an I/O operation is performed to each expected device to see if the device is actually there. If it is, the volume label is read and placed into the UCB. If the volume is not there, NIP marks the UCB unavailable. If the device is in error, the operator is notified.

   Each path is tested to determine the paths available for I/O operations.

4. NIP finds and sets up pointers to the Master Catalog (see Figure 8.5). The SYS1.NUCLEUS data set on the system residence volume contains the volume serial number and device type of the master catalog. NIP looks up the volume in the UCBs and reads the Volume Table of Contents (VTOC) of the volume to find the master catalog. The master catalog in MVS is a normal VSAM catalog. It is special because it contains the system data sets.

   Until the catalog is opened, the system data sets (such as SYS1.NUCLEUS) must reside on the same volume which the IPL started from. After the master catalog is open, MVS modules can access any data set listed in the master catalog.

5. NIP initializes the consoles. The operator will note that the consoles "beep" as they are initialized. After this time, MVS can communicate with the operator through the operating system console. Note that the "old" MVT communication rules apply: Each message reply must be answered with **R nn,abcde**, where "R" is the operator "reply" command and "nn" is the message number, and "abcde" is the reply to the outstanding message. Most MVS operators are used to the con-

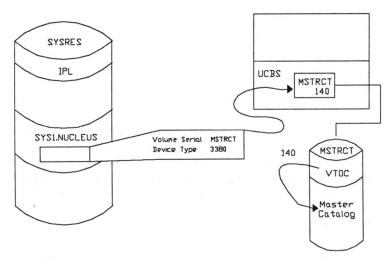

Figure 8.5   Locating the Master Catalog. In the SYS1.NUCLEUS data set on the IPL volume is the volume serial and device type of the Master Catalog. NIP finds the volume mounted on device 140 and opens the Master Catalog for future use.

vention permitted by the JES subsystem where only the "nn,abcde" is required. This shorthand notation is not available in the IPL process until after JES is initialized.

The primary console as specified in the Systems Generation process is tried first. If found, the Master Console is assigned to that console. If the first console is not available, the others are tried in order of specification until one is found. If no console is found that MVS can use, MVS cannot continue so the Processor Complex is placed into a disabled wait state.

Make sure your operations staff is aware of the console selection order — and their locations — so they will not have to play "hide and seek" in the event of a multiple console failure! Operators probably know where the consoles they use, but are they aware of the location of the console in the shift supervisor's office or in the Systems Programming area?

6. NIP requires input from the operator in the form of system parameters to determine what will be initialized and to provide parameters for the many MVS functional subsystems. For example, the Common Service Area (CSA) size is determined by system parameters.

Each release of MVS adds or changes these system parameters. See *System Programming Library: Initialization and Tuning Guide* (e.g., GC28-1149 for MVS/XA) for complete information on these parameters. If you are responsible for the initialization and tuning of MVS at your data center, you should read this book at least once a year to ensure you have specified what your data center currently needs. Each release of MVS adds and changes parameters which have defaults — defaults are generally not good for your installation. Defaults assume your data center is average — the worst of the best or the best of the worst.

NIP asks the operator to **SPECIFY SYSTEM PARAMETERS** for this initialization. MVS parameters are specified in the SYS1.PARMLIB data set. The default parameter list — member IEASYS00 is always read by NIP.[2] The operator can reply in two forms:

a. No parameters. The operator just presses the "enter" key which indicates to NIP to use member IEASYS00 of SYS1.PARMLIB to define all system parameters for the IPL. IEASYS00 may point to other members (e.g., IECIOSxx) but not to other IEASYSxx members.

b. One or several parameters in the form of KKKK=nn. "KKKK" is the system parameter (e.g., SYSP=, IPS=, ICS=) and "nn" is any two alphanumeric characters which are added to the member name in SYS1.PARMLIB. A reply of IPS=01 would load IEAIPS01 to specify tuning and performance parameters.

The default suffix is always "00." If MVS requires a parameter, and none is specified, MVS will look for mmmmmm00, where mmmmmm is the prefix name which is required. If no IEAICS parameter were specified, IEAICS00 would be searched for in SYS1.PARMLIB to identify the installation control specifications.

Each NIP initialization module has defaults defined in case the installation does not specify a member for the initialization routines to use. I recommend that an installation not depend on defaults. Someone at the data center should know and understand the MVS parameters.

---

2. In at least one version of MVS, MVS would not IPL without an IEASYS00 member in SYS1.PARMLIB.

7. NIP sets the volume "mount attributes" of each online DASD volume. Member VATLSTxx of SYS1.PARMLIB is used to determine if the volume should be:
   a. Permanently resident.
   b. Reserved.
   c. A storage volume.
   d. A public volume.
   e. A private volume.
   These attributes will be described later.
8. The Systems Resource Manager (SRM) is initialized. Members IEAIPSxx, IEAOPTxx, and IEAICSxx are the main members of SYS1.PARMLIB which are used. SRM will be introduced in another chapter.
9. The Auxiliary Storage Manager (ASM) is initialized. The Page and Swap data sets are opened and verified. A minimum of one PLPA, one COMMON, and one LOCAL data set are required. ASM parameters are specified in IEASYSxx members.
10. The Program Manager initializes the various areas for MVS modules:
    a. Pageable Link Pack Area (PLPA) contains all the modules from the SYS1.LPALIB data set (and others if MVS/XA 2.2 or later is used). These are MVS modules used by access methods, SVC modules, and any other module which the data center deems "common" and available for all to use.

    There are several types of IPL, determined by the operator adding CLPA to the IPL parameters: **Cold start** is the term used when "CLPA" is part of the operator reply. All modules are read from "SYS1.LPALIB" into virtual storage and paged out to the SYS1.PLPA data set. Many installations follow the IBM recommendation of only performing a cold start infrequently. I recommend installations *always* perform a cold start. MVS rarely needs to be IPLed. If your data center only IPLs once a month, and you apply maintenance twice a year, then it is possible you could go seven months without reading SYS1.LPALIB. I feel it is best to cold start and reread the modules.
       i. **Quick start** is the term used when the operator (or SYS1.PARMLIB) uses the CVIO parameter to just clear the VIO pages and not load all the PLPA modules.
       ii. **Warm start** is the term used when neither the CLPA nor the CVIO parameters are used for the IPL.

b. **Fixed Link Pack Area** (FLPA) contains modules which the data center has determined are used often enough to be fixed into Central Storage. The page frame in which these modules exist is "fixed" in Central Storage and is not available for paging.

c. **Modified Link Pack Area** (MLPA) is an area in which the data center can specify modules from any data set to be loaded into virtual storage. These modules will be in virtual storage for as long as this IPL of MVS lasts. These are usually accounting modules and other modules written in-house.

11. Several address spaces are initialized:

a. **PCAUTH** is the cross memory address space which controls cross memory access.

b. **TRACE** is the MVS trace address space. Supervisor services are traced in this address space in case a failure occurs.

c. **GRS** is the Global Resource Manager to manage serialization of logical resources.

d. **DUMPSRV** is the address space which manages system abnormal dumps.

12. NIP initializes multiple CPUs in the Processor Complex (see Figure 8.6). MVS has been IPLed on a two-CPU Processor Complex. At the proper point, NIP signals the other processor to start processing. There are two System/370 architecture pieces to support multiple processors:

a. **Prefixed Save Area.** The first 4,096 bytes of storage contain the PSWs and control information for MVS to communicate with the hardware. In a tightly coupled environment, all of the 16 Mb or 2 Gb virtual storage is available to both CPUs, but the first 4,096 must be unique to each CPU in the complex.

MVS obtains a 4-Kb Central Storage frame at NIP time and sets another special register — the **PREFIX register** — with the address of the obtained page. Any references to the first page frame by MVS, an application program, or the I/O subsystem will be interpreted by DAT to be this relocated page.

Each CPU has its own copy of the "first" page of memory. Note that this is not part of the virtual memory paging system but a special feature of the hardware to support tightly coupled processing.

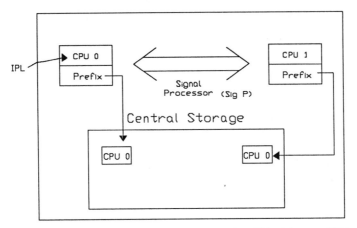

Figure 8.6   MVS multiprocessing initialization. MVS is IPLed in one CPU. After initialization, MVS uses a System/370 instruction — SIGP — to "wake up" other CPUs in the Processor Complex. Each CPU will create its own "first page" somewhere in Central Storage.

b. **Signal Processor (SIGP).** Each CPU in a Processor Complex has a number associated with the CPU. MVS uses a special instruction to communicate from one CPU to another in the Processor Complex: SIGP has a CPU number as an operand. Some of the SIGP communication requests are:

i.   Initialization — prepare a CPU for work. Note, as MVS is starting up, the hardware frame shows 100 percent utilization in the target CPU as it is initializing. The 100 percent busy should stop in 20–30 seconds.

ii. Start, Stop, and Restart. Reconfiguration of the CPU, either online or offline. An operator command, CONFIG, can vary CPUs on and offline.

iii. External Call. As part of normal operation, MVS will **shoulder-tap** other CPUs to inform them there is work to be done (Address spaces are now dispatchable).

iv. Emergency signal. When a processor fails, the machine check handler will issue a SIGP to the other processors to notify them to take over the other work.

13. NIP ends and turns control over to the **Master Scheduler**.

The Master Scheduler is now in sole posession of the first Address Space. This Address Space is numbered "one," not "zero" as you might expect. Several other address spaces are initialized:

1. CONSOLE — The console messages which go to the various operator consoles in the computer room are initialized.
2. ALLOCAS is the allocation address space in which data set allocations are recorded.
3. SMF is the System Management Facilities address space. SMF collects data records from various parts of MVS.
4. LLA (LINKLIST Lookaside) is the address space introduced in MVS/XA to provide information in virtual storage from directories of load libraries. LLA speeds up the "load" function of program management (explained in the chapter on Program Management.) MVS/ESA expands the LLA function by utilizing a feature called **Virtual Lookaside Facility** (VLF), which is used to load "the most active" modules into virtual storage rather than fetching the modules from DASD. (VLF can be used for any data string that is normally online to MVS, not just load modules.)

   MVS/ESA also adds a new term for LLA — **Library Lookaside**. The Library Lookaside system services can control libraries outside the Linklist libraries. The managed libraries need not be load libraries — heavily used partitioned data sets of any type can be controlled. The data center can dynamically add, remove, and refresh pointers to members in the libraries.

   Changes in an LLA managed library (new or replaced members) are not available to the MVS system until an "F LLA,REFRESH" operator command is issued.
5. CATALOG is the address space introduced in the later versions of MVS/XA to move CATALOG control blocks into a separate address space.
6. The Master Scheduler initializes the version of JES (JES2 or JES3), which was generated for this copy of MVS.
7. JES initialization programs set up to start jobs and TSO tasks.
8. The system is now ready for business.

In the chapter on virtual storage, you learned that all versions of MVS have common areas available to all address spaces. One of these areas — the prefixed save area (PSA) — contains pointers to MVS control blocks. Probably the most important is the pointer to the Communications Vector Table (CVT).

The CVT is an anchor control block. It contains information about the MVS system, but it also points to almost all other MVS control blocks. Many subsystems, like JES and VTAM, have their own version of the CVT — a large block of virtual storage which points to many other blocks or queues.

8.3. DYNAMIC ADDRESS TRANSLATION (DAT)

One of the most important services of MVS is to support DAT. Dynamic Address Translation (DAT) gives MVS applications several benefits:

1. Programs only use Central Storage (their working set) as they actually need it. The operating system can overcommit Central Storage and execute more jobs concurrently than if they were entirely resident. The multiprogramming level can be raised to a higher level than Central Storage would allow.
2. Central Storage fragmentation is reduced.
3. It is possible to design systems without consideration for the amount of Central Storage available.
4. In theory, long-running programs will only use the amount of Central Storage needed at any instant, not the largest amount of Central Storage ever needed for the job. (In practice, a little more or less Central Storage needed at any instant is available.)
5. Reliability is increased: Each task has its own address space and cannot "look" into the address space of another.

DAT is the System/370 hardware feature that makes Virtual Storage possible. Let's review some virtual storage concepts:

1. A block of Central Storage is a called a **FRAME** and contains 4,096 bytes.
2. A block of virtual storage is called a **PAGE** and contains 4,096 bytes.
3. A block of Auxiliary DASD storage is called a **SLOT** and contains 4,096 bytes.
4. Active pages are in Central Storage.
5. Inactive pages are in Auxiliary Slots.
6. Moving pages between Central Storage and auxiliary storage is called **paging**.

DAT allows MVS to maximize utilization of Central Storage. With "DAT on," the operating system can interrupt a program at an arbitrary moment and store the instructions and/or data on auxiliary storage to free frames for another program. MVS can dynamically relocate programs and/or data anywhere in addressable Central Storage without modifying their instructions or data.

An address space is a TSO session, batch job, or started system task. The unit of work in MVS is an address space (there may be multiple tasks in the address space). Each address space is assigned a number from 1 (the MASTER address space) to the largest number of address spaces allowed by the installation.

Each address space is made to appear as if the address space is the only user of the computer. We will see that some parts of the "virtual address space" are unique to each address space and some parts are shared by all of the address spaces. Each address space can address the full limits of the architecture: 16 megabytes for MVS/370 and 2 gigabytes for MVS/XA and MVS/ESA.

DAT is implemented in the microcode of the Processor Complex. There are two versions of DAT used by MVS: The first is for MVS/370, the second for MVS/XA and MVS/ESA. In the case of the 303x family of Processor Complexes, the microcode which was loaded did not have a multiple choice option for microcode selection — the data center got MVS/370 microcode. The 308x and 309x Processor Complex has an option on the system configuration frame to select one of two types of microcode when the Processor Complex is initialized or powered on.

The Processor Complex microcode and the version of MVS — MVS/370, MVS/XA, or MVS/ESA — must be coordinated. That is, each version of the microcode maps one-to-one with versions of MVS.

8.3.1. Virtual Storage Addresses

Figure 8.7 shows how DAT maps an address space. The virtual address is segmented into values that are used with the MVS control blocks to locate a page in Central Storage.

In a 16-Mb architecture (MVS/370), each address space can address 16 Mb. The address is a 24-bit value.

MVS/370 divides the 16 Mb into 256 segments (zero to 255, of course) with each segment being 64 Kb. Each segment is divided into 16 pages (numbered zero to 15). Within each page are 4,096 bytes (0 to 4,095).

A MVS/370 virtual address is 24 bits long. The address itself can be divided into three pieces: segment, page, and displacement within a page.

In the example, virtual address x'0FB002' is a location in a program. The segment is 15 (x'0F'), the address is in the 11th (x'0B') page, and the displacement in the page is 2 (the third byte in the page).

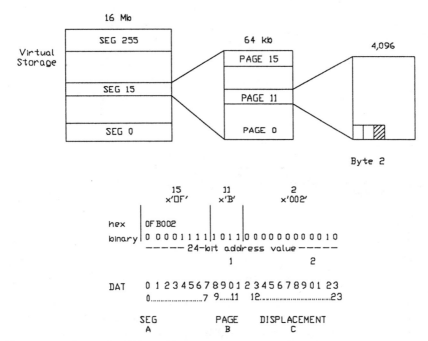

Figure 8.7   Dynamic Address Translation — System/370. The 24-bit address in MVS/370 is interpreted by the hardware in three pieces: A is a 64-Kb segment, B is a 4-Kb page, and the displacement is the byte offset within the page.

8.3.2.   MVS Virtual Storage Software

The MVS service which assigns virtual storage is GETMAIN. The MVS service which releases virtual storage is FREEMAIN. Virtual storage is assigned to a program explicitly or implicitly. If the program issues a GETMAIN request, that is an explicit request. If the program issues an OPEN request, that is an implicit request — the storage is obtained for the address space by MVS OPEN modules to support the I/O operation.

Creation of an address space is started with a GETMAIN for a region size called a GETPART. The "REGION=nnnnK" parameter on the JOB or EXEC JCL card is used for the size of the GETMAIN. MVS/370 creates a segment table (SEGTAB) and a page table (PAGETAB) for each address space. Figure 8.8 shows these tables. The segment table has one entry for each of the 256 segments. The page table has one entry for each of the 16 pages. The segment table entry points to the page table. The page table entries either contain

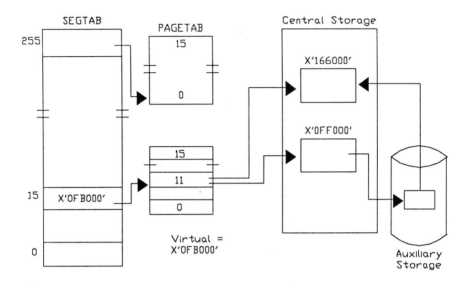

Figure 8.8 MVS/370 Segment and Page tables. Each address space has a set of tables to describe the relationship of virtual addresses to real addresses. In this example virtual address x'0FB000' is translated to read address X'0FF000' until the page is stolen and paged out to Auxiliary Storage. When it is paged into x'166000', only the page table entry needs updating for DAT to work.

the address of the Central Storage page frame or are marked *invalid*, which means the page is not in Central Storage.

If a page is not in Central Storage, it could be on Auxiliary storage (the page was in Central Storage at one time but was paged out), or the page could never have been referenced. When a page is referenced the first time, a Central Storage page is allocated.

Let's look at the creation of an address space and use of virtual storage:

1. The address space is started. MVS selects an available address space number and creates segment and page tables. The pages of the address space do not exist at creation time as with MVT or DOS. The address space is only control blocks which are created and placed on MVS "chains": Actual Central Storage pages are assigned as needed.

2. The program is loaded:
    a. The loader routines of MVS request virtual storage (GET-MAIN). MVS assigns a virtual address of x'0FB000', for ex-

ample. With MVS/370, addresses assigned to application programs are generally about 1Mb. This is because the MVS/370 nucleus usually occupies the first megabyte of virtual storage. The virtual storage of the Nucleus and other fixed areas are automatically made available in the page and segment tables so the application program can access programs and data in the Nucleus.

b. The loader gets the size of the program. In this example, the program will fit in a single 4,096-byte page. The Central Storage has not been assigned yet, so a Central Storage page is allocated at x'000FF000', for example. The address space page tables are updated with the address of the page frame. If more than one page were required, then all pages would be obtained at the same time. All page frames required for the program are "locked" into storage (a requirement for I/O) and the loader starts I/O operations to read in the program.

c. Using information loaded with the program, areas in the program are changed to reflect the virtual address x'0FB000'.

3. The program starts. The program moves some constants or data within the program. The move commands work because the virtual address of x'0FB000' is translated to address x'0FF000' by DAT using the SEGTAB and PAGETAB control blocks. The instructions and data are in the same Central Storage page frame.

4. The program waits for some event. MVS needs the central storage page frame at x'0FF000'. The page is moved to a slot on Auxiliary Storage. The page table entry is marked invalid.

5. The wait ends. MVS turns control over to the program. Note MVS stole the page frame, knows it is gone, and is nevertheless turning control over to the program.

6. The System/370 hardware interrupts MVS with a page exception. The page frame that was needed is not in storage. Why did MVS do this to the program? The MVS services which stole the page — the Real Storage Manager — keeps control blocks separate from the MVS Dispatcher. It is not feasible to check to see if page frames which are going to be needed are available. It is easier to just dispatch the address space and let the hardware find the missing pages.

7. MVS reads the page frame into storage, frame x'0FF000' is not available, but frame x'166000' is available. The page table entry is marked with this real address.

8. MVS again turns over control to the program. Now the program can execute instructions because the hardware can translate virtual address x'FB000' into real address x'166000'. *MVS did not have to change the program when it relocated its page!* To do the translate, DAT uses the control blocks to "look up" the real address (see Figure 8.9):

   a. When MVS dispatches the address space, it loads Control Register 1 (one of the special registers — Segment Table Origin Register, or STOR) with the address of the segment table for this address space.

   b. DAT uses the STOR to convert the virtual address into a real address:

      i. DAT moves the STOR into the hardware Storage Address Register (SAR).

      ii. DAT multiplies the segment number by four (the length of a SEGTAB entry) and adds that to the SAR.

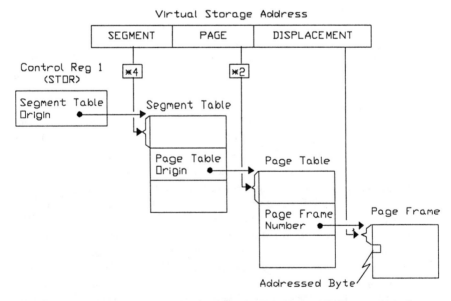

Figure 8.9   Dynamic Address Translation. DAT uses the MVS control blocks and the virtual address to develop a Central Storage address. This is done for each address accessed by an instruction. Intermediate calculations are performed using the Storage Address Register (SAR), not shown.

  iii. DAT loads the address pointed to by the SAR into the SAR. The SAR now contains a pointer to the page table origin.

  iv. DAT multiples the page number by two (the length of a page table entry) and adds this to the SAR. The value pointed to is the page table entry.

  v. The displacement from the virtual address is added to the page address, and a Central Storage address is now available.

Each time the System/370 DAT hardware successfully translates a virtual address into a real address, DAT saves the address in another special hardware buffer called the **Translation Lookaside Buffer** (TLB). DAT checks this buffer before beginning the translation process — if DAT is to translate an address that is in the buffer, DAT can bypass the translation process. The process is successful because most instructions are near the next instruction and most instructions access nearby data. The term for how successful this process is, is **locality of reference**. All virtual operating systems benefit from TLB processing — MVS/370, MVS/XA, MVS/ESA, VM, etc.

These actions by DAT are the reason the application program, in a virtual storage environment, need not be concerned about Central Storage. The microcode does the work to translate virtual addresses to real addresses. Did you note how much work MVS had to do to if the page was not in Central Storage? MVS would have to do an I/O operation to let one instruction execute or to access one operand! There is a lesson here:

Paging is wasteful. Paging consumes both CPU and I/O resources and should be avoided, if possible. The advantages of paging outweigh the disadvantages, but any asset can be allowed to deteriorate into a liability.

8.3.3. DAT with MVS/XA and MVS/ESA

Dynamic Address Translation for both MVS/XA and MVS/ESA works exactly like MVS/370 with the exception that it supports address spaces of 2 Gb (the virtual address is 31 bits wide.) See Figure 8.10.

MVS/XA divides the 2 Gb of virtual storage into 2,048 1 Mb segments (11 bits). Each megabyte segment has 256 page frames (8 bits) and each page is 4,096 bytes (12 bits).

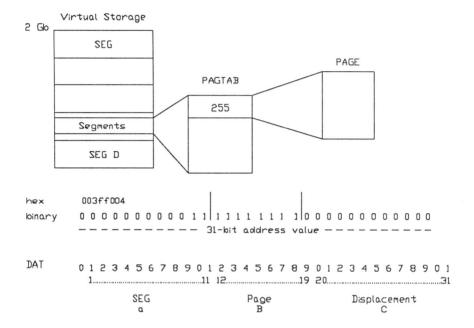

Figure 8.10   DAT for MVS/XA and MVS/ESA. The 31-bit virtual storage address is divided into 11 bits for the 2,048 segments, 8 bits for the 256 pages, and 12 bits for the 4,096 bytes in a page.

8.4. MULTIPROCESSING

Up to this point, we have viewed MVS from the perspective of a single CPU in a Processor Complex, but MVS can coordinate the work of more than one CPU in several types of multiprogramming configurations:

1. Tightly coupled processing is multiple CPUs running concurrently with the same copy of MVS. A 3084 or 3090-600 are examples of a tightly coupled Processor Complex. Tightly coupled processing is putting all of the data center's eggs in the same basket — if something happens to MVS or the hardware, all processing is stopped. In Figure 8.11, six CPUs are running the workload in the tightly coupled example. If the operating system or the Processor Complex is disabled, then all that power is lost.

3090-600

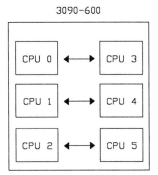

Tightly Coupled Multiprocessing

3090-400 'TSO'   3083 'BATCH'

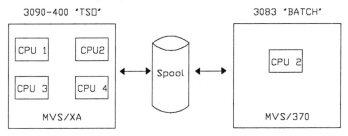

Loosely Coupled Multiprocessing

Figure 8.11 Multiprocessing. In a tightly coupled multiprocesisng environment, the MVS operating system is in control of multiple CPUs inside the same Processor Complex. In loosely coupled multiprocessing, two Processor Complexes are running different copies of MVS.

2. Loosely coupled multiprocessing is multiple Processor Complexes running different copies of MVS (see Figure 8.11). "TSO" is one Processor Complex running MVS/XA. "Batch" is another Processor Complex running MVS/370. Loosely coupled processing requires shared DASD and the same version or a compatible version of JES. Either JES2 or JES3 can be on both Processor Complexes. (JES2 cannot read/write to JES3 Spool volumes and JES3 cannot read/write to JES2 Spool volumes.) In the chapter on JES we will explore Network Job Entry which allows multiple JES to communicate.

In the example, four CPUs are available for one set of work (TSO), and one CPU is available for another set of work (BATCH). If one version of MVS or the Processor Complex it is using is disabled, then the other continues, usually without interruption.

Loosely coupled is more expensive due to software costs but adds a level of reliability. If one copy of MVS is terminated on purpose or by abnormal termination, the other one usually continues unhampered. Loosely coupled is putting eggs in several baskets.

In a loosely coupled configuration, jobs submitted on one processor may execute on any processor that is sharing the same direct access spool volumes.

8.5. ENQUE AND LOCKS

The MVS supervisor provides two techniques for serializing the use of resources: These are for ENQUEing and Locking. ENQUEing is serialization which all MVS users should understand and use. ENQUEing protects resources (e.g., data sets) within a single MVS system or across loosely coupled processors.[3] Locking serializes the use of MVS resources (e.g., control blocks that define Central Storage page frames) and is used only within a single MVS system (there is no reason for MVS to protect its control blocks from another copy of MVS — they do not share CPU or Central Storage page frames).

This serialization is not like the protection afforded by the security system of MVS — RACF or OEM equivalent. RACF allows or disallows usage of a resource. Serialization ensures the resource will not be contaminated by two or more address spaces updating the resource and making the resource invalid. Serialization is, therefore, a temporary lockout mechanism. The duration of a lockout should be very short — portions of seconds (ENQUE device allocation) or several minutes (ENQUE on data set names).

8.5.1. ENQUE

ENQUE is serialization of resources by a "gentlemen's agreement" that the user of a resource will issue ENQ, DEQ, and/or RESERVE

---

3. Loosely coupled resource protection requires the data center to take additional steps to provide protection. MVS global resource serialization (GRS) or OEM products are needed to pass the ENQUE from Processor Complex to Processor Complex.

macros at appropriate places in the use of the resource. Versions of MVS before 1.3.0 had no method to propagate the ENQUE across loosely coupled systems. Other vendors provided that service.

Starting with MVS/370 1.3.0, a new function called Global Resource Serialization (GRS) was added to the MVS 3.8 base code. At first, the OEM serialization programs were more efficient, so many installations set GRS to local-only mode and continued to use one of the OEM products. Today, that distinction is clouded as IBM has improved GRS. If you are planning to implement loosely coupled systems, benchmark all products.

There are three items of information provided to the MVS serialization supervisor. These are:

1. The resource name:
   a. **Qname**, the "major" name — an alphanumeric field of eight characters.
   b. **Rname**, the "minor" name — a 1–255 byte field.
2. **Scope**, which is the range of serialization:
   a. **STEP** serializes within a job step.
   b. **SYSTEM** serializes within a single copy of MVS.
   c. **SYSTEMS** serializes across loosely coupled MVS systems.
3. Type of request:
   a. **Exclusive** indicates the resource will be changed and is needed by this task only.
   b. **Shared** indicates this task will only "read" the resource and as such can be held as shared by a number of tasks.

The access to requested resources is obtained or queued depending on the type of request, the status requested, and the status of the resource when the request was made.

Figure 8.12 contains a decision table showing the rules used by MVS to determine the action when an address space issues an ENQUE. For example, let address space 10 (ASID 10) begin to use data set USER01.PDS.CNTL. No one else is using the data set. ASID 10 wants to update the data set and specifies DISP=OLD. ENQUE sees the status for the data set is "free" and the request is for "exclusive." The row/column intersection says to "honor" or allow the address space to continue. MVS creates a control block to indicate that ASID 10 has USER01.PDS.CNTL and has it exclusively.

Now address space 20 requests an ENQUE on data set USER01.PDS.CNTL and wants to read the data set but not update it (that is, the request is for shared access). ENQUE sees the status of

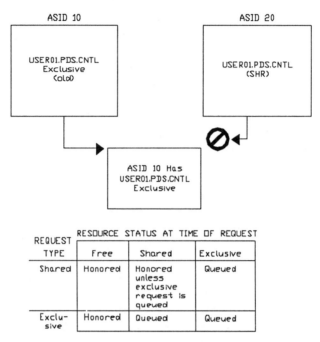

Figure 8.12   ENQUE rules. ENQUE uses a decision table to determine the action taken when an address space requests a resource.

the data set is "exclusive." Even though ASID 20 only wants to read the data set, ASID 20 is "queued" or placed in a wait state until ASID 10 finishes with the data set and issues a DEQ macro to free the resource.

It is possible to issue an ENQUE request and not wait if the resource is in use. This technique may be required to prevent lock-outs or to notify the operator that there is a problem. Enque Lockout Prevention is documented in *Systems Programmer's Problem Solver*:[4]

The ALLOCAS address space contains the Qnames and Rnames for this copy of MVS. If this copy of MVS is connected in a loosely coupled environment, then GRS communicates ENQUE requests to other copies of MVS in the network.

---

4. William Mosteller, *Systems Programmer's Problem Solver*, QED Information Sciences Inc., Wellesley, MA 02181, 1989.

8.5.2. Locks

The MVS architecture allows for multiple CPUs to be "independently" processing. *Locks are the method MVS uses to serialize processing inside a tightly coupled processor.* The serialization is used to control access to system queues or control blocks. Serialization is generally requested while the queues are changed. Without serialization, multiple CPUs accessing the same central storage would not work.

Early MVS reliability and availability problems occurred when components of MVS did not handle serialization properly. In multiple CPU environments, the component in one CPU would access a resource without a lock and change it as the same component in another CPU was trying to use the component.

A lock is simply an area in common virtual storage (usually "fixed" in Central Storage). It contains bits to indicate whether the lock is in use and if so, who owns the resource. There are two classes of locks:

1.   Global: across all address spaces in this copy of MVS.
2.   Local: across all tasks in a single address space.

There are two types of locks:

1.   Spin: where the processor will be executing a tight instruction loop waiting for a lock (commonly called a "spin loop"). The loop includes an instruction that will test a value and set the area of storage *with the same instruction.* Examples of such instructions are Test and Set, Compare and Swap, and Compare Double and Swap. Test and Set is really a System/360-compatible function. MVS uses Compare and Swap and Compare Double and Swap for management of common areas.
2.   Suspend: where the task waiting can give up control while waiting.

In Figure 8.13, address space 10 is executing and issues a GET-MAIN for some virtual storage. The program tries to clear the virtual storage, and an interrupt goes to MVS to allocate a Central Storage page frame to match the virtual storage:

1.   The MVS Real Storage Manager (RSM) attempts to get (and succeeds in getting) the Real Storage Management Global Lock (RSMGL), which is a global spin lock.

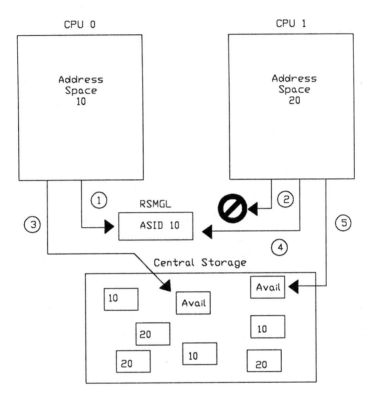

Figure 8.13 MVS locks. In this figure address space 10 is executing in CPU 0. Address space 20 is executing in CPU 1. ASID 10 needs to allocate a Central Storage page frame. MVS RSM gets the RSMGL, searches for a page frame to allocate. ASID 20 needs a page frame. CPU 1 will "spin" until CPU 0 frees up the lock. ASID 20 can then get a page frame.

2. In CPU 1, address space 20 tries the same thing, but the RSM code does not get the lock, so the CPU goes into a "spin" waiting for the lock to come free. A "spin" is 100 percent CPU busy executing a few instructions while the MVS code in the CPU is waiting for the lock to become free.

3. RSM in CPU 0 allocates an available page frame to Address Space 10.

4. After RSM frees the lock from ASID 10, ASID 20 falls through the instruction loop and obtains the RSMGL.

5. RSM allocates an available free page to ASID 20 and frees the RSMGL.

The internal lock hierarchy is beyond the scope of this book, but it is introduced to you because sometimes locks come out of the shadows, and the result is a deadlocked Processor Complex. The machine room operator usually sees a stopped processor with messages on the console, which indicate that one of the CPUs is in a **spin loop**. This means one CPU has detected that another CPU has been waiting for one of the MVS locks for longer than a preset time period (usually under a second.) The problem may be an MVS problem, a hardware problem, or some delay which caused MVS to lose track of "who's on first." I have recovered from several of these spin loops (more with MVS/XA than MVS/370). The secret is to look at the message and thoughtfully reply to the message. (That's a hint.)

Unfortunately, the message only stays on the screen for several minutes. MVS then gives up and goes into a **disabled wait state**. The wait state is only a continuation of the problem. Take the action, then restart the Processor Complex by selecting the proper response on the hardware console for the Processor Complex.

8.6. TIMING SERVICES

The MVS Timer supervisor routines support the System/370 time of day clock, the clock comparator, and the CPU timer. The services are requested by the following assembler language macros:

1. TIME returns the time of day and the date.
2. STIMER sets an exit to be taken to program code:
    a. When some specified interval has expired:
        i.   the interval of time the task was running in the processor.
        ii. the wall clock interval (the task need not be running).
    b. At a specific time of day.
3. TTIMER requests the amount of time left in this request or cancels a STIMER exit.

8.7. SYSTEM OPERATOR COMMUNICATION

Every MVS system has a 327x terminal for communications with the data center operations staff. This section describes those functions.

8.7.1.   Operator Messages (WTO, WTOR)

Operator messages come from almost all parts of MVS. The largest number come from the MVS operating system itself. JES produces many messages. Applications can also write messages to the system operator. The MVS messages are discussed in the appendix "MVS Messages."

When applications or systems programmers want to communicate with the console operator, they use MVS services. The COBOL programmer uses DISPLAY UPON CONSOLE and the Assembler programmer uses the WTO and WTOR macros. The programmer can set bits (MSGTYP) to place the message in a subclass for the MONITOR command or set bits (MCSFLAG) to indicate the type of console which the message(s) should be displayed on.

It is folly for most programmers to use this. The number of lines printed to the operator's console in a MVS system is too large for operators to respond to messages.

If you must stop a job in the middle of a series of job steps, a program can be written to issue a message and wait for a reply (WTOR). The program has only one input (PARM field) and issues a WTOR to pass this parameter to the operator. It must be fully documented and tested. Operators will need training on the program's use.

The Action Message Retention Facility allows up to 1,000 messages to be retained. Most operators do not like this feature and disable it as soon as possible after IPL. To stop the facility, use the operator command "CONTROL M."

MVS Message name conventions are documented in OS/VS2 System Codes (e.g., *MVS/Extended Architecture Message Library: System Codes — GC28-1157*). The prefix is the first three characters of a message number, and the actual message may be documented in one of several dozen manuals.

Many people in the MVS community do not bother to look up messages because they are not familiar with the manuals and naming conventions. That is a pity because IBM has done a very good job creating documentation. MVS documentation is really the tools of our trade. What would you think of a carpenter who was working on your house who did not know how to use his hammer or saw? Would you feel comfortable? How can your superiors and co-workers feel comfortable with you if they never see you in the manuals? To get you started, the appendix titled MVS Messages is a synopsis of common MVS names.

8.7.2. Automated Operations

MVS displays messages and asks for replies in order to control the operation of Data Base/Data Communications systems (e.g., IMS or CICS), batch jobs, and interactive TSO sessions. Most installations have operator personnel monitor the MVS consoles to read, interpret, and reply to appropriate messages.

That is a thankless task. Watching a terminal is no fun, but it is important. Automated Operations is a concept that has evolved which has a "watcher" (usually a Personal Computer with a program that "reads" MVS messages) and a "replier" (the same program — different parts) that responds based on the data center's specifications.

For example, if MVS sends a message "OK to update SYS1.PARMLIB?," and the address space is not an authorized address space, then the reply is automatically "no, do not allow the update."

The Message Processing Facility (MPF) is one MVS service which assists in the process of inspecting MVS messages. MPF is provided with MVS SP 1.3 and above and gives the data center the ability to define and suppress nonessential messages to decrease message volume. MPF is activated with a SET MPF=xx command and deactivated with a SET MPF=NO. The xx is appended to MPFLST to get a member of SYS1.PARMLIB which contains the message IDs or prefixes to bypass the console (i.e., send only).

8.7.3. Alternate Console Support

Alternate Console support allows the data center to place MVS operator consoles at strategic places such as tape and printer areas. These consoles should never be outside the computer room for security reasons.

MVS/370 1.3 and above allows optional channels to be generated for consoles. This saves UCB area and reduces the confusion about consoles.

8.7.4. Disabled Console Support (DCS)

The MVS services that display information on the operator console are available to all address spaces. As such, the console support runs "enabled for interrupts" — the PSW has the appropriate bits turned on that allow all types of hardware interrupts.

DCS is a feature of MVS which allows portions of MVS that are running disabled for interrupts to communicate with the operator. One example of where DCS would be used is the case of a "hot I/O," where an I/O control unit continually presents interrupts. MVS must disable for interrupts to stop the device. MVS must also tell the operator that a problem has happened.

DCS can display information on the operator console outside the normal operation. The Master Console is cleared and the message is displayed. The operator is given a choice of several recovery actions. *No task in the system continues until the action is taken.*

A subtle problem can occur in your data center if your Master Console is on a channel path with devices that are "likely" to cause hot I/O situations. If a hot I/O occurs on the channel path that the Master Console is attached to, then DCS will not work. The moral? Plan your consoles so the master is on a channel which is not likely to get hot I/Os from other devices.

8.8. MANAGING ADDRESS SPACES

In addition to the above services, which most computer users see, is the task of controlling the work flow in the hardware. The MVS component which performs this task is collectively known as the **supervisor**.

The general subdivisions of the supervisor are:

1. **Interrupt processing.** The System/370 has hardware and software conventions to switch control from one task to another to achieve multiprogramming. Remember, multiprogramming is the illusion that several, or thousands, of computer users feel that their work is being processed by a computer as if they were the only user.

2. **Task creation.** The method by which MVS keeps track of work is by the address space, but within the address space are subdivisions of the work.

3. **Dispatching work.** After the work is created, and the mechanism for switching among the tasks needing resources, MVS must turn control over to them in an orderly manner. The **dispatcher** is the MVS program which accomplishes this task.

8.8.1. Interruption Processing

System/370 interrupts are events which change the sequence of instructions which are executing on a given CPU in a Processor Complex. There are six types of interrupts, shown in Figure 8.14:

1. **Supervisor Call (SVC) Interrupts** are planned transfer of control from an application program to the supervisor. Each SVC processes a particular service. Examples are:
   a. SVC 0 (EXCP) — request an I/O operation
   b. SVC 4 (GETMAIN) — request some virtual storage. Several versions of GETMAIN exist in addition to SVC 4.
   c. SVC 19 (OPEN) — request a file be opened.
   d. SVC 20 (CLOSE) — request a file be closed.
   e. SVC 35 (WTO/WTOR) — request a record be written to the console operator.
2. **I/O Interrupts** are unplanned and occur when the channel needs to notify MVS that an I/O operation has finished processing.
3. **External Interrupts** are unplanned and occur for several external reasons. Examples are:
   a. A time interval has elapsed. The MVS STIMER processing has set an alarm clock and the alarm is ringing.

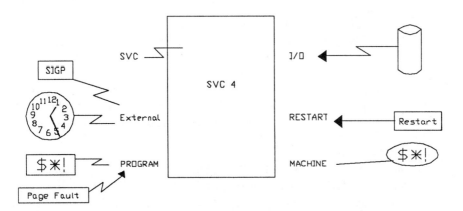

Figure 8.14   Types of Interrupts. There are six types of interrupts. Only SVC interrupts are planned by an application issuing a Supervisor Call to perform a service. All the others are asynchronous and interrupt what is executing on the CPU.

   b. SIGP processing. Another processor is "shoulder tapping" this CPU.
4. **Restart Interrupts** are unplanned and occur when the operator selects the restart option on the hardware console or when a SIGP restart is received.
5. **Program Interrupts** are unplanned and are caused by:
   a. Invalid operations by programs (application or system).
   b. Page faults. DAT has recognized a referenced page is not valid and is asking MVS to load the page into Central Storage.
   c. Monitor Call interruptions are unplanned and are indications from the System/370 Program Event Recording (PER) hardware that an event has occurred. PER will be treated in another chapter.
6. **Machine Check Interrupts** are unplanned and indicate the System/370 Processor Complex has detected one or more components have failed.

Program Status Word (PSW)   The PSW in each CPU points to the next instruction which will be executed by the CPU. There is only one current PSW for each CPU, but there are three types to keep track of:

1. The **current PSW** is the PSW which is used by the CPU for executing instructions. Bits in the PSW indicate the STATE of the CPU:
   a. **Enabled** is a state which indicates one of the interruptions above can occur. If a PSW is "enabled" for I/O processing, then the I/O portion of the System/370 Processor Complex can interrupt this CPU.
   b. **Disabled** is a state which indicates one of the above interruptions cannot occur. If the current PSW is "disabled" for I/O processing, then the I/O portion of the Processor Complex cannot interrupt this CPU.
2. **NEW PSW** is associated with each of the six types of interruptions. There is an I/O NEW PSW, a PROGRAM NEW PSW, etc. The NEW PSW points to the MVS module that handles interrupt. For example, the PROGRAM NEW PSW points to a MVS module that looks at problems the hardware has determined it cannot handle.
3. **OLD PSW** is associated with each of the six types of interrupts. There is an I/O OLD PSW, a PROGRAM OLD PSW, etc.

The OLD PSW contains the address of the program that was interrupted. For example, the PROGRAM OLD PSW contains the address of the instruction that the hardware could not execute.

The OLD and NEW PSWs are really locations in the Prefixed Save Area in the first 4,096 bytes of storage. Remember, this block exists in some other Central Storage frame other than x'0000000' if the Processor Complex has multiple CPUs.

Either MVS or hardware can change the "current" PSW. The hardware stores the current PSW and loads the new PSW to "state change" from one module to another. MVS uses a machine instruction **Load Program Status Word** (LPSW) to make the transition when MVS wants to transfer control to another program and change the state (e.g., from supervisor mode to problem mode.)

Interrupt Handlers are the MVS programs which get control when an interrupt is processed. The following occurs:

1. The hardware detects an interrupt condition. The Processor Complex determines if it can interrupt this CPU. (The interrupt is enabled.)
2. If it cannot (disabled for the interrupt), it delays the interrupt. The Machine Check interrupt is rarely disabled (the bottom is falling out of this CPU, no need to disable it).
3. If the interrupt is enabled, the hardware stores the CURRENT PSW in the OLD PSW position in the PSA and loads the PSW from the NEW PSW position (see Figure 8.15).

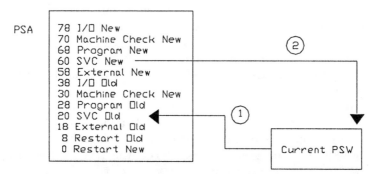

Figure 8.15   State change. When an interrupt occurs, the System/370 hardware swaps PSWs. The CURRENT PSW is stored in the OLD postion. The NEW PSW is moved into the CURRENT PSW.

4. The next instruction executed is the **First Level Interruption Handler** (FLIH). The FLIH:
   a. Saves the registers of the executing program.
   b. Determines the type of interrupt.
   c. Begins actions to process the request or recover from the failure.
5. The FLIH may give control to a **Second Level Interruption handler** (SLIH) to continue processing.
6. The interrupted task may have been **nonpreemptive** — of such importance that the interruption handler will return directly to the task interrupted. Normally, the interruption handler turns control over to the Dispatcher. Note the next task that is dispatched *may* be, but is not necessarily, the same task which just lost control.

8.8.2. Units of Work

Task Control Blocks (TCBs) TCBs are created by the ATTACH SVC, which calls supervisor services which creates the TCB, places the TCB in the chain of active work for the address space, and branches to program management routines. These routines find, load, and execute the program.

Each Address Space has several Task Control Blocks. A TCB represents a system utility or a system program executing to support a user program. The common TCBs are:

1. **Region Control Task** (RCT) is responsible for the entire address space. Note old MVT terminology. MVT had "regions" to run programs. MVS has address spaces, but MVT used an RCT to control and the name came forward to MVS.
2. **DUMP** is responsible for dumping the address space, if the address space terminates abnormally.
3. **Started Task Control** (STC) is the TCB for the program which starts the address space.
4. **Application TCBs:**
   a. For batch jobs, an **initiator TCB** and finally the TCB for the application or utility program.
   b. For operator started tasks (STC), the TCB for the program on the execute card in the procedure.
   c. For a TSO user, the **Terminal Monitor Program** TCB, which executes the TSO commands you enter at the terminal.

5. **Other TCBs** as generated by the program. Some programs generate many TCBs — notably OEM database management systems. Some programs generate very few TCBs — notably CICS. If a CICS region has a thousand terminals, then one and only one TCB will be used to dispatch the work for all those terminals.

A task can be in one of three states:

1. **Ready.** The task has work to do and the TCB is marked ready to be dispatched.
2. **Active.** The task has control of the CPU and is executing instructions. The instructions may be the COBOL or other language which the application was written in, or it may be in systems or access method code.
3. **Waiting.** The task is waiting for one or more events to occur.

Let's look at a sample of the flow that a task might experience from task creation to the end of the task (Figure 8.16):

1. The task is created — a job step starts, or the task is created. The TCB is entered on the ready queue.
2. The task is ready for work. If there are higher priority tasks which have control of the CPU, then the TCB remains on the ready queue.
3. The task is active. MVS has used the LOAD PSW instruction to begin executing the task. The task is using the CPU.

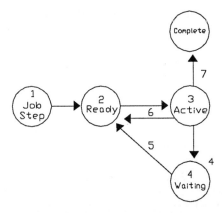

Figure 8.16   States of a task in MVS. An MVS task can be ready, active (executing instructions in one of the CPUs), or waiting for an event to complete.

4. The task issues a voluntary wait such as waiting for an I/O operation or waiting for a resource.
5. The wait has ended. The MVS routine which was processing the request has completed. The TCB is placed again on the ready queue.
6. The task did not give up voluntarily. Any of the five above interrupts could cause this.[5]
7. The task comes to the end of the work it was assigned. It "returns" to the MVS routines which attached it.

Service Request Blocks (SRBs) System tasks can request a service routine to execute in this address space or in another address space. SRBs are created with the assembler SCHEDULE macro. An SRB can be:

1. **Global**, which has the highest priority of any address space and executes in another address space.
2. **Local**, which has the priority of the address space and executes in and for the address space which issues the SCHEDULE macro.

SRBs are nonpreemptive. From above, if an interruption occurs while the SRB is executing, then control will be given back to the routine.

8.8.3. Dispatcher

The dispatcher maintains a **queue of address spaces** (ASIDs), which are in the system. The queue is in dispatching order — the highest priority and next to get control of the CPU is on the top.

The dispatcher chooses SRBs or TCBs to be executed. The task will control the processor until:

---

5. A compute bound task, which is not otherwise externally interrupted, is eventually interrupted by expiration of a timer set by MVS before the task is dispatched. The duration of the maximum time slice given to a task is calculated by SRM from the mean-time-to-wait value adjusted by the relative speed of the Processor Complex. This ensures that no task can monopolize the CPU.

1. The task enters a wait, or
2. An interrupt (I/O, Machine Check, Program, SVC, or External) occurs.

If there are no tasks to be executed, then the dispatcher loads the registers and environment of IEEVWAIT: a wait PSW with all zeros. All registers are zeros.

You will see more about how MVS controls the work in the system in the chapter on Control and Decision Making.

8.9. MVS CREATION AND MAINTENANCE

In the "good old days," new users of MVS would order the operating system from IBM, receive a box of tapes, restore the tapes to DASD, and spend several weeks generating, customizing, and preparing MVS for the data center. Today, new users of MVS order MVS, restore several tapes, customize MVS by changing some parameter libraries, change the I/O device configuration, and start running. The difference is in packaging. IBM provides customized installation and maintenance.

8.9.1. SYSGEN

Before we look at maintenance, let's look at the components of the MVS SYSGEN and I/O configuration process. The SYSGEN process is used to define all the options for MVS. There are two types of SYSGEN:

1. **Full generation.** In a full or complete SYSGEN, all options of MVS can be selected.
2. **I/O generation.** An I/O generation is used to redefine the devices connected to the Processor Complex that MVS can access. The output of an I/O generation is the portion of MVS (in the Nucleus) that contains the Unit Control Blocks (UCBs) and other control blocks to define the devices. IBM now calls the collection of these control blocks **MVS I/O configuration data.**

The I/O configuration data is combined with the rest of the MVS Nucleus to form a load module (IEANUC0x) in the SYS1.NUCLEUS data set. Each different I/O configuration requires a different

IEANUC0x load module. Remember that the I/O configuration is for MVS use only. The hardware (and MVS) needs to have an Input/Output Configuration Program (IOCP) built.

Starting with MVS/XA Version 2.2, the MVS Configuration Program is used to define I/O devices to MVS. This program creates members IEANCTxx, IOSIITxx, IOSUCBxx, and IEFEDTxx in SYS1.NUCLEUS, where "xx" is the configuration number. The operator then specifies the appropriate configuration to be used at IPL time (on the hardware console of the Processor Complex).

One of the components of either method of device specification is the **Eligible Device Table** (EDT). The EDT is a table of installation-defined terms that point to devices. It is a grouping of I/O devices that can be accessed by UNIT=nnnn, where "nnnn" is some installation-specified name. For example, the installation could define devices 920 through 92F as "TAPE" — the devices are 3480 tape drives. If a user coded "UNIT=TAPE" on a JCL card (or dynamic allocation request), then MVS would search for a device in the range of 920-92F to satisfy the request.

One common specification for almost all MVS installations is SYSDA for several DASD devices which can be used for temporary, non-specific devices used to store data from job step to job step.

8.9.2. Maintenance

Nine times a year, IBM issues error corrections, or **Program Temporary Fixes** (PTFs), which fix problems with MVS system programs. Approximately 1,500 fixes are combined onto a **Program Update Tape** (PUT), which is shipped to registered owners of MVS.

Periodically, IBM also combines all maintenance into an operational replacement for all of MVS — called **Custom-Built Installation Process Offering** (CPIPO). CBIPO can be used to provide the first MVS system for a data center, or it can be used to entirely replace the MVS system for the data center.

IBM supplies a program — **System Modification Program Extended** (SMP/E) — to help install MVS programs:

1. New MVS products. For example, VTAM is a product separate from MVS. In order to use VTAM, the modules must be installed in the libraries with MVS. The MVS **Custom-Built Product Delivery Offering** (CBPDO) is a package for adding products or service to an existing MVS system.
2. New releases of existing products.

3. PTFs on the PUT tapes or received separately to fix problems as the problem is detected. The term "preventive service" is used for applying maintenance before the problem is detected in your data center. The term "corrective maintenance" is used for applying PTFs which are the result of having the problem in your data center.

The reader should refer to the documentation for SMP/E which is installed on their system. Examples are manuals *System Modification Program Extended User's Guide* (SC28-1302), *System Modification Program Extended Messages and Codes* (SC28-1108), and *System Modification Program Extended Reference* (SC28-1107). An excellent introduction to software management in an MVS/XA environment is *International Technical Support Centers, Software Management in an MVS/XA Environment* (GG24-3204).

The VSAM data set which is used by SMP/E to maintain the MVS system is called the **SMP Consolidated Software Inventory** (SMPCSI). SMP/E maintains two groups of system libraries:

1. **Distribution Libraries** (DLIBs) contain all the modules, macros, and source programs which IBM distributes as part of the MVS system. The libraries are not used to run MVS, but are used to create the operating system libraries which the data center uses to run MVS.
2. **Operating System Libraries** (Target Libraries) are libraries which are built as part of the System Generation (SYSGEN) process.

When one or more modules are packaged together, they are called **SYSMODs**. Each SYSMOD is assigned a unique 7-character alphanumeric identification called a **SYSMOD ID**. The data center can — and should — apply all local modules and modifications by creating local SYSMODs or **USERMODs**. It is imperative that the data center create USERMODs if the modification is to an IBM module or exit. If IBM replaces or updates its module the local modification will be lost unless SMP/E has been notified a local modification exists.

8.10. MVS SUMMARY

MVS is a very powerful and complicated Operating System. If MVS does not work, the data center probably has a very expensive hardware configuration that is useless. The data center should make every effort to ensure that MVS runs. With MVS libraries and data sets spread out over several or dozens of DASD volumes, anything that happens may prevent MVS from running.

The answer for me since the early 1970s has been a one-pack system. In the early days of VM, we created a one-pack MVT system to test changes to the operating system. The idea grew until it was also used for a Disaster Recovery volume. Use JCL to copy all data sets needed for MVS to a single DASD volume. The operation takes about one hour, and you will have a single volume which you can IPL MVS on a real or virtual machine.

Some of the key points presented in this chapter are:

1. The hardware must be prepared for MVS. The microcode is selected to match the version of MVS — MVS/370, MVS/XA, or MVS/ESA.

2. The hardware is initialized with a configuration — IOCP — which tells the hardware about the devices attached to the Processor Complex. This is called a Power On Reset.

3. The system is reset, Central Storage is cleared to binary zeros and MVS is initialized — Initial Program Load (IPL).

4. The hardware loads MVS from a DASD device that has been created by the Systems Generation (SYSGEN) process. The volume can either contain all of MVS (not likely in production operation) or contain enough of MVS to load all the routines to run MVS. The volume may contain pointers to systems catalogs and other MVS data sets on other volumes.

5. The portion of MVS that actually initializes MVS is called the Nucleus Initialization Program (NIP). The data center can have all customization parameters in a data set (SYS1.PARMLIB), or the operator can override the parameters and change MVS as it is starting up.

6. MVS switches to "virtual" addressing mode by turning on the Dynamic Address Translation (DAT) hardware.

7. MVS supports multiprogramming (multiple tasks executing under a single operating system) and multiprocessing (multiple tasks executing concurrently).

8. MVS software provides services such as console processing, locking and enqueing services, and interruption handling.

9. MVS maintenance comes from IBM periodically. The data center can either select to put maintenance on in small doses (PUT tapes) or completely replace the MVS system (CBIPO).

The next chapter addresses differences between MVS/370, MVS/XA, and MVS/ESA, now that you know something of their common organization. We will then return to MVS services with the chapter on the Job Entry Subsystem (JES).

9

MVS XA and MVS ESA

9.1. WHY YOU SHOULD BE CONCERNED WITH THE DIFFERENCES

There are three versions of MVS — MVS/370, MVS/XA, and MVS/ESA. This chapter discusses the differences so you can understand them and either make good conversion decisions or profit from their advantages.

The selection of an operating system to use, or the decision to move from one to another, should be made on the basis of the needs of your company. Selection and implementation require many months of evaluation and work and should be part of the midrange planning of your company.

This chapter should help you understand the differences between the MVS systems. Once you understand the differences and how they can affect your company, you can make cost-justified decisions for your company. Different operating systems affect how much the hardware (Processor Complex and associated I/O devices) can produce.

The decisions I am talking about are *million dollar decisions*! New System/370 Processor Complexes cost millions of dollars. In at least three large data centers, I have seen the correct decision (cost effective while providing ample processing) save the company $4,000,000 over a four-year period. These companies chose a 3084 Processor

Complex over a 3090-200. But the decisions cannot, and must not, be made strictly on cost. Just as many companies have made the cheap decision and wound up spending as much or more because they were not prepared or able to make the "cheap" decision work.

You may not even get to make the decision. It may be made for you by current or previous decision makers. If you are going to make a workable situation out of adversity, then you need to understand the MVS relationships to make decisions that will help.

Before we investigate the differences between MVS/370 and MVS/XA, and between MVS/XA and MVS/ESA, let's look at two areas of consideration for the data center: **capacity management** and **constraints**. There are a number of definitions of capacity, but one good one is:

> Capacity management is the process of ensuring that adequate data processing resources are available to meet the corporate business plan in a cost-effective manner.

What if your company has a 3081 Processor Complex, and it needs to increase the CPU capacity? You determine that a 25-30 MIPS processor is needed. A 3084 is a less expensive alternative than a 3090-200. You can select the 3084 if you are using MVS/XA. You cannot select the 3084 if you are running MVS/370 — MVS/370 cannot operate a 3084 in single-image mode. Decisions like these will continue to be made. With your help, you can influence profitable decisions.

A definition of data processing constraints is:

> Constraint exists when your company is prohibited from making a decision or taking an action because of the architecture of the data processing system.

You are constrained if your company wants to combine two applications in a single CICS region and cannot do it. You may want to combine them to improve the productivity of your accounting department and you discover that the private area of virtual storage is not large enough.

If you are comparing two operating systems, you should examine what they will do differently for your data center. The following discuss the major differences of these operating systems. Whether the differences make a positive or negative impact on your data center is for you to determine. Remember:

FIXING A PROBLEM THAT DOES NOT EXIST DOES NOT
HELP ANYTHING (except your vendors' sales figures).

9.1.1. System Capacity

The System/370 Processor Complex has a certain defined capacity.
Each CPU can operate at a certain speed. There are a fixed number
of Central Storage frames available and there are a fixed number of
channels and I/O operations. System capacity is a flexible com-
modity, however: the same Processor Complex with the same mix of
work to be done will respond differently, depending on the architecture of the operating system and the tuning done by the staff of the
data center. The migration from MVS/370 to MVS/XA was designed
to get more usable capacity from a Processor Complex.

System Capacity can be thought of in terms of CPU resources,
Central Storage page frames, and I/O subsystems. Figure 9.1 shows
a time line of a task using these resources:

1. The task becomes ready and waits to be dispatched.
2. The task waits for Central Storage to become available.
3. The task uses CPU resources.
4. The task waits for I/O operations to start.
5. The task waits for I/O operations to complete.
6. The above continues (loops) until the task is complete.

9.1.2. Constraints

The MVS/370 constraints are reached at various times by various
data centers, but a general order of when a data center will "discover" constraints is:

1. **I/O Subsystem.** Data centers grow by adding Direct-Access
   Storage Devices (DASDs). Usually, they can add more external
   storage space than the channels can efficiently process. The
   303x series had a limit of 16 channels. The 3033 AP and MP
   could process more data than 16 channels could deliver. The
   43xx series of Processor Complexes usually reach channel
   capacity as they add I/O devices.
2. **Central Storage.** Multiple Virtual Storage (MVS) was
   designed with 24 bits for Central Storage and virtual addresses; users were stuck with the 16 megabytes. Even with the

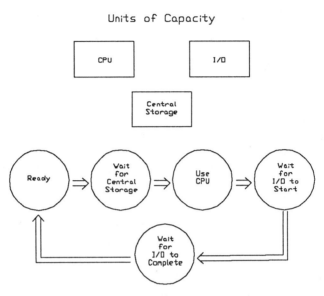

Figure 9.1   Time line of a task. A task proceeds from a ready state, to waiting for Central Storage, to using CPU resources, to waiting for an I/O to be started, to waiting for an I/O completion. This loop is repeated until the task completes the work which is assigned.

larger 303x and 308x Processor Complexes, Central Storage was depleted quickly.

IBM did release a modification to MVS/370 to allow **Extended Real Addressing**. By adding a 25th bit for Central Storage addressing to some parts of MVS, 32 megabytes of Central Storage could be configured on the 4381, 3033, and 3081. This spelled relief for a while. A 26th bit was added, so now MVS/370 can support 64 megabytes of Central Storage. (The extra bits are stored in the Page Frame Table Entry (PFTE) for the page.)

3. **Virtual Storage.** It usually does not take long for a data center to outgrow 16 megabytes of virtual storage in MVS/370. Even with MVS/XA, the "below the line" virtual storage becomes constrained.

CPU vs. I/O Speed Gap   In the 1970s, we used Processor Complexes which could process 2–3 million instructions per second (MIPS). The DASD devices then could deliver a physical block of data into Central Storage in the 30–60 millisecond time frame. Today, we have single CPUs which deliver 15–20 MIPS and Processor Complexes

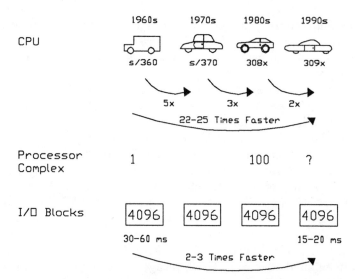

Figure 9.2 The CPU–I/O gap. As Processor Complexes got faster and faster, the I/O subsystem did not keep up. The top part of the figure shows that each "generation" was several times faster, and today we have processors 22 to 25 times faster than in the 1960s. (These are times for a single CPU, not multiprocessor total speed.) Yet the speed of the I/O subsystem to deliver a 4,096-byte block into Central Storage has only become two to three times faster.

which deliver over 100 MIPS. *That's 8–30 times faster!* Figure 9.2 shows the relative speed of yesteryear and today. DASD today can deliver the same block in 15–20 milliseconds. *That's only two times faster!* I/O devices continue to be constraining devices.

The purpose of MVS/XA and MVS/ESA is to allow higher I/O rates and minimize waits on I/O — if they can't make I/O faster, do it better.

Central Storage Constraints There was a beer commercial many years ago which said something like "When you're out of . . ., you're out of beer." That could be paraphrased in the MVS world as "when you are out of Central Storage, you are finished." Nothing hurts so much as being out of Central Storage.

You will only get faint clues when you are running out of Central Storage. At least with the beer, you could look in the refrigerator and tell what your capacity was at any given moment. That is not true with Central Storage.

Over the last 10 years, I have observed several data centers run out of Central Storage. All of the data center management missed the problem creeping up on us. In a fine-tuned autopsy, the only clue we could find was the MVS Unreferenced Interval Count (UIC) started creeping up over a period of several months (like three!) just before we hit the Brick Wall.[1]

SRM gets control every second and inspects each Central Storage page frame. If the page has been referenced or changed, a counter is incremented by 1 (second). Over a period of time, SRM averages these numbers. The result is the Unreferenced Interval Count (UIC).

The UIC counter can be from 0 to 255. The reader should know why the upper limit is 255 — it is because the counter is one byte, and one byte can contain a number from 0–255 (0–x'FF').

In Figure 9.1, note the next thing needed after MVS dispatches a task is Central Storage. If your goal is to ensure proper online response time for your data center, and you want to save your data center major performance problems, keep the UIC between 150 and 255 during peak periods. The average page frame in the system would go untouched (and not moved to/from DASD) for over two minutes. That may sound like a lot, but it isn't.

Virtual Storage Constraints When MVS/370 was first introduced in the mid-1970s, MVS used 8 megabytes, and the private area used 8 megabytes. At that time, most of the applications were batch. Today, virtual storage requirements have grown because of requirements for additional:

1. Buffers for applications.
2. VTAM storage to define terminals spread over the entire geographic area of your company.
3. Graphics and engineering applications.

The MVS system was changed to allow the data center to control how much virtual storage is available to the user. Unfortunately, as MVS function grew, so did the virtual storage requirements of the operating system. The result was a squeeze on virtual storage.

Reliability, Availability, Serviceability While Reliability, Availability, and Serviceability is not really a capacity, performance, or constraint

---

1. The term "Brick Wall" is used to indicate a performance problem which does not creep up. It strikes like hitting an invisible brick wall.

topic, it is a major selling point for MVS/XA and MVS/ESA. They can be viewed as performance considerations of a data center because the worst performance problem is a system which is "down."

Reliability is "does the software/hardware break?" A number of measures of reliability exist:

1. **Mean Time Between Failures (MTBF).** The average number of hours or days (hopefully not minutes or seconds!) is calculated and tracked.
2. **Failures per megabyte transferred.** This is a popular one to be used for DASD or tape.

Availability is "did anyone notice the thing broke?" The industry has a number of interesting ways to measure availability. The most popular is **percentage available**, but is this really useful? What if you told your users a system will be available 95 percent of the time? In a single day, this would allow 72 minutes of outage. What if that 72 minutes occurred between 10:00 A.M. and 11:12 A.M. each day? Most people would notice.

Serviceability is "how long did it take to fix the broken thing?" The measure here is **Mean Time To Repair** (MTTR). Your goal is to measure MTTR in hours, not days.

9.2. DIFFERENCES BETWEEN MVS/370 AND MVS/XA

In the fall of 1981, IBM announced the upgrade of the System/370 to Extended Architecture and MVS/XA as the operating system to be used in XA mode. *MVS/XA consists of two pieces — hardware and software.* For many installations, the announcement of MVS/XA was just in time to relieve many of the above constraints.

9.2.1. Virtual Storage Differences

In both MVS/370 and MVS/XA, the virtual storage used by MVS is determined by the parameters specified by the installation. Figure 9.3 shows much of MVS was moved above the line. MVS/XA uses roughly one megabyte less virtual storage below the 16-megabyte line than MVS/370. MVS/XA uses a large amount of virtual storage above the line.

The following are some of the factors which determine the virtual storage size differences:

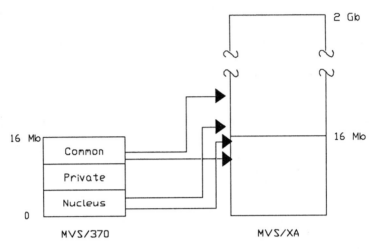

Figure 9.3   Virtual Storage differences. The conversion from MVS/370 to MVS/XA moves some areas from below the 16-megabyte line to above the 16-megabyte line. Private virtual storage also has a part below the line and a part available above the line.

1. **Size of Central Storage.** In MVS/370, the Page Frame Table Entries (PFTEs) are stored below the line. In MVS/XA, they are moved above the line. To support 31 bits for Central Storage requires four bytes for chain pointers in MVS/XA versus two bytes in MVS/370. The virtual address in the control blocks is expanded from three bytes to four bytes. (The result is an extra 4 Kb of PFTEs for each megabyte of mapped virtual storage.)

2. **Number of paging and swapping devices.** MVS maintains control blocks — called Paging Channel Command Words (PCCW) areas — for each paging device and for each swap device. If you think about the paging process, the entire I/O operation must be set up and ready for the whole time MVS is in control. MVS cannot afford "opening" and "closing" system data sets!

   Figure 9.4 is a table of the size of each PCCW and Swap Channel Command Words (SCCW). Because each 3380 paging device requires 7.5 Kb of virtual storage, MVS/370 may typically allocate 50–100 Kb below the line while MVS/XA has these areas above the line.

   MVS allocates some number of PCCWs for each paging device. In many cases, the default is not enough. One of my first modifications to MVS/370 was to triple the default num-

Device Type	PCCW (bytes)	SCCW (bytes)
3330	2048	1560
3340	2048	1560
3350	2816	1560
2305-2	3328	1560
3375	4608	1560
3380	7424	1560
3380-11	2816	1560

Figure 9.4 Paging and Swapping Virtual Storage. Each device which has a swap or page data set has virtual storage allocated for control blocks. The size is given by the device type.

ber. It is not unusual to have 100 Kb of virtual storage allocated to PCCWs. In MVS/XA, of course, these are moved above the 16-Mb line.

3. **Amount of paging activity.** As MVS gets paging requests, it builds control blocks to keep track of the requests. These blocks are called Page Control Blocks (PCBs). Although each PCB is only 64 bytes, they are never freed. The number of PCBs is dependent on the maximum number of pages going out of or coming into the machine. If you ever swap an address space with 1,000 page frames (e.g., CICS), it will require 64 Kb of virtual storage just for one swap. It is not uncommon to have 90–125 Kb of virtual storage for PCBs.

4. **Fixed Link Pack Area** (FLPA). In MVS/370, there are two copies of a "fixed" module. One is in the Pageable Link Pack Area; one is in the fixed area. The reason is MVS loads the LPA completely, then checks to see if you want to fix any modules. I do not know why they did not just fix the pages in which the LPA resides. Instead, they load the fixed modules again near the nucleus and fix the new pages. Of course, MVS could not free the module in the LPA because it was in the middle of other system modules in PLPA. In MVS/XA, only one copy exists in the nucleus, and in most cases the module is in the extended nucleus, above the line.

5. Last, but not least, is local tailoring. If you get MVS distributed in CBIPO format, remember it is an "average" system. Many of the MVS/370 tuning efforts pay off in MVS/XA. The data center can usually save a megabyte of virtual storage in either MVS/370 or MVS/XA by deleting unused functions such as Graphics Access Method (GAM), Basic Telecommunications

Access Method (BTAM), and DUMP exits.

The best discussion of virtual storage tuning is in *MVS Virtual Storage Tuning Cookbook* (G320-0597), published by the Dallas Systems Center as a Technical Bulletin.

9.2.2.   Storage in the Processor Complex

The Processor Complex has two types of storage inside the hardware box. Central Storage is storage that is addressable by all address spaces operating under MVS. Expanded Storage is addressable by some address spaces.

Central Storage Differences   The move from MVS/370 to MVS/XA has a *large negative* impact on Central Storage. Said another way, the same Processor Complex running MVS/XA will have less Central Storage available to the data center users than if the data center were running MVS/370. MVS/XA requires from 1 1/2 to 2 megabytes of Central Storage for itself plus "40–60 Kb" per resident address space. The first rule of conversion from MVS/370 to MVS/XA is:

Ensure you have at least 2 megabytes of Central Storage "unused" before conversion.

(You may want to vary several megabytes of Central Storage offline in MVS/370 mode to observe the effect on your data center processing.)

In MVS, fixed frames are required for the areas shown in Figure 9.5:

1. The Hardware Save Area (HSA). The HSA is loaded at Power On Reset of the Processor Complex and is the area of communications between MVS and the hardware. The area is approximately the same for MVS/370, MVS/XA, and MVS/ESA.
2. Nucleus — PSA. The Prefixed save area is part of the nucleus in MVS/370 (and is wasted in a tightly coupled processor) and a separate area for MVS/XA. The PSA is 4,096 bytes per CPU.
3. Nucleus — Fixed BLDL Table. The FBLDL is created just after the nucleus in the MVS/370 and is a separate area in MVS/XA.
4. Nucleus — Fixed Link Pack Area. The FLPA contains modules which are used so frequently (STIMER, PURGE) that their pages are usually fixed in a well-tuned MVS system. In

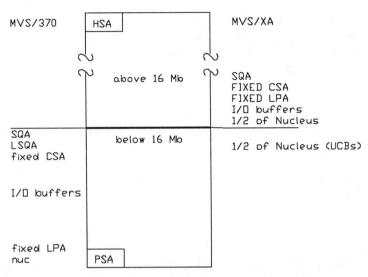

Figure 9.5 Central Storage usage. MVS/XA uses more Central Storage but gives relief to below 16 megabytes.

MVS/370, the data center had to specify these to be fixed. In MVS/XA, these and other modules are moved to the nucleus.

5. Nucleus — load module. The MVS nucleus consists of the load module itself which contains routines which must be in Central Storage and never paged, the Auxiliary Storage Manager (ASM) control blocks, and the Unit Control Blocks (UCB). Depending on the options generated, the nucleus is approximately one megabyte of fixed frames.

6. The Pageable Link Pack Area (PLPA). Both MVS/370 and MVS/XA will have PLPA frames in Central Storage because PLPA frames are frequently used by many address spaces. In most cases, you will see two megabytes of storage for PLPA modules.

7. Modified Link Pack Area (MLPA). MLPA is an extension of PLPA. In MVS/370, the modules were loaded after NIP with the "regular" loader. If a module did not fit in a page, then another block was allocated, and the space in between was "wasted." Another early MVS modification was to modify this routine to "pack" the modules. MVS/XA fixes this problem and packs the modules.

8. The Common System Area (CSA) and System Queue Area (SQA). CSA and SQA contain MVS control blocks that are

shared among address spaces. It is not unusual to see 1–3 megabytes of Central Storage for CSA and SQA.
9. Address space frames. Each address space has several Central Storage frames associated with it:
   a. Local System Queue Area (LSQA) frames. Control blocks for the address space are fixed in storage for the duration of the time the address space is in storage.
   b. Pages are fixed for the duration of an I/O operation by the address space.

MVS/XA relieves some pressure on the frames below the 16-megabyte line:

1. Fixed frames for about half of the nucleus, SQA, and LSQA can be anywhere in Central Storage for the 31-bit modules.
2. The I/O subsystem can perform I/O operations above the 16-megabyte Central Storage line, so IOS does not have to move pages from above 16 megabytes to below 16 megabytes just to perform the I/O operation.

Expanded Storage Expanded storage on the 309x Processor Complexes can be used in several ways to relieve the additional requirements for Central Storage.

1. Hold stolen Central Storage page frames. The first usage of Expanded Storage was to "store" Central Storage page frames, thus eliminating the need to move the page frames to Auxiliary Storage in a page or swap operation. Before Expanded Storage, MVS only had Auxiliary Storage to hold page frames which were "stolen" from address spaces. Expanded Storage is very similar to a Solid State Paging Device, only instead of being at the end of a channel, it is inside the Processor Complex.
2. Hold logically swapped LSQA. With MVS/ESA and RMF Version 4.1 a new term was identified — **Disabled Reference Storage** (DREF), which are the System Queue Area (SQA) and local system queue area (LSQA) page frames of a swapped out user. These page frames were previously kept in Central Storage as they contained the information needed to swap in a swapped out address space.
3. Using data space for Buffers. With MVS/ESA, Expanded Storage can be used to hold large numbers of buffers for a data space.

4. HIPERspace buffers. With MVS/ESA, HIPERspace pages never reside in Central Storage. Data in HIPERspace can not be referenced directly; it must be moved into an address space before it can be used by an address space.

9.2.3. CPU Utilization Differences

Trace Table Processing One of the things the systems designers of MVS/370 noticed was that the trace processing of MVS used considerable resources. In some measurements I performed, it was as high as 3 percent of a CPU, but this is not surprising. One of my first modifications to CICS was to turn off the CICS trace to get a marked improvement in CICS response time on a System/370 155. Trace processing stores information in a wraparound table which is printed if an abnormal termination happens. The trace is used to give clues of what happened up to the point of the problem. This storing of information requires CPU resources and Central Storage resources.

In tightly coupled multiprocessing environments, it becomes even more complex. If a task is dispatched in CPU1, the trace buffers are stored in the CPU cache. If the task is dispatched in another CPU (such as CPU4), CPU1 has to move the trace entries to Central Storage (called "casting out"). CPU4 can then "fetch" the addresses.

To resolve the problem, MVS/XA trace is implemented in software and hardware. Each processor has its own trace buffer. The entries are controlled by the microcode.

Another situation with MVS/370 was that the Generalized Trace Facility used the same system resources as the trace table and actually disabled the trace while GTF is running. Thus, a GTF trace of a teleprocessing line could prevent diagnostics from being captured if a system failure occurred while GTF was running. MVS/XA does not disable tracing when GTF is running.

I/O Processing I/O processing uses CPU resources. The MVS system performs several thousand instructions to process an I/O. If MVS has to "redrive" an I/O to select another path, additional CPU cycles are used. Fewer I/O interrupts result in lower CPU utilization. The Input/Output Supervisor executes as one of the top priority tasks because IOS gets control when an I/O interrupt is detected. The movement of the redrive functions and path selection to the microcode lowers CPU requirements of MVS/XA.

9.2.4. I/O Resources

Each I/O subsystem has an architectural limit to the number of I/O operations which can be supported *at a certain response time.* The key here is "response time." In the case of magnetic tapes, the channel subsystem can be driven to 100 percent busy, because a one-minute delay to a two-hour job is not significant. A 15-second delay to a terminal transaction, however, is unacceptable.

In the case of DASDs, the problems associated with Rotational Position Sensing Miss (RPS MISS) can cause a channel which is too busy to actually get worse as the devices try to reattach to the channel.

I/O Operations in MVS/370 MVS/370 initiates an I/O operation for a specific path: channel, control unit, head of string, and device. The I/O can only "talk" over that path. But wait. Didn't we tell the microcode in the MVS/370 IOCP that the device had two paths? The answer is yes, but the microcode (XA) and operating system (MVS/XA) was not ready yet. It is typical of IBM to deliver hardware before a function is made available in the software.

Let's look at the exact things which happen in an I/O operation in MVS/370 (see Figure 9.6):

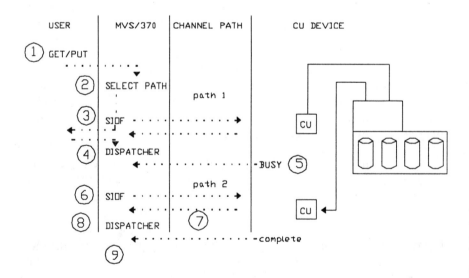

Figure 9.6   I/O operations in MVS/370. The I/O operation is started. If the path selected is busy, the MVS software must be involved to redrive the I/O operation.

1. A user issues a GET/PUT or READ/WRITE. The application code calls the MVS supervisor.
2. MVS Input/Output Supervisor (IOS) selects a path — in this case path 1.
3. A System/370 instruction — Start I/O Fast Release (SIOF) — is issued, which goes through the channel to some point on the channel path and returns. The SIOF instruction completes before the channel path has been completely investigated. The SIOF instruction replaced the System/360 Start I/O (SIO) instruction because the CPU was tied up while the electrical signal went several hundred feet out the channel and back.
4. The MVS dispatcher gets control and starts to do other work.
5. The channel, control units, or device decides the path is busy and interrupt the processor.
6. MVS selects another path and issues another SIOF — this time down path 2.
7. This time the I/O operation continues to the device and data is transferred.
8. The MVS dispatcher gets control and starts to do other work.
9. Finally the I/O interrupt comes in to say some productive work has been done.

I/O Operations in MVS/XA MVS/XA initiates an I/O operation. The channel subsystem returns immediately, and the channel takes care

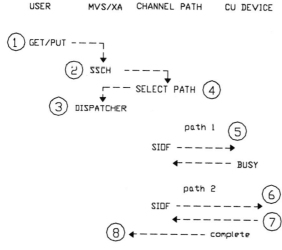

Figure 9.7   I/O operation in MVS/XA. With MVS/XA, the Channel subsystem selects paths and redrives I/O operations if necessary. The CPU is only interrupted if the I/O is complete or terminates with an error of some kind.

of the process until it is complete. The XA version of the microcode can use the information in the IOCP. Let's look at the exact things which happen in an I/O operation in MVS/XA (see Figure 9.7):

1. A user issues a GET/PUT or READ/WRITE. The application code calls the MVS supervisor.
2. MVS Input/Output Supervisor (IOS) issues a Start Sub Channel (SSCH) to pass the I/O request to the channel subsystem in the Processor Complex.
3. The MVS dispatcher gets control and starts to do other work.
4. The channel subsystem selects the path.
5. The channel path and associated control units and devices decide the path is busy and interrupt the processor.
6. The channel subsystem selects another path and issues another SIOF — this time down path 2.
7. This time the I/O operation continues to the device and data is transferred.
8. Finally the I/O interrupt comes in to say some productive work has been done.

Number of I/O Devices MVS/370 supports a theoretical maximum of 1,917 devices because each device must have a Unit Control Block (UCB), and there is a table of pointers to the UCB which has two bytes for the address of an UCB.

The number 1,917 is correct if you only have card readers and printers defined in the system, because they are the smallest UCBs. If you take an average size of a UCB including DASDs and tapes, the number is more like 1,100 devices.

In MVS/XA, the theoretical and maximum is 4,096 devices because the UCB pointers are now 3 bytes long. The 64-Kb storage limitation is removed. The change to 3 bytes was necessary to move the UCB from the first part of Central Storage to just below the 16-Mb line.[2]

---

2. Remember three bytes can contain an address up to 16 megabytes. Two bytes can support an address up to 64 Kb. Now you know the rest of the story — why MVS/370 was limited to less than 2,000 devices or so — 64 Kb divided by 32 bytes per UCB = 2,048 more or less.

Dynamic Path Reconnect One of the features of the 3380 standard device is **Device Path Selection** (DPS). Three-fourths of the benefit of DPS (alternate controller selection, two-path transfer, and Volume reserve) are available to all operating systems. The fourth, and most important, benefit is only available to Extended Architecture operating systems — Dynamic Path Reconnect.[3]

DPR is a combination of 3380 architecture and MVS/XA software and hardware. All must be in place to receive the benefits of DPR. For an idea of how DPR helps, look at Figure 9.8 and review an I/O to a 3380 AA4 device:

1. Queue the request for the UCB. Perform an I/O operation for the highest priority task.
2. Wait for a free path to the device:
   a. Channel (4 selected first)
   b. 3880 Control Unit (10)
   c. Head of String (49x)
   d. Internal Path to the device.
3. Seek the arm to the desired cylinder.
4. Set Sector — wait for the sector to get close.
5. Wait for a path (RPS delay if not reconnected).
6. Search, then read/write.

DPR comes into play during step 5 above. In MVS/370, the "path" is limited to the path which was first used for this I/O operation — path 490 in Figure 9.8. In MVS/XA, *all paths are simultaneously used* to get to the Processor Complex. In Figure 9.8, both path 490 and path 990 are tried at the same time to reconnect. With two paths (or four paths with 3990 control units and xJ4 or xK4 devices), the probability a path will be available is clearly much better. The average response time will be lower with a lower probability of a RPS miss.

---

3. Device Level Selection (DLS) and Device Level Selection Extended (DLSE) are extensions of DPR for Extended Capability (e.g., AD4) and enhanced subsystem (e.g., AJ4) models and are discussed in the chapter on Direct Access Storage Devices (DASD).

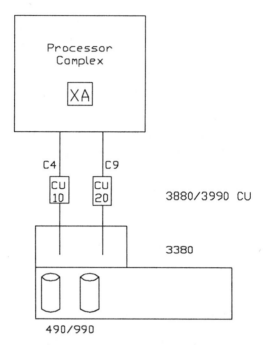

Figure 9.8   Dynamic Path Reconnect (DPR). With DPR device 490 can try to reconnect to the Processor Complex either through path 490 or through path 990.

9.2.5.   RAS Differences

Each new release of MVS increases the Reliablity, Availability, and Serviceability (RAS) because IBM fixes the bugs in the programs. Additionally there are some changes to the architecture to eliminate problems:

1. The nucleus is moved from the first frames in the machine. If there are errors in the first frames and you are trying to IPL MVS/370, then the system will not come up. If the same thing happens to MVS/XA, then the system *should* come up. I say "should" because I have seen at least one instance where a 3084 had Central Storage errors and the system would not initialize. I suspect the errors were in the highest Central Storage and the HSA could not be initialized. Now, if they could fix that bug!

2. Finer granularity in page protection. We have learned MVS/XA has page protection on 4-Kb boundaries rather than the 64-Kb segment protection that MVS/370 uses.

3. The system trace facility has been improved in MVS/XA. If the developers have a better idea what led up to a problem, they are more likely to find a fix to the problem.
4. The system dumping process has been improved. There are more fields, more control blocks are formatted, and you really can find almost everything in a system dump which is needed to fix a problem.

9.2.6. When to Upgrade from MVS/370 to MVS/XA

Now comes the hard part. When should your installation convert from MVS/370 to MVS/XA. While I cannot make that decision for you from this distance, I can suggest things to consider that I and my colleagues have used over the years to plan and convert.

The Cost of the Upgrade As with any change to your software and hardware configuration, you are encouraged to get an accurate cost differential between the "new" software — MVS/XA — and the "old, out-of-date" software. Only by knowing the price can you determine if it is cost-effective.

Do not forget the cost of the software you have purchased from other vendors. They usually want additional dollars depending on the hardware you have. In some cases, "only the new product" will support MVS/XA, so you will have to pay for an upgrade to the OEM product as well as pay for the difference between MVS/370 and MVS/XA.

Virtual Storage Problems Do you have virtual storage constraint?

You Have Split DB/DC Applications: One clue to virtual storage problems will be hidden in your Data Base/Data Communications (DB/DC) environment. People there will be making decisions to circumvent problems. The clue usually is multiple CICS or IMS regions or CICS Multiple Region Option (MRO). The two reasons for having multiple DB/DC systems are:

1. Security or availablity of a system forces two regions. The users of SYSTEM A require they be separate from the users of SYSTEM B.
2. There are constraining problems.

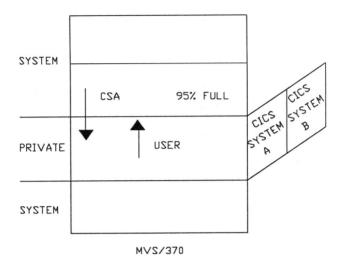

MVS/370

Figure 9.9   When to upgrade from MVS/370 to MVS/XA. As the pressures grow on virtual storage, there are several clues that indicate trouble is brewing.

CSA: A second area which shows constraint is that CSA is running at 95 percent full. As VSAM and VTAM usage grows, forcing the MVS upper boundary down, the user regions are usually growing up toward the boundary. Figure 9.9 shows this two-way push. Remember, it takes an MVS IPL to change the line between private and MVS common areas.

Private Area Problems: As the application programs run out of virtual space, you will notice the number of abends growing which relate to virtual storage — x0A abends in particular.

I/O Constraining Problems   In MVS/370, the block multiplexor channels to DASDs should not be allowed to exceed approximately 30–35 percent busy during peak periods. This "rule of thumb" is based on studies of RPS miss and channel queuing. Channel busy times greater than 30–35 percent result in wildly erratic and usually unacceptable device response times.

With the support in MVS/XA for Dynamic Path Reconnection, the channel can be allowed to peak at approximately 50 percent busy. Figure 9.10 shows the path busy concept.

Single Image on 3084, 3090-400, or Larger   Finally, there are the "you can only get to there from here" reasons to select MVS/XA. You could choose to run a 3084 in partitioned mode and use MVS/370 on both

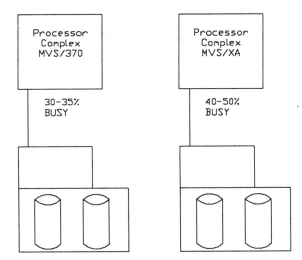

Figure 9.10   Channel Busy Rule of Thumb. In an MVS/370 environment, no channel should be allowed to exceed 30–33 percent busy for peak periods. In an MVS/XA environment no channel should be allowed to exceed 40–50 percent busy for peak periods. The exception in both MVS/370 and MVS/XA is tape channels, which can operate at much higher channel busy rates.

sides. IBM does not charge for multiple MVS licenses on partitioned mode Processor Complexes — not yet — but others do. Usually when you add up multiple Processor Complex charges from your OEM vendors, the total cost is less with MVS/XA.

9.3.   DIFFERENCES BETWEEN MVS/XA AND MVS/ESA

In 1988, IBM announced expanded versions of the 3090 series of Processor Complexes. These 309x E/S models contained the microcode to support ESA/370. The software that uses the new hardware functions is called MVS/ESA. Limited distribution began in the fourth quarter of 1988.

It should not come as a surprise to the reader that new function in MVS requires new hardware. The dividing line between hardware and software becomes more fuzzy with each passing year. Let's look at the changes in the hardware. Keep in mind what we learned with the 3380 and dynamic path recovery — IBM creates the hardware before they announce the function. IBM calls MVS/ESA *a base for future applications.*

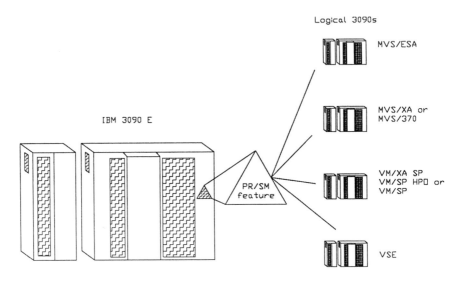

Figure 9.11   Processor Resource/Systems Manager (PR/SM). The 309x Expanded models can have optional microcode which allows the physical hardware to be logically divided into smaller units.

9.3.1.   Processor Complex Changes

A number of changes to the hardware (Processor Complex) and software (MVS/ESA) combine to make up what we know as MVS/ESA. As you read these descriptions, look for clues to future IBM announcements. Remember, the 3081 was announced with totally new microcode — new commands, new ways of doing operator functions. Then MVS/XA was announced!

3090 Processor Resource/Systems Manager (PR/SM)   The 3090 Processor Resource/Systems Manager (PR/SM) is not a part of MVS/ESA, but was announced at the same time as MVS/ESA. In Figure 9.11, a 3090 processor can be logically divided into partitions.[4] Each partition can be IPLed to run any of the IBM operating systems.

---

4. As of this writing, there can be six partitions on each side (a total of 12 if the Processor Complex is split). The number can change as the microcode changes.

The concept has been available for years on IBM equipment. The hardware could be physically split apart, but had to be split on predefined boundaries. The 3084 can be physically partitioned to two 3081 equivalents. The 3090-400 can also be split into two 3090-200 equivalents.

What has not been available is the partitioning on other boundaries. For example, before PR/SM, a 3090-400 could not be split with one CPU on one side and three CPUs on the other side. OEM plug-compatible Processor Complexes could logically partition before PR/SM.[5] VM has for a long time been able to logically partition the hardware it controlled. The similarities between the concepts of VM and PR/SM give credence to the theory that 3082 and 3092 Processor Controllers are really little VM machines.

Note, also, that PR/SM supports DOS/VSE. This is the first announcement of VSE support on the 309x. The data centers converting from VSE to MVS should find this particularly interesting.

The term for the PR/SM split of the Processor Complex is **Logical Partitioning** (LPAR). The console operator can reconfigure the physical resources through the use of the IOCP. CPUs, vector facilities, Central Storage, Expanded Storage, and channel paths can be configured. The CPUs can be dedicated or shared among partitions or a combination of the two options. If the CPUs are shared, there is a PR/SM scheduler to control the time slices each logical partition is allowed to have of the CPU resource.

Central Storage and Expanded Storage are assigned to the logical partitions in 1-Mb increments. Channel paths can be initially assigned through the IOCP or dynamically assigned by the system operator.

VM/XA has a feature called **Multiple Preferred Guests** (MPG) which uses the PR/SM hardware to logically divide up the hardware among multiple virtual machines or guest Operating Systems. Because the VM/MPG uses the same hardware as the LPAR com-

---

5. AMDAHL has had its Multiple Domain Facility (MDF), which is very similar to PR/SM, for several years.

mands, you should not run VM/XA under a Processor Complex which has LPAR active.

438x and 309x Expanded Models The 438x and 309x E/S models have the microcode to support MVS/ESA. In the 438x Processor Complex, Central Storage is subdivided into Central Storage and Expanded Storage.[6]

9.3.2. Virtual Storage Changes

MVS/ESA has the same two gigabyte virtual storage as MVS/XA. What is added is the ability to address other two gigabyte address spaces. This addressability is different from cross-memory facilities offered by all versions of MVS — **Dual Address Facility** (DAS) and **Cross-Memory Services Facility** (XMS). The secondary address spaces do not map MVS areas. The whole two gigabytes can be used for data. Before we look at the new address spaces, let's summarize the "old services."

Base Cross-Memory Facilities Both DAS and XMS have been available since early versions of MVS/370. The drawback is that they are only usable by assembler language programmers. See Figure 9.12 for some of the uses of DAS and XMS.

Dual Address Space Facility (DAS): DAS is a set of MVS (MVS/370 or MVS/XA) instructions which enable direct data movement and program execution between two address spaces. Some of the functions of DAS are:

1. Data movement from one address space to another via instructions which do not require interruption and redispatch of the other address space.
2. Direct execution of code resident in the private area of a second address space.

---

6. The 9370 family has announced "enterprise systems" support (for VM) but not MVS support as of this writing. It may be announced by the time you read this. Remember, though, the 9370 is a fairly small Processor Complex in terms of CPU power and MVS is a workhorse of an operating system. The 9370 may be too small to run MVS/XA or MVS/ESA as the operating system.

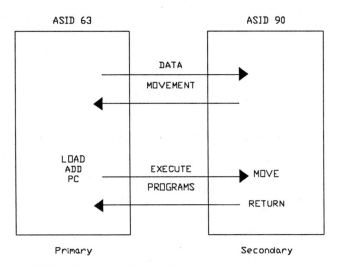

Figure 9.12 Dual Address Facility and Cross-Memory Services. Even in MVS/370, the user could use data in a second address space. The first address space is called the "primary" address space, and the second address space is called the "secondary" address space.

3. Ability to switch to a higher authorization level (e.g., supervisor state or to a protection key other than the current address space).
4. Authorization to access data in another address space.
5. Authorization to execute code in another address space.

Cross-Memory Services Facility (XMS): Cross-Memory Services Facility is:

1. A set of control structures and macros within MVS.
2. Services which invoke the DAS instructions.
3. Services which manage the cross-memory environment.
4. Enabling of DAS instructions directly within an address space.

The next two sections explain the new MVS/ESA address spaces.

DATA SPACES MVS/ESA Data Spaces are two gigabyte virtual storage address spaces which do not contain program instructions except where instructions are treated as data. Figure 9.13 shows some of the items which they may contain:

1. Data buffers from files.

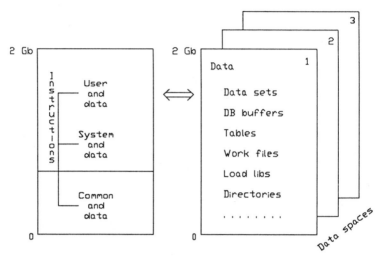

Figure 9.13   Data spaces. MVS/ESA introduced a new type of 2-Gb address space. The 2 Gb cannot contain instructions (except instructions treated as data — load modules that are moved in and out) and does not have all the common storages mapped, so the entire 2 Gb can be data.

2. Program tables and arrays.
3. Other data structures such as DB2 data sets and Data in Virtual (DIV) objects.
4. Work files such as SORT work space.
5. Load libraries.
6. Partitioned Data Set directories.

Data Spaces are byte addressable. Access is very similar to data which is in the address space using a Data Space. Application programs can access a Data Space via **Data Windowing Services**, announced for FORTRAN, PL/I, COBOL, C, PASCAL, and assembler language programs.

A Data Space can be defined as **private** (the Data Space is only available to one address space) or **shared** (more than one address space can use the data). Shared address spaces can only be created by authorized programs.

HIPERspaces The HIgh PERformance Space is a second MVS/ESA improvement. HIPERspaces use Expanded Storage and paging devices for a resource which can be accessed by data center users. A HIPERspace is a contiguous area which can exist in one of two places:

1. Partially in expanded storage, partially on virtual storage. These are called **standard** HIPERspaces.
2. All in expanded storage. These are called **Expanded Storage Only** (ESO) HIPERspaces and can only be used by "authorized" MVS address spaces.

The data stored in HIPERspaces must be accessed in four Kb (4,096-byte) blocks. A HIPERspace can be up to two gigabytes in size, although there are MVS/ESA services to link Data Spaces.

An application can read and write to this storage using new system services. There are two types of HIPERspaces:

1. Authorized program area. This type of HIPERspace can only be used on processors with Expanded Storage.
2. Application program area. This type of HIPERspace is available to applications through the Data Windowing services and will be in Expanded Storage if the 309x E/S or 438x E has Expanded Storage available. If not, it will be supported from the Auxiliary Storage.

Systems Services MVS/ESA has not forgotten its own requirements. One only has to look at the hundreds of cylinders of executable code in MVS to realize there is a need to manage load modules. These services can be organized into several general areas:

1. Data Windowing Services. High level languages can scroll through large **permanent Data Sets** or large **temporary data sets**. In Figure 9.14, the program executing in address space 10 can scroll through a "Data Set" represented by address space 20.
2. Authorized program load modules. MVS system programs and other authorized programs can store "objects" such as load modules in Data Spaces. These "objects" would normally "reside" on DASD and be limited to the transfer rate and contention from I/O devices. Figure 9.14 shows program A being loaded into a Data Space (15). When address space 10 issues a load for the module, it is retrieved directly from address space 15.

   Other savings are realized as this service loads and keeps the module in a different format than the one on the Partitioned Data Set. When a module is called for, it can be moved to the requesting address space and "relocated" much more efficiently than if the module was coming from DASD.

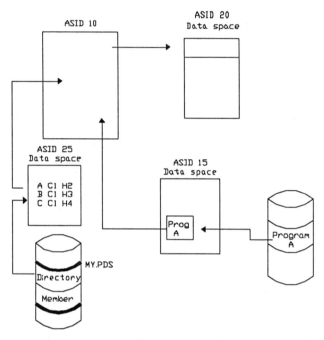

Figure 9.14   System services. MVS/ESA provides three services — data windowing, program fetch data spaces, and dynamic PDS directory buffering.

3. Directory services. A library service can be called to identify active modules and keep their directory entries available in Data Spaces. This is available in MVS/XA for the LINKLIST (Linklist Look Aside) but is expanded for production load and nonprogram libraries. Of course, selective refreshment of the directory entries is allowed so you can get to new modules added after the system has been initialized. You do have to remember to do the refresh! In Figure 9.14, Data Set MY.PDS is a partitioned Data Set. The director has three members — A, B, and C. The library is specified to be included with directory services. When the address space 10 issues a load or get for member A, the PDS directory entry is searched from a Data Space — ASID 25.

9.3.3. Systems Managed Storage

For years, IBM has been promising to get the data center out of the business of DASD volumes, cylinders, and tracks and into the business of creating Data Sets. Just think of how much DASD IBM could sell if it had all the Systems Programmers and Analysts creating Data Sets instead of managing them!

MVS/Data Facility Product Version 3 (part of MVS/ESA), Data Facility/Hierarchical Storage Manager (DF/HSM), Data Facility/Data Set Services (DF/DSS), Data Facility/SORT (DF/SORT), and RACF provide the function of **Data Facility Storage Management Subsystem (DFSMS)**

Introduction Each year, the data center spends more people resources managing the data which is important to its company. DFSMS is designed to separate the logical view of data from the physical way the data is stored on the hardware.

The separation is a very important concept. For those of us who went through 2314 to 3330, 3330 to 3350, and 3350 to 3380 conversions, we are looking forward with glee to the operating system handling allocating, retrieval, and archiving of data without our interference. I will caution you: *Data Sets must be cataloged in an ICF catalog.* If your data center permits tape and Data Sets to be accessed without using the catalog — volume serial number and unit — then you will probably not be able to use these new features.

Classes and Groups There are three types of "classes" to define the attributes of a Data Set:

1. **Data Class** gives the logical record length (LRECL), Data Set organization (DSORG), space requirements, and VSAM options.
2. **Storage Class** gives the logical Data Set characteristics such as the block size and what kind of performance you request the physical device will give to data requests.
3. **Management Class** gives the information about the backup and recovery options you request. If archived, how long should it remain archived before it is scratched?

The **Storage Group** gives information about the groups of I/O devices similar to generic specifications today, but expanded:

1. The volumes associated with this group.
2. The space thresholds of these volumes.
3. The management information associated with this group of volumes.

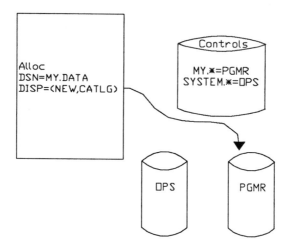

Figure 9.15 Data Facility Systems Managed Storage. Data sets can be allocated by a new function of MVS/ESA. If DFSMS is specified, the allocation is intercepted and the data set is allocated based on installation controls. Only the data set name (DSN=) and disposition (DISP=) are used. In this example, the system administrator said any data set that begins with "MY" will be allocated to the "PGMR" volumes.

Automatic Class Select (ACS) The data center can allocate Data Sets through a process called **Automatic Class Select**. DFSMS will intercept the allocation and assign the data to volumes based on the filters assigned by the data center. Figure 9.15 shows **MY.PDS** getting allocated to one set of DASD because the data center has specified that Data Sets which begin with "MY" should go to the "SLOW" pool of DASD. Now seems a good time to bring up naming conventions. No one likes to think they are getting "branded" or labeled. Everyone wants the "best." Be careful selecting names. Instead of "slow," you could use terms meaningful to your business (e.g., PGMR for programmer space).

Centralized Control Centralized control finally gives the data center the ability to enforce class definitions such as block size. In MVS/370 the data center did have the ability to write assembler language "exits," but few data centers took this opportunity to enforce standards. Now this power is performed through panels on screens.

A side benefit to centralized control is that the only parameters — like VSAM — needed are Data Set name and disposition. By using RACF controls, the data center can control who gets to the "fast" volumes.

9.4. SUMMARY

When selecting an MVS version and System/370 Processor Complex, do so based on the needs and growth plan of your company. CPU speed, I/O throughput, Central Storage, and virtual storage can constrain system growth, and although MVS/XA and MVS/ESA relieve constraints, they are larger and more costly than MVS/370. Your goal should not be to have the biggest and the best but to maintain high standards of Reliability, Availability, and Serviceability (RAS).

The differences between MVS/370 and MVS/XA relating to virtual storage constraint originate in MVS/XA's use of the Extended Architecture to reallocate much of the supervisor's data areas from below the 16-Mb line to addresses above it. Consequently, applications regain addresses below the line, and MVS/XA is free to increase the capacity of a system by its increased addressability.

This comes with cost, however: MVS/XA requires about two Mb more Central Storage than does MVS/370.

Other 370/XA enhancements are used by MVS/XA to improve throughput and increase capacity: Expanded storage acts as an alternative repository to the I/O subsystem; the I/O subsystem can resolve busy paths without the attention of a CPU; MVS/XA can support more I/O devices; DPR can get data from I/O devices to the CPU by investigating all return paths simultaneously. Further, IBM has improved the RAS of MVS/XA over MVS/370.

370/ESA and MVS/ESA expand the architectures further. They permit an application in one address space to directly reference (in a controlled manner, of course) other address spaces containing code and data without going through the overhead of a supervisor call. Thus, even if 31-bit addressability were to constrain as 24-bit addresses once did, provision exists to reference additional address spaces. Management of load modules is improved as well.

MVS/ESA also brings long-promised improvement to Data Set management with DFSMS, in which users specify the access and storage characteristics with meaningful names rather than locations and sizes with (too often arbitrary) numbers.

DFSMS gives the data center much control over the ways Data Sets are allocated and permits it to transparently modify them to suit changing requirements — without having to chase down users' JCL.

10

Job Entry Subsystems (JES)

10.1. INTRODUCTION

The Job Entry Subsystem (JES) is the part of MVS which manages batch jobs and SYSOUT under MVS. There are two flavors. The first is JES2. The second is JES3. Each has its own merits. The data center is probably running JES2 or JES3 based upon the opinions and preferences of the systems programmer who started the data center. If you are converting to MVS from VSE or just starting a data center, then you have a unique opportunity. Make your decision between JES2 and JES3 carefully. Once the selection is made, *very few installations switch from one to the other*.

Figure 10.1 illustrates the basic functions of JES. There are many similarities between the JES2 and JES3. They both receive ("read") batch jobs to be processed by MVS. Instream data (SYSIN) is stored until the job starts executing and OPENs/READs the file. Both support writers to print on local and remote printers. They both support readers to read the batch jobs from local users and remote users of the data center. They both support TSO. Both JES subsystems write accounting information to SMF. Both support remote computing — Network Job Entry (NJE).

The two JES subsystems differ in how they handle work flow, how they interface to MVS, and operator interaction. Later sections in this chapter will discuss the work flow management.

One of the largest differences between JES2 and JES3 is console communications. All JES3 consoles communicate with all Processor Complexes which comprise the node. JES2 consoles are an integral

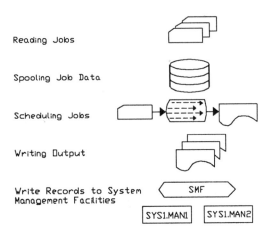

Reading Jobs

Spooling Job Data

Scheduling Jobs

Writing Output

Write Records to System
Management Facilities

Figure 10.1   JES basic functions. Both JES2 and JES3 support reading jobs, spooling data, and job management.

part of MVS and can only communicate with other copies of MVS via the $DM command.

JES2 and JES3 are *subsystems* to MVS. They are able to handle the above functions because they "register" with MVS that they will handle the functions. The subsystem interface (SSI) is the MVS method used to communicate between JES and MVS. Figure 10.2 shows the logical view of a Subsystem Interface. JES is started after the Master Scheduler is completely initialized. In fact, the only thing that can start after the Master Scheduler is a JES. If JES abends, the only thing that can be started next is a JES. In other words, a *JES must be running for tasks to start and stop.*

JES really is in two parts. The first part is a separate address space which does the work of establishing an environment for other address spaces to use JES services and managing jobs. The second part is a set of service routines which are available to all address spaces — in the Pageable Link Pack Area.

When JES starts up in its own address space, initialization routines establish control blocks in the Common System Area (CSA) and start initiators (separate address spaces). The JES service routines perform two types of services:

1. Provide Subsystem Interface (SSI) functions which may or may not cause activity in the JES address space to allocate new areas of the spool volumes and other functions to complete the work required for spooling.

Subsystem Interface

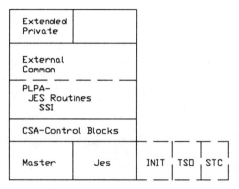

Figure 10.2   Subsystem Interface. JES must start just after the Master
Scheduler is initialized and establishes communications between MVS and JES.

2. Provide the spool access method modules. The normal mode for
   spool access is actually VSAM macros and calls. Most users,
   however, use QSAM or BSAM forms, which convert GETs and
   PUTs (or READs and WRITEs) to VSAM calls. The MVS component that does the conversion is called the SAM compatibility interface.

   The reason most users use the SAM interface is that the application can be changed, with JCL, from SYSOUT to most
   other MVS devices. The user can print an output file or build a
   data set on a device to be edited or passed to another MVS
   program.

Another common feature of the JES subsystems is the ability for
batch jobs to submit other jobs during execution — the Internal
Reader function. In production applications, this is one of the most
beneficial and time-saving features of JES. A job, after it completes a
procedure successfully, can execute a "step" to submit the next job
(or jobs) in the series. It is not as sophisticated as a job scheduling
system, but it works.[1]

---

1. Thanks to Richard Milazzo, Jim Thompson, Tom Horvath, and Michele
   Berger for demonstrating these techniques in a successful production environment.

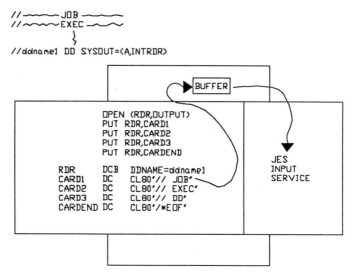

Figure 10.3　JES internal reader. An application program (or CICS) DD card allocates a SYSOUT spool data set. Instead of being printed or punched, the data is fed into the JES input service.

Figure 10.3 shows the internal reader in action. Generally, SYSOUT=(A,nnnn) requests a special output writer whose program name is "nnnn." One such "special" writer is "**INTRDR**."

When the program issues an Assembler "PUT" macro or COBOL "WRITE" statement, it goes to the JES spool just like other spooled output, but upon close, the spooled output is processed by the JES reader. The following are actions required for using the Internal Reader:

1. Open the data set. It should be defined as physical sequential (DSORG=PS). Opening the data set establishes the connection to the JES reader function.
2. Code a WRITE (BSAM), PUT (QSAM), or COBOL WRITE statement to send records to JES.
3. Notify JES that the job is ready for processing:
    a. Issue a CLOSE macro. The CLOSE normally finishes an output data set and prepares it for output on a system output device. In this case, JES places the output in a queue for the JES input service.
    b. Code /*EOF as the last record. JES will simulate the close function and make the job available for input service. The

end of file function gives a clue as to why and when to use VSAM macros to write to JES. The VSAM equivalent to /*EOF is **ENDREQ**, which is what the TSO SUBMIT command uses. **ENDREQ** returns the job identification (JOBnnnnn) of the job just passed to JES.

Other possibilities are:

c. Code /***DEL** as the last record of the job to cancel the job and send it immediately to output processing. In JES3, the file will be reopened when another record is written to it.

d. Code /***PURGE** as the last record of the job to cancel the job and purge the output. PURGE is a JES2 option only.

e. Code /***SCAN** as the last record of the job to scan for JCL syntax but not execute the job. SCAN is a JES2 option only.

Another common feature of both JES systems is **spin data sets**. Normally, all print and punch data sets are held until the batch job completely ends execution. If the DD card that specifies the SYSOUT parameter also contains **FREE=CLOSE**, the JES subsystem will begin processing the "spin" data set as soon as the program issues a CLOSE macro. The data set will be separated from the job by having a separate spool allocation bit map.

If a data set has a separate allocation bit map, then when the data set is completely printed, the space on the spool volume can be freed. The benefit is that long-running jobs can have their print data sets start to print even before the job finishes.

For an example of when to use this feature, assume a job in step 5 prints a large report on special forms. Step 6 will back up all the data sets processed by the job — occupying, for example, three dual capacity 3380s. If step 5 specified "FREE=CLOSE," the data center could start printing the output while the job continued on to back up the files.

Readers are cautioned that dynamically allocated (a DD card is not used, but an MVS service — SVC 99 is used) SYSOUT data sets need bits properly set to get a separate spool allocation bit map.

10.2. JOB ENTRY SUBSYSTEM 2 (JES2) MULTIACCESS SPOOL

JES2 can operate with one copy of MVS or communicate between multiple copies of MVS. The interconnection of from two to seven copies of MVS running on separate Processor Complexes is called

Multiaccess Spool (MAS). MAS refers to multiple copies of MVS accessing the same JES spool volumes. The collection of all the copies is called a **node**. Jobs submitted on any Processor Complex in the node may run on any Processor Complex. Alternately, Jobs submitted in the node may be limited to run on only certain Processor Complexes in the node.

Because all copies of JES2 have all the functions, as opposed to the JES3 arrangement, if one Processor Complex in the node fails, the others continue processing as if "nothing" had happened. (This is not quite true — the others do notice that a member has fallen.)

When two or more Processor Complexes share spool volumes, it is recommended that the checkpoint volume be isolated on a volume and that an alternate checkpoint be allocated (probably on one of the other spool volumes). I recommend that data centers always have duplexed checkpoints — even if you only have a single Processor Complex. You are using approximately one to five cylinders to guarantee that your entire data center input and output will be saved if you lose the primary checkpoint volume. I feel that is a cost-effective decision.

I even go further and do what Bill Mosteller taught me — keep a checkpoint data set on *every* spool volume. The advantages are that you always have a primary and secondary checkpoint data set to use. If you have problems with your DASD hardware, recovery is complex enough without having to figure out where checkpoints and alternates can be placed. Only one secondary is used at a time.

Figure 10.4 is an overview of the JES2 configuration. The Processor Complex on the right — labeled BATCH — is optional. You can run JES2 with just one Processor Complex. The figure shows that if two Processor Complexes are running multiaccess, then their only points of communication are the spool and checkpoint volumes.

10.2.1.   JES2 Initialization

Initialization options determine what will be done to start JES2. Definition of the Input/Output devices, remote facilities, tuning parameters, job classes, and SYSOUT classes are specified to the initialization process.

Once the data center has defined the valid options, the user community can specify which one to use. For example, job classes are specified in the CLASS=x parameter on the JOB card (Job Control Language) or created by the data center automatically in SMF exits.

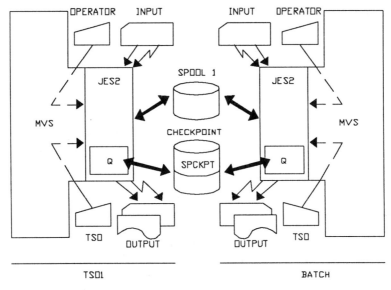

Figure 10.4 JES2 configuration. The JES2 logical configuration consists of operator consoles, local printers and readers, Spool volumes to hold input and output data, checkpoint volumes for an "index," remote reader and printers, and support for TSO.

SYSOUT classes are specified by the SYSOUT=x parameter of the DD card.

There are several types of initialization:

1. **Cold Start** results in the loss of all jobs and all SYSOUT and all SYSIN on the spool. The spool is wiped clean. (What actually happens is that the checkpoint is initialized.) The "cold" start can have a parameter — **FORMAT** — which will write records to each cylinder allocated for the SPOOL. A "cold" start can be done in a matter of seconds; a "cold format" is finished in 15–20 minutes depending on the release of JES and the number of SPOOL volumes. To see what happens, look at Figure 10.4 again. The complex on the left is named "TSO1," and the complex on the right is named "BATCH." Assume neither system is running. IPL either one — TSO1, for example — and respond "cold" to the JES request for parameters. The checkpoint data set on DASD volume SPCKPT will be formatted with the parameters specified in the JES2 parameter library. If "cold,format" were entered, the volume SPCKPT would be formatted (1–5 cylinders are all that is needed for the checkpoint

data set), and *all the cylinders* (885 for single capacity 3380, for example) would be written on SPOOL1.

Once spool volumes have been formatted, they do not have to be formatted again until you change the JES specifications to change the physical block size of the record written to the track. JES will check the physical block size and, if incorrect, format the spool volume that has inconsistent block sizes. "Cold" starts should be authorized only by those who fully understand the ramifications.

2. **Single System Warm Start** (SSWS) is the term used for starting a single system in a multiple access spool. The operator replies "warm" to the request for options. JES2 will requeue all jobs that were previously running, if any, and initialize JES2.

   In Figure 10.4, assume both TSO1 and BATCH are running. BATCH is re-IPLed, and "warm" is replied to the JES message. The result is an SSWS by BATCH.

3. **All System Warm Start** (ASWS) is the term used for starting a single system in a multiple access spool where this system starting is the only one running at the time of warm start. JES2 performs many housekeeping functions at this time that it could not do if others were using the common spool. The reply is the same — "warm" — only JES notices that no other Processor Complex is using the spool.

   In Figure 10.4, assume that neither TSO1 nor BATCH are running at all — say after a long weekend. The operators "IPL TSO1" and reply "warm" to JES2. TSO1 is doing an All System Warm Start.

4. **Hot Start** is the term for initialization of JES in a Processor Complex where JES has abended or otherwise terminated. JES starts up and notices that other work is already going on. What really happens is that JES2 finds its control blocks already in virtual storage. When JES "hot" starts, all work is allowed to continue. In fact, JES2 can be taken out of the system on purpose and restarted. Since much of the initialization is skipped over, many parameters cannot be changed.

   In Figure 10.4, assume both TSO1 and BATCH are running. The JES in BATCH abends for some reason and is restarted. The restart is a hot start.

5. **Quick Start** is the term used for second and subsequent Single System Warm Starts (SSWSs) of other JES2 systems on other Processor Complexes. It is faster than the first SSWS.

   In Figure 10.4, assume neither TSO1 nor BATCH are running. TSO1 is IPLed. When BATCH is initialized, it will be a "quick" start. You can tell if a JES2 start will be quick or warm by issuing an operator command — **$LSYS**. If the system that is going to be started shows as **DORMANT**, then you get a warm start because JES2 cleans up the jobs and things which were active when the system went down. If the system shows as IDLE then the start will be quick. The JES is marked "idle" if the operator has issued an **$ESYS** command to reset and recover a JES system that will be out of service for a period of time.

JES2 initialization is shown in Figure 10.5. The initialization has the following general steps:

1. JES2 loads the modules it will need.
2. JES2 checks for and initializes necessary printers, card readers, and DASD devices.
3. JES2 establishes tables in virtual storage that will be used by JES2, MVS, and the address spaces that use JES2 services.
4. JES2 looks at the parameters and goes to check if other versions of JES2 are running — this information is on the checkpoint data set.
5. JES2 establishes the Subsystem Interface (control blocks in virtual storage).

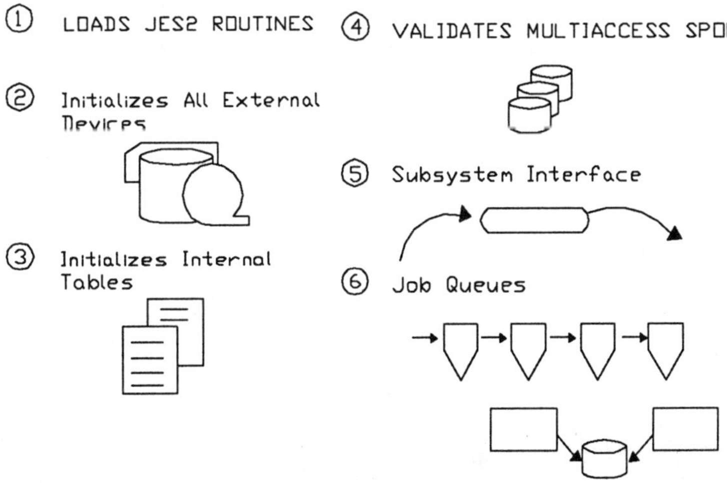

Figure 10.5   JES2 Initialization. JES2 programs initialize pointers and customize the installation with the JES2 parameters.

6. JES2 looks at the queues of work to be done and starts processing.

10.2.2.   Input Processing

Input processing is the part of JES2 code that reads a job into the system. A remote RJE terminal or a "REAL" device (e.g., card reader) may be used. An **"internal" reader** allocated from a batch job, a started system task, or a TSO session may also be used for a software reader interface. Once the whole job has been read, it is placed on a queue for the next phase.

Figure 10.6 shows a job being processed by INPUT and placed on the SPOOL volume.

10.2.3.   Conversion Processing

The converter scans the Job Control Language (JCL) for syntax errors and creates an encoded representation of the job called internal text. If all looks well, then the job is placed on the next queue: job

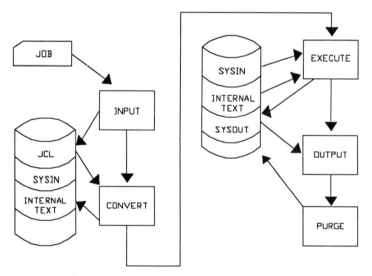

Figure 10.6   JES2 processing. JES2 accepts jobs, places the JCL on the spool volumes, and passes SYSIN to executing jobs and accepts SYSOUT from jobs as part of the EXECUTE process. OUTPUT processing writes reports to local or remote printers. PURGE cleans up all the control blocks.

transmission or execution. If there is an error, a strange cryptic message is included with the JCL, and the job bypasses GO, does not collect $200, and goes to the Output processor.

Generally the converter can detect errors to the left of the equal sign on a JCL card. For example, if the user had coded **UNTT=3380** then the converter would detect the invalid operand on the DD card — UNIT should have been specified. If the user coded **UNIT=TPAE** (where the data center had defined "TAPE" to mean 3480 magnetic tape drives but not "TPAE"), the converter would not detect that error until the execution began. Another example is "data set not found." MVS will not terminate a job if it cannot find a data set until the job actually starts execution.

The immediate turnaround of JCL errors is a great step beyond Operating Systems previous to MVS. With unmodified versions of HASP under MVT, you could submit the job now and wait several hours for the job to start up and *then* get the JCL error of a missing comma. Only certain JCL errors, such as syntax errors, are discovered by the Converter. If a data set is specified as OLD or SHR and it does not exist, this process will not catch that error.

The input stream is also scanned for JES2 Control Statements. JES2 control statements begin with a "/*" in columns one and two, they cannot be continued, and they cannot exist in a cataloged procedure. For historical reasons, "card" is sometimes used rather than "statement." Be sure to see the MVS documentation for the system you are using. One example is *MVS/370 JCL User's Guide* (GC28-1349). Examples are:

1. /*$command — contains, if authorized, MVS or JES2 commands to be executed. The commands must be before the JOB statement.
2. /*JOBPARM — specifies information to JES2 such as the number of cards or lines to be output, room number, etc.
3. /*MESSAGE — sends messages to the operator at input time. This is a nice idea but rarely works. At input time, the operator usually is not concerned with the job.
4. /*NETACCT — specifies an account number to be used for cross-network jobs.
5. /*NOTIFY — routes the job's notify messages to a userid.
6. /*OUTPUT — specifies processing options for SYSOUT data set(s). This card is useful for 3800 parameters and copies/routing information. This card cannot exist on cataloged procedures, so most JCL coders use the JCL "//OUTPUT" card instead.

7. /*PRIORITY — assigns a JES selection priority to the job. This priority determines which jobs will be selected by JES to next be started in an initiator. This "priority" should not be confused with dispatching "priority" which is set by the Systems Resource Manager (SRM) after the job starts executing.
8. /*ROUTE — specifies destination information for output or the node for the job to execute.
9. /*SETUP — indicates volumes needed for executing a job. Unfortunately, these are processed at INPUT time, not when the job starts executing. (See "/*MESSAGE.")
10. /*SIGNOFF — ends a remote job stream to terminate an RJE session.
11. /*SIGNON — starts a remote job stream by initiating communication between JES and a remote processing station.
12. /*XEQ — routes the job to another NODE for executing.
13. /*XMIT — routes a job to another NODE for executing, but in addition JES2 will not process or check the data following this card, only transmit it.

Remote NODEs may be in the same machine room or miles away. If the job has been "routed" (via control card) to another node, then the JCL is bundled up and sent to that node.

If a job is shown as in "awaiting converter-interpreter" status, then the node (or system in the node) is not active.

10.2.4. Execution Processing

JES2 keeps track of each job by building a **Job Queue Element** (JQE) to represent the job. The JQE has the job name, the job number, the job class, the Priority, Input and Output routing, and pointers to other control blocks.

A job may have 1 of 38 possible job classes. A–Z are the first 26 possibilities, 0–9 are 10 more, and "Started Task" and "logon" are the 37th and 38th.

On the execution queue, a job is selected by these criteria:

1. Is there an initiator available with this job class? If an initiator has more than one job class assigned, then jobs are selected in order by job class. For example, if initiator 10 has job class "AB" assigned, class "B" jobs will be selected only if there are no class "A" jobs.

2. Is the priority of the job the highest priority in the queue for this job class?

As the job executes, the Job Entry Subsystem performs simulated Input/Output operations for SYSIN and SYSOUT data sets. At the completion of the job, JES places the job on the next queue — output processing.

10.2.5. Output Processing

As a job produces output, **Job Output Elements** (JOEs) are built. Each unique output data set with different characteristics is represented by a JOE. JOEs are kept in a table called the **Job Output Table** (JOT)

Output data sets are written to print and punch files in the JES2 SPOOL. They can be routed to local and/or remote locations. *Only after all spooled data sets are processed can the job proceed to the purge queue.*

This sometimes causes confusion to the data center. In Figure 10.7, job A has four output data sets: LOG, JCL, messages, and a report. The report is a million lines of output. After the million line

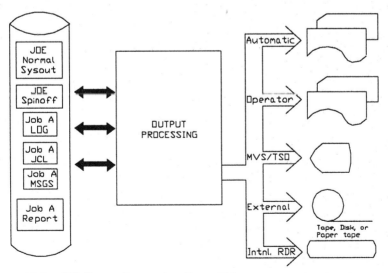

Figure 10.7   JES Output Processing Flow. JES2 processes SYSOUT data sets either when the job ends (normal) or when the data set is closed (spinoff).

report is printed, the LOG, JCL, and messages are still waiting to be printed. *None of the spool space is released* until all output, including the million print lines, is completely processed. To recapture all the spool space, the data center must print or dispose of all parts of the job.

External Writers run in their own address spaces and communicate through the Subsystem Interface to get lines from the spool to "print" on their own. External Writers may "print" the data set to tapes, mass storage media, or other virtual printer. One excellent use of external writers is to archive production JCL and output. It normally is not needed, but if there are problems with the production run, the application or user department may want to see the run's JCL and messages.

Functional Subsystems run like external writers. The Print Services Facility (PSF) program product is an example. The computer operator interfaces with a printer attached to PSF just like any other JES writer. The only difference is that the operator must issue the set MODE=FSS command to the printer. If the operator watches carefully, a started system task is created to operate the printer.

The PSF printer subtask uses a Functional Subsystem Interface (FSI) to get lines and pages to print on its printer. The reader is cautioned that when the printer is stopped and the address space is terminated, it removes one of the available address spaces from the number MVS allows. Said another way, if you allocated 300 address spaces for MVS and started and stopped PSF 290 times (leaving 10 for MVS and associated address spaces), then you could not start any more TSO sessions, initiators, etc.

10.2.6. Print/Punch Processing

Print/Punch processors select JOEs from the JOT by priority within class, set printers up, if necessary, and print the output. JES2 allows the data center to specify device characteristics for output devices. The Print/Punch processors write spooled I/O to real printers and remote facilities. Special forms and multiple copies may be specified.

The selection of printer output is a complex topic beyond the scope of this book. See your JES manual for the parameters which control special forms and other criteria.

10.2.7. Purge Processing

After all processing required for this job is complete, the direct access space on the JES2 spool is released and the job number becomes available for a new job. JES2 will not actually reuse the job number until it has wrapped around the maximum number of jobs. The default is 9,999 jobs.

In IBM JES environments, after PURGE takes place, there is no trace of the job. In some non-IBM environments, the PURGE process only places the job's resources on an available queue. If the area has not been used, the data center and its users can "retrieve" PURGED, but not overlaid, job information. I wonder why IBM has never adopted this philosophy.

10.3. JOB ENTRY SUBSYSTEM 3 (JES3)

In a JES3 environment, one of the Processor Complexes is "different." Every JES3 node has one and only one **Global** processor. The other processors are called **Local** processors. Figure 10.8 shows one global and two local processors. The Global manages the entire node. There must be a Channel-to-Channel (CTC) connection be-

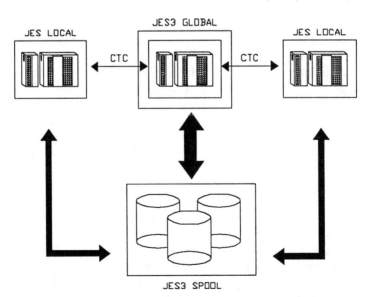

Figure 10.8 Basic JES3 configuration. The JES3 GLOBAL Processor Complex passes work to the JES3 LOCAL Processor Complexes.

tween the Processor Complexes. The JES3 subsystems communicate using the CTC.[2] Every JES3 (as in JES2) system must have a channel path to all the SPOOL volumes.

In a JES3 environment, all SYSIN and SYSOUT devices, as well as all remote telecommunication lines, are connected to the Global processor. Everything is run by the Global. JES3, on the Global, performs all input, conversion, interpretation, allocation setup, output, and purge for every job in the complex.

When an initiator on one of the locals needs to look for work, it does not go directly to the spool volumes but sends a message across the CTC. If work is available, the Global sends back a message identifying the job and where it can be found on the spool.

10.3.1. JES3 Initialization

JES3 initialization is similar to JES2. Options are specified, through parameters, in the JES3 initialization deck. The "deck" (historical term) is a data set on DASD. Figure 10.9 shows the process of initialization. Routines are loaded, if needed, into virtual storage. JES3 reads the initialization parameters and prepares devices, spool volumes, virtual storage tables, and consoles.

10.3.2. Input Processing

Figure 10.10 shows the JES3 job flow. Jobs are read from local or remote devices and TSO users. The Global places the jobs on the spool. Input processing supports TSO submit and readers of all types. There are two phases:

1. Input processing separates jobs, data included with the job, and control statement.

---

2. A Channel-to-Channel Adapter is a special connection inside a Processor Complex that connects directly to another Processor Complex. IBM also has a 3088 which emulates CTC connections. JES3 is one of the few pieces of IBM software that use CTCAs.

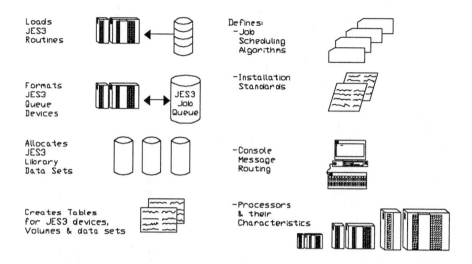

Figure 10.9   JES3 initialization. JES3 loads programs that are not already in virtual storage, initializes queues and data sets, reads and sets up installation standards.

2. Control statement processing builds JES3 control blocks which will be used throughout the job. Defaults are applied for missing parameters.

10.3.3. Interpreter Service

The Interpreter — like in JES2 — converts JCL statements into control blocks on the spool. These control blocks are what MVS will need to start and run the batch job. Cataloged Procedures are interpreted and merged into the JCL by substituting text in the statements. This process is called symbolic substitution — symbols in the JCL or cataloged procedures are used to create final JCL specification. Like JES2, JCL syntax errors are detected and the job is directed to OUTPUT if there are errors.

The following are JES3 control statements:

1. //**command enters JES3 operator commands from the SYSIN data set.
2. //*DATASET begins an input data set in the input stream.
3. //*ENDDATASET terminates an instream data set.

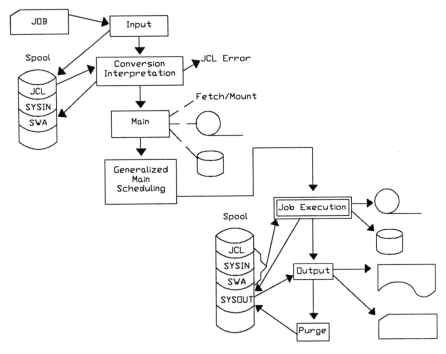

Figure 10.10   JES3 job flow. The JES3 input processor reads jobs onto the Spool. The Conversion/Interpretation routines translate the job into control blocks to be executed. Job execution reads SYSIN and writes SYSOUT to the spool. When all execution is done, and SYSOUT has been completely processed, PURGE processing erases all traces of the job from the spool.

4. //*ENDPROCESS ends a nonstandard job.
5. //*FORMAT gives instructions to JES3 for SYSOUT processing.
6. //*MAIN defines processing parameters for this job.
7. //*NET passes to JES3 relationships between predecessor and successor jobs.
8. //*NETACCT specifies the account number for network jobs.
9. //*OPERATOR sends messages to the MVS console operator.
10. //**PAUSE stops the input reader.
11. //*PROCESS starts a nonstandard job.
12. //*ROUTE specifies the execution node for a job.
13. /*SIGNOFF terminates a remote job stream session.
14. /*SIGNON begins a remote job session from a remote RJE terminal.

10.3.4. Main Service

Main service is a part of job scheduling which facilitates job initiation.

Main Device Scheduling (MDS) One major difference between JES2 and JES3 is that JES3 takes over the device allocation functions from MVS, whereas JES2 leaves device allocation to MVS modules. JES3 not only allocates devices to jobs *before* the job starts, but *premounts volumes* so the job does not have to wait to start. MVS control blocks are set up to let MVS go through allocation routines, but MVS "finds" all the volumes already mounted and allocates the devices to the job. The reason JES3 performs this preallocation is:

1. MVS allocates for each step. The MVS reasoning is that if step 1 needed three tape drives and steps 2 through 10 only need one, then the three tape drives should be freed for others to use. JES3 goals say a batch job should never wait for allocation. JES3 will hold the minimum or maximum number of devices needed for any one step of the job for the duration of the job, depending on parameters set by the installation.
2. Minimize wall clock time of a job. If all the allocation is done before the job starts, then the job will not be delayed at all for operator intervention to vary devices online, mount volumes, etc.
3. MVS does not know which resources are shared with other copies of MVS. If there are 16 tape drives in a facility, and Processor Complex TSO1 has 14 tape drives allocated, Processor Complex BATCH still "thinks" it has the full 16 available.
4. Maximize use of I/O devices. Jobs are selected and routed to Processor Complexes that have the resources, so the data center never gets device allocation waits or "waiting for volume" messages.

Generalized Main Scheduling (GMS) GMS controls the workload on a Processor Complex and maximizes system throughput. The following are considerations that JES3 can be instructed to use in determining scheduling, monitoring, and controlling jobs:

1. Job priority.
2. Group interaction of jobs.

3. Explicit and implicit specification of Processor Complex.
4. Job class mix.
5. I/O rate mix.
6. Initiator availability.
7. Sequence of jobs within a group.

What is the purpose of the JES3 setup? What problems does it solve? JES3 is really ASP grown up to MVS (just as JES2 was HASP grown up to run on MVS). The two serious problems in those old systems were Central Storage and MVT itself. If a job waited in MVS, it used not only the devices allocated, but all the Central Storage that the job would need for the life of the job. In MVS, the job gets swapped out and only uses minimal Central Storage.

The second problem with MVT was that if a job waited, MVT had many resources ENQUEed. Other tasks were delayed. With MVS, there are many improvements to the scheduler. These problems are not as important today.

Main Servicing Main Servicing executes on the Global or Local to process the job as it is running. SYSIN is read from the spool, SYSOUT is written on the spool. Write to Operator (WTO) and Write to Operator with Reply (WTOR) messages are routed back to the Global to be placed on the system consoles and on the spool for later printing with the job.

10.3.5. Output Service

Output service is similar to JES2 — it processes SYSOUT data sets. Figure 10.11 shows the logical view of Output processing. Output can be routed locally, to remote facilities, or to TSO sessions. There are two phases: Scheduling is performed based on the characteristics of the SYSOUT data set, and writing is controlled by several types of processes:

1. Hot writers are started by the operator and wait for certain types of work — Class A, for example.
2. Dynamic writers are started by JES3 when it needs to print a certain type of output. Many data centers do not like to use dynamic writers, because they "seize" printers and call for spe-

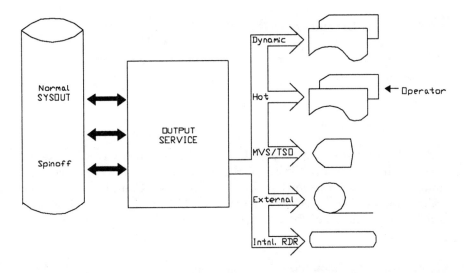

Figure 10.11   JES3 output service. JES can route output to local or remote printers or display the output for TSO sessions.

cial forms or other setups based on demand — not on the data center's wishes.

10.3.6. Purge

When all processing and external writing has been completed, JES3 can "Purge" the job. During Purge, all areas allocated on the spool volumes to hold input or output messages, JCL, and control information are returned to the "available" queue.

10.4. JES2 AND JES3 COMPARISON

JES2 uses non-Centralized Processor Complex management techniques where information about the workload mix is shared on common DASD volumes. JES3 uses centralized Processor Complex management techniques where one Processor Complex is the king of the hill, and the other copies of JES3 are "slaves." This section will compare the two subsystems on a functional basis.

10.4.1. Task Creation and Control

"Tasks" to JES are the services that the subsystem provides for the benefit of the jobs in the system.

10.4.2. Input/Output

JES2 does SYSIN and SYSOUT processing in each Processor Complex in the node. JES3 limits SYSIN and SYSOUT for every job that enters the complex from the GLOBAL Processor Complex. JES3 does allow the LOCAL to support 3800 and 3820 printer tasks but only under the direction of the GLOBAL.

10.4.3. Device Allocation

All JES2 device allocation is controlled by the MVS routines. JES3 is designed to manage a node as a single entity. The Global JES3 Processor Complex controls all allocation and "fools" MVS into following the JES3 "recommendations."

10.4.4. Job Processing

JES2 initiators interrogate and select work from the spools from every Processor Complex in the node. JES2 uses the hardware functions of RESERVE and RELEASE to share DASDs to allow all Processor Complexes in the node to read and write from the same checkpoint data set. Only JES3 GLOBALS can "start" jobs. JES3 also has features called **Dependent Job Control** and **Deadline Scheduling**.

Dependent job control allows the user to specify, through JES3 control cards, a "tree" of jobs. For example, if jobs A1, B1, and C1 are submitted, job A1 could specify "run job B1 if job A1 completes successfully" and "run job C1 if job A1 does not complete successfully."

Deadline Scheduling allows a user to specify a time by which they would like the job to finish. JES3 and installation specifications try to ensure that the job will be started in time to finish "on time."

10.4.5. Console Services

Each MVS system must have at least one console — to IPL and communicate with the operator. In a JES2 controlled environment, all consoles are MVS consoles. JES2 uses MVS console services to communicate with the operator. In a JES3 environment, most consoles are controlled from the GLOBAL Processor Complex.

JES2 has the ability to submit commands to the system based on time of day.

10.4.6. Spool Management

JES2 accesses the primary checkpoint volume using Shared DASD techniques — read with "share," write with "exclusive." The JES2 checkpoint access techniques using CCWs are one of the most sophisticated in the industry. JES3 spools are controlled by the GLOBAL Processor Complex and the contention and sharing of spool volumes is not a major consideration.

10.4.7. Protection Philosophy: RAS

If one JES2 Processor Complex fails, the work continues in the other Processor Complexes. If one JES3 LOCAL fails, the work continues in the other Processor Complexes. If the JES3 GLOBAL Processor Complex fails, the GLOBAL must be switched to a LOCAL Processor Complex.

10.5. NETWORKING

Both JES2 and JES3 support **Network Job Entry** (NJE). NJE is the feature of JES that connects one node (group of Processor Complexes connected by JES) to another node and transmit batch jobs, operator commands, messages, SYSOUT data, and accounting information between the nodes. Why is this necessary? If your company has several data centers, the company may need to transmit data from one location to another.

Perhaps the payroll is processed in one location and the checks are printed at all locations. You would need to send the check print file to the other location or node.

Perhaps the company wants a company-wide capacity and performance evaluation. One large manufacturing company I worked for had four data centers. One data center was very much overloaded and could not get the work finished. The other three had excess capacity. By shifting batch work load from one center to the other, all work was processed in a timely manner for $1,000,000 less per year in expenses. This solution could not have been accomplished without centralized monitoring and NJE.

Communications between the nodes is accomplished over Channel-to-Channel adapters at the same physical location or over phone lines using Binary Synchronous Communication (BSC) or Synchronous Data Link Control (SDLC).

If a job is read by JES, the default node is the node that reads the job. The job can contain control cards to route the job, SYSOUT, or messages to another node. If the job is destined for another node, the userid and password information must be valid on the other node. All of the job received by the Input Processor is passed to the destination node.

JES2/NJE can "participate" — receive, process, and transmit jobs — with JES3 or even VM networks. Figure 10.12 shows one sample

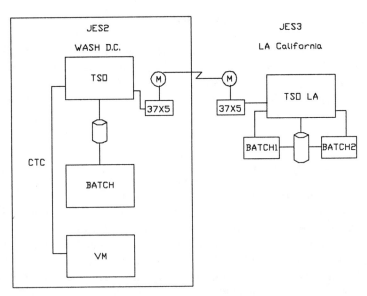

Figure 10.12   JES Network Job Entry. The example shows a JES2 node with two Processor Complexes (TSO and BATCH) communicating with a JES3 node in Los Angeles and a VM system running on a separate Processor Complex. A Channel-to-Channel (CTC) adapter connects the MVS and V systems.

configuration of networking. The data center has a JES2 node running shared spool on two Processor Complexes. At the same location, a Virtual Machine (VM) system is operating on a third Processor Complex. The company has another data center in Los Angeles. Batch jobs can be transmitted to California to be processed. Why? Maybe the three-hour differential can be used to run batch jobs at night. Maybe the California location has the databases for all states west of the Mississippi.

Both JES2 and JES3 support an older architecture of remote job processing. JES2 supports Remote Job Entry (RJE) and JES3 supports Remote Job Processing (RJP).

10.6. CONCLUSION — WHICH JES IS FOR YOU?

JES2 is a decentralized management of a data center complex. Most facilities choose JES2. If the system you are designing is a single Processor Complex, with mostly online processing, then JES2 is the choice.

JES3 is a centralized management of a data center complex and costs more. The entire complex is managed by a single copy of JES. JES3 will use more Central Storage. JES3 will use more CPU cycles. JES3 is the system of choice if most of the processing you will do is batch oriented, and the total amount of work requires multiple Processor Complexes.

Do not forget that people get the work done. If you have a staff and/or user group that is familiar with and understands one of the two systems, that should weigh heavily on your choice. There are exceptions to every rule. Some single Processor Complex data centers successfully run JES3 and some Multiple Processor Complex (six to eight) data centers successfully run JES2.

JES3 is a more complicated system for the data center personnel. Maybe the additional complexity results in more function for the data center users. One indication that JES3 is more complex is that JES3 seems to have more fixes (APARs) than JES2. While I have not seen published figures from IBM, I have heard estimates that 90 percent of MVS data centers use JES2 and 10 percent use JES3.

10.7. JES SUMMARY

Your Job Entry Subsystem controls the jobs that execute under MVS. JES operates in a separate address space and controls local and remote printers. Because it is the interface point for the data center user, JES conventions that have been set up by the data center must be known before you can run jobs at a data center.

JES also provides a number of services for the user. Job submission and printing are important. Internal reader functions are valuable in a production environment. Entire systems can be created which will start up new jobs on successful completion of a series of tasks.

JES2 is a multiple access spool system. Said another way, all copies of JES in all Processor Complexes have full access to the checkpoint data set and to all information stored on the spool volumes. JES3 is a master–slave spool system. One Processor Complex is king-of-the-hill and controls all other Processor Complexes.

Both versions of JES provide:

1. Input processing functions which read jobs, store instream data sets and set up data on the spool volumes.
2. Conversion processing which creates the MVS control blocks needed to run a batch job, TSO session, or started systems task and performs checking of the Job Control Language (JCL).
3. Execution processing which provides services to the data center to manage the execution of batch jobs.
4. Output processing executing jobs under MVS to spool SYSOUT data sets.
5. Print/Punch processing which manages the physical tasks of printing data sets on printer (and maybe punching cards!).
6. Purge processing which cleans up the JES spools.

In order to utilize JES output processing for programmers, operators, and systems programmers, something else is needed. Neither MVS nor JES supplies a spool display system. There are a number of fine spool display packages. IBM provides the **System Display and Search Facility** (SDSF) (5798-DWX). OEM vendors such as Fischer International Systems Corporation — **Input/Output Facility** (IOF). — provide a similar function. There even is a "free" one (QUEUE) available from SHARE Inc., Chicago, IL.

11

Access Methods and Data Set Management

11.1. TYPES OF ACCESS METHODS

Access methods are the MVS programs or routines that get control when a program issues an OPEN, CLOSE, GET, PUT, READ, or WRITE macro or high level statement. Access methods give MVS programmers and analysts a very flexible environment to develop systems.

11.1.1. Sequential Access Method (SAM)

SAM files have records placed in a physical rather than logical order. Sequential files are created one record after the other. Magnetic tape, cards, and printed output are sequential files. Direct-access devices may contain sequential files. Sequential files are usually written and read, one after the other.

MVS defines five types of record formats. Figure 11.1 shows the different types. Remember from the chapter on DASD that "records" have count, key, and data organization. We are showing here only the part of the physical recording media that is of interest to the data center user or programmer/analyst.

Fixed Unblocked   In a fixed unblocked file, all records are the same length (hence "fixed"). Each physical block contains one logical record. The physical and logical sizes are the same.

Fixed Blocked   In a fixed blocked file, each physical block contains an **integral number** of logical records. All logical records must be the same size. If you divide the physical block size by the number of records, you get an integer (whole number, no fractions).
Two reasons exist for blocking tape or DASD files:

1. Maximize the efficiency of the storage media. Efficiently blocked files have fewer gaps. Fewer gaps mean more of the magnetic medium is used for data.
2. Speed up data transfer. MVS and the access methods expend resources (CPU, Central Storage, and channel time) to read a block. If these resources can bring in twice as much data, the resources required hardly increase.

Variable, Unblocked   In a variable, unblocked file, every logical record in the file can be a different length. Because of this, there is a four-byte **record length** (RL) in front of each logical record. Each physical block also has a four-byte **block length** (BL) as its first four bytes. In Figure 11.1, the sample has a logical record size of 100. The RL is x'64', or decimal 100. The BL is x'68,' or decimal 104. Because

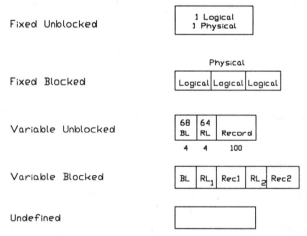

Figure 11.1   Sequential files. Sequential files are written block by block from the start of the file to the end of the file. The logical records may be blocked (more than one logical record per physical record) or unblocked (one logical record to one physical record).

it requires eight bytes of "lengths" for each variable record, this format is not recommended: Variable blocked is more efficient.

Variable Blocked   In a variable blocked file, each physical record contains more than one logical variable record. The example has two logical records in the physical record. There are two record lengths, but the block length is "shared" by the two logical records.

Undefined   Undefined records are of any length. The length is determined by the programs that read and write the records. With advanced assembler language using execute channel program, the program can read a block and determine how many bytes were read after the block is read into storage.

11.1.2.   Indexed Sequential Access Method (ISAM)

ISAM records can be read or written in sequence according to a key that is part of the record. ISAM files must be on direct access devices, although copies of the files may be unloaded (sequentially) onto magnetic tape. An index or set of indices maintained by MVS gives the location of each record. The user can go directly to a single record or sequentially process the file.

There are three types of areas in an ISAM file:

1.   Indices. The cylinder index is the highest level of index and is always present. Records in the cylinder index point to track indexes. There is only one cylinder index for the file. Optionally, one to three **master indices** can be created if the cylinder index is too large (over four tracks).

   Figure 11.2 shows the contents of a cylinder index and the reason why ISAM is such a problem to a data center. The index has a pointer to the highest key and the absolute track address of the track on which the key exists. If the data center or user wishes to move this data set, it must use ISAM access methods, not dump/restore techniques, *because the contents of the record* describe the physical address of the data. In order for a dump/restore or archive program to back up and restore this data set, the *data set must be restored to exactly where it was dumped from.* These restrictions are almost impossible to meet in an active data center.

2.   Prime data area. The prime area holds records. The prime area must be formatted with hardware keys.

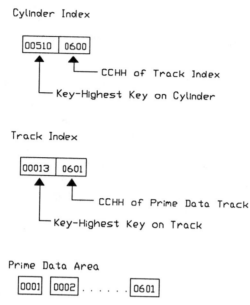

Figure 11.2   Indexed Sequential Organization. An ISAM file consists of a cylinder index, a track index, Prime Data Area, and an Optional Overflow Area.

3. Overflow area. The two types of overflow areas are cylinder and independent overflow areas. Records are written to these overflow areas as additions are made to the file. Cylinder overflow areas are tracks within the cylinder. It is best for performance if the extra added records can be written to the cylinder overflow, because the access method does not have to move the DASD read/write head to get to the independent overflow area.

The independent overflow area is at the end of the prime area. There is no index into the overflow area. These records are read sequentially until the proper record is found. As records are added to the independent area, the read/write heads move over ever-increasing distances, and the channel path gets more congested.

I do not recommend building any new files using ISAM under MVS because there are major performance problems with ISAM. I recommend that the data center disable ISAM (remove the access method modules from MVS) to prevent its use unless there are production ISAM files. In that case, I recommend VSAM emulation of ISAM.

11.1.3. Basic Direct-Access Method

Basic Direct-Access is provided by MVS to minimize the time required to locate records in a file. MVS does not provide automatic buffering and overlap of Input or Output scheduling for BDAM files. When the program "reads," MVS goes and gets the record requested.

The major problem here is that part about not buffering. Physical blocks are read and written. If the application needs to have several logical blocks in a physical block, the program must keep track of where in the block it is looking at logical records.

The BDAM organization implies that each record has a definite, computable relationship to the key or contents of a record. If the program needs to find record "Johnson," the program must be able to convert "Johnson" to something that can be used to access a record on a DASD track. There are several types of references:

1. **Relative Track Address**. The user presents to the system a three byte binary number — TTR — where:
   a. **TT** is the position of the track relative to the first track in the data set. The first track is TT=0, the second track is TT=1, and so forth.
   b. **R** is the number of the physical block relative to the first physical block on the track. The first block is "1." (Why wasn't it zero?!)
2. **Relative Track and Key**. The user presents a two byte relative track number and a key that the system uses to search the track for the record which has the specified key. This key is the external one, not the one inside the record.
3. **Relative block address**. Here the program presents the system with a three byte relative block number. The first block has a relative address of zero.
4. **Actual address — MBBCCHHR**. Here the user presents the system with the eight-byte "actual" address of the record that is needed. The CCHHR is cylinder, head, and record that we learned from the chapter on DASD. The **M** is the extent number (from 1 to 16) within the data set. The **BB** is actually from a very old DASD — the data cell. The data cell had 10 "bins," and the channel architecture was changed to allow a two-byte hexadecimal value for the bin specification. I know — two bytes can contain up to 64-Kb "bins." One byte could contain up to 16 "bins," but this was way back in the 1960s. Now the reader sees what I mean about IBM carrying baggage forward forever!

A **Directly Addressed File** exists when every possible key in the file converts to a unique address. It is possible to locate any record in the file directly. The records must be fixed length, and the keys must be numeric. In the example in Figure 11.3, a key of "3" would be the third block in the file.

An **Indirectly Addressed File** exists when the one-for-one layout would waste too much space. In Figure 11.3, the keys go from 0001 to 0002 to 0003 and then jump to 0500. If some mapping method were not devised, 497 records would be "wasted." Indirect access is used with keys that are alphanumeric. There are many conversion techniques available for converting the key to a relative address to be used to access the file. These techniques are complex and must be included in every program that reads or writes records to this file.

One of the major drawbacks of BDAM records is that they are probably *unmovable*. They may not be relocated from place to place on a single direct access volume or from one volume type to another. The reason is that the method of looking into the file may contain "absolute" addresses. BDAM files are the nemesis of a data center trying to upgrade direct access devices.

11.1.4.   Partitioned Access Method

PAM files have the records grouped into independent segments called members. Each member has a name, and the name may be up to eight characters, the first of which must be alphabetic. In Figure

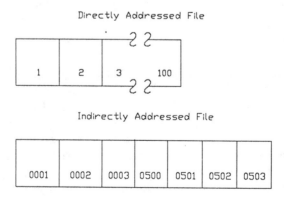

Figure 11.3   Basic Direct-Access Method. BDAM is an access method that minimizes the services provided by MVS while expending minimal resources to do I/O to a file.

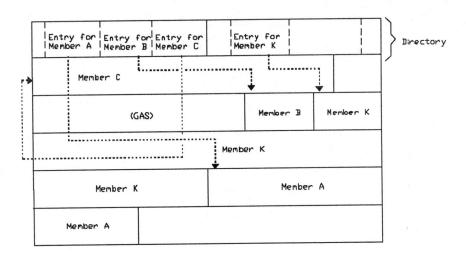

Figure 11.4   Partitioned Access Method. A partitioned data set is really two data sets in one. The first one is the directory, which points into the second one, which contains the members. The clear space is "gas," or space between members that have been deleted or replaced.

11.4, the first section of this data set is called a "directory." A partitioned data set is actually two data sets in one. The first — directory — consists of 256 byte fixed length records which contain information about each member or possible member. The directory always has 256-byte physical records regardless of the record format of the PDS itself.

The member names are sorted in ascending alphabetical order in the directory. The size of the directory is fixed at the time of allocation and cannot be changed unless the file is copied to another file with a different sized directory.[1]

Figure 11.5 shows the skeleton of a directory entry. The directory contains the name of the member, a relative location (so the data set can be moved) of the first block of the member, and optional data. ISPF keeps statistics on a member in the optional area of the directory entry.

---

1. Several OEM utilities can change the size of a PDS directory. One "free" utility is available from SHARE Incorporated, Chicago, Illinois. The PDSAA utility on the SHARE "CBT" tape will expand the PDS directory.

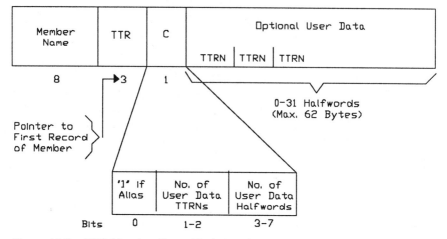

Figure 11.5   PDS Member Entry. Each member entry in a PDS directory contains at least the member name and a TTR pointer to the first record of the member. Optional data areas are used by the linkage editor and SPF for statistics and information about the member.

The second part of the data set is for the members, that is, the data itself. As one member is updated, it is copied forward (to the end of the data set) and the space for the old member is unused. This causes "gas" in partitioned data sets. As any high school physics student knows, gas can be turned into a solid by compressing it. The process of using IEBCOPY to "compress" a PDS in place removes the extra space in the member area of the data set.

11.1.5. Virtual Storage Access Method

Virtual Storage Access Method (VSAM) supports both sequential and direct processing. It was designed to replace ISAM. VSAM is a component of MVS (and DOS/VSE). In Virtual Machine (VM), the CMS/VSAM support is based on DOS/VSE.

VSAM Design Objectives   The VSAM organization was originally presented to replace all data set organizations. This did not occur. VSAM accounts for a large part of the data sets created, but sequential and partitioned data sets remain as popular as ever.

VSAM is designed to let programmers and analysts concentrate on the logical view of data as in Figure 11.6. The design objectives of VSAM are:

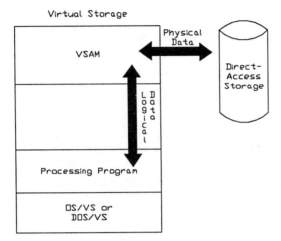

Figure 11.6   VSAM. VSAM is an access method designed to be positioned between the program and the hardware. VSAM should relieve the programmer from physical data storage concerns.

1. Operating system independence. The data should be portable from DOS/VSE to MVS/370 to MVS/XA to MVS/ESA.
2. Device independence. The access method should allow the data sets to be moved from device to device, yet exploit the random nature of DASD.
3. Data integrity. The access method should be insensitive to unscheduled operating system outages.
4. Data security. Changes to user files and catalogs should only be performed by "authorized" users and data should not be "lost."
5. File performance. Insertion activity should not slow down as more inserts are done (ISAM problem).

VSAM Features   How well did VSAM live up to its objectives?

Data portability: VSAM can be moved from one operating system to another, but in practice few data centers move data among DOS/VS, MVS/370, MVS/XA, and MVS/ESA Processor Complexes.

Device independence: VSAM is independent of track sizes. VSAM stores records of all types of data in a fixed length area of DASD called a **control interval** (CI). By having fixed physical blocks, the units of transfer are quickly copied to almost any DASD volume. In Figure 11.7, the top sample has track 1 contain four physical records

Physical
Records

Control Interval				Control Interval				Control Interval			
Track 1				Track 2				Track 3			

Control Interval				Control Interval				Control Interval			
Track 1			Track 2			Track 3			Track 4		

Figure 11.7   VSAM Control Intervals. VSAM Control Intervals are fixed-length areas that are written to DASD. Note that the top view has four blocks per track and four blocks per CI. (One CI = one track.) In the bottom view there are three blocks per track but four blocks per CI. One CI does not equal one track.

on each track. A track is also a control interval. The bottom sample has a control interval spanning tracks.

Data integrity: How well does VSAM protect data integrity? VSAM has a low vulnerability during record insertion. The potential remains to lose records, but the probability is lower than ISAM. Data sharing is limited. The user must understand VSAM data sharing in order to share a file among many users. VSAM implements **Software End-of-File**, which defines where the "add" process was and makes it possible to recover the file if the system or program "crashes" or abends.

Security/change control: How well does VSAM rate in security and change control? VSAM provides centralized control over:

1. File creation
2. File access
3. File deletion
4. Space occupied by files

VSAM provides a multilevel password facility, but it is not recommended that you use VSAM passwords. Use a comprehensive security product such as RACF.

VSAM provides an excellent audit trail of actions taken on data sets. VSAM writes records to the System Management Facility

(SMF) each time an address space creates, deletes, or changes a VSAM data set. SMF type 60-68 records are created by VSAM. Types 60-63 are for audit purposes. Type 64 is for each open.

Consistent performance: How well does VSAM give consistent performance to overcome the problems with ISAM insertions? VSAM has several free space options which can reduce record insertion delays.

VSAM performs an "amoeba-split," which allows insertion of records yet avoids a disorderly file when free space is exhausted. The term "amoeba" is used to describe the split of a CI like the small single cell animal — the amoeba. Look at Figure 11.8. Record 58 is to be inserted into the CI, but the CI has no room. The CI is split, and record 58 is inserted in the file. The records are in sequence within a CI, but CIs are out of sequence. The index in the keyed sequential data set (KSDS) keeps them in order.

IDCAMS — VSAM utility program: IDC Access Method Services (IDCAMS) is the IBM utility to manage VSAM data sets. It is also called "Access Method Services." The major functions of IDCAMS are:

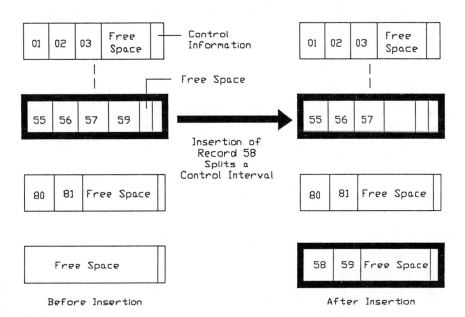

Figure 11.8 VSAM Insertion — CI Split. In this example, record 58 is to be inserted into a "full" control interval.

1. Create "objects" which are:
   a. System catalogs to keep track of:
       i.   User files.
       ii. MVS page spaces and swap data sets.
   b. User files.
2. Move data from one device to another:
   a. For file load and unload.
   b. For file backup and recovery.
   c. For catalog backup and recovery.
   d. For file copy.
3. Miscellaneous functions:
   a. List file characteristics.
   b. List file contents.
   c. Delete file/catalog.
   d. Alter file characteristics.
4. Assign and remove security for:
   a. Catalogs.
   b. User files.

Uses for VSAM   VSAM is the choice for most data centers for high performance, random access applications. VSAM is ideal for CICS, IMS, and batch databases, but VSAM is also used by IBM for a large part of the data that MVS creates and/or uses.

Critical MVS functions: VSAM is used for many MVS functions, and each release of MVS finds new uses for VSAM data sets. The critical MVS uses of VSAM are:

1. The master catalog. MVS cannot operate without the master catalog. It contains the pointers to the systems data sets and pointers to other catalogs which contain pointers to all the data center data sets.
2. Page and swap data sets. These are VSAM data sets but are a "special" type of VSAM. Special parameters tell IDCAMS to format the page and swap data sets so that the Auxiliary Storage Manager can use them for 4,096-byte page slots.
3. The SMF data set is a VSAM data set. SMF record sizes vary widely, so VSAM is an ideal data set method. Some SMF records are several hundred bytes. Some SMF records are thousands of bytes long.

File Support for Systems Programming Aids: VSAM is the IBM strategic direction for data set management. The following are a sample of the IBM products that use VSAM for their data:

1. Information/MVS — the IBM product that contains information on MVS such as announcements, questions and answers, APARs and PTFs, and technical discussions.
2. Information/Management — the IBM product that provides a data center with a tool to capture management information about a data center.
3. Information/Access — the IBM product that provides a data center with access to IBM databases for APARs and PTFs.
4. Network Problem Determination Application (NPDA) — the IBM product that provides information and a database for network management. NPDA is merged with NETVIEW.
5. Interactive Problem Control System (IPCS) — the part of MVS that allows the data center to manage problems and inspect MVS dumps.
6. System Modification Program Extended (SMP-E) — the part of MVS that manages modification to MVS.

File Support for High-Performance Applications: VSAM is also used for system files for the major IBM data base and file managers such as IMS/DL1, CICS, and DB2.

VSAM Performance Comparisons VSAM is a complex topic. This section introduces the reader to concepts required to understand VSAM performance considerations.[2]

Background: Figure 11.9 shows the types of VSAM data sets and the "regular" MVS data sets that the VSAM data set emulates.

VSAM ESDS vs. Sequential: ESDS files do not have a prime index associated with them. When a record is added, VSAM returns a "relative byte address" (RBA). The programmer analyst must keep track of the RBA if direct addressing is needed to a ESDS file.

You can use direct addressing with ESDS by preformatting the data set with null or blank records, then you could determine the location where a record should be read from or written to within the file. The record's key must be converted to/from an RBA.

In Figure 11.10, a file is loaded with records whose contents seem to be out of order. The order may have some other meaning such as the date and time they were received.

---

2. A complete discussion is included in VSAM Performance, Design, and Fine Tuning by Jan Ranade. ISBN 0-02-948631-9.

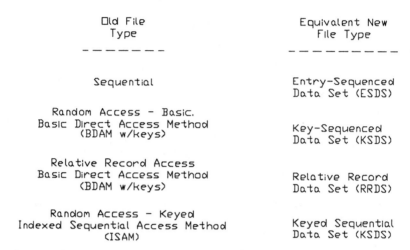

Old File Type	Equivalent New File Type
Sequential	Entry-Sequenced Data Set (ESDS)
Random Access - Basic. Basic Direct Access Method (BDAM w/keys)	Key-Sequenced Data Set (KSDS)
Relative Record Access Basic Direct Access Method (BDAM w/keys)	Relative Record Data Set (RRDS)
Random Access - Keyed Indexed Sequential Access Method (ISAM)	Keyed Sequential Data Set (KSDS)

Figure 11.9   Comparison of VSAM functions. VSAM functions are similar to "regular" access method functions. The only function not replicated is partitioned.

You should not use ESDS just to replace sequential processing. Traditional SAM is generally faster, has the possiblity of loading more data on a track of DASD, and is easier to use. So why use ESDS? One reason is that an ESDS file can have an alternate index. An alternate index is a secondary index into the data. In our example, the alternate index could keep the A1-A19 records in sort order, while the ESDS file could keep the order of when the records were received.

VSAM RRDS vs. BDAM Relative Record: A Relative Record Data Set has no index. The file contains a string of fixed length slots. Each record is written and read based on the record number. In Figure 11.11, record 3 is in the third slot. Each Control Interval contains a fixed number of slots, so VSAM only has to calculate the CI number and can then find the record.

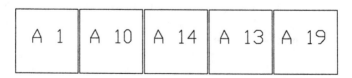

Figure 11.10   VSAM ESDS. ESDS files are created one record at a time, and each record is placed at the logical end of the file. In this example, the first record has a value of "A1." The second is "A10." The third one received is "A14." The fourth one is "A13."

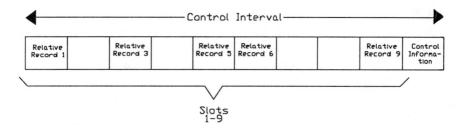

Figure 11.11   VSAM Relative Record Data Set. An RRDS has reserved spaces for each record.

VSAM KSDS vs. ISAM: A Keyed Sequential Data Set (KSDS) is always defined with an index. Figure 11.12 shows the logical view of a KSDS file. The index consists of an index set, which may contain more than one level. Index records contain information about the next lower level. The lowest level of the index is called the **Sequence Set**. The sequence set contains pointers to several control intervals. The sum of the Control Intervals pointed to by a single sequence set is called a **Control Area**.

VSAM uses **vertical pointers** from the highest level to the Sequence Set to get the address of a Control Interval for the VSAM record. VSAM uses **horizontal pointers** in a sequence set when it is reading sequentially and needs the next key in a collating sequence.

Understanding the relationship of VSAM indices and Sequence Sets is vital to understanding VSAM performance. VSAM "reads" the highest level ("A" in Figure 11.12), then "reads" the next level — a Sequence Set ("B" in Figure 11.12).

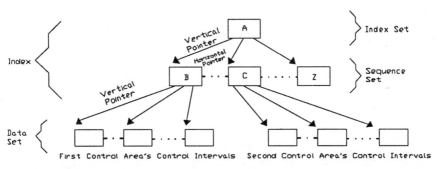

Figure 11.12   VSAM Keyed Sequential Data Set (KSDS). A KSDS has one or more levels of index that point to the data in Control Intervals. A program can access the data either sequentially or directly.

If there were two record buffers for VSAM to read the index, then "A" could be read, "B" could be read, and a read of "C" would have to overlay or bump out one of the two. If, in the example, there were 26 VSAM index buffers, then the entire index could be read into virtual storage, and it would not need to be read in again!

As with anything, there is more involved than this — buffer refresh is an example — but the reader can see that more VSAM index buffers have got to help performance.

VSAM performance compared to ISAM should be:

1. Better by about 4:1 for record inserts.
2. Better by about 2:1 for random direct-access reads.
3. About the same for sequential reads.
4. About the same, maybe a little slower than ISAM, for file loading.

Alternate Indexes (AIX) An Alternate Index (AIX) performs the same function as a prime index of a data set. The data set itself is referred to as a **base cluster**. The base can be a KSDS or an ESDS. The AIX is similar to a cluster. It contains an index component and a data component. The index is identical in format to any other KSDS. The data component contains pointers to the base cluster.

In Figure 11.13, the base cluster has two alternate indexes. The first alternate is ordered by the owner's name. Path 1 is the com-

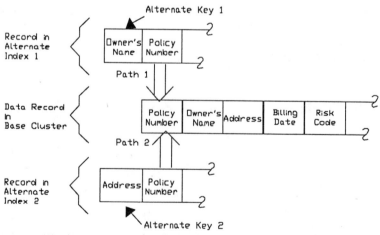

Figure 11.13 VSAM Alternate Indices. The base cluster of this file (possibly a file of customers of an insurance company) can be accessed by the policy number (base), the owner's name (Alternate Index 1), or the owner's address (Alternate Index 2).

Operation	− − −Device Type− − −		
	3350	3380S	3380E
Sequential:			
Read 6K	26	15	18
Write 6K	33	23	26
BDAM Random:			
Read 6K	41	20	23
Read 3K	38	19	22
VSAM Read:			
Default	138	76	86
Optimized	44	22	24
ISAM Read:			
Default	137	105	114
Optimized	68	52	59

Figure 11.14   VSAM Data Set Performance. The relative performance of the different types of DASD as compared to the different access methods is shown. The numbers are given in milliseconds. The 3380S (AA4) is the 3380 with Dynamic Path Selection (which runs under MVS/XA and MVS/ESA only). The 3380E is either the Extended (AD4) or Enhanced (AJ4) model. These are only approximate numbers, and the values will vary from data center to data center.

bination of alternate 1 and the base cluster. The second alternate is ordered by the owner's address. Path 2 is the combination of alternate 2 and the base cluster.

Device Type Considerations   VSAM is designed for and performs best with the IBM 3380 class of devices. There are several benchmark studies available. One is the IBM publication, *DASD Access Method Performance Considerations (GG22-9241).*

Readers are advised to do their own benchmarks. What really counts for your data center is that the device performs for your work load. I recommend that you take your programs, your data, and try them on different device types. You may be surprised at the results.

Figure 11.14 shows what you may expect from the various devices using various access methods. It is not unusual that the 3380 is faster than the 3350, because the data transfer speed of the 3380 is twice as fast as the 3350. What may seem a little strange is that the 3380 Standard (e.g., 3380 AA4) is slightly faster than the 3380 Extended (e.g., 3380 AD4) or the 3380 Enhanced (e.g., 3380 AJ4). The reason is that the "E" models have microcode that does extra work to determine paths to use. The "E" models will probably respond better in an active system, but if they are the only device on a path, they should respond slightly slower.

The larger track and larger size of the 3380 make it an ideal DASD to place data base data sets.

Note that if VSAM or ISAM file access is optimized on a 3350 and not optimized on a 3380, then the older 3350 device gives better I/O service time than the 3380 device with VSAM defaults!

VSAM Warnings   There are several major situations with VSAM that should be watched by the builder of VSAM data sets. The first one is a wasteful "bother." The second one is a major data center disaster.

VSAM Optimizes DASD Space: The VSAM defaults are designed to optimize the space taken on Direct Access Storage Devices (DASD). The reader is cautioned to watch all defaults carefully. This admonition applies to all "computer defaults." Remember what "average" is! (The worst of the best and the best of the worst.) VSAM applies defaults to create CI sizes based on the size of the minimum and maximum record and other criteria. You should never let VSAM specify CI sizes for either the index or the data component.

Maximum VSAM Data Set: The maximum VSAM object is dictated by the size of the pointer used to keep the maximum relative byte of the file — four bytes. The size is roughly what can be contained on eight 3380 single capacity actuators or 4.3 billion bytes. The penalty for exceeding this size is traumatic:

1. In MVS, the data set gets a "data set full" message; no more records can be added to the file.
2. In DOS/VSE, the data set wraps — the next record added overlays the first record of the file. The program gets one error similar to "data set full." The user usually just adds space to the file and restarts. Unfortunately newly added records overlay the first records in the file.[3]

---

3. It will probably be fixed by a program temporary fix (PTF) by the time you read this. It is only mentioned here to convince the reader that *every* error message has the potential for disaster.

The solution to this is to break the file into two or more parts. This requires that all programs which access the file look at multiple files based on the key value. The reprogramming effort could take months.[4]

You should watch the maximum size of your files — do not allow them to exceed VSAM maximums.

VSAM Publications Each version of MVS (the Data Facility Product, or DFP, is the component of MVS that contains VSAM) brings many new manuals for the software that builds and maintains VSAM data sets. The reader is cautioned to be sure that the manuals you are using for commands and messages *exactly match* the version of MVS that you are using. As with all IBM systems however, what worked before generally will work now. One "old" manual that you might find very useful is *VSAM Primer for the Integrated Catalog Facility in an MVS Environment* (GG24-1563). The manual was published in 1982, but it is full of practical examples of VSAM coding techniques. Just be careful to verify for yourself that the techniques are still valid.

Other books have been written on VSAM, and the reader is invited to obtain and read them.[5]

11.1.6. Data in Virtual (DIV)

Data-in-Virtual (DIV) is a programming facility introduced in MVS/XA Version 2 Release 2. DIV is a new method of storing and accessing data and is best suited for data which is processed as an array, table, or a list.

---

4. Thanks to Sue Courter, Kathy Calabrese and staff for demonstrating how to do it right. I taught this in a class and they reprogrammed just in time. We hit the limit, but it only took hours to install the new programs (they were tested and ready for production!). This is much different from a large state agency which lost one of its largest files for months! What if your largest file was out of service for months?

5. One of the best is Jay Ranade and Hirday Ranade *VSAM Concepts, Programming, and Design.* MacMillan, New York, NY, 1987. ISBN 0-02-948630-0.

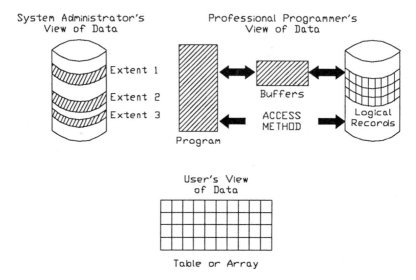

Figure 11.15   Data-in-Virtual (DIV). There are three views of data shows here. DIV is more like the user's view — a table or array of data.

Views of Data   Figure 11.15 shows the three views of data which are used by three types of MVS users. The first is the systems administrator's view — hardware and physical storage is the key to this view. The second is the programmer/analyst view of data. Programs, buffers, and logical records are the key topics. The third is a user's view — the entire table of information (look at the popularity of the Personal Computer spreadsheet as a clue to how users view data).

Linear Data Sets or Data Objects   With MVS/XA Version 2 Release 2, which supports DIV, IDCAMS can be instructed to build a **Linear** data set. A Linear data set is a VSAM data set, but the application program does not use VSAM macros to access the data. A Linear data set must be cataloged in an Integrated Catalog Facility catalog. VSAM catalogs and CVOLs do not support Linear data sets.

Once the data set has been defined, a program can use an assembler language macro **DIV** to access the data. High level languages (such as FORTRAN and PL/I) can access DIV by calling common assembler routines. The following are the DIV macro functions:

IDENTIFY: specifies the DD statement which points to the Linear data set containing the data.

ACCESS: indicates if the data object will be changed or just read.

MAP: specifies the virtual storage that is to hold the data object contents. The parameters are "ID=," which is the value from the IDENTIFY, and AREA=, which is a word holding the area address.

SAVE: writes *only the changed part* of the file back to the data set.

RESET: tells DIV to stop processing and to not save any changes since the last save.

UNMAP: tells DIV that you are finished with a map.

UNACCESS: tells DIV that you are finished with the data object.

UNIDENTIFY: tells DIV that you are finished with the DD statement (like "close").

DIV Summary DIV is a whole new feature provided by MVS/XA (Version 2 Release 2 and later). Usually when a new feature is offered by MVS it takes several years to catch on. The reader is invited to experiment with DIV functions to see how it can solve problems in a better way for your data center. An overview is provided by *An Introduction to Data-in-Virtual* (GG66-0259). This manual not only gives an explanation of DIV, but also gives examples on how to use DIV with high level languages. FORTRAN, COBOL, PL/I, PASCAL, and Assembler language can access DIV data sets.

11.2. DATA SET DEFINITION AND ACCESS

We now turn to the MVS structure of data. MVS provides services to create and access "data sets" which are areas on DASD or tape that are the files of information kept by the data center and its users.

IBM uses the terms **Total Storage Management** (TSM) or **System Managed Storage** (SMS) when it talks of data in the computer center. These are collective, futuristic terms for data. They imply that MVS will, eventually, manage allocation and file movement without detailed help from the end user.

Today, data sets still must be allocated and used in some organized fashion. SMS may not be in use in very many data centers for some time, so let's investigate what we have now so we can understand what SMS will do for us.

11.2.1. DASD Volume Table of Contents (VTOC)

The Volume Table of Contents is the "data set" on each MVS DASD volume that contains the name of every data set that is on the volume. The VTOC is a keyed data set and is basically unchanged since the earliest days of System/360 architecture. Even DOS used VTOCs to keep track of DASD volume space allocation.

With IBM's announced System Managed Storage (SMS), VTOCs will eventually disappear. The VTOC is a very limiting structure, but like most of MVS you should know the past so you will be able to cope with the future.

The first track — cylinder 0 head 0 — on every DASD has a fixed set of records:

1. The first record is a 24-byte record. If the volume is an IPL volume, it contains the IPL bootstrap. If it is not an IPL volume, it contains information that will place the Processor Complex in a disabled wait state if it is ever selected for an IPL action.
2. The second record is a 144-byte record. If the volume is an IPL volume, it contains the Bootstrap "program" (really just Channel Command Words.)
3. The third record is a standard label for the volume. It must contain the volume serial number starting at the eighth byte and a pointer to the VTOC starting at the 19th byte.
4. The fourth record is either the IPL record or does not exist for standard MVS volumes.

VTOC Placement Figure 11.16 shows a typical DASD volume and the pointer to the VTOC. VTOCS can be moved (by DFDSS or OEM dump restore programs), so you should monitor heavily accessed volumes and make corrections. The VTOC can be anywhere on the volume, but some usual locations are:

At Front of the Volume: Many volumes have the VTOC starting at cylinder 0, head 1. The reason for this is that the VTOC is inspected each time an OPEN is issued for a data set on the volume. The VTOC is read to determine the location of the data set. The front is recommended for volumes with a few large data sets and for which total number of data sets is less than 40.

At One-Third of the Volume: Some systems programmers design the VTOC to be about one-third of the way into the volume. In the case of a 3380 single capacity, this would be about cylinder 300, head 0. As the volume fills with data sets, the space for allocation of a new data set is some point into the volume. One-third seems to work well for relatively busy volumes.

At the One-Half Point: Some very busy volumes due to allocation get better performance when the VTOC is at the halfway point. On average, the VTOC will have to be read and then a data set located.

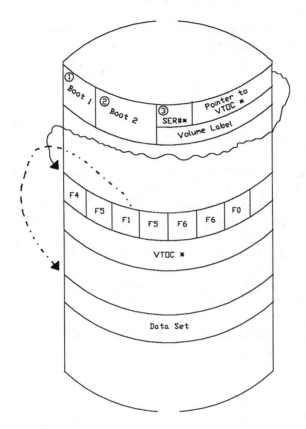

Figure 11.16 DASD VTOCS. The Volume Table of Contents of a DASD is pointed to by a fixed location on a DASD volume (cylinder 0, head 0, record 3). The VTOC contains pointers to data sets on the volume.

If the VTOC is at the midpoint, then an average of one-fourth of a volume would have to be spanned by head movement (one-half of one-half).

VTOC Size Much debate exists on the size of a VTOC. For a long while, it was important to have the VTOC *end on a cylinder boundary* — that is, have the last track of the VTOC be the last track of a cylinder. On a 3380, there are 15 tracks per cylinder. If the VTOC started on cylinder 0 head 1, it should be 14 tracks and end on cylinder 0 head 14. Remember, cylinders are numbered relative to 0, so the numbers are 0 to 14.

At some point in the development of MVS, this became less of an issue. Recent measurements show that having the VTOC end on a cylinder boundary is not that important for allocation.

I believe it is best to allocate either a track (for volumes with less than 20–40 data sets) or multiples of cylinders for volumes with a large number of data sets. Remember, you cannot dynamically enlarge the VTOC: you would have to rebuild the volume — remove all data sets, rebuild the VTOC, and restore all the data sets.

VTOC Contents The VTOC contains several types of records. All records in the VTOC are 140 characters long and are in two parts. The records are documented in the MVS SPL Debugging handbooks (for example, *MVS Extended Architecture Debugging Handbook Volume 3* — LC28-1166.) There are assembler language macros that can be used to provide mapping for the fields of the VTOC records — IECSDSL1, for example, for MVS/XA.

The first part of a VTOC record is a 44-byte physical key (separate from the data portion) which contains either the record type, data, or a data set name. The second part is a 96-byte data component. The records are called **Data Set Control Blocks** (DSCB)

Before we discuss this further, you will need to know several terms:

1. **Contiguous** refers to a set or group of consecutive items. If we needed 10 tracks, the tracks could be supplied by providing tracks 3 through 12. That allocation contains contiguous tracks. MVS could also supply tracks 1 through 5 and tracks 8 through 12. That, too, represents 10 tracks, but they are not contiguous.
2. **Extent** refers to contiguous data space on DASD. In the above example, one extent would be the tracks 3 through 12, but when MVS supplies tracks 1–5 and 8–12, that is represented by two "extents." The VTOC is always a contiguously allocated single extent data set.
3. **Cylinder allocation** refers to allocating data sets in whole cylinder units. To understand cylinder allocation and what it means, let's look at how the DASD hardware implements "protection." There are Channel Command Words (CCW) to tell the hardware to "interrupt" MVS if a cylinder boundary is crossed. The hardware's only protection feature is to notify MVS (via I/O interrupt) that a CCW string attempted to cross a cylinder boundary.

Look at an example: An application allocates a five-track data set and MVS allocates cylinder 1 heads 10–14 on a 3380 device. The last track is head 14, which is also the last track on a cylinder. MVS will allow multitrack operations because MVS can also tell the hardware to interrupt the CCW execution if any CCW attempts to cross a cylinder boundary. The CCW string could attempt to read or write to cylinder 1 head 5, but MVS checks the CCW string for those types of violations.

In another example, the application allocates a five-track data set and MVS allocates cylinder 1 tracks two through six. MVS will not allow multitrack operations because MVS cannot tell the hardware to stop the execution if it crosses track boundaries. In this case a search of a PDS directory will interrupt the Processor Complex at the end of every track of the directory.

4. A **multitrack** operation is where MVS allows multiple track CCWs to be used. Examples of multitrack CCWs are search and read operations. If the VTOC contains 53 DSCBs per track and MVS starts a search for a data set with a SEARCH ID= command, it should be able to read through the entire VTOC with one CCW string — if multitrack operations are allowed.

   Multitrack is allowed when either the VTOC (or data set) is allocated in *whole cylinders* or the extents of the data set (or VTOC) *end on a cylinder boundary*.

5. A **track-by-track** operation is where MVS only allows a single track at a time to be read and/or written. Track-by-track operation is forced with VTOCs or data sets allocated in track increments where the last track of an extent is not the last track of a cylinder.

I will present the types of DSCBs in the order that they might be in the VTOC. I do not know why the record numbers were created in this manner — maybe the room was *too* smoke filled!

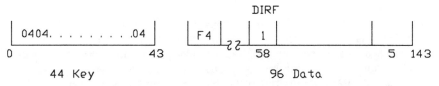

Figure 11.17   Format 4. The Format 4 DSCB must be the first record in a VTOC. It describes where the VTOC is located and keeps other information about the volume.

Figure 11.18 Format 5. The Format 5 describes all the free space on a DASD volume. Each free space is accounted for by the starting relative cylinder (from cylinder 0, head 0) and the number of cylinders and/or tracks that are in the free area.

Format 4 — VTOC: The Format 4 is always the first record in the VTOC, and there is only one Format 4. The record's physical key is x'040404...04'. The record describes the VTOC — the location on the volume and absolute addresses of the VTOC. Figure 11.17 shows part of the Format 4. Note that at byte 44 is x'F4' or printable character "4." Each record has its own type at this location to make it easy to determine the type from a printed listing.

One important bit — byte 58 bit x'04' — is called the **DADSM Interrupt Recording Facility** (DIRF) bit or DOS contamination bit.[6] The DIRF bit is turned on by DOS when DOS accesses a volume, because DOS allocates space and does not support MVS space management — it does not update the Format 5 free space blocks. MVS notices the bit turned on and recalculates space on the volume. MVS turns on the DIRF bit when it creates **indexed VTOCs**. The DIRF bit "on" indicates that the Format 5 (free space) is not valid.

Format 5 — Free Space: The second type of record on a volume is usually the free space DSCB. When a volume is initialized, there are only two allocated DSCBs — one Format 4 and one Format 5. The Format 5 is only valid if the VTOC is not "indexed."

Figure 11.18 shows the layout of a typical Format 5. Note that the DSCB is divided into five-byte "free space" extents. The relative

---

6. Remember from the chapter on Processor Complexes that MVS bits are defined left to right starting at zero. The x'04' bit turned on is "bit 5." I prefer to refer to the bits by their hexadecimal value because if you display the field, it will be represented in the hexadecimal '04' representation. IBM refers to the bit as "bit 5" in most documentation.

track number is two bytes (maximum of 65,536 tracks on a volume!). The number of free cylinders is also two bytes (same maximum), and the number of free tracks is one byte (255 tracks maximum).

The 140-byte Format 5 records are divided to allow 8 free space extents to be accounted for in the 44 byte key area and 18 free space extents to be accounted for in the data area. The last five bytes are a pointer to another Format 5, if more than 26 extents are needed to define the free space. MVS combines adjacent free space extents into one extent. Format 5 DSCBs are returned to the available pool (Format 0) when the Format 5 no longer contains free extents.

Format 1 — Data Set: The Format 1 record describes a data set and the space it occupies — up to three **extents**. Figure 11.19 shows that the key area is the data set name. That is the reason for the 44-byte key. MVS can issue a special channel command — **search key equal** — to find whether a data set exists on a particular volume. MVS does not have to read and examine each block in the VTOC.

If the VTOC (or any data set, for that matter) *ends on a cylinder boundary*, then multitrack operations can be issued and one entire cylinder of the VTOC can be searched for a data set with one CCW string.

Again, the 45th byte is x'F1', indicating a Format 1 type of record. The rest of the data area contains information about the data set — LRECL, BLKSIZE, extent information, and a pointer to other DSCBs, if necessary.

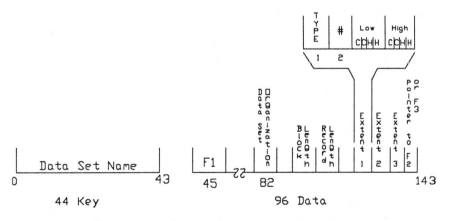

Figure 11.19   Format 1. The Format 1 contains the data set name as the 44-byte key and information about the data set, including pointers to the first three extents.

Now is a good time to explain how IBM describes an extent (each extent is ten bytes long):

1. First byte: extent type indicator.
2. Second byte: extent number.
3. Third through sixth bytes: lower limit of the extent in CCHH format, where CC is the cylinder number and HH is the head number.
4. Seventh through tenth bytes: upper limit of the extent in CCHH format.

Format 3 — Extents: Format 3 contains information about extents 4 through 16 of a non-VSAM data set. Only one Format 3 is used for non-VSAM data sets. VSAM data sets cataloged in an ICF catalog can have up to 128 extents and can have Format 3 records chained together. Figure 11.20 shows a typical Format 3. Note that the "key" area contains 4 bytes of x'03' to indicate it is a Format 3 and room for the 4th through 7th extents. The data portion contains room for nine additional extents.

Note also the last 5 bytes are marked "reserved." The MVS limit of 16 extents for a data set is enforced for non-VSAM data sets, yet there is no technical reason why non-VSAM data sets cannot have more than 16 extents. Again, upward compatibility hurts as it helps.

Format 2 — ISAM: Format 2 DSCBs are extensions to a Format 1 and describe Indexed Sequential Access Method (ISAM) data sets. See Figure 11.21. This block contains the addresses and extent information of the index(es), the overflow record areas, and, if necessary, a pointer to a Format 3 for more than three extents.

Format 0 — Empty: A Format 0 is a null, or empty, record. The record type is called Format 0 because the record is all hexadecimal

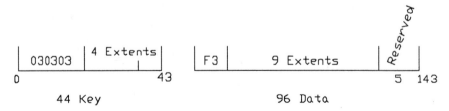

Figure 11.20   Format 3. If a data set requires four or more extents, a Format 3 is built for the data set. The Format 3 contains extent information for extents 4 through 16.

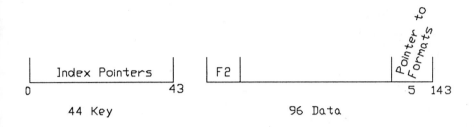

Figure 11.21   Format 2. Every ISAM file must have a Format 2 DSCB to describe what part of the data set is the index portion and where the overflow records are to be kept. If necessary, Format 2 will point to a Format 3 for additional space.

zeros. A Format 0 can be used to build any of the other types. When there are no more Format 0 records, you cannot add data sets to the volume and you cannot expand any data set on the volume from three extents to four or more extents.

Format 6 — Shared: In previous IBM operating systems, cylinders could be shared by data sets. The reasoning was that if data sets were on cylinder boundaries, they could have better performance. If the data set did not need a whole cylinder, it could "share" with another data set. This was just too complex, and support is dropped for split cylinders by MVS.

If the user wishes to access the VTOC, you can write assembler language programs using READ or EXCP to read the VTOC. You can use the CAMLIST macros or you can use the CVAF macros with certain later versions of MVS. The user is cautioned that IBM may change the VTOC functions. They may not change the existing VTOC structure, but they may create a new type of initialization for Systems Managed Storage that eliminates the VTOC.

Search for Data Set   Figure 11.22 shows the process MVS goes through to search for a data set. In this example, data set "YOUR.DATA" is on volume DATA01. MVS starts in the Master Catalog and finds a pointer to the user catalog on volume USERC1. The name of the user catalog is CATALOG.VUSERC1. In the user catalog is a pointer for *every data set that begins with "YOUR."* MVS finds a pointer for "YOUR.DATA" to volume DATA01. MVS reads the VTOC and finds the extents for the data set.

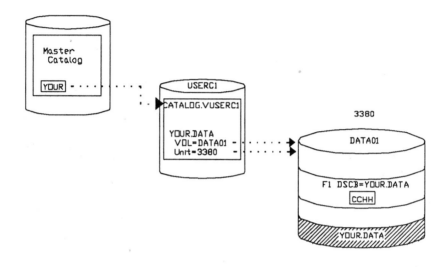

Figure 11.22   Search for Data Set. MVS begins to look for data sets in the Master Catalog. The search continues through user catalogs to the VTOC of the volume that contains the data set.

11.2.2.   Indexed VTOCs

MVS also provides services to build an index for the VTOC. Remember that the 140-byte VTOC record — including a 44-byte, separate key area — is not an efficient method to store data. It is an even worse method to retrieve data. As data centers grew and more and more data sets were created, the VTOC became a bottleneck. IBM developed a second method to keep track of data set names and extents.

The Indexed VTOC is a parallel, duplicate method to keep track of data sets and free space on a DASD volume — it duplicates the data in the VTOC. Duplicate data is beneficial because the Indexed VTOC can be used to find a data set on the volume or allocate new space for a data set on the volume much quicker than with the VTOC only.

Up to MVS/ESA and **System Managed Storage**, every volume had a VTOC and may have an Indexed VTOC. Volumes controlled by Systems Managed Storage do not contain VTOCs.

The Device Support Facility (DSF) program is used to create the Indexed VTOC, which is a separate "sequential data set" containing four record types.

VTOC Index Map (VIXM) The VIXM is a record that contains a bit for each record in the Indexed VTOC. If a bit is on for a specific record, then that record is "in use." If a bit is off for a specific record, then that record is available for use.

VTOC Pack Space Map (VPSM) The VPSM contains bits to indicate which tracks and/or cylinders are in use or available for allocation on the volume. This is the same function provided by the Format 5 above. In fact, when an Indexed VTOC is active, this record is the only accurate indication of free space on the volume. The DIRF bit is on to warn other users to use the indexed VTOC.

VTOC Map of DSCBs (VMDS) The VMDS is a bit map that shows which DSCBs in the VTOC are available (bit is zero) and which DSCBs are allocated (bit is one). To allocate a new data set, DADSM only needs to read a few records. Early MVS systems consumed many channel resources to find the next available Format 0 to be used for a new data set. Once it found the exact track address, it built the Format 1 and searched for an available Format 0 again! One of my performance modifications to MVS (fortunately not needed any longer — it was difficult to maintain) was to keep, in storage, the track location of the next Format 0 that was available for use.[7]

VTOC Index Entry Record (VIER) The VIER contains the data set name of each data set on this volume and the address (CCHHR) of the Format 1 DSCB for that data set. VIER records are read by MVS when it is looking for a data set on a volume. Then the Format 1 is read to get explicit data about the location and attributes of the data set.

When to Index Your VTOCs As a general rule, you should create In-dexed VTOCs for all your volumes. Individual situations can dictate that you should not use Indexed VTOCs. The classic example is the volume that has relatively few data sets and does not get alloca-tion/deallocation requests very often. Your data center may have some volumes with only one or two data sets such as part of a multi-volume VSAM data set. It is not necessary to index that VTOC. You

---

7. The guidance of Howard Wolvington was vital to this effort.

may not want to index your VTOCs if your DASD accounting and management software do not support indexed VTOCs.

11.2.3.   Allocation

How are data sets created? A large number of MVS modules are the software support for data set creation and deletion. The term **allocation** is used for this function. The part of MVS that is responsible for allocation of data sets on DASDs is called **Direct-Access Device Management** (DADSM). DADSM routines are primarily concerned with:

1. Allocating primary space for new data sets on DASDs.
2. Allocating secondary space (extending the data set) for programs that have written to the end of the current allocation and would like to write more.
3. Releasing DASD space:
   a. Freeing all the space associated with a DASD data set if the data set is scratched.
   b. Freeing space *at the end of the data written* if the user has specified **RLSE** for the data set.

Finding Space for the Data Set   Allocation   routines   assign   units, volumes, and data sets based on JCL DD statements and dynamic allocation requests. Serialization is performed on three levels:

1. For the device, while allocation is in progress.
2. For the device, for the duration of the JOB/STEP (e.g., a tape drive).
3. For volumes, such as tapes, for the duration of the job step.

Allocation of direct access data sets can be controlled by assigning volume attributes in the SYS1.PARMLIB member VATLSTxx.[8]

1. **Mount** attributes can be:

---

8. See *System Programming Library: Initialization and Tuning* (e.g., GC28-1149 for MVS/XA).

  a. **Permanently resident**, where the volume cannot be dismounted.

  b. **Reserved**, where the volume remains mounted until the operator issues an unload command.

  c. **Removable**, where the volume can be dismounted by MVS at any time it is not allocated.

2. **Use** attributes can be:

  a. **Public**, where the volume is eligible for allocating temporary data sets.

  b. **Private**, where the volume is eligible for allocating a data set only when the volume is explicitly or implicitly specified.

  c. **Storage**, where the volume is eligible for allocating both temporary and permanent (nontemporary) data sets when no specific volume is requested and Private is not specified. If Public volumes are present, temporary data sets are sent to those volumes.

Data set allocation is the first step in using the resources of the computer center. MVS provides the freedom to defer specifications such as buffer length, block size, and device type until a job is submitted for processing. This allows programs to be created to process data with widely different applications. Allocations can be done by Job Control Language (JCL) using DD statements, by **Dynamic Allocation** (assembler macros that do not need DD statements to access a data set), or by the TSO ALLOCATE command.

Creation of a DSCB for New Data Sets New data sets that are to be created on DASDs must have the SPACE parameter specified. The SPACE parameter provides the following type of information:

1. The type of allocation:

  a. **CYLINDER** means that the space should be in units of cylinders. In the case of the IBM 3380, which has 15 tracks per cylinder, a two-cylinder allocation would obtain 30 tracks. Additionally, CYLINDER allocation states that the data set must begin and end on cylinder boundaries.

  b. **TRACK** means that the number of tracks specified are to be provided but may start at some track that is not at the beginning of a cylinder.

  c. **BLOCK LENGTH** means that the allocation is in number of blocks times this block length. For example, if a 3380 track can hold 10 4,096-byte blocks and the number of blocks wanted is 150, then 15 tracks should be allocated. If the user also wants to have the data set begin and end on cylinder boundaries, the **ROUND** parameter will tell DADSM to allocate one Cylinder. (ROUND is used to get cylinder allocation for performance while specifying space in terms of block length and number of blocks.)

2. The **primary** and **secondary** allocation specification.

    a. Primary allocation amounts are the space that DADSM is to find before the task can start. *The primary allocation amount is also required for secondary volumes.* DADSM will be successful if the amount given can be obtained *within the first five extents.* When a data set is first allocated, it would be nice to get the entire primary allocation as the first extent. Unfortunately, in the real world, volumes become fragmented. For example, imagine that an allocation is attempted for 100 cylinders, but the largest free extent is 50 cylinders. Remember from our discussion on Format 1 and Format 3 DSCBs, each extent must be contiguous, because the extent description only has a start address and number of cylinders/tracks. In this example, assume there also is a 30-cylinder and a 20-cylinder free space. DADSM would assign the 50, the 30, and the 20 cylinder to satisfy the 100-cylinder request. To summarize, when DADSM allocates space, it:

        i. Finds the smallest contiguous area that satisfies the request.

        ii. "Builds" noncontiguous area from no more than five available extents.

        iii. Stops and forces an ABEND B37 if the primary space cannot be found.

    b. Secondary allocation amounts are what is specified by the requestor for DADSM to use to get space if the requestor is writing to the data set *and there is no more room in the current file allocation space.* The program can Abend in several situations:

        i. No secondary space was specified.

        ii. The volume that the data set is on does not have any free space.

        iii. The data set has reached the maximum number of extents (16 in the case of non-VSAM data sets).

It may seem that a file can become as large as the primary and 15 times the secondary, but that is not always true. If the primary requires five extents to get the requested space, then the file can only grow to one Primary allocation and 11 secondary extents on one volume.

11.2.4. System Catalogs

After allocation comes the process of finding the data set at a later time. Pen and paper worked when there were a few 2311 devices on the computer room floor, but now DASD comes in multiple gigabyte increments. The system catalog is the central repository for the name of the data set, the volume on which it exists, and the unit attributes of the volume.

Catalog Benefits and Types   Data centers running MVS can find, account for and manage every data set in the installation. Storage management is a real possibility under MVS at the data set level. Some operating systems do not have system catalogs (e.g., VSE and VM) and the data center has difficulty managing data sets.

There are several benefits of cataloged data sets:

1. The data set can be accessed without knowing where the data set exists. This is very important if the data set might move from device to device (not enough room to expand on the current device).
2. Device independence can be achieved, unless the data set has attributes which are unique to the current device.
3. The end user can let the system manage the data set names. Generation Data Groups (GDGs) can be created to allow the system to manage how many versions of a data set exist. GDGs are very useful for periodic data collection and then gathering all the data sets together at a later time without knowing when the data was collected.
4. VSAM data sets must be cataloged.

Figure 11.23 shows several types of system catalogs. All catalog searches begin at the MVS SYSTEM Catalog (Master Catalog), which is either a VSAM or an Integrated Catalog Facility (ICF) catalog. If the Master Catalog is a VSAM catalog, it can contain pointers to other VSAM catalogs (USERCATS) or OS CVOLs. If the Master Catalog is an ICF catalog, it can contain pointers to VSAM catalogs, OS CVOLs or other ICF catalogs. *All master catalogs in MVS should be ICF catalogs.*

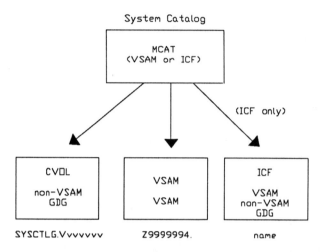

Figure 11.23 Catalog overview. There are three types of MVS catalogs. The CVOL is a very old (from MVT) catalog structure and should not be used today. The VSAM catalog was the first MVS catalog and has several problems associated with it. The Integrated Catalog Facility (ICF) catalog is the one that should be used in all MVS data centers.

A user catalog (USERCAT) must be cataloged in the Master Catalog in a user catalog record. A CVOL must be defined in the Master Catalog. The CVOL name on the disk is **SYSCTLG**, but the name cataloged in the master catalog is **SYSCTLG.Vxxxxxx**, where xxxxxx is the volume serial of the CVOL.

The master catalog contains the full catalog entry for some data sets, such as the paging, swap, SMF, and other data sets. An entry fully defined in the master catalog is generally not available to another copy of MVS.

OS CVOLs CVOLs were the catalogs in the MVT environment. When MVS was introduced, the CVOL support was continued for upward compatibility. The MVS Master Catalog has always been a VSAM catalog, but some facilities are still using CVOLs because it is always difficult to convert catalogs. Come on folks, convert!

CVOLs are a tree structure of cataloging non-VSAM data sets. The time to access a data set is *dependent on the data set name*, the format of the CVOL, and the size of the CVOL. For example, to locate "NAME.A", which is on 3350 PACK01 and is cataloged in a CVOL on PACK02:

1. Examine the names of all open catalogs for "NAME." If MVS finds an open catalog, it can go directly to the CVOL.
2. Search the Master Catalog for "NAME.A." This fails.
3. Search the Master Catalog for "NAME." This is successful and returns an ALIAS entry of "NAME" whose related entry is "SYSCTLG.VPACK02."
4. Examine the names of all open catalogs for "SYSCTLG.VPACK02." This fails the first time because there are no open catalogs.
5. Search the Master Catalog for "SYSCTLG.VPACK02." This is successful and returns a non-VSAM entry, "SYSCTLG.VPACK02," on VOLSER PACK02 and device type "3350."
6. Allocate and open the SYSCTLG data set, the CVOL on PACK02. This requires a search of the master catalog.
7. Search the CVOL on PACK02 for "NAME." Find the pointer to the next record in CVOL PACK02.
8. Read and reread records until "NAME.A" is found. Up to this point, CVOLs are similar to accesses to ICF catalogs. The key in this last point is "reread." I have seen MVS do several dozen reads inside a CVOL to find a complex data set name. CVOLs need to be reorganized often or they get out of hand.

Whew! The rule of thumb for data set names to minimize the problems with catalogs is: *Define data set names with as few qualifiers as possible.* Minimizing qualifiers is a good idea for all catalogs (including the VSAM catalogs below) as well as any hierarchical chain.

VSAM Catalogs VSAM catalogs were the first truly MVS catalog. Unfortunately, they had many problems. This section is included for historical purposes and as a helpful hint to those of you still using VSAM catalogs that it is about time to convert.

VSAM user catalogs held pointers to VSAM data sets and could contain pointers to non-VSAM data sets. If the VSAM data set did contain pointers to non-VSAM data sets, the recovery of a damaged VSAM catalog became a very complicated process. The recovery was so difficult that I recommended that non-VSAM data sets, including Generation Data Group (GDG) data sets, be cataloged in CVOLs (Ugh!). VSAM catalogs were reserved for VSAM data sets. Figure 11.24 shows the IDCAMS control card statements which create a VSAM catalog.

```
DEFINE USERCATALOG -
        (NAME(user.a) -
        FILE (volser) -
        VOL (volser) -
        CYL (4 1))      -
        CATALOG(SYS1.name)
```

Figure 11.24   Defining VSAM catalogs. An IDCAMS DEFINE USERCATALOG command is used to create a system catalog.

ICF Catalogs ICF catalogs are the best MVS Master and User catalogs. VSAM data set information, non-VSAM data set information, and even Generation Data Sets can be safely and efficiently stored in in ICF catalogs. Figure 11.25 shows the IDCAMS control statements to create a VSAM ICF catalog. The only difference between this and Figure 11.24 is the "ICFCATALOG" parameter to IDCAMS.

11.3. DATA SET CAUTIONS

I believe that the most important thing we do as data processing professionals is to protect the data we process. The data sets we create for our companies contain information vital to the business of our business. If it is not vital, why are you processing it? Even a blind dog with a note in its mouth can detect whole data sets that are missing. What is difficult to detect, and correct, are incorrect or missing pieces of data.

11.3.1. Lost Data If Abend

The access method places logical records into output or physical buffers in virtual storage. As the buffers fill, the physical blocks are written to the I/O device. When the program issues a "CLOSE"

```
DEFINE USERCATALOG  -
        (ICFCATALOG  -
        NAME(user.a)  -
        FILE (volser) -
        VOL (volser) -
        CYL (4 1))    -
        CATALOG(SYS1.name)
```

Figure 11.25   Defining ICF catalogs. The ICFCATALOG parameter is added to tell IDCAMS that an ICFCATALOG is to be formatted.

macro, all the buffers are written to the output device and some "end-of-file" is indicated. If the program abends, these buffers may be in virtual storage and not get written to the device. MVS does not issue "CLOSE" macros for any open file if a task abends.

What does this mean to the programmer/analyst? I have seen programs abend after writing hundreds of records to the file only to have the records "disappear" from the file. If a program abends, you should assume that data has been lost.

VSAM has a unique method of identifying files that were open when a program abends. When a VSAM file is opened, a bit is set "on" indicating the file is open. If the VSAM data set was opened for output, the next VERIFY generates a condition code (97) to indicate the file was not closed properly. Data may still be lost, but VSAM notifies the next job of the problem.

11.3.2. Control Records and Cross Footing

The computers we use are very good for counting. It amazes me that systems produce reports to ensure the data was correctly edited and the fields are proper — correct alphanumeric fields and types, for example — yet only the sophisticated systems track the records from data entry to report.

These control records should be passed from the beginning of a job stream to the end of the job stream and printed out for verification. The count of records and total value of the updates should be passed from job step to job step. All "missing" data should be identified and the reason for the differences identified and corrected.

Probably the worst example of abuse of this was an accounting system that I was given the responsibility to manage. I discovered that the error listing was so large that the listing was routed to a "scratch" tape, and the tape was never used again. No one even looked at the errors! It took months, but the situation was reversed. Most users were amazed that their monthly bills were vastly different yet now consistent and accurate.

11.4. SUMMARY

Data set access methods supply applications with various ways of organizing and accessing data sets. They all supply OPEN, CLOSE, GET, PUT, READ, and WRITE services, but the options and effects of these vary among access methods.

SAM files are sequential with records of fixed, variable, or undefined length; they may be unblocked (one record per block) or blocked (more than one record per block.)

ISAM files may be accessed sequentially or, through a keyed index, randomly. ISAM stores absolute disk addresses in the index data set, so it is difficult to relocate ISAM files; VSAM can emulate ISAM function without this disadvantage, so ISAM itself should not be used.

BDAM allows random access with low access method overhead, but much of the data management burden rests with the application using it. This freedom gives an application enough rope to hang itself — and maybe the data center along with it.

Partitioned Data Set (PDS) files contain one or more named members, each of which is accessed like a sequential file. All members in a PDS file have the same record format. Modifying PDSs can result in wasted space, which may be reclaimed periodically with the IEB-COPY utility.

VSAM was to replace all other access methods, but SAM and PAM remain in common use, even by MVS software itself. Unlike ISAM and BDAM, which store absolute disk locations, VSAM stores relative Control Interval and offset locations and is less dependent on file placement. VSAM datasets are portable across VSAM installations, and VSAM performance may be better than that of other access methods for the same tasks.

VSAM offers sequential, indexed sequential, and random access and can log accesses to SMF. The IDCAMS utility provides data management services for VSAM data sets. VSAM is used by many IBM data management subsystems and is IBM's strategic direction for data management.

DIV is a departure from previous data set access method services and is the first in a trend toward unifying data set access with the virtual storage architecture. Eventually, applications will access entire data sets as separate address spaces, but DIV gives access within the application program's own address space.

Access methods are primarily concerned with the organization inside data sets; MVS also supplies ways to organize the collection of data sets as well. The ways are somewhat dated and varied, but IBM is trying to unify their approach with Total Storage Management or System Managed Storage.

VTOCs contain information about data sets stored on DASD volumes. A VTOC records data set names, placement, and storage allocation on a volume. An Indexed VTOC is an optional, parallel structure giving more efficient access to the same information.

Catalogs are means to get to data sets (tapes and VTOCs). The systemwide Master Catalog is the first access point. If the full data set name is found in the Master Catalog, then the system knows which volume to address. If not, and the first part (qualifier) of the data set name, the alias, references a User Catalog, then that is searched for the data set name.

There are three types of catalog organization: CVOL, from OS/MVT; VSAM; and ICF. The latter is the preferred catalog type and can reference the other two. In particular, an MVS system's use of System Managed Storage depends on its being cataloged with ICF.

Our most important professional responsibility is to protect our data. Maintaining a well-organized catalog structure, checking production results (especially after abends), searching for reported errors, and tracking data throughout its life cycle are means to that end.

We next look at MVS facilities for managing the programs that manipulate our data sets.

12

Program Management

12.1. OVERVIEW

MVS program management performs three functions for program modules. The first is to search for and schedule the module to be in storage. The second is to synchronize exits to routines during Supervisor functions. The third is to fetch modules into storage after a LINK, LOAD, XCTL, or ATTACH supervisor call has been issued. This chapter is a discussion of the searching and fetching functions.

The third function is accomplished by a **relocating loader**, which is the basis for the success of program management in MVS. The program can be compiled or assembled anywhere (usually location 0), and the relocating loader will change the contents of the program to reflect the location at which the program is loaded into virtual storage.

12.1.1. MVS Program Management

MVS program management functions consist of the following general functions:

1. Finding and "loading" a module into virtual storage if a LOAD macro has been issued. Figure 12.1 shows a load process. Module A issues a LOAD macro, and the address of the module is returned in a general purpose register. (The LOAD macro generates a Supervisor Call (SVC) 8.) The program must save

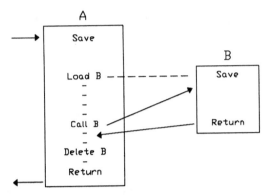

Figure 12.1   LOAD operation. Module A can issue the MVS macro "LOAD," which causes program B to be brought into virtual storage. The address of module B is returned to program A in a general purpose register (zero). The DELETE macro frees the storage occupied by the module.

the address of the module to be used when the program needs to go to the module with a CALL macro. *Module B does not get control until the CALL macro branches to it.*

2. Linking to a module if a LINK macro has been issued. Figure 12.2 shows a LINK operation. Module A issues a "LINK" Supervisor Call (SVC 6) which causes module B to be found or loaded, and execution begins immediately in module B. When module B is finished and issues a "RETURN" macro, control passes back to module A. This is repeated for module C in the figure.

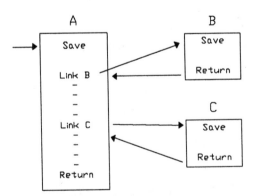

Figure 12.2   The LINK operation. Module A "links" to module B. After returning from module B, module A does some more processing and "links" to module C.

JES initiators link to programs specified on the EXEC card. For example, if the JCL said

//stepname EXEC PGM=myprogrm

then the initiator would issue a LINK for "myprogrm." *Note:* SVC 6 will will cause an abend 806 if the module is not found.

3. Transferring control to a module if an XCTL macro has been issued. When the Systems Analyst is preparing the flow from module to module, it may be necessary to leave a module completely and go to another one. Transfer control is referred to in MVS as XCTL. Figure 12.3 shows one way that XCTL could be used.

4. Deleting a module if a DELETE macro has been issued. The MVS way to "get rid" of a module in virtual storage is to "delete" the module. In Figure 12.1, the program issued a LOAD macro which loaded the program into virtual storage. After all the possible "calls" have been performed, a DELETE macro should be issued to clean up virtual storage.

5. Allowing modules to establish entry points that can be used if a Link, Load, or XCTL is requested. The program issues an IDENTIFY macro and points to the area that will receive control from program fetch. The program can have the linkage editor create additional "names" for a program. The linkage editor "Alias" command is used.

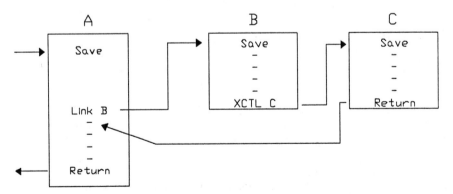

Figure 12.3   XCTL function. In MVS, one module can transfer control (XCTL) to another module. In this example, module A has linked to module B, but in module B it is determined module C must finish the process. An XCTL macro is issued with loads and transfers control to module C. Return is back to module A.

12.1.2. Program Fetch

Program management invokes "program fetch" to bring modules into storage. The first step in program fetch is to issue a Build List (BLDL) macro to find the location of the module in the correct library. BLDL reads the directory of a specific Partitioned Data Set and gets information about the physical location of the load module on DASD.

Each version of MVS gives us better BLDL processing. MVS/XA introduced LINKLIST Lookaside (LLA), which loaded the PDS directory of the libraries in the LINKLIST into virtual storage. Instead of performing I/O operations to read the directories, it "reads" the directory entry from virtual storage.

MVS/ESA gives the data center the ability to expand this "lookaside" function to other libraries — even non-load module libraries.

The second part of program fetch is to load the module into virtual storage. This process is highly tuned — up to 64Kb Central Storage is fixed, one I/O operation is started, and Program Controlled Interrupt (PCI) is used to get the module into storage as fast as possible for MVS/370 systems. MVS/XA systems gave up using PCI and depend on the module having correct length and pointers in the module to avoid the need for PCI.[1]

12.1.3. Relocating Loader

Figure 12.4 shows the processing done for loading a program. A particular application or program is developed in **source code** then **assembled** or **compiled** into language which the System/370 understands. The output of the compiler is called the **object code**, which

---

1. Program controlled interrupt is a feature of the System/370 which enables a program to get control *during* an I/O operation in order to modify the channel program. MVS/370 used this feature to speed up loading programs. It is not always successful. The channel does not wait. If the program can be dispatched and complete its work before the channel needs the next channel command word, then it works. If the channel "beats" the CPU, then it does not work. Relative timings are one of the few aspects IBM *does not* promise as upward compatible, so depending on it begs trouble.

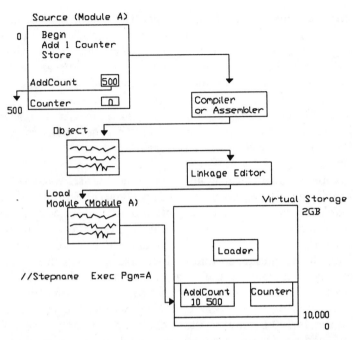

Figure 12.4   Relocating loader function. The source for program "A" is compiled and transformed into "object" code. The MVS Linkage Editor reads the object code and creates a load module. The initiator loads program A, which causes the contents of program A to be altered based on the point in virtual storage where program A is loaded.

is the instructions in the source converted to System/370 machine instructions in binary codes. The linkage editor converts object code to executable load modules. The program can then be **loaded** into the computer to execute the instructions. There are three types of loading which are possible:

1. **Absolute** loading in which the program, at source and compile time, identifies exactly where in the computer the program will execute. For example, the source code could specify a particular address, such as x'4000', as the start of the program. The drawback of this technique is that the program must be loaded at x'4000' in the computer to be able to be executed. If two programs have the same address, then they cannot be run at the same time. Early DOS operating systems used this technique because there was a limit of two programs running at any one time: foreground and background. MVS does not use absolute loading.

2. **Static relocation** loading in which the loader does some work as it is bringing in the program to *change the contents of the program* by relocating the program to the location in the computer that the program was being loaded. For example, the source code could have an address such as x'4000' as the start of the program, but the loader could change the start address to x'9000' by adding x'5000' to all the places in the program that addressed data in the program. This method's drawback is the program, once loaded and relocated, could not easily be moved.

3. **Dynamic relocation** is an expansion of static relocation. The translation of program references to Central Storage addresses is *delayed until the last possible moment*. A relocating loader changes the contents of a program based on the virtual address which the program is loaded into, and the instructions are System/370 instruction formats which use base registers to point to 4,096 byte pages and displacements within the page.

In Figure 12.4, the source for a program contains the address of a counter (called "ADDCOUNT") within the program. The counter is 500 bytes into the program. After compiling, linking, and loading, the area called "ADDCOUNT" has been changed from "500" to 10,500 because the program was loaded at location 10,000. The loader went into the module, found the pointer to the counter, and added the address that the program was loaded, to the pointer. (This example is running under MVS/XA, so the program might be loaded at location 10,000. In MVS/XA, the nucleus straddles the 16-megabyte line.)

Remember, a program only references virtual storage addresses. It can be interrupted at any point, swapped out by the Auxiliary Storage Manager (ASM), and reloaded (swapped in) into a different set of Central Storage addresses without modification.

Memory allocation is performed by the loader while loading in a program or combination of programs. The particular combination of programs can be decided *just prior* to loading.

12.2. WHERE ARE THE MODULES?

When a batch job or TSO session is executing, many MVS modules are needed to perform the services (OPEN, CLOSE, READ, WRITE, and others). MVS modules reside in only a few load libraries. (User or application modules may, of course, reside in any load library.)

12.2.1. SYS1.LPALIB

SYS1.LPALIB contains the most frequently accessed of the modules which the system and the end user need to execute system functions. I/O drivers, SVC modules, and TSO commands are here. Every module in LPALIB is available to a program to load and call.

12.2.2. SYS1.LINKLIB

SYS1.LINKLIB contains most of the utilities and the modules which are either not reentrant or are not normally shared by more than one user at a time. Examples are SORT modules, COBOL and PL/I compilers, and IEBGENER. SYS1.LINKLIB is the first of several load libraries which are collectively called LINKLIST libraries. The data center must specify SYS1.LINKLIB, a library for modules written or maintained by the data center and called something like SYS2.LINKLIB, and other libraries. The compilers and sort libraries are examples of these "other" libraries.

12.2.3. SYS1.SVCLIB

SYS1.SVCLIB was a very important library in MVT systems, but today only contains exit or "appendage" routines. It is kept around mostly because of compatiblity reasons.

12.2.4. SYS1.CMDLIB

SYS1.CMDLIB contains the TSO command processor modules.

12.2.5. SYS1.NUCLEUS

SYS1.NUCLEUS contains the modules that initialize and define the system as a result of the System Generation (SYSGEN) process.

12.3. MVS MODULE NAMING CONVENTIONS

MVS module names are usually eight characters long. The eight characters may be of two formats (see Figure 12.5). One is

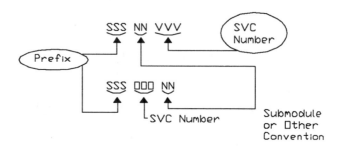

Figure 12.5   MVS module names. One of the most common naming conventions IBM has is for the first three characters of the program name to indicate the portion of MVS which the module comes from. The figure gives you a sample of Supervisor call naming conventions.

sssnnvvv, where "sss" is the subsystem prefix with which the module is associated. For example, if "sss" is "IEF" then the modules are job allocation modules. The middle "nn" is usually a version number or submodule name, and the "vvv" is the SVC number or other designation. It is easy to see, with only eight characters, it is very difficult to have informative naming conventions.

Another "convention" is **sssooonn**, where "sss" is a prefix, "ooo" is the SVC number, and "nn" is a suffix. Examples are IFG019xx (Open: SVC 19), IFG020xx (close: SVC 20), and IFG055xx (EOV: SVC 55)

12.4.   MODULE SEARCH

MVS is composed of thousands of modules. There are tens of thousands of messages. There are tens of thousands of abend codes. *There is a madness in this method.* This is a naming convention which dates back to 1965. It is not a good naming convention, is not always followed, but we might as well learn it. When in Rome, do as IBM does.

Figure 12.6 shows a flow chart of the program search logic. For those readers who are not familiar with flow charts, here are some rules about the figures in a flow chart:

1. The person drawing the flow chart tries to go from the top of the page to the bottom of the page and from left to right. Sometimes the top-to-bottom and left-to-right is reversed if it makes the figure easier to read.

2. Ovals (START) are entry points to the figure.

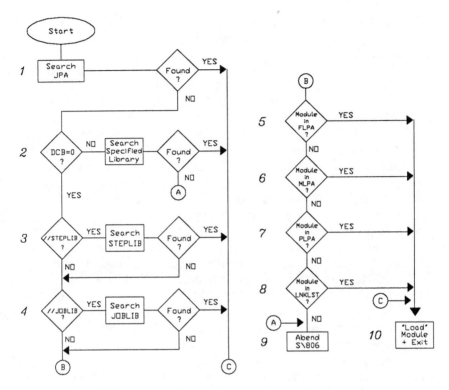

Figure 12.6   How MVS searches for a module. The flow chart traces the decisions MVS uses to find and/or load a module.

3. Rectangle boxes are processing boxes. The contents of the rectangle describe the type of processing. In the first example, "Search JPA" indicates MVS will search the control blocks that make up the JPA. If the module name is found, the address will be loaded and the flow chart says to proceed to circle with a "C" inside.
4. Circles with arrows pointing into them are entry points from other areas on the flow chart. Circles with arrows pointing out of them are "branches" or "jumps" to other areas on the flow chart.
5. A diamond with arrows coming into and from the points is a decision block. The content of the diamond is a question which can be answered, usually with a "yes" or "no."

Figure 12.6 shows the order that MVS Program management searches for a load module:

1. Job Pack Area (JPA). If the module has already been loaded and can be reused, return the address of that module.
2. DCB≠0. A load command may specify a specific library that must be used to find the module. If the library contains the module, the module is "loaded" into storage and the address is returned. If the module is not found, terminate the request — the user asked to use a specific library.
3. Step library. If there is a STEPLIB DD card search in that library (or concatenated libraries) for the module. If it is found, load it and quit searching. If it is not found, go on to the next step.
4. Job library. If there is a JOBLIB DD card, MVS searches the libraries that are pointed to by the JCL.
5. Fixed Link Pack Area (FLPA). MVS searches modules that are loaded into Virtual Storage and then have their pages locked into Central Storage. The control blocks searched are called the **LPA Queue**. If the module is found, its address is returned.
6. Modified Link Pack Area (MLPA). MVS searches modules that are loaded into Virtual Storage by the SYS1.PARMLIB parameters. MLPA modules are also on the LPA Queue.
7. Pageable Link Pack Area (PLPA). MVS searches modules that are loaded into Virtual Storage by MVS that are in the SYS1.LPALIB data set (or other partitioned data sets for MVS/XA 2.2 and MVS/ESA). The searching is accomplished by inspecting the Link Pack Directory which contains Link Pack Directory Entries (LPDA).
8. LNKLIST. Member LNKLSTxx of SYS1.PARMLIB contains the names of the data sets that the data center wants to use as a "last resort" to find programs that are requested.
9. If the module is not found, the program is ABENDed with a code of 806.
10. If the module is found, the module is "loaded" and control is returned to the calling program.

Now let's turn to some of the above areas to understand when MVS would find a module in these areas.

12.4.1. Job Pack Area

The following elements comprise the Job Pack Area (JPA; see Figure 12.7):

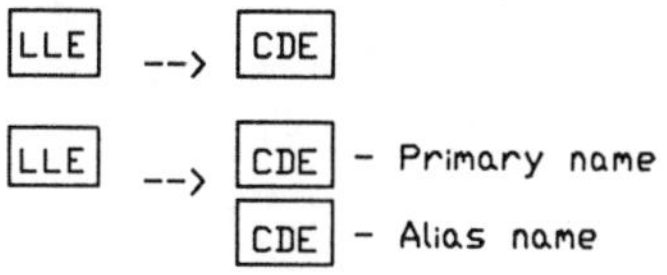

Figure 12.7   Control blocks for modules in the JPA. The control blocks used by MVS are the Load List Element (LLE), which contains pointers to the Contents Directory Entry (CDE), which contains the module name. In this example, one module has a second name or "alias."

1. Modules already loaded. Virtual storage contains the modules loaded by this address space. The JPA modules reside in the private area of an address space, and these programs are only available to this ASID.

2. The job pack area queue, which is a chain of control blocks called Contents Directory Entries (CDEs). Each CDE contains the name of the module, the address of the entry point for the name, and use count (how many current users are "in" the module). If the module has an alias (another entry point), then there are two CDEs — one for the "major" name (first name of the module) and one for the "minor" name (alias or secondary entry point to the module).

3. The load list, which is a chain of control blocks called Load List Elements (LLEs). There is an LLE and a CDE for each module which has been explicitly loaded. This queue of modules available within the address space is the first queue the load routine searches.

4. The Link Pack Directory Entries (LPDE) represent a particular load module which is loaded into the Pageable Link Pack Area (PLPA).

12.4.2. Link Pack Area

Five elements comprise the Link Pack Areas (see Figure 12.8):

1. The Pageable LPA refers to virtual storage containing all the modules which reside in the 'SYS1.LPALIB' data set.[2]

---

2. MVS/XA — MVS SP 2.1.1 added the capability to use additional data sets and define them in the LPALSTxx member of SYS1.PARMLIB.

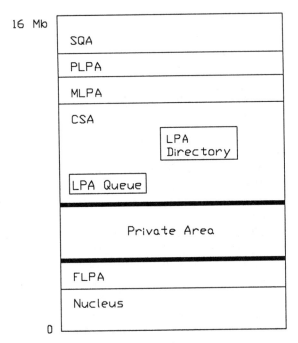

Figure 12.8   Link Pack Area (LPA). The LPA is really a combination of areas built by MVS as it is initializing and control blocks which hold pointers to the modules.

As the name indicates, the virtual storage occupied by PLPA is pageable — the module may be in Central Storage or it may be on auxiliary storage. *They are not paged out.* MVS loads the PLPA page data set at IPL time (when CLPA — Create LPA — is specified), and the pages are only paged in if needed. Referenced pages remain in Central Storage because the Central Storage page is "referenced" often.

Large Virtual Storage Constraint relief can be realized by cleaning out 'SYS1.LPALIB'. If the system programmer has old versions of modules which have been changed (usually names like "OLD0001C" or "ZZZ0001C"), then virtual storage is being wasted by having two copies of these modules in virtual storage.

Whole unused functions can still be in the LPA. If the data center does not have any use for ISAM, the ISAM modules can be removed. For example, module IGC019GA is a QISAM load function module. It is about 4,000 bytes. If this module were removed from LPA, then your system would not have to load

and pass over it for all module search activity. Complete discussion of this and other modules you may want to remove is
in *MVS Virtual Storage Tuning Cookbook* (G320-0597).

2. The LPA directory is a chain of control blocks, called LPDEs.
    Each LPDE contains an entry point for each LPA module and
    alias name.

3. The Modified LPA is an optional list of modules which are in-
    cluded in the LPA for performance or other reasons. MLPA
    was designed to allow the data center to "temporarily" add
    modules for the duration of an IPL without having to reload
    the PLPA.

    At IPL time, "MLPA=nn" is specified either by the operator
    or in member IEASYSxx of SYS1.PARMLIB, to tell MVS which
    modules to load. Use MLPA with caution. If the module
    belongs in LPA, put it there. Some uses that data centers have
    made for MLPA specifications are:

    a. Reduction of paging. If several DB/DC systems (such as
        CICS or IMS) are running, then making one copy of
        reentrant routines available to all of the DB/DC jobs, saves
        virtual storage and paging resources. For example, all
        CICS modules are usually in one program library. If the
        very active CICS modules are moved to the Link Pack Area
        (or selected from alternate LPA libraries with certain ver-
        sions of MVS), and CICS is instructed to use the LPA
        members, then all CICS modules will use the same copy of
        the module in common storage.

    b. Add modules for performance reasons. A common practice
        is to add TSO command modules so TSO performance is
        improved. This reduces search time for often-used modules.

    c. 308x Processor Complex and XA migration. The pageable
        LPA is protected from modification by the hardware. Lots
        of IBM modules and many accounting and other data cen-
        ter modules have violated reentrant requirements. The
        MLPA is outside the LPA protection. Use of the MLPA
        should just be a temporary work-around for system abend
        0C4s. The modules should be permanently fixed and moved
        to PLPA.

4. The Fixed LPA is an optional extension of the Link Pack Area.
    These modules do not reside in the upper part of virtual
    storage (MVS 370) but reside down with the Nucleus. Many
    DB/DC SVC modules require Fixed LPA residence because
    they are old code which was written for OS/MVT. In OS/MVT,
    all storage was fixed and real.

5. The LPA Queue is a queue of Contents Directory Entries (CDEs) of modules in the FLPA, MLPA, and currently active PLPA modules. Another name for this queue is the "active LPA queue," and it is designed to reduce the search time to find a module.

12.4.3. Auxiliary Storage Libraries

Auxiliary storage libraries are load libraries which contain modules that are not in virtual storage. These are the Linklist libraries and job and step libraries.

12.5. PROGRAM PROPERTIES TABLE (PPT)

The Program Properties Table (PPT) is where the installation can assign special properties to programs by placing their names in this table. The program can be given special attributes such as noncancelable, different storage keys, and be marked not swappable. See Figure 12.9 for examples of the naming conventions for MVS/370.

Starting with release 2.0 of MVS/XA, the data center can use a member of SYS1.PARMLIB (SCHEDxx) to modify the PPT to suit its requirements.

12.6. TASK MANAGEMENT

MVS has two types of tasks: the Task Control Blocks (TCBs) and the Service Request Blocks (SRBs). TCBs represent work within an address space such as user programs, utilities, and system programs which are operating on behalf of, or performed for, the user task.

```
Module  IEFSD060
CSECT  IEFSDPPT
Macro  SGIEFOPT
```

Figure 12.9 Program Properties Table (PPT). In MVS/370, macro SGIEFOPT is changed and assebled into module IDFSDPPT, IEFSDPPC is a csect of IEFSD060. With MVS/XA at Release 2, the SCHEDxx member of SYS1.PARMLIB, option PPT, can be used to modify the PPT.

SRBs represent work requested by one address space that is executed in another address space.

TCBs are created when the user explicitly or implicitly issues an ATTACH macro. Look at Figure 12.10. Three types of work are shown — batch jobs, Started Tasks (STCs), and TSO address spaces. The Address Space Control Block (ASCB) points to an Address Space Control Block Extension (ASXB) in the Private portion of virtual storage. The ASCBs are in the System Queue Area (SQA) because all ASCBs must be available to all address spaces.

In the example, there are five programs "running." The Region Control Task controls the address space. The DUMP task takes over if any abend is scheduled. The Started Task Control module is executed when the operator issues a start for the initiator. The JES Initiator code is linked to, and, finally, the program called for in the job step is given control.

For a started task other than the initiator, everything is the same, except control is transferred to the program specified on the EXEC card of the started task procedure.

In a TSO session, the Terminal Monitor Program (TMP) is given control to execute the user's TSO commands.

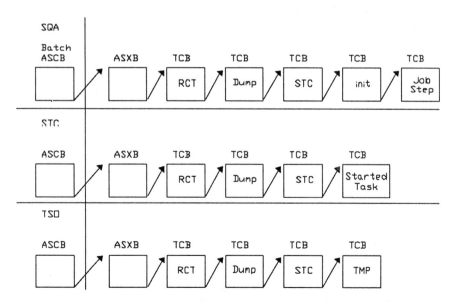

Figure 12.10   Task management. The three types of work — batch jobs, Started Tasks, and TSO sessions — all have TCBs associated with each piece required to give control to the user program.

How did all these tasks get started? What MVS function is controlling them? Task management performs services for both problem (that is, application) and system programs. The MVS assembler macro names are included in the following list of MVS task management functional areas:

1. Create and delete subtasks: (ATTACH/DETACH).
2. Control the execution of a task.
   a. Changing the dispatching priority of a subtask (CHAP).
   b. Allowing a task to wait for an event (WAIT, EVENTS).
   c. Notify another task of a completion of an event (POST).
   d. Serialization of tasks (ENQ, DEQ, RESERVE).
   e. Provide program interruption interception (SPIE, STAE, ESTAE).
3. Provide informational services (EXTRACT, TESTAUTH).

12.7. SUMMARY

MVS program management locates and schedules modules for execution, synchronizes exits during supervisor functions, and fetches other modules into storage on request. The LOAD, CALL, LINK, XCTL, DELETE, and IDENTIFY assembler macros invoke these functions.

Program relocation may be accomplished at several points: by a linkage editor after source program compilation or assembly, by the loader during program fetch, or by the program itself during its execution.

Program fetch obtains load modules from several sources: the LPALIB, LINKLIB, SVCLIB, CMDLIB, NUCLEUS library, and application libraries, all of which are partitioned data sets (PDSs). MVS has an algorithm for locating a given module name in the libraries and in shared areas of virtual storage (JPA and LPA, for example). The PPT can give programs operational properties.

Task management manipulates TCBs, representing work in an address space, and SRBs, representing requests for work from other address spaces. The ATTACH, DETACH, CHAP, WAIT, EVENTS, POST, ENQ, DEQ, RESERVE, SPIE, STAE, ESTAE, EXTRACT, and TESTAUTH assembler macros obtain task management services.

Programs manipulate data sets using access methods, but they also communicate with terminal peripherals, also through access methods; these are the subjects of the next chapter.

13

Communications Software and Access Methods

13.1. INTRODUCTION

Most access to applications which run under MVS use the 3270 Information Display System or Cathode Ray Tube (CRT) for displaying alphanumeric and graphic data. The family consists of:

1. Display stations with the ability to display between 480 and 3,564 characters.
2. Matrix printers with a maximum speed of up to 400 characters per second or laser printers that print 20 pages per minute.
3. 3274 or 3174 control units (or "cluster controllers") which control four to 32 display stations and/or printers. The 3274 control unit has connections for up to 32 devices via coaxial cable. All devices have to be 327x terminals or printers or intelligent terminals (PCs) that emulate 327x equipment. The 3174 control unit is a more modern version of the 3274 and can support Local Area Network (LAN) connections, ASCII terminals, bisynchronous terminals, and X.25 connections in addition to 327x terminals and printers.

The devices can be attached to the Processor Complex either "locally" or "remotely."

13.1.1. Local Attachment

Local attachment is the term used for 3270 devices which are attached to control units which have direct channel attachment to the Processor Complex. The term "local" is used because there is a channel cable length limit of 400 feet between the Processor Complex and the control unit.

Local Devices — 3274 Model D The first type of local attachment is the "D" unit. It attaches on the channel and uses 32 addresses on the channel for the 32 terminals or printers.

Local Devices — 3274 and 3174 Model C The second type of local attachment is the "C" or "SNA" attachment. This control unit uses one channel address to serve 32 terminals or printers; the one channel is multiplexed between them.

13.1.2. Remote Attachment

Remote attachment is the term used for 3270 devices which are attached to 3274 and 3174 control units that connect to the Processor Complex over a telephone line or via satellite. The term "remote" is used because there is no channel cable which attaches the device to the Processor Complex and the control unit.

The hardware, that does attach to the channel of the Processor Complex, is the 37x5 Communications Controller. The software which is loaded into the 37x5 is either Advanced Communications Facility for Network Control Program (ACF/NCP) or the Emulation Program (EP).

Point-to-Point Point-to-point refers to only two "devices" sharing a communication line. Remember that the control unit is one "device." The communications controller attaches to a phone line and one "device" is at the end of the phone line.

Multipoint Multipoint refers to more than two "devices" sharing a communication line. The communications controller attaches to a phone line and at a remote location one or more terminals and/or printers are attached. At another location *on the same telephone line* (party line!), other terminals and/or printers are attached.

Leased Line Attachment. One type of attachment to the 37x5 is by leased line (technically called "nonswitched" lines.) A leased line is one which you obtain from your local telephone company that is "directly" connected to the remote facility. You do not have to dial a leased line: The line is active at all times. Leased lines may be operated in point-to-point or multipoint mode.

The leased line is "always" ready. This type of line is selected if the time the line is active monthly is sufficiently high to justify the cost of a leased line. The leased line may cost from several hundred dollars to thousands of dollars per month. For example, if the leased line cost $1,000 per month and dial telephone service cost $25 per hour, then a leased line would be selected if the remote facility needed to access data at least 40 hours or more per month.

Each line must be evaluated and reevaluated periodically to ensure cost effective operation.

Dial Line Attachment Dial lines (technically called "switched" lines) are lines which must be dialed. Dial lines are point-to-point only. Usually someone at the remote location picks up a telephone, dials a telephone number in the computer center, and waits for a high-pitched tone called a "carrier." The line is then activated and data can be transferred.

It is possible to have the central site dial the remote locations and establish communication. It is possible to have the remote site automatically dial the central site.

Tuning Remote Attachment In most cases applications designers can affect remotely attached applications by their design. They can minimize (or not make worse) the remote response time. Some things to keep in mind when designing applications which will be used by customers or fellow employees are:

1. Send to the screen as few characters as possible. By this I mean design screens which have the same information in the same place. Send updates to the screen, not whole replacements, where possible.
2. Transfer as few bytes as possible. Read only updated fields from the screen. Keep track of what was displayed on the screen and pass this information from program to program.
3. Investigate control units which have RAM storage to store screen prototypes. The newest 3x74 control units and OEM replacements are beginning to get storage to hold information in the control unit.

13.1.3. Distributed Processing

MVS is an excellent base for Distributed Processing. The user can use any of a number of microcomputers, minicomputers, or even mainframe computers to offload data and/or processing. Examples are:

1. IBM's Personal Systems (Personal Computers or microcomputers) can be used to *upload* data from the PC to MVS or *download* data from MVS to the PC or to communicate peer-to-peer with other PCs and larger machines.
2. Application Systems 400 (midrange computers) can be used to process data at a remote location and upload and download data from the remote department. AS/400s are a combination of the older architecture of the System/36 and the System/38 midrange computers from IBM. The AS/400 may be more than midrange computers, as they were announced with upper limits of 96 Mb of Central Storage and 27.2 Gb of DASD!
3. 9370 and 43xx (mainframe computers) can be used to process data at a remote site and communicate the data and or control information to be used by MVS applications.

The **Systems Application Architecture** (SAA) is a statement of intent to be followed by implementation support for a common user interface, common programming interface, and homogeneous communications facilities to standardize these aspects of application programs across the full line of IBM machinery into the 1990s.

13.2. NETWORK ARCHITECTURE

A network is the combined software and hardware which supplies MVS with communication facilities for terminals to access MVS batch jobs, Data Base/Data Communications (DB/DC), and TSO sessions. Network architecture is concerned with how the data center can support terminals at local and remote locations. The following are important goals of a good network architecture:

1. Design a uniform structure.
2. Establish and honor Software and Hardware Protocols.
3. Develop one network for all functions (homogeneity).
4. Provide for multiple Processor Complexes in the network.
5. Provide easily modified network configuration.

6. Develop transparency of the network to application programmers and end users.

Once the goals of the network have been established, the functions which a good network architecture provide are:

1. Hardware and software that are structured into layers (modular construction).
2. Common data formats established for communication between the layers.
3. Protocols established for communications between layers.
4. Functions defined for each layer.
5. Functions which set up a logical path before communication can take place between two Network entities are defined.

13.2.1. Components

This section discusses the generic components that are needed to attach terminals to MVS. The components of a network architecture are designed around the functions needed to tie a terminal into an application.

Components Needed for Local Attachment The first component needed is the application software to provide the data to be formatted on the terminal.

Second is access method software to build the correct code for the terminal after the application has built the information to be placed on the terminal; that is, the access method helps hide the peculiarities of each type of terminal from the application.

Third is a device controller which accepts commands from the channel to do something specific on a device. A controller is designed to work with devices of the same type and characteristics.

Components Needed for Remote Attachment For remote terminals, the same first three components are needed, but the terminals are connected by modems.

13.2.2. Network Intelligence

The process of controlling communications activity can be located entirely in the central computer or scattered (distributed) throughout the network. Logic Functions and interfaces are located in any one of the points of the network:

1. Terminals.
2. Terminal Control Units.
3. Concentrators.
4. Line Control Units.
5. Front End Processors.
6. Central computers (host Processor Complexes).

13.2.3. Evolution of Communications

Before Network Architectures existed, an application which wanted to display its information on terminals had to completely control the terminal. Some "situations" which arose from this difficult architecture were:

1. Hardware was often developed for specific applications.
2. Standard interfaces did not exist.
3. Separate networks existed for different applications.
4. Excessive costs were incurred:
    a. Maintenance had to be done one on one.
    b. Changes required large programming efforts.
    c. Upgrades required large efforts by the data center.
    d. Interconnection of terminals and applications was almost nonexistent.
    e. Migration to newer terminals was difficult.

The first terminal applications contained the software to drive the terminals in the application software itself. Examples of these terminals were 1052 and 2260 local devices. This software performed all functions to get application information to and from the terminal. One of the author's first applications was to write EXCP level code for a large legal information retrieval system. Each Input/Output operation required the "application system" to write every character on the terminal.

This is also called "roll your own" applications. The drawbacks were many. Each type of terminal required the software to know down to the bit level how the terminal worked. The same task in the processor which was doing database access was "talking" to the terminals. The devices generally were within 100 to 200 feet of the processor. Later, the architecture was expanded to cover many buildings, some even miles away with digital to analog converters — modems. Figure 13.1 shows the two types of "communication" — local and remote.

The major benefit of the program controlling the terminals was speed. This type of software could read and write to the terminal faster than any other architecture. There was no middleman. Some applications had the database encoded in the code required by the terminal. Therefore, the final output could be read from the database and sent to the terminal without conversion.

As line cost increased, it became important to develop efficient line usage. **Switched (dial up)** lines were used with 2740-1 and 2741 devices. **Multidrop (multipoint)** lines were used with 2740 and 327x terminals. (Multidrop means more than one terminal per line.)

The road to true network architecture progressed with the development of Basic Telecommunication Access Method (BTAM) controlling the terminals. Figure 13.2 shows a BTAM flow. BTAM allowed more flexibility in the types of terminals that could be connected to an

Terminals began with local attachment

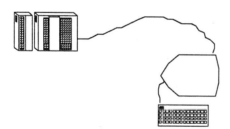

Evolution to remote terminals

Figure 13.1   Terminal attachment. In the beginning, terminals were only attached to System/370 Processor Complexes locally. Eventually, terminals were attached from remote locations by Modulator-Demodulators (MODEMs).

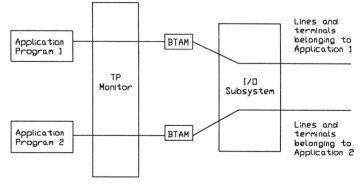

Figure 13.2   BTAM as the TP monitor. BTAM was only a set of access method modules that the application could use to control I/O to specific lines and/or terminals.

application. BTAM controlled the interface with the I/O subsystem. The application only had to build the calls and buffers for BTAM.

The drawback came when the application no longer knew the type of terminal out on the end of the line. Applications were tied to "line mode" queries. These read and wrote lines of data at a time. Sure, some emulated full screen applications, but it was messy.

With the advent of the Telecommunications Access Method (TCAM) and the Virtual Telecommunications Access Method (VTAM), multiple applications could access the same group of lines. Figure 13.3 shows "advanced" telecommunications. A single terminal

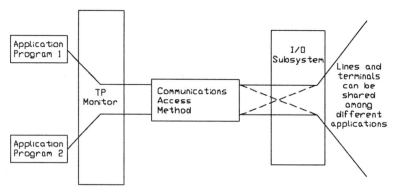

Figure 13.3   TCAM or VTAM as the Access Method. TCAM and/or VTAM is a more complete communications access method. The application asks for and receives information from the terminal, but the nature of the interaction with the terminal is known only to the access method.

could access multiple applications. We will see later that this gave the application programmer much flexibility.

Larger and more complex networks separated the software to control the network from the application software. **Front end processors** are more sophisticated device controllers. The next step was to move network control functions to a remote location and then funnel all activity on a single line to a **remote front end** or **concentrator**. Figure 13.4 shows how a Front end processor can be placed locally (in the same building as the Processor Complex) or at the end of a phone line.

13.2.4. Integration

Integration of the Network into the operating system requires several types of functions. A Software I/O Driver must be available to receive the terminal input and output. A Line Control module must be available to control the communication lines. A Network control module must be available to handle network commands. An Application Subsystem Interface must be available to interface with the COBOL, CICS, TSO, or IMS modules. A communications controller module must be available to start, stop, and control the local and remote communications controller.

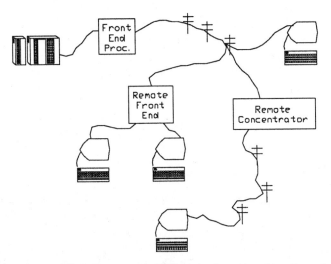

Figure 13.4   Front End Processors. IBM and others developed specialized control units called front end processors to control terminals located remotely to the data center. The Front End Processor may be located in the same building as the Processor Complex or at the end of a telephone line.

13.2.5. Flexibility

Systems Network Architecture was developed to create flexibility. Not every user wants to access the same data. Each user has his/her own requirements for the data center. Flexibility in the type of applications means that the network might support:

1. Data entry.
2. Message switching.
3. Remote job entry.
4. Inquiry and data retrieval.
5. Process control information.

Each of these applications could be accessed from the same physical terminal.

13.2.6. Addressing

Front end processors can be addressed by asynchronous or bisynchronous commands. Each terminal port requires a channel address in the form of cuu, where "c" is the channel and "uu" is the unit address. Each address must be on a byte multiplexor channel — which limits the number of terminals to 256 per channel. Usually only two- or three-byte multiplexor channels are supported on Processor Complexes. Three channels support 768 terminals, a very limiting architecture.

Systems Network Architecture (SNA), using Synchronous Data Link Control (SDLC) addressing can service a large number of terminals for each address.

13.2.7. Routing

Routing applies specifically to IBM **Advanced Communications Function** (ACF) release 3 levels. ACF software allows the definition of more than one route between two subareas in a network, one of which must be a host subarea.

ACF release 3 allows the definition of multiple active SDLC links between two adjacent NCP nodes. These can be parallel links and are limited only by the maximum for which the 37x5 has been configured. Routes can be:

1. Explicit, which is a sequence of physical network elements, that may include host nodes, NCP nodes, and transmission groups.
2. Virtual, which is a logical connection between two communicating subarea nodes.

13.3. TERMINAL TO APPLICATION INTERFACES

An application program (such as a payroll program) uses VTAM macros to request connection to a terminal in the network and to transfer data between itself and the connected terminal.

Connection is the process of making a network path available for communication between a program and a terminal. Attachment may be in:

1. **Record mode**, designed for use with intelligent network devices such as control units. Data is independent of the path or communication link control. The data stream can be variable length and all 8-bit combinations can be valid data.
2. **Basic mode**, supporting non-SNA devices using start-stop BSC line control and local 3270 terminals. This mode supports a response mode of operation where each transaction has only a transmission and response portion.

13.3.1. Introduction to Telecommunication Access Methods

A Teleprocessing monitor (TP) is a special set of programs which act as a second command level to MVS for application and network control. TP monitors provide the support for Access Methods such as TCAM and VTAM which interface applications to the network.

TP monitors can be imbedded in a special operating system or can be part of a Data Base Management System (DBMS) package. TP monitors can also be standalone.

Some TP monitors use queuing to disk so the number of accesses per second may be limited to the speed of accessing the disk. Some TP monitors use virtual storage to queue terminal transactions, so the amount of common virtual storage may limit the number of transactions per second.

Teleprocessing Monitor Functions The major functions of a Teleprocessing monitor are to:

1. Manage the flow of data on each communications line.
2. Control the terminals.
3. Dynamically allocate line buffers.
4. Handle terminal data flow and Processor Complex to terminal control.
5. Use data center tables to define the configuration of lines and terminals and map these definitions so the application to use the lines and terminals.
6. Detect and recover from communication line errors.
7. Recognize permanent errors in the configuration and reconfigure, if possible.
8. Provide interfaces to DB/DC and high level languages.
9. Provide test and debug facilities for online application programs.

Software   MVS is responsible for the scheduling and execution of all programs in the computer and for controlling access to all I/O units connected to the CPU. When a program needs data from the I/O device, MVS suspends execution of the program and initiates the I/O module responsible for initiating I/O from the device. While the I/O module is executing, MVS selects and executes some other program.

The Teleprocessing monitor is responsible for priority and scheduling of the Teleprocessing requests from application tasks to be presented to MVS for execution.

13.3.2.   Basic Telecommunications Access Method (BTAM)

The Basic Telecommunications Access Method (BTAM) was one of the first MVT access methods for terminal access. BTAM is used today for large OEM applications that perform many of these terminal handling functions in application code. All the application needs is a method to have MVS do the I/O functions for them. BTAM characteristics are:

1. Device and line control are combined. Terminals are treated as a single entity.
2. Each application program owns and manages its own lines and terminals.
3. Neither lines nor terminals can be shared with another address space or application.
4. Each application program reads a message from a device into a predesignated buffer.

5. The application program issues a WRITE for output.
6. No message editing is performed by BTAM.
7. The application program issues low level (assembler) WRITE macros. A WAIT macro is issued until the I/O is complete.
8. Devices and data lines are referred to by the physical address generated in the MVS system.
9. User-written exits can be provided to map symbolic names to physical addresses for read and write operations.
10. All device and line control information must be a part of the buffer, and it must be unique to the destination terminal.

13.3.3. Telecommunications Access Method (TCAM)

IBM introduced TCAM as a replacement for BTAM. The improved function of TCAM enabled customer networks to grow.

TCAM handles many different types of terminals. TCAM has its own control program for queueing and traffic scheduling.

Figure 13.5 shows the three general types of communication in a TCAM environment. The first one shows terminal A sending in the question to the application asking "What is the month?" The application program researches and routes the answer "June" back to terminal A.

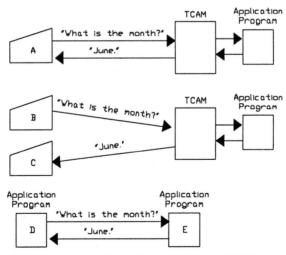

Figure 13.5   TCAM communications. The three types of TCAM communication are terminal to application, terminal to terminal, and application to application.

The second application has terminal "B" asking the question, but terminal "C" gets the answer. The third application has application program "D" asking the question, and application program "E" responding back to application program "D."

The following are characteristics of TCAM:

1. Allows line and device sharing between applications.
2. Employs a set of message queues between applications and the communications network.
3. Permits message switching.
4. The TCAM Message Control Program (MCP) performs network control functions.
5. MCP establishes connections and performs recovery, handles queuing, routing, acknowledgements, and correlates received acknowledgements with sent requests.
6. Handles logical connection (session) management and path control.
7. Supports application programs' use of high level GET and PUT macros.
8. Supports application program line and device independence.
9. Supports user-specified message handler code to analyze, validate, and edit data messages.

Figure 13.6 shows the logic flow of TCAM. The user "writes" to a buffer in the common system area (CSA). TCAM moves the buffer through the network to and from the terminal.

13.3.4.   Virtual Telecommunication Access Method (VTAM)

This section is an introduction to VTAM and the Systems Network Architecture (SNA). The concepts are presented in a general manner because complete treatment of the topic is beyond the scope of this book. Several places to continue your study of SNA are:

1. *Advanced Communications Function — Primer* (GG24-1547).
2. *Systems Network Architecture: Concepts and Products* (GC30-3072).
3. *Advanced Communications Function Products Installation Guide* (GG24-1557).

VTAM is a full-function telecommunications Access Method. VTAM supports the IBM 37x5. The software loaded into the 37x5 is

TSO/TCAM Logic Flow

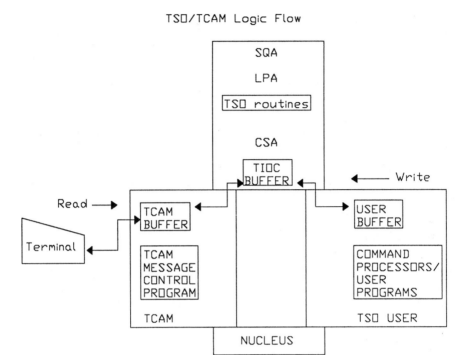

Figure 13.6   TCAM logic flow. In a TCAM network, the application "writes" to a TCAM buffer, and TCAM moves the buffer to the terminal. The buffers, called **TIOC** buffers, are allocated at the start of TCAM and are stable as long as the system is running.

the **Network Control Program** (NCP). In the Processor Complex, the **Synchronous Data Link Control** (SDLC) protocol is used to talk to the NCP. VTAM has the ability to work with any file access method or structure, including the structure inherent in most database management systems.

The characteristics of VTAM are:

1. VTAM allows applications programs to share resources, devices, and lines directly without queueing. In Figure 13.7, Application "A" can have terminals "1" and "4" communicating with it. At the same time, terminals "2" and "3" can be communicating with application "B."

    With Multiple access monitors, special 3x74 control units, or Personal Computers, a single terminal can be communicating with multiple applications at the same time.

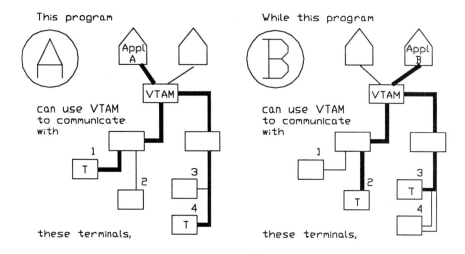

Figure 13.7   VTAM Resource Sharing. Application "A" can be communicating with the terminals "1" and "4" while application "B" can be communicating with terminals "2" and "3."

2. Control the allocation of resources.
3. Establish, control, and terminate connections between applications programs and terminals.
4. Transfer data between applications programs and terminals.
5. Permit operation of the network to be monitored.
6. Permit dynamic reconfiguration of the network.
7. Uses dynamic storage allocation.
8. Is designed to be more efficient than TCAM.

Figure 13.8 shows the buffer movement between the address space which is talking to the terminal and the terminal itself. The buffers are still in CSA but are moved by instructions in the user's address space. The CSA VTAM buffers are in CSA below the line in MVS/XA with VTAM Release 2 and above the 16-Mb line in MVS/XA with VTAM Release 3.

The application program writes to **Logical Units** (LUs) defined in VTAM. These logical units are mapped to **Physical Units** (PUs):

1. **Logical Unit (LU).** The Logical Unit (LU) provides the addressing which an application uses to talk to a point of access in the network. The end user has a logical unit (or multiple

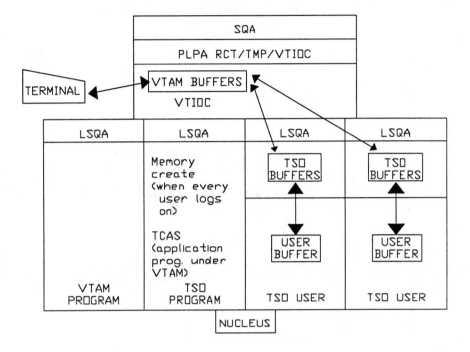

Figure 13.8 VTAM Buffer Movement. In a VTAM environment, the application program "writes" to buffers in its own address space and/or CSA. VTAM routines transmit the data to and/or from the terminal.

LUs) to access the network. The LU is associated with the application (such as CICS), and the connection is made.

2. **Session.** The LUs are connected in a session which is the connection of two logical units. Buffers are allocated for the communication between the logical units.

3. **Physical Unit (PU).** The Physical Unit is a set of SNA hardware which provides services used to control terminals, controllers, and processors. Each terminal, controller and processor is a physical unit. Figure 13.9 shows the VTAM logical unit and physical unit associations. In this example, application (1) moves a screen image (2) to a VTAM buffer (3). VTAM (4) moves the buffer through the 37x5 (5) to the cluster controller (6) and finally to the terminal (7) which is attached to application (1).

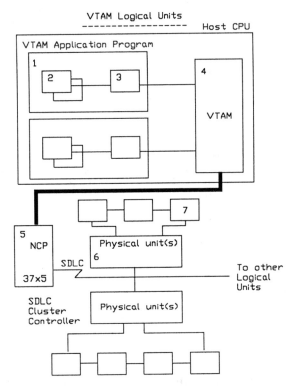

Figure 13.9   VTAM Logical and Physical Units. VTAM applications communicate to "logical" units, and VTAM converts the logical unit address to "physical" unit addresses.

13.4. SUMMARY

Application programs not only manipulate data sets but also must communicate with people and with applications on other computers.

People interact with applications using various kinds of display stations, printers, and more esoteric devices located locally or remotely with respect to an MVS system. Various communication line topologies dictated by economics further complicate communications management.

Once, applications handled communications unaided. As communications increased in complexity, the burden overwhelmed applications, and access methods such as BTAM were developed and refined to contain the complexity. TCAM overcame many of BTAM's limitations, but TCAM could only connect a host MVS system with a terminal.

The need for distributed processing, in which arbitrary connections between hosts (peer-to-peer), terminals and host, and terminals and host through intermediate hosts required rethinking communications architecture. VTAM is the current TP access method and handles interconnections like these.

VTAM is, however, not an end — local area networks (LANs) and communications between peers located in separate LANs pose problems for VTAM, so enhancement or replacement of VTAM is likely. Protocols used in VTAM, LU6.2 in particular, shall live on.

IBM has not stopped with SNA, a network architecture to unify its disparate product line, but has continued the trend by announcing SAA to unify the appearance and development of applications on these interconnected machines.

Communications, networking, and standard interfaces are exciting things to which one book, much less one chapter, cannot do justice. We return, therefore, to the mundane and look at the MVS utilities we use to keep our MVS systems running in the distributed world.

14

Utilities

14.1. INTRODUCTION

Several types of utilities are provided in a typical MVS data center. Remember, the primary goal of a data center is the management of data for the corporation. It is not surprising, then, that most utilities are concerned with data manipulation.

What is a utility? It is a generalized program which can be used by members of the data center and the data center users to perform data processing functions. These functions are so commonly used that it is cost effective to purchase them or write them with programming staff at the data center. There are several types:

1. **Application utilities** are programs provided by IBM to create, change, or delete MVS data sets and control system data sets. The utilities presented here are programs which normally run as executable steps in batch jobs. For interactive use, most data centers have standardized on ISPF as the primary editor in an MVS environment. Some of the batch utilities are duplicated in ISPF panels.

   Most batch utilities are documented in the MVS utilities manual (e.g., *MVS/XA Data Administration Utilities* — GC26-4018). Be careful to match the manual to the version of MVS which you are using. MVS utilities are included in MVS as a part of the **Data Facility Product** (DFP).

2. **Sort/Merge** is covered in a separate section because it is very important and has a large part to play in data center management.

3. The Access Methods Services program **IDCAMS** is introduced here but is too diverse to be covered in this book. You are encouraged to investigate the fine books on VSAM.[1]

4. **System utilities** are generally used by the Systems Programming staff of a data center, but they supply several functions which are very useful for application programmers. Unfortunately, no one teaches this to the applications staff!

5. **Device Support Facilities** (DSF) is a program that IBM supplies to perform maintenance on DASD. DSF is included with MVS.

6. **Data Facility Data Set Services** (DFDSS) is a program that IBM supplies to backup and restore DASD. IBM charges extra for DFDSS.

7. **Data Facility Hierarchical Storage Manager** (DFHSM) is an example of a utility that archives and manages data sets for the end user. IBM charges extra for DFHSM.

OEM utilities (utilities written by "Original Equipment Manufacturers") are programs written by vendors other than IBM. The field of OEM utilities is not covered in this book. You are encouraged to investigate these utilities because your data center will find them cost-effective.

Before we cover utilities, we will review JCL. Those of you who are experts at JCL can fast forward these pages to the next part.

14.1.1. JCL for Utilities

This book is not a JCL manual, but you must know some JCL for me to discuss utilities. This review of JCL covers the important topics.

JCL consists of "card image" (80 columns wide) data which contains instructions to MVS on how to run batch jobs. Only columns 1

---

1. One of the best is Jay Ranade, *VSAM Performance, Design, and Fine Tuning*, Macmillan, New York, NY 1987. (ISBN 0-02-948631-9)

through 71 are used by MVS. Column 72 may be used for a continuation indicator, and columns 73 through 80 may be used for optional identification or sequence numbers.

All JCL begins in column 1 and 2 with "//." The next character indicates the type of JCL card. A "*" (thus, a "//*") is a comment card and is ignored. A blank in the third column is either the end of the JCL stream (a NULL) or a continuation from a previous JCL card. Any other character in column 3 begins a name field.

Lowercase letters are not allowed in JCL. Including them will cause the entire job to be flushed and not executed.

There are four areas on a JCL statement:

1. The **name** field is a one to eight character area which contains alphanumeric characters. The first character must be an alphabetic (A–Z) or so-called "national" character (@, $, or #). In this book, the use of lowercase letters indicates you can pick any of these combinations of letters.
2. The **operation** field names the type of JCL statement:
   a. **JOB** statements delineate units of work for JES. The JOB statement indicates and defines the beginning of a batch job. All the cards from the JOB statement to a null statement (or another JOB card) are part of the batch job.
   b. **EXEC** statements delineate job steps or programs which are to be executed as part of the job. There must be at least one EXEC statement in a job.
   c. **DD** (Data Definition) statements describe data sets which can be used by the program that is executed by the program or series of programs specified on the EXEC card.
3. The **operand** field contains parameters separated by commas and terminated by the first nonquoted blank.
4. The **comment** field contains comments to explain the card to a human reader (such as the author!).

In Figure 14.1, each JCL card is numbered for reference to the explanations following; these numbers are *not* part of the cards! Characters in uppercase are keywords and should be entered as is. Lowercase characters are to be changed according to the rules of the data center. The meaning of each card is:

1. The JOB card (cards 1–6):
   a. The JOB statement has a "jobname" starting in column 3. This jobname will be used by MVS to give a name to the Address Space Identification Block (ASID). The "acct" field

NAME	OPERATION	OPERAND	COMMENT

1. `//jobname`   JOB   (acct),   this is a comment
2. `//`   'programmer name'
3. `//`   REGION=4096K,
4. `//`   TIME=(5),
5. `//`   NOTIFY=tsoid,
6. `//`   MSGCLASS=c
7. `//jobstep`   EXEC   PGM=IEFBR14
8. `//*SYSUDUMP`   DD   SYSOUT=*
9. `//SYSPRINT`   DD   SYSOUT=*
10. `//SYSUT1`   DD   DSN=data.set.name,
11. `//`   DISP=disp
12. `//SYSUT2`   DD   DSN=data.set.name,
13. `//`   DISP=disp
14. `//SYSIN`   DD   DUMMY
15. `//`

Figure 14.1   Sample JCL. There are four fields on a JCL card. The name field is like a label, the operation field identifies the type of JCL card, the operand field supplies positional or keyword parameters, and the comment field is for the analyst to document the card.

is a data center defined group of characters which allow the person who creates the job to tell the data center which account should be charged with the resources that the job requires.

When the operator issues a "DISPLAY ACTIVE" command, the jobname from the JOB card is displayed.

The first positional parameter field — the accounting field — is included on the first JOB card. A positional parameter is determined by its position on the card, rather than by a name associated with the parameter. The accounting field is completely dependent on the rules of the data center. There are no MVS requirements.

The last character in the operand field of this example is a comma, indicating a continuation onto the next card. Subsequent continuation cards will end the operand field with a comma. The last continuation card will not have a comma as the last character in the operand field.

b. The second card (2) is a continuation card (column 3 is blank) and contains a second positional parameter — the programmer or department name. This field is used by JES for an identification of the person who submitted the job. Note that the continuation begins in column 16 of the card. This is one of the strangest rules in JCL. JCL is generally freeform but has some very restrictive rules. Continuations can begin in column 4 (columns 1–3 must contain two slashes and a blank) through 16. If your continuation begins in column 17 or later, MVS will issue an error message and the job will fail.

Note the positional parameter is enclosed in quotes. The quotes are required because there is a blank between "programmer" and "name" in this example. If the name field had been continuous characters, then the single quotes would not be necessary. I recommend you always include single quotes in this field.

c. The third card (3) is "REGION=4096K." After the first two positional parameters, any of the **keyword** parameters can be coded. A keyword parameter is one which consists of a one to eight "word" and an equals sign. The REGION= parameter can be on the JOB card or the EXEC card. I recommend that the REGION parameter should only be on the JOB card and not on any EXEC card.

d. The next card (4) — "TIME=(5)" — is a parameter to indicate the time in CPU minutes you expect the *entire job to use*.[2] One of the most confusing things to even experienced data processing experts is the TIME= rules. The TIME= on the JOB card specifies the *cumulative CPU time* which can be used by *all steps* (EXECs) in the job. Each step has a default TIME limit in MVS. If the JOB card has TIME=60, and the default TIME= for each step is 30 minutes, then when a single step exceeds 30 minutes, the job will abnormally terminate.

e. The next card (5) — "NOTIFY=tsoid" tells MVS the completion of this job should be sent to the TSO userid identified by "tsoid."

f. The next card (6) — "MSGCLASS=c" is used to instruct MVS into which JES output class the output of the job should be placed. This card does not end with a comma and thus terminates the JOB card.

2. The next card (7) is an EXEC card. The program executed is IEFBR14. The name of the step is "jobstep."

---

2. Two "times" are used in MVS — wall clock and CPU time. Wall clock is the elapsed time as observed by a clock such as may be on the wall. CPU time is the time MVS measures that a program or group of programs are actually using the CPU.

3. The next card (8) is an example of a comment card. I have chosen a card that would otherwise provide a JES SYSOUT data set for a named file of "SYSUDUMP." Because it is a comment card, though, MVS will ignore the card. In some cases, errors in utilities will not require you get MVS to print an "abnormal termination" dump of virtual storage. Occasionally, the dump will be useful. Keeping the SYSUDUMP card as a comment card is a good technique in case it is needed in the future.

4. The next card (9) is not needed all the time, but almost every utility uses SYSPRINT as a data set to print messages and reports. It is used so often that many people place a SYSPRINT in every job stream. It may not be very efficient, but it beats strange condition codes and cryptic messages because the output message data set is not there. Note the specification of SYSOUT=*. This tells MVS to allocate a JES spooled data set to the same class as the job messages and JCL. This technique is very helpful when the output of the job will be viewed by one of the spool display programs.

5. The next two cards (10,11) are for a named file **SYSUT1**, which is a common input name for IBM utilities. The minimum fields required are data set name (DSN=) and data set disposition (DISP=).

Some utilities do not need data set names on their DD cards. They only require UNIT=, DISP=, and VOLUME=. The utility uses this DD card to allocate the areas on the volume which are necessary for the operations indicated in the control cards.

In some cases you will use **UNIT=SYSALLDA**.[3] All MVS systems have a generic value of SYSALLDA to point to every Direct Access Storage Devices (DASD) in the configuration. I use SYSALLDA for input or read only JCL cards because I have always worked in a data center with more than one device type.

SYSALLDA always works in JCL. SYSALLDA only works sometimes in control cards. (Control cards are data input to many utilities.) For example, IEHLIST and IEHMOVE control

---

3. Do not confuse SYSALLDA with the popular name — SYSDA given, by many data centers, to volumes mounted as "public" — for temporary data sets (created and scratched within the same job).

cards at MVS XA 2.2 and, later, allow SYSALLDA. In some earlier versions, SYSALLDA was not allowed as a parameter in IEHLIST or IEHMOVE. The only way to know is to try the parameter in your installation.

6. The next two cards (12,13) are for a named file **SYSUT2**, which is a common output name for IBM utilities.

7. The next card (14) — SYSIN — is a second common input file for IBM utilities. The example shows a "DUMMY" file specification. When the utility tries to read and process the file, it goes immediately to the end of file routine. Some utilities have defaults and do not need control cards, so a dummy file is acceptable. Generally, however, the SYSIN file contains control cards or commands to the utility. The following shows the cards needed for a SYSIN file. The "/*" indicates the end of the instream data set to JES:

//SYSIN DD *
control cards here
/*

8. The last card (15) is a NULL card to indicate the last card of a job. Many programmers and analysts leave off the NULL card. Although it is not necessary, it is good practice to always include the NULL card.

14.2. MVS APPLICATION UTILITIES

Application utilities are a collection of the programs that IBM provides that are likely to be used by application programmer, systems analysts, and systems programmers. The community of data center users may also use these programs, but their use will probably be limited to sophisticated information center users.

14.2.1. IEFBR14

One of the first programs I learned to use was the IEFBR14 "utility." It was explained that IEFBR14 could do any data set manipulation you needed. It would allocate a data set, scratch it, or catalog the data set. I was amazed. Figure 14.2 contains two examples of IEFBR14. The first one is to create a data set, and the second one is to delete the data set.

IEFBR14 is unusual because the program itself does nothing. The name of the program comes from the assembler language branch instruction used to exit a procedure or program. In fact, the first ver-

Example to create a data set:

```
//jobname    JOB  (acct),"programmer name",REGION=4096K,TIME=(5),
//           NOTIFY=tsoid,MSGCLASS=c
//jobstep    EXEC PGM=IEFBR14
//SYSUT1     DD   DSN=data.set.name,DISP=(NEW,CATLG),SPACE=(TRK,1),
//           VOL=SER=volser
//
```

Example to delete a data set:

```
//jobname    JOB  (acct),"programmer name",REGION=4096K,TIME=(5)
//           NOTIFY=tsoid,MSGCLASS=c
//jobstep    EXEC PGM=IEFBR14
//SYSUT1     DD   DSN=data.set.name,DISP=(OLD,DELETE),SPACE=(TRK,1),
//           VOL=SER=volser
//
```

Figure 14.2   IEFBR14. One IBM "utility" can be used to create, delete, or catalog data sets.

sion of the only program only consisted of two hexadecimal characters: x'07FE', or branch unconditionally to the address in general purpose register 14. Register 14 contains the address of the initiator module which attaches or calls every batch job.

The program was only two bytes long: 07FE. At some time in the MVS progression of releases, MVS *doubled the size of the module to four bytes.* The entire program was now x'1BFF07FE' — clear register 15 (the return code) and return immediately to the initiator.

IEFBR14 works because the data set allocation and deallocation routines handle the information in the JCL, and all that is needed is for a program (any program) to execute to allow allocation to create and deallocation to dispose of data sets.

While IEFBR14 can scratch and allocate data sets, it is *not recommended* for production JCL job streams. If a data set is in a DD card, the data set must exist if DISP=OLD is coded. Let's examine a job that is part of a series of production jobs. Previous jobs have taken backups of a production data set and validated (edited) the transactions which are to be applied to the production master data set.

1. This production job has three steps:
    a. Step 1 deletes the data set which will be created using IEFBR14. The JCL contains DISP=(OLD,DELETE) for the old production data set.

b.   Step 2 sorts input transactions which are to be applied to the file.

c.   Step 3 merges the backup production data set and the transactions. The JCL contains DISP=(NEW,CATLG) for the new production data set.

2. Suppose the job abends in step 2 — the sort step — for some reason.

3. The job must be very carefully restarted in step 2 — bypassing the first step. If the first step is attempted, the job will end with a JCL error because the data set is specified as DISP=(OLD,DELETE) and the data set is not there.

If the IDCAMS utility had been used in step 1 instead of IEFBR14, control cards could have been passed to request deletion of the data set. If the data set were not there, then the IDCAMS step would end with a condition code, not terminate the whole job with a JCL error. IDCAMS can even be instructed with control cards to set the condition code equal to zero.

The instructions for restarting this job are much clearer if IDCAMS is used instead of IEFBR14 — "if the job abends in step 1 or 2, restart the job!" Your production job streams should be made as simple and recovery should as easy as possible. Where possible, recovery actions should not require JCL changes.

14.2.2.   IEBGENER

I have researched several data centers and IEBGENER was the most frequently used program at those data centers. Unlike IEFBR14, IEBGENER actually opens data sets and moves data. The name comes from the function — generate data. Some functions IEBGENER can perform are:

1. Copy a sequential file. A sequential file could be a Physical Sequential file or a single Partitioned Data Set member. Figure 14.3 is an example of this most popular of all the functions. The file described in SYSUT1 is copied to the file described in SYSUT2. The SYSIN file is a "dummy" data set. When IEB-GENER opens the SYSIN data set, it immediately gets an end-of-file indication, and IEBGENER takes all of its defaults — copy SYSUT1 to SYSUT2. Otherwise, SYSIN could contain control cards to alter the behavior of IEBGENER.

```
// Jobname       JOB  (acct),'programmer name',REGION=4096K,TIME=(5),
//                    NOTIFY=tsoid,MSGCLASS=c
// jobstep       EXEC PGM=IEBGENER
//*SYSUDUMP      DD   SYSOUT=*
//SYSUT1         DD   DSN=data.set.name,DISP=disp
//SYSUT2         DD   DSN=data.set.name,DISP=disp
//SYSPRINT       DD   SYSOUT=*
//SYSIN          DD   DUMMY
//
```

Figure 14.3   IEBGENER. The major purpose of this utility is to move data.
Most data centers use the program to copy data from one data set to another.
In the above example, the data set in SYSUT1 is copied to the data set
described in SYSUT2.

2. Print the contents of a file. The file could be copied to a JES
   SYSOUT data set, or parts of the file could be printed.
3. Reorganize a file by expanding or changing fields in a record.
4. Change certain attributes of a file such as the record length or
   block size.

IEBGENER requires the attributes of the SYSUT1 file be exactly
the same as those of SYSUT2. These include the record format
(RECFM=FB on input must be RECFM=FB on output) and logical
record size (e.g., LRECL=133). The physical block sizes can be different. IEBGENER can be used to "reblock" a file. A file with
LRECL=133, BLKSIZE=1330 can be copied to a file with
LRECL=133, BLKSIZE=13300.

There is a major problem with IEBGENER in MVS/370. IEB-
GENER forced the number of buffers to two, which throttled the I/O
processing. MVS/XA and later versions may have removed this
restriction. Some OEM software companies created IEBGENER front
end processors, which detected from the JCL if a plain copy was to
be done, and did the copy with a larger, more efficient number of I/O
buffers. These OEM utilities claimed severalfold improvements over
IEBGENER. SYNCSORT Incorporated has an example of one of
these OEM utilities — SYNCGENR.

14.2.3. IEBCOPY

IEBCOPY is a utility program used to make copies of and maintain
partitioned data sets. The three major functions of IEBCOPY are:

1. Compress a partitioned data set. The members of a partitioned data set are moved together (compressed) to remove the space left behind by changing existing members.

   Figure 14.4 is an example of compressing a data set. Note that the disposition of the data set has been changed to OLD. The SYSIN DD card has been changed from "DUMMY" to "*" to indicate an instream (JES-controlled) data set. The control card points the input data set (INDD=) and the output data set (OUTDD=) to the same DD card.

   Warning: When IEBCOPY compresses a data set in place, it unloads the directory to the work data set and starts moving members around in the data part of the PDS. Unless IEB-COPY successfully completes, *the data set is damaged.* The directory is invalid! Many installations go to the trouble of copying the file out to another data set, compressing in place, and then scratching the copy. If the job fails, the backup copy is used to restore the damaged data set. Another technique is to copy the full PDS to a new name and rename the old PDS to a temporary name and rename the new PDS to the old name.

2. Copy a partitioned data set from one data set to another. The data set may be another on a DASD or on tape. If IEBCOPY moves the data set to tape, it is said to be *unloaded.*

   Two "work" data sets — SYSUT3 and SYSUT4 — are also allocated. IEBCOPY requires these work data sets to store intermediate data for some of its functions. You should always have them in your JCL. They can be temporary data sets. The data sets do not have to be very large. You can specify one track with secondary extents.

```
//jobname      JOB  (acct),"programmer name",REGION=4096K,TIME=(5),
//                  NOTIFY=tsoid,MSGCLASS=c
//Jobstep      EXEC PGM=IEBCOPY
//*SYSUDUMP    DD   SYSOUT=*
//SYSUT1       DD   DSN=data.set.name,DISP=OLD   data set to be compressed
//SYSPRINT     DD   SYSOUT=*
//SYSUT3       DD   SPACE=(TRK,(1,1)),DISP=(,DELETE)
//SYSUT4       DD   SPACE=(TRK,(1,1)),DISP=(,DELETE)
//SYSIN        DD   *
     COPY INDD=SYSUT1,OUTDD=SYSUT1
/*
//
```

Figure 14.4   IEBCOPY. One of the most used functions of IEBCOPY is to compress a data set. This example shows how to do it. Note the addition of two work data sets — SYSUT3 and SYSUT4.

3. Merge partitioned data sets. Two or more partitioned data sets can be merged into a third data set.

IEBCOPY has control cards — INCLUDE and EXCLUDE — which allow the user to copy certain members.

IEBCOPY is a very important part of conversion from MVS/370 to MVS/XA, because IEBCOPY is used to copy, reblock, and most importantly, fix up the RLD records in a load library. The **ALTERMOD** (alter load modules in place) and **COPYMOD** (copy and alter load modules) statements will remove problems with non-XA modules.

Once the conversation to MVS/XA is complete, you should not forget COPYMOD. The data center can rebuild load modules to fit the device on which the load module data set is allocated. All vendor libraries should be copied with COPYMOD to ensure the load module really is blocked at the proper size. Some vendors (including IBM) create load modules which will fit on the smallest DASD device supported — the 2314 at 7,000 bytes!

Even worse, vendors may use the "DC" operand for the Linkage editor and force 1,024 (1 Kb!) blocks. That really slows down the load of those modules.

14.2.4. IEBDG

IEBDG gets its name from Data Generator; thus, the major function of IEBDG is to create a sequential or ISAM file. Because ISAM is no longer a viable access method, and IEBGENER will perform data generation functions, IEBDG is rarely used in most data centers but is used often enough that you should know what it does.

IEBDG allows you to use the defaults of SYSUT1 as input and SYSUT2 as output or define the DD names in a control card. Figure 14.5 contains an example of IEBDG, creating a data set with the output defaulting to the SYSUT2 data set.

14.2.5. IEBEDIT

IEBEDIT is a program to scan a file and break up the file into jobs or jobsteps. IEBEDIT was very important in the early days of MVS when the system generation process created many jobs in a single data set. Today, the ISPF editor is much better to use, and IEBEDIT is rarely used in most data centers.

```
// Jobname          JOB  (acct),"programmer name",REGION=4096K,TIME=(5),
//                       NOTIFY=tsoid,MSGCLASS=c
// jobstep          EXEC PGM=IEBDG
//*SYSUDUMP         DD   SYSOUT=*
//SYSUT2            DD   DSN=data.set.name,DISP=disp
//SYSPRINT          DD   SYSOUT=*
//SYSIN             DD   *
      DSD   OUTPUT=(SYSUT2)
      FD    NAME=NAME1,LENGTH=10,FORMAT=AN
      FD    NAME=COUNT,LENGTH=10,FORMAT=ZD,INDEX=1
      CREATE QUANTITY=10,NAME=(NAME1,COUNT)
      END
/*
//

OUTPUT OF UTILITY:

ABCDEFGHIJ0000000001
ABCDEFGHIJ0000000002
ABCDEFGHIJ0000000003
ABCDEFGHIJ0000000004
ABCDEFGHIJ0000000005
ABCDEFGHIJ0000000006
ABCDEFGHIJ0000000007
ABCDEFGHIJ0000000008
ABCDEFGHIJ0000000009
ABCDEFGHIJ0000000010
```

Figure 14.5   IEBDG. The example will generate a sequential file with two fields. The first field — 10 characters — is in columns 1–10 and contains "ABCDEFGHIJ." The second field — 10 characters — is in columns 11–20 and contains "0000000001" on the first card and "0000000010" on the tenth card.

Figure 14.6 shows an example of IEBEDIT. IEBEDIT will read the data set indicated by SYSUT1, look for the beginning of a job with a name of JOB1, and place all JCL from that point until the next job in the data set indicated by SYSUT2.

14.2.6. IEBISAM

IEBISAM is a utility to load, unload, and print ISAM data sets. Because ISAM is not a recommended access method any longer, this utility has decreased in importance.

The functions IEBISAM can do are:

1. Copy an ISAM data set from one DASD volume to another.
2. Create a backup of an ISAM data set to magnetic tape or another DASD volume.

```
//jobname      JOB  (acct),'programmer name',REGION=4096K,TIME=(5),
//                  NOTIFY=tsoid,MSGCLASS=c
//jobstep      EXEC PGM=IEBEDIT
//*SYSUDUMP    DD   SYSOUT=*
//SYSUT1       DD   DSN=data.set.name,DISP=disp
//SYSUT2       DD   DSN=data.set.name,DISP=disp
//SYSPRINT     DD   SYSOUT=*
//SYSIN        DD   *
     EDIT START=JOB1
/*
//
```

Figure 14.6   IEBEDIT. All the steps in JOB1 will be copied from one data set to another.

3. Create an ISAM data set from an unloaded data set. This feature also is the "compress" function because to "compress" an ISAM data set, you first unload the data set, scratch and reallocate the data set, and then reload with IEBISAM. Figure 14.7 is an example of an unload.
4. Print an ISAM data set.

14.2.7.   IEBPTPCH

The IEBPTPCH utility is used to:

1. Print a sequential file or member of a partitioned data set.
2. Punch (to a card punch) a member of a partitioned data set.
3. Format the printed or punched output. The data fields of the input record could be repositioned, and packed decimal fields could be unpacked and made printable.

```
//jobname      JOB  (acct),'programmer name',REGION=4096K,TIME=(5),
//                  NOTIFY=tsoid,MSGCLASS=c
//jobstep      EXEC PGM=IEBISAM,PARM=UNLOAD
//*SYSUDUMP    DD   SYSOUT=*
//SYSUT1       DD   DSN=data.set.name,DISP=disp
//SYSUT2       DD   DSN=data.set.name,DISP=disp
//SYSPRINT     DD   SYSOUT=*
//
```

Figure 14.7   IEBISAM. This example will unload an ISAM data set pointed to by SYSUT1 and place the unloaded data in the data set pointed to by SYSUT2.

This utility is not used much by data centers today, and the reasons are that IEBPTPCH does not access VSAM data sets, and the control cards require some study to use. Two PRINT keywords that are useful are **STARTAFT** and **STOPAFT**. These can be used to print a small portion of a file in the middle or at the end of a file.

Figure 14.8 is an example of a simple print of all the members of a partitioned data set. Note that the RECORD FIELD is required or IEBPTPCH takes its default, which is to put a space between each 8 characters in a data set.

14.2.8. IEBUPDTE

IEBUPDTE is a utility to manipulate 80-byte records (cards). IEBUPDTE is limited to 80-byte logical records and is used for source program maintenance in batch mode. ISPF is much better at source editing, changing and maintenance, so IEBUPDTE is generally not used by data centers to maintain 80-byte card image records.

One of the few uses which remain for IEBUPDTE is that some OEM vendors send changes to their source in IEBUPDTE format. There are several drawbacks to using IEBUPDTE to maintain remote copies of source. Unless IEBUPDTE is used to completely replace a member (as in Figure 14.9), then the receiving member must have the same sequence numbers in columns 72–80 that the vendor has at the vendor's data center.

Figure 14.9 is an example of placing an entire PDS member in a data set from a sequential data set. In this instance, the "input" is in SYSIN and the output is placed into the data set pointed to by the SYSUT2 DD card.

```
//jobname      JOB  (acct),'programmer name',REGION=4096K,TIME=(5),
//                  NOTIFY=tsoid,MSGCLASS=c
//jobstep      EXEC PGM=IEBPTPCH
//*SYSUDUMP    DD   SYSOUT=*
//SYSUT1       DD   DSN=data.set.name,DISP=disp
//SYSPRINT     DD   SYSOUT=*
//SYSIN        DD   *
    PRINT TYPORG=PO,MAXFLDS=99,MAXNAME=99
    RECORD FIELD=(80)
/*
//
```

Figure 14.8   IEBPTPCH. This example will print all of the members of a partitioned data set described by SYSUT1.

```
//jobname        JOB  (acct),"programmer name",REGION=4096K,TIME=(5),
//               NOTIFY=tsoid,MSGCLASS=c
//jobstep        EXEC PGM=IEBUPDTE
//*SYSUDUMP     DD    SYSOUT=*
//SYSUT2        DD    DSN=data.set.name,DISP=disp
//SYSPRINT      DD    SYSOUT=*
//SYSIN DD *
  ./ ADD NAME=NEW1
    THIS IS GOOD
/*
//
```

Figure 14.9 IEBUPDTE. This example shows IEBUPDTE replacing an entire member of a partitioned data set.

14.2.9. IEHLIST

IEHLIST is a program to list entries in a CVOL (non-VSAM) catalog, to list entries in the directory of a partitioned data set, or to list entries in the Volume Table of Contents (VTOC) of a DASD device. IEHLIST requires the volume serial number of any DASD to be inspected be included in the SYSUT1 data set.

Figure 14.10 shows an example of the JCL and control cards necessary to list the VTOC of a volume. IEHLIST is one of the utilities that does not need a data set name in the utility DD card. A little known shortcut for MVS is to use **UNIT=SYSALLDA** on JCL cards which could be changed often to different device types. SYSALLDA is a generic name that can be used for all DASD device types in the facility. In some versions of MVS, IEHLIST allows VOL=SYSALLDA=vvvvvv in the control card.

```
//jobname        JOB  (acct),"programmer name",REGION=4096K,TIME=(5),
//               NOTIFY=tsoid,MSGCLASS=c
//jobstep        EXEC PGM=IEHLIST
//*SYSUDUMP     DD    SYSOUT=*
//SYSPRINT      DD    SYSOUT=*
//SYSUT1        DD    VOL=SER=vvvvvv,DISP=OLD,UNIT=SYSALLDA
//SYSIN         DD *
        LISTVTOC FORMAT,VOL=SYSALLDA=vvvvvv
/*
//
```

Figure 14.10 IEHLIST. This example shows IEHLIST JCL and control cards to print the VTOC on volume vvvvvv, a 3380 device. SYSUT1 must contain the volume serial of the DASD, UNIT=, and DISP=OLD.

By using SYSALLDA, the coder of the utility need not be concerned with the unit that the device volume "vvvvvv" is mounted on. Many data centers have more than one type of DASD. For example, the data center may have 3350s and 3380s; or it may have 3375s and 3380s. Generally the JCL for IEHLIST is changed from time to time to look at another data set or volume VTOC. The user only needs to change the volume serial and submit the job.

You should try SYSALLDA at your data center. If it works, you can use it if you find it a time-saving feature. If it does not work, ask your system programmer or IBM Systems Engineer why.

14.2.10.   IEHMOVE

IEHMOVE is a utility to move or copy data sets. IEBCOPY does a better job of moving partitioned data sets, so IEHMOVE is rarely used except by some OEM vendors who must support a wide range of MVS systems.

The move function of IEHMOVE will copy a data set to another medium and *scratch* the old data set on the "from" medium or source. The copy function of IEHMOVE will copy a data set to another medium and leave the old copy in place.

IEHMOVE has INCLUDE and EXCLUDE parameters which allow the user to control which members of a partitioned data set are moved or copied.

Example 14.11 is one common use of IEHMOVE to "copy" or "load" a data set from a magnetic tape. The tape could be received from

```
//jobname      JOB   (acct),"programmer name",REGION=4096K,TIME=(5),
//                    NOTIFY=tsoid,MSGCLASS=c
//jobstep      EXEC  PGM=IEHMOVE
//*SYSUDUMP    DD    SYSOUT=*
//SYSPRINT     DD    SYSOUT=*
//SYSUT1       DD    UNIT=SYSDA,SPACE=(CYL,(10,5)),DISP=(,DELETE)
//indd         DD    DSN=data.set.name,DISP=OLD
//OUTDD    DD  VOL=SER=vvvvvv,DISP=OLD,
                    UNIT=SYSALLDA,SPACE=(CYL,(5,1,9))
//SYSPRINT     DD    SYSOUT=*
//SYSIN DD *
 COPY PDS=data.set.name,TO=3350=vvvvvv,FROM=3400-6=(tttttt,3),
              FROMDD=indd,RENAME=new.data.set.name
/*
//
```

Figure 14.11   IEHMOVE. The example of IEHMOVE will restore a data set to a DASD volume (vvvvvv) from a tape data set volume (tttttt).

almost any MVS location, and the data set can be restored at your data center if the sending data center is using some form of MVS. IEHMOVE was the "universal data mover" of the MVS environment.

With most data centers using MVS/370 or MVS/XA, however, and with the relative ease of use of IEBCOPY, IEBCOPY has risen to the most popular method of movement of data — especially partitioned data sets.

Note the SYSUT1 data set is a "work" data set. The **DISP=OLD** must be coded on the input and output DD cards to prevent the inadvertent deletion of a data set during the move or copy functions.

14.2.11. IEHPROGM

IEHPROGM is used to modify data in catalogs or in DASD VTOC. Specifically, IEHPROGM can accomplish the following tasks:

1. IEHPROGM can be used to scratch or rename non-VSAM data sets or members of partitioned data sets. Again ISPF is much faster and easier to use than IEHPROGM at allocating and scratching non-VSAM data sets. In batch mode, IDCAMS can do all the functions of IEHPROGM.
2. IEHPROGM catalogs and uncatalogs data sets. IEHPROGM must be used to catalog and uncatalog data sets in a CVOL catalog. IEHPROGM builds or deletes an index or alias in a CVOL. IDCAMS requires all VSAM data sets to be cataloged but can do the equivalent of uncataloging using the "NOSCRATCH" option.
3. IEHPROGM creates generation data groups (GDG). IDCAMS can also create GDGs. The following IEHPROGM control card will build a GDG:

   label BLDG INDEX=name.name2,ENTRIES=nn,what

   In the above control card:
   a. **label** is any one to eight character label for the user to identify the operation.
   b. **BLDG** is the command.
   c. **INDEX=name.name2** is the name of the generation data group.
   d. **ENTRIES=nn** specifies the number of entries to be contained in the GDG index. The number can be from 1 to 255. Guess why the number is 255? Maybe the field is one

byte, and in hexadecimal, the largest number is x'FF' or 255.

   e. **what** is either:

      i. **EMPTY**, which indicates all entries be removed from the GDG when it overflows. In other words, if you are keeping five versions, when you create the sixth one, the first five are deleted.

      ii. **DELETE**, which indicates the data set is to be scratched after it overflows. In other words, if you are keeping five versions, when you create the sixth one, the first one is deleted. DELETE is usually what you want to specify.

4. IEHPROGM can add and delete passwords from the MVS PASSWORD data set. In the early years of MVT, IBM added "security" to data sets by implementing a feature called "password protection" for data sets. The "password" is maintained in a system data set — PASSWORD. Note it is only a one level data set name — it is not "SYS1.PASSWORD." With only one level, the data set must be cataloged in the Master Catalog (there is no high level pointer to point to another catalog.)

There are a number of reasons why password protection should not be used. It is not secure (almost anyone can determine passwords). It is not available to multiple systems in loosely coupled environments.[4] The password data set MUST be on the systems residency volume.

IBM has replaced the password feature with RACF. Other OEM vendors have excellent security systems. Many data centers have completely removed the password feature because it only causes trouble in a RACF or other secured environment.

The rule of thumb you should follow is, if you do not need security at all, use nothing. If you need any security at all, benchmark and select one of the add-on security environments.

5. IEHPROGM can scratch all the temporary data sets from a volume if the data sets are not in use. This function should be

---

4. One of my early modifications to MVS was to change the modules that reference the PASSWORD data set. I changed the name to "SYS2.PASSWORD" so the same password data set could be used in a loosely coupled environment. It can be done — it is just a pain.

```
//jobname      JOB   (acct),'programmer name',REGION=4096K,TIME=(5),
//                   NOTIFY=tsoid,MSGCLASS=c
//jobstep      EXEC  PGM=IEHPROGM
//*SYSUDUMP    DD    SYSOUT=*
//SYSUT1       DD    VOL=SER=vvvvvv,DISP=OLD,UNIT=SYSALLDA
//SYSPRINT     DD    SYSOUT=*
//SYSIN        DD    *
   SCRATCH VTOC,VOL=SYSALLDA=vvvvvv,SYS
/*
//
```

Figure 14.12 IEHPROGM. This example shows one of the few uses left of IEHPROGM — to scratch temporary data sets from DASD volumes.

done at every data center or else the temporary volumes will get filled up with temporary data sets. Figure 14.12 shows an example of IEHPROGM which will scratch all the temporary data sets which are not in use. Temporary data sets have the format of

SSSyyddd.Thhmmss.RA000.jobname.ddname

where "yyddd" is the year and date, "hhmmss" is the time, "jobname" is the name of the creating job, and "ddname" is the ddname in the job step.

Temporary data sets are normally scratched at the end of the job, but certain abends — including system abends — will leave the data sets behind, filling up the temporary volumes.

14.2.12. IEBCOMPR

IEBCOMPR is a utility used to compare two sequential or partitioned data sets. Each logical record is compared in both files. You can use IEBCOMPR if you need to compare two data sets (source programs or JCL, not load modules), and the output data sets should be identical. Figure 14.13 is an example of comparing two sequential data sets.

IEBCOMPR suffers from one major flaw. Once the two data sets get out of sequence, IEBCOMPR will treat the entire rest of the two data sets as unequal. Said another way, if one logical record is inserted in one file, then the rest of the files are "unequal," even

```
//jobname      JOB  (acct),'programmer name',REGION=4096K,TIME=(5),
//                  NOTIFY=tsoid,MSGCLASS=c
//jobstep      EXEC PGM=IEBCOMPR
//*SYSUDUMP    DD   SYSOUT=*
//SYSUT1       DD   DSN=data.set.name,DISP=disp
//SYSUT2       DD   DSN=data.set.name,DISP=disp
//SYSPRINT     DD   SYSOUT=*
//SYSIN        DD   *
    COMPARE TYPORG=PS
/*
//
```

Figure 14.13   IEBCOMPR. This example compares two sequential data sets.

though all the records before the insert may be identical and all the records after the insert may be identical.

The IBM field developed program Source Compare Facility (5796-PLZ) is a far superior compare program — it will detect and flag insertions and deletions. You are more likely to see the changes to a source file.

14.3. SORT/MERGE

MVS is not delivered with a Sort/Merge program. The data center must purchase one. The IBM DF/SORT is an excellent one. SYNCSORT Inc. has an excellent sort. Other OEM vendors provide cost effective Sort/Merge programs. If you are evaluating Sort/Merge at your environment, be sure to build a test environment of your data and benchmark the various vendors against the data you are going to sort.

The Sort/Merge program will take records in an input file, sort the records, and place the records in the output data set. The SORT uses work files (SORTWKxx DD cards) and sorts can be done in place: The output file can be the input file.

If the file is very large, it may be broken into small files, sorted, then merged into one large file. Figure 14.14 shows an example of sorting a file. The input is in DD statement SORTIN, and the output will be in the file referenced by SORTOUT.

The SORT requires one or more work data sets — **SORTWKxx**, where xx is any number from 01 to 99. These data sets cause the most confusion and create the most wasteful environment. The data sets are temporary data sets, only needed for the duration of the

```
//jobname        JOB  (acct),'programmer name',REGION=4096K,TIME=(5),
//                    NOTIFY=tsoid,MSGCLASS=c
//SORT      EXEC PGM=IERRC000
//SORTMSG   DD   SYSOUT=*
//SYSOUT    DD   SYSOUT=*
//SORTWK01  DD   UNIT=SYSDA,SPACE=(CYL,(pp,ss)),DISP=(,DELETE)
//SORTWK02  DD   UNIT=SYSDA,SPACE=(CYL,(pp,ss)),DISP=(,DELETE)
//SORTWK03  DD   UNIT=SYSDA,SPACE=(CYL,(pp,ss)),DISP=(,DELETE)
//SORTIN    DD   DSN=data.set.sortin,DISP=disp
//SORTOUT   DD   DSN=data.set.sortout,DISP=disp
//SYSPRINT  DD   SYSOUT=*
//SYSIN DD *
          SORT FIELDS=(39,8,CH,A,21,17,CH,A)
          RECORD TYPE=V,LENGTH=(18,,121,52)
/*
//
```

Figure 14.14   SORT. The sort utility can be invoked by using several names. In this example IERRC000 is used for the program name. SORT could also be used as a program name because SORT is an alias of IERRC000. The data set pointed to by SORTIN will be sorted and placed in the data set pointed to by SORTOUT. The file will be sorted on an alphabetic key, which is 8 characters long and starts in column 39 of the data set. A second sort field ("key") of length 17 starting 21 characters into the record is used to order records within the primary key.

SORT step. Unfortunately, most programmers and analysts do not pay much attention to the size of the data sets.

The SORT should print statistics on the SYSPRINT data set which show the number of tracks/cylinders which were allocated and the number actually used. Programmer/analysts should monitor these and adjust their JCL to reflect what is needed.

The SORT program should be able to allocate secondary extents on its own. If the analyst underallocates, the SORT should attempt to continue.

One useful SORT application is to SORT the daily SYSLOG on the job number and date and time. The output can be used to look at all the MVS messages which a job had associated with it during execution.

14.4. IDCAMS

In the early days of MVS, IBM introduced the Virtual Storage Access Method (VSAM). VSAM was designed to replace all other access methods in the MVS environment. Over the years, VSAM has not been able to replace all the other access methods, yet each year, VSAM grows in its share of the market.

Although IDCAMS is the utility which IBM provides to control VSAM data sets, IDCAMS can be used with all access methods except partitioned data sets. The AMS in IDC-AMS comes from **Access Methods Services.**

The discussion of IDCAMS presented here is not intended to be complete. You should get the Access Methods Services manuals that are part of the documentation for the version of MVS on which you are operating. AMS changes with each release. *Be sure you have the correct documentation.*

As stated before, the subject of VSAM is beyond the scope of this book. I will introduce you to the types of things IDCAMS can do. Before I do that, let's look at IDCAMS basics. Figure 14.15 shows the JCL required to execute IDCAMS. IDCAMS is a very large program and requires at least a megabyte of virtual storage. I recommend you always run IDCAMS in at least a four-megabyte address space.

One of the control cards shown with IDCAMS in several publications is the //STEPCAT DD card. The STEPCAT card and/or the CATALOG control card parameter are used to force catalog access to a specific system catalog.

```
//jobname      JOB   (acct),'programmer name',REGION=4096K,TIME=(5),
//                   NOTIFY=tsoid,MSGCLASS=c
//jobstep      EXEC  PGM=IDCAMS
//*SYSUDUMP    DD    SYSOUT=*
//ddname       DD    DSN=data.set.name,DISP=disp
//SYSPRINT     DD    SYSOUT=*
//SYSIN        DD    *
    DEFINE CLUSTER
          (NAME (aaaa.bbbb.cccc)                     -
           FILE (ddname)                             -
           VOLUMES (vvvvv1 vvvvv2 vvvvv3)            -
           RECORDS (primary secondary)              -
           RECORDSIZE (average maximum)             -
           INDEXED or NONINDEXED or NUMBERED        -
           KEYS (length,offset))                    -
        DATA (NAME(aaaa.bbbb.cccc.DATA))            -
      INDEX (NAME(aaaa.bbbb.cccc.INDEX))
/*
//
```

Figure 14.15 Access Methods Services (IDCAMS). IDCAMS is a utility program which is used to manipulate all access methods except partitioned. IDCAMS does not rely on DD cards as much as other utilities because IDCAMS uses dynamic allocation where possible. The SYSIN DD statement contains the control cars which drive the IDCAMS functions.

You should not use either of these two options unless you are a Systems Programmer defining or manipulating catalogs.

The reason is simple — the catalog structure in a data center is a treelike structure. MVS likes to start at the master catalog (top of the tree) and work down until it finds the data set. If you fool mother MVS by forcing MVS to start in a catalog (a branch halfway down the tree) that MVS did not find by starting at the master catalog, then it is possible for you to create data sets that MVS cannot find later.

Another reason is that the ICF catalog structure is designed to move catalog entries easily. The data center can position catalog entries easily for the best overall system performance. If your JCL has JOBCAT, STEPCAT, or CATALOG statements, then the data center management must find and correct your statements when changes are made to the catalog — almost an impossible task.

IDCAMS also has the ability to specify passwords. You can specify passwords for catalogs, data sets, etc. Again, like the discussion on the MVS passwords, the VSAM password is only part of the solution, and with security, a partial solution is similar to being partially dead. It does not work. Select RACF or an OEM product like it and implement security properly.

14.4.1.   IDCAMS Control Card Basics

IDCAMS requires control cards. There are no defaults, like with IEBGENER, which would copy a file from SYSUT1 to SYSUT2 as the default. IDCAMS is completely different from the other MVS utilities, so the control cards are substantially different. Some of the differences are:

1. Either a space or a comma separates parameters of an ID-CAMS command.
2. A hyphen (-) is used to continue a command's parameters to the next line in the SYSIN data set. This makes sense because spaces can be used to separate parameters, so there need be no comma at all, much less an "ending comma."
3. Parentheses are used to indicate a parameter's value. For example, to specify space, code CYLINDERS(100 15). Other utilities use the equals sign, but that is sometimes confusing, as in the VOL=SYSALLDA=vvvvvv parameters.

14.4.2. Defining Data Sets

The IDCAMS DEFINE statement is used to create data sets on DASD. DEFINE must be used to create a VSAM data set, because the JCL processor cannot create a VSAM data set with the parameters in JCL. Non-VSAM data sets can be created either with JCL or with IDCAMS DEFINE parameters. Figure 14.15 shows an example of the DEFINE statement with several subparameters:

1. **DEFINE CLUSTER** defines a VSAM data set. Its subparameters are enclosed in a single pair of parentheses.
   a. **NAME (aaaa.bbbb.cccc)** is the fully qualified data set name of the cluster.
   b. **FILE(ddname)** is the label of the DD statement which identifies the volume on which the primary space will be allocated.
   c. **VOLUMES(vvvvv1 vvvvvv2 vvvvv3...)** identifies all the candidate volumes that could contain this VSAM data set. Use more than one volume only when you reasonably can expect the data set to exceed the space of a single volume. Unused candidate volumes for VSAM cause many problems for the data center in the area of archiving and restoring VSAM data sets.
   d. **RECORDS** or **TRACKS** or **CYLINDERS (primary secondary)** give the space allocation for the data set. Primary is the number of units to be allocated as the data set is created. Secondary is the number of units to be allocated each time when, while writing to the data set, the previous extents are filled.
   e. **RECORDSIZE (average maximum)** is the average and maximum logical record size you will use to write records to the file.
   f. **INDEXED** or **NONINDEXED** or **NUMBERED** to create key-sequenced files (INDEXED), entry sequenced files (NONINDEXED), or relative files (NUMBERED).
   g. **KEYS (length offset)** gives the length of a key and the offset into the logical record of the key.
   h. **DATA** and **INDEX** parameters give a name to the data and index components of a file. I recommend that the last part of the name be "DATA" for the data component and "INDEX" for the index component. The names will stand out when listing the VTOC of a volume.

2. **DEFINE NONVSAM** defines a non-VSAM data set, such as a sequential data set.
3. **DEFINE USERCATALOG** creates a VSAM catalog. Figure 14.16 shows a typical job to define a user catalog.
   a. **NAME (ddname)** specifies the name of the catalog.
   b. **FILE(ddname)** points to a DD statement which points to a DD statement that points to the volume that will contain the catalog.
   c. **VOLUME(vvvvvv)** gives the volume serial number of the volume to contain the catalog.
   d. **CYLINDERS (primary secondary)** gives the number of cylinders for the catalog. Although you can specify a catalog which is a certain number of RECORDS or TRACKS in size, I believe a catalog should be at least one cylinder. Smaller sizes are a symptom that you may have too many small catalogs.
   e. **ICFCATALOG** indicates the catalog should be built in Integrated Catalog Facility (ICF) format.
4. **DEFINE SPACE** creates a "regular," or non-ICF, data space for suballocated VSAM data sets. Suballocated VSAM data sets and non-ICF VSAMs are not recommended, so you should not use this type of DEFINE.

```
//jobname     JOB  (acct),'programmer name',REGION=4096K,TIME=(5),
//                 NOTIFY=tsoid,MSGCLASS=c
//jobstep     EXEC PGM=IDCAMS
//*SYSUDUMP   DD   SYSOUT=*
//ddname      DD   DSN=data.set.name,DISP=disp
//SYSPRINT    DD   SYSOUT=*
//SYSIN       DD   *
  DEFINE USERCATALOG                          -
     (NAME (catalog.vvolume)                  -
      FILE (ddname)                           -
      CYLINDERS (primary secondary)  -
      VOLUME (vvvvvv)                          -
      ICFCATALOG                              -
      )
/*
//
```

Figure 14.16 IDCAMS DEFINE USERCATALOG. One of the most important functions of IDCAMS is to define catalogs.

14.4.3.   Printing Data Sets

IDCAMS can also print VSAM and other data sets. The PRINT command is used. Figure 14.17 shows an example of printing the entire VSAM Volume Data set. The MVS systems programmer might choose to do this for a volume which is being cleaned off to remove the volume from service. ICF VSAM catalogs have pointers to any volume that has or has had a VSAM data set in the catalog. These pointers should be removed before the volume is removed from service.

14.5.   MVS SYSTEM UTILITIES

The group of utility programs most likely to be used by the systems programming staff of a data center will now be discussed. The reader is reminded that applications and operational personnel may find these utilities useful.

Several of these utilities are documented in the Service Aids manual (e.g., *MVS/Extended Architecture, System Programming Library, Service Aids* — GC28-1159).

14.5.1.   AMASPZAP

AMASPZAP is a program which will verify and change data on a direct access device. It is also very handy to format (dump) load module data sets on DASD. Even the VTOC can be changed. This program should be controlled very carefully and should only be used

```
//jobname      JOB  (acct),"programmer name",REGION=4096K,TIME=(5),
//                   NOTIFY=tsoid,MSGCLASS=c
//jobstep      EXEC PGM=IDCAMS
//*SYSUDUMP    DD   SYSOUT=*
//SYSPRINT     DD   SYSOUT=*
//name1        DD   DSN=SYS1.VVDS.Vvvvvvv,DISP=SHR,UNIT=SYSALLDS,
//                   VOL=SER=vvvvvv,AMP=AMORG
//SYSIN        DD   *
       PRINT INFILE(name1)
/*
//
```

Figure 14.17   IDCAMS PRINT. This example shows an IDCAMS job which will print a VSAM file. One "special" VSAM file is a VVDS on each volume which has or did have VSAM data sets. The Print command has a parameter "INFILE" to point to the DD name of the file to print.

```
//jobname    JOB  (acct),'programmer name',REGION=4096K,TIME=(5),
//           NOTIFY=tsoid,MSGCLASS=c
//jobstep    EXEC PGM=AMASPZAP
//*SYSUDUMP DD   SYSOUT=*
//SYSLIB    DD   DSN=data.set.name,DISP=disp
//SYSPRINT  DD   SYSOUT=*
//SYSIN     DD   *
   NAME membername csectname
   VER 0010,47F0
   REP 0010,4700
/*
//
```

Figure 14.18   AMASPZAP. AMASPZAP, or "super zap," is a program which is
used to modify DASD tracks by reading the DASD record, verifying data,
changing the data, and rewriting the data to DASD. In this example, member
"membername," csect "csectname" in data set "data.set.name" will be changed.
The "NAME" control card points to the member to be changed. The "VER"
control card verifies the contents of a displacement (x'0010) into the module
contains a certain hexadecimal value (x'47F0'). The "REP" control card
specifies the displaement and the value to be substituted (x'4700").

by Systems Programmers to maintain and fix the operating system.
Figure 14.18 shows an example of changing a module.

One of the most beneficial uses of AMASPZAP is to remove VSAM
data set components if the catalog has not been updated correctly. If
the VSAM catalog does not contain a pointer to the cluster, data, and
index components of a VSAM KSDS, then VSAM cannot delete the
space in the VTOC. If the VSAM bit is turned on in the VTOC, then
IEHPROGM and/or JCL deallocation routines cannot delete the data
set. The only recourse is to use AMASPZAP to turn off the VSAM
and data protection bits and use deallocation or ISPF DELETE functions to eliminate the data set.

14.5.2. AMBLIST

AMBLIST (see Figure 14.19) is a service aid which lists load
modules and the Link Pack Area (LPA). It must be used to map
SYS1.NUCLEUS because the Nucleus is "scatter loaded" and the

```
//jobname     JOB   (acct),"programmer name",REGION=4096K,TIME=(5),
//            NOTIFY=tsoid,MSGCLASS=c
//jobstep     EXEC  PGM=AMBLIST
//*SYSUDUMP   DD    SYSOUT=*
//library     DD    DSN=data.set.name,DISP=disp
//SYSPRINT    DD    SYSOUT=*
//SYSIN       DD    *
   LISTLOAD OUTPUT=XREF,DDN=library,MEMBER=membername
/*
//
```

Figure 14.19 AMBLIST. AMBLIST is a utility to list load libraries to print attributes of load modules. This example will list member "membername" from the library stored in data set "data.set.name." The output will be a cross reference listing similr to the one obtained from the linkage editor.

output from the linkage editor does not reflect the contents of Central Storage.[5]

14.5.3. AMDPRDMP

AMDPRDMP formats stand-alone dumps, SVC dumps, and SYSMDUMPs. It can be used to print GTF and VTAM records. The original MVS version of AMDPRDMP was executed as a batch job, and program AMDPRDMP was executed directly as the step program. With MVS/XA, the dump program was converted to a series of commands executed under the terminal monitor program (IKJEFT01). Figure 14.20 shows an example of both.

14.5.4. IEBIMAGE

IEBIMAGE creates and maintains modules to support the IBM 3800 printing subsystem (see Figure 14.21). IEBIMAGE stores the modules in the **SYS1.IMAGELIB**. JES uses the modules stored in SYS1.IMAGELIB to control the printing on the 3800 printer.

---

5. The linkage editor can read programs or load modules and either place them into one large "program" or create a number of different configurations. One such configuration is mainly used for the MVS nucleus — scatter loading.

```
     MVS 370

//jobname     JOB   (acct),"programmer name",REGION=4096K,TIME=(5),
//                  NOTIFY=tsoid,MSGCLASS=c
//jobstep     EXEC PGM=AMDPRDMP
//*SYSUDUMP   DD    SYSOUT=*
//SYSUT1      DD    DSN=data.set.name,DISP=disp
//SYSUT2      DD    DSN=data.set.name,DISP=disp
//SYSPRINT    DD    SYSOUT=*
//SYSIN       DD    *
     PRINT STORAGE=(fromaddr,toaddr)
/*
//

     MVS XA

//jobname     JOB   (acct),"programmer name",REGION=4096K,TIME=(5),
//                  NOTIFY=tsoid,MSGCLASS=c
//jobstep     EXEC PGM=IKJEFT01,PARM=AMDPRDMP
//*SYSUDUMP   DD    SYSOUT=*
//SYSTSIN     DD    DUMMY,DCB=(RECFM=F,LRECL=80,BLKSIZE=80)
//SYSTSPRT    DD    DUMMY,DCB=BLKSIZE=80
//INDEX       DD    SYSOUT=*
//SYSPRINT    DD    SYSOUT=*
//PRINTER     DD    SYSOUT=*
//SYSUT1      DD    UNIT=SYSDA,SPACE=(CYL,(25,5))
//TAPE        DD    DSN=SYS1.DUMPxx,DISP=SHR
//SYSIN       DD    *
     PRINT STORAGE=(fromaddr,toaddr)
     END
/*
//
```

Figure 14.20   AMDPRDMP. AMDPRDMP is a utility to format virtual storage in system dump data sets and trace data sets. In these examples, the utility will print a block of storage from "fromaddr" to "toaddr" if the storage is available in the dump.

The user is cautioned that to set up and make full utilization of the 3800 in native mode takes a long time and is very manpower intensive. IBM gives 5-day classes to learn how to set up the 3800 in APA mode.

14.5.5. IEHATLAS

IEHATLAS is a system utility used with DASD when a defective track is detected (see Figure 14.22). The utility can be used to locate

```
//jobname      JOB  (acct),"programmer name",REGION=4096K,TIME=(5),
//                   NOTIFY=tsoid,MSGCLASS=c
//jobstep      EXEC PGM=IEBIMAGE
//*SYSUDUMP DD   SYSOUT=*
//SYSUT1     DD   DSN=SYS1.IMAGELIB,DISP=SHR
//SYSPRINT   DD   SYSOUT=*
//SYSIN      DD   *
   control cards here
/*
//
```

Figure 14.21   IEBIMAGE. IEBIMAGE creates members of SYS1.IMAGELIB which JES uses to control the 3800 printing subsystems.

and assign an alternate track. Records which can be read can be "saved" and written to the alternate track.

A very complex use of IEHATLAS is to provide an exit to I/O routines (called a SYNAD exit), which will invoke IEHATLAS when the program tries to read or write a record on a DASD track. IEHATLAS will attempt recovery of the data.

Most data centers wait for an error to happen and use DSF to recover the data if possible.

14.5.6.   IEHINITT

IEHINITT is a program to place standard IBM labels on magnetic tape (see Figure 14.23). It is most often used by the operations staff

```
//jobname      JOB  (acct),"programmer name",REGION=4096K,TIME=(5),
//                   NOTIFY=tsoid,MSGCLASS=c
//jobstep      EXEC PGM=IEHATLAS
//*SYSUDUMP DD   SYSOUT=*
//SYSUT1     DD   UNIT=SYSALLDA,VOL=SER=vvvvvv,DISP=OLD
//SYSPRINT   DD   SYSOUT=*
//SYSIN      DD   *
   control statements here
/*
//
```

Figure 14.22   IEHATLAS. IBM's old IEHATLAS utility is used to locate and assign alternate tracks on a DASD. Most of these functions are now provided by DFDSS. IEHATLAS can be called by complex assembler language programs that wish to do their own on the fly recovery of data checks.

```
//jobname      JOB  (acct),'programmer name',REGION=4096K,TIME=(5),
//                  NOTIFY=tsoid,MSGCLASS=c
//jobstep      EXEC PGM=IEHINITT
//*SYSUDUMP    DD   SYSOUT=*
//SYSPRINT     DD   SYSOUT=*
//*   DEN=4 IS 6250 BPI
//*   DEN=3 IS 1600 BPI
//label        DD   DCB=DEN=4,UNIT=(tape,1,DEFER)
//SYSIN        DD *
label    INITT SER=nnnnnn,OWNER=company,NUMBTAPE=1
/*
//
```

Figure 14.23   IEHINITT. This example of IEHINITT will write a label on a magnetic tape. The LABEL DD statement points to the unit which IEHINITT will use.

to initialize a batch of new tapes to add to a tape library. Some programmers use this program to initialize tapes they want to send to other data centers.

In some cases, the tapes sent out come back. In other cases, the tapes sent are not returned. It is recommended that any tape sent from the data center be a new tape which has not been assigned a label which falls within the range of the permanent tape library. Some of the reasons are:

1. If the tape is not returned, there is a "hole" in the library.
2. If a "scratch" tape is selected and sent, it may contain company confidential data which you should not or, by law, must not release. Payroll information is a good example. There are computer systems on which it is possible to inspect tapes after their logical end of volume (two tape marks). MVS is one such system.

14.5.7.   IFCEREP1

IFCEREP1 is the IBM program which prints and formats information from the SYS1.LOGREC data set. (Remember, SYS1.LOGREC contains information about errors that occur in software and hardware and have been reported to MVS.) Figure 14.24 shows an example of the type of JCL which is used to execute IFCEREP1. Parameters to control the execution of IFCEREP1 can either be

```
//jobname       JOB   (acct),"programmer name",REGION=4096K,TIME=(5),
//              NOTIFY=tsoid,MSGCLASS=c
//jobstepn      EXEC  PGM=IFCEREP1,REGION=4096K,PARM=CARD
//*             ACC=N             DO NOT ACCUMULATE TO ACCIN DATA SET
//*             CUA=(CUA,CUA)   SELECT RECORDS FOR ADDRESS
//*             DATE=(YYDDD-YYDDD I YYDDD,YYDDD) DATE TO USE
//*             DEVICE=(3380 I 3330I 33XX)       DEV TYPE
//*             DEVSER=(SERIAL,SERIAL)           VOLSER
//*             EVENT=(N I Y)                    ONE LINE ABSTRACTS
//*             HIST=YIN                         USE ACCIN DD AS SYSIN
//*             MERGE=YIN                        MERGE SERLOG AND ACCIN
//*             PRINT=SU        SUMMARY ONLY
//*                    PS       PRINT FULL RECORD & SUMMARY
//*                    PT       PRINT FULL RECORD ONLY
//*                    NO       NOTHING
//*             TABSIZE=NNNK    SORT TABLE SIZE
//*                TIME=(HHMM-HHMM I HHMM,HHMM)  TIME OF DAY
//*                TYPE=C          CCH
//*                     D          DDR
//*                     E          EOD
//*                     H          MIH
//*                     I          IPL
//*                     M          MCH
//*                     O          OBR
//*                     S          SOFTWARE
//*                     T          MDR
//SERLOG        DD    DSN=SYS1.LOGREC,DISP=SHR
//ACCIN         DD    DSN=EREP.TSO2.MONTHLY(0),DISP=SHR
//DIRECTWK      DD    UNIT=SYSDA,SPACE=(CYL,(10,10))
//ACCDEV        DD    UNIT=SYSINT,SPACE=(CYL,(1,1)),DSN=SYS056.TEMP.ACCDEV,
//              DISP=(,CATLG),DCB=(RECFM=V,LRECL=2000,BLKSIZE=6420,DSORG=PS)
//TOURIST       DD    SYSOUT=A,DCB=BLKSIZE=133
//EREPPT        DD    SYSOUT=A,DCB=BLKSIZE=133
//SYSIN         DD    *
 PRINT=PS
 ACC=N
 TABSIZE=384K
 ZERO=N
 TYPE=S
 DATE=(88199-88199)
 HIST=Y
 TIME=(0000-2400)
ENDPARM
SHARE=(999999.B3X,999991.B3X,999992.B3X,999993.B3X)
/*
//
```

Figure 14.24   IFCEREP JCL. This version of EREP will print software failures which have been logged into the SYS1.LOGREC.

given through the PARM field of the EXEC statement, or PARM=CARD can be coded to have IFCEREP1 read the data set pointed to by a //SYSIN DD card.

The first consideration, when running IFCEREP1 to extract data only, is to specify ZERO=N to prevent IFCEREP1 from clearing the LOGREC data set. Only production jobs should clear LOGREC.

14.5.8.   IFHSTATR

IFHSTATR is a system utility which is used to format and print information from SMF type 21 records. Type 21 records provide error statistics by volume serial number. A type 21 is written when:

1. A volume is dismounted from a tape or DASD drive.
2. A volume is dismounted as part of error recovery — Dynamic Device Recovery (DDR).
3. A tape drive is varied offline.
4. IFCEREPx is run to gather statistics on devices.

One of the problems with type 21 analysis is that multiple records may exist for a single volume. As you can see from above, there may be several records on a single mount of a tape or DASD. The program analysis must take this into consideration. Figure 14.25 shows the template for a job to run IFHSTATR.

14.5.9.   Stand-Alone Programs

Almost all MVS utilities run under the MVS operating system. There are times, however, when the MVS operating system cannot operate. What is needed then is a program that can be IPLed (like an operating system) but only runs one program in the Processor Complex. The term used for these programs is **stand-alone programs**.

```
//jobname    JOB  (acct),'programmer name',REGION=4096K,TIME=(5),
//                NOTIFY=tsoid,MSGCLASS=c
//jobstep    EXEC PGM=IFHSTATR
//*SYSUDUMP  DD   SYSOUT=*
//SYSUT1     DD   DSN=data.set.name,DISP=disp
//SYSUT2     DD   DSN=data.set.name,DISP=disp
//SYSPRINT   DD   SYSOUT=*
//SYSIN      DD   *
   control statements here
/*
//
```

Figure 14.25   IFHSTATR. Utility IFHSTATR is used to evaluate SMF type 21 records which have statistics on volume errors. SYSUT1 is the input data set which contains the SMF data. SYSUT2 is the output, or report, data set.

```
//jobname      JOB  (acct),'programmer name',REGION=4096K,TIME=(5),
//                  NOTIFY=tsoid,MSGCLASS=c
//jobstep      EXEC PGM=IEBGENER
//*SYSUDUMP    DD   SYSOUT=*
//SYSUT1       DD   DSN=SYS1.ASAMPLIB(ADRDMPRS),DISP=SHR
//SYSUT2       DD   DSN=data.set.name,DISP=(NEW,CATLG,DELETE),
//                  DCB=(RECFM=F,BLKSIZE=80,LRECL=80),
//                  LABEL=(,NL)
//SYSPRINT     DD   SYSOUT=*
//SYSIN        DD   DUMMY
//
```

Figure 14.26   Stand-alone tapes. This example will place the stand-alone program on a magnetic tape. Note that the tape must be unblocked.

Examples of stand-alone programs are DSF (to initialize volumes), DFDSS (to restore DASD volumes), and the stand-alone dump program (to dump all of Central Storage and virtual storage for diagnosis of a problem that prevents MVS from continuing).

The stand-alone program can be placed on a disk or on a tape. *Either a DASD or a tape can be IPLed!* For either, the address of the device is specified on the hardware console of a Processor Complex that is not running any operating system, and "IPL" is selected.[6]

If you want to place the stand-alone program on disk, the DSF program is used to write the IPL text on the disk volume. Figure 14.26 shows an example of how to produce a stand-alone tape using the IEBGENER utility. This works for any stand-alone program that is available to the data center in card-image format as a stand-alone program. In the case of the stand-alone dump program, the card-image format is produced by the installation after assembling macro **AMDSADM2**. The tape must be unblocked with each record 80 bytes (card images, of course!) and the tape must be nonlabeled.

---

6. Remember, only one "operating system" can be in control of a processor complex at one time. Even with VM, the VM system controls the processor complex. Other operating systems are running as guests, and the "IPL" is only simulated. If you IPL a stand-alone "operating system," you will terminate whatever was running the processor complex. The hardware does not care if your company's entire network was operational.

14.6. DEVICE SUPPORT FACILITIES (DSF)

Device Support Facilities (DSF) is supplied by IBM to provide service functions, error detection, and media maintenance on DASD. DSF became important with the 3380 device. IBM transferred responsibility for media management from the local Customer Engineer to the data center. IBM still replaces the hardware — cards and HDAs — but the data center is responsible for understanding and running DSF for diagnostics.

Complete information should be researched in the *Device Support Facilities User's Guide and Reference* (e.g., GC35-0033 for Release 8.0)

There are always two versions of DSF. One runs as a batch job under MVS. The second is a stand-alone version. If MVS cannot operate, then one of the functions which may have to be done is to initialize (DSF) and restore (DFDSS or OEM product) enough volumes to allow MVS and its subsystems to initialize.

14.6.1. Initialization — INIT

The first thing you will use DSF for is to initialize DASD volumes which have been obtained for the data center. After installation, the Customer Engineer turns over to the data center a DASD HDA which is not usable. It is a little like getting a new car from the dealer that you have to place the spark plug wires on, fill up with gas and oil, and ensure that the car starts.

For most versions of DSF, there are three types of initialization:

1. **MINIMAL.** A MINIMAL initialization is performed with the keywords NOVALIDATE and NOCHECK. A volume needs to have as a minimum the following:
   a. Write IPL bootstrap and IPL records if necessary.
   b. Format the VTOC with a VTOC header record (FORMAT4), a free space indicator (FORMAT5), and empty VTOC records (FORMAT0).
   c. Index data set (SYS1.VTOCIX.V33001), if requested.
2. **MEDIAL.** A MEDIAL initialization is performed with the keywords VALIDATE and NOCHECK. The volume is formatted as in MINIMAL and, in addition, all tracks are formatted with Home Addresses and Record Zeros.
3. **MAXIMAL.** A MAXIMAL initialization is performed with the keyword CHECK(n) (prior to release 9.0) or VALIDATE DATA

(release 9.0 and later). The volume is formatted as in MEDIAL and, in addition, all tracks are checked by writing a bit pattern on the surface of each track to ensure that what is written can be read. The versions which use "CHECK(n)" take several times longer than the versions which use VALIDATE and DATA.

I believe that *every* volume that is placed into service should have a MAXIMAL level of initialization. Think about the surface of a triple capacity 3380 volume. Almost two gigabytes of data can be recorded on the surface. If data sets are allocated and scratched at random, the last cylinders may not be written to for several months or even years. If the area has been shipped from the factory or damaged at any time, shouldn't you learn about that *as the volume is placed into service?* Up to MVS/XA Release 2.2, I always specified CHECK(3), because that seemed to take a reasonable time (1.5 hours per single capacity 3380). With Release 2.2, IBM changed the specification to VALIDATE DATA. Figure 14.27 shows two examples of initialization of a DASD device.

14.6.2.   Surface Analysis — ANALYZE

The ANALYZE command of DSF is used to test a DASD device to see if the Actuator is working and to read the tracks to see if there are errors in reading the data. ANALYZE can be run while the

```
//jobname     JOB  (acct),'programmer name',REGION=4096K,TIME=(5),
//                  NOTIFY=tsoid,MSGCLASS=c
// jobstep     EXEC  PGM=ICKDSF
//*SYSUDUMP   DD   SYSOUT=*
//ddname1     DD   DSN=data.set.name,DISP=disp
//ddname2     DD   DSN=data.set.name,DISP=disp
//SYSPRINT    DD   SYSOUT=*
//SYSIN       DD   *
    /*     Use this version for 3380's with DFP and MVS XA 2.2   */
       INIT UNITADDRESS(cuu) PURGE NOVERIFY    -
            VTOC(0,1,14) VOLID(vvvvvv) VALIDATE DATA
    /*     Use this version for 3380's with pre MVS XA 2.2       */
       INIT UNITADDRESS(ccu) PURGE NOVERIFY    -
            VTOC(0,1,14) VOLID(vvvvvv) CHECK(3)
/*
//
```

Figure 14.27   DSF INIT. This example shows initialization of a 3380 DASD with a VTOC placed at cylinder 0, head 1. The VTOC will be 14 tracks to end the VTOC on a cylinder boundary.

volume is allocated to one or more MVS tasks. Response from the volume may degrade as DSF runs its tests. The following checks are made:

1. Verify that the drive can read and write. ANALYZE performs I/O operations on the CE track (not available to the data center) to verify the actuator can read and write data.
2. Verify the drive can SEEK properly. ANALYZE moves the heads to a specific location on the volume and verifies (by reading the Home Address) that the arm actually moved to where it was directed.
3. Verify the drive can detect address marks.
4. Verify the drive can switch read/write heads
5. Verify rotational position sensing is working.
6. Verify the drive can detect and skip over defective areas on a track.

ANALYZE should be performed against any volume which gives any I/O error indication. The output will help pinpoint if the problem is permanent or temporary and point to an action plan to correct the problem. Figure 14.28 is an example of a whole volume ANALYZE.

14.6.3.   Recovery of Data Errors — INSPECT

The INSPECT command of DSF is used to perform the following functions on *a portion of a volume* (see Figure 14.29):

```
//jobname     JOB   (acct),'programmer name',REGION=4096K,TIME=(5),
//                  NOTIFY=tsoid,MSGCLASS=c
//jobstep     EXEC  PGM=ICKDSF
//*SYSUDUMP   DD    SYSOUT=*
//ddname1     DD    VOL=SER=vvvvvv,UNIT=SYSALLDA,DISP=OLD
//SYSPRINT    DD    SYSOUT=*
//SYSIN       DD    *
    ANALYZE  DDNAME(ddname1) NOSPEED  SCAN
/*
//
```

Figure 14.28   DSF ANALYZE. DSF will read and write to protected areas on the volume to ensure the volume is working properly. Because no LIMITS or CYLRANGE has been specified, the whole volume is checked.

```
//jobname     JOB   (acct),'programmer name',REGION=4096K,TIME=(5),
//                  NOTIFY=tsoid,MSGCLASS=c
//Jobstep     EXEC  PGM=ICKDSF
//*SYSUDUMP   DD    SYSOUT=*
//ddname1     DD    VOL=SER=vvvvvv,UNIT=SYSALLDA,DISP=OLD
//SYSPRINT    DD    SYSOUT=*
//SYSIN       DD    *
  INSPECT DDNAME(ddname1) CHECK(3) FROMRANGE(X'0084',X'000A') -
          NOASSIGN TORANGE (X'0084', X'000A') PRESERVE SKIP    -
          VERIFY(vvvvvv)
/*
//
```

Figure 14.29   DSF INSPECT. In this example, DSF is going to read cylinder x'84' head 10 and try to read the data on that track and rewrite it with skip displacements. The "NOASSIGN" indicates an alternate cylinder should not be assigned.

1. Checks the surface of a track to determine if there is a data check.
2. Writes skip displacements on the volume if the volume supports skip displacements.
3. Assigns an alternate track.
4. Reclaims a track after an alternate track has been assigned improperly. Usually a track does not "get better." What may happen is a hardware electronic card may fail and give invalid indications. Alternate track(s) could be assigned thinking the problem was on the surface of the medium. After the hardware is fixed, the data center may want to reclaim the track because it was not really broken in the first place.
5. Prints a map of defective tracks on a volume.

14.6.4.   Building Indexed VTOC — BUILDIX

The BUILDIX command of DSF will convert a DASD volume to or from indexed VTOCs. Figure 14.30 is an example of building an indexed VTOC.

14.6.5.   Resetting Control Units — CONTROL

MVS and the 3880/3990 control units have microcode to detect problems with writing on DASDs. I have experienced the situation

```
//jobname    JOB  (acct),"programmer name",REGION=4096K,TIME=(5),
//               NOTIFY=tsoid,MSGCLASS=c
//jobstep    EXEC PGM=ICKDSF
//*SYSUDUMP  DD   SYSOUT=*
//ddname1    DD   UNIT=SYSALLDA,VOL=SER=vvvvvv,
//           DSN=SYS1.VTOCIX.Vvvvvvvv,DISP=(NEW,KEEP),
//           SPACE=(ABSTR,(10,1))
//SYSPRINT   DD   SYSOUT=*
//SYSIN      DD   *
    BUILDIX DDNAME(ddname1) IXVTOC
/*
//
```

Figure 14.30   DSF BUILDIX. The BUILDIX function will build an indexed VTOC in the previously allocated data set. The data set name must begin with "SYS1.VTOCIX." Note SPACE is allocated using ABSTR, which will place the data set at absolute track 1 (cylinder 0 head 1), and the data set will be 10 tracks in length.

where the channel program was asking to write on device 140 at cylinder 1, head 1, record 1, but the control unit took it upon itself to write the same record, not only on device 140, but on device 141, and device 142, and so forth, until the last device on the string was written. That was a strange and devastating problem. (The problem was on non-IBM second generation DASD.)

The newer control units attempt to detect and stop such odd and destructive behavior. The control unit microcode apparently has the ability to discover problems and disable itself. I have never seen this happen.

The CONTROL command with the ALLOWWRITE parameter is used to "turn on" writing for the control unit, after the failing storage control unit has been repaired, that is. Figure 14.31 is an

```
//jobname    JOB  (acct),"programmer name",REGION=4096K,TIME=(5),
//               NOTIFY=tsoid,MSGCLASS=c
//jobstep    EXEC PGM=ICKDSF
//*SYSUDUMP  DD   SYSOUT=*
//ddname1    DD   UNIT=SYSALLDA,VOL=SER=vvvvvv,DISP=OLD
//SYSPRINT   DD   SYSOUT=*
//SYSIN      DD   *
    CONTROL ALLOWWRITE DDNAME(ddname1)
/*
//
```

Figure 14.31   DSF CONTROL. The CONTROL function is designed to turn on a 3880 control unit after a failure has disabled write functions.

example of this feature. You should not do this without consulting with your IBM Customer Engineer.

14.6.6. Rename Volumes — REFORMAT

DSF is also used to give new volume serial names to DASDs. Additionally, IPL data can be added to a volume. REFORMAT is useful on volumes which already have data on the volume.

The reader is cautioned about changing the volume serial on a DASD. Volume serial numbers are kept in the system catalog(s) and their extensions, so if a DASD volume serial is changed, it is likely that the catalogs would need to be changed as well.

The ability to add IPL data is important. For instance, you may want to add a stand-alone dump program to a volume. REFORMAT is function to use. Figure 14.32 is an example of REFORMAT.

14.7. DATA FACILITY DATA SET SERVICES (DFDSS)

Data Facility Data Set Services (DFDSS) is the IBM program whose function is to manage data on DASDs. DFDSS is not included with MVS as part of the system but is included here to describe the function which is performed by DFDSS and several OEM dump/restore programs.

There are always two versions of a dump/restore program. One runs as a batch job under MVS; the other is a stand-alone version. If MVS cannot operate, then one of the functions which must be done is

```
//jobname     JOB  (acct),'programmer name',REGION=4096K,TIME=(5),
//                  NOTIFY=tsoid,MSGCLASS=c
//jobstep     EXEC PGM=ICKDSF
//*SYSUDUMP   DD   SYSOUT=*
//ddname1     DD   VOL=SER=vvvvvv,DISP=OLD,UNIT=SYSALLDA
//ipldd       DD   DSN=aaaa.bbbb.cccc,DISP=OLD
//SYSPRINT    DD   SYSOUT=*
//SYSIN       DD   *
 REFORMAT DDNAME(ddname1) IPLDD(ipldd) OWNERID(yourshop) PURGE NOVERIFY
/*
//
```

Figure 14.32   DSF REFORMAT. Volume "vvvvvv" will have the IPL program contained in data set "aaaa.bbbb.cccc" added to the first cylinder. After this job executes successfully, you can IPL ("load") a System/370 from this volume.

to restore enough volumes to allow MVS and its subsystems to initialize.

This section will introduce the available functions and give examples of some of the most important ones. For complete details, you should see *Data Facility Data Set Services: User's Guide and Reference* (SC26-3949).

14.7.1. Dumping Data from DASD to Tape — DUMP and COPYDUMP

Probably the most important function of DFDSS is to dump data from DASD to tape. Dumping could be used to transport data from your data center to a backup site. Dumping could be used to back up data sets periodically (each night) to protect a data center users in case they inadvertently scratched important data sets.

Figure 14.33 shows an example of a full dump of volume "vvvvvv."

14.7.2. Restoring Data from Tape to DASD — RESTORE

Once the data has been successfully dumped to tape, you should test the dump to be sure it was successful. The method to do this is to actually restore the data to an empty volume (if full volume dump was performed) periodically. More than one data center has been caught off guard by not being able to restore data from a dumped volume.

Figure 14.34 is an example of a full volume restore. If the volume is critical to MVS — a system volume or a catalog volume — you

```
//Jobname     JOB  (acct),"programmer name",REGION=4096K,TIME=(5),
//                  NOTIFY=tsoid,MSGCLASS=c
//jobstep     EXEC PGM=ADRDSSU
//*SYSUDUMP   DD   SYSOUT=*
//ddname1     DD   UNIT=SYSALLDA,VOL=SER=vvvvvv,DISP=OLD
//ddname2     DD   DSN=data.set.name,DISP=disp
//SYSPRINT    DD   SYSOUT=*
//SYSIN       DD   *
  DUMP INDDNAME(ddname1) OUTDDNAME(ddname2) ALLDATA(*) ALLEXCP -
  TOLERATE(ENQUFAILURE)
/*
//
```

Figure 14.33 DUMPing data. DFDSS can dump all the data on a DASD volume. The parameter TOLERATE(ENQUEFAILURE) will continue the dumping operation, even if a data set on the volume is being used.

```
//jobname     JOB  (acct),'programmer name',REGION=4096K,TIME=(5),
//                 NOTIFY=tsoid,MSGCLASS=c
//jobstep     EXEC PGM=ADRDSSU
//*SYSUDUMP   DD   SYSOUT=*
//ddname1     DD   DSN=data.set.name,DISP=disp
//ddname2     DD   UNIT=SYSALLDA,VOL=SER=vvvvvv,DISP=OLD
//SYSPRINT    DD   SYSOUT=*
//SYSIN       DD   *
  RESTORE INDDNAME(ddname1) OUTDDNAME(ddname2) REPLACE TOLERATE(ENQF)
/*
//
```

Figure 14.34   Restoring data. DFDSS can be used to restore data dumped by DFDSS.

should also use the stand-alone version to restore the tape to a volume periodically. The "REPLACE" parameter is used to tell DFDSS the restore should not be terminated if the volume contains data sets that have an expiration date.

The TOLERATE ENQF keyword specifies data sets are to be processed, even if another address space "seems" to have the data set allocated.

Early versions of DFDSS could not restore to unlike DASD (dumped from 3350 and restore attempted on 3380). Later versions can restore to unlike DASD. *Be sure you test your restore requirements.*

14.7.3. Printing DASD Tracks — PRINT

One of the most overlooked features of DFDSS is to print the data on DASD tracks. For example, VSAM indexes, VTOCs, Partitioned Data Set directories, and VSAM VVDS do not have standard print or dump utilities to inspect the contents of these "data sets." DFDSS needs only the cylinder and head of the "data set" to print them.

In Figure 14.35, assume the index component of a VSAM file is at cylinder 10 head zero through 5. This example will print the index.

14.7.4. Copying Data from Volume to Volume — COPY

The COPY command allows the user to copy from one DASD to another and, in the process, copy from one device type to another.

```
//jobname      JOB  (acct),'programmer name',REGION=4096K,TIME=(5),
//                  NOTIFY=tsoid,MSGCLASS=c
//jobstep      EXEC PGM=ADRDSSU
//*SYSUDUMP    DD   SYSOUT=*
//ddname1      DD   VOL=SER=vvvvvv,UNIT=SYSALLDA,DISP=OLD
//SYSPRINT     DD   SYSOUT=*
//SYSIN        DD   *
   PRINT TRACKS(x'10',x'00',x'10',x'05')   INDDNAME(ddname1)
/*
//
```

Figure 14.35   DFDSS print. The DFDSS print command is used to print data sets or in this case specific tracks of a DASD volume.

Figure 14.36 is an example of copy operation. In this copy operation, the whole volume is copied, including the volume serial number. This operation would be used to move a whole volume from one device to another, to prepare for maintenance, or to clear the volume to allow it to be upgraded from single to dual or triple capacity.

14.7.5.   Reorganization of DASD (Removing Fragmentation) — DEFRAG

DEFRAG attempts to reduce free space fragmentation (Format 5 VTOC DSCBs) by relocating *single extents* of data sets to combine free space into larger contiguous areas of DASD space. One extent is moved at a time. DEFRAG does not compress multiple extent data sets into fewer extents.

```
//jobname      JOB  (acct),'programmer name',REGION=4096K,TIME=(5),
//                  NOTIFY=tsoid,MSGCLASS=c
//jobstep      EXEC PGM=ADRDSSU
//*SYSUDUMP    DD   SYSOUT=*
//ddname1      DD   VOL=SER=vvvvvv,SYSALLDA,DISP=OLD
//ddname2      DD   VOL=SER=vvvvvv,SYSALLDA,DISP=OLD
//SYSPRINT     DD   SYSOUT=*
//SYSIN        DD   *
     COPY INDDNAME(ddname1) OUTDDNAME(ddname2) -
          ALLDATA(*) ALLEXCP CANCELERROR COPYVOLID
/*
//
```

Figure 14.36   DFDSS COPY. The DFDSS copy in this example will copy all the data from the volume pointed to by "ddname1" to the volume pointed to by "ddname2."

14.8.   DFHSM: INCREMENTAL BACKUPS

There are a number of incremental backup systems. The IBM program is called Data Facility Hierarchical Storage Manager (DFHSM). OEM vendors also have excellent backup systems. The functions of all these programs are similar. The implementation is usually vastly different. You should decide how you want to do backups and investigate vendors' offerings.

The following is a general plan of action which should be considered for creating incremental backups:

1. Implement data set naming conventions. This is not an option, it is a mandatory requirement, not only for incremental backups, but for all of MVS. Not having strictly enforced data set names is like jumping off a 100-story building. The question is not *if* you will be in trouble, but *when* you will be in trouble.
2. Decide on the software which will be used.
3. Write a task plan. DFHSM has a checklist which serves as a good basis for the task plan. Each installation is different. The plan must be customized to your data center.
4. Install and test the software.
5. Decide on how long you will keep archived data.
6. Decide on the parameters for each class of data: How long will DFHSM wait after a data set goes inactive before it archives the data set. Some data sets may be used monthly. If you set these to 30 days, DFHSM will archive them just in time to be needed online for the monthly batch JOBS — not a pretty sight.

```
//jobname     JOB   (acct),"programmer name",REGION=4096K,TIME=(5),
//                  NOTIFY=tsoid,MSGCLASS=c
//jobstep     EXEC  PGM=ADRDSSU
//*SYSUDUMP   DD    SYSOUT=*
//ddname1     DD    DSN=data.set.name,DISP=disp
//SYSPRINT    DD    SYSOUT=*
//SYSIN       DD    *
 DEFRAG      DDNAME(ddname1)
/*
//
```

Figure 14.37   DFDSS DEFRAG. DEFRAG attempts to reduce free space fragmentation by relocating data set extents. DFDSS moves one extent at a time and does not attempt to combine extents.

7. Implement with users. A phased approach is always recommended — place some users under DFHSM, evaluate, and move to larger users.
8. Evaluate the project. One of the most important steps is to see how you accomplished the task plan. Are there any ways to improve future task plans?

14.9. SUMMARY

Utilities are programs designed to perform tasks related in function or in the type of data manipulated. Their general applicability makes them different from applications programs. Application utilities manipulate data sets and augment applications systems. Some of the useful ones follow:

IEFBR14 does "nothing" as a placeholder in a JCL EXEC statement and is used for the side effects of the job step's JCL.

IEBGENER copies and prints, reorganizes, and changes attributes (e.g., reblocks) files, and can generate test data.

IEBCOPY copies and maintains partitioned data sets.

IEHLIST lists entries DASD Volume Table of Contents.

SORT/MERGE utilities such as DF/DSORT and SYNCSORT are important to a data center and should be carefully benchmarked and evaluated prior to purchase.

IDCAMS for VSAM is too complex to describe fully here but is well worth investigation by the reader.

System Utilities, though aimed at systems programmers, are sometimes useful to application programmers. Examples are:

AMASPZAP can display and modify either a load module, given its PDS and member name, or arbitrary areas of a DASD given cylinder, head, and record addresses.

AMDPRDMP formats various storage dumps.

IEBIMAGE supports the IBM 3800 printing subsystem.

IFCEREP1 formats and prints the SYS1.LOGREC data set.

Some utilities can run stand-alone, such as DSF to initialize DASD volumes, DFDSS to restore DASD from tape copies, and stand-alone dumps. Stand-alone means that the program is loaded like an operating system into a Processor Complex and performs functions without the assistance of MVS.

DSF provides service functions, error detection, and media maintenance for DASD. The introduction of DSF transferred media maintenance functions from IBM Customer Engineers to the data center.

DFDSS utilities, though not free, perform a variety of dataset management functions: dumping, restoring, printing tracks, copying volumes, defragmenting DASD, and taking incremental backups.

Utilities can save a great amount of time and trouble; it is worth learning about these from IBM and OEMs, getting useful ones and using them regularly.

In the next section, we will look at miscellaneous MVS topics, beginning with a more in-depth look at the Input/Output System.

Part

D

Controlling MVS Efficiency and Throughput

Part D of *MVS: Concepts and Facilities* includes in-depth information about the I/O subsystem. Direct-Access Storage Devices (DASD) and channel commands are discussed. The material in the previous parts is brought together to show you how to tune applications to make the most cost-effective decisions in systems and applications.

MVS control and decision making — from JES to the Systems Resource Manager — are introduced. Understanding job selection and dispatching priorities is important to understanding MVS.

Finally, MVS monitoring, tracing, and security are covered.

Chapter

15

Input-Output in Depth

15.1. I/O OPERATIONS ON DASD

The chapters up to now have given the reader the information about the hardware and software makeup of an MVS computer center. This chapter brings many of the concepts together and gives the reader techniques to use to solve the 54-hour and 13-hour problems introduced at the start of the book.

This chapter also includes information about what to do when things do not go as planned. DASD errors do not happen very often with current hardware, but when today's DASD has a problem, it interrupts transfer of megabytes of data!

15.1.1. Review of Input/Output Operations

Figure 15.1 shows the logical view of an I/O operation initiated by an application program such as one written in COBOL. (COBOL is an application programming language.)

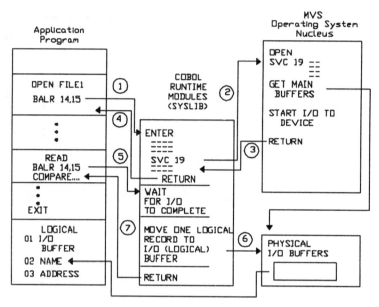

Figure 15.1   I/O from the application program viewpoint. An application program OPENs a file and read/writes to the file. During the open a "state" change occurs to let MVS get control to perform supervisor services for the address space.

1. The program issues an OPEN, which branches into a COBOL program.
2. An SVC 19 (OPEN) is issued which performs a "state" change[1] and "branches" into the MVS Operating System modules.
3. Buffers are obtained and the control blocks are filled in. The first I/O operation is started to fill the buffers. The OPEN module *does not wait* for the buffer to be filled. Control returns to to the COBOL runtime module.
4. COBOL returns control to the application program.

---

1. A state change is accomplished by a System/370 instruction which causes the System/370 hardware to branch into the operating system supervisor code. A "new PSW" is loaded. When the MVS operating system gets control, it needs to be in **supervisor state** to perform **privileged instructions,** so when the hardware loads the "new" PSW, the supervisor state is in effect.

5. When appropriate in the program, a READ is issued. The program branches into the COBOL program and access method code to wait for the I/O started at OPEN time.
6. The data from the physical buffer is moved into the logical record.
7. Control is returned to the application program.

Figure 15.2 is another view of an I/O operation but includes the hardware and software components. The OPEN routines complete control blocks to point to the Unit Control Block (UCB), which has the volume for this data set. The application program issues a READ (or WRITE or GET or PUT) for a logical record. The access method

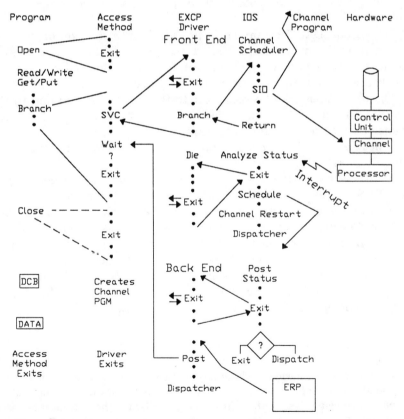

Figure 15.2   An I/O request including the hardware. This view of an I/O operation includes the hardware. Many things could possibly go wrong while the I/O is in progress.

requests a physical buffer via the EXCP interface (SVC 0). This is called the "front end" of an I/O operation.

If another task has an I/O operation running on the device, the request is queued. If not, the I/O operation is started with a Start I/O (SIO) operation for MVS/370 or a Start Subchannel (SSCH) for MVS/XA. (This is the first possibility for hardware error. The channel, control unit, or Head of String may be broken — in which case the *path is in error.*)

If the path is functional but busy, the request is queued until later. If the path is available, the channel fetches the Channel Command Word (CCW) to begin execution. This example is an I/O to a DASD. The first command is to move the arm of the DASD to the area on the volume which has the data. This is called seeking. (**Seek Checks** are the second possibility for problems. The arm may not be able to move.)

The second DASD command is to wait for the rotation of the disk to get near the data. This is called set sector. The device is looking for a certain record. (A **record not found** condition indicates the hardware did not find the record it was asked to retrieve or find.)

The drive then tries to reconnect to the head of string and to the control unit and channel. If reconnection is successful, then data transfer is started to Central Storage.

If not successful, *the drive waits a whole revolution.* This is called an RPS miss.

An RPS miss is *not an error.* RPS misses are not logged in any file. RPS misses are handled differently by all vendors and differently within some vendors' equipment. For example, one vendor had microcode which would allow up to three RPS misses and would then keep trying to reconnect without waiting for the proper sector. This can cause erratic response time observations. Response time may vary widely for the same work load. Some hardware will obediently keep waiting for the proper sector and retrying forever. This causes large **outliers**[2] which are very long response times.

---

2. The term "outliers" refers to statistical observations which are far outside what should be "normal." These observations could be a cause for concern and should be monitored, but mostly they bias the statistical study. Many performance analysts either throw away or discard these abnormal observations. One statistical method — 95th percentile — eliminates the top five percent of the observations to overcome the outlier bias.

If the data is not transferred successfully, then a **Data Check** has occurred. The hardware will attempt a retry on its own to retransfer the data. The retry count is usually proprietary information to both IBM and the OEM vendors but is approximately 10 retries before the hardware gives up and notifies MVS.

MVS retries approximately 10 times (this is 100 retries — 10 for the hardware times 10 for the software) to get a successful completion. If neither the hardware nor MVS can successfully complete the operation, then the Access Method is "notified" that the I/O was in error. If the Access Method has error recovery routines, these routines may attempt some recovery operation.

After the data is transferred correctly, the hardware "interrupts" the CPU and the "back end" of MVS I/O operations wraps up the I/O access: The application program is then given control to process the data.

Figure 15.3 shows the breakdown of the time spent to do an I/O operation. The request may wait on several resources:

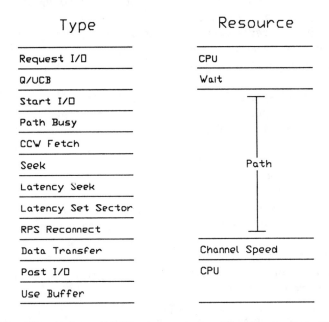

Type	Resource
Request I/O	CPU
Q/UCB	Wait
Start I/O	
Path Busy	
CCW Fetch	
Seek	Path
Latency Seek	
Latency Set Sector	
RPS Reconnect	
Data Transfer	Channel Speed
Post I/O	CPU
Use Buffer	

Figure 15.3   Time to do an I/O. The components of the time to do an I/O operation can be spent waiting in the CPU for resources, in the channel path to the device, or in the device while transferring data. Although these are not drawn to scale, you can see channel speed is one of many parts of the response time of an I/O operation.

1. Logically wait on the device (Q/UCB): The address space may be queued to get to the Unit Control Block. For most devices, only one I/O operation can be started at a time.
2. Wait for data transfer to begin:
   a. The MVS Input/Output Supervisor issues a "start" to the device.
   b. The path may be busy. In MVS/370, the MVS supervisor will queue and restart the I/O. In MVS/XA and MVS/ESA, the channel subsystem will queue and restart the I/O without bothering MVS.
   c. The channel fetches the Channel Command Words (CCWs) to begin the operation.
   d. For DASD, the arm is moved (seeked) to the appropriate cylinder; this takes time.
   e. The device waits for the head to be near the requested record.
   f. Wait time may be extended for RPS misses.
3. Physically wait for data transfer: the data is transferred to Central Storage at the speed of the device.
4. Wait for redispatch: MVS performs cleanup and/or error recovery operations and places the address space on the dispatchable queue.

The channel speed of the device and associated control units is a relatively small portion of the time an address space could wait for an I/O operation to complete.

15.1.2. I/O Errors

The hardware could detect errors at any point along this path. The hardware will retry errors and attempt to complete the operation successfully. Some hardware errors are noticeable by the end user. The errors which affect production should be prevented if possible or corrected if not. (Uncorrected errors can grow up to become disasters.) Hardware error categories are:

1. Programming errors, such as asking for an invalid record format or giving an incorrect record specification. These errors are usually not recoverable. Something has happened to the data set, and it is usually not fixed by retrying the operation.
2. Data error on a read or write operation. The data center should manage these errors.

Some of the characteristics of errors which need to be examined are:

1. Recoverability of error:
   a. Recovery from **temporary errors** is by correcting the data or retrying the I/O operation. If the hardware cannot complete successfully, the software will retry in an attempt to get a successful I/O operation. For example, if a channel error is indicated, an alternate channel will be tried. In some cases, the hardware actually tells the software where the error is and how to fix it. The Error Checking and Correction Code (ECC) is used to "fix" the record in Central Storage.
   b. **Permanent errors** cannot be recovered by retrying the operation. The data set will usually have to be restored or rebuilt. Your data center does have a "recent" copy of the data set, and you have kept all the updates since that copy was made, correct?
2. Duration of error:
   a. An **intermittent error** changes with time. The error may occur and "go away," or it may seem to move from spot to spot on a DASD volume.
   b. A **continuous error** is one which does not change with time. It requires a "fix" from outside the system.
3. Seek and overrun errors are timing problem errors.
4. Equipment errors are usually mechanical or electrical problems.

Error Considerations There are several possible times when errors might occur. The first is on the write of the data, in which the data does not get recorded properly on the surface of the disk. With the first generation of DASD (2311-2314), it was recommended to use an access method facility — write verify — to have the access method read the block after writing to ensure the data was actually recorded on the surface. With 3330s and later generations, this double work is no longer recommended because the devices became so reliable that the performance degradation was not worth the effort.

The possibility exists that the data, once written correctly, cannot be read successfully at a later time. These failures could be:

1. **Soft failures,** which means the control unit and/or the operating system use recovery routines to retry the failure, and on one of these successive tries, actually gets to read the record *without detected failure.* Soft failures are estimated to take

0.500 seconds to complete — quite a bit longer than the normal 0.040 to 0.060 seconds.

2. **Hard failures**, which means the software and hardware failed in all attempts to read the record, and the only exit is to pass a failure code back to the requesting program. Hard failures have been timed on 3380 devices to take *1.03 seconds* to complete all retry attempts.

There are several ways in which the data center personnel can work around DASD problems. One is available if part of a track is bad (skip displacements). One is available if an entire track is bad (alternate tracks).

Skip Displacements: The surface of the disk platter may contain areas which are either impossible or hard to read and write data on the track. The surface of the track could have a scratch or other defect which prevents correct recording. A skip displacement is used by MVS to indicate to the *device* that, while reading or writing a block, it is to skip over certain spots on the recording surface.

Figure 15.4 shows a spot in the middle of the data portion of Record 1. Once the track has been flagged, the data can be rewritten and read, and the device automatically skips over the bad spot.

Skip displacement information is kept in the Record zero (R0) field of the track. The number of bytes into the track and the number of bytes to skip are recorded for each skip area. No additional software processing is required once the skip displacement has been defined. *There is no performance penalty* for I/O operations which require the actuator to skip over a bad spot.

Each track has a limit to the number of skip displacements. The 3380 track is limited to seven skip displacements, and the 3350 is limited to three.

Alternate Tracks: Each DASD surface has a number of reserved tracks for assignment if one of the primary tracks becomes useless for recording. These are called alternate tracks and are usually assigned closest to the spindle by the DASD firmware. *A performance penalty is paid* for using alternate tracks. The operating system tries

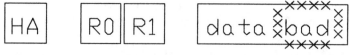

Figure 15.4   Surface defects. DASD platters are metal disks with a magnetic coating. If the surface is not able to record information, then the bad spot can be "skipped" by assigning skip displacements.

to read or write the primary track. The I/O result is a permanent error, and the Home Address is read to find the address of the alternate track. The head is positioned to an alternate track, and the data is read. Several I/O revolutions are required for alternate track processing. *Do not allow alternate tracks to be used for highly active data sets.*

Now that I have said that, I must be the bearer of bad news — there is no easy way for you to ensure your highly active data set(s) is not on alternate track(s). The data center must keep track of alternate tracks as they are assigned!

15.2. ACCESS PATTERNS

The way a program accesses data in a physical block is important to the health of the MVS system. There are Central Storage and channel considerations. Some rules of thumb are:

1. Read just what your application needs. The block size should approximate how much data you need.
2. Read sequentially if possible: You should fully utilize the data in a page frame before you go to another. Do not jump back and forth unnecessarily in a large logical record or from logical record to logical record.

In Figure 15.5, the program is reading a file of customer records. The analyst has room for the name and account number (100 bytes) and a very large area for the history of this customer. When the

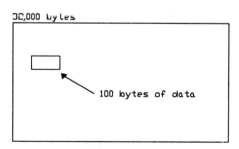

Figure 15.5   Access patterns. The application should have a physical block large enough to contain all the data needed, but not too large to cause real storage or channel problems. The application using this physical block has defined a 32,000-byte block yet only needs 100 bytes of data for the online query.

customer calls in, the online system needs the 100 bytes, the customer name, and account number, but to get this "piece," the program has to read all 32,000 bytes of the block.

MVS would have to allocate 32,000 bytes of Central Storage, and the channel would have to transmit 32,000 bytes of data just so the program can display the customer name and account number. That is a waste.

What should be done? Select a block size which will efficiently transfer data into storage based on the needs of the processing:

1. Use large block sizes for batch processing.
2. Use small block sizes for online interactive programming.
3. Use large block sizes to conserve DASD space (to make a 3380 hold the same as a 3330, use a block size of 80 bytes!).

I realize all online files must be processed by batch for update, backup, etc. Later in this chapter, you will see how we have our cake and eat it too!

15.3. CHANNEL COMMANDS

Channel commands are the communication medium used by MVS running in the Processor Complex to direct the Storage Control Unit (SCU), which controls the I/O device. Each SCU responds to Channel Command Words (CCWs) valid for that SCU and device.

CCWs are sometimes built by application programs, but access methods and MVS build most CCWs. The CCWs are built in virtual storage. Once built, the CCWs are passed to MVS to complete the I/O operation. Let's review an I/O operation from channel program construction to execution:

1. The application program builds a channel program and asks MVS to start it.
2. MVS gets control via supervisor services and ensures the I/O operations are valid.
3. MVS fixes the Central Storage page frame which contains the virtual address of the I/O buffer.
4. MVS copies the CCWs from the application area to a new area, then translates virtual addresses to the real addresses in the fixed frames.

5. MVS prefixes the modified application CCWs with control CCWs to limit the scope of the I/O operation. MVS ensures the application channel program makes valid references but, with the Set File Mask control CCW, directs the channel to notify MVS if the application tries anything funny (such as referencing DASD areas outside an opened data set).
6. If MVS/370 is executing, MVS looks to see if the device is busy. If it is, MVS places the I/O request on a pending start queue. If the device is available, MVS issues one of several System/370 I/O operations — Start I/O or Start I/O Fast Release.
7. If MVS/XA or MVS/ESA is executing, the Processor Complex handles I/O pending problems, so a Start Subchannel (SSCH) instruction is executed.
8. MVS places the I/O request on a list of **pending interrupts**.
9. MVS returns control to the requestor. The requestor can wait or continue processing. The I/O request may not be completed for several milliseconds.

15.3.1. CCW Translation

Figure 15.6 shows another view of Channel Commands. The I/O subsystem does not operate using virtual storage addresses (there is no DAT feature for I/O addresses), so MVS must convert the data ad-

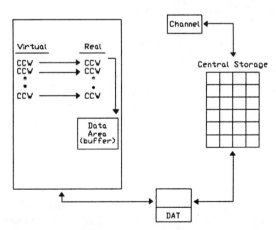

Figure 15.6 Channel program translation. The MVS access methods build Channel Command Words (CCWs) to read/write to data areas or buffers. Channels need real addresses in the CCWs, so MVS translates CCWs from virtual addresses to real addresses. (This is why I/O buffer pages must be fixed.)

dress portion of the CCW to the real storage address where the data is to be stored or fetched.

Up to now, we have viewed a buffer as a contiguous area which contains all the logical records in a physical record. What if a user requested 12,288 bytes to be read, however, and the first 4,096 bytes were in one page frame and the rest were in other noncontiguous page frames? The answer is the data address of the CCW could point to an **Indirect Data Address Word** (IDAW). Figure 15.7 shows the virtual CCWs translated to "real" CCWs, but in the process, the "pointers" to the buffer can be indirect addresses. Each IDAW describes a 2-Kb[3] block of Central Storage and contains the Central Storage address for the block.

In this example, the virtual CCW built asks to read 12,228 bytes. The start I/O points to an **Indirect Address List** (IDAL). The list contains pointers to the Central Storage addresses of the buffer.

A different CCW is required if the Central Storage addresses are above the 16-Mb line. Format 0 mode CCWs are used when the data area addresses are 24 bits (3 bytes) long. Format 1 mode CCWs are used when the data area addresses are 31 bits (4 bytes minus one bit) long. In Figure 15.8, the address part of the CCW of both the Format 0 (MVS/370, MVS/XA, and MVS/ESA) and the Format 1 (MVS/XA and MVS/ESA only) CCWs are shown.

15.3.2. Types of Channel Commands

There are several types of Channel Command:

WRITE CCWs Write operations initiate transfer from Central Storage to the I/O device. Data is fetched in ascending order. Examples are:

---

3. DAT was originally designed to permit selection of either 2-Kb or 4-Kb pages. Studies have shown that there is little advantage to 2-Kb page sizes in virtual memory architectures, so 4-Kb pages are used exclusively. The 2-Kb addressability of IDAWs may be considered a vestige of upward hardware compatibility.

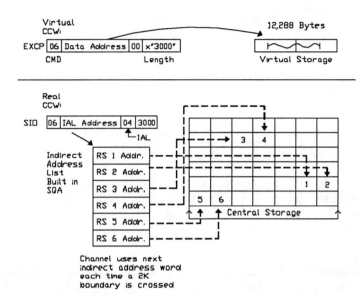

Figure 15.7   Use of Indirect Address List. The CCW is built in virtual storage, but MVS must make a copy of the CCW and substitute addresses to point to the central storage frames.

1. **Write Count, Key, and Data** commands write data, then format the rest of the track. The device is busy for the rest of a rotation. These are also called "formatting writes."
2. **Write Data** commands only update the data area of a specific record.

READ CCWs   Read operations initiate transfer of data from the device to real storage. Examples are:

1. **Read Count** transfers the count area of a record from the track to Central Storage. This CCW is used by MVS to determine the size of a block on DASD.
2. **Read Count, Key, and Data** transfers all three sections of a physical block to Central Storage.
3. **Read Multiple Count, Key, and Data** reads the selected record and all the rest of the records on the track.

SENSE CCWs   Sense operations initiate transfer of information about the device from the device to storage. The information concerns both unusual conditions detected during the last operation and the status of the device.

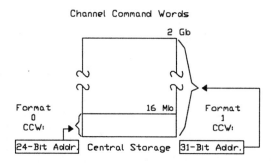

Figure 15.8   Format 0 and Format 1 CCWs. MVS/370 uses only Format 0 CCWs, because it addresses only 16 megabytes of virtual storage. MVS/XA and MVS/ESA use either Format 0 or Format 1 CCWs because they need to access up to 2 gigabytes of virtual storage.

1. **Sense** CCWs transfer 24 bytes of sense information describing the status of the device from the SCU to Central Storage.

2. **Device Reserve** sets a bit in the HOS which indicates that this channel path has control of the *entire volume or actuator* and *transfers 24 bits* of sense information from the SCU to Central Storage. Among other things, this sense information indicates whether the reservation request was honored. Device Reserve is used by MVS (when the UCB is marked "shared") to gain control of a volume when it is going to change information on the volume that might be read by other Processor Complexes in the data center. (Device Reserve is to I/O devices as the Test and Set instruction is to memory.)

3. **Device Release** turns off the reserve bit in the HOS and transfers 24 bytes of sense information from the SCU to Central SSorage.

CONTROL CCWs   Control commands set up the device in some manner. Examples are:

1. **Seek** commands move the read/write arm to a selected cylinder.

2. **Set Sector** transfers a sector number (usually 0 to 127 for the 128 sectors) to say "ok to free up channel until you get to a specific spot in the rotation of the disk."

3. **Read Sector** asks the device to write back the one byte sector number of a particular record. MVS uses this value as the argument of a Set Sector when the next Read/Write operation is requested.

4. **Transfer-in-Channel** operations causes the next channel command to be fetched from a different location in Central Storage. This is a branching or decision-making facility in channel programs.
5. **Set File Mask** (SFM) transfers a mask byte to the SCU to govern the remainder of the channel program. The mask byte can inhibit or permit selected operations. Only one SFM may appear in a channel program; the second yields a channel check.

DIAGNOSTIC CCWs Diagnostic commands are used by the IBM utilities for functions not normally used by applications that run under MVS. Examples are commands used to assign skip displacements.

15.4. TUNING DASD I/O — 13-HOUR AND 54-HOUR JOBS

We now turn to the topic of how you can tune DASD I/O. This is a very complex subject which could be the topic of a whole book! You have to begin somewhere, so let's begin.

You can control the number of physical buffers accessed by a single I/O read or write. On the left side of Figure 15.9, the default number of buffers — five — are shown. CCWs are built to read and write approximately three buffers with one Start I/O or Start Subchannel. If we allocate 20 buffers for the access method to use, then we could get the CCWs to read and write 10 blocks at a time — on average. You will soon see how that can be done. Remember that you are ultimately influencing the access method's behavior — building and using buffers and CCWs.

15.4.1. Tuning VSAM — the 13-Hour Job

I stated earlier that the 13-hour job is a daily job that was taking too long. The job consumed approximately 5 percent of the Processor Complex and was observed waiting on a DASD. It was important to finish the batch job in less than six hours. A bigger Processor Complex would not help. The channels were 5–15 percent busy. The problems were with VSAM defaults.

VSAM defaults to one index buffer and two data buffers: Each read request results in three physical reads. The job could be sped

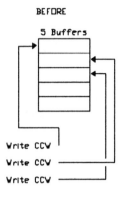
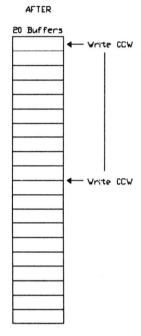

Figure 15.9 Building and executing CCWs. MVS access methods build and execute CCWs based on the number of available buffers. If the default of five buffers is allocated, the access method will read or write two to three blocks per I/O operation. If 20 buffers are specified, the access method will read or write 10 blocks per I/O operation.

up if the VSAM index could be read into Central Storage and remain there.

The VSAM parameters specifying the number of index buffers (BUFNI=10) and the number of data buffers (BUFND=10) were added to the JCL for the files by application programmers. Figure 15.10 shows the result of changing the default VSAM buffers — the daily job was *reduced from 13 hours elapsed time to 4 hours!*

The Buffer Space parameter (BUFSP) could have been used instead. BUFSP is mutually exclusive with BUFNI/BUFND. If BUFSP is coded, it supersedes any BUFNI/BUFND. BUFSP specifies the bytes of storage to use for buffers. Given the choice, use the more relevant BUFNI/BUFND.

The analyst, however, was not satisfied. Program changes were made to further reduce the I/O. The file was rebuilt to reduce the I/O requirements even further.

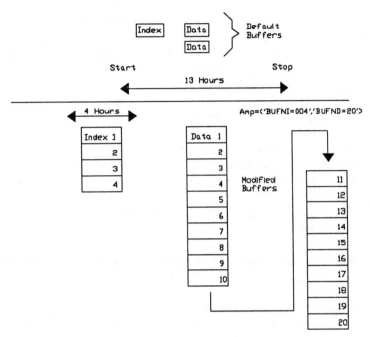

Figure 15.10   Tuning VSAM: JCL. By changing the IDCAMS buffer specification, this batch job elapsed time went from 13 hours down to 4 hours.

15.4.2. Tuning Tape Access — 54-Hour Job

There are several considerations for the MVS user when using tape data sets. The most obvious one is that the tape suffers from the same problem as the disk data sets suffer from — gaps between blocks. Shorter records result in more gaps. More gaps effectively shorten the tape. They also elongate processing time.

I introduced a problem of the 54-hour job in previous chapters. The reader now has enough information to solve the problem. Your company has a 54-hour job, too — just waiting for you to solve it using these techniques. Oh, the job may not take exactly 54 hours. It is probably buried somewhere in your production system. Would you advertise that you have a job out of control and using too many resources? Of course not!

If you remember, the 54-hour job wrote a tape file. The tape blocks are required to be 4,096 bytes long because the **receiving machine** — a microfiche recorder — requires that size. Here is what happens:

1. The application program reads several disk files and builds print lines to be placed on microfiche. The microfiche machine reads a round (3420 type) tape and produces microfiche. The program writes a round tape file.
2. As a physical block fills with logical records, MVS access methods (WRITE) builds CCWs for each 4,096-byte block. See Figure 15.11 — each block is passed to IOS to write to the tape drive, one or two at a time.
3. The MVS Input/Output supervisor uses CPU, Central Storage, and I/O resources to write the block onto the tape.
4. The tape drive must start up, write one or more blocks, and stop "on a dime."
5. The above repeats until the entire file is converted to microfiche records.

What could the application programmer or system designer do differently to make this job more efficient?

JCL Changes   The first place to attack is where all the work is being done — writing the blocks of tape. The MVS JCL manual has, buried in the Data Definition (DD) section, the DCB parameter "part two" options called BUFNO and OPTCD.

BUFNO= in JCL communicates to the MVS access method that it should allocate more than the default number (five) of buffers. For example, you could specify DCB=BUFNO=20 on the JCL to get 20 buffers. This was tried without success (under MVS/370).

```
Default MVS-5 buffers        OPTCD=C, BUFNO=20


Write CCW -->  Block 1       Block 1   <-- Write CCW
Write CCW -->  Block 2       Block 2   <-- Write CCW
               Block 3       Block 3   <-- Write CCW
               Block 4       Block 4   <-- Write CCW
               Block 5       Block 5   <-- Write CCW
                             Block 6   <-- Write CCW
                             Block 7   <-- Write CCW
                             Block 8   <-- Write CCW
                             Block 9   <-- Write CCW
                             Block 10  <-- Write CCW
                                  . . .

                             Block 20
```

Figure 15.11   OPTCD=C, BUFNO=20. The default number of buffers is 5. By using DCB=(OPTCD=C,BUFNO=20), you can affect the CCWs built for each I/O instruction — in this case 10 blocks are written at one time.

One of the uses of OPTCD is to control the number of consecutive buffers accessed by a single I/O operation. OPTCD=C signals the access method to use **chained scheduling**. Chained scheduling works as follows:

1. The number of buffers you ask for is divided by two. With OPTCD=C and BUFNO=20, the number of buffers passed to MVS is now approximately 10.
2. When writing, your program fills up half the buffers, and the access method *then* writes out the first half while your program is filling the second half. In Figure 15.11, the first 10 CCWs are passed to IOS with one request. (The same thing happens on read requests.)

This situation requires short (4 Kb) tape blocks and does waste space on the tape, but we are getting most of the benefits of large block sizes — 40,960 bytes are being transferred with each request. Expected results are:

1. CPU utilization will be smaller.
2. The cost of your computing will be less. Most billing algorithms charge for each I/O. Fewer I/O requests result in a smaller bill. (This is not cheating because you are using resources more efficiently and should be rewarded.)
3. Your job will take less elapsed time to run.

DCB=(OPTCD=C,BUFNO=20) was coded on the JCL statement for the output tape, and the elapsed run time of the microfiche job dropped dramatically — from 54 hours down to 20 hours.

Program Changes   The analyst took up the challenge and changed the program. The program was writing names and addresses on the microfiche for the 1,200 vendors in the file (see Figure 15.12). As transactions were read, the vendors' names and addresses, were looked up in the file and written to microfiche. The programmer built a table to hold the names. This eliminated most of the disk I/O operations, and the 54-hour job was further *reduced to 6 hours*.[4]

---

4. Thanks to Jim Thompson for demonstrating these techniques.

1,200
Vendor Names
Table
Program
Transactions

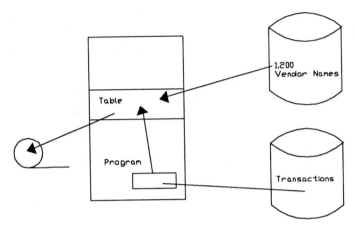

Figure 15.12 Program changes. The program was changed to read in the active vendor names into an in-storage table. As transactions were read, the table in real storage was used instead of the VSAM disk file.

Yes, you can tune I/O operations, but the best programming change you can do is to eliminate I/O operations. The motto in Figure 15.13 says the fastest I/O operation is NONE AT ALL!

You should note that, in some versions of MVS (notably MVS/XA Release 2.1.3 and above), the parameter OPTCD=C is not necessary. If you specify more than five buffers, MVS will assume chained scheduling. This was not true with previous versions. It is always proper to specify OPTCD=C. Remember upward compatibility!

15.5. SUMMARY

Fortunately, it is not necessary for you to deal with the intricacies of channel programming to effect major improvements in I/O efficiency. As the solutions to the 13- and 54-hour jobs show, judicious use of DD statement parameters such as BUFNI, BUFND, BUFNO, and OPTCD can have marked effect.

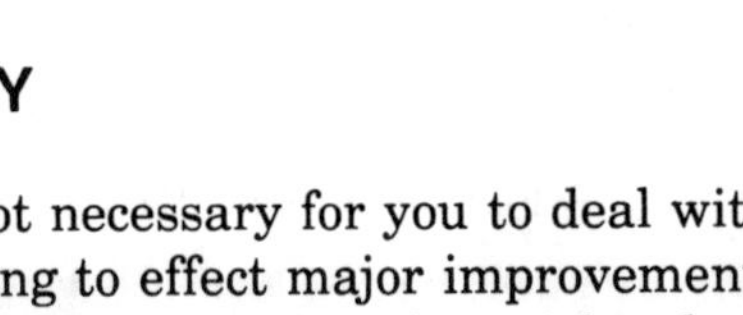

It is far better to
do nothing than
to do something
efficiently.

Figure 15.13 I/O adage. The fastest and most efficient I/O is not to an I/O device but to virtual storage.

Perhaps you think it was unfair, even stupid, of me to put so many pages and chapters between the statement of a problem and its solution. Perhaps you think I wanted to entice you to read the parts between by giving you something to look forward to! (Would that be terrible of me?)

The reason I committed this apparently heinous crime is that it would not have been enough to tell you to "code this" and "make that number bigger." Requesting lots of big buffers can backfire if they end up creating more overhead than they prevent, but you understand that now, and why. Efficiency is a balance of power.

In my mind, this book is successful if it causes you to say to yourself every time you see or code a DD statement, "this is going to result in a channel program, and with this DCB and AMP, I am initiating a complex interaction between a lot of hardware and software." You are, in effect, telling an access method how to write its channel programs, and it will do what you say.

Programmers (and users!) have longed for a "Do What I Mean" instruction, program statement or command. The first step to this is to know what you mean.

I do not want you to write channel programs: I do want you to understand them.

We have taken a look at the interactions between software and hardware to effect I/O on an MVS system. Normally, an application calls upon the access method to perform an I/O operation. The access method arranges for data buffers, builds a channel program, and asks MVS to cause the channel to execute it.

Once the channel has control of the I/O operation, there are several occasions for error, some of which are recoverable, some not. (A data center should never ignore device errors, even those from which MVS or the hardware recovers.) Provisions exist in DASD for skipping over bad spots on the medium (skip displacement) and for assigning alternate tracks; use of the latter incurs a performance penalty.

When an access method (or application) requests execution of a channel program, MVS must do some preparation. Pages must be fixed in Central Storage, virtual addresses in CCWs must be translated (by software) to real addresses, and the channel must be instructed to disallow operations which might compromise the integrity of data outside that for which the requestor is allowed access.

CCWs exist to read and write data, obtain and change device status, control movement of and access to a device, and perform diagnostic functions.

CCWs are but one of the things MVS regulates on behalf of the system. In the next chapter, we see how MVS gives shares of other resources, such as the CPU, among the applications running on the system.

16

Control and Decision Making

16.1. BEFORE AND AFTER JOB EXECUTION — JES

Before job execution, JES receives and processes a job and schedules when the job will be available for MVS to give it CPU, Central Storage, and I/O resources. MVS has a number of points at which it makes decisions about Processor Complex resource allocation. After job execution, JES schedules and completes disposition of spooled output.

16.1.1. Before Job Execution

The Job Entry Subsystem (JES) controls a job before it begins execution by considering the resources it requires, the initiators available to execute it, and the job's relative priority within the system.

Resources Batch jobs are submitted by data center users to be processed. The JES input processor reads the Job Control Language (JCL) for the job and places the job onto a queue of jobs. If the data center has loosely coupled Processor Complexes, the user may request that the job execute on a specific Processor Complex. If JES networking is installed, the user may request that the job execute on a particular NODE. In a JES2 environment, the /*ROUTE XEQ, the /*XEQ, or the /*JOBPARM SYSAFF= cards are used to specify this. In a JES3 environment, the /*XMIT or the //*MAIN SYSTEM= cards are used to specify the node.

The names used with the above cards are called resources. Each Processor Complex has a resource name associated with the Processor Complex. A job is selected for processing if the resource(s) associated with a Processor Complex match the resource(s) requested by a job. For example, if a job requests to run on the Processor Complex labeled BATCH1, then JES will only allow the job to be started on that Processor Complex. Each Processor Complex may have several resource names associated with it, so names can be assigned Processor Complexes to indicate general classifications of resource availability.

For example, the "BATCH1" Processor Complex may share the resource name "VECTOR" with all others also having a Vector Facility installed.

JES Initiators JES passes the batch job to initiators which operate in a separate address space to run the batch jobs. Initiators are MVS modules that use the Subsystem Interface (SSI) "job select" routine to read jobs. Figure 16.1 shows two initiators. Initiator 01 in address space ID (ASID) number 15 has been set by the operator (or COMMNDxx member of SYS1.PARMLIB) to "CLASS=A." Initiator 02 in ASID number 16 has been set by the operator to two job classes — "B" and "A."

In this example (JES2), the initiator in ASID 15 will process any job which can run on this Processor Complex and has "CLASS=A" assigned it. The assignment of a class to a job can be done either by the submitter coding "CLASS=A" on the job card or by MVS operating system SMF Exits which look up the resources the JCL describes and automatically assign a class. The latter arrangement is better because the data center controls how resources — CPU, I/O, Virtual/Central Storage, and DASD space — are used.

If this example were a JES3 subsystem, the data center could specify in the start up deck something like "only run 3 Class A jobs on Processor Complex TSO."

The order of class specification is very important. The initiator in ASID 16 was set to CLASS=BA. As long as there are Class B jobs, no Class A jobs can be selected by this initiator. In Figure 16.1, if Initiator 01 (Class A) were busy with a job and jobs PRINT01 and PRINT02 were submitted, then job PRINT02 would start in Initiator 02 (CLASS BA.) The initiator selects jobs by class based on a first

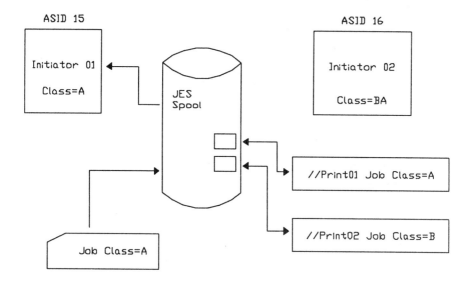

Figure 16.1   Control: JES. JES reads jobs and selects the job based on "resources" (is the job eligible for this Processor Complex?) and JOBCLASS (is a qualifying initiator available to process the job?)

come, first served by class. In this case, all Class "B" jobs would be selected before any Class "A" jobs were selected by Initiator 02.

Selection Priority The submitter of a batch job can specify a "priority," either on the job card (PRTY=x) or on a JES2 control card (/*PRIORITY). Both JES2 and JES3 implement priority aging. As a job waits in the queue for execution, the priority is raised to enhance the chances of the job being selected.

In JES2, the priority is increased as it waits to be started. JES2 keeps raising the priority until the job is selected for execution.

JES3 increases a job's priority based on the number of times it is has been passed over for selection. A job may be passed over because devices are not available, another job has volumes needed by this job, or because there is not enough storage available.

16.1.2. After the Job Executes

After the job terminates, JES is responsible for printing the output generated. The job class is no longer important. The SYSOUT class and priority are. If a printer is not set to the SYSOUT class, the output will not be printed. The higher the print priority, the faster the job is selected for output processing.

Many data centers set JES to assign priorities according to the number of print lines. Smaller numbers of lines get higher priority; larger numbers of lines get lower priority.

16.2. DURING JOB EXECUTION — SRM

The Systems Resource Manager (SRM) is the collective group of MVS modules whose objective is to control distribution of resources as the data center dictates to maximize throughput and to prevent shortages of CPU cycles, I/O availability, and Central Storage. The SRM has five functional groups of functions:

1. The **Interface Function** is the means by which other MVS modules communicate with the SRM and through which the SRM directs the other parts of MVS.
2. The **SYSEVENT function** analyzes communications to the SRM and translates the communications to actions which the SRM should perform.
3. The **control function** performs swapping[1] analysis, obtains swap recommendations from other SRM components, and translates them into specific swapping decisions.
4. The **resource-use algorithms** consist of processor, I/O, and storage management functions, which monitor these resources and make swapping recommendations. The monitoring determines the multiprogramming levels (MPL). SRM decides to raise, lower, or keep the MPL the same.
5. The **workload manager** function maintains statistics on each address space and its consumption of resources. These statistics influence the control function's swapping decisions.

---

1. Swapping is moving the address space out of Central Storage and onto auxiliary storage. The address space cannot use resources until it is swapped in.

16.2.1.   Reactive Manager

The SRM is a reactive manager, which is to say that decisions are made only if shortages "appear" to occur. If no shortages are detected, the SRM will not take any corrective action.

SRM can be compared to a bean counter, where "beans" are resources such as Central Storage, CPU cycles, and I/O accesses. SRM attempts to ensure the jobs and TSO sessions in the system are given beans based on data center's specifications. The larger the system, the more beans SRM has to account for.

SRM does not give out the beans. Jobs and TSO sessions take whatever number of beans they need and can get their hands on. SRM only looks around and counts the beans which are used. SRM does not even know when someone takes an I/O bean, a Central Storage bean, or a CPU bean, but if SRM looks and does not find enough beans of each type, SRM may take actions to get some beans back.

SRM can collect almost all the beans from an address space by swapping out the address space (some Central Storage beans remain to point to the address space on auxiliary storage). All the beans are returned when the address space completes.

The data center specifies, in member SYS1.PARMLIB(IEAICSxx), who are the good guys and who are bad. Member SYS1.PARMLIB(IEAIPSxx) specifies how much each address space gets.

There are one major and four minor decisions which the SRM is designed to make:

1. Which ASIDs should be in storage (swapping)? (Major decision)
2. How many frames should each have (storage isolation)?
3. What should be the dispatching priority of the address spaces in storage?
4. Which devices should be selected at device allocation time for nonspecific device requests (UNIT=SYSDA, for example)?
5. Which ASID should get priority when starting Input/Output (I/O) operations?

The reference for SRM is *System Programming Library: Initialization and Tuning* (e.g., GC28-1149 for MVS/XA), but let's take a brief look at SRM definitions.

16.2.2. SRM Definitions

Transaction A transaction is the SRM basic unit of work. Each batch job or started task is one transaction. For a TSO user, a transaction may be a command or the amount of work consumed from when the terminal user hits "enter" on the terminal until the terminal is waiting for the user to respond again. For a 3270 user, this is usually the period of time the keyboard is locked.

Figure 16.2 shows two examples of a transaction. A batch job with two steps is a single transaction. A TSO terminal user issuing a command "LISTC" and waiting for a response is a transaction.

CICS and IMS have "transactions," too, but these transactions are performed inside the respective address spaces. SRM does not control these transactions, other than applying controls to the CICS or IMS address spaces.

Service Unit (SU) A Service Unit (SU) is a number calculated by SRM to determine how much "service" an address space has received for this transaction. Figure 16.3 shows the calculation. A Service Unit is the numeric sum calculated by adding together:

1. the CPU time used by a transaction (the sum of the Task CPU time (TCB) and the Service Request Block (SRB) CPU time), each multiplied by coefficients (a and d);

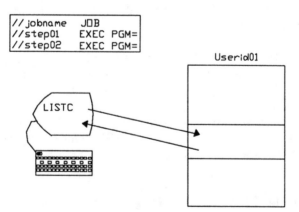

Figure 16.2 Transactions. An SRM transaction is either a complete job or a TSO command issues at a terminal. Do not confuse this with a CICS or IMS "transaction," though — SRM and application transactions are on different levels.

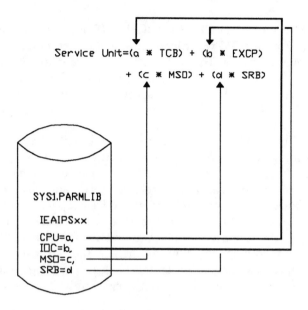

SERVICE RATE: su/second
ABSORPTION RATE: su/second while swapped in

Figure 16.3   SRM definitions. As the transaction gets service, the service rate is the sum of the Service Units per second "absorbed," or used, by the address space. A Service Unit is the CPU time used (SRB and TCB), the I/O requests (EXCP), and the Central Storage usage, each multiplied by a specified coefficient.

2. the number of I/O operations (EXCPs)[2] multiplied by a coefficient (b);
3. and the number of Central Storage page frames used multiplied by an coefficient (c).

The coefficients a, b, c, and d are called the Service Definition Coefficients (SDC) and are part of the Installation Performance Specifications (IPS). SCDs are specified in SYS1.PARMLIB member

---

2. "EXCP" comes from Execute Channel Program, the MVS macro which uses SVC 0 to request MVS to start a channel program. All access methods eventually issue an SVC 0 to call the MVS Input/Output Supervisor.

IEAIPSxx using keywords CPU=a, IOC=b, MSO=c, and SRB=d. The SU is the basis of all SRM work load management recommendations. Each component of service (I/O, CPU, or Central Storage) is weighted to allow the IPS builder to increase the relative importance of certain resources. CPU could be specified as most important by making the CPU SDC larger than that for the other resources.

Service Rate The number of service units per second that a transaction is consuming (i.e., how fast it is running) is deceptively simple. The number of seconds a transaction is swapped out is included in this calculation: this increases the probability the address space will be swapped back in. For example, if an address space accumulates 100 service units in 100 seconds, the rate is one service unit per second. If the address space is then swapped out for 100 seconds, the 100 service units divided by 200 seconds is 0.5 service units per second, which makes the job seem to be less of a "hog" and more likely to be scheduled to receive further service units.

Absorption Rate The absorption rate is the number of service units/seconds consumed by a transaction over the time the transaction is resident (swapped in). Absorption rate is a measure of how fast the transaction is capable of running.

Domain A domain is a collection of address spaces which will compete for access to the system. Domains are defined with the SYS1.PARMLIB IEAIPSxx DMN keyword. Domain numbers are arbitrarily chosen from 1 to 128 to identify the domain. (Although the following example uses domain numbers 1, 2, and 3, other numbers could have been used.)

In Figure 16.4, three domains are shown. Domain 1 has been chosen for partial control. The CNSTR=(8,25) indicates between eight and 25 address spaces can be in storage trying to get access to CPU, storage, and I/O resources. This means that if there are fewer than eight address spaces in the domain, SRM does nothing with them. Between eight and 25, SRM exerts some control. If any more than 25 address spaces are in the domain, SRM causes the excess to be swapped out.

The second domain has no SRM control. The CNSTR=(8,8) indicates if there are eight address spaces or less in storage, then they should be allowed to stay in storage. The data center usually ensures there are no more than eight address spaces running (such as CICSs).

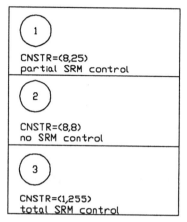

Figure 16.4 SRM Definitions — Domains. Domains are not controlled by SRM, partially controlled by SRM, or completely controlled by SRM, depending on the defined constraints.

The third domain has "total" SRM control. From one to 255 address spaces can be in Central Storage. The data center could specify zero as the minimum number of address spaces, but unless there are specific reasons to do so, it is not good practice to let SRM have domain specifications of zero. The reason for this is that if SRM starts to swap address spaces in the domain, it may degrade into **thrashing** — a term used when large volumes of resources are consumed by MVS to move address spaces into and out of storage without giving the address space a chance to perform meaningful work. By having a minimum of one address space, you ensure that one will be left in storage. The risk is that you could overcommit MVS and not give MVS enough control over the tasks. My response to that is if you do not have enough resources for one address space in each domain, you are configured wrong.

Most data centers do not specify a value as high as 255 for the maximum number of address spaces. You should calculate the most you can afford to have in Central Storage at the same time and set the number to that value.

It is possible and sometimes advisable to create a domain with CNSTR=(0,0). I call this "domain 99" and establish performance group (described below) 99 to be in domain 99. If an operator sets an address space's performance group to 99, using a command like

RESET jobname,PERFORM=99

SRM immediately swaps out the address space and leaves it there until the address space is assigned to a different performance group. The "99" convention is easy to remember and gives the operator a quick way to suspend an address space if it proves necessary.

Performance Group   MVS creates address spaces for TSO users, started system tasks, and batch jobs. Each address space has a group of control blocks and up to 16 megabytes of virtual storage (for MVS/370) or 2 gigabytes of virtual storage (for MVS/XA and MVS/ESA). There is an address space identification number (ASID) assigned to each address space. Each ASID is assigned to a performance group. This assignment is made by one of the following:

1. The PERFORM parameter in JCL.
2. The PERFORM parameter in the LOGON procedure.
3. IEAICSxx parameters.
4. The TSO User Attribute Data Set (SYS1.UADS). UADS keeps information on TSO users such as the identification and password (except in RACF (or OEM equivalent) data centers.

Prior to MVS/SP, there were no controls on performance group selection by batch jobs, and TSO performance groups were controlled by SYS1.UADS definition. With MVS/SP, the PARMLIB member IEAICSxx was added to control the performance groups which may be used. If the data center uses IEAICSxx, then all of the other methods are ignored.

I recommend that your data center always specify IEAICSxx members for control. I have found you must change the IEAICSxx even when you are using CBIPO to start up MVS. CBIPO is an excellent packaging tool, but IBM cannot know your business. At one large data center, I found TSO users waiting for resources behind batch jobs (running large sorts!). By a simple IEAIPSxx and IEAICSxx change, I reduced the *average* response time from over 5 seconds to *less than 1/2 second!*

Subsecond response time! No additional hardware. No additional software. No IPL. Two MVS commands (SET IPS=xx and SET ICS=xx). It was wonderful!

IPS stands for Installation Performance Specifications; ICS stands for Installation Control Specifications.

The domain for each performance group is defined in the IEAIPSxx PGN keyword: PGN=2,(DMN=1,...). In Figure 16.5, the entry means all work in performance group 2 will be assigned to domain 1 when it enters the system. Domain 2 is assigned as the transaction takes longer to complete. Domain 3 is assigned when the translation takes even longer to complete.

Performance Period Performance groups are divided into performance periods which are defined in SYS1.PARMLIB member IEAIPSxx's PGN keyword. Performance periods allow a transaction to be given different service based on the resources used up to a point in the life of a transaction. The concept is easiest to explain in terms of TSO commands. Look at Figure 16.5. For TSO you might divide your TSO work into three types defined as follows:

1. Period 1 — trivial commands, giving the best service with a high probability of access to the system. Period 1 could be assigned a duration of 1,000 service units.
2. Period 2 — longer commands, giving good service, but the user may have a lower level of service and fewer of these transactions running concurrently. Period 2 could be assigned a duration of 5,000 units — 1,000 in period 1 and 4,000 in period 2.
3. Period 3 — longest commands, compiles, and applications. These are run at still lower service. There is no need to specify duration for the last period — the transaction will stay here until it completes.

```
Performance Group
   'PERFORM=' in JCL
   Logon Proc
   IEAICSxx
   SYS1.UADS

Performance Period--IEAIPSxx

   PGN-2, (DMN-1...) /* trivial */
          (DMN=2...) /* longer */
          (DMN=3...) /* batch-like */



Performance Objective

   WKL=(1,5,9,10)
   OBJ=1,SRV=(3000,3000,3000,3000)
```

Figure 16.5   SRM Definitions — Performance. The Performance Group is assigned in one of several ways. Most MVS data centers use IEAICSxx to specify performance groups. Performance periods are specified to give different treatment to trivial (short commands), longer (medium SU consumers), or "batchlike" transactions. Performance objectives allow the data center to specify what happens as the transaction consumes more and more resources.

All work starts in the first performance period and moves to the subsequent periods as the service usage limits of a period are exceeded. If your data center has a standard that certain types of work should be run in batch, a method of enforcing this would be to use a fourth period whose service could be below batch. As a general rule, three periods are enough for a single Performance Group.

Performance Objective Performance objectives are defined in SYS1.PARMLIB member IEAIPSxx with the WKL keyword and the OBJ(SRV) keyword. Each performance period in the installation performance specification (IPS) is assigned to one of the defined performance objectives. The objective defines relative priorities to be given to each performance period in a domain. The objective maps the service rate to a number called the work load level. If SRM needs to lower the multiprogramming level (MPL) of a domain, address spaces with the lowest workload levels within the domain are selected for swap out.

16.2.3. Input from Other Managers

Figure 16.6 shows the logical view of the interaction of SRM and the workload managers.

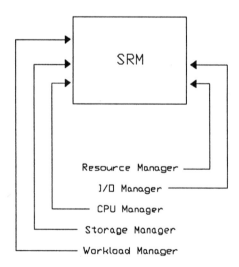

Figure 16.6   SRM Input from other managers. SRM gets inputs from all of the resource managers.

Resource Manager The resource manager measures the resources used over several intervals and recommends to SRM control modules that the MPL should be raised, lowered, or remain the same.

I/O Manager The I/O manager biases the decision for which device to use in the cases where MVS has several possibilities for device selection. Specific allocation requests — cataloged data sets — use the device that contains the data set, of course. The I/O manager consists of two parts:

1. **Device Allocation.** As MVS (in JES2 environments) decides on which device to use, consideration is given to current I/O channel rates to select the device which will give the most balanced channel activity. Some of the rules followed are:
   a. If a tape drive contains the requested tape (a data set on the tape has been passed from a previous job step), select the drive.
   b. If a tape drive is requested, eliminate as candidates all ready devices and devices with passed volumes. These drives may be needed later by this or other jobs.
   c. Choose the candidates on the lowest utilized logical channel (for MVS/370).
   d. If a DASD is requested, choose the device with the lowest allocated user counts.
   e. For all others, choose randomly.
2. **I/O Load Balancer Swap Analysis.** The I/O manager monitors channels and recommends swap out or swap in, depending on the address space usage of the logical channel. If an address space is using too much of a channel, it may be recommended for swap out.

CPU Manager The Automatic Priority Group (APG) programs use three types of dispatching priorities: fixed, rotate, and mean time to wait. (Another section will cover dispatching priorities.)

Storage Manager The page replacement function maintains an up-to-date indication of which frames have gone unreferenced for how long. The Real Storage Manager (RSM) is invoked to increment the Unreferenced Interval Count (UIC) for each Central Storage page. Statistics such as the highest, lowest, and average UIC are gathered for use by the Storage Manager.

The Real Page Shortage Prevention function is invoked by SRM when the available frame queue falls below the available frame queue low threshold. Pages are stolen from all users and the system pageable area until the available frame queue is within specifications.

The Auxiliary Slot Shortage Prevention function is invoked to check for a shortage of DASD page slots. Exceeding the first threshold prevents the creation of new address spaces. Exceeding the second causes a batch address space which is acquiring auxiliary storage slots to be swapped out.

It sounds like the above paragraph would cause more auxiliary storage to be used for the swap out. The address space is referencing too many pages, and the only way to stop an address space is to swap the address space out. Most of the pages are probably already on auxiliary storage anyway. (That there is a shortage of slots in the first place indicates that a problem exists, either with the system configuration or with the job mix.)

The SQA Shortage Prevention function is invoked by the virtual storage manager (VSM) when a shortage of SQA is detected. Creation of address spaces is prevented until the shortage is relieved.

Pageable Real Storage Shortage Prevention is invoked by the Real Storage Manager (RSM) when the percentage of fixed frames to total frames exceeds a predefined limit. This function will prevent creation of address spaces until the Central Storage shortage is relieved.

Workload Manager The workload manager is a collection of routines which monitor the rate at which system resources are consumed by individual address spaces and provides swap recommendations based on specifications.

16.2.4. Installation Specifications of SRM Parameters

Installation specifications are recorded in SYS1.PARMLIB by the Systems Programmer and take effect at IPL time. These may be selected or overridden by the operator: The first message after a normal IPL of MVS is message IEA101A, and the reply to this may be one of:

1. **Take all defaults.** All MVS defaults are taken by replying with a "null" response of just pressing the "enter" key on the console (or "return," or "end-of-block (EOB)," depending on the

terminal). Member IEASYS00 of SYS1.PARMLIB is read, and any parameters supplied in the member are used to initialize SRM.

2. **Override defaults.** Other PARMLIB members may also be specified by the operator. For example, the operator can reply **R 00,SYSP=(xx),ICS=yy**. Lowercase letters (xx and yy) are any two alphanumeric characters. IEASYS00 is always read by the Nucleus Initialization Program (NIP). The IEASYSxx members are used to point to one of several alternate parameter lists (e.g., IEAOPTxx, IEAICSxx).

Complete specifications of the IPL parameters are in the MVS Initialization and Tuning manuals. Each version of MVS has its own version. For example, the MVS/XA version is *MVS/Extended Architecture System Programming Library: Initialization and Tuning* (GC28-1149.) Be sure you have the manual which matches your version and release of MVS.

SRM parameters are specified in IEASYSxx as keywords IPS=x1, OPT=x2, and ICS=x3:

1. IEAIPSx1 — defines the workload, where "x1" are any two alphanumeric characters.
2. IEAOPTx2 — sets SRM constants, where "x2" are any two alphanumeric characters.
3. IEAICSx3 — defines performance groups that are valid for started system tasks, TSO sessions, and batch jobs, where "x3" are any two alphanumeric characters.

In Figure 16.7, the operator has replied to use members IEASYS01 and IEASYS02 (TSO members contain IPL specifications.) Member IEASYS00 is always read. Member IEASYS02 has a parameter, **ICS=01**, which tells SRM to read member IEAICS01 for its parameters.

16.3. MVS CONTROL MECHANISMS

The Systems Resource Manager (SRM) controls the tasks in the system by setting and changing the dispatching priority of tasks, swapping address spaces into and out of Central Storage, and isolating and manipulating the maximum number of Central Storage page frames which an address space can have.

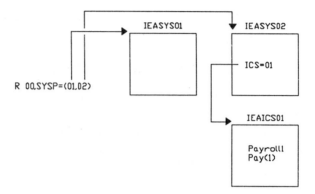

Figure 16.7   System Installation Specifications. The System operator, at IPL time, specifies the members of SYS1.PARMLIB to be used for the IPL of MVS. Some of the members included in the specification include SRM parameters. IEAICSxx defines the performance groups of jobs, Started Tasks (STC), and TSO sessions. IEAOPTxx sets SRM constants. IEAIPSxx sets workload characteristics.

16.3.1.   Dispatching Priority

MVS arranges address spaces in two queues. The first queue contains ASIDs available for processing. These are called **dispatchable** address spaces. The second queue contains ASIDs which are not available for processing. These are called **nondispatchable** address spaces. In both cases, the ASIDs are arranged in descending dispatching priority. Dispatching priority is a number from 0 to 255, or x'00' to x'FF'. The higher the dispatching priority, the more likely the address space will get to use the CPU.

The data center specifies the dispatching order of tasks either specifically or generically. In SYS1.PARMLIB(IEAICSxx), the data center specifies the performance group for a task. A task may be identified by complete name or by using "wild cards." In Figure 16.7, member IEAICS01 has a fully qualified batch name for PAYROLL1. Any job submitted with a job name of PAYROLL1 will get a specific performance group. Any job which starts with the letters "PAY" in the first three positions will be assigned a different performance group. The data center can also use the account codes (from the JOB card in the JCL for batch jobs or in SYS1.UADS for TSO sessions) to specify performance groups in MVS/XA and MVS/ESA.

In SYS1.PARMLIB(IEAIPSxx), dispatching priorities are assigned by the keyword **DP=txy**:

1. The first parameter, "t," is the type: Fixed, Rotate, or Mean-Time-to-Wait. Fixed priority ("F") assigns a dispatching priority, which does not change over time. Rotate priority ("R") has several address spaces at the same dispatching priority, and MVS rotates them so each address space has some percentage at the top of the single priority number.

    Mean-Time-to-Wait (M) was developed by the original HASP programmers. They noticed that if a region (in the operating system, a "region" was the equivalent of today's "address spaces") had a dispatching priority higher than other address spaces, and the region used a large amount of CPU time, then the other regions could not get very good throughput. By rotating the dispatch priority based on the following, throughput could be substantially increased:

    a. A MVS timer service (STIMER) was set for some number of milliseconds — 200, for example.

    b. A region was dispatched. If the region did not voluntarily give up control by the time the STIMER expired, the region was said to be "CPU-bound," and the dispatching priority would be lowered by some value.

    c. If the region voluntarily gave up control before the time slice expired, then the region was said to be "I/O-bound," and the dispatching priority would be raised by some value.

2. The second parameter, "x," is the APG range of 16 values. Figure 16.8 shows the APG range of dispatching priorities. In this example, 6–15 are specified. Note the top APGRNG (15). The possible dispatching priorities are 240–255.

3. The third parameter, "y," is the position in the fixed queue and is only specified if "t" is "F." (This value varies, depending on the release of MVS.)

Hex	Decimal	APGRNG	set
F0–FF	240–255	15	9 <--
E0–EF	224–239	14	8
D0–DF	208–223	13	7
. . .	. . .	. .	. . .
70–7F	112–127	7	1
60–6F	96–111	6	0

Figure 16.8 Dispatching Priority. The MVS dispatching priority is divided into "APG" ranges. In this example, the APGRNG=6–15 has been specified.

Hex	Decimal	APGRNG	DP=txy	type
FF	255	15	F94	fixed
FE	254	15	F93	fixed
FD	253	15	E92	fixed
FC	252	15	F91	fixed
FB	251	15	F90	fixed
FA	250	15	R9	Rotate
F9	249	15	M9	MTW
F8	248	15	M9	MTW
F7	247	15	M9	MTW
F6	246	15	M9	MTW
F5	245	15	M9	MTW
F4	244	15	M9	MTW
F3	243	15	M9	MTW
F2	242	15	M9	MTW
F1	241	15	M9	MTW
F0	240	15	M9	MTW

Figure 16.9   One APG Range. The APG range has 16 possible dispatching priorities. The three groups are Fixed, Rotate, and Mean-Time-to-Wait.

Let's look at APGRNG 15 in Figure 16.9. There are three ways to specify the 16 possibilities:

1. **Fixed.** If "DP=F90" were specified, the address space would always run in dispatching priority 251, or x'FB'.
2. **Rotate.** If "DP=R9" were coded, the address spaces would always be at the same dispatching priority — 250, or x'FA' — but MVS would rotate their position on the queue with others in R9 so that each got a share of the resources. Some data centers use rotate with CICS or other data base address spaces. Each address space gets a time slice at the top of the queue.
3. **MTW.** If "DP=M9" were specified, the dispatching priority would vary from 240 to 249. MVS would look at the average time an address space waited and raise the number if it had waited some time and lower the number if it were "hogging" the resource. I have been very successful specifying that CICS address spaces be in a Mean-Time-to-Wait group.

Figure 16.10 shows some "special" dispatching priorities. If the address space is in virtual storage and available for execution, the dispatching priority is a value from x'02' through x'FE'. If the address space is "logically swapped," then MVS sets the dispatching priority

Where	Who	Dispatch Priority
In Storage	ASID 10 ASID 20	02-FE 02-FE
Logically Swapped	ASID 30	01
Physically Swapped Out	ASID 40 ASID 50	FF FF

Figure 16.10   Special Dispatching Priority. MVS also assigns some special dispatching priorities. X'01' indicates the address space is logically swapped (in storage, but waiting on some future event). X'FF' indicates the address space is physically swapped out or is some MVS system address space which is at the highest dispatching priority.

to x'01'.[3] In the example, ASID 30 is logically swapped out. If the address space is physically swapped out and not available for dispatch, the dispatching priority is set to x'FF'. Some MVS address spaces are set to dispatching priority x'FF' to be the highest task in the system. Most of these address spaces are "nonswappable" — so important to MVS that SRM will not or cannot swap the address space out.

16.3.2. Swapping

The SRM's major decision is which address spaces will be in main storage. SRM maintains three counters for each domain. The minimum is the value set by the data center as the minimum number of address spaces that are allowed in Central Storage that represent this domain. The Maximum is the value set by the data center as the largest number of address spaces allowed.

The **Target MPL** is computed by SRM and is the value that affects swapping. If the number of address spaces in Central Storage is

---

3. Logically swapped is the term used for address spaces that have been placed into a wait (e.g., waiting for a terminal to respond). It is likely that the address space will become active shortly so MVS places the address space on a queue that remains in Central Storage but is not on the active queue.

less than or equal to the target MPL, then SRM does nothing. If the number is more than the target, then SRM selects one address space to swap out. SRM asks the Auxiliary Storage Manager (ASM) to transfer the address space to the system paging or swap data sets or both.

SRM uses three types of objectives for a domain:

1. **DOBJ** — Domain Objective. The DOBJ is used when the data center wishes to control the number of address spaces based on the total service consumed by all the address spaces within a domain. Batch and long-running transactions are good candidates for DOBJ.

2. **AOBJ** — Average Objective. AOBJ is used when a data center wishes to control the number of address spaces based on the average service consumed by all the address spaces that are in this domain and in Central Storage. TSO and other low resource–consuming address spaces are good candidates.

3. **FWKL** — Fixed Workload. FWKL is used when the data center wishes to allocate a certain portion of the resources to a domain. TSO first period and other high-priority short transactions are good candidates for FWKL.

16.3.3.   SRM Central Storage Control

SRM has several methods of controlling which address spaces are allowed to use Central Storage.

Page Stealing.   One of the functions of SRM is to ensure that enough Central Storage page frames are available according to data center specifications. The methodology used by SRM to locate pages to steal — the oldest unreferenced page(s).

Each address space needs Central Storage to execute. Central Storage is divided into 4,096-byte (4-Kb) page frames. Each page has an additional area associated with page. The area is called a Storage Protection Key or "key." The key contains four types of information:

1. Access control bits (ACC), for protection against fetching.
2. Fetch protection bit, to indicate restricted use.
3. Reference bit, to indicate the page has been used by a program.
4. Change bit, to indicate the page has been changed. Some part of the 4,096 bytes has been changed since the last time SRM inspected all of Central Storage.

SRM routines periodically check and clear the referenced and changed bits. Information on each page frame is kept to determine the oldest pages in all of Central Storage. If SRM needs to steal Central Storage frames, it uses this information to steal the oldest page.

Storage Isolation. Storage isolation is the mechanism by which the data center can specify minimum number of pages, maximum number of pages, and page rates for specific performance groups.

Figure 16.11 shows several address spaces and the Central Storage page frames they own. The system only has six Central Storage pages. (This figure is only for demonstration purposes. No MVS system uses only six pages!)

SRM parameters can be specified to provide a minimum and maximum number of page frames for an address space. For example, if the data center specified that ASID 10 should have four page frames, and it only has three, but needs another page, one of the other address spaces would have its oldest page frame stolen. The "oldest" is the page frame with the largest Unreferenced Interval Count (UIC). (The UIC is the count of seconds since the page has been referenced or changed.)

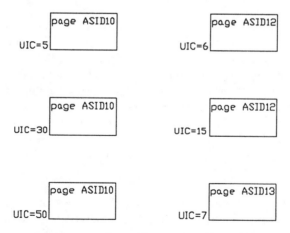

Figure 16.11   Storage Isolation. Storage Isolation is the name given to the MVS facility which dedicates a certain number of page frames to an address space. Good candidates for Storage Isolation are System address spaces, CICS and IMS address spaces, and TSO address spaces. Each frame has an additional hardware "key" which contains the protection key and the access, fetch, referenced, and changed bits.

SRM would pick the second page frame owned by ASID 12. It has an UIC of 15, which is the oldest in the system that is not isolated. It would not pick the page frame owned by ASID 13 because the UIC is 7.

SRM does not "give" pages to an address space. It can steal pages and place them on the available frame queue. The ASID will page fault and "get" the pages it needs. SRM will stop stealing page frames when the address space which is isolated has a number of page frames between its minimum and its maximum.

Note that Storage Isolation can cause problems. In Figure 16.11, the oldest page used by ASID 10 is 50 seconds old. It may never need the page, yet we stole a page from ASID 12 to honor a request from the greedy ASID 10. **Storage Isolation should be used with caution.**

16.3.4. MVS under VM and/or PR/SM

The above discussion describes MVS running "native" on a Processor Complex. There are special considerations for MVS when either another Operating System (e.g., VM) is controlling MVS or when hardware (PR/SM) is controlling MVS.

CPU Considerations If VM is "dispatching" MVS, then there will be times when MVS has control and VM preempts MVS. MVS does not know it has had the CPU resources taken away. MVS uses the Store Clock instructions to get timings, and the time VM has control will be included in what MVS thinks it has had control. There are a number of hardware **Assists** to overcome this problem.

With the 3090 PR/SM hardware, resources in a Processor Complex can be logically divided among several Operating Systems, and (for the most part) MVS will recognize what portion of the CPU it is getting.

I/O Considerations If VM is controlling the Processor Complex, MVS may issue a start I/O instruction, but VM will have to handle the actual I/O operation unless some special Preferred Guest or hardware Assists are in control. It may seem like a trivial matter, but running MVS under VM is very difficult if the MVS system is doing a large number of I/O operations per second.

Virtual to Real Translation. If MVS is running under VM, and VM controls all Central Storage, then MVS cannot directly control

Central Storage, too. The early solution was to have VM support **Shadow Page Tables**, which increased the efficiency of the DAT hardware.

With Preferred Guest microcode and PR/SM, some portion of Central Storage can be allocated to MVS, and MVS can control its "share" of Central Storage.

Tuning Considerations In the early days of running MVS under VM, it was necessary to disable almost all SRM controls except demand paging to get MVS to run properly. With PR/SM, there are hardware functions to partition the resources to various Operating Systems, but there are MVS considerations also.

For example, if the SRM parameters are set up to run on a 128-Mb Processor Complex, and the same system is placed on a PR/SM machine which only has 64 Mb partitioned for MVS to use, then the SRM parameters may have to be adjusted.

16.4. SUMMARY

Different decisions are made using different processes when a job is executing than before and after execution: SRM controls the former and JES the latter.

When a job (list of JCL statements) is submitted, JES may select a node for execution (based on a network resource name) and inserts the job into a job queue.

Jobs are assigned to inactive initiators based on two parameters: job class (a single alphabetic character) and selection priority. (JES2 and JES3 have different ways of specifying these parameters.) An initiator may be set to favor one job class over another. The set of jobs qualifying for an inactive initiator compete for that initiator based on their selection priority. (A job's selection priority increases while it waits in the job queue, a process called "aging." This ensures that those with relatively low selection priority eventually get to an initiator.)

Once a job is assigned to an initiator, job class and selection priority have no effect on execution progress; this is where SRM takes over.

Once execution completes, JES uses the SYSOUT class (not the job class) and the selection priority to assign spooled output to printers. (JES may be configured to alter the SYSOUT class based on the number of output lines.)

SRM recommends controls of execution progress to the MVS paging, swapping, dispatching, and I/O subsystems once jobs are started in initiators. The "bean counter" analogy seems to characterize the important functions of SRM:

1. SRM is a reactive king: he only sees what is happening *after it has happened*.
2. SRM cannot make beans. There is a finite number of beans in a data center.
3. Only the IBM salesman (or your OEM salesman) can make more beans by selling the data center more hardware.

If SRM is going to enforce the bean rules, SRM must get notification of events which are important to bean counters.

The resources an executing job uses along with its domain and performance group determine the "flow" of resources it receives. (Performance groups allow a data center to determine which kinds of jobs will compete with each other for resources.)

SRM is thus a mechanism whereby parameters to MVS resource administration modules are dynamically changed to maintain efficient progression of work in MVS.

The data center can specify parameters to SRM itself to influence its decisions. These parameters can make or break response time and throughput for that data center's particular job mix. Careful selection of IPS and ICS parameters can have a greater effect than a more powerful and faster model of Processor Complex!

Changing SRM parameters can be a lot like giving your teenager the car keys and different amounts of money and time each night when you have no idea of the effect they will have.

The Scientific Method you learned in high school biology is applicable (though too often ignored or forgotten) in most relations with a computer but is most crucial in system tuning efforts: Measure the current situation, change one variable, measure the new situation, determine what changed.

The next chapter describes tools at your disposal to make these essential measurements.

17

Monitoring,
Tracing, and Security

17.1. MONITORING FACILITIES

MVS has some of the most sophisticated monitoring facilities of any
operating system ever created. This is a two-edged sword. Almost
any data you need is available. Too much data may be available.
Your data center will certainly need a data reduction system for
monitoring data. The Statistical Analysis System (SAS) is almost a
requirement for every MVS data center. Most MVS data centers require statistical analysis of large volumes of data and I have used
SAS since the early 1970s to process MVT, VM, and MVS data.
Morino Associates (MICS product) and Merrill Consultants (MXG
product) both have outstanding SAS-based products to reduce the
volumes of MVS data.

17.1.1. System Management Facilities (SMF)

The System Management Facility (SMF) is a standard feature of
MVS. SMF is the name of a group of MVS modules and data center
"exits" which collect data about the MVS system, jobs, and TSO sessions, and write the records to system files to record the data.

(The term "exits" refers to modules written in assembler language
which are included in MVS at IPL time and to which MVS grants

control as it processes tasks. These exits can change existing SMF records, add new records, or change the way MVS manages the address space. Exits are well-defined interfaces by which a data center may customize software from IBM and third parties without worrying that the changes will "corrupt" the distributed software; use of the term is not limited to the discussion of SMF.)

The SMF data set contains records which have a common prefix of information including an SMF type code. The type may be from 1 to 255. Some record types are written by MVS. Other record types are reserved for the data center to use. For example, the group of SMF records which contain data about user programs (types 4, 34, 5, 35, 20, 30, and 32) are used to account and charge for resources consumed by a job or TSO session.

Some data centers have discovered files associated with SMF are the largest "database" in the data center. Each batch job and TSO session may generate a number of these SMF records. If the data center tries to keep many months of these records without condensing them, the volume of data can grow out of control.

The volume of data generated is also dependent on the options specified in SYS1.PARMLIB member SMFPRMxx and on the interval which is specified to write records. SMF records of type 30 and 32 are interval records, and if the time value is low (1–15 minutes), the volume of data could be very large. Most installations transfer SMF data from the SYS1.MANx data sets to tape each day. If you collect all MVS records, this could amount to many reels of tape per day.

The Resource Management Facility (RMF) collects data and has SMF record the data. RMF records (types 70–79) have another interval specified in the SYS1.PARMLIB member ERBRMFxx.

The overhead of collecting SMF data occurs in many MVS modules, and even if the records are not recorded, the overhead to build the records remains. If you do not want a series of records, such as type 60–69 for VSAM, you can either "turn off" the record type in PARMLIB or modify the modules which actually build the records. The former is the easiest to do. The latter is the one which will save the most CPU resources but is expensive in terms of maintenance for the modifications — each time IBM changes the module, the data center will need to rework the modification. (This is why exits exist, to prevent this maintenance overhead, but exits are not designed into every part of the system!)

The data center can also control the SMF data by operator commands:

1. **SET SMF=xx**, where "xx" is the suffix of the PARMLIB member. For example, if the operator typed "SET SMF=02," SMF would load member SMFPRM02 from SYS1.PARMLIB to determine the SMF options. If for some reason you need to cancel and restart SMF, or if the SMF address space ABENDs, issue "SET SMF=xx" to restart SMF. This command should only be performed under the direction of someone who understands the ramifications.

2. **SETSMF** **parameter(value)**, where "parameter" is a parameter the installation wants to add to the current execution of SMF. Any parameter can be specified except ACTIVE, PROMPT, SID, or EXITS. This command also should only be performed under the direction of a someone who understands the ramifications.

3. **DISPLAY SMF,(S or O)**, where "S" indicates that the status of the SMF data sets are to be displayed, and "O" indicates that the status of the current options are to be displayed. This command can be used by MVS operators to see the status of the SMF data sets.

SMF contains the monitoring data which can be captured and analyzed over a period of time to watch the growth pattern of the data center. For this reason, most data centers ensure that SMF records are collected continuously. The types of information available are:

1. System-related data:
   a. Configuration data. Each DASD, tape drive, and Processor Complex is counted and the addresses are recorded.
   b. Paging activities. Demand paging is "bad" in that it slows down processing. If the processing is for batch jobs, the data center users probably do not notice. If the paging causes a delay in online terminal response time, then someone should correct the situation to improve the productivity of the end user.
   c. Workload data. The types of applications, the programs executed, and the resources used are collected.
2. Job and TSO data:
   a. CPU time. The amount of CPU used by the task is collected.
   b. SYSOUT processing. The number of print lines and punched cards (if anyone is still punching cards) of each task is recorded.

    c. Data set statistics. Data set information is collected — (e.g., how often the data set is used and which address space used it).

SMF formats this information into records and writes the records into several disk data sets. The SMF data sets are VSAM clusters with names of "SYS1.MANx," where "x" is 1–9 or a–z. In Figure 17.1, two data sets are shown for the "TSO" system. SYS1.MAN1 is being written to and SYS1.MAN2 is the next data set to be used. It switches from "MAN1" to "MAN2" when "MAN1" is full.

SMF exits allow the installation to impose control on the jobs processed. These exits are invoked at specified times — job initialization, specific events during the job, and for unusual events such as when the time limit expires.

Each SMF record is "time stamped" — the date and time are in the first few bytes of the record. The time stamp becomes very important if the data center expects to do anything with the data. The time-of-day clock is set at system initialization time and is updated by a hardware clock. There is a time of day clock in each processor (two for MP/AP/Dyadic).

In a loosely coupled environment (two or more Processor Complexes in a data center), it is difficult to synchronize the times. Do you and your neighbor have the same time on your wristwatches? Probably not. You may not even have the same minute much less second. In Figure 17.1, two Processor Complexes are running MVS. The Processor Complex labeled "TSO" has its clock set to 10:01 A.M. The Processor Complex labeled "BATCH" has its clock set to 10:00 A.M. A very short job submitted on TSO and executed on BATCH may seem to end before it was submitted! There is no MVS mechanism to synchronize clocks in a loosely coupled environment.

If there are multiple data centers in different time zones connected by network job entry, synchronization is hard to maintain. If the clocks are not synchronized, a job could end before it begins. The job could start at 10:00 A.M. Eastern time and execute in California at 7:01 A.M. How would you charge for a job that used negative three hours?

The MVS mechanism to overcome this is to synchronize all the clocks to Greenwich Mean Time (GMT). The clocks are all set to the local time in Greenwich, England. The local time is calculated using member PARMTZ (up to MVS/XA Version 2 Release 2) or member CLOCKxx (MVS/XA Version 2 Release 2 and MVS/ESA) of SYS1. PARMLIB, each of which contains the difference between GMT and local time in hours. The data center would still have a problem if the

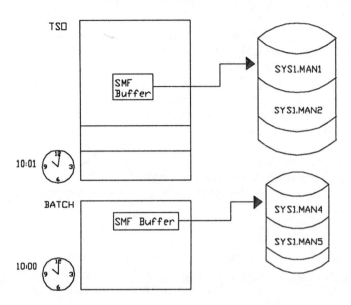

Figure 17.1 SMF. The SMF system collects records in SMF buffers in common Virtual Storage. As the buffers fill up, they are written to the SMF data sets on DASD.

clock used to set the eastern clock were a few minutes faster than that used to set the western Processor Complex.

17.1.2. Types of SMF Records

SMF is the recording secretary for a number of subsystems. Task level statistics are gathered about each address space in MVS. System level statistics are gathered by MVS about how the system is running and device/control unit statistics are gathered about specific devices.

Task Level Statistics — PA-2 and CMF Task level statistics are gathered by a number of subsystems. In many cases, SMF is the place the records are stored for evaluation. One example is the Performance Analyzer 2 (PA-2), an IBM Field Developed Program (FDP). PA-2 was introduced in CICS 1.2. It was supported through CICS 1.5 but was replaced by CMF. The CICS Measurement Facility (CMF) was introduced in CICS 1.5 as part of the CICS product base. Both of these products collect information about a CICS address space and place records in SMF while CICS is running. Figure 17.2 shows CICS passing CMF records to SMF for recording.

CMF contains information about the system and individual transactions. One of the problems with CMF is that transaction counts are maintained in an area which is available to the transaction programmer. The data may be changed by the programmer by mistake in some releases of CICS.

System Level Statistics — RMF The Resource Measurement Facility (RMF) collects data from MVS, formats the data into records, and writes the records to the SMF data set. There are three kinds of "sessions":

RMF Monitor I Session: The Monitor I session is a started system task which constantly monitors and records information you wish to collect all the time. Although you can get prints directly out of Monitor I, most data centers spool the data to SMF and process it after the SMF dataset is dumped to tape. Think of Monitor I as a background data collector.

The RMF address space sets timer interrupts and samples data from MVS control blocks in common storage. The MVS interrupt processors capture information for RMF to use in its records. Figure 17.3 shows the interval timer interrupting RMF.

The RMF monitor is usually started by the COMMNDxx member of SYS1.PARMLIB at IPL time. The address space is a data collector only. Figure 17.4 is an example of the JCL for the started task.

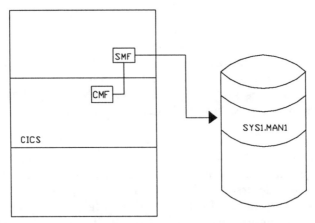

Figure 17.2   Task Level — CMF. One example of task level statistics is the CICS CMF system. As CICS transactions are generated, records are buffered and transferred to SMF for storage on the SYS1.MANx data sets.

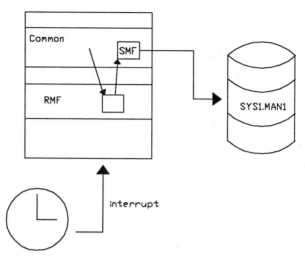

Figure 17.3   System Level — RMF. The RMF address space sets timer interrupts to sample MVS control blocks and write out (through SMF) the type 70–79 records.

The parameter field of the EXEC card for RMF has a parameter **MEMBER(nn)** to indicate the member of PARMLIB which RMF should use for its initialization parameters. The nn is appended to "ERBRMF" to form the member name. For example, **PARM='MEMBER(01)...'** would cause RMF to read member ERBRMF01 in the data set pointed to by the IEFRDER DD statement. The library usually is, but does not have to be, SYS1.PARMLIB. Figure 17.5 shows a sample member. Be sure to check the manual corresponding with the version of RMF you are using for your MVS system.

```
//jobname  JOB   (acct),"programmer name",REGION=4096K,TIME=(5),
//            NOTIFY=tsoid,MSGCLASS=c
//IEFPROC  EXEC  PGM=ERBMFMFC,REGION=4096K,
//            PARM='MEMBER(nn),SYSOUT(x)'
//IEFRDER   DD    DSN=SYS1.PARMLIB,DISP=SHR
//MFMESSGE  DD    DUMMY,
//      DCB=(RECFM=VBA,LRECL=125,BLKSIZE=1693)
//RMFSCZZ   DD    DUMMY
//SYSABEND  DD    SYSOUT=x
```

Figure 17.4   JCL to run RMF. The parameter "MEMBER(nn)" tells RMF which member to use in the IEFRDER data set to get parameters for the RMF session.

RMF Monitor II Session: Monitor II can be thought of as an immediate problem solving monitor. The Monitor II session is a snapshot of the system taken at a specific time. There are two types of Monitor II sessions: The first is available from a local 327x console or from a TSO display console; the second is a background session which is started by modifying the RMF address space.

RMF Monitor III Session: Monitor III was originally called the **Workload Delay Monitor**. Monitor III is a contention oriented real-time monitor. This means RMF attempts to analyze the data sampled and reduce the data to something meaningful to the analyst. Monitor III provides continuous realtime monitoring and displays the resource contention which it finds. Monitor III can be thought of as an online problem solving tool which can display MVS activity for variable time periods in the recent past.

In RMF Monitor III, a task is said to be in one of three **states**:

1. Using a resource. The task could be using the CPU or performing I/O to a device.
2. Idle. The task is in a voluntary wait state.
3. Delayed. The task is queued for one or more resources such as the CPU, I/O device, Central Storage, JES, ENQUE, or HSM.

RMF Post Processor: The RMF Post Processor reads records which Monitor I has placed into the SMF file and produces summary reports using Monitor I and Monitor II data.

```
/* NORMAL RMF MONITOR I SESSION OPTIONS      */
/*                                           */
/*                                           */
   CHAN              /* phys-log channels    */
   CPU               /* CPU and queues       */
   CYCLE(1000)       /* OBS.  EVERY 1000 MS  */
   DEVICE(DASD)      /* COLLECT DASD STATS   */
   EXITS             /* for FOR VIRT STOR MON*/
   INTERVAL(15M)     /* 15 MINUTE REPORT int */
   NOOPTIONS         /* OPER CAN'T CHANGE    */
   PAGESP            /* PAGE/SWAP            */
   PAGING            /* PAGING Rte/frm/slots */
   RECORD            /* RECORD ON SMF        */
   NOREPORT          /* NO REPORTS PRODUCED  */
   NOSTOP            /* CONTINUOUS RUNNING   */
   WKLD(PERIOD)      /* PERIOD DOMAIN OBJ    */
   SYNC(59M)         /* SYNC TO before hour  */
   DEVICE(DASD)      /* COLLECT DEVICE STAT  */
   ENQ(DETAIL)       /* ENQUE -detail        */
```

Figure 17.5   RMF parameters. This example shows the typical parameters for RMF. Comments may be placed between "/*...*/" characters. In this example, RMF will sample every 15 minutes because the parameters contain "Interval(15M)."

System Availability Management (SAM): IBM also sells a separate program product that interfaces with RMF. SAM monitors system failures and system stalls and writes records into the Information/Management system to track the events and the times of the outages.

RMF Record Types: Each SMF record has a record type associated with the record so that programs that read the SMF files can distinguish between the records. RMF creates type 70–79 records. If you wish to understand RMF and the RMF field descriptions, then I recommend the IBM World Trade Systems Center document, *RMF — Field Description and Analysis* (GG24-1564). You would think from the title that the records would simply be described. Instead, it is the most comprehensive reference on RMF, SRM, and MVS tuning concepts IBM has published. The objectives of the manual are to explain fields, how to use the data in performance evaluation, how to use the data in a tuning effort, and to provide an understanding of the MVS and System/370 environment.

Unfortunately this manual has not been upgraded for every release of RMF. It is still a good manual, though, because much of every version of MVS is carried forward to the next version.

Let's look at the RMF data (types 70–79) stored in the SMF data set.

1. **Type 70, CPU activity**, is written for each RMF interval specified in the RMF parameter data set. A record is written when the RMF session terminates (usually the latter does not happen as most installations keep the RMF started task running all the time). It contains information about each CPU, its status, and the amount of wait time which has taken place this interval. The CPU busy time is calculated as the wait time percent subtracted from 100 percent.

2. **Type 71, paging activity**, is written for each RMF interval and when RMF terminates. It contains information about the paging subsystem, Central Storage, and external page storage.

3. **Type 72, workload activity**, is written for each RMF interval and when RMF terminates. One record is written for each performance group and contains information on each period, the transactions, the active time, and the resources consumed by these performance groups.

4. **Type 73, channel activity**, is written when channel activity measurement is requested. There is a section for each physical and logical channel (logical channels are only valid in MVS/370).

5. **Type 74, device activity,** is written for each interval and, when the session is terminated, for each device specified in the device option. It contains an entry for each device which has been online at least once during the interval.
6. **Type 75, Page/Swap Data Set Activity,** is written at the end of each RMF interval. One record is written for each page or swap data set for the interval.
7. **Type 76, trace activity,** is written at the end of each RMF interval. One record is written for each field name sampled during the interval. The record contains minimum, maximum, and sum of the squared values of the field. The final value is recorded.
8. **Type 77, ENQUE activity,** is written at the end of each RMF interval and at the end of the session. It identifies the resources ENQUEed upon during the interval and the contentions which occurred.
9. **Type 79, Monitor II activity,** is written when a record is requested. It contains a prefix record and subtypes for each type of Monitor II activity.

RMF Data Volume: The data volume can be very large if you are collecting DASD or trace records. DASD records in even a modest size data center can be over 32 Kb each.

IDCAMS LISTDATA (3880-xx Cache) The 3880-11 and 3880-21 (3880-x1) paging cache control units and the 3880-13 and 3880-23 (3880-x3) application cache control units have two methods to monitor the efficiency of cache (read hits):

1. Manually by using IDCAMS LISTDATA commands.
2. Automatically by purchasing the IBM cache RMF Reporter (5789-DQD) to automatically record cache measurement statistics in RMF.

The manual method is used by running IDCAMS, specifying "LISTDATA," and getting a listing of some numbers. The LISTDATA does not zero the counters — they are zeroed when the control unit is IMLed. The LISTDATA is run at the end of the selected monitoring period, and a manual calculation is performed to calculate the read/write hit ratios.

The manual method was the only method available when cache devices were introduced. Such a reporting mechanism did not provide adequate support for cache devices. In Figure 17.6, the WTO option signals IDCAMS to send a message to the operator console describing the status of the cache.

IDCAMS seems to be the focal point for maintenance of control units. The 3990 control unit can develop hardware problems which cause it to take itself offline, "permanently." The 3990 can only be "reset" by IDCAMS.

17.2. TRACING FACILITIES

MVS Reliability, Availability, and Serviceability (RAS) has improved many times over during its lifetime. One of the reasons for this is that MVS developers have devised a number of ways to capture information on problems. Much of the information comes from systems programmers in the field — people like you, perhaps. The MVS tracing facilities are among the most comprehensive in the industry. They are also the most complex but worth learning how to use.

17.2.1. Failure/Recovery

Address space failure can come from the three resources needed to run a task:

1. **CPU processing.** Failure in the processor can be invalid instruction execution or operating system detected error.
2. **I/O processing.** Failure can be from the movement of data or from the operating system detecting the error.

```
//jobname    JOB   (acct),'programmer name',REGION=4096K,TIME=(5),
//           NOTIFY=tsoid,MSGCLASS=c
//LISTDATA EXEC   PGM=IDCAMS
//DD1        DD    VOL=SER=vvvvvv,DISP=SHR,UNIT=3350
//SYSPRINT DD     SYSOUT=*
//SYSIN      DD    *
   LISTDATA STATUS FILE(DD1)   WTO
   LISTDATA COUNTS VOLUME(vvvvvv) UNIT(3350) SUBSYSTEM LEGEND
/*
//
```

Figure 17.6 Example of how to run IDCAMS LISTDATA. The STATUS subcommand gives information about the size of cache configured available, and indicates if cache is offline. The COUNTS subcommand gives information on cache effectiveness — Read Hits and Write Hits.

3. **Central Storage.** Failure can come from the hardware or by the operating system detecting a logic error.

Recovery is implemented by a chain of pointers to routines which "handle" any failure. The chain begins with recovery routines which the programmer installs. The chain ends with a "the buck stops here" routine in the operating system.

Recovery is complex. Recovery involves software, firmware (microcode), and hardware. Recovery requires *thoughtful considera- tion.* As Bill Mosteller says in his book, *System Programmer's Prob- lem Solver,*[1] senior systems programmers can save their computer center many hours of outage caused by complex problems.

Three MVS subsystems monitor and detect errors:

1. **EREP** is the generic name of the routines which monitor and collect data about errors.
2. **SLIP** is the trapping mechanism of MVS.
3. **DUMP** is the data collection media for MVS problems.

Types of Failures   *CPU Processing:* One type of error concerns the processing of instructions. The problem may be hardware-detected or software-detected.

Hardware problems: Instructions are executed unless the Proces- sor Complex hardware discovers an error in the instruction sequence which violates the Principles of Operation. One example is an 0C7 — data exception. Perhaps the program tried to increment a decimal number which was not properly formatted.

The Program Check First Level Interrupt Handler (FLIH) routine passes control to Recovery Termination Modules (RTM — super- visory routines) to correct or overcome the error. If the user has an error recovery routine, this routine is entered in an attempt to retry the operation which failed.

In Figure 17.7, the program is trying to add to a field which should be packed binary but is not. The CPU cannot continue processing these instructions. A **state change** takes place. Control is passed to recovery routines if they exist. If not, the task is abnormally ter- minated (Abended). MVS places an entry in SYS1.LOGREC record- ing the Abend, and an entry is in the trace table.

---

1. QED Information Sciences, Inc., Wellesley, MA 02181, 1989.

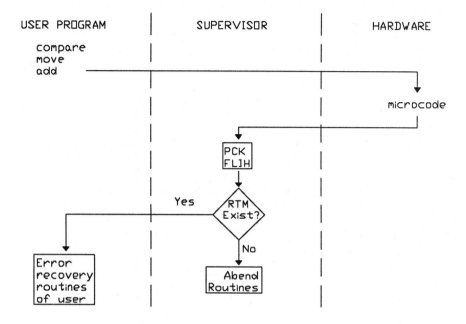

Figure 17.7   CPU Processing — hardware errors. In this example the user program attempted to perform an "add" instruction. The hardware and microcode could not successfully complete the instruction.

Software problems: If the operating system detects errors in supervisory components, the system will enter the same error recovery routines used during a hardware failure.

In Figure 17.8, the user has asked for some virtual storage, but the storage is not available. The GETMAIN SVC cannot continue, so it calls the error recovery routines if they are provided. If not, MVS abnormally terminates (Abends) the task. Both the GETMAIN request and the Abend are noted in the trace table.

I/O Processing: Errors can be detected when a task requests a physical block to be read from or written to an I/O device. Either MVS software or the hardware could detect the error:

Software-detected problems: Input/Output processes are begun by building control blocks, asking the supervisor to initialize the control blocks (OPEN), and then reading and writing the records. Supervisor errors are issued for logic problems such as asking for a file which is not available or asking for a new file without specifying a block size.

Many of these errors have Abend numbers in the form of **x13** because the open SVC is SVC 19 (decimal), or x'13' (hexadecimal). Look

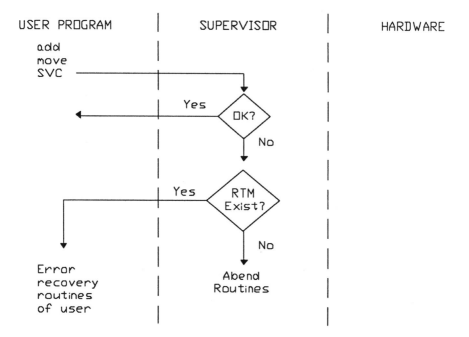

Figure 17.8   CPU Processing — software. In this example, the MVS software has detected a problem with the Supervisor Call (SVC) which has been issued by the user program.

at an example of a program that wants to read a file. In Figure 17.9, if the user program asks to open a nonexistent file (2), MVS would detect the error (3), and causes the task to ABEND with a code of **213-nn**, where nn is a number from 1–99. The ABEND is noted in the trace table and in SYS1.LOGREC.

If the file exists and the user is allowed to read the file, MVS starts a read operation (4) to read in the first physical buffer. The start I/O operation must return (5) before MVS (or any other task in the CPU) can continue. This operation only asks to start the I/O. MVS returns control to the program (6).

When the device is finished transferring the first block(s), the channel interrupts the CPU (7) and MVS "posts" the fact that the first block is in storage.

The program issues a "read" command (8), which goes to the access method to wait (9) for the block(s) to be successfully in storage. The program can then process the data (10)

Hardware-detected problems: Data transfer errors may also cause abnormal terminations. These errors result in 001 Abends. The Wait

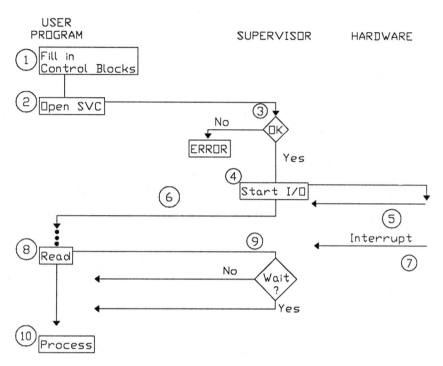

Figure 17.9 I/O processing — software. I/O operations have many areas for errors to occur. In 2, above, the Open may not be able to be successfully completed. Once the I/O operation has started, it may return with an error. The error may be in one of the hardware boxes or the error may be a logic error.

SVC (SVC 1) is the last two digits of the Abend. In Figure 17.9, at location 5, the device could present status to indicate the I/O did not complete successfully.

Central storage: Just as hardware can have errors outside the processor, there can be errors inside the processor. These are called **machine checks.** Some of the errors are observed by the data center and some only by the user. Some errors may be uncorrectable, resulting in termination of the task. Some errors will only be logged for fixing later.

Environmental Recording Editing and Printing (EREP) SYS1.LOGREC is the data set MVS uses to write entries for each type of failure. In Figure 17.10, the MVS system places records in the LOGREC buffer from all address spaces. Most records are placed there by the First and Second Level Interrupt Handlers.

The EREP system formats and prints these records. Each type of failure has a record type associated with it:

1. CCH are channel errors.
2. DDR are device errors which were permanent.
3. EOD errors are written at the "end of day" for statistics on the devices in the system.
4. MIH are missing interrupt records.
5. OBR are outboard (channel) error records. OBR records are used to measure tape and DASD reliability. They indicate "hard" failures (the data did not get transferred) and "soft" failures (the data was transferred to Central Storage but had to be "fixed"). Figure 17.10 shows the MVS routines recording the data in LOGREC buffers and writing them to SYS1.LOGREC. A batch job is started, executing program IFCEREP1. IFCEREP1 reads the SYS1.LOGREC data set and produces reports about the errors.
6. Software records are program checks and system Abend records.
7. MDR records are miscellaneous data records which are statistics dumped from devices to gather information kept in the control units and heads of string. MDR records are generated

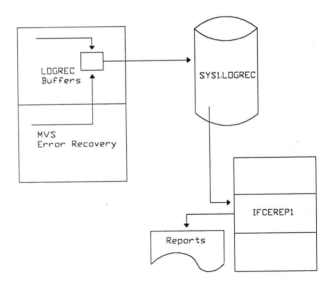

Figure 17.10 LOGREC and EREP. MVS routines place records in the SYS1.LOGREC data set as errors are detected by the various MVS routines. The IBM IFCEREP1 program reads and prints reports about the records.

when a counter overflows in a control unit or when the operater enters the "Z EOD" command to terminate MVS.

Dumping Facilities Figure 17.11 shows some of the dumping facilities in MVS. In MVT systems, the SYSABEND card told MVT to print the nucleus, and the SYSUDUMP card told MVT to only print the user task region. That was the only control provided or needed. In MVS, SYSUDUMP and SYSABEND are treated alike.

MVS system generation parameters and member IEADMP00 of SYS1.PARMLIB (for MVS/370) or operator command CHNGDUMP (for MVS/XA and MVS/ESA) specify the virtual storage areas dumped for various types of requested dumps.

SNAP Dump: An assembler language program can issue the SNAP macro to cause a dump of all or parts of virtual storage to be "printed" to a data set. The program continues execution after the SNAP macro.

SYSABEND/SYSUDUMP: An assembler language program can abnormally terminate — Abend — an address space by issuing the ABEND macro. The address space is terminated and processing does not continue unless recovery routines get control, fix the problem,

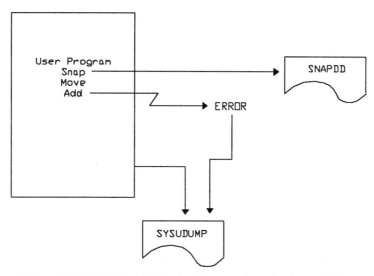

Figure 17.11 DUMP Facilities. This example shows a program which issues a SNAP macro to print some or all of the contents of the Virtual Storage available to the address space. The program continues. At some later time, the program attempts to do an "add" instruction which fails, and MVS prints the contents of Virtual Storage on the SYSUDUMP data set.

and continue. Output is placed either on the dataset specified by the SYSABEND DD card or the SYSUDUMP DD card.

SVC Dump: Supervisor services executing on behalf of an address space create an **SVC dump** when problems occur which warrant it. MVS writes the dump to one of the system dump data sets — SYS1.DUMPxx. These dumps are created without regard to a SYSUDUMP or SYSABEND card.

Stand-Alone Dump: If MVS cannot continue at all, there is a stand-alone program which can be IPLed to get information concerning the problem. The reader might, correctly, wonder how information can be presented on the running operating system if another "operating system" must be IPLed to take the dump.

The answer lies in a System/370 feature called **Store Status**. The store status saves the current Program Status Word (PSW), all the registers, and control information in the microcode area of the Processor Complex. A Store Status is done either explicitly (the operator issues a command on the hardware console for the System/370 Processor Complex) or implicitly (the microcode on the System/370 issues the "Store Status").

The operator IPLs the Stand-alone Dump program (from DASD or tape) which writes some Central Storage to an area on the device from which the Stand-alone IPL program was loaded. (The areas are used for work areas for Stand-alone dump.) It reads and saves the information from the Store Status and writes all Central Storage and virtual storage address spaces to the output of the dump. The data set for system dumps are generally on tape.

Note: SYS1.DUMPxx data sets can be scratched and reallocated at any time, but until the next IPL, the system will continue to use the area of the disk as specified by the data set definition at the last IPL. This could cause some weird problems. It is best if you scratch and reallocate these data sets just prior to re-IPLing.

17.2.2. SLIP — non-PER

Serviceability Level Indication Processing (SLIP) is a diagnostic aid designed to intercept or trap certain system events. SLIP can be set to detect certain events and describe what actions are to be taken when the event occurs. *SLIP should only be used by one who knows the ramifications* because if misused, SLIP can seriously degrade system performance or cause MVS to ABEND.

Most data centers use the COMMNDxx member of SYS1.PARMLIB to automatically invoke a series of SLIP commands to ignore certain dumps and set software traps for intermittent problems.

Complete information about SLIP commands can be obtained from the Systems Commands manual for the version of MVS you are running. For example, *MVS Extended Architecture Operations: Systems Commands* (GC28-1206) is used for MVS/XA. Sample information is given to spark your interest to go read the book!

This section discusses the "non PER" SLIPs. A later section discusses "Program Event Recording" (PER) SLIPs. The "non PER" SLIPs can be used by the system programmer to control the amount and type of information to be made available, but it should not be inferred that the non-PER SLIP is safe. If the match limit (MATCHLIM) is not set, the system could be hurt by large dumping volume. Non-PER SLIPs can even put the whole Processor Complex into a disabled wait state.

SLIP traps are set by operator command. The active SLIP traps can be displayed by **DISPLAY SLIP**. If you are having a problem getting a SYSUDUMP, or you need the storage of the entire address space to diagnose a problem, you can use the slip traps to capture your documentation. In the appendix "ABEND codes," there is a "SLIP Trick" described to get an address space dump.

Event Filter Keywords Event filter keywords define the type of event or events which the trap is to monitor. All other events are ignored. One or many of these keywords can limit the events for this particular SLIP:

1. **ADDRESS** gives the virtual address range in which the error must occur.
2. **ASID** is the address space identifier. Up to 16 may be specified.
3. **ASIDSA** is an address space with storage alteration. This is for cross memory processing.
4. **COMP** specifies a system or user ABEND code associated with the error. SLIP cannot trap ABEND codes 13E, 33E, or x22.
5. **DATA** specifies the address and logical expression for the compare. For example "DATA=(2R,EQ,80)" says general purpose register 2 is equal to 80 hexadecimal.
6. **ERRTYP** specifies one or more error events. The type "ALL" indicates all types of errors.
7. **JOBNAME** specifies the one to eight character name of the job, TSO userid, or started task which must be in control for the match test to succeed.

8. **JSPGM** specifies a one to eight character name for the job step program to be a match.
9. **LPAEP** specifies the module's entry point name in the link pack area.
10. **LPAMOD** specifies a one to eight character name of the LPA module which must be in control.
11. **MODE** specifies the mode the system must be in for a match. These are DIS (disabled), GLOC (holding global lock), GLOCSD (holding a global suspend lock), GLOCSP (holding a global spin lock), HOME (executing in a cross memory address mode of "home"), LLOC (holding the local lock), LOCK (holding any lock), PKEY (problem program key), PP (problem state), RECV (recovery routine in control), SKEY (system key of 7 or less), SRB (SRB mode), SUPER (supervisor state), SUPR (supervisor control mode), TCB (task mode), TYP1 (type 1 SVC mode), or ALL (all of above).
12. **NUCMOD** specifies a module in the nucleus.
13. **PVTEP** specifies an entry point in a private area module.
14. **PVTMOD** specifies the one to eight character private area load module which is in control for a match.

Action Related Keyword **ACTION** is the action related keyword, and it specifies what you want the system to do when the event occurs. There are several operands for ACTION:

1. **IGNORE** indicates resume normal processing. IGNORE is used to exclude a subset of events being trapped by a more general trap.
2. **NODUMP** denotes that no dump should be created for this event. For example,

   SLIP SET,ACTION=NODUMP,COMP=806,END

   would prevent dumps for system ABEND 806. Most data centers have this in their system to minimize SYSUDUMPs and SYSABENDs.
3. **NOSUP** says do not suppress the dump. If the system has a dump suppression, but wants a dump for some reason, this parameter will force the dump.
4. **RECORD** specifies force recording in LOGREC.
5. **STDUMP** indicates the system trace records should be created and an SVC dump scheduled.

6. **STRACE** indicates the SLIP system trace records are to be written if the system trace is active.
7. **SVCD** indicates the system is to schedule a system (SVC) dump to go to SYS1.DUMPxx.
8. **TRACE** indicates SLIP should generate a GTF SLIP record.
9. **TRDUMP** indicates trace records should be generated while the trap is enabled and an SVC dump is to be scheduled when the trap is disabled.
10. **WAIT** indicates the system is to be placed into a 01B wait state. *Use this with extreme caution.* If this trap goes off, it will cause system interruption.

Trap Control Keywords These keywords allow the system programmer to enable or disable the trap and control how many times the trap should match.

1. **DISABLE** sets the trap initially inactive. It waits to be enabled.
2. **ENABLE** indicates the trap is to be defined initially as active.
3. **MATCHLIM** specifies the SLIP trap is to be disabled after this number of entries. The value is one to 65535.

Dump and Trace Tailoring Keywords These keywords allow the system programmer to specify what should and should not be included in dumps written to SYS1.DUMPxx and to specify what information should be included in trace records.

1. **ASIDLST** specifies the address space identifiers of the address space(s) to be dumped. This is useful for systems that have two or more address spaces that make up a subsystem (e.g., IMS).
2. **LIST** specifies the start and ending addresses which are to be dumped. Relative addressing (10 percent, for example) can be used.
3. **SDATA** specifies the kind of system control information to be dumped.
4. **SUMLIST** specifies the start and ending address of areas to be included in a summary dump.
5. **TRDATA** specifies the type and contents of GTF records for ACTION=TRACE or ACTION=TRDUMP.

Specialized SLIP Keywords These keywords are maintenance information for SLIP.

1. **END** indicates the end of the SLIP specifications.
2. **ID** is the name of this SLIP trap. This name is used in operator communication.
3. **DEBUG** is a diagnosis aid and is specified if the SLIP trap is not doing what you want. This directs SLIP to record each time the trap is checked and not just when it finds a match.
4. **RBLEVEL** indicates which request block the system is to use for error detection traps.

17.2.3. MVS Information Traces

Collection facilities are available to trace minute details of the activity in an MVS system. SYSLOG is absolutely necessary, but the others should be used with care as they generate a large volume of records.

System Trace and Master Trace MVS has built-in facilities to trace Supervisor Calls (SVCs), I/O interrupts, Program Checks, External Traces, and even branch commands. The TRACE system command and member SCHEDxx of SYS1.PARMLIB control the size and types of traces which can be recorded. Figure 17.12 shows the trace table entries for an application program. The OPEN SVC, WAIT SVC, and I/O interrupts create entries in the trace table.

SYSLOG The SYSLOG data set is a JES spool file which contains all messages that are displayed on the system console. In most data centers, this volume is very large. The data should be dumped to tape each day at the same time. The problem comes with what to do with all the data. You may write a program or use the Statistical Analysis System (SAS) to strip off periods of time or all records for a specific task.

Another utility to use with SYSLOG is the SORT. If you sort the daily SYSLOG data set by job name and number, you can see all the messages that a job produces.

Because the SYSLOG data set is a JES spool file, it is best to start a writer task to "print" the file to a DASD data set. This writer should be started about once per hour (or whatever your data center needs.) The data set can be written to tape each day. Daily tapes can be combined into weekly tapes, and weekly tapes into monthly tapes.

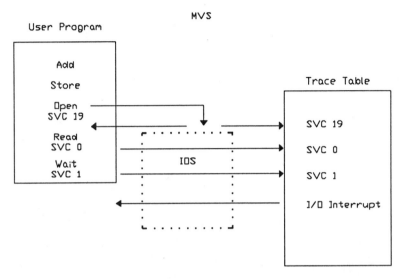

Figure 17.12 Traces. The MVS trace tables have information which can be recorded by MVS as it gets control, voluntarily or involuntarily, from the user program. In this example, the user program issues an OPEN macro which issues SVC 19. The trace table has an entry for the SVC. As the program issues a READ macro, an SVC0 (EXCP) is issued, and an entry is placed in the table. When the I/O interrupt occurs, IOS places an entry in the table.

Generalized Trace Facility (GTF) The Generalized Trace Facility has been around since the early days of MVT. This facility accumulates information from each component of MVS as it is starting and ending.

A GTF address space is started, and GTF is instructed to monitor certain events. GTF then enables "hooks" in predefined places in the MVS system and waits for events. Tracing is done either internally (in buffers located in virtual storage) or externally (to DASD or tape). Figure 17.13 shows the GTF address space running. It is trapping information from the "user program" address space. Data written to DASD may "wrap." When GTF fills up the first extent, it will begin writing over at the start of the DASD extent.

CCWTRACE: CCWTRACE was an IBM Field Engineer (FE) aid developed to trace I/O operations and, in addition, to collect the channel command words (CCW) controlling the I/O operation. CCWTRACE started (and was very successful) in VM/370. MVS now has the command.

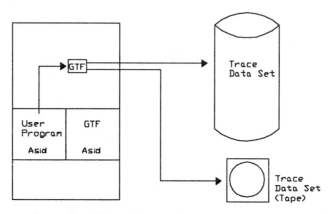

Figure 17.13   Generalized Trace Facility (GTF). GTF is started as a separate address space. GTF activates "hooks" in the MVS software and microcode which traces events for one or several addresss spaces. The data can then be written to a DASD file or a tape file.

One of the best uses of CCWTRACE is to monitor the pattern of I/O operations of a job. You can determine:

1. The size and number of physical blocks in the I/O operation.
2. The pattern of reads and writes to calculate the read/write ratios for cache operations.
3. The pattern of read operations after a direct search. Does the application read the rest of a whole track or just a few blocks? This information could be used to determine the efficiency of certain cache controllers for your specific applications.

VTAM Traces: VTAM traces are the least disruptive types of traces. GTF does not intercept any operations — it only waits for its trace to be called to record some "user" information. One common VTAM trace is to trace a particular problem in an online system. CICS VTAM accesses are traced in the following manner:

1. GTF must be active.
2. Issue the following VTAM modify command:
   F VTAM,TRACE,TYPE=(BUF/IO),ID=luname,MODE=EXT
3. Perform the task you want to trace, such as CICS transactions.
4. Stop the trace:
   F VTAM,NOTRACE,TYPE=(BUF),ID=luname,MODE=EXT
5. Stop GTF.

SLIP — PER Program Event Recording (PER) is a System/370 facility that can trace down to the instruction level. Three SLIP keywords enable the PER feature of the hardware. These keywords are:

1. **IF**, which indicates an instruction fetch PER trap.
2. **SA**, which indicates a storage alteration PER trap.
3. **SB**, which indicates a successful branch PER trap.

These keywords *dramatically increase* the CPU consumption of all tasks in the system and cause a major degradation to the system. PER traps should only be used when absolutely necessary.

Several special operands are available only to PER slip traps.

1. **RANGE** specifies the start and end address of a PER trap.
2. **PRCNTLIM=p**, where "p" is a number from 1 through 99, specifies the maximum percentage of the system time that can be spent on PER SLIPs. If you think that SLIP will use an unacceptable amount of time, specify a percentage which is relatively low — 20 percent — and watch the system. If you specify this parameter, however, you may miss the event you are trying to trap.
3. **Recovery** forces PER traps to initiate a process which either saves the system or lets it ABEND.

17.3. SECURITY

MVS was released by IBM in 1974 and was the largest and most complex operating system ever produced. Since then, it has grown several times larger. The predecessor of MVS — MVT — relied on the PASSWORD facility to provide security. Passwords could be applied to non-VSAM data sets, VSAM data sets, and TSO Logon userids, but these were too cumbersome and not really secure. I do not recommend you use these password facilities.

I do recommend you use one of the full-function security systems. In fact, I think you are operating a few bricks short of a full load if you do not have a full-function security system.

IBM developed the Resource Access Control Facility (RACF) as an add-on to MVS. OEM developers created ACF2 and Top Secret (both now owned by Computer Associates International). These security systems provide the security tools which the data center needs to implement a security system.

There is no such thing as total security. Someone can always breach security. The confidence provided by the security system can be deceptive. Some MVS maintenance can cause system integrity errors, permitting exposure of the operating system to unauthorized access even with a RACF-like system in place.

While IBM has excellent testing and verification process, it has a major problem with these exposures. It cannot (and should not) publicize the problem. For example, if PUT tape 8802 contained a module which let anyone logon under a certain circumstance, IBM could not publish a warning "If you have 8802 maintenance, and you . . . ." Any facility at that level would be open for violations.

So, IBM creates the fix and ships it in the next available release tape. In our example, if you installed tape 8802 in June 1988 and did not apply more maintenance until February 1989, then your data center would be vulnerable from June 1988 until February 1989.

IBM is not the only one to open the data center to violations. OEM software manufacturers usually provide an SVC as part of their database or other subsystem. In at least one instance, an OEM vendor left the interface of that SVC such that anyone could get into Supervisor State and Protection Key zero with only minimal knowledge. *If a program achieves supervisor state, even RACF-like protection is worthless.*

A method of extending the security offered by MVS is to **encrypt** the data. IBM provides cryptography hardware and software to change the EBCDIC representation of the data to a nonreadable form. The user must provide a "key" to decode the data. Even so, that key must be in storage sometime, however brief, to decrypt the data, and a program that can achieve Protection Key zero could possibly steal the key.

Security is never absolute: The probability of a compromise may approach, but is never, zero. Securing a system is the act of moving that probability closer to zero than it was before.

17.3.1. Preparing for Security

The data center and its users should decide on the security required for the data and facilities provided by the data center. Almost always, a security system such as RACF should be in place, if for no other reason than to protect the investment the data center has in the MVS operating system. The following are a few of the considerations which should be covered in preparing for security in a data center:

1. Obtain agreement on the goals of a security system:
   a. With management. The management of the data center and/or the company as a whole should decide broad security goals. All security costs something. Near-total security will cost the company a huge amount of money. No security will open the company up to potentially large expenses and possibly legal violations and law suits. Somewhere in between is a security system which management is willing to pay for and live with.
   b. With data processing. The data processing department should require security to prevent unauthorized access to programs and files.
   c. With the user department. If the user department understands it is making decisions and investing time and money in the information coming from the programs and files at the data center, it should be willing to pay some of the "costs" of a security system.
2. Identify and train the key members of the security team.
3. Develop and publish a security policy, including procedures for all to use. Technology such as RACF is only part of the answer. Remember that your primary security resources are the people — the technology exists not only to elicit the machinery's assistance but also as a means of galvanizing support from the people entrusted with the machinery.
4. Develop and publish an implementation plan.
5. Implement.
6. Monitor. This is usually forgotten in most data centers. Violations occur in any security environment and many fall into the "ok if it happened before" category. Examples are application programmers who forget to change production names to test names and are ABENDed because they cannot update production files. In some cases, people and departments are attempting — or succeeding — to access data they should not. If the data center does not have a security administrator *and allocate time* to monitor security, then the security is not complete.

Classification of Job Functions   The job classifications of your company are a good place to start defining security job classifications. Systems Programmers, Operators, Production Control, Application Programmers, User departments, and hardware and software vendors have different needs and responsibilities. These area definitions are a good place to start defining job functions.

Your personnel department may want to mention security in job descriptions, even for those positions not specifically charged with maintaining it, so newcomers are automatically sensitized to the desire for a secure environment after it has been established.

Classification of Data   Each type of data in the corporation should be grouped into classifications to provide a policy for the data. Each organization is different, but the following give guidelines for areas you might use for your data:

1. System libraries. The MVS and data center libraries must be protected to ensure the operating system and data center data sets are not modified without authorization.
2. User department data. Each department should define the data and requirements. The payroll data should probably not be accessed by anyone except the department and selected others. Accounts payable data may have a wider audience.
3. Program libraries. These libraries contain the software investment of the corporation. They should probably be protected from read or write access, not only to protect the integrity of the programs themselves but also to ensure that they are not used as "Trojan horses" to threaten the integrity of the the rest of the system.

Obtaining Agreement   Obtaining agreement is a very simple process. The following are a list of the key items needed:

1. The security policy must be a top priority of upper management. Top priority means a verbal, written, and funded commitment.
2. All members of the security committee must understand the policy and understand the need for the policy.
3. Resources (time and money) must be available to implement the policy.

17.3.2.   Data Security Policy

The policy should begin with a brief statement of the corporate intent. It should clearly state the policy is part of the contract with the user department. Security is a two-edged sword. The policy should state what the corporation is trying to accomplish with the security system.

The data security policy should come from the highest levels of the corporation. Security is a bother. Security is expensive in both system and people resources. Security prevents some people from doing things they might want to do, but do not have the corporate direction to do.

Security should be delegated to the responsible areas. The systems programmers should protect MVS and the associated operating system functions. The accounts payable department should protect the accounts payable files. Audit trails should be in place to ensure multiple administrative safeguards are in place.

17.3.3. Implementation

Implementation Plan   Implementation of a security system should be accomplished by a team of representatives from all departments. It will be difficult to have a team accomplish this complex task, but if it is not a team effort, then problems will certainly occur. The following is a sample scenario for a phased implementation of security:

1. Decide on and install the security system. The IBM MVS system is the Resource Access Control Facility (RACF). OEM software vendors have security systems which will work in place of RACF.
2. Define groups and/or departments — wide areas of responsibility.
3. Define security administrators who will accept responsibility for their department's security implementation.
4. Set up a security subsystem which includes the above organization. Create names for each group.
5. Define system protection and implement. This is the easiest to check and a very important first step to security.
6. Define applications to start protecting. If the system has a "warning" feature — where the task is warned with a message and not actually cancelled — this is a good feature to run in production to see the effect of the security before it is fully implemented.
7. Implement protection for all departments.
8. Monitor security violations.

Resource Access Control Facility (RACF) Flow   RACF is a combination of modules which interface with MVS subsystems (allocation, JES, etc.) to ensure TSO LOGONs and batch jobs are authorized to operate at the data center. The key interface is the RACHECK macro. In Figure 17.14, the user's address space asks for a resource such as data set allocation. The "application," in this case, is Direct-Access Storage Management (DADSM). DADSM issues a RACHECK macro to have RACF (or the equivalent OEM program product) look up the request and allow the access or disallow the access.

Figure 17.14 shows the logical view of RACF processing:

1. The user address space asks for a service — for example, opening a data set.
2. The OPEN routines issue a RACHECK macro which calls MVS modules to check the RACF ID against the **profile** of the resource.

   The profile is usually loaded into virtual storage by MVS routines and identifies the classification of the resource and specifies the access limitations to impose on it. Whenever the profile is changed, it must be "refreshed" for the changes to take effect.

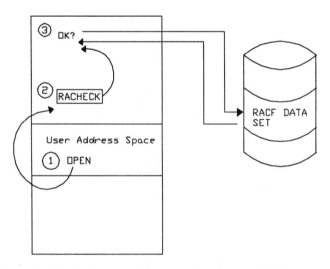

Figure 17.14   RACF. The user's address space isses an OPEN request. DADSM issues a RACHECK macro to see if the user can access the data set. If the user can access the data set as outlined in the RACF profiles in the RACF data set, the access is slowed. If not, DADSM is instructed to Abend the task with a 913 Abend.

3. The RACHECK MVS modules look in virtual storage or read parameters from the RACF data sets. The user is either allowed to access the resource or denied access.

The resource does not have to be something real like a data set. It can be a made-up name to control access to a system. For example, the resource "payroll" could be created to allow or disallow access to the payroll system in CICS. The security routine could issue a RACHECK macro to see if a particular user could access the payroll system.

17.4. SUMMARY

SMF collects data about the MVS system, jobs, and TSO sessions. The volume of data collected can be large and is determined partly by parameters in the SMFPRMxx member of SYS1.PARMLIB. System-related data, including configuration data, paging activity, and workload information, can be used to evaluate performance of the system. Job data, such as CPU time, spool processing, and data set statistics (including VSAM-generated information), can be used for billing and for security audit purposes.

SMF records include a record type which identifies the information each contains. A variety of subsystems generate and analyze information through the SMF data gathering mechanism.

One of these, RMF, can be used to continuously collect data about resource utilization, analyze archived data for any time period, or combine both functions by abstracting realtime data and calling attention to resource contention. The most comprehensive reference on RMF is the *RMF — Field Description and Analysis* (GG24-1564) publication of the IBM World Trade Systems Center.

Three MVS subsystems monitor, detect, and report errors: EREP reports those such as I/O errors (hard and soft), ABENDs and program checks, and device statistics; SLIP can be used to detect certain events and can be directed to do something at the time an event is detected, bringing the data gathering closer to the source; and the DUMP facilities permit post-mortem analysis of problems. (Dumps can be taken on request by either application or supervisor programs, upon an ABEND, or stand-alone if MVS cannot continue at all.)

Minute details about MVS system operation can be obtained through trace tables, SYSLOG, and GTF. Traces can generate a huge amount of data; they should be used cautiously after an adequate amount of planning to make sure the data collected is useful and not wasted. SLIP with PER support can trace down to the instruction level to help diagnose those really tricky problems.

Predecessors to MVS had piecemeal security provisions. MVT relied on the PASSWORD facility but was cumbersome and not very secure. RACF is superior to and more flexible than simple password protection. Through use of the RACHECK macro, RACF can be integrated into any application and can be used to regulate access to nontangible and abstract "resources."

Any security scheme, including RACF, is no better than the entire system's ability to prevent programs from unauthorized entry into supervisor mode. Although encryption is available in MVS, encryption and decryption require system resources and usually require keys which cannot be completely hidden from supervisor mode access.

For that reason, a data center needs to develop a comprehensive security plan involving management, DP, and user departments so that people can fill in the gaps. Even if you think your company does not need heavy security, it would not have the machinery in the first place if it had no value to the company. Protect the investment in machinery and data by addressing the issues, and do not rely solely upon hardware or software security.

17.5. CONCLUSION

If you have reached this point, you either skipped to the last chapter to see the ending, or you slugged it out. Either way, congratulations! Unfortunately I have some good news and some bad news. The good news is that you are well on your way to understanding the most exciting operating system architecture ever created.

The bad news is more like a challenge: the half life of information in this industry is about 18 months. In 18 months, all you know today will be out of date. In 36 months, you will only have 25 percent current information. I feel you can be successful if you use the techniques presented in this book to carry you forward to the Twenty-first Century. They certainly have aided me for two decades. Good Luck and God Bless!

Glossary

This glossary is intended to be an aid to the student of MVS. As the reader can see from the discussion of the term used for storage in the Processor Complex, a Central Storage by any other name is still a Central Storage. Further definitions may be found in the IBM *Dictionary of Computing* (previously, *Vocabulary for Data Processing, Telecommunications, and Office Systems)* (GC20-1699).

Many of the terms have more general meaning than is expressed here, and other reference works can be consulted. The scope of definitions contained here is, for the most part, limited to the use of terms in an MVS data center.

Above the Line: An address greater than 16 Mb. Normally refers to Virtual Storage but can also apply to Central Storage. "Above the Line" is referenced in 31-bit mode. See also **Below the Line**.

Access Method: MVS subroutines that provide the machine instructions to input and output physical data blocks to devices attached to the Processor Complex. Access Method modules calls are created by high level language commands (e.g., READ or WRITE) or assembler macros (e.g., GET or PUT). Access Methods (e.g., QSAM, VSAM) build Channel Programs and manage buffers. Most access method subroutines execute in in the address space of the task. Some Access Methods, such as VTAM and TCAM have separate address spaces which process data requests.

Actuator: The portion of Direct Access Storage Devices (DASD) that contains the read/write heads and the disk platters that contain the data. The actuator is the portion of DASD that is addressable to the data center by volume serial number. In some DASDs, a single Head Disk Assembly (HDA) will contain two actuators. See also **HDA**.

Address Space: An executing batch job, system task, or TSO user. Each address space has its own 16 Mb (MVS/370) or 2 Gb (MVS/XA or MVS/ESA) virtual storage. Each address space has its own Segment Table and its own Page Tables for its Private Area but shares the Page Tables for the Common Area with all other users. The exceptions are MVS/ESA data spaces which do not map Common Areas in the data space (e.g., HIPERspaces).

AMODE: Addressing Mode. An attribute, assigned by the Linkage Editor program, of an entry point of a Load Module. With AMODE=24, MVS program management will pass control to the entry point in 24-bit mode. The 24-bit mode program may change to 31-bit mode. With AMODE=31, MVS/XA or MVS/ESA will pass control to the entry point in 31-bit mode. The program can access any storage area without changing its mode.

APAR: Authorized Program Analysis Report. A report of a problem caused by a suspected defect in a current unaltered release of an MVS program. IBM controls APARs.

APG: Automatic Priority Group. The early MVS method of controlling dispatching priorities of address spaces.

ASCB: Address Space Control Block. The control block which represents an Address Space to MVS. ASCBs reside in the System Queue Area. Each ASCB contains an "ASID" number which uniquely identifies the address space at any instant of time.

ASID: Address Space Identifier. The number associated with the Address Space Control Block which is assigned as the Address Space is started. The ASID number can be any number from 1 through the maximum number of address spaces allowed by the data center. MVS keeps a table of ASIDs and assigns them as STCs, batch JES initiators, and TSO address spaces are created. See also **ASCB**.

ASM: Auxiliary Storage Manager. The MVS modules which manage the Page and Swap data sets. ASM builds channel program to transfer pages in and out of Central Storage.

ASP: Attached Support Processor or Asymmetric Multiprocessing System. The predecessor of JES3 that ran under the MVT operating system.

Assembler: A program that processes source statements (which may correspond one-to-one with System/370 machine language instructions) into object code (System/370 machine language). The IBM Assemblers (ASMF, ASMG, and ASMH) allow "Macros" which are single assembler statements that result in multiple assembler statements. IBM supplies many macros as part of MVS. IBM users can create their own macros. Most IBM "system generations" are the result of IBM macros which generate individual modules or whole systems.

Authorized: A program which resides in special MVS program libraries. Authorized programs may change its execution state from Program to Supervisor State.

Availability: The amount of time a computer system can perform functions for its end users. Availability is usually expressed as a percentage of time. Availability is dependent on Reliability. If a system fails the clock stops counting for availability to the user.

Auxiliary Storage: The term used for MVS paging devices (Local and Swap) which contain Central Storage page frames that are not in use.

BC MODE: Basic Control Mode. The name of the microcode that allows MVS/370 systems to run on the System/370 Processor Complexes. See also **EC MODE**.

BCS: Basic Catalog Structure. The portion of ICF catalogs originally introduced with DF/EF for user catalogs. The BCS contains pointers to volumes that contain a specific data set. See also **VVDS**.

BDAM: Basic Direct Access Method.

Beejay Switches and Lights: In a Device Level Selection 3380 (e.g., AD4), refers to the bank of indicator lights used to identify actuator ready state and switches to manage availability of the actuator. Beejays replaced a sole light and switch originally located on the control panel which applied to the entire string. Effective use of Beejays enables restoration of service if a critical actuator can not sustain a ready state.

Below the Line: An address less than 16 Megabytes. Any MVS program can access memory with addresses in this range for programs, data, and I/O buffers. See also **Above the Line.**

BJ switches and lights: See **Beejay switches and lights.**

BLDL: Build List. BLDL is the MVS Macro instruction which calls MVS supervisor service modules that search the directory of a partitioned data set. A list of information about members is returned from the directory. Information returned can be later passed to the MVS Load supervisor service modules to bypass the directory search. This is an efficient method if the module is to be "loaded" several times (e.g., CICS programs). See also **BPAM.**

BLOCK: A physical group of logical records. Blocks are separated by gaps on the recording medium. Each block may contain one or more records. A block is the physical unit of transfer between storage and an I/O device. Blocks usually contain a group of logical records. Hardware is more concerned with blocks, whereas software is more concerned with records.

Block Multiplexor Channel: A part of a Processor Complex channel subsystem that can keep track of more than one device transferring blocks and interleave blocks on the channel to different devices.

BPAM: Basic Partitioned Access Method. The MVS access method which is used to update partitioned data sets. PDS members can be read and written with QSAM but only if a single member is accessed sequentially. BPAM must be used to update PDS directory entries.

BSAM: Basic Sequential Access Method. An MVS Access Method which is used to read from or write sequential files. BSAM does not block or deblock records (like QSAM does).

Buffer: A Virtual Storage area that is used to receive data from a device or provide the area for data going to an I/O device.

Byte: The smallest unit of storage in MVS. Eight bits.

cache: A Random Access Memory used to buffer data from larger storage media. Whenever data is requested, the microcode first checks to see if the requested data is in the cache. If it is in cache (a "hit"), the block is provided from cache. If it is not (a "miss"), a much slower access to the larger memory is required. The target of the cache may be DASD, tape devices or be larger, slower Random Access Memory (e.g., Central Storage in a Processor Complex).

Cache Fast Write: The term for an output operation in which the data buffer is written to the cache storage in a 3990 control unit, and the I/O instruction is "completed" to the Processor Complex. Nonvolatile Storage is not used.

CBIPO: Custom-Built Installation Process Offering (MVS). All of MVS is included on several tapes. MVS has been "generated" and all applicable maintenance has been applied. CBIPO is a "ready to IPL" system.

CCHH: Cylinder (two bytes) and head (two bytes) of an address of a track on DASD.

CCH: Channel Check Handler. MVS modules which handle errors on I/O channels.

CCW: Channel Control Word. In System/370 Processor Complexes, a separate computer, called a Channel, performs Input/Output operations. The channel is directed by Channel Programs, which are composed of one or more Channel Control Words. CCWs are eight bytes long and contain operation code, a virtual or Central Storage address of data for the channel, the length of the data for the channel, and option flags. Format 0 CCWs support a 24-bit data address. Format 1 CCWs support a 31-bit data address and are used in MVS/XA and MVS/ESA.

Central Storage: A term for the random-access, read/write memory inside a Processor Complex.

Channel: A channel connects the Processor Complex with the input and output control units. In the 308x architecture, the channel is part of the External Data Controller (EXDC). In the 309x architecture, the channel is a part of the Channel Control Element (CCE).

Channel Selection Algorithm: Most MVS devices are configured with two or more channels to access the device. The MVS Input Output Supervisor (IOS) (for MVS/370) or the channel microcode (for MVS/XA and MVS/ESA) decide which channel to try first, the order of channel access and the next channel to try if the first selection is busy. This process is called a Channel Selection Algorithm.

One algorithm is **Sequential** which indicates that the first path defined is always the first to be tried. Other paths will be used only if the first path is busy. Another algorithm is **Reverse Sequential** which is the opposite of Sequential. The last path is used until that path is busy. Another is **Last Channel Used** (LCU) in which the last successful path is remembered and reused until it is busy. The one IBM most often uses is **Rotate** which indicates paths are tried in order that they are defined. The utilization should be evenly distributed over all channels.

CICS: Customer Information Control System. CICS accepts transaction codes from teleprocessing terminals and calls programs to process the transaction. CICS provides services needed by those programs to accomplish the task including storage allocation, program management, terminal buffer control, and file management.

CKD: Count, Key, and Data record format (of a DASD track). CKD is a data-recording format which has self-defining record formats on the track. CKD devices are supported by MVS. Another type of track format is Fixed Block Architecture (FBA), which is not supported by MVS but is in the literature (Device Support Facilities) which must be read by MVS systems programmers.

CLPA: Create Link Pack Area. An IPL parameter used to copy SYS1.LPALIB to virtual storage. CLPA IPLs are slower than non-CLPA IPLs because all modules in SYS1.LPALIB must be loaded from the system residence volume into virtual storage, and paged out to the PLPA paging data set.

CMS: Cross Memory Services. An enhancement introduced in MVS at Version 1, Release 1.2 which provides supervisor services needed for the Dual Address Space (DAS) facility. CMS adds macros which use the PC (program call) instruction to call MVS services in the PCAUTH address space. CMS should not be confused with VM/Conversational Monitor System (VM/CMS), the TSO equivalent for interactive access in a VM environment. CMS is sometimes abbreviated XMS.

Common Area: Virtual Storage shared by all address spaces in MVS. See also **CSA, Nucleus, PLPA, PSA,** and **SQA.**

Control Block: A contiguous piece of virtual storage, usually divided into defined fields, in which information is kept for communications between MVS tasks. Control blocks are pointed to by lists pointers or queues. For example, Address Space Control Blocks (ASCBs) contain information such as Address Space Identifiers (ASIDs) and addresses of page tables of address spaces.

Control Program: Another term for "operating system."

Control Unit: A device that controls input and output operations to one or more devices. Examples of DASD control units are 3880 and 3990.

Core: A term for Central Storage, referring to ancient random access memory devices constructed from iron cores through which tiny wires were woven. This memory was magnetized one way or another to represent binary "1" and "0" values. Although "core memory" exists (or should exist!) only in museums today, the term is still used to refer generically to the primary storage in a computer.

Coupling: A term used to indicate how the MVS operating system is configured to interface with MVS executing on another CPU. In "loosely coupled," the CPUs may request that each other perform tasks, but each has its own operating system and its own Central Storage. The request is placed on a CTCA or shared DASD. In "tightly coupled," more than one CPU shares the same Central Storage and the same copy of the operating system. The request can be placed in virtual storage or directly requested via SIGP instructions.

CPU: Central Processing Unit. The part of a Processor Complex which executes the machine instructions.

Cryptographic: Hardware or software which encode and decode data and modules for the purpose of data security. Data passed through cryptographic systems is said to be encrypted. Encrypted data can not be read with normal techniques. The letter "A" does not exist as x'C1' but as some other character. Data is converted to and from the encrypted format with a "key."

CSA: Common Storage Area or Common Service Area. A part of Virtual Storage. Subsystems (e.g., VTAM, IMS) use CSA for data areas. For MVS/XA and MVS/ESA, part of CSA is below the line and part (ECSA) is above the line.

CTCA: Channel to Channel Adapter. A device which allows data to be transferred between two System/370 channels (attached to two different Processor Complexes). CTCAs are usually used by IBM subsystems (e.g., JES3, GRS, and VTAM) but can be used by other programs. A single CTCA is usually not shared by multiple MVS tasks. There are hardware limitations to the number of CTCs which can be attached to a Processor Complex. See also 3088 Multisystem Channel Communications Unit.

CVOL: Control Volume. CVOLs were the MVT catalogs for saving data set information and are supported in MVS for upward compatibility. No MVS system should allow CVOLs at this late point in time.

CVT: Communications Vector Table. An MVS control block in the Nucleus from which almost any other control block in MVS can be found. The Address of the CVT can be obtained from a fixed location in Virtual Storage (in the Prefixed Save Area) so every MVS task can find the CVT. Another term used for the CVT is an "anchor" control block. The CVT contains pointers to other control blocks and thus "anchors" their addresses.

DADSM: Direct Access Device Space Management. The name applied to MVS modules which allocate DASD space for data sets, delete data sets and maintain information in the VTOC of DASD volumes. See also **DFP**.

DAS: Dual Address Space Facility. An architectural provision of System/370 which provides modules in separate MVS address spaces the ability to share data without having to use CSA for intermediary storage. Address spaces can share modules without scheduling SRBs to have the program run in the other address space. DAS is very efficient. See also CSA.

DASD: Direct Access Storage Device. An I/O device which allows modules to read or write specific blocks anywhere in a file. Most DASDs today have rotating magnetic disks to store the data. Some "DASD" (e.g., STC 4705) use random-access memory chips to emulate a DASD device.

DASD Fast Write: A form of write to a 3380 device attached to a 3990 model 3 control unit that has the control unit write physical block(s) to cache storage and Nonvolatile Storage in the control unit. The Processor Complex is notified the I/O operation is complete before the physical block(s) get to the 3380. Data integrity is ensured by the 3990 control unit. Even if power goes out, the control unit "remembers" to write the physical block(s) to the 3380.

DAT: Dynamic Address Translation. The term used for the combination of MVS software and control blocks and the System/370 hardware to use a mulit-level table lookup to convert virtual address to addresses in Central Storage as instructions are executing.

DATA: Any representations such as characters or analog quantities.

Data Set: The area of data on a recording medium that contains data in one of several formats. The format is determined by the access method that defines and writes to the data set. The term "data set" is used in IBM nomenclature where the term "file" is commonly used in that of other vendors.

Data Streaming: A hardware communication protocol which allows channels to support a 3 Mb/second rate (and higher for E/S models). Data-Streaming originated with DASD devices but later became available with 3480 and 3422 tape drives.

DBMS: Data Base Management System — a software subsystem which provides the nucleus of modules to maintain a a well-organized set of data. The data center usually must code programs to access the data in the data base.

DB/DC: Data Base/Data Communication. MVS subsystems which give data center users at teleprocessing terminals read and/or update access to data bases. DB/DC is often used to refer to CICS, IMS, or several OEM data base systems.

DCB: Data Control Block. The MVS control block that contains information about a data set. The program and access method use the DCB to hold information about the data set. Data Control Block is the most often used meaning for the contraction DCB. Another meaning for DASD is Detection Code Bytes.

DDR: Dynamic Device Reconfiguration. The MVS modules that get control for Input/Output device errors and will swap mountable magnetic media (mostly tapes) from one device to another if the error is not recoverable. If the error cannot be recovered, DDR will transfer control to the application recovery routine, if any, or ABEND the task.

Deadly embrace: A condition in which two or more MVS tasks are waiting for a resource such that neither can continue. A deadly embrace may be direct, involving two processes, or indirect, in which multiple waits prevents any of the participants from proceeding. This condition can be avoided with proper use of locks and queueing.

DEB: Data Extent Block. The MVS control block that contains information about the location of a data set including the cylinders and heads if on DASD.

DEQUE: The MVS function that removes a task from the list of users of a resource created by ENQUE. See also **ENQUE.**

DF/DS: Data Facility/Device Support. A program-product successor to early MVS data management support which was replaced by Data Facility Product (DFP). DF/DS introduced indexed VTOCs, and user exits for DASD space allocation. DF/DS was later shortened to DF and added to IBM program products such as HSM (DFHSM) and sort (DFSORT).

DF/DSS: Data Facility/Data Set Services. A program-product successor to the free MVS IEHDASDR disk dump/restore program. DF/DSS was introduced with MVS Version 1 Release 1.1.

DFHSM: Data Facility Hierarchical Storage Manager. An IBM program product which manages DASD data sets. Data sets not referenced within a period of time specified by the installation are migrated to less expensive storage (tape or compressed disk files). If a user attempts to access a data set which has been migrated, execution is suspended while DFHSM retrieves the data set and puts it back on DASD.

DFP: Data Facility Product. The collection of MVS modules which provide the Input/Output and data management function for MVS. See also **DADSM.**

Disabled: When a CPU does not accept interruptions (such as notifications of completed I/O or timer interrupts) it is "disabled." Normally, MVS disables while it processes an interrupt. During the time MVS is disabled, no other activity can use the CPU. If an I/O operation was issued by the lowest priority task in the system, then the interrupt prevents even the highest tasks from operating. Low priority tasks can interfere with high priority tasks by causing interrupts which increase disabled time.

Dispatchable: The property of a task whereby it is ready for execution and not waiting on some external event, such as completion of I/O or allocation of requested resources.

DLIB: Distribution Library. The tape dump of a DASD device that contains all the MVS modules which is sent from IBM when a customer orders MVS.

DLS: Device Level Selection. A term used with 3380 DASD for the AD4, AE4, AJ4, and AK4 (and associated B units) because they can simultaneously service any two I/O actuators. There are no internal path limits as there are with Standard 3380 devices (e.g., AA4).

DLSE: Device Level Selection Enhanced. A term used with 3380 DASD for the AJ4, and AK4 (and associated B units) because they can simultaneously service any four I/O actuators. Four path DLSE access requires two Heads of String be connected.

DPS: Dynamic Path Selection. The term used for IBM 3380 devices that allow two actuators to be serviced by a single head of string.

DREF: Disabled Reference Storage (DREF). The SQA and LSQA pages for a swapped out user that are stored in Expanded Storage by MVS/ESA on a 309x or 43xx Processor Complex with Expanded Storage while the address space is swapped out.

DSF: Device Support Facilities. The IBM utility that manages Direct Access Storage Devices (DASD).

DSN: Data Set Name.

DYADIC: A term for "Multiprocessor" which IBM uses for Processor Complexes with multiple CPUs (e.g., 3081). A DYADIC has two CPUs, and both CPUs have I/O capability. The system can continue to run if one of the CPUs fail, but, unlike previous multiprocessors, the system cannot be partitioned and run as two uniprocessors.

Dynamic Path Reconnect (DPR): A DASD device, operating in DPR mode, may reconnect (after releasing control for seek or set sector operations) to *any* channel connecting it to the Processor Complex which initiated the request. Non DPR devices must reconnect to the same channel through which the I/O request was originally started. 3380 Extended devices that are driven by MVS/XA and MVS/ESA use Dynamic Path Reconnection.

EBCDIC: Extended Binary Coded Decimal Interchange Code. The code that IBM uses to represent characters and control values on System/370 Processor Complexes. EBCDIC uses the 256 possible 8-bit patterns to represent characters (printable) and control codes (non-printable).

EC MODE: Extended Control Mode. The term used for the microcode which support MVS executing in MVS/XA and MVS/ESA mode. See also **BC MODE**.

ECB: Event Control Block. The MVS control block used to communicate between MVS and application or system modules for timer interventions, Input/Output requests, or other "events" at some future time.

EFLPA: Extended Fixed Link Pack Area. The MVS/XA and MVS/ESA area in Virtual Storage for the "above the line" extension of the Fixed Link Pack Area (FLPA).

EMLPA: Extended Modifiable Link Pack Area. The MVS/XA and MVS/ESA area in Virtual Storage for the "above the line" extension of the Modified Link Pack Area (MLPA).

Enhanced Processor Complex: The term for the 3090 "E" and "S" models which have faster cycle times than the "standard" models and support MVS/ESA.

ENUCLEUS: Extended Nucleus. The MVS/XA and MVS/ESA area in Virtual Storage for the "above the line" extension of the Nucleus.

ENQUE: Modules running under MVS can issue an ENQUE macro to ask for and receive access to a resource (e.g., a data set). ENQUEs are vital to protecting resources but can be a performance bottleneck or cause data integrity problems if the resource is improperly used.

EOV: End of Volume on a data set. EOV is an MVS service that gets control when a program has a read outstanding for more data and the current volume does not have any more data or has a write outstanding and there is no more room to put the data on the current volume. EOV either finds another volume or returns to the program to say it has reached the end of the data set.

EP: Entry Point. Usually of a module.

EPLPA: Extended Pageable Link Pack Area. The MVS/XA and MVS/ESA area in Virtual Storage for the "above the line" extension of the Pageable Link Pack Area (PLPA).

EREP: Environmental Recording and Editing Program. EREP is used to display information saved in the MVS SYS1.LOGREC data set. LOGREC contains information concerning errors and statistics collected by MVS.

ERV: ENQUE Residency Value. The MVS parameter which prevents an address space from being swapped out while it holds an exclusive ENQUE. ERV values tell MVS to try to service an Address Space that is holding a resource that another task needs.

ESDS: Entry Sequenced VSAM Data Set.

ESQA: Extended System Queue Area. The MVS/XA and MVS/ESA area in Virtual Storage for the "above the line" extension of the System Queue Area (SQA).

EXCP: Execute Channel Program. The assembler macro used to request MVS Input Output services is EXCP. A channel program is passed to EXCP to be executed on a specified I/O device. The MVS EXCP modules translate channel programs, and verify channel programs. The completed channel program is passed to the Input/Output Supervisor to complete the I/O operation. The count of the number of EXCPs to a file is the count of the number of physical I/O operations to the file. EXCP counts are usually used for charging or billing for I/O services.

EXCPVR: Execute Channel Program Virtual=REAL. A lower level (less overhead in MVS) of EXCP for which the program has created the channel program containing Central Storage addresses, bypassing the need for channel program conversion.

EXDC: External Data Communicator. The EXDC portion of the 308x Processor Complex that performs I/O operations requested by the MVS in the Processor Complex. When operating in MVS/370 mode, Start I/O and Start I/O Fast Release instructions initiate input or output to a device. When operating in Extended Architecture Start Subchannel instructions initiate input or output to a device. EXDC functions include queueing requests when physical paths are busy and gathering statics for MVS.

Exit: An interface that permits customization of a system or subsystem. An Exit is one or more modules written by the data center and included in MVS program libraries. MVS is notified that the exit is there either by PARMLIB statements or by replacing a "dummy" module. A dummy module is one provided by IBM that is always called, but does no processing. At the specified point of execution the subsystem branches to the exit to perform some function or alteration of normal processing. Exits are preferable to direct modification of MVS because the interface should not change, reducing the maintenance required for customization.

Extended Architecture: Enhancements to System/370 Processor Complexes which include 31-bit virtual and Central Storage addressing and a Dynamic Channel Subsystem.

File: A set of related logical records that can be accessed individually or as a whole. See also **Data Set**.

Fixed Head: The portion of some DASD actuators which can access data without moving the read/write head. Some units, such as the 2305, have all their storage accessible through fixed heads; others, such as 3350, offer an optional fixed head feature for several (two for 3350) cylinders under fixed heads with the rest accessed by movable heads. The 3380 was originally announced with a fixed head option but was not shipped with fixed heads.

FLIH: First Level Interrupt Handler. The name applied to MVS modules that get control from the Processor Complex for External, Supervisor Call, Program Check, Machine Check, and Input/Output interrupts. Most interrupt handlers have secondary modules in MVS called Second Level Interrupt Handlers.

FLPA: Fixed Link Pack Area. A part of MVS Virtual Storage that contains modules that may be used by many different address spaces at once. MVS allows a data center to specify that certain modules from the Link Pack Area should be "fixed" in Central Storage because the module will be accessed so often that the data center does not want MVS to consider paging out the module. FLPA is also used by OEM software for modules that are not designed to move around in Central Storage. See also **PLPA**.

Front-End Processor: A computer used to accept, check, translate, compress, or decompress data before transfering to or from a mainframe for further processing. Most references are to teleprocessing controllers such as the 37x5 Communications Controller.

FRU: Field Replaceable Unit. A part of hardware that can be replaced at the customer's location. In most cases a FRU refers to parts that the IBM Customer Engineer replaces to fix errors in the hardware. As IBM transfers this function to the data center, employees of the data center will be replacing cards and other FRUs.

GDG: Generation Data Group. A special data set naming convention that has MVS append sequence numbers to the name and keep track of generations (father, son, grandfather, etc.).

Gigabyte (Gb): 1,073,741,824 bytes. Two to thirtieth power. The number of bytes that can be addressed with a field 30 bits wide. MVS/XA and MVS/ESA provide 31-bit addressing, or 2 Gigabytes.

GRS: Global Resource Serialization. The IBM facility to pass ENQUE requests from address space to address space in tightly coupled environments and from Processor Complex to Processor Complex for loosely coupled MVS environments.

GTF: Generalized Trace Facility. The name for MVS modules which writes records that trace information from the MVS environment. GTF may be used to trace I/O operations, Supervisor Calls, subsystem (VTAM and VSAM) trace records, and other internal data. The overhead of running GTF *may be* high (up to 20% of the CPU) if the data collected is a large volume.

HASP: Houston Automatic Spooling Priority System. The predecessor to JES2 that was used under Multiprogramming with Variable number of Tasks (MVT). Although JES2 is now used for the name of the subsystem, the messages still have "HASP" as the first bytes of many messages.

HDA: Head Disk Assembly. The portion of Direct Access Storage Devices (DASD) that contain the physical media that has data recorded on surfaces of a spinning disk. HDAs may be hermetically sealed to prevent atmospheric contaminants from damaging the heads and recording surfaces, unlike removable disk drives which attempt to filter air circulated throughout the mechanisms. Oddly the 3380 devices are not completely sealed HDAs.

Head of String (HOS): The first drive of a DASD "string" (one or more devices bolted together and electrically dependent on the HOS) that has the connections to the Control Unit. The HOS supervises and sends commands to all the DASD units in its string. When a HOS can be accessed through more than one control unit, this is called String Switching.

HIPERspace: An address space that can exist under MVS/ESA that contains only data.

Hit Ratio: The result of dividing the number of Input/Output accesses that are "found" in the cache storage of a control unit by those which are not. The result is usually expressed as a percent. When a "hit" occurs, the I/O does not have to go all the way to the drive to read or write the physical block.

HSM: Hierarchical Storage Manager. See **DFHSM**.

ICF: Integrated Catalog Facility. The term used by IBM for the third generation of VSAM catalogs. See also **BCS** and **VVDS**.

IDAW: Indirect Data Address Word. In System/370, the I/O subsystem only accesses Central Storage addresses. An option for CCWs allows the data address field to point to an I/O buffer or to a list of IDAWs which in turn point to pieces of the I/O buffer. The mechanism of IDAWs permits construction of an I/O request which uses what appears to be a contiguous I/O buffer in Virtual Storage but is actually discontiguous due to mapping of virtual pages into Central Storage page frames.

IDCAMS: The IBM utility which reads control statements and performs data set functions such as creation, deletion, cataloging, and uncataloging. IDCAMS also backups and restores VSAM data sets. The contraction IDCAMS is derived from IDC (the message suffix for the modules) and the first letters of Access Method Services.

Initiator: A set of MVS modules to which JES assigns jobs. Each initiator operates in its own address space and takes control of the address space before and after each job step executes.

IML: Initial Microprogram Load. IML is loading the microcode into the Processor Complex to enable the Processor Complex to process instructions. Different microcode is required for different versions of MVS. For example, MVS/370 and MVS/ESA (used for both MVS/XA and MVS/ESA) are IML options on the 309x Processor Complexes. Once a Processor Complex is IMLed, an Initial Program Load (IPL) can be used to load the operating system (e.g., MVS).

IMS: Information Management System. One of IBM's large DB/DC application systems. IMS is used for data center written programs to process transactions entered at teleprocessing terminal. IMS provides the services needed by those applications to retrieve and update data in DL/I data bases and return a response to the terminal which invoked them. IMS modules run in two or more Address Spaces. Applications run in Message Processing regions. IMS control programs run in the IMS Control Region, which is in a separate MVS address space. See also **CICS**.

Interrupt: An interrupt is the System/370 process of suspending a program running on a CPU by the machine hardware and execution of an operating system routine (see FLIH) to deal with the event associated with the interrupt. One example is the I/O completion interrupt. The channel signals the Processor Complex that a channel program's execution has been completed, and the Processor Complex interrupts the program in execution, saves its status, and passes control to the Input/Output Supervisor (IOS) FLIH. IOS checks and processes the information from the I/O request, and transfers control to the MVS dispatcher to dispatch the next task. The interrupted program will be dispatched at its point of interruption when its turn comes in the dispatching order.

I/O: Input/Output. The process of transferring data from Central Storage to a device such as a disk or tape.

IOCP: Input/Output Configuration Program. The MVS program which reads the data center's description of the I/O configuration and writes it to the EXDC. The IOCP is required for the 308x and 309x Processor Complexes. On previous Processor Complexes, the I/O configuration was only described in the operating system.

IOGEN: The term used to describe the I/O configuration to the MVS Input/Output Supervisor. A set of Assembler macros are prepared by the data center which describe the I/O units, the options, and the paths (channels and control units) that are attached to the devices. The input "deck" is the same as the one for IOCP. The output of the Assembler is linked into the Nucleus. MVS is now ready to run. See also **SYSGEN**.

IOS: Input/Output Supervisor. The name of the MVS modules which send channel programs to the Processor Complex I/O subsystem. IOS issues the Start I/O instruction or Start I/O Fast instruction (for MVS/370) or the Start Subchannel instruction (for MVS/XA and MVS/ESA) to begin execution of a channel program. Another part of IOS is the FLIH which is entered when the channel program is completed to perform post-I/O actions. IOS queues requests for later execution if the request cannot be started immediately (e.g., the device is busy with a request from some task in this Processor Complex. In MVS/370, requests are queued on the Logical Channel Queue (LCH) so that MVS can select alternate paths. In MVS/XA and MVS/ESA, requests are queued on the UCB, because the EXDC manages the physical paths.

IPCS: Interactive Problem Control System. The MVS system to inspect data in MVS address space or full system dumps.

IPL: Initial Program Load. The term used when the MVS Operating System is loaded into a Processor Complex.

ISAM: Indexed Sequential Access Method. A very old access method which supports both sequential and direct (random) access by key to records in its files. ISAM has been superceded by VSAM.

ISPF/PDF: Interactive System Productivity Facility/Program Development Facility. The full screen product which drives 3270 class terminals. ISPF contains an editor and many utility programs. ISPF runs under TSO (and VM/CMS). ISPF contains support to facilitate writing applications and developing "dialogs" with 327x terminals.

JCL: Job Control Language. The term used to for a structured language, used by MVS to execute a unit of work (TSO session, batch job, or system task). Batch jobs begin with a JOB card and one or more "steps." The program to be run is specified on an EXEC card. Files are specified on DD (Dataset Definition) statements.

JES: Job Entry Subsystem. The name used for the MVS modules which read batch jobs, interprets their JCL, schedule execution, spool the print and punch output they generate, and finally produces that output at the appropriate destination. JES drives all printers, card readers, and punches attached to an MVS system. JES also supports remote batch workstations over teleprocessing lines. There are two versions of JES. All MVS systems must run either JES2 or JES3.

JES2: Job Entry Subsystem-2. IBM rewrote portions of HASP (a program product under MVT) for MVS and called the new subsystem JES2. We do not know what happened to JES1. Many of the JES2 messages begin with "HASP" which indicates how much of HASP was not re-written for MVS.

JES3: Job Entry Subsystem-3. IBM rewrote portions of ASP (a program product under MVT) for MVS and called the new subsystem JES3. JES3 was designed to loosely couple multiple Processor Complex into a single complex. JES3 processors communicate over CTCAs with one machine being the Global and the remainder being Locals.

Kilobyte (Kb): 1,024 bytes.

KSDS: Key Sequenced VSAM Data Set.

Latency: The time it takes for a rotating Direct Access Storage Devices (DASD) to reach the desired angular position on an I/O device.

Logical Channel Queue (LCQ): A queue of MVS/370 IOS control blocks which represents all physical paths to a set of I/O devices. LCQs are most important in MVS/370 systems. I/Os requests in MVS/370 systems, which cannot be started at once, are queued on the LCQ because MVS/370 could use any path to try to start an I/O operation and the LCQ contains pointers to all possible paths for a device. MVS/XA and MVS/ESA retain the term but delayed I/O requests are queued on the UCB because the Processor Complex channel subsystem selectes the channel from possible paths.

Linkage Editor: The IBM program which takes the output (object code) of assemblers and compilers and builds a load module.

Load Module: A member of a Partitioned Data Set which is created by the Linkage Editor. The Load Module is read by MVS Program Fetch into virtual storage for execution. Load modules contain relocation instructions (used by the Linkage Editor and Program Fetch), the machine instructions that make up the program, and other control information. A Load Module may or may not be a complete program. Some Systems Analysts create subroutines that must be linked together to operate successfully.

Lock: A term used for MVS macros and supervisor services that serialize access certain MVS resources in a tightly coupled multiprocessing environment. A lock is a word in Central Storage whose value is changed only with special instructions. Two types of locking is performed. Spin locks that are not available result in the program looping until the lock is free. Suspend locks place the program in a queue waiting for the resource to become free.

LOGREC: SYS1.LOGREC. The MVS data set that contains records for errors and statistics.

Loosely Coupled: See **Coupling**.

LPA: Link Pack Area. The MVS Virtual Storage which holds modules that can be used by multiple Address Spaces at the same time. The LPA is created from the SYS1.PLPA data set. See also **PLPA, MPLA,** and **FLPA**.

LPAR: Logical PARtition. The VM/XA feature that allows a 309x Processor Complex to be logically partitioned to divide up the Processor Complex for multiple System Control Programs. MVS (or other operating systems) can be IPLed in those logical partitions.

LPSW: Load Program Status Word. The System/370 instruction that forces a "state change" of the CPU, usually for the purpose of transferring CPU control to another program.

LSQA: Local System Queue Area. Virtual Storage in the Private Area where MVS control blocks are built that are only needed for this Address Space. One example of the type of control block is the address space's Segment Table and the Page Tables. These control blocks are usually fixed in Central Storage.

Megabyte (Mb): 1,048,576 bytes. Two raised to the twentieth power.

MCH: Machine Check Handler. The collective names of the MVS modules which obtain control when the Processor Complex detects an error that it cannot fix without damage. The MCH attempts to overcome the error by varying off some logical part of the Processor Complex or by abnormally terminating some address space. One part of MCH which is used in Operator documentation is **Alternate CPU Recovery** (ACR) which is the modules that vary CPUs offline that have failed.

MCS: Multiple Console Support. The name of the MVS modules which support 327x consoles which communicate directly with

MVS or JES. One group of modules in MCS is the Device Independent Display Operator Console Support (DIDOCS) which actually handle the 327x display terminals.

MFT: Multiprocessing with a Fixed number of Tasks. One of the first System/360 operating systems. Central Storage was divided up into "partitions" of fixed sizes. Jobs would be assigned to partitions at least as large as the REGION= requested in their JCL. MFT was replaced by OS/VS1. See also **MVT.**

Microcode: The lowest level of instructions for a Processor Complex, I/O control unit, or device. For example, the 308x family has 108-bit microinstructions which have no resemblance whatsoever to the instruction set of the System/370. This "microprogram" implements the System/370 instruction set that is defined in the Principles of Operation. See also **IML.**

Microsecond: One-millionth of a second.

MIH: Missing Interrupt Handler. The MVS modules that detect and notify the console operator if an I/O operation does not terminate in a period of time.

Millisecond (ms): One-thousandth of a second.

MIPS: Millions of Instructions per Second. A commonly used measure of CPU power. The measure fluctuates widely depending on the workload being run and the individual announcing the measurement. Some detractors use Meaningless Indicator of Processor Speed or Marketing's Indication of Product Superiority. It has been noted that measuring the speed of a Processor Complex is like counting the number of steps taken in a foot race and the winner is the one who takes the most steps. In defense of MIPS, there is no standard method of measuring the capability of a CPU.

MLPA: Modified Link Pack Area. The Virtual Storage in MVS which is reloaded at every IPL, rather than just IPLs in which the CLPA option was specified. MVS looks in MLPA before PLPA so it is a good place to store new modules to test or to keep separate from MVS modules with the same name.

MP: Multiprocessor. More than one CPU in a Processor Complex.

ms: Millisecond (1/1000th of a second). Milliseconds are usually used to measure I/O service times.

MTW: Mean Time to Wait. A term used by the Systems Resource Manager (SRM) to group one or more tasks and attempt to give each task an equal share of resources (e.g., CPU, Central Storage, and I/O).

Multiplexer Channel: A part of a Processor Complex channel sub-system that can control a number of I/O devices simultaneously.

Multiprocessing: Refers to a technique or computer system capable of supporting more than one concurrently executing instruction stream. Multiprocessing really does more than one instruction at once; multiprogramming merely gives the illusion of doing so.

Multiprocessor: A Processor Complex having more than one CPU with a single Central Storage.

Multiprogramming: Refers to a technique or computer system capable of sharing a single CPU's instruction stream with more than one thread of execution by periodically interrupting an executing program and allowing another to continue.

Multitasking: Often used as a synonym for "multiprogramming," but in the MVS sense, specifically refers to the condition of having more than TCB within a single address space.

MVS: Multiple Virtual Storage.

MVS/SP Version 2: See **MVS/XA.**

MVS/SP Version 3: See **MVS/ESA.**

MVS/ESA: MVS/SP Version 3. The version of MVS/SP designed to run on System/370 Processor Complexes with ESA/370 microcode loaded in the Processor Complex.

MVS/XA: MVS/SP Version 2. The version of MVS/SP designed to run on System/370 Processor Complexes with Extended Architecture or ESA/370 microcode loaded in the Processor Complex.

MVS/370: MVS/SP Version 1. A generic term for all versions of MVS which do not support Extended Architecture.

MVS 3.8: The "free" version of MVS. This term almost always implies the latest version of the free MVS base code with all free SUs (selectable units) applied. MVS 3.8 is also the "base" of all MVS versions. When you receive MVS/ESA, you are running MVS 3.8 with lots of additions!

MVT: Multiprocessing with a Variable number of Tasks. One of the early Operating System for the System/360 Processor Complex. MVT supported multitasking. Regions were variable size and not set by the operations staff. See also **MFT**.

NIP: Nucleus Initialization Program. The part of MVS that begins the initialization of MVS.

NJE: Network Job Entry. A JES term used to describe the movement of jobs and data from Processor Complex to Processor Complex. Unlike operating systems can be at either end.

Nonvolatile Storage: A part of the 3990 model 3 control unit which saves data that the control unit has told MVS is successfully written. See also DASD Fast Write.

Nucleus: That part of a system control program which is always resident in Central Storage. The nucleus forms the central core of the "personality" of the operating system and is often where the ultimate security of that system lies. (Other literature calls this the "kernel" of an operating system.)

OEM: Original Equipment Manufacturer. The term applies to non-IBM software and hardware suppliers such as AMDAHL, Computer Associates, SYNCSORT, Morino Associates, CANDLE Incorporated, and many, many others.

OS: Operating System. Operating Systems provide service routines which make the task of program development easier. IBM named its multiprogramming operating system for the System/360 "OS," and some people persist in calling "MVS" by the old name, "OS." The old IBM "OS" systems were usually qualified to distinguish their memory management philosophy: OS/MFT, OS/MVT, OS/VS1, OS/VS2.

Page: A group of 4,096 bytes with contiguous addresses in storage by which the System/370 DAT hardware manages virtual memory. In general, unqualified use of the term "page" refers to such a block of memory in a virtual address space; "page frame" refers to the space a virtual page may occupy when resident in Central Storage, and "page slot" to the space it may occupy on secondary, backing storage (usually DASD).

Paged In: An address space that is resident in Central Storage. "Resident" means that some of the address spaces pages are in Central Storage. Rarely are all pages for one address space in Processor Complex.

Paged Out: An address space that is not resident in Central Storage but on Auxiliary Storage.

Page Fault: When a task references a virtual address which is not currently assigned to a Central Storage address via the DAT tables the hardware interrupts processing by causing a special type of program check called a page fault. MVS gets control and suspends the task. If the page is on Auxiliary Storage, the desired page is scheduled to be read in from Auxiliary Storage. After the page is successfully in Central Storage, the user is then allowed to continue as if nothing had happened. If the page has been allocated but never used, MVS allocates a Central Storage page frame.

Page Protection: MVS/XA implemented Page Protection for certain common areas to improve the Segment Protection hardware of MVS/370. A bit in the Page Table Entry for a page is set to prevent any instruction from storing data in the page regardless of the protect key of the program attempting to do the store. Page Protect improves MVS reliability by protected portions of MVS from itself. If storing is attempted, the task is ABENDed.

Page Table: The area shared by MVS and the DAT feature of System/370 to implement Virtual Storage to Central Storage conversion.

Parity: An extra bit added to characters to help spot errors in transmission and reception. The parity bit is set to make the total number of "1"s in the character odd or even (depending on whether odd or even parity has been specified). If a character is received with the wrong total of "1"s, including the parity bit, then the receiving system knows it has found an error. Note that parity checking can detect single-bit errors, but double-bit errors might pass undetected without help from other error detection architectures.

PARMLIB: SYS1.PARMLIB. A Partitioned Data Set, usually in 80 byte card-image format, which holds parameters. MVS uses the SYS1.PARMLIB data set to hold members that define execution options for MVS subsystems (e.g., VTAM and JES).

PCI: Program Controlled Interrupt. A System/370 architecture component that allows a CCW string to indicate that the channel should disconnect and try to allow the CPU to change the CCW string *while the channel is still processing*. The theory was that the CPU could alter channel programs to an advantage before the channel needed a specific CCW. It was used for Program Fetch in MVS/370. It is not widely used in MVS/XA.

PDS: Partitioned Data Set. An MVS data set composed of a "directory" and "members." The directory is at the start of the data set and is a preformatted area that contains pointers to the members. Each member could be considered a sequential file (in fact members are terminated with an "end of file" marker). PDSs generally reside on DASD but may be transported in "unloaded" format by the IEBCOPY and IEHMOVE utilities.

PER: Program Environment Recording. The System/370 feature that is used by the MVS Generalized Trace Facility (and VM TRACE and CCWTRACE) modules.

PID: Program Information Department. The IBM division that gathers MVS programs and mails them to the companies that license MVS.

PLPA: Pageable Link Pack Area. An area of Virtual Storage which holds modules used by more than one address space at a time. MVS initialization reads all of SYS1.PLPA (common, reenterable modules such as TSO, VSAM, JES, and access method modules) into Virtual Storage (if CLPA is specified) and pages all of it out to the PLPA page data set. Any common page can be read in directly from the page data set without relocating the module. PLPA is usually three to four megabytes in size.

PPT: Program Properties Table. The MVS data area that contains information about programs; the PPT is used by the LOADER function.

Private Area: Virtual Storage which a job, system task, or TSO session does not share with other Address Spaces.

Problem State: Problem State exists when a bit is on in the Program Status Word (PSW). When that bit is off, the program is running in Supervisor State. A program in Problem State cannot issue the machine instructions designated in the Principles of Operation as "privileged" (e.g., I/O instructions). See Supervisor State.

Program Fetch: The generic name of MVS modules that load modules into Virtual Storage. Program Fetch locates the program in a Partitioned Data Set (usually STEPLIB/JOBLIB DD cards or LINKLST libraries), determines where the module can be loaded (above or below the line), allocates Virtual Storage to hold the program, reads the module from DASD, and "relocates" any addresses imbedded in the module by adding the starting location of the program to area in the program.

PSA: Prefixed Save Area or Prefixed Storage Area. The first 4,096 bytes of Central Storage. Values in the PSA usually have fixed, hardware-defined uses. One example is an I/O instruction. MVS stores the address of the channel program to be executed in the word at location 72 (decimal). The channel hardware knows where to start looking for the CCWs. A second example is the address of the CVT: 16 (decimal).

PSW: Program Status Word. The PSW is an 8-byte control register which contains the address of the next instruction to be executed and information about the task (e.g., problem or supervisor state, protection key, etc.).

PTF: Program Temporary Fix. A modification to IBM-supplied programming supplied in machine-readable form. Most PTFs fix MVS bugs (program errors). IBM has been know to introduce function with a PTF.

PUT: Program Update Tape. A set of Program Temporary Fixes (PTFs) periodically sent to registered users of IBM programs or operating systems.

QSAM: Queued Sequential Access Method. An MVS Access Method used to read and write sequential files. QSAM creates (at OPEN) and manages physical buffers for logical records passed to the QSAM read and write routines. Many application files, even today, are maintained with QSAM. QSAM is the same as "SAM or "SAM-E."

RACF: Resource Access Control Facility. An IBM program product which controls user access to resources such as data sets and TSO Logon IDs.

RAM: Random Access Memory. Another term for Central Storage. RAM is usually considered to be accessible for both reading and writing. See also ROM.

RAS: Reliability, Availability, and Serviceability. The term IBM uses for most of the improvements of MVS over other operating systems.

RCT: Region Control Task. The name of the MVS modules which control swap in and swap out of an address space. The term "region" is of historical significance and comes from MVT. MVT had a "SWAP" feature for TSO users and a "Roll in/Roll Out" feature for batch.

Read Hit: The term used when a block is to be read from a device and the record is available in cache, thus saving the time required to read the block from the slower magnetic medium. See also **Write Hit and cache**.

Read Miss: The term used when an attempted read cannot be satisfied from cache memory and requires a physical access to the "slower" memory (Central Storage or DASD). "Read Misses" take longer than "Read Hits." In most cases the microcode places portions of the area being read in the cache to anticipate subsequent requests. See also **Write Miss and cache**.

Real Storage: The read/write RAM inside a Processor Complex. IBM uses the terms Central Storage, Random Access Memory,

Core Storage, Main Storage, and Processor Storage interchangeably. Central Storage may become the most prevalent term.

Reconnect: When a DASD device processes certain CCWs (e.g., Set Sector), the channel is released while the device completes the CCW. Reconnect is the term used for the device regaining control of the channel to complete the channel program.

Record: A collection of related bytes that is the smallest unit of a file. Logical records are the size the Systems Analyst specified in creating the file. Physical records are the size of the block physically transmitted to the device.

Reentrant: The property of a program or subroutine which allows more than one thread of execution to use a single copy of the program in storage. In System/370, reentrant modules do not allocate static storage in fixed locations but use the GETMAIN and FREEMAIN services to obtain work areas for each thread of execution that invokes it. A reentrant module is also serially reusable.

Reliability: The probability that a system will not fail during any given period of time. Highly reliable systems rarely fail and if they do fail, the time to recover is relatively short. See also **Availability**.

RJE: Remote Job Entry. Sending data from a remote terminal to a mainframe for batch processing by MVS. Current MVS architecture supports Network Job Entry (NJE), which is a better system for file and job transfer.

RMF: Resource Measurement Facility. An MVS Program Product which gathers information about utilization of hardware and software resources and writes SMF records. RMF consists of modules for a Started System Task (data collector), modules to display real time information on TSO 327x terminals, and batch modules (postprocessor) which formats reports from RMF records.

RMODE: Residency Mode. A parameter passed to the Linkage Editor, and a bit in the directory of a load module which tells Program Fetch where in Virtual Storage a program may be loaded. RMODE=ANY indicates the program may be loaded anywhere in Virtual Storage. RMODE=24 indicates the program must be loaded into Virtual Storage with addresses below 16 Mb.

ROM: Read Only Memory. Area in the Processor Complex that can be read but not written to. Usually refers to the area microcode is loaded. See also RAM.

RPS: Rotational Position Sensing. The ability of a DASD device to disconnect from the channel while certain CCWs are executed. RPS was first introduced for the 3330 Set Sector command. The 3330 released the channel which started the I/O request until the disk reaches the angular position ("sector") specified in the CCW. The device then attempted to "reconnect" to the channel so it may execute the next CCW (usually the Search) in its channel program. All subsequent DASD architectures support RPS.

RPS Miss: Rotational Position Sensing Miss. When a DASD device has released the channel and cannot regain control in time to read/write a block, the device must wait an entire revolution before it can try again. The I/O operation is penalized approximately 17 ms for each RPS miss. RPS Misses start becoming a problem at 30% channel busy for MVS/370 and 40% to 60% channel busy with MVS/XA and MVS/ESA.

RSM: Real Storage Manager. The name of the MVS modules which control Central Storage. RSM manages unused page frames, assigning them for page faults. When it runs low, RSM "steals" frames from Address Spaces nominated by the SRM. RSM requests the Auxiliary Storage Manager (ASM) to move pages in or out of Central Storage.

SAM: Sequential Access Method. The name of the collection of access method modules which process sequential data sets. These modules are linked to when a sequential data set is opened and a GET or PUT macro is executed.

SAM/E: Sequential Access Method — Enhanced. The IBM program product supplement which offers improved performance for sequential access I/O requests. SAM/E has been included free in MVS for some time.

Seek: One of the CCWs for IBM DASD. SEEK commands move the read/write head to the cylinder specified in its argument. IBM

DASD channel programming conventions require all I/O requests to begin with a SEEK, even those for devices without moving heads (e.g., 2305). Some coders discovered that SEEKs were not absolutely necessary, but IBM has begun to enforce the rule. SEEK disconnect from the channel for pre-3380 devices. The 3880 processes the SEEK and Set Sector at the same time for 3380 devices.

Segment Protection: A MVS/370 facility which adds a bit in the Segment Table Entry to indicate that the segment is read-only. Attempts by any task to store into a protected page will fail with a program check. In MVS/XA and MVS/ESA, segment protection has been replaced by page protection.

Selector Channel: A part of a Processor Complex channel subsystem that can only process one device at a time.

Serviceability: How quickly a system may be repaired. Serviceability reflectes how little MVS is out of service for maintenance interruptions.

SIGP: Signal Processor. A MVS/370 instruction which allows a CPU to force another (or itself) to perform one of a number of operations. The MVS External Interrupt Handler is programmed to enter a subroutine specified by the signalling CPU. Examples of the types of signalling done by MVS is to dispatch tasks in other CPUs, pass emergency failure information, and start and stop CPUs.

SIO: Start I/O. A System/370 instruction used to tell a channel to begin executing a channel program. The address of the I/O device is passed in the instruction, and the address of the first CCW in the channel program is passed in the PSA. "SIO" is used to refer to both the SIO and the SIOF (Start I/O Fast Release) instructions.

SLIH: Second Level Interrupt Handler. The name of the MVS modules that get control after the First Level Interrupt Handler routines have processed an interrupt.

SLIP: Serviceability Level Indication Processing. An MVS tracing facility.

SMF: System Management Facility. The MVS data collection facility for information about executing tasks (e.g., batch jobs). The SMF records are written out to special system data sets whose names are of the form "SYS1.MANx."

SMP/E: System Modification Program/Extended. The IBM programs that maintain MVS and other program products. SMP maintains a data base to record all maintenance on the system and what dependencies exist between the maintenance. SMP also maintains holding libraries for system maintenance which has been received from a PTF tape but not yet made a permanent part of the system.

SMS: System Managed Storage. The MVS/ESA implementation of storage management that implements allocation by data center specifications, not JCL.

SP: System Product. A designation added to certain product names when they have become fully supported and engineered. As large as IBM is, it develops much software of an experimental nature and is sometimes forced to release the experiments under pressure from their clients. IBM has attached "SP" to product names to indicate their commitment to support the product for some time to come. Examples are "MVS/SP" and "VM/SP."

SPOOL: An acronym for Simultaneous Peripheral Operation On-Line. The term originated with HASP under MVT. The term Spool Volumes refers to DASD volumes which contain JES SPOOL data sets. JES uses DASD to minimize program delays while a program waits for card readers, card punches, and printers.

SQA: System Queue Area. The MVS virtual storage used to create control blocks which must be both fixed and globally addressable. Examples of control blocks are the Address Space Control Blocks (ASCBs), which identify the active address spaces. SQA is fixed in Central Storage as it is allocated. Only Authorized modules may allocate storage in SQA.

SRM: System Resources Manager. The SRM monitors resources used by address spaces and takes actions based on the Installation Performance Specifications (IPS). SRM monitors percent CPU busy, page fault rate and other system statistics and attempts to keep them within the values set in IPS. The system Multiprogramming Level (MPL) is changed up or down by swapping READY users in or out. The IPS contains parameters set by the installation to control this process.

SSCH: Start Subchannel. A machine instruction for System/370 Processor Complexes running in MVS/XA or MVS/ESA mode. SSCH causes the CPU to signal the channels to begin execution of a channel program on the device associated with the subchannel address specified in the instruction.

SSD: Solid State Device. An I/O device which emulates a 2305-2 or a 3380 in which data is saved in Random Access Memory rather than rotating magnetic media.

SSI: Subsystem Interface. A MVS architecture that allows subsystems such as JES to start and stop processing requests from some or all address spaces.

String: A group of two to eight I/O units that are attached as a single unit. Each unit may have one or more logical units.

Subsystem: A defined group of MVS modules which control access to their Address Space through the Subsystem Communications Vector Table (SSCVT) and processes request from the IEFSSREQ macro. MASTER, JES, IMS are formal subsystems. The term is also applied to groups of modules (e.g., CICS, ASM, 3850 Mass Storage Subsystem) that perform specific functions.

Supervisor State: Indicated by a bit being off in the PSW. If the bit is on, the currently executing program is running in Problem State. If the bit is off, it is in "Supervisor State." A program in Supervisor State can issue any machine instruction supported on the computer — I/O instructions, state changes such as Load Problem Status Words, and other "privileged" instructions. See Problem State.

STARTIO: The name of the assembler macro used by I/O DRIVERs to call the MVS Input/Output Supervisor to start an I/O operation. STARTIO can only be used when running in key 0, supervisor state. The caller must supply an IOSB (I/O Supervisor Block) which points to a channel program that does not require translation. An SRB is scheduled back to the requesting address space when the I/O completes.

STC: Started Task Control. One of the types of address spaces in MVS. The address space is created by an operator START command.

SVC: Supervisor Call. A System/370 machine instruction which causes a state change machine interruption. The current PSW is stored at a fixed location in the PSA and the Supervisor Call New PSW is loaded from another PSA location. The Supervisor Call First Level Interrupt Handler gets control and enters the MVS routine designated by the operand (a number from 0 to 255) specified on the SVC instruction. SVCs allow a Problem State program to invoke a function which runs in Supervisor State; thus SVC gives controlled access to supervisor mode.

SYSGEN: System Generation. The process used to customize MVS to the data centers requirements. Assembler macro statements are prepared to specify options for the system. The file of macros is input to the Assembler in the "stage one" job, which produces as its output a large job stream. This job stream, is called "stage two." The stage two job updates MVS system libraries (e.g., replaces the MVS Nucleus in SYS1.NUCLEUS). Very few MVS installations do full SYSGENs any more. See also **IOGEN**.

SYSRES: System Residence. The DASD volume that contains some or all of the MVS modules.

System/370: Any Processor Complex which supports the architecture of MVS. The architecture is defined in the IBM publication IBM System/370 Principles of Operation (e.g., GA22-7000 for MVS/370).

TCB: Task Control Block. The MVS control block which contains all information about a single task (e.g., a program.)

Terabyte (Tb): 1,073,741,824 bytes. Two raised to the fortieth power.

Tightly coupled: See **Coupling**.

TSO: Time Sharing Option. IBM's subsystem for interactive access to MVS services was introduced with MVT. In those days almost all processing was accomplished by batch jobs. TSO was a very expensive (in terms of Central Storage and other resources) and was not used by every MVT facility. MVS removed many of the limitations and TSO is no longer an option. TSO is required and used by every MVS installation. Most MVS installations use ISPF as the driver for TSO functions because ISPF is much easier and more productive for end users.

UCB: Unit Control Block. The MVS control block that describes each I/O Unit. Normally there is one and only one UCB for each device. Exceptions occur with multiple exposure devices (e.g., 2305 and 3880-x1) which have one UCB per exposure. The Input/Output Supervisor (IOS) inspects and modifies the UCB. UCBs are created by the IOGEN process. The UCB also points to several other control blocks or extensions.

UCW: Unit Control Word. The special register in the channel subsystem that stores the status of each I/O request as it progresses from start to completion. This is the hardware equivalent of the UCB. Some of the information kept in the UCW are the number of bytes yet to be transferred to or from the device as part of the operation of the current CCW. UCWs may be shared (e.g., 3420 tape devices) or non-shared (all the rest).

UIC: Unreferenced Interval Count. The count of the number of seconds since a page has been accessed. The system wide UIC is used by SRM to determine the "stress" on Central Storage.

UP: Uniprocessor. A Processor Complex with only one Central Processing Unit.

Upward Compatible: MVS has maintained the philosophy that if an application program runs in MVS at one level, it will run at the *next higher level*, providing it does not violate "application interfaces."

VIO: Virtual Input/Output. One of the most expensive DASD operation is to allocate small data sets. Most work is done finding space, creating VTOC entries, and making entries in the catalog. VIO was introduced to replace these expensive with "inexpansive" paging support for small data sets. MVS simulates DASD I/O devices in Auxiliary Storage; VIO is part of the paging subsystem. The application program allocates a VIO file with JCL UNIT= parameters (established by the data center) and proceeds exactly as if it was using a real DASD file. The program opens the data set using any non-VSAM access method. The access method builds channel programs and issues the EXCP assembler macro. EXCP notices that the request is being made against a virtual unit and transfers control to the VIO processor.

Virtual: Not real. If you can kick it with your foot, it is real; if you cannot kick it, it is virtual. System/370 hardware supports Virtual Storage. The 3850 Mass Storage Subsystem supports virtual 3330 DASD.

Virtual Storage: The mechanism by which the hardware of a Processor Complex makes a correspondence between logical addresses and either Central Storage addresses or disk storage. Virtual Storage does not need to have a page of Central Storage to hold it — hence the term "virtual."

Volume: A portion of data that is a recognizable unit to the data center and the user community, such as a DASD volume or a tape volume.

V=R: Virtual=Real. A JCL parameter which informs MVS that the Virtual Storage assigned to this address space must match, one for one, the Central Storage assigned to this address space. V=R address spaces must have all of their REGION= space allocated from Central Storage at the time the address space is started. The data center specifies how much V=R space is to be allowed in SYS1.PARMLIB member IEASYSxx. If the value is over specified, Central Storage page frames are wasted. If the value is under specified, the system must be IPLed to specify more V=R space.

VSAM: Virtual Storage Access Method. An MVS access method for DASD data sets which supports entry-sequenced, relative record, and key-sequenced files. VSAM replaces the ISAM access method. VSAM is clearly the access method of choice from IBM. The VSAM volume pooling considerations (until MVS/ESA and SMS the data center needed to purchase OEM software to eliminate the need to specify volume serial numbers when allocating VSAM), recovery considerations, and performance considerations make VSAM a difficult access method to understand and use. The benefits outweigh the difficulties.

VSM: Virtual Storage Manager. The name assigned to the MVS modules which allocate and free Virtual Storage in response to program requests using the GETMAIN and FREEMAIN macros. VSM supports 255 "subpools." The subpool number indicates the area to which the storage is assigned (e.g., subpool 245 will be assigned in SQA subpool 0 will be assigned in the user private area). Central Storage page frames are not allocated when Virtual Storage is allocated. Central Storage page frames are allocated when a module tries to store information into the virtual address. Thus, over allocating Virtual Storage is not necessarily bad.

VSPC: Virtual Storage Personal Computing. An IBM subsystem which supports timesharing under MVS and VS1. VSPC is designed to support multiple users from a single address space and therefore save resources expended for timesharing. Individual user programs and storage are saved in VSAM data sets. Functions (e.g., compilers, edit, submit, and data set maintenance) provided are more limited than TSO provides. VSPC is not widely used with MVS.

VS2: Virtual Storage/Two. Another name for Multiple Virtual Storage (MVS). VS2 was also the name used for SVS. IBM seems to consider both SVS and MVS to be the virtual storage implementation of MVT. See also **OS**.

VTAM: Virtual Telecommunications Access Method. The IBM subsystem which controls local and remote terminals for application programs or allows communication VTAM supports Systems Network Architecture for MVS.

VTOC: Volume Table of Contents. An area on each DASD volume which contains data set names and pointers to all extents of all data sets (including itself) on the volume. The VTOC may contain records which describe free space available on the volume unless the VTOC is "indexed" in which case free space is maintained in another special data area (VVDS). The VTOC can be positioned anywhere on the DASD surface and its starting point is located by reading cylinder zero, head zero, record three. VTOCs are not used with System Managed Storage DASD volumes.

VVDS: VSAM Volume Data Set. Each volume that is under the control of DF/EF or DFP VSAM catalogs contain a VVDS. The VVDS contains information about VSAM or non-VSAM (with System Managed Storage) data sets on the volume.

Wait State: It is possible for MVS to stop communicating with the outside world. When MVS stops moving tapes, printers and DASD it is said to be in a "Wait State." The wait may be "disabled" or "enabled." A disabled wait exists when the PSW contains bits to disable all interrupts and the address portion contains a wait state code. One example of a disabled wait state occurs during IPL. If MVS cannot find any consoles that are defined and usable, MVS will cause the processor to enter a disabled Wait State. If MVS has no work to do, it enters an enabled wait state. An enabled wait state exists when the PSW instruction address is all zeros, all interrupts are enabled and the "wait state" bit is on. The operator can issue commands, but nothing happens. This condition may be caused by certain JES commands ($P for JES2) which prevent all new work from starting. It may also be caused by one or more vital MVS subsystems (e.g., VTAM or JES) abnormally terminating.

Working Set: MVS SRM routines calculate the amount of Central Storage that an address space needs to execute. The value is not exact (SRM can not predict what an address space will require). The value changes with the load in the system and the type of work done in the address space. The value is used in page in, page out, and swap decisions.

Write Hit: Refers to the situation where a record is written to a cache device and the record is already in the cache. The cache version of the record is overlaid, and the record is or is not written to the target depending on the cache management algorithm. See also **Read Hit** and **cache**.

Write Miss: Refers to the situation where a record is written to a cache device and the record is not in the cache. The record is written to the target depending on the cache management algorithm. See also **Read Miss** and **cache**.

WTO: Write To Operator. The MVS assembler macro that issues messages to be displayed on the Operator Console.

WTOR: Write To Operator with Reply. The MVS assembler macro which provides the function of displaying a message to the operator and returning an operator-supplied reply back to the program that sent the message. The program has the option of waiting for the reply or continuing processing. (The wait is accomplished with the WAIT assembler macro.)

XA: Extended Architecture. MVS/XA introduced the ability to address two gigabytes (31 bit addressing) of virtual and Central Storage, improved I/O processing, and improved the Reliability, Serviceability, and Availability of the operating system.

XMS: Cross Memory Services. Also abbreviated "CMS" and "XMS" (to prevent confusion with the VM/Conversational Monitoring System).

24-Bit: The mode in which only 16 Mb of Central Storage or Virtual Storage may be addressed because only the 24 bits of any address are used. See also **Below the Line** and **AMODE.**

31-Bit: The mode in which 2 Gigabytes of Central Storage or Virtual Storage may be addressed because 31 bits of any address are used. See also **Above the Line** and **AMODE.**

B

DASD Statistics

The following tables of DASD statistics list representative IBM DASD devices that attach to the System/370. The first table contains the capacity statistics. The table includes bytes per actuator and not bytes per physical drive as you may see with vendor tables of this type. With the increasing variety of devices, bytes per physical drive becomes meaningful only to the data center operation as it responds to user needs and acquires the megabytes of storage required for the least cost analysis and acceptable performance.

The second table lists the performance statistics for representative DASDs. The most interesting aspect of this table is the comparison of the seek and response time differences between the generations of DASD.

Tables 3, 4, and 5 show information about the block sizes of selected DASD. The reader will be surprised that your "big" 3380 may not be very big if you select the wrong block size.

The reader is cautioned to remember the end of file marker which is a single "count" record with a data length of zeros. If a track is filled with data and an end of file is written, this eight-byte record must be placed on the next track. Take the example from Table 3 of a PDS directory on 3380. If you specify 46 directory blocks (the number per 3380 track), you would expect the entire directory to fit on a single track. It does. The end of file, however, is on the next track. In the case of a PDS, this is not very important. In the case of a file that you would expect to perfectly fit on one 3380 track, it will require two tracks.

The last tables show information about the hardware structure of selected DASD. Complete information on these devices can be obtained from the device description manuals. Examples are: *IBM 3880*

Storage Control Models 1, 2, 3, and 4 Description Manual (GA26-1661), *IBM 3380 Direct Access Storage Description and User's Guide* (GA26-1664), *IBM 3375 Direct Access Storage Description and User's Guide* (GA26-1166), *3350 Access Storage Models A2* (GX20-1983), *3375 Direct Access Storages* (GA26-1666), *3330 Series Disk Storage* (GX20-1920), *IBM 3380 Direct Access Storage Introduction* (GC26-4491), and others.

Table 1
DASD Capacity Statistics[1]

Device Type	Actuators per Unit	HDA	Bytes per Actuator	Bytes per Track	Tracks per Cylinder	Cylinders per Volume
2311	1	1	7,250,000	3,625	10	200
2314	2	1	29,176,000	7,294	20	200
2321	N/A		400,000,000	2,000	20	200,000
3330-1	2	1	100,018,280	13,030	19	404
3330-11	2	1	200,036,560	13,030	19	808
3340(35)	2	2	34,944,768	8,368	12	348
3340(70)	2	2	69,889,536	8,368	12	696
3344	2	2	279,558,144	8,368	12	2784
3350	2	1	317,498,850	19,069	30	555
3375	2	2	409,868,928	35,616 *	12	959
3380 AA4 B04	4	2	630,243,900	47,476 *	15	885
3380 AD4 BD4	4	2	630,243,900	47,476 *	15	885
3380 AE4 BE4	4	2	1,260,487,800	47,476 *	15	1,770
3380 AJ4 BJJ	4	2	630,243,900	47,476 *	15	885
3380 AK4 BKJ	4	2	1,890,731,700	47,476 *	15	2,655

* The largest block supported by MVS access methods is 32,760 bytes. The user must write at least two physical blocks on each track.

---

1. Permission is granted to make one copy of this appendix to hang in your work space. Printed from Bob Johnson's *MVS: Concepts and Facilities*, McGraw Hill, New York, NY 10011, 1989. ISBN 0-07-032673-8

Table 2
DASD Performance Statistics[2]

Device Type	Average Latency (ms)	Minimum Seek (ms)	Average Seek (ms)	Maximum Seek (ms)	Data Transfer Rate (bytes/sec)
2311	12.50	25	75	135	136,000
2314	12.50	25	60	130	312,000
2321	12.50	95	173	600	55,000
3330-1	8.33	10	30	55	806,000
3330-11	8.33	10	30	55	806,000
3340	10.10	10	25	50	885,000
3344	10.10	10	25	50	885,000
3350	8.33	10	25	50	1,198,000
3375	10.10	4	19	38	1,859,000
3380 AA4 B04	8.33	3	16	30	3,000,000
3380 AD4 BD4	8.33	3	15	28	3,000,000
3380 AE4 BE4	8.33	3	17	31	3,000,000
3380 AJ4 BJ4	8.33	2	12	21	3,000,000
3380 AK4 BK4	8.33	2	16	29	3,000,000

Effect of Blocksize on Space Utilization

Tables 3 and 4 give the reader an idea of the effect of the physical blocksize on the amount of space that is actually used. The first one gives the number of blocks that can be placed on various DASD tracks. The second shows block sizes and percent of space actually used. In some cases, you cannot control the block size — PDS directory entries and VTOC records.[3] Where you can decide the physical block size, you are urged to select the largest practical size. The

2. Permission is granted to make one copy of this appendix to hang in your work space. Printed from Bob Johnson's *MVS: Concepts and Facilities*, McGraw Hill, New York, NY 10011, 1989. ISBN 0-07-032673-8
3. Remember that the PDS directory is 256-byte blocks for each directory entry even if the block size of the library is 20,000 bytes! For VTOC entries, each physical block is 140 bytes — 44 of which is a separate hardware key!

column for 3380 devices is for all 3380 models. The track size for every model is the same.

The following tables were calculated by simple multiplication. For example, take the case of 800-byte records on a 3380 volume. The number of 800-byte blocks that will fit onto a 3380 track is 36 (from the component description manual for the 3380). Multiply by 800 bytes to get 28,800 actual data bytes stored on the track. Divide by 47,476 bytes per track if the track was filled. The result is displayed in line one of Table 3 — 60.66% of the track is usable.

Use these techniques to evaluate the next generation of DASD after you have evaluated the average block size of the data sets in your data center. The exercise will tell you exactly how the new devices will benefit you.

Table 3
Selective Small Physical Blocks[4]

	3350	3375	3380
Number of 800-byte records/trk:	19	30	36
% of volume used: (no key)	78.94	67.39	60.66
No. of 512-byte records	20	40	46 *
% of volume used: (no key)	53.70	57.51	49.61
No. of 256-byte PDS directory entries:	36	43	46 *
% of volume used: (8-byte key)	48.33	31.31	24.80
No. of 140-byte VTOC records:	47	51	53
% of volume used: (44-byte key)	34.51	20.06	15.63

* This is not an error. You get the same number (46) of 512 byte records with no separate key as you do with 256 byte records with an eight byte key.

---

4. Permission is granted to make one copy of this appendix to hang in your work space. Printed from Bob Johnson's *MVS: Concepts and Facilities*, McGraw Hill, New York, NY 10011, 1989. ISBN 0-07-032673-8

Table 4
Selective Physical Block Sizes[5]

| Block Size | % of Space available actually used | | | |
	3330	3350	3375	3380
80	37	30	17	14
3024	93	95	85	83
4096	94	86	92	86
6233	96	98	88	92
13030	100	68	73	82
19069	–	100	54	80
23476	–	–	66	99

Table 5
LRECL and BLKSIZE

The following table lists various device types and popular logical records sizes and recommended block sizes to maximize the use of DASD space.

Device Type	LRECL	BLKSIZE	Records per Track	Maximum BLKSIZE
3330	80	12,960	162	13,030
3350	80	19,040	238	19,069
3375	80	17,600	220	17,600
3380	80	23,440	293	23,476
3330	121	12,947	107	13,030
3350	121	18,997	157	19,069
3375	121	17,545	145	17,600
3380	121	23,474	194	23,476
3330	133	12,901	97	13,030
3350	133	19,019	143	19,069
3375	133	17,556	132	17,600
3380	133	23,408	176	23,476

5. Permission is granted to make one copy of this appendix to hang in your work space. Printed from Bob Johnson's *MVS: Concepts and Facilities*, McGraw Hill, New York, NY 10011, 1989. ISBN 0-07-032673-8

Table 6
3380 (AA4 TYPE) Internal Paths[6]

This table gives the internal paths for 3380 "standard" architecture. The best performance will be gained if the reader does not put data sets that are likely to be accessed at the same time on the same internal path. For example, if you were going to allocate two MVS swap page data sets, you would put them on device zero and two. Do not use device zero and one because three or more Swap I/Os are started "at the same time" and device one would wait completely for device zero to finish.

```
path 1: xx0, xx1, xx8, xx9
path 2: xx2, xx3, xxA, xxB
path 3: xx4, xx5, xxC, xxD
path 4: xx6, xx7, xxE, xxF
```

Table 7
Valid Set Sector CCW Arguments

The following table lists valid arguments for the Set Sector Channel Command Word for several models of DASD:

Device Type	Number of Sectors	Range
3330 & 3350	128	0-127
3340 & 3344	64	0-63
3375	196	0-195
3380	222	0-221

For any of these devices, an argument of "255" causes the Storage Control Unit (SCU) to present channel end and device end as an ending status. No operation is performed.

---

6. Permission is granted to make one copy of this appendix to hang in your work space. Printed from Bob Johnson's *MVS: Concepts and Facilities*, McGraw Hill, New York, NY 10011, 1989. ISBN 0-07-032673-8

C

MVS Messages

MVS messages are displayed in a number of places: on listings, on operator consoles, on remote consoles, on printers. The messages of most interest to the operations staff of a data center are displayed on the operator console and in the SYSLOG data set and are generated from the Operating System, JES, the Data Facility Product, and application programs and systems running under MVS.

The messages of most interest to Programmers, Analysts, Systems Programmers, and end users are displayed on the printed output such as SYSPRINT, of MVS programs.

Different versions of MVS — MVS/370, MVS/XA, MVS/ESA — have different message formats. The reader should consult the IBM manual that matches the version of MVS that is running on the Processor Complex of the data center. Examples are *MVS/Extended Architecture System Messages* (GC28-1376 and GC28-1377) for MVS messages that begin with **ADY** through **ITV** and *MVS Message Library JES2 Messages* (GC28-1353) for JES2 messages that begin with $HASP.

The System Log, or SYSLOG data set, is a JES SYSOUT data set which contains all messages that are routed to any operator console. MVS provides filtering exits and SYS1.PARMLIB members to prevent messages from being physically displayed on consoles. This filtering does not prevent the messages from being written to the SYSLOG data set.

Messages have several formats, but the most common are:

1. MVS, JES2, and DFP produce two types of messages. The difference between the two is the time stamp and the identity of

the address space that is issuing the message (the second one below).

   a. **f message** where "f" is a character to indicate to the operator what to do with the message:

      i. | (vertical bar), which indicates the operator can delete the message.   The required action has been accomplished

      ii. **(blank)** no character indicates an informational message.

      iii. - (dash) indicates the message is informational only.

      iv. * (asterisk) indicates a specific action is requested by MVS or a program.

      v. @ sign indicates a specific action is required by a problem program.

   b. **message** is the message from the address space. If the message is from an IBM module, it will begin with three characters that identify the program area or subsystem that the message is coming from. If the message is from an OEM program product or from modules written in the data center, then the message may not begin with any particular characters.

2. **hh.mm.ss jobident f message**, where:

   a. **hh.mm.ss** is the time the message is issued.

   b. **jobident** is the job identification. Snnnn is a Started System Task. Jnnnn is a batch Job. Tnnnn is a TSO userid.

   c. **f** is the same as above.

   d. **message** is the same as above.

3. JES3 uses the **format hhmmsst jobident f message**, which has the same meanings as for MVS and JES, but are in a slightly different format.

MVS and its associated subsystems produce thousands of messages. Each version of MVS adds and changes messages according to the functions provided by the version of MVS. The general categories of messages can be determined by the first three characters of the "message number" which is the eight to ten characters at the beginning of the message.

Most message numbers end with a suffix which is significant:

1. **A** indicates the operator must perform some specific action.
2. **D** indicates the operator must choose an alternative.
3. **E** indicates that the operator must perform some action "as time permits."
4. **I** indicates that the message is informational in nature.

D

ABEND Codes

Introduction

Abend codes can be any number from 1 through 4095. ABEND codes are produced from two sources: **User Abends** are four-digit decimal (three-digit hexadecimal) ABEND codes set by a task running in an address space, such as an application program, in which an "Abend" macro is issued to terminate the task. **System Abends** are four-digit decimal (three-digit hexadecimal) Abend codes set by the MVS operating system when a system routine detects that a system utility or application program has violated some rule.

User ABENDs

Some application software abnormally terminate, and when they do they create the code as part of the specifications of the application program. OEM software also have Abends in their programs and they choose codes based on their specifications. User application program and OEM Abend codes are not documented anywhere in IBM documentation because IBM did not write the "user" program.

So there could be three places for a person to look for an Abend code: in MVS documentation, application documentation, or OEM documentation.

All the Abend codes should be ONLINE and SEARCHABLE. The IBM products Information Library and Library MVS provide such online searchable information.[7]

System Abends

System Abend codes are documented in the MVS System Codes manual for the version of MVS that you are using. For example, manual GC28-1157 *MVS/Extended Architecture Message Library: System Codes* is the manual to use for MVS/XA.

Always look up the Abend code and associated messages. It is sometimes amazing how much time can be saved using the clues in the code descriptions.

The value of the code tells the area of MVS that originated the Abend. This appendix will list the generic types of Abends and some hints as to what caused the Abend, but the reader is cautioned to get the manual that matches the Operating System and read it.

Abend Codes 001 to 0FF

Abend codes 001 to 04F are data management Abends.

1. **001 and 002** are for I/O operation problems (EXCP) such as I/O errors or block/record size problems. The Abend may also be caused by attempting to read after the end of the file. A DD statement may be missing. The LABEL specification may be wrong on tape.
2. **013 - 047** are Open/Close/EOF problems. One special type is 028 Abends, which are paging error problems.

---

7. Information Library (product 5665-277) and Library MVS (product 5665-294) can be used to store your application manuals. While it does not contain full text for all IBM manuals, it can be used as a good beginning to an online documentation system. It would be nice if OEM vendors shipped their manuals in machine readable text that could be added to such a system.

Abend 052 - 0FF

1. Abend codes **052 - 0BF** are supervisor Abends.
2. Abend codes **0C1 - 0DF** are logic problems that are detected by the System/370 hardware as violations of the Principles of Operation, then passed onto the program by the supervisor. Thus a hardware 004 program check Abend is converted into a 0C4 system Abend. Some reasons for COBOL programs (or others) to Abend are:
   a. **0C1 — Operation Exception**. The hardware has detected an instruction that is not valid. Abends may be caused by missing DD statements, a misspelled DDNAME, a COBOL PERFORM being exited improperly, etc.
   b. **0C2 — Privileged Operations**. The hardware has detected an instruction that is only allowed in "privileged" mode — usually MVS modules. The Abend may be caused by an incorrect or missing DD card.
   c. **0C3 — Execute Exception**. The System/370 EXECUTE instruction cannot have as the target of the EXECUTE instruction another EXECUTE instruction. This Abend is used by Systems Programmers to force dumps that can be captured by the SLIP system to get complete address space dumps.[8]
   d. **0C4 — Protection Exception**. The System/370 and MVS architecture has trapped access (read or write) to virtual storage areas that are protected or not available to the task. Abends may be caused by attempting to read an unopened data set, attempting to reference an output area before the data set has been opened, or incorrect subscripting, for example.
   e. **0C5 — Addressing Exception**. The virtual storage address is not available. Abends may be caused by:
      i. Subscript values exceeding the maximum or table areas overlapped.
      ii. Incorrect LINKAGE SECTION data definition — passing parameters in the wrong order, omission of a parameter, or incorrect lengths.

---

8. Thanks to Dave Halbig for this tip!

596 MVS: Concepts and Facilities

iii. Arithmetically manipulating a field which has not been initialized.

  f. **0C6 — Specification Exception.** The instruction is valid but the specification of parameters to the instruction is invalid. Abends may be caused by:

    i. PERFORMed procedure not executed properly.

    ii. Attempting to reference an I/O areas before an OPEN and READ.

    iii. Incorrect LINKAGE SECTION.

    iv. Incorrect variable length records.

    v. Attempting to WRITE to a file opened as INPUT.

  g. **0C7 — Data Exception.** The instruction and specification of the parameters are ok, but when the hardware tried to act on the data, the data was in an invalid format. Abends may be caused by:

    i. Data field not initialized properly.

    ii. Omission of USAGE clause or erroneous USAGE clause.

    iii. Incorrect LINKAGE SECTION.

    iv. Input record fields that should contain numbers are "blank."

    v. Literals are destroyed in the literal pool.

    vi. Improper REDEFINES clauses.

    vii. By design. Some programs and complete systems execute improper instructions just to "cause" a dump in COBOL.

  h. **0C8 — Fixed-Point Overflow Exception.** Abends are usually caused by a programming error.

  i. **0C9 — Fixed-Point Divide Exception.** Abends are usually caused by a programming error.

  j. **0CA — Decimal Overflow Exception.** Abends are usually caused by a programming error.

  k. **0CB — Decimal Divide Exception.** Abends are usually caused by a programming error.

  l. **0CC — Exponent Overflow Exception.** Abends are usually caused by a programming error.

  m. **0CD — Exponent Underflow Exception.** Abends are usually caused by a programming error.

  n. **0CE — Significance Exception.** Abends are usually caused by a programming error.

  o. **0CF — Floating Point Divide Exception.** Abends are usually caused by a programming error.

3. Abend codes 0Ex are problems with virtual I/O data sets.
4. Abend codes 0Fx are more system logic Abends.

Abend Codes 100 to EFF

These Abend codes are divided into categories such that the first digit is a sequence number and the last two digits are the SVC number.

1. **x00** Abends are problems encountered by the Execute Channel Program (EXCP) SVC. These problems are associated with an input/output operation.
2. **x01** Abends are for SVC 1 (WAIT) problems.
3. **x02** Abends are for SVC 2 (POST) problems.
4. **x03** Abends are for SVC 3 (EXIT) problems and indicate something was not cleaned up after a program thought it was done.
5. **x04, x05, x0A** are for virtual storage (GETMAIN or FREEMAIN) so 80A is not enough central storage.
6. **x06, x07, x08,** and **x09** for module load problems. Abend 806 is the eighth type of Abend issued for module load.
7. **x0B** are for timer problems.
8. **x0D** are for problems with an Abend macro being issued in which Abend discovered problems.
9. **x13** for open data set problems because nineteen (x'13') is the SVC for OPEN.
   a. **213** can be caused by a missing data set or specifying DISP=OLD for a new output data set.
   b. **413** can be caused by the volume serial number not being specified on an input data set or an I/O error reading the volume label.
   c. **813** can be caused by incorrect volume serial number or incorrect data set name specification.
10. **x14** for close data set problems because twenty (x'14') is the SVC for CLOSE. So Abend 214 is a problem associated with an attempt to close a data set.
11. **x37** (decimal 55) is end of volume, so D37 is associated with a write attempt after filling a data set or a volume. You have run out of space.

Abend Codes xF0 to xFF

These Abends indicate that there are/were errors from system failures, JES2 or JES3 errors.

Abend Codes Fxx to FFF

These Abend codes are for errors that are detected by user SVC routines. The 'xx' is the hexadecimal SVC number.

Index